MW00785783

THE COMPLETE BOOK OF
CATS

THE COMPLETE BOOK OF CATS

BREEDS • NUTRITION • HEALTH CARE

A comprehensive encyclopedia of cats and cat care with a fully illustrated guide to 120 breeds and over 1350 photographs

ROSIE PILBEAM

Contributing Editor: Alan Edwards
Photography by Robert and Justine Pickett

LORENZ BOOKS

Contents

Introduction

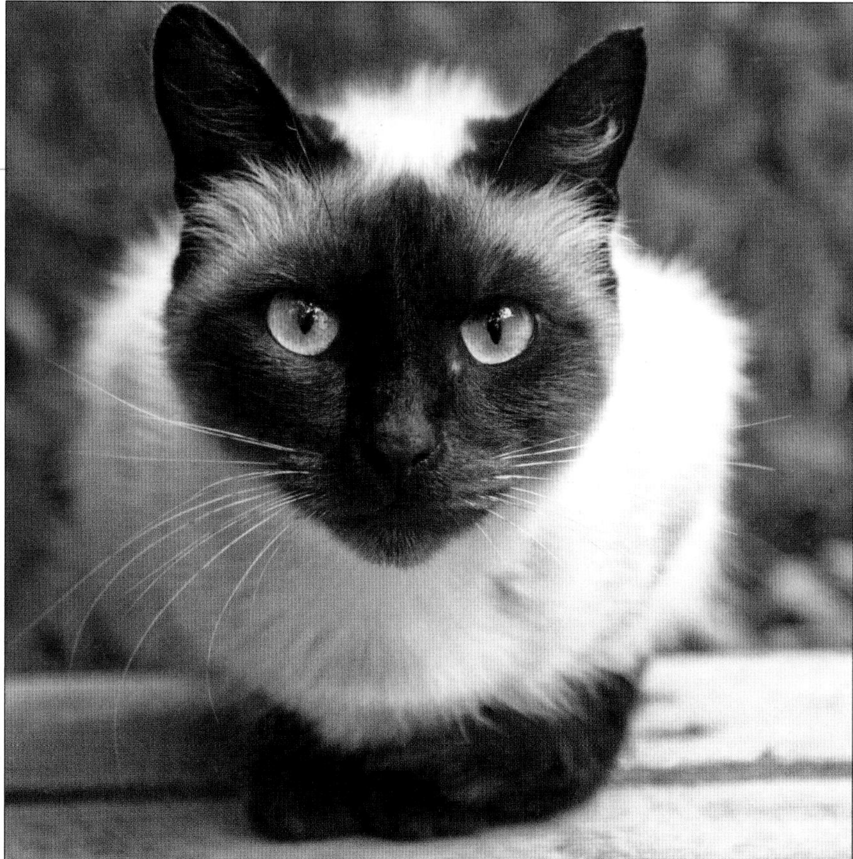

The cat is universally acknowledged as the second most popular domestic pet, after the dog. But if we take domestic cats (*Felis catus*) as a whole, both pets and feral, the statistics are reversed with approximately seventy-five million cats worldwide compared to seventy million dogs. It is estimated that if we look at the group Felidae, which includes collectively both wild and domestic species, there are 220–600 million cats in the world. This is a very loose estimation as it is extremely difficult to accurately count such large numbers of undomesticated felines.

Given these numbers it is quite surprising how much is still unknown about cats. Scientists continue to try to unlock the mysteries of feline anatomy and physiology. Despite the fact that cats have been domesticated for thousands of years, it was only in 2005 that neuroscientist Dr Joseph Brand discovered that cats cannot taste sweet things. In 2010 Dr Roman Stocker led a group of researchers using high-speed cameras to set out to find how a cat drank. Until this point it was assumed that it was the same way as dogs, but this was proven to be untrue.

▼ *The author's cat, Baby, who invited himself into the house three years ago and still won't let anyone touch him.*

Modern technology has made huge impacts upon the world of felines in a manner that would astound our grandparents. Microchips, trackers and electronic cat flaps help to keep our pets secure in a fast-paced world. Close-circuit cameras allow us to watch our pets even when we are at work. Laser beams and DVDs provide catty entertainment while advances in pet nutrition offer a vast choice of age-specific diets.

Gone are the days of a few boiled cods' heads and a saucer of milk for puss. Veterinary science has proved that there is a direct link between some illnesses, their cause or recovery, and nutrition. Nowadays there is a greater understanding of the stress that our cats are under as their environment alters, and in many cases, shrinks. In a more restricted environment simple things such as cleanliness can promote good health and prevent disease and sickness. Behavioural issues now indicate that all is not well in the cat's world and not that you just own a crabby cat.

▲ *In relation to their size, cats have the largest eyes of any mammal and approximately 32 muscles in their ears.*

On the whole cats now live in a safer, healthier environment but, for the majority, at the cost of being unable to do what is a cat's natural behaviour. The lack of hunting opportunities, trees to climb and territories to patrol can make life very sedentary and boring. This adds a greater responsibility on owners who must now provide alternative occupations for their cats to ensure a happy and fulfilled life. Life has changed greatly for cats since they first chose to share their lives with us, but for humans the cat is still almost as enigmatic as when the ancient Egyptians worshipped them as gods.

Routine care of any animal is vitally important. A daily physical check can alert the owner to any problems from weight loss to runny eyes.This can also act as a pleasurable connection time with your pet. Having a knowledge of basic first-aid treatments and minor ailments can be a great asset. Washing and cleaning wounds can prevent infection and understanding the need to prevent parasitic infestation will promote a healthy life for your cat. It is equally important cat owners should not delay in seeking veterinary advice for more serious problems.

▲ *Despite the fact that cats are capable of producing over a hundred different vocal sounds, most choose only to use a few.*

▼ *Domestic cats spend 70 per cent of their lives sleeping. That is 13–16 hours of every day. Their genetic makeup is 95.6 per cent the same as a tiger.*

Health items covered in this book are intended for the reader's reference only and to enable the owner to have a better understanding of the complaint. The best animal husbandry advice that has ever been given to me is the following statement – 'if in doubt give the vet a shout'.

Owners have also changed the cat world by protecting existing breeds and introducing new ones. There are over 120 cat breeds and the list continues to grow. Although cats do not vary greatly in size from breed to breed, temperament, looks and how much attention they will need from their owner should be carefully considered when thinking of buying a cat. The breeding of healthy cats is the greatest of responsibilities. Looks, originality, coat colours and buyer appeal must always take second place to health and soundness. This simple fact must never be overlooked or under-rated. Most breeders strive hard to undertake this and produce healthy kittens that go on to live happy contented lives as much-loved companions, contributing greatly to their owner's lives. Owning a non-pedigree cat may be all you desire, but you may well consider entering your cat in a show or breeding from it, and all cats need regular care, whether pedigree or not.

► *Good nutrition is vital if the lactating queen is to adequately feed her kittens and not lose body condition.*

Most people have seen a dog show, be it the local village attraction or a televised national event, but are unaware that cat shows even exist. International and national cat registries, cat clubs and breed societies all run these events and list them on their websites. In many cases, classes are available for kittens, domestic pets and breed champions with the majority of classes being reserved for registered pedigree cats. There are generally two types of show, open or closed. In open shows the owners and spectators can watch the judging taking place. Closed shows prohibit access to anyone, barring the officials, until judging has been completed. A cat show is an excellent way of looking at and gaining information on the breeds. Not every cat is happy in a formal show situation, or owner keen to take part, but a visit as a spectator is an interesting day out for most cat lovers.

As a result of the Covid 19 pandemic, 2020 saw the first-ever online cat shows. These virtual shows are not as formal as those outlined above and are judged purely on pictures of the exhibit. Pet owners have delighted in them and it looks as if this type of fun show may well continue into the forseeable future.

▼ *Cat shows are very social events offering the opportunity to chat with like-minded people.*

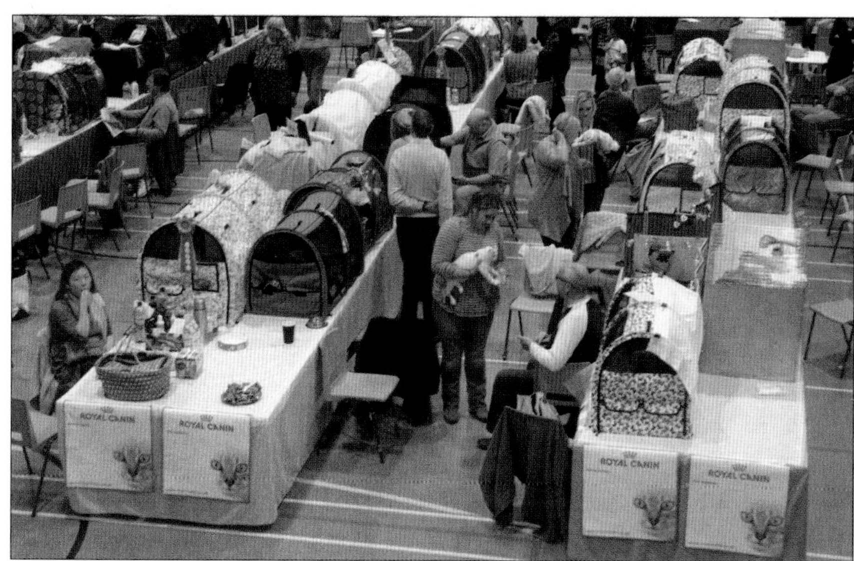

The decision to breed from your cat needs careful consideration; the welfare of the cat being as important as the owner's contemplations. Regardless of gender the cat will have to be restricted so accidental litters do not occur. Free-roaming entire males can be aggressive towards neighbouring felines and fighting males are likely to spread FIV and FeLV. An entire male will spray (territory mark) and this pungent smell makes it unlikely that it will be welcomed inside the home. An un-neutered female can have a first litter when she is only a kitten herself and go on to have up to three litters a year. She will have to be confined to ensure that this does not happen.

The huge number of cats and kittens in shelters must make one wonder if it is ever correct knowingly to breed with a mixed breed cat. In this situation, timely neutering is strongly recommended.

► *There is no substitute for the advice from a veterinarian surgeon; annual check-ups occur at vaccination time.*

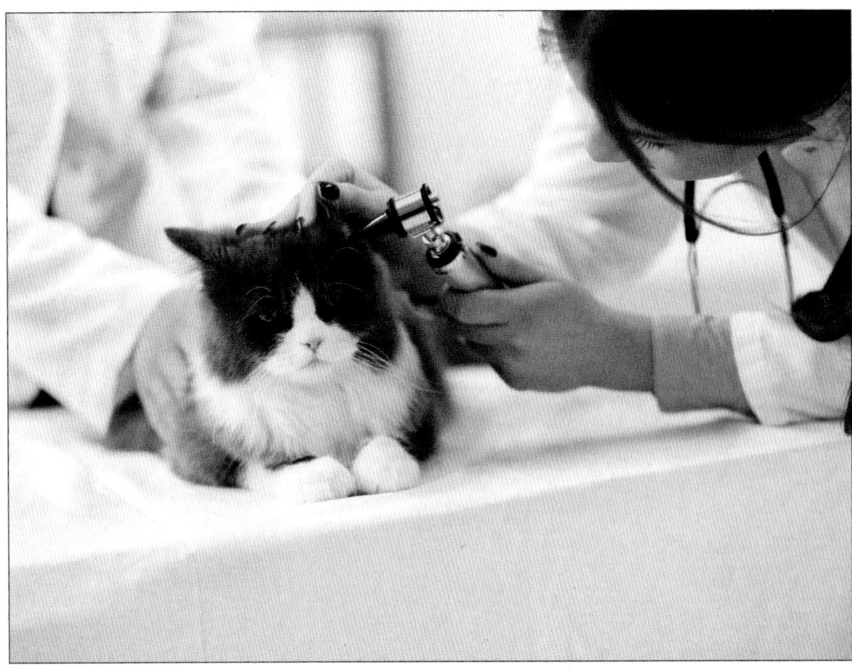

In the case of pedigree cats only those who correctly represent the breed standard should be promoted in a breeding programme. Judges at shows and experienced breeders will be able to advise you on the suitability of your cat. Having a litter to make money is never a good or right reason to breed with your cat. Possibly the only viable reason to breed from your pedigree pet is because you want a kitten yourself.

If you do decide to breed, early preparation is important. Gradually change your cat onto a suitable diet and ensure that all health checks have been undertaken. It is essential that vaccinations are up to date. Introduce the cat to the new routine of visiting the vet and get it used to being examined. Keep careful records of when matings take place and calculate when litters are due. Check registration papers have been transferred and correctly completed. Birth is always a magical experience to witness but it doesn't always go to plan and can result in large vet fees.

Kittens need to stay with their mothers until they are at least twelve weeks old. This is a huge time and financial commitment for the owner. Finding good homes for kittens is not an easy task either, and this too should be taken into considered when deciding whether to breed at all.

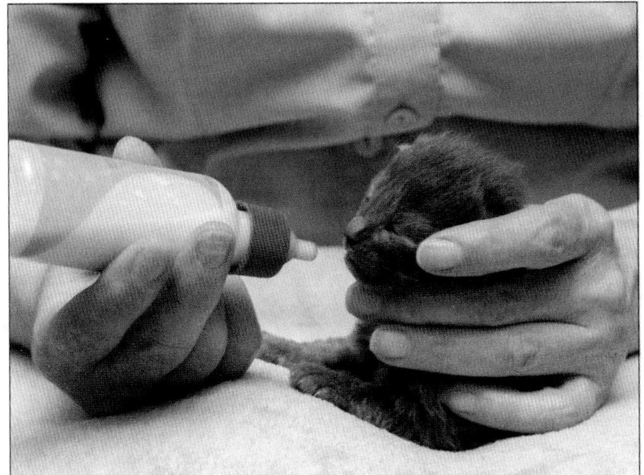

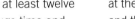

◄ *This little one needs some extra help. Bottle-feeding kittens is a huge undertaking.*

IN THIS BOOK

This book is divided into four sections for ease of reference. The first looks at the fascinating history of the cat and their interaction with humans and examines the structure, senses and physical make-up of this alluring creature. It is here that you will learn how a cat really does drink. The second section deals with looking after your pet including nutrition, grooming, general care and common ailments and injuries. The third section on cat breeds is an illustrated directory of more than 120 breeds from around the world including unrecognized breeds and hybrids. For every type of cat a 'Breed Box' panel summarizes the animal's eye and coat colours, grooming requirements, exercise needs and temperament. Showing and breeding from your cat are also covered. The final section covers natural and holistic cat care, such as massage, osteopathy and acupuncture.

CATS IN THE HUMAN WORLD

The historical journey of the cat from early tree dweller to pampered pet is uncertain in parts. Scientists are still piecing together the development of this animal into the feline that we see today. It is easy to understand why cats were often regarded as mystical animals as they travelled from wild rodent killer to one of the most popular pets globally. The cat's strategy of sticking close to people, in most cases, proved to be a winner. Food stores collected by humans provided safe shelter for these clever felines, alongside a ready supply of rodents to eat. Gradually the cat's position shifted from vermin controller to much-loved family member. A recent survey showed that 42.7 per cent of American pet-owning households had at least one cat. This percentage of pet cat ownership is similar across all the continents with the exception only of Antarctica. One third of all pet cats are chosen from rescue centres with only a tiny percentage coming directly from breeders.

◄ *There are more pictures and posts relating to cats on social media than any other animal. This shows just how much they have entered into our world.*

The origin of cats as a species

Our pet cats are members of the Felidae family. The exact forefather of the domestic cat is hard to pinpoint. It is agreed that the first cat probably evolved from the prehistoric *Proailurus*. Living in Eurasia, this creature is believed to have been slightly larger than a domestic cat. It had a long tail and is thought to be a climber and lived mainly in trees. What is not so certain is whether the *Proailurus* was the first 'cat' or the last precursor to the cat.

Jumping forward in time, it is known that roughly 20 million years ago there was a prehistoric cat, *Pseudaelurus*. This animal had a slender body, short legs and looked rather like a weasel. The *Pseudaelurus* is the common ancestor of the three subfamilies of Felidae. These families are Pantherinea (lions, tigers, leopards and jaguars), Felinae (lynxes, cougars, cheetahs, ocelots and domestic cats) and Machairodontinae (the sabre-toothed tiger or smilodon).

► *The Korat is an ancient breed from Thailand and has remained unchanged for thousands of years.*

All members of the Machairodontinae sub-family are now extinct but most people can visualize a sabre-toothed tiger from pictures seen in books. These animals are characterized by their long, curved canine teeth that extended from the mouth even when it was closed. These teeth could grow up to 17.78cm (7in) long. Just like today's domestic cat, sabre-toothed tigers were carnivorous and excellent hunters. They preyed on deer and bison but would tackle a small woolly mammoth if the opportunity arose. Their exact diet is unknown. The reproductive cycle of Machairodontinae had similarities to the modern domestic cat as well. They only bred in the warmer and lighter months, although the gestation period could have been as long as eight months. The colour of their coats is not known, but it is thought that it was similar to that of a lion. There is no certainty as to the

▼ *Longhaired cats from ancient Persia would have looked vastly different to the modern Persian breed below.*

▼ *Cats remarkably similar to the Egyptian Mau would have seen the building of the pyramids.*

▲ *Early longhaired mutations are thought to have originally occurred in Russia, Turkey and Persia (Iran).*

reason why this group of animals died out. Various reasons have been proposed, the most commonly held belief being that they had to compete with man for a diminishing food source. It is known that man preyed on the sabre-tooth and used them as part of their diet. It is possible that climate change could have had an influence too. They lived worldwide and existed for around 42 million years before they died out. There were many species of sabre-toothed tiger; it is important to note that not all were part of the Machairodontinae sub-family and so not all related to the domestic cat.

All felids, including the domestic cat, share common traits. They only eat meat, have no taste receptors for sweetness, often live in social groups and many are nocturnal. In reality, there is little difference between a 'big cat' and a 'moggy' other than the size. A number of scientists, including Warren E. Johnson and Stephen J. O'Brien, both from the National Cancer Institute, have used DNA to look at the lineage of cats. They looked at all cats, domesticated and wild, big and small, and discovered that there are thirty-seven species. All have proven to have evolved from *Pseudaelurus* and, therefore by extension, to *Proailurus*.

It was commonly thought that the domestication of the house cat started roughly 3,600 years ago, by the Egyptians. Recent scientific research now considers that there is a possibility that domestication started a long time before. There is some evidence, from Egypt, Iraq, Israel, Lebanon, Syria and Jordan, that cats and man could have formed a bond much earlier. This may have been as much as 10,000 years ago. In 2004 a Neolithic grave was excavated in Shillourokambos, Cyprus. The burial site contained the skeletons of both a human and a cat, lying close together. The cat was much larger than a modern house cat and resembled the African wild cat. This grave is 9,500 years old. No one can ever be sure if the cat was a domestic pet, the ingredients for a meal, a gift to the gods or as a protector in the next life.

Thousands of years ago, or in modern times, mystery surrounds the cat. From its origins to its anatomy, there is much that we still do not know. But the relationship between cat and human has a long and intertwined history.

▼ *There are many examples of cats with aristocratic Siamese-type heads in ancient Egyptian art (see page 18).*

Journey from the wild

Members of the cat family Felidae range from the great, roaring cats such as the lion and tiger to the small domestic cat. They are separated into different genuses (family sub-divisions), not because of their size, but because of differences in their anatomy. These enable members of the genus *Panthera* to roar, while the small cats in genus *Felis* cannot do so. There is a third genus for the cheetahs because they have non-retractable claws. Early in the 1900s there were more than 230 different species of cat in the family as a whole, but now there are fewer than 30. Many became extinct because cats have always been hunted and killed by humans for their fine pelts.

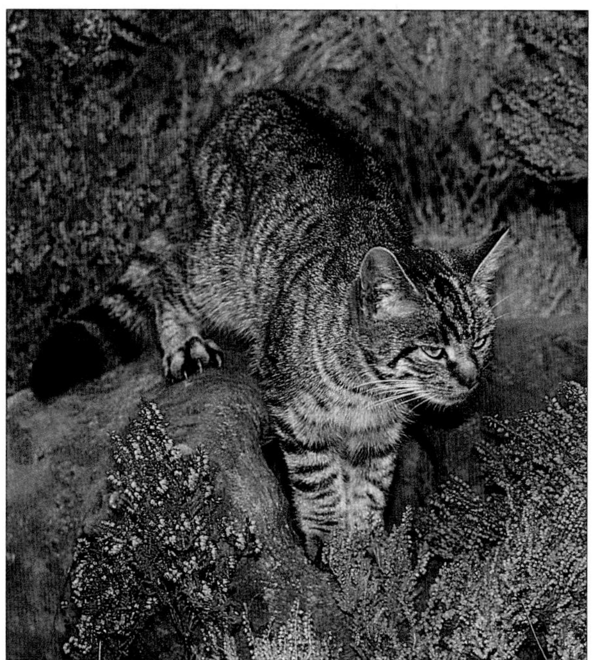

◄ ▼ *The European wild cat (left) was thought to be the ancestor of today's domestic cat because of its tabby markings, but this is now considered unlikely because of its instinctive wariness of people. The more likely contender is the African wild cat (below).*

ORIGINS OF DOMESTIC CATS

There is a close relationship between the wild and the domestic cat, but it is uncertain which wild sub-species of the *Felis* (small cats) genus actually made the leap into domesticity. Wild cats are widely distributed and vary considerably in appearance and habits. Northern cats, for example, developed dense, almost woolly coats, while in warmer, southern climes, a fine, body-hugging fur was the norm. Experts ended up with three major contenders for the ancestor of the domestic cat: the European wild cat and its Asian and African equivalents.

For many years, the Europeans believed that it was their wild cat (*Felis sylvestris sylvestris*), which is still found in localized parts of the Scottish Highlands and northern continental Europe. Their assumption was based on the cat's colouring and tabby markings that are common in non-pedigreed cats of today. However, even if the young offspring are reared by humans, they remain very wary,

Cat ancestry

The wild ancestors of today's domestic cat were among the first carnivores that evolved during the late Eocene and early Oligocene periods of pre-history over 35 million years ago. But it was another family of carnivores, the dogs, Canidae, that became the first animal companions of human beings. Stone Age man took advantage of the dog's superior sensory powers to help him hunt, and this provided a sound basis for an ongoing relationship. It was not until people graduated into a more settled agricultural way of life that cats became part of the typical domestic scene.

Small feline skeletons have been found in Stone Age archaeological sites, usually with the remains of other small wild animals such as badgers, which suggests that the cats were killed for their meat or pelts. The first evidence of cats actually living in some tentative relationship with humans was found in a New Stone Age site in Jericho in the Middle East, dating from about 9,000 years ago.

However, it is unlikely that domestic cats, living in a relationship with humans similar to that of today, emerged until around 3,500 years ago in ancient Egypt.

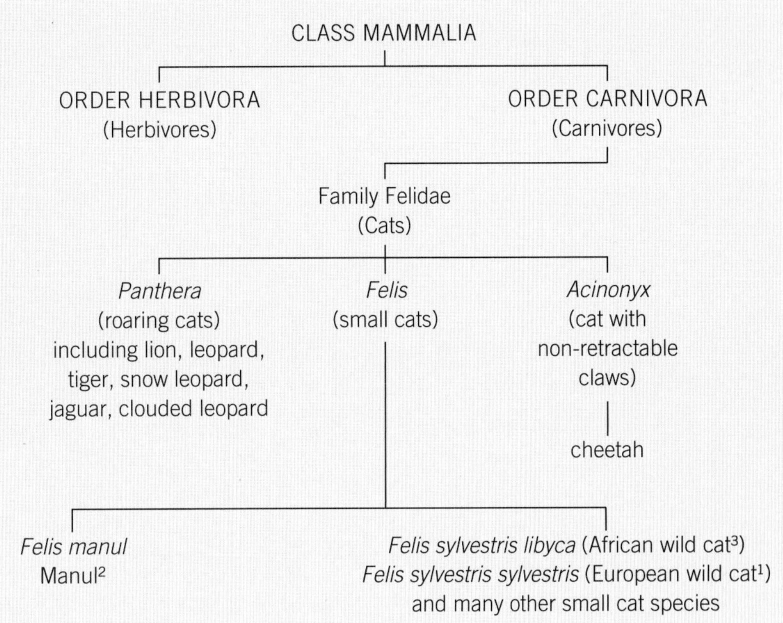

[1] May have bred with the early domesticated cats that reached Europe

[2] A possible ancestor of longhaired cats

[3] The most likely ancestor of most domestic cats

▲ *The leopard is in a different genus from the small cat not because it is bigger, but because the anatomy of its larynx enables it to roar.*

▲ *The cheetah is in a separate genus because it has non-retractable claws. It is closely related to the puma (also known as the mountain lion or cougar), which can retract its claws.*

◀ *The lion is another roaring cat of the genus* Panthera. *However, it is quite clearly in the same family as the domestic cat, with its flexible, muscular body, a typically short, rounded head, and large eyes.*

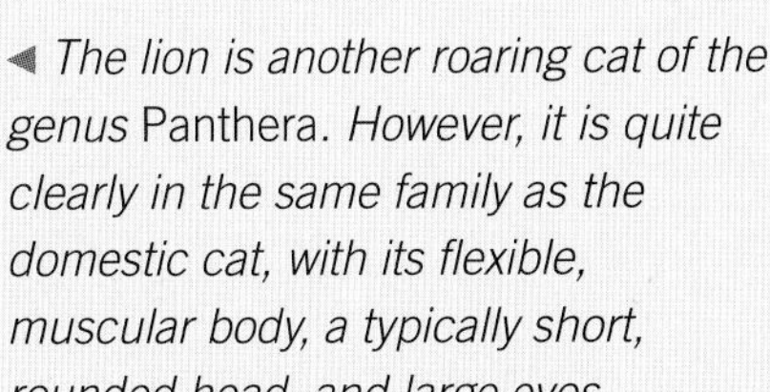

▶ *Every member, big and small, of the cat family is built to be an efficient killer. The tiger, the largest of the* Panthera *species, is one of the most powerful predators of all.*

and do not abandon their wild behaviour patterns. This inherent anti-social streak makes them unlikely to have been inclined towards domestication.

On the other hand, the African wild cat (*F. sylvestris libyca*), which still survives in Africa, western Asia and southern Europe, not only has the same number of chromosomes as the domestic cat but is relatively sociable. Both this sub-species and the Asian desert cat (*F. sylvestris ornata*) often live on the outskirts of human settlements and are fairly easily tamed. Significantly, remains of the African wild cat have been found in caves lived in by ancient man, and it is generally accepted as the ancestor of most of today's domestic cats. *F. sylvestris libyca* (abbreviated to *F. libyca*) is, in fact, very similar to the Abyssinian breed of today – lithe, long-faced with large ears, and with a ticked, or agouti (dark-tipped) tan coat.

► *The golden fur of today's Abyssinian is ticked with a darker brown – very similar to that of the African wild cat from which it is probably descended.*

THE PATH TO DOMESTICATION

Our ancestors may simply have hunted and killed these cats, both as a food source and for their pelts. However, as humans were developing an agrarian society based on crops that would have attracted rodents, it is also possible that the kittens were tamed and used to control pests. This would also have been in the cat's interests – keeping the scavenger population under control provided a regular concentration of well-fed prey.

In 1865, Francis Galton, a British scientist who specialized in the study of heredity and intelligence, defined the essential qualities of the early domestic animal. It would need to be useful, easy to tend, able to breed

◄ *The African wild cat* (Felis libyca) *is still found today in the wild in Africa, western Asia and southern Europe. It does not seem to be intimidated by people and often lives near human settlements.*

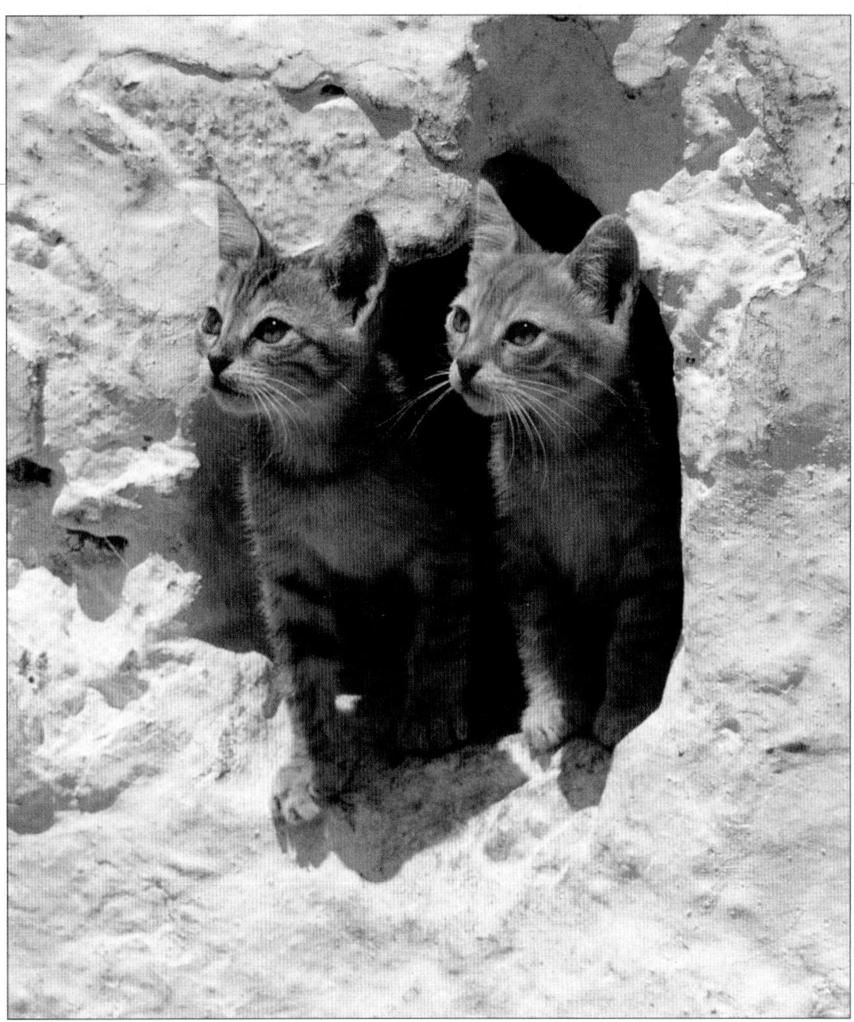

► *Feral cats, like these on a Greek island, tread a fine line between the wild and the domesticated; they invariably live – and breed prolifically – in towns and villages.*

freely, and above all (in the case of the dog and cat, for example), be comfort-loving and have a liking for humans. There is also a hypothesis that the process of domestication from wild, savage feline may have been accelerated by genetic mutation. Genes, the building blocks for a living creature, include patterns for behaviour as well as the size and general conformation of the adult. A fault in the genes that control behaviour patterns could, at some time, have created a cat that was temperamentally unwilling to leave a juvenile (kittenish) dependency state.

▼ *The Asian leopard cat* (Felis bengalensis bengalensis) *is a wild species that has been crossed with a domestic cat to produce a new pedigree, the Bengal.*

This, coupled with a ready supply of food from the human farmers, created an environment in which the mutual advantages of domestication were explored. The kitten-cat gained warmth, comfort and a secure environment in which to breed, and its offspring were valued as an ongoing supply of rodent exterminators. This made the spread of the genetic fault creating the socially valuable domesticated cat inevitable.

The domestication process may well have been accelerated as the African wild cat spread from warm southern and eastern regions and cross-mated with its northern European relation. It has been found recently that cross-matings of these sub-species produce animals with coat qualities that resemble those of the modern domesticated cat. It also seems that in such cross-matings, the genetic trait for domestication in one sub-species can strongly affect a more savage temperament in the other. The most recent example of this is the domestic cross with *F. bengalensis bengalensis* (Asian leopard cat) to produce the pedigree variety known as the Bengal. Successive generations enhanced the domesticated qualities of this new breed. (The registration organizations for pedigreed cats in some countries, notably the Cat Fanciers' Association in the United States, do not recognize this breed or any other developed from cross-matings of domestic cats with wild cats, although The Governing Council of the Cat Fancy in the United Kingdom does.)

EGYPTIAN REFINEMENT

Compared with the dog, the domestication of the cat is relatively recent. It probably occurred only 5–8,500 years ago, compared with the dog's 50,000-year relationship with humans. During excavations of the 8,000-year-old human settlement of Khirokitia in Cyprus in 1983, a single feline jawbone was found. Cyprus has never had endemic wild cats, so it is possible that this cat was a domestic animal. The proximity of Cyprus to Africa suggests that it could have been related to the African wild cat *F. sylvestris libyca*.

However, overwhelming evidence points to ancient Egypt as the first area in which the cat was elevated to a role beyond that of rodent exterminator. The cat established a niche for itself in ancient Egypt as early as 3500 BCE.

▲ *Ancient Egyptian murals depict cats well settled into domestic life. This one has tabby stripes on its back – the most common fur pattern that is also seen on the African wild cat.*

▲ *A mummified cat discovered in an Egyptian tomb dating from between 1000 and 332 BCE. More than 300,000 cat mummies were discovered at one archaeological site in 1890.*

► *This polished bronze statue of Bastet, the cat goddess of ancient Egypt, dates from the 6th century BCE and stands 34cm (13½in) high.*

Several wall paintings in tombs built at the time of the New Kingdom (1560–1080 BCE) depict the cat as being part of everyday Egyptian life. On the death of a household cat, Egyptian families went into deep mourning, even shaving off their eyebrows as a sign of their grief.

The cat was also revered as a symbol of fertility. Bastet (also known as Bast and Pasht), daughter of the

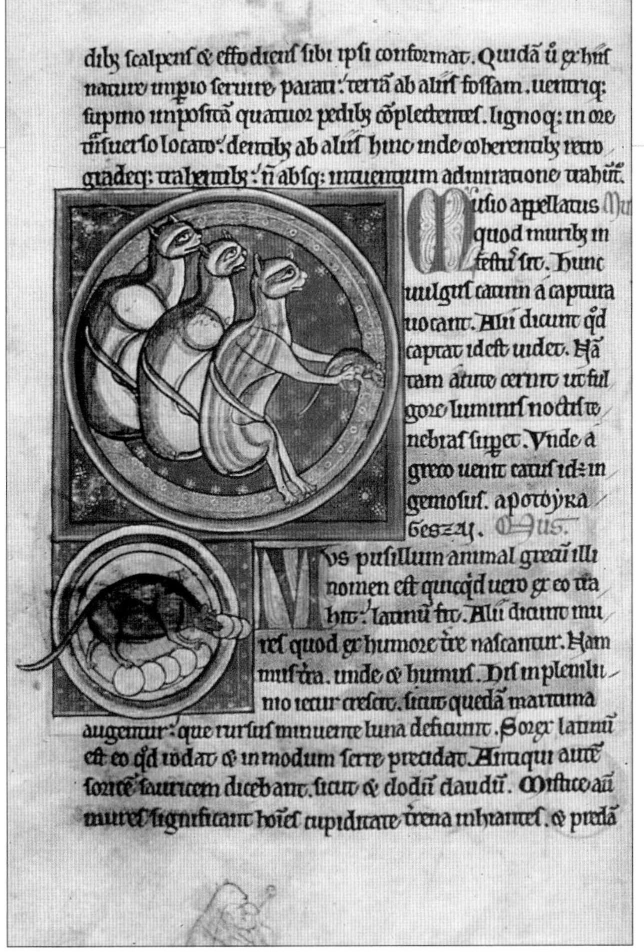

► *A cat is featured in a 13th-century bestiary (a book of beasts). Although widely feared and reviled at this time, cats were still useful mousers, and in England, were protected by the Church to some extent.*

sun god Re, or Osiris, and goddess of fertility, was originally depicted as a lion, but later assumed the shape of a small cat. It is from her name that the word puss is thought to derive.

In 1890, archaeologists discovered more than 300,000 cat mummies buried in an underground sanctuary dedicated to Bastet at Ben Hassan. Beside the cat mummies were mummified mice – food for the cats' journey into the afterlife. Cats were also domesticated in the Far East in ancient times, probably around 2000 BCE. They may have arisen from the Asian desert cat (*F. sylvestris ornata*) and be the forebears of the longhaired domestic cat.

WESTERN DOMESTICATION

The domesticated cat in the West spread with the expansion of the Roman Empire. Romans smuggled cats out of Egypt and took them to their northern conquests, where they were used to control rodents. Cats also enjoyed some degree of veneration by the Romans. The 1st-century BCE Greek historian Diodorus describes an incident in which a Roman charioteer in Alexandria, who ran over and killed a cat, was stoned to death by an angry mob.

Monks travelling to the Far East took cats with them, where they would have bred with the Asian domestic cats. The earliest domestic cat bone discovered in Britain dates back to between AD 10 and AD 43, before the Roman conquest. In Chelmsford, England, Roman roof tiles impressed with cats' paw prints have been found.

The Romans saw the cat as a symbol of liberty, but it was with the fall of the Roman Empire that the cat lost popularity. Earlier beliefs were

► *By the time this cat was depicted in a 14th-century bestiary, the cat population in the West was declining due to human persecution. This in turn helped the rodent population quickly spread, and with it the virus that carried the Black Death through Europe.*

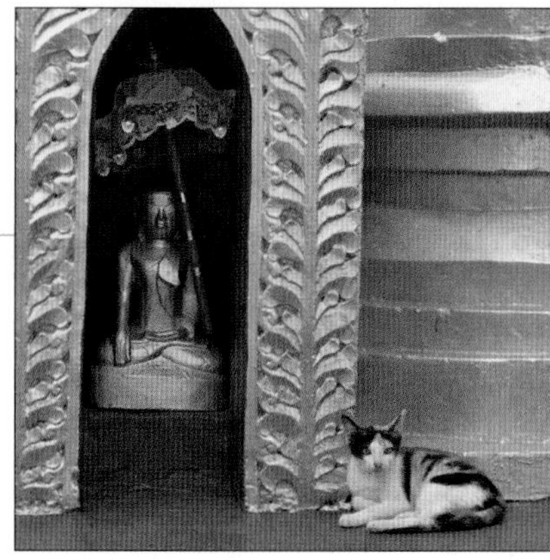

▲ *Buddhists show loving kindness to all animals, providing sanctuary to this wild cat at Kakku Temple, Myanmar.*

adapted to fit in with the cat's gradual loss of image. The Nordic goddess of love, Freya, for example, had always been depicted surrounded by cats, but later became a frightening witch whose cats were the denizens of hell. For around 700 years after the first millennium, throughout Europe the cat was often associated with witches and evil. In the town of Metz in France, hundreds of cats were burned alive on the second Wednesday in Lent, as a ritual sacrifice of witches.

In parts of the post-Roman world, the cat disappeared completely from the archaeological records. Luckily, in Britain it was still highly valued as a mouser, and until the 10th century – the beginning of the Middle Ages – it enjoyed some protection from the Church. However, in continental Europe, its fur was used to line and decorate garments, including the trimmings on the gowns of lawyers. In times of famine, cat flesh was added to the soups and stews of hungry farming folk.

EASTERN APPRECIATION

During this time cats may have lost favour in Europe but in Japan they were considered a symbol of good fortune. Legends tell of a Japanese gentleman of property who was distracted by a cat that appeared to be waving at him. He moved towards it and seconds later a lightning bolt struck the exact spot that he had been standing. It was considered that the cat had saved his life. This gave rise to the Maneki Neko, a symbolic cat sitting with a raised paw. These ornaments are seen to this day and are said to bring good luck and fortune to the owner. It is, in part, from this story that the modern-day 'Hello Kitty' brand was developed.

▼ *In Nordic mythology Thor gave Freya, the goddess of love, a chariot that was drawn by two male cats.*

▲ *Asian Leopard cats are beautifully marked but are shy, nervous and nocturnal so are not suitable as pets.*

During the Song Dynasty in 12th-century China, long haired lemon and white cats were greatly valued as pets. They feature in paintings, and writings explained that it was possible to buy fish and beds for them from specialist vendors in the markets. Black cats were regarded as a symbols of sickness, death and misfortune and so avoided. During the Cultural Revolution Chairman Mao is quoted as saying "It doesn't matter what colour a cat is. As long as it catches a mouse it is a good cat".

In both Japan and China cats were vital rodent control in areas that produced silk worms. Mice could devastate silk worm populations causing extreme hardship for the farmers that raised them. The actions of cats were also used to predict weather changes and even the best place to catch fish. The Japanese island of Tashirojima is home to a shrine built over the grave of a cat that was killed by a local fisherman.

► *Daily visitors bring good luck charms to the Gotokuji Temple in Toyko, adding to the thousands of Maneki Neko cats already there.*

In Hindu mythology cats are associated with fertility. The goddess of birth and protector of children, Shashti, is depicted riding a cat while she suckles one child and holds the hand of another. Figures of this type have been dated as early as 500 BCE. Shashti is also the goddess of food grains, so it is easy to understand why she should be associated with cats. In Asian countries cats are not normally kept as household pets within Hindu homes. They tend to live on the streets in semi-feral populations. Shelter and food is often provided by local residents so that the cats remain in the area and kill rodents. The killing or harming of cats is prohibited in Hinduism and considered a grave sin. Anyone doing so must travel to Kashi, worship on the bank of the Ganga River, and donate a small cat made of gold. This means that the feral population is virtually protected and growing rapidly. Neutering needs to be considered to prevent further problems.

In Russia, cats have been considered as good luck for centuries. This is thought to be especially true if the owner allowed the cat to enter a new house before the humans as it would bring good fortune to the home.

▲ *The Bengal was bred to be as close as possible to a scaled-down version of a wild cat.*

► *The African wild cat is believed to be an early ancestor to the modern domestic cat.*

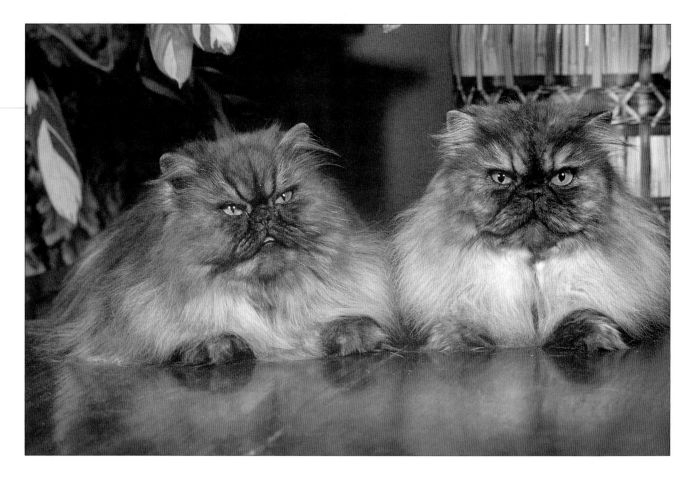

AMERICA AND AUSTRALIA

DNA evidence suggests that there were no indigenous domestic-type cats in either America or Australia. Therefore all must have been brought over by boat.

Cats in South America appear to have been from Iberian stock, while those in North America seem to have a European origin. The European cats were brought to the New World during the 1600s and 1700s by settlers and traders. Most cats in North America can trace their origins back to those owned by early colonists. Nowadays approximately 42% of households in the United States of America have at least one cat.

Records show that cats were not brought to Australia until 1804 and that by 1820 there was a feral colony living around Sydney. Feral cats are now considered as one of the country's most invasive species and have been implicated in the extinction of several mammal and marsupial species. It is now estimated that there are between 2.1 and 6.3 million feral cats living on mainland Australia and surrounding islands.

Domestic cats have been resident in Tasmania for only 200 years.

THE RISE OF THE DOMESTIC CAT

From the 1600s, the cat did once again find some favour as a domestic pet. The French Cardinal Richelieu was known to like cats, which he had with him while he worked. A French harpist left a large part of her fortune to her cats, together with instructions that they be properly cared for. By the 1700s, cats were sometimes featured in portraits of the Romantic era as favoured companions, and the poet Thomas Gray wrote his *Ode on the Death of A Favourite Cat Drowned in a Tub of Goldfishes.* There was even a cat fair held in the city of Winchester, England in 1598.

▲ *Persian cats were among the first exotic breeds to be developed in the West, their popularity boosted by the enthusiasm of European royals such as Queen Victoria of England.*

▼ *The Maine Coon Cat was a valuable mouser in the north-eastern United States, and was a major winner at America's first cat show in Madison Square Garden, New York in 1895.*

► *Domestic cats now compete with dogs as favourite pets. In the United States the cat population is around 95.6 million compared with 90 million dogs; in Britain, there are 10.9 million pet cats against 9 million dogs.*

▲ *The Turkish Angora of today is very different from its late-19th-century ancestor that, together with a Persian cat, founded many of the modern longhaired cat breeds.*

However, it was not until the 1800s that serious interest was taken. Country fairs in the United States included exhibitions of Maine Coon Cats from the 1860s. A cat show proper, with Maine Coons featuring strongly, was held in Madison Square Garden in New York in 1895. The first British cat show – with benched cats in individual pens – was held at London's Crystal Palace in 1871. It was organized by the writer and notable cat artist Harrison Weir. The early shows were inspired by a growing interest in the glamorous pedigreed breeds. It became necessary for some sort of registration body to record the parentage of the cats, and to set some sort of standard that would list the desirable and undesirable traits for each breed. This was the role of the National Cat Club, founded in the United Kingdom in 1887, which marked the beginning of the cat fancy as it is known today. Harrison Weir was its first president.

Local clubs and clubs for specific breeds were soon formed. Today, there are active cat fancies in most countries, recent additions being Russia and Malaysia. At the early shows, the main varieties seen were Persian longhairs, domestic shorthairs, Siamese, Foreign Blue (now known as Russian Blue), Manx and Abyssinian. During the 1900s, as travel became easier, wealthy enthusiasts imported cats from other countries and different breeds quickly spread across the world. Breeding suffered a setback during the world wars, and some breeds, such as the Abyssinian and Russian Blue, nearly became extinct. From the late 1950s, the cat fancy and knowledge of genetics grew, and many new breeds and colour varieties within breeds were developed.

▼ *Although cats are described as domestic pets, as a species they can return to the wild and survive (although a highly bred individual might struggle). This creates a feral (wild) population like these residents on Cooper Creek, South Australia.*

Human-feline interaction

Owning a cat has many benefits besides that of their original use as rodent control.

EMOTIONAL HEALTH BENEFITS

Cats provide companionship and stability in life and help to overcome feelings of loneliness. Cats will initiate contact with their owners both physically and vocally. This in turn reduces anxiety and stress in the owner and is especially apparent in older people, or those that have recently suffered from a bereavement. Caring for a cat takes the focus away from immediate problems and improves one's emotional state.

Many cat owners state that they prefer to discuss problems with their pet than with another person and, in a recent survey, a large proportion felt that their cat understood them better than their family or friends. This feeling of empathy is believed to help people relate to other people, as well as their cat. Cats are now used to help assist teaching children who have social interaction and communication problems. They have also been instrumental in assisting autistic children to understand and relate to emotional feelings.

Over thousands of years cats have developed a sound that is half purr and half howl. This triggers the same receptors in the human brain as that of the cry of a newborn baby. Instinctively we will look to the cat and see if we can tend to its needs. This gives purpose and a feeling of responsibility, routine and structure that may have been missing in the lives of some people.

Cats are also a great way of making friends as cat ownership is often a common denominator. As they are no respecter of boundaries, your cat may well introduce itself to a new neighbour before you do. They also help to maintain friendships as they provide an easy topic of conversation.

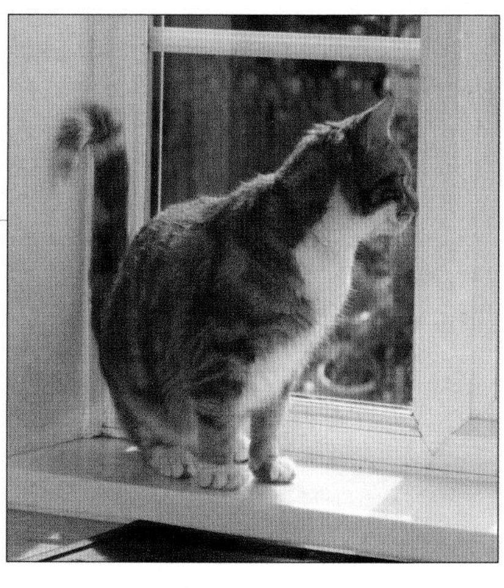

▲ *Cats will wait patiently watching for their owners to return from work or outdoor commitments.*

PHYSICAL HEALTH BENEFITS

People who own a cat generally have decreased blood pressure and anxiety. It is this reduction in anxiety that can significantly reduce the risk of heart attack or stroke. Owners that do suffer a heart attack recover more quickly and live longer than those without a pet. Studies have shown that owning a cat can also help to lower cholesterol and triglycerides and be as effective as medication if combined with moderate

▼ *The 25–39 age group tends to spend more money on their cats; this could be because their pets are younger in age.*

▲ *Rubbing round the owner's legs in greeting ensures that the cat has also scented its own property.*

► *Young children and adolescent cats will play happily together for hours, each entertaining the other.*

exercise and a diet containing fewer carbohydrates and less processed food.

Sitting with a cat purring on your lap is more than just a pleasant, comforting experience. Recent medical research also shows that the frequency or pitch of a cat's purr helps to heal bones and muscles after injury.

Playing with a cat increases levels of serotonin and dopamine, which promotes a greater feeling of calmness and relaxation. Cat owners are less likely to suffer from depression than non-pet owners. Cat ownership can also help ease the symptoms of Post-Traumatic Stress Disorder and Bipolar Disorder.

Cat owners, regardless of age, make fewer visits to doctors, are discharged from hospital sooner, have a better immune system and are more resistant to above average levels of stress.

Studies show that children brought up with cats from birth are less likely to suffer from asthma, eczema and allergies in later life. It is thought that this is because the child will have higher levels of some immune system chemicals and so have a stronger immune system activation. This contradicts the old advice that allergy-prone families should avoid furry pets. It has been noted that children raised in a home with a cat miss fewer days from school due to their increased immune function.

Research also shows that these children have a greater empathy towards others, a better understanding of body language, generally have a and are more likely to take part in social activities.

The information above is backed by extensive medical research studies, although, in some cases, there is limited understanding of the reasons why cats have such a positive effect on our health and wellbeing. All of the physical and emotional benefits of cat ownership occur regardless of age, gender, social status or income.

◄ *A purring cat is therapeutic, lowering the owner's stress levels and blood pressure.*

► *Owners derive pleasure from choosing tasty meals and treats for their cat. Organic or additive-free products and nutritionally enchanced foods are popular.*

Cats and children

▲ *A mother teaches her toddler to gently stroke a cat. Children are enchanted by a cat's purr.*

Cats make lovely companions for children but careful thought must be taken before you choose to introduce one into the family home. For a parent it is a total commitment as the bulk of care will fall upon them. Not only will they be responsible for the cat but also for teaching the child how to interact with its furry friend. If the parent has any doubt about their ability to undertake this task then the best advice is not to get a cat.

If the decision is made to get a cat, a kitten is the best choice as both feline and child can grow up together. Care should be taken in selecting the best breed or individual as a placid cat will adapt better to a busy and active household.

Toddlers should never be left alone with a cat as they may accidentally frighten or hurt their pet. A frightened cat will defend itself by scratching or biting. Therefore any interaction between toddler and cat must be supervized at all times.

Children should be taught how to correctly pick up a cat and that if the animal struggles then they should let it go. Knowing that a cat that lays its ears back or lashes its tail is not happy, and needs to be left alone, is an important lesson too. When playing with the cat appropriate toys must be used. Enticing the cat with wiggling fingers is not wise and may lead to scratches.

It is not a good idea to allow the cat to sleep in the bedroom of a small child. This can be prevented by simply closing the bedroom door. Although health risks are small, parasites and ringworm fungus could be transmitted from cat to child. Suffocation by a sleeping cat is possible in the case of a baby.

Simple precautions such as placing cat food and litter trays out of reach and providing the cat with a 'safe place' to retreat to are common sense. With careful introduction and consistent supervision children often form a very special, lifelong bond with their feline pet.

▲ *Children should be encouraged to wash their hands after handling the family pet.*

◄ *Responsibility and empathy are just two of the many skills that a child can learn when assisting in the care of a cat.*

Cats and the elderly

All animals provide companionship and a cat is an ideal choice for an older person. Relatively cheap to buy and feed, they do not require an ongoing range of costly equipment. Unlike a dog they don't need daily walks and are happy to spend most of the day curled up on a lap or sleeping on the bed. But owning a cat will still promote a feeling of responsibility and routine. This is often missing in the life of an older person, especially if a spouse has died and grown-up children are leading their own lives with families of their own. Feeling unneeded can lead to a lack of self-esteem, loneliness and even depression.

Kittens are hard work and may not be the best choice for an older owner. Rescue shelters are full of adult cats requiring homes and the staff will be able to advise on the temperament of each individual. A placid cat, without costly medical problems, who enjoys human company is the ideal.

Feeding, grooming and cleaning the cat's litter tray requires activity but are not too strenuous for an owner with reduced mobility. Playing with a cat can be done from a chair by using a toy on a stick. A wide variety of these toys are now available to entertain and amuse both owner and cat.

Cats can offer unconditional love and their company may fill a void in the life of someone who is alone. Owners can chat to and confide in them, without fear of being thought stupid, thus reducing any feelings of isolation. Touching or stroking a cat is a means of communication that the pet will return by jumping on a lap or purring. Animal ownership is also a real icebreaker and talking about the health or antics of a cat to like-minded people will help to make friends.

Veterinary insurance is important for owners on reduced incomes or a pension. It is also a good idea to arrange with a friend or family member that they will care for the cat if it should outlive its owner.

▲ *The regular routine of feeding and caring for a cat can help fight off depression which is, sadly, common among the elderly.*

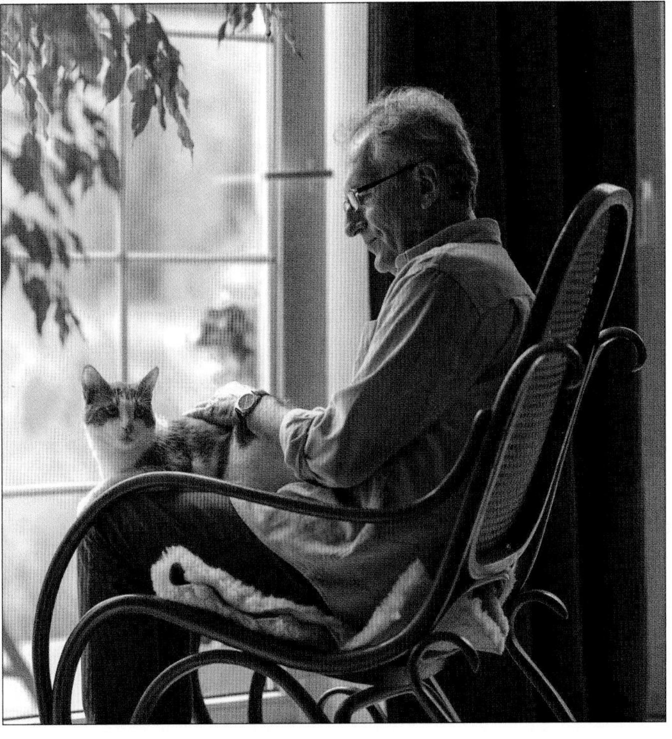

▲ *Caring for a cat gives a sense of purpose and provides companionship.*

► *Stroking or grooming a cat helps to keep elderly arthritic joints supple and flexible, as well as benefiting the owner's cardiovascular system.*

Legal rights and responsibilities

Although many people consider cats as independent animals and therefore above the law this is not the case. The owner or keeper of a cat is subject to many regulations. An owner is a person who is regarded as having legal ownership of the cat but may not be caring for it at the time. A keeper is a person who may have care of the cat on a part-time basis, for example while in a cattery, but not the actual owner of the cat.

Firstly, under various animal welfare legislation, a cat that is not classified as feral has rights that it can expect from its owner or keeper. These cover the right to be fed and watered, provided with shelter and a suitable environment, to be free from pain and given veterinary treatment when required, have physical and mental stimulation and not be subjected to cruelty. In the majority of cases if these conditions are not provided a prosecution could be brought. Most cat owners and keepers care for their charges well but a few should re-examine their responsibilities.

Depending on the country, cats can fall under the laws of nuisance. This doesn't mean that an offence has been committed if a cat repeatedly uses a neighbour's garden as a litter tray. But it does cover situations where cats cause such a nuisance that a neighbour is unable to use their garden at all. An example would be that a cattery was next door and that the smell or noise was so bad that people were unable to sit in or enjoy their garden.

If a large number of cats are kept in a residential house, local council or environmental officers may force the

▲ *Many countries attach legal responsibility to those who feed strays, including having to have the cat neutered.*

◄ *It is important to register your cat with a veterinary surgery before any need for treatment.*

◄ *It is your responsibility to provide your cat with a warm, clean and dry place to sleep.*

▼ *Cats need to be fed properly with a balanced diet. Failure to do so may lead to illness and in turn prosecution.*

▼ *Landlords, in some circumstances and countries, can evict tenants if the property smells of urine.*

owner of the building to apply for a 'change of use'. If this is not granted an order can be issued to reduce the number of cats in the residence.

A cat is regarded as 'property' and it is an offence to steal it from the owner. Equally it is against the law to kill or injure a cat. Cats are still regarded as the property of the owner even if they have strayed away from home. They are also covered by legislation guiding the sale of goods. If a cat is bought from a breeder who states it to be a certain type or breed and it turns out not to be as described, the purchaser has a right of complaint. In extreme cases, the purchaser could take the breeder to court. This also covers cats who are sold with a known but undisclosed inherited disease, although this can be harder to prove.

Owners are responsible for 'severe' damage caused by their cat to other animals, property or people. If a cat repeatedly attacks the pet of a neighbour then steps should be taken to prevent this happening. The neighbour can expect any vet bills to be paid. Laws of damage also cover injury to people from severe scratches through to death by contracting a disease from the cat. These laws do not cover anything that could be regarded as normal feline behaviour. So killing a neighbour's pet bird would not be considered an offence unless it was already agreed that the cat was subject to the law of 'nuisance'.

Sadly if a cat is injured or killed by a car, the driver, in all but deliberate cruelty cases, is not legally responsible and doesn't have to report the accident. It is unlikely, but not without precedence, that the driver would be able to make any claim against the owner of the cat for any damage or injury. Cats are not subject to the law of trespass and are regarded as having the 'right to roam'. This is because it is not considered possible or practical to restrain them. It would be illegal to attempt to stop a cat accessing your garden by putting out poisons or traps for example.

Cats are subject to quarantine rules and travel regulations. Owners should ensure that these are adhered to before moving their pet from one country to another (see pages 118–19).

Legislation varies greatly from country to country. Equally, each case is different. Therefore the information given on these pages should be used for guidance only. If a dispute arises involving a cat, professional legal advice must be sought.

▼ *It is compulsory to microchip cats in Australia, Greece, France, Belgium and some parts of Spain.*

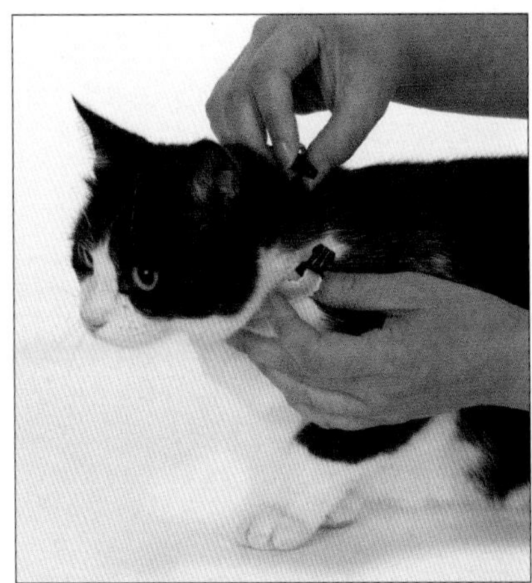

UNDERSTANDING THE CAT

There are marked parallels between humans and cats: we are both social creatures who are able to communicate verbally. It would be easy to assume that there are few biological differences other than shape and movement, but this is simply not the case. There are aspects of a cat's anatomy and physiology that are frankly astounding and much that we still do not understand. Anatomy is the term used to define the study of the structure of the body while physiology refers to the study of cells, soft tissue and organs. Both have been studied for many decades by scientists and veterinarians and their findings are the building blocks of our feline knowledge. A basic awareness of how our remarkable feline pets 'work' will help an owner to better understand the needs of their cat.

◄ *Cats are capable of rational thought and problem solving, and have both long- and short-term memory capacity, although they do not always let us know this!*

The structure of a cat

The primary function of the cat's skeleton is to support the body, protect the soft organs and to provide a system of levers for locomotion. It also produces vital red blood cells. The average cat skeleton consists of around 250 bones. This is forty more bones than in a human skeleton. The number of bones in the tail varies between species; this, and additional polydactyl toes, affects the overall bone count.

A cat's bone is made up of one third protein and two thirds minerals. This combination provides strength and some flexibility. Bones contain soft marrow, some of which produces blood cells. Marrow bones can produce hundreds of thousands of blood cells per second. This is vital as some white blood cells survive only a few hours and red blood cells only last for about three months. A cat that is highly active is more likely to have dense bones as they are putting them under constant pressure by running and jumping. A less energetic feline will have a more delicate bone formation.

► The bones of a cat's skeleton are held together by bands of a strong fibrous material called ligaments.

▲ An agile cat is capable of jumping six times its own length and five times its own height.

The skull is made up of approximately twenty-nine dense bony parts. Unusually, the eye sockets are very large in comparison. At the front of the skull is a heart-shaped hole where the nose is located. The jaw is strong and contains the teeth. At the front are six incisors and two canine teeth, while the teeth at the back are premolars and molars. The lower jaw is called the mandible and it is not uncommon for this to fracture, at the point that forms the chin, after a traumatic incident. Common causes are falling from a tree or high fence or being hit by a road vehicle.

The vertebrae bones in a cat's back are looser than those of most other animals. This enables them to twist and turn when jumping and helps them to be able to land on their feet. They have three more back vertebrae than their owners. These additional bones allow greater flexibility, which is why a cat can curl up and get into small spaces.

▼ CAT SKELETAL STRUCTURE

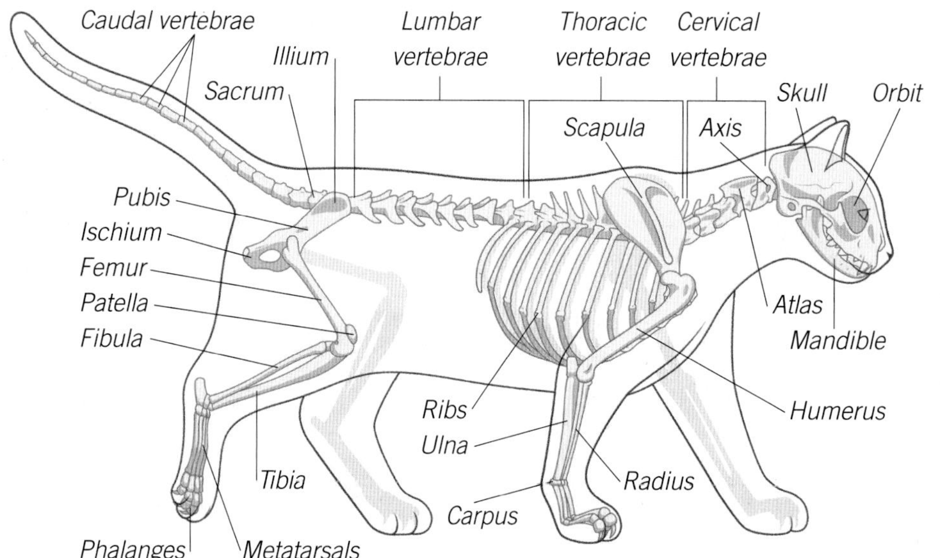

► *Cats have thirteen pairs of ribs, each of which are attached to a thoracic vertebrae.*

The tail is made up of nineteen to twenty-three caudal vertebrae, except in the case of Manx cats and breeds with shorter tails. This is roughly 10% of the bones in a cat's body. These bones are held together by muscles, tendons and ligaments which aid its mobility. The tail acts as a counter-balance and this helps the cat when leaping from object to object or walking on narrow surfaces. Surprisingly, cats without tails seem to manage these feats equally well. The average tail length for a male cat is 27.75cm (11in) and 24cm (9.5in) for a female. The spinal cord doesn't extend all the way into the cat's tail but injury to the tail can cause serious nerve damage.

Bones at the wrist (carpus) are very loosely jointed. This allows a cat to rotate their paws inwards. This can be seen when a cat plays with a toy, climbs a tree or is washing its face. A cat is a digitigrade walker. This means that they walk on their toes and the central pad of the paw. It appears as if they are walking on tiptoe. They share this action with dogs and many other mammals. As less of the foot touches the ground there is less friction and this conserves energy. All digitigrades are able to move swiftly and almost soundlessly. This is a huge advantage for a hunter as they are able to creep up on their prey and kill by stealth. Unlike a dog, the cat is able to retract its claws when walking, which is why we seldom hear their feet clicking when they walk on a solid, hard surface.

The legs of a cat appear short in proportion to the length of their body. The sharp angle of the hind limbs, coupled with powerful, strong muscles, act like a spring. This provides power for leaping, climbing and sprinting. The front legs are often shorter than the hind and are extremely flexible. A cat is able to stretch them wide apart so they can wrap them round a prey and hug it to their chest. This ability is also helpful when climbing trees.

▼ *Bone disease is relatively rare but can be inherited. If worried, visit the vet for advice and help.*

▲ *Although cats have collar bones (clavicles), they are not attached to other bones.*

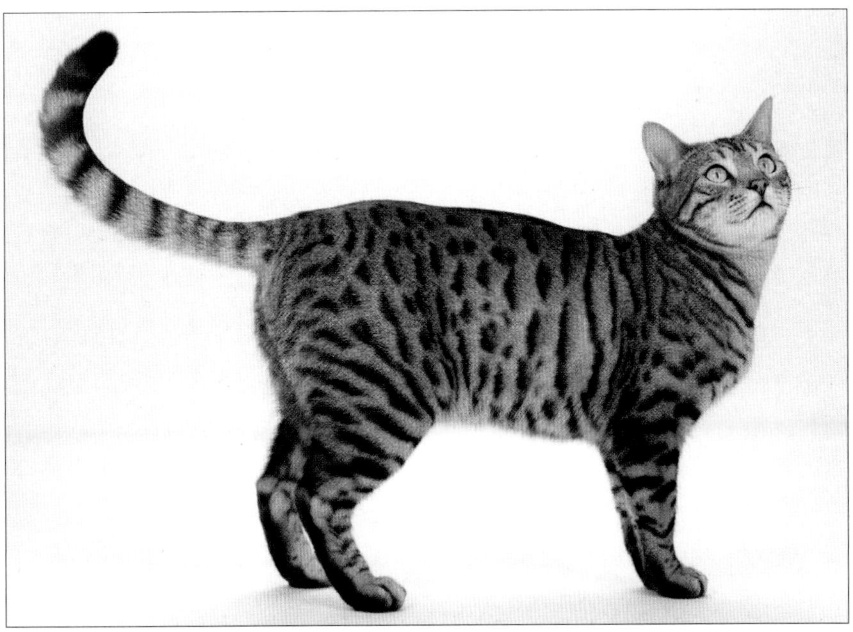

▼ *ANATOMY OF A CAT*

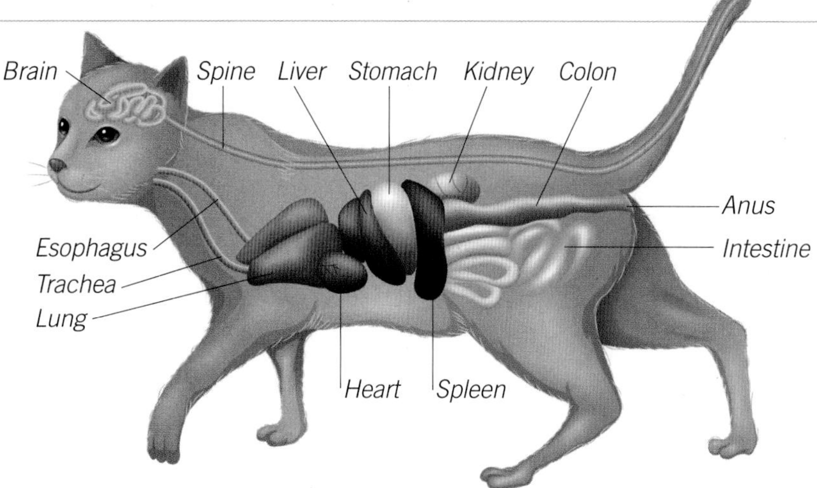

The pads on a cat's paws are full of touch receptors; not only do they communicate how hot or cold a surface is but they can 'feel' the location and speed of prey. The skin of each pad is strong enough to resist damage from most natural terrains. Between each paw pad are glands that secrete an oil that only cats can smell. This is used to mark their territories. When they knead their paws while sitting on an owner's lap they are marking the owner as their territory too. Cats also sweat through their paws and this helps to regulate body temperature. The skin colour of the pads is related to the coat colour. Black cats have black pads, ginger cats have ginger-coloured pads and grey cats have grey pads. Multi-coloured cats often have pads of differing colours.

Cats, wild or domestic, are able to retract their front claws. The exception to this rule is the cheetah which can only partially retract its claws. They share this ability with some of the viverrid family, including the African civet and the genet. This saves on wear and tear and keeps the claws sharp for catching and killing prey. When the cat wants to use its claws, it contracts a tendon that extends them up and out. Claws curve at the ends and this assists in holding prey. The claws grow continuously throughout the cat's life but get worn down and dull over a period of time. When this happens the outer sheath is shed, exposing a new, sharp claw covering beneath.

Like dogs, cats have a small pocket in the side of the ear. This is called the cutaneous marginal pouch or Henry's pocket. No one is quite sure who the Henry in question was or why it got this name. Neither is there any conclusive proof as to what this pocket is for, but it is believed that it may, in some way, enhance a cat's hearing. It is possible that it improves the ability to hear high-frequency sound, but this is not scientifically proven.

▼ *There are five metacarpus bones and fourteen phalanges in a cat's paw. These are some of the smallest bones in the skeleton.*

► *A feline pelvis looks as if it is one bone but in reality it is six bones that are fused together.*

Understanding your cat's anatomy

The cat's skeleton provides support and protection for the vulnerable internal organs. The entire feline skeleton is strong but light, as befits its function as a hunter.

The coat normally comprises a dense, soft undercoat covered by coarser hairs which are known as guardhairs. The density of the fur adds a further level of protection to the skin (epidermis) from which it grows.

Skin consists of many layers of cells. These are constantly reproducing to compensate for the loss caused by sloughing of the cells which die and are shed from the surface as scurf (dander).

Tail Tail bones are joined by a complex machinery of small muscles and tendons, making the tail capable of a great range of movement. This enhances balancing potential and has also developed as a barometer of the cat's emotional state.

Head is that of a typical predator, with a strong skull protecting the brain. It is capable of a wide range of movement due to the very flexible neck.

Eyes Deep, large eye sockets facing forward protect the eyes. Binocular vision gives the depth of focus needed by a hunting animal in order to judge distances accurately.

Ears Large, cup-like outer ears collect a vast range of sound. This is helped by tiny muscles which give the ears great flexibility of movement. The inner ear assists with balance.

Back The back muscles are well developed to allow the cat to carry heavy weights over long distances. The spinal column ranges from the closely positioned bones of the chest to the longer, heavier lumbar vertebrae which support the weight of the body organs.

Pelvis is fused to the vertebrae of the lower back, and these are also linked to the progressively smaller bones of the tail.

Teeth are those of a typical predatory carnivore – canine teeth, or fangs, for killing; incisors for gripping; heavy, sharp molars for chewing and tearing. This process is helped by a very flexible lower jaw arrangement which allows sideways movement so that the tearing process becomes very efficient.

Front legs are capable of some rotation so that the pads can be presented to the face, for use in the washing process.

Paws are long so that the cat actually walks on its fingers and toes which are supported by the sensitive fleshy pads. Claws are capable of being retracted.

Back legs Movement is restricted to backwards and forwards only. The way in which the knee opposes the position of the elbow at the front, allows for the enormous spring which gives the cat the ability to pounce.

The sense of sight

Humans and their feline pets see the world in a different way. The eyes of both have a layer of tissue called the retina which contains photoreceptor cells. These cells convert light into electrical signals which, via nerves, are sent to the brain and are transmitted into images. Photoreceptor cells fall into two categories, rods and cones. Rods make it possible to see at night, peripheral vision and brightness. Cones enable day vision and the ability to see colour. Cats have a high number of rods and many fewer cones. In humans, the reverse is true. So a cat can see much better at night than its owner, while the human can see colours more clearly.

The cat only needs one sixth of the light a human requires to be able to see well. At the back of the retina they have a configuration called the tapetum. This acts as a mirror allowing light to pass through the rods and cones and be redirected back again. It is light hitting the tapetum that makes cats eyes appear reflective in the dark. The distinctive shape of the pupils of a feline also assist in good night vision ability. A cat's pupils are elongated which enables them to open wider and take in more light than the round pupils of a human. In the wild, cats are more active at dawn and dusk. This is termed crepuscular. Good low light vision is vital for cats as most rodents, a large part of their natural diet, are also crepuscular. Rodents are more active at night, making them easier for cats to find and hunt.

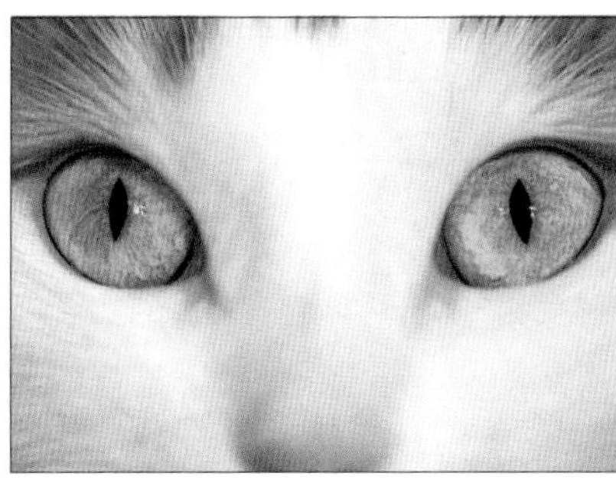

▲ *The pupil is the dark hole in the middle of the eye. It expands or contracts to regulate the amount of light entering the eye.*

▲ *When the pupil is wide open the eyes are termed as dilated. This happens in low light or when the cat is shocked, in pain or excited.*

Cats have a wider field of vision than their owners. They have a peripheral vision of 200 degrees while a human only has that of 180 degrees. Like all predators their eyes face forward and the vision from each eye overlaps that of the other. But the human far outshines the cat in clarity of vision. We can clearly see items up to a hundred metres away but the cat would need to be less than six metres away from the same object to see it as sharply.

For many years it was thought cats could not see in colour, just in black, white and shades of grey. This has subsequently proved to be untrue.

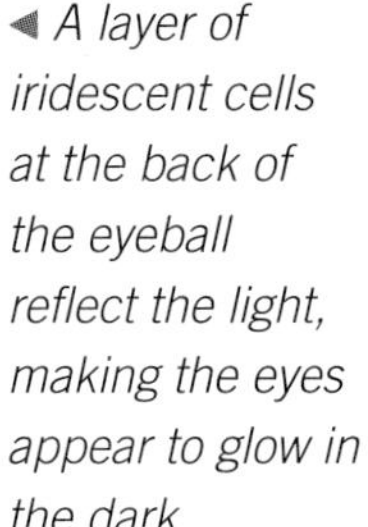

◄ *A layer of iridescent cells at the back of the eyeball reflect the light, making the eyes appear to glow in the dark.*

► *A cat's eyes are extremely delicate and even minor injuries can cause blindness.*

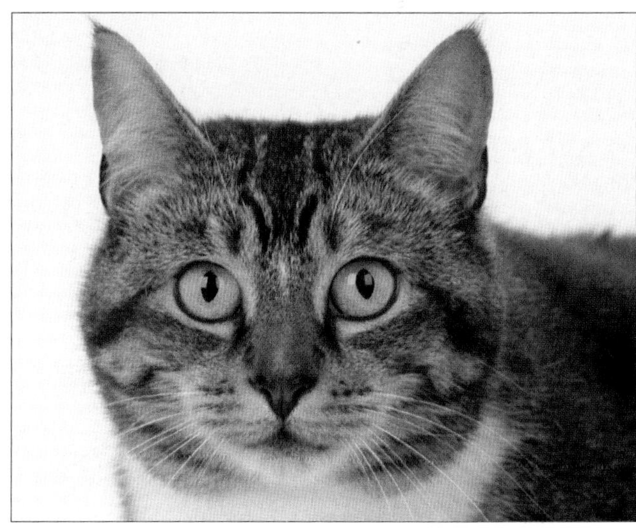

► *A cat's vision is sharpest a metre away from their face.*

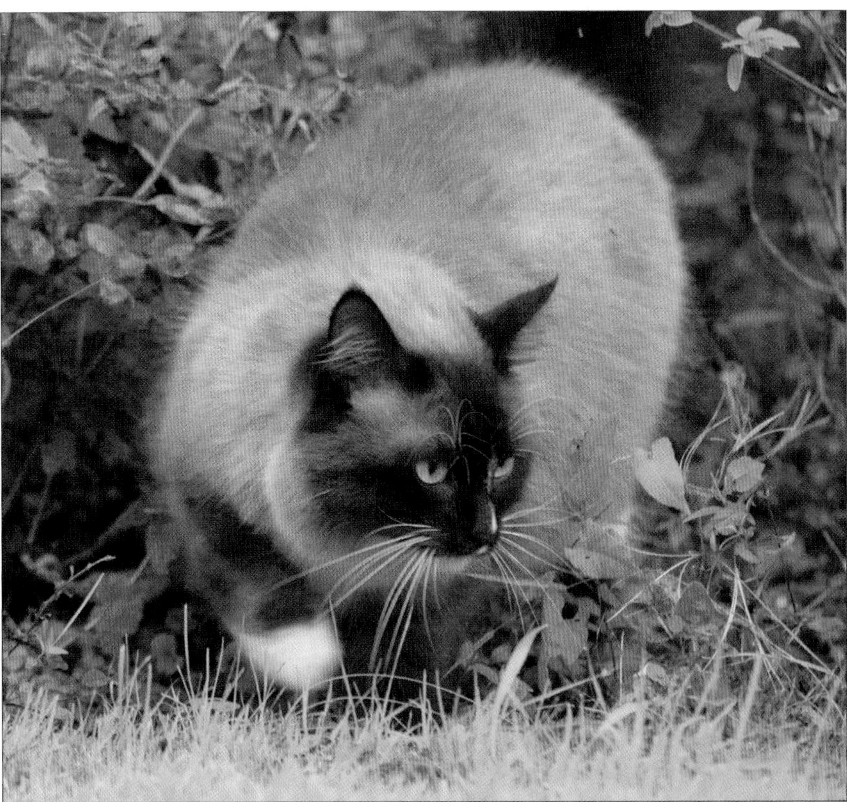

▲ *Blue eye colour is genetically linked to coat colour and is caused by a lack of pigmentation. This is not a cause of blindness.*

Cats do see colour but not the same rainbow range we do. The colour is far more muted and not with the same hue, brilliance or intensity as a human being. They can certainly see blues and greens but vision of red-based colours is similar to that of a person who is colour-blind. It is assumed that reds and pinks look more like a variation of green, while purple would appear as a shade of blue. For an animal that, in the wild at least, would hunt in low light or in the dark, this lack of definition of colour poses no problem.

Cats have a third eyelid, the nictitating membrane, that moves horizontally across the eye from the inner corner to the outer. It is a thin, transparent cover that can be seen when the cat's true eyelids open. This membrane helps to lubricate the eye and remove dust and debris. This removes the need for the cat to constantly blink to flush and clean the eye. Not having to blink is a great asset to a hunter as they never have sight of their prey blocked, not even for a millisecond. The nictitating membrane is sometimes visible when a cat is sleepy and it partially closes across the eye when a cat is ill.

Cats are capable of using their eyes as a method of communication. They are able to 'squint' and do this when expressing the fact that they are happy and content. This is equivalent to a cat smile. Your pet will constrict its pupils to narrow slits when showing aggression or anger. Large dilated pupils often indicate that your pet is excited. If your cat stares at you this could either be a plea for attention, an expression of dominance or an indication of hostility.

▼ *Research conducted by the University of Texas suggests that cats, when shown a picture of their owner, only recognized it 50% of the time.*

The sense of hearing

Cats have the most incredible sense of hearing. They can hear within a range of around 20-6500 hertz. This is 1.6 octaves above a human and 1 octave above a dog. This enables them to hear high-pitched sounds, even that above a dog 'silent' whistle, which humans are unable to register. Not only can they hear sounds we can't but they can receive noise over a greater distance. This can be as much as four to five times further away than for a human.

Hearing is vital for all members of the cat family as it enables them to perceive and pinpoint prey. They can detect tiny variations in sound, as little as one tenth of a tone, which can tell them the type and size of the prey. In a domestic pet this means that they really can recognize the sound of your car and be at the door ready to greet you. They can locate the position that a sound is coming from in about six one-hundredths of a second. This ability is particularly important for wild and feral cats who have to hunt to feed themselves. Feline mothers also have the capability to hear faint cries from their young kittens when they have strayed too far from the nest.

The external ear, or pinna, catches sound and acts as a funnel directing the sound waves into the ear canal. The pinna contains twelve muscles, making them very mobile. Cat ears are able to rotate up to 180 degrees, enabling them to locate the smallest squeak or movement. In addition, they are able to move independently of each other so one ear may be facing forwards while the other is rotated back. When a cat is listening its ears constantly flick backwards and forwards to catch the faintest noise. While they are doing this they are not only hearing but also locating the precise position that the sound is coming from.

The inner ear houses the vestibular apparatus. This is an organ that is responsible for balance. It is made up of chambers and canals filled with tiny hairs, crystals and fluid. As the cat

► *Your pet will turn its head in the direction of a sound and is able to recognize your voice.*

▲ *Cats can hear a mouse squeaking from quite some distance and a cockroach scurrying about inside a wall.*

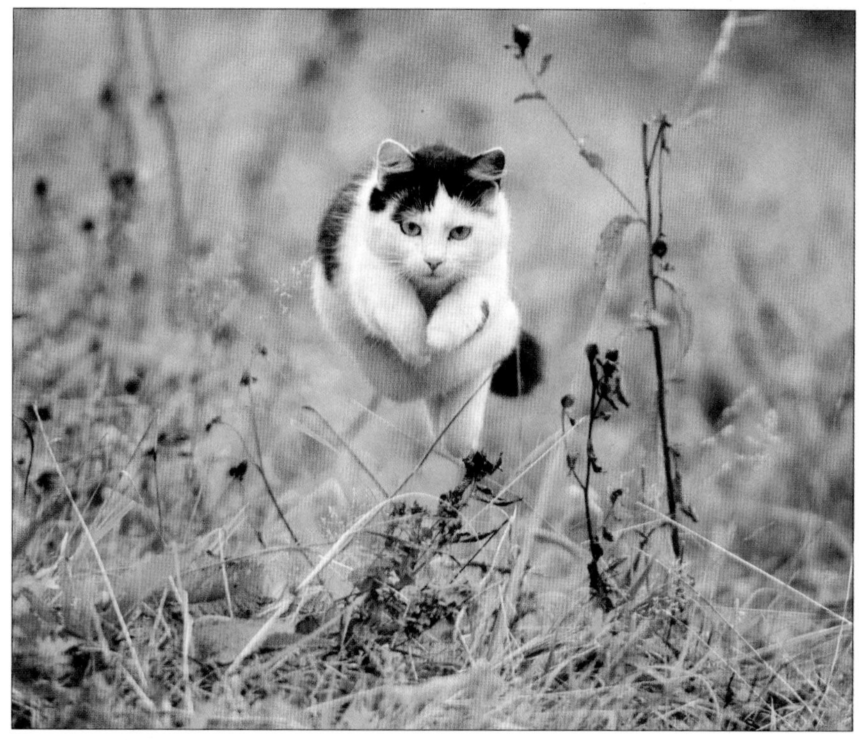

◄ *A cat's enhanced hearing capability is one of the reasons they are such successful hunters.*

▲ *Cats hear a higher frequency than humans and dogs. They really can hear a pin drop.*

▲ *The gene that produces white coat and blue eyes does so by suppressing pigment cells including those in the tissue in the middle ear.*

moves, the levels within the organ tilt, rather like a spirit level, enabling a cat to work out which way is horizontal or vertical. When your pet loses its balance this vital organ kicks in, enabling it to right itself. The vestibular apparatus and the balancing tail are the reason why most cats will land on their feet when they fall.

The cat's hearing ability diminishes when the eardrum starts to thicken with age. This has a catastrophic effect on their hunting ability and also on their recognition of sounds alerting them to danger. Deafness might also be due to outer ear trauma, infection, injury, disease or damage to the inner ear. The latter can be caused by subjection to over-loud noise.

Deafness may be hereditary. This is not necessarily specific to breeds but more likely related to the dominate gene responsible for producing white hair. Incidents of deafness are most commonly seen in white coated cats that have blue eyes. Those that have one blue eye and one of another colour are often deaf in the ear on the blue-eyed side. Owners who believe that they have a deaf cat should check to see if their pet can hear a higher frequency sound like a silent-type dog whistle. Blow the whistle softly from the other side of the room and see if there is any response. However canny cat owners will all be aware that cats only hear what they want to hear and most can be selectively deaf when it suits them. The only way to be sure if there is impaired hearing is to have a veterinary hearing test.

Your pet cat never stops listening; they even scan for sound when they are asleep. This, and the fact that everyday noise sounds louder to them, has implications to the cat in our home. The background radio or television might sound deafening. Try turning the volume down a bit. Music may contain sounds that grate on their hearing. Some fluorescent tubes, computers, laptops and even light dimmer switches admit high frequency noise that may cause some distress.

▼ *The folded ear mutation does not appear to affect hearing and these cats will still swivel their ears in the direction of sound.*

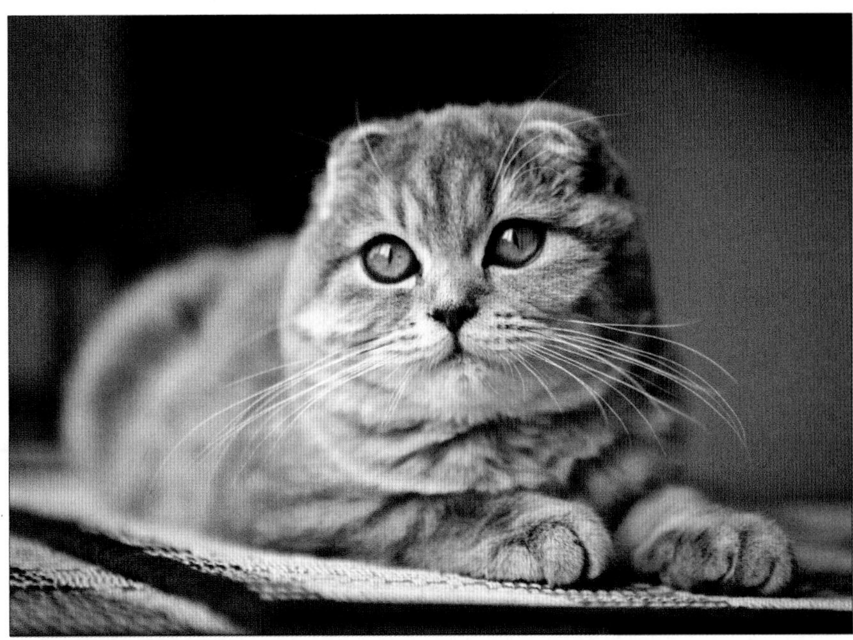

The sense of taste

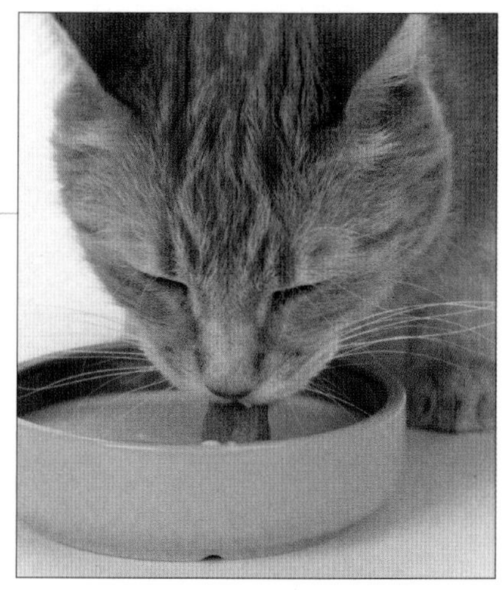

► *Taste buds are located on the tip, round the edges, and at the back of the tongue, leaving the rest of the surface for moving food.*

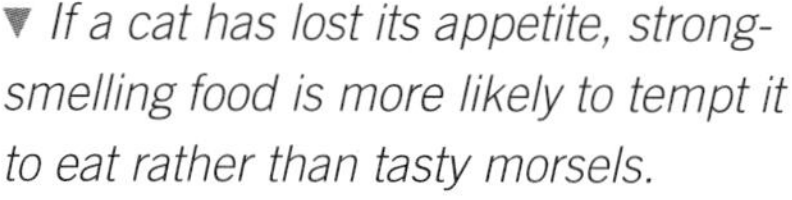

▼ *If a cat has lost its appetite, strong-smelling food is more likely to tempt it to eat rather than tasty morsels.*

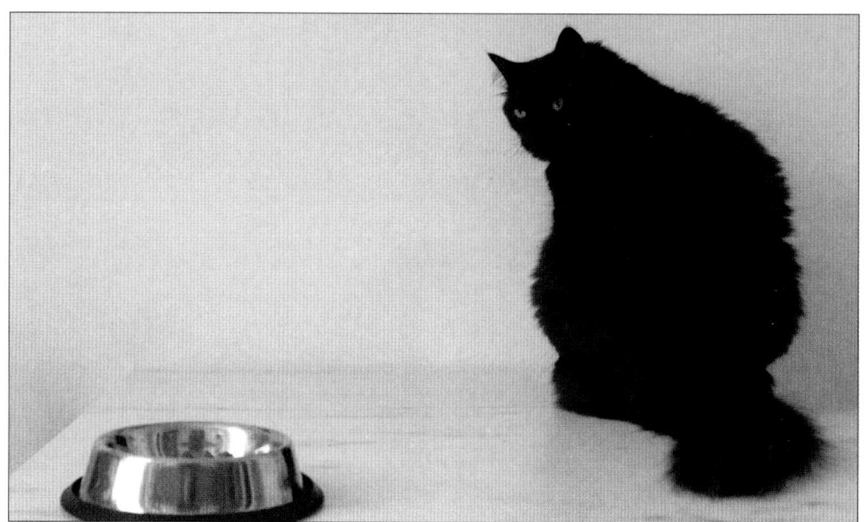

Cats have a very different sense of taste to humans. They are unable to taste some of the flavours that we take for granted. A human has about 9,000 taste buds while a feline only has 473. This apparent deficiency is countered by their superior smell receptors.

Surprisingly, cats cannot taste sweetness. This applies equally from the lion to the domestic tabby. They appear to be the only mammal that lacks this ability. Initially it was thought that all meat eaters didn't have receptors to taste sweetness, but this has been found to be untrue. It seems that cats have been genetically designed not to be able to taste this flavour as they lack the ability to process sugar-forming carbohydrates and sugars. Many cat owners refuse to believe that their pets can't taste sugar because ice-cream and marshmallows are favourite treats that are much relished. In the case of ice-cream what the cat is really tasting is the fat contained in it. A love of marshmallows is harder to explain but it is quite possible that their pet is smelling rather than tasting the sugar.

They do, however, have twelve different receptors in the tongue for tasting bitterness. These act as a natural, built-in defence against eating toxic prey, such as toads. The gall bladder in mammals is very bitter to taste, which is why this small dark organ is always left uneaten when a cat kills a mouse or rat. A cat's dislike to a bitter taste has been exploited by manufacturers of anti-lick products.

Cats can't taste spice but are able to detect salt. Salts are found in blood and therefore in meat. The strongest attraction to our feline pets is the savoury taste of meat. This is termed the umami taste. All cats prefer eating food at the same temperature as their tongue, which leads to the assumption that meat tastes better or stronger when warm. Taste preferences develop when very young. It is interesting to note that a kitten introduced to a range of different tastes at an early age will be a much less finicky eater.

◄ *Studies show that cats may be drawn to texture rather than taste when choosing favourite food.*

The sense of smell

Cats have a much better sense of smell than humans. In fact, it is about fourteen times as strong. They have twice as many smell receptors in their nose and, by comparison, the nasal organ is larger than that of a person. They also have a sensory organ in their mouth called the vomeronasal or Jacobson organ. This organ comprises of two fluid-filled sacs and is located on the roof of the mouth, behind the teeth, and connects directly to the nasal cavity. By drawing air into the mouth past this organ they are able to smell an odour more deeply. When a cat is doing this they partially open their mouths, pull up their upper lip and appear to wrinkle their muzzles and grimace. Opening the mouth enlarges the ducts that connect the Jacobson organ to the nasal cavity. This facial expression is generally thought of as a 'sneer' although some people liken it to a 'smile'. This action is called a 'flehmen response' and is very visual. It is interesting to watch how often your cat does this.

The ability to have a keen sense of smell is very important when hunting – to detect the presence of prey – because a successful kill means food. For the domestic cat smelling food is what tempts it to eat. For all cats the smell of food triggers hunger. In older cats this sense may have diminished so eating can often be encouraged by offering stronger-smelling food. This is a helpful strategy when tempting cats suffering from upper respiratory infections, as this condition will severely curtail the cat's sense of smell. Cats also use smell to assist in navigation and are able to detect the presence of another animal long before they see it, or hours after it has left the area.

In addition, the cat uses its sense of smell to perceive pheromones or sexual odours in the surrounding environment. This is the reason why every tomcat in the neighbourhood knows which house contains a female cat on heat. Male cats will also mark territorial boundaries which are 'sniffed out' by other felines.

▲ *A male cat is able to sniff the sex pheromones produced by a female in heat up to a mile away.*

▲ *Unfamiliar smells in a cat's environment can lead to stress, be it a stranger or a scented cleaning agent.*

► *A cat's sense of smell is the primary way he or she distinguishes friend from foe and recognizes familiar people and objects.*

The sense of touch

▲ *There are approximately twenty-four moveable whiskers on a cat's upper lip plus a few extra ones on the cheeks.*

As cats are not able to see any object directly in front of their faces very well they rely on their whiskers to help provide them with information.

Whiskers are thickened hairs, called vibrissae, and are commonly seen under the chin, above the eyes and on the muzzle. Less noticeable are the tactile hairs present on the jaw line and on the back of the front legs.

All whiskers are embedded deeper into the cat's body than the normal coat hairs. At the base of each whisker is an organ called a proprioceptor, which is able to send information to the nervous system and brain.

The whiskers provide the cat with a variety of information. They assist in helping the cat to judge widths so that, even in the dark, a cat will know if it can fit through a gap. These tactile hairs respond to vibrations in the air helping the feline to track prey when it is hunting. This is particularly important as the cat is nocturnal by nature and needs to be able to hunt in the dark.

Whiskers also send information on distance measurements. This enables a cat to jump from one object to another with ease. It is also the reason why cats are able to leap gracefully onto the narrowest of shelves without knocking anything off it. The whiskers above the eyes cause the cat to blink if they touch anything and so protect the eyes. This is essential to prevent injury if hunting in undergrowth.

Like the coat hair, whiskers grow and shed but should never be cut or trimmed. This is unnecessary and cruel, and can cause pain due to their sensitivity. If the whiskers are clipped not only does the cat lose its 'radar system' but its equilibrium will be drastically affected. They will have difficulty walking in a straight line and may fall over. The cat will become disoriented and unable to work out if it will fit through a gap and possibly get stuck. They will misjudge distances, run into things and be unable to flee from danger.

▲ *Whiskers are more than twice the thickness and root three times deeper in the tissue than normal coat hair.*

◄ *When a cat is interested or engaged in normal daily activity the whiskers pull forward and fan out.*

Do cats have a sixth sense?

For thousands of years cats have been revered, either as gods or evil spirits. They have been accredited with mystical powers and predictive abilities to foresee disasters. Cat owners today give anecdotal evidence of an amazing sixth sense that their pet seems to possess. There is no scientific evidence either positively or negatively to prove that they have an additional sense. But many of a cat's apparent psychic abilities have a natural explanation.

Some owners are sure that cats are able to see ghosts. They certainly can see images that we cannot. Scientists have recently discovered that cats, plus some other mammals, see in ultraviolet light. The lens of a human eye blocks this light but it can travel through a cat's transparent lens so reaching the retina. From there nerves transport signals to the brain to be interpreted. It is known that seeing with ultraviolet light enhances the patterns on flowers for bees and makes urine trails visible to rodents. No one is currently sure how it alters the cat's visual world. But one thing is certain, next time your cat stares and spooks at something invisible to you, it is looking at an image in the natural world as opposed to the spirit world.

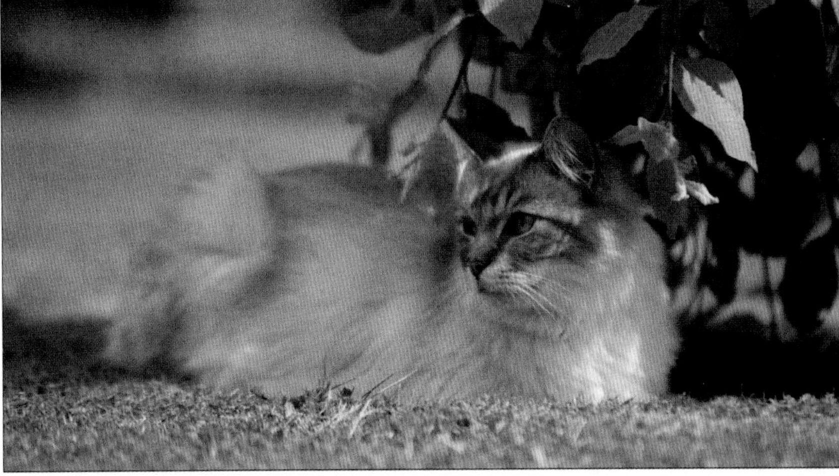

▲ *It is thought that cats can read facial movements, smiles or frowns, and deduce if you are in a good or bad mood.*

▶ *For centuries cats were associated with witchcraft, but their mystic abilities are all based on scientific footings.*

Cats are credited with the ability to sense if a person has a serious illness or is dying. They similarly appear to recognize human pregnancy even in the early stages. It is not a mystic talent but more to do with their sense of taste-smell detecting tiny chemical changes in the human body. This seems to cause them to change their behaviour and become more loving to the person in question.

◀ *The ability to foretell a storm by sensing changes in air pressure made the cat revered by fisherman.*

Much evidence documents cats alerting owners to pending floods, storms and earthquakes. There is a scientific explanation for this. The inner ear of the cat is very sensitive to changes in atmospheric pressure. It is interesting to note that cats often diligently wash behind their ears prior to a thunderstorm. Whiskers and feet also detect the smallest vibration and tremor. Undeniably cats are miraculous but it is due to a remarkable feat of nature as opposed to suspected clairvoyant skills.

BEHAVIOUR AND INTELLIGENCE

The average cat is considered to be fairly intelligent, but compared with dogs its repertoire of party tricks appears paltry. Dogs, as pack animals, will obey understood commands in order to seek the approval of, or a reward from, the owner, who is considered to be the dominant pack leader. The cat is a more solitary animal and may well understand what it is supposed to do but choose not to comply. Possibly this refusal to take part in what they probably consider a pointless task shows a greater intelligence. Without doubt cats are able to problem-solve, communicate their needs, adapt to their environment and interact within a social group. They also have dependable memories, with research showing that they can retain learned information for up to ten years.

◄ *Both child psychologists and feline behaviourists agree that the intelligence of an adult cat is similar to that of a child of two to three years of age. It is a shame that the intellect of our furry friends is sometimes gravely under-estimated.*

The art of communication

What a cat is inclined to do and what it can do are quite different. By nature and inclination, for example, cats move gracefully, daintily and sedately, yet their bodies are designed for speed and movement. When establishing a relationship with your cat, bear in mind that it will do what you ask not because it considers you dominant, but because it feels inclined to do so.

A well-balanced cat is used to being handled by its owner, and is alert, independent and inquisitive. If a cat is timid, dependent and constantly seeking attention, it may have suffered misuse or lack of socialization when it was young (6–16 weeks).

LEARNING FROM YOUR CAT

Communication is a two-way process; if you are alert and observant, you will notice subtle nuances in your cat's voice and body language. Listen to your pet in the context of its activity at the time and you may be able to link certain sounds with meanings such as hunger or contentment. Vocalization and vowel sounds – miaowing – vary from cat to cat. Siamese tend to be very vocal and 'talk' to their owners, other cats speak hardly at all. Purring – which can be done breathing in or out and for remarkably long, unbroken periods – is generally an indication of contentment. Kittens start to purr from approximately one week of age; they purr when they are feeding and their mother knows that all is well. It is believed that each kitten has a distinctive and unique purr so that the queen is able to instantly recognize which of the offspring is communicating. Communication by purring continues into adulthood. Generally assumed to be a sign of pleasure, cats also purr when in pain or are injured. Some scientific studies suggest that the low frequency vibrations produced by a 'purr' may be a natural healing mechanism. It is possible that these vibrations aid healing and strengthening of bones and are nature's way of providing pain relief. The domestic cat and some other species of the Felidae family are unique in their ability to purr. Although lions can make a purr-sounding noise, they and other members of the big cat (Patherinae) family are not able to produce a true purr.

Domestic cats often combine a meow and purr together. This vocalization is called a 'solicitation purr' and is used when a cat wants attention. It is the noise that many cats make when they are asking for food. Many owners will respond rapidly to this sound in the same way that mothers respond to the sound of a baby crying.

► *A well-balanced cat – confident, alert and relaxed.*

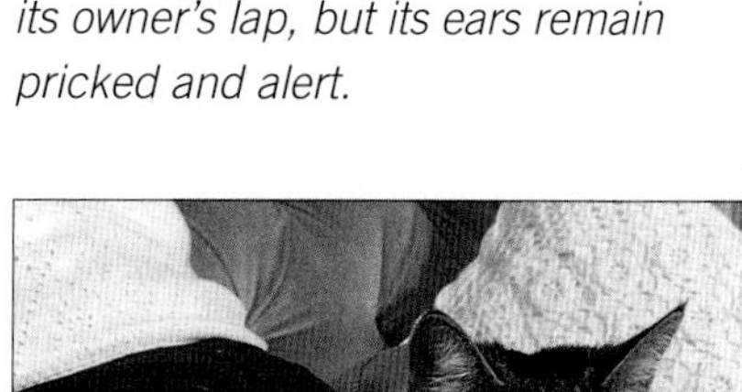

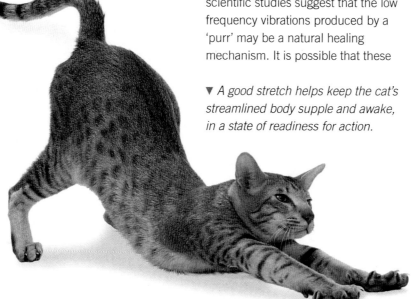

▼ *A cat may be comfortably settled on its owner's lap, but its ears remain pricked and alert.*

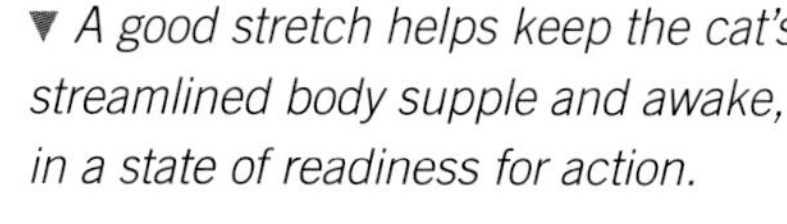

▼ *A good stretch helps keep the cat's streamlined body supple and awake, in a state of readiness for action.*

▲ *Cats have a range of vocal sounds which they use to express their need for food, play, comfort and attention.*

► *Rubbing up against a human's leg is a form of welcoming similar in type to two cats rubbing faces in greeting.*

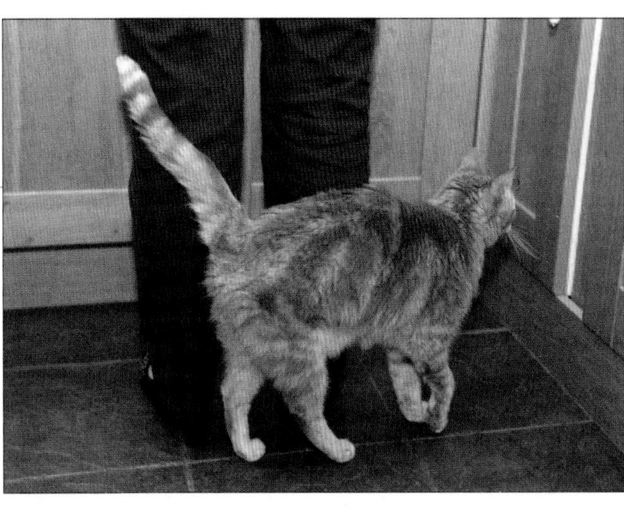

Fear, anger and dissatisfaction are expressed by spits, hisses and snarls. The pitch of a growl drops when a cat is hunting to become a low hypnotic rumbling. Some cats 'chitter' and salivate in anticipation or excitement when they catch sight of something to hunt. Strained, high-intensity yowls are reserved for inter-cat communication, and are especially noticeable in a female on heat.

BODY LANGUAGE

When a cat feels good, its ears are erect and forward-pointing, and its whiskers are relaxed. At rest on a familiar lap, it may purr and 'knead' its paws, opening and closing them. If its whiskers bristle forwards, ears turn back, pupils narrow to slits, and fur, particularly along the spine and tail, stands on end, the cat is spoiling for a fight. The fur extension may be accompanied by an arched back so that the cat looks as big and menacing as possible. Wide eyes and flattened whiskers and ears are signs of fear. Whiskers are highly sensitive organs of touch and cats sometimes use them to make friendly contact with another cat.

Watching a cat's tail will help you to understand its emotions. An anxious cat will either keep their tail completely still or move the tip slowly from side to side. Fearful cats may bring the tail underneath the body or slash it vigorously from side to side. Angry cats hold their tails up in a rigid, stiff manner with the hair fluffed out. If a cat is feeling relaxed or happy the tail is still or held high with a slight curl at the top similar to a question mark. A quivering upright tail is a sign of excitement while a hook at the base of the tail signals defensive aggression.

Sudden licking of the lips, when no food is involved, indicates a stressed or uneasy cat. Excessive grooming, washing or scratching of the body denotes the same emotion.

When assessing a cat's body language, it is important to look at the cat as a whole and not concentrate on just one aspect. All cats express themselves slightly differently and observant owners will soon be able to read their own cat's moods and emotions.

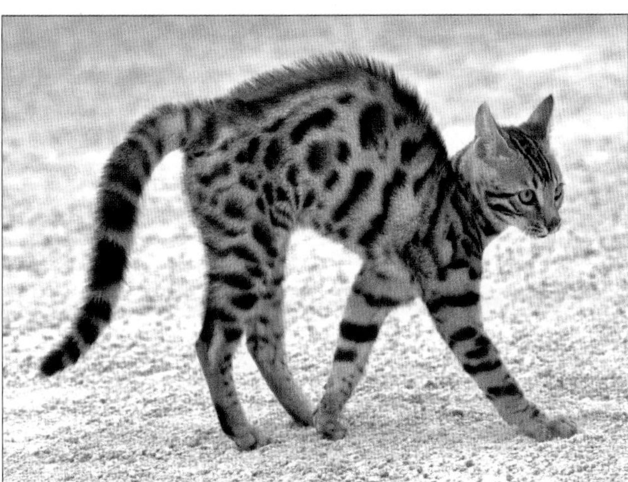

◄ *An arched back with a raised ridge indicates either aggression, stress or fear.*

► *This stance expresses confidence and contentment. A little twitch of a vertical tail means happiness.*

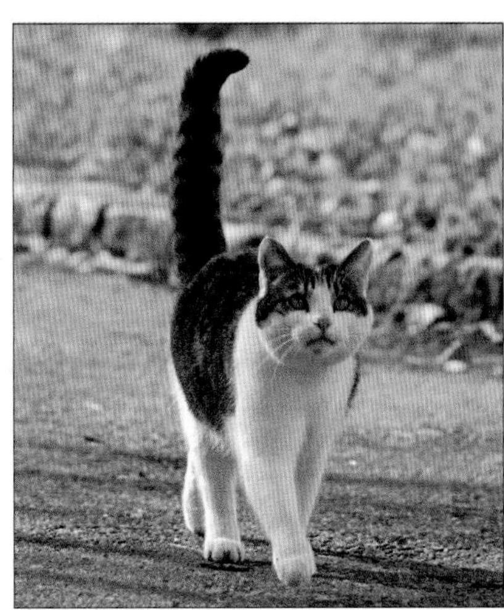

Basic instincts

Cats are nocturnal and may spend up to 16 hours in any one day resting, if not actually asleep. As hunters, they are conserving their energy for the quick bursts of power needed to pursue their targets. Their overwhelming instinct when they go out is to hunt small creatures. This can even be detected in the play of young kittens with toys and leaves. Hearing, sight and smell are geared to the demands of stalking and hunting and these senses are much more acute than they are in humans. Tactile whiskers supplement the other senses, acting as sensors to feel close objects.

Cats are sociable and will establish a relationship with other animals or become part of the neighbourhood cat community if they are allowed outside. This community is hierarchical, with the unneutered (unaltered) males and females reigning supreme, and highly territorial.

Both male and female cats gently assert their territorial rights by rubbing their heads against objects and humans. They leave traces of a scent that is secreted by glands located at various parts of the body, but particularly around the ears, neck and at the back of the head. The scent is also released from between the paw pads when a cat scratches a tree to sharpen its claws.

The most basic of all instincts in animals is that of flight or fight. Cats are no exception. This is a response

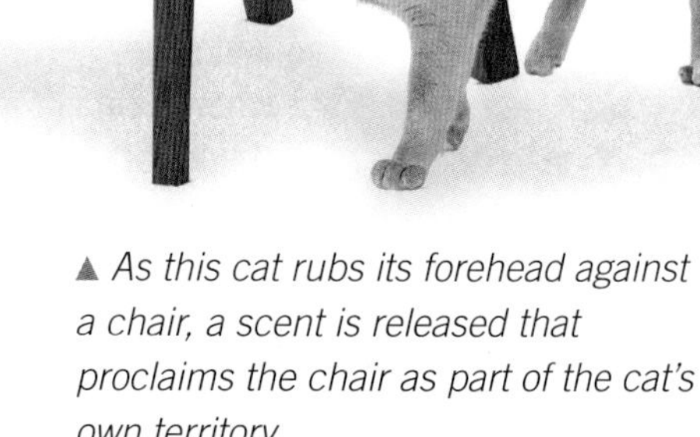

▲ *As this cat rubs its forehead against a chair, a scent is released that proclaims the chair as part of the cat's own territory.*

▲ *At still only a couple of weeks old, this kitten has not begun to acquire trust or domesticated patterns of behaviour; it is still in its feral state, expressing fear and aggression at intruders.*

◄ *A cat pounces. Its specially adapted eyes, with their wide angle of vision, are able to make the most of limited light, enabling a cat to detect the slightest movement in dim light.*

triggered by the adrenal medulla to any situation that could be considered a threat to survival. This action is also called hyperarousal or acute stress response. Physiological changes occur that give the body temporary increased strength and speed to either fight or flee from danger. These changes include diverting blood flow from other parts of the body into the muscles. Blood pressure, heart rate and blood sugars are increased to give the body additional energy. Blood clotting functions speed up so, that in the case of injury, wounds do not bleed excessively. Additional speed and strength is gained from increased muscle tension. When cats are in a state of hyperarousal they will also dilate their pupils and the hair on their bodies will often stand on end to dissipate heat.

It depends on each cat's fear sensitivity threshold as to when this basic instinct is triggered. Actions that individual cats take in a perceived dangerous situation are variable but generally they will only fight if flight is impossible. Owners will know exactly how difficult it is to catch a frightened cat. The ability of the animal to accelerate in speed and perform a complex sequence of turns is truly amazing. Although the flight instinct is a response to fleeing from danger it sometimes appears as if the cat 'runs blind' and puts itself into a more dangerous position, for example in the path of a travelling car. On other occasions the flight seems more calculated, for instance running and climbing a tree away from danger. Only when they are cornered and there is nowhere else to go will a cat normally exhibit signs of aggression.

Occasionally a third option is seen when in a state of hyperarousal, that of freezing. Opinions differ as to the meaning or use of this action. It could be a moment of indecision, a frozen state due to overwhelming fear, or the fact the cat might consider that if it is immobile it is less likely to be seen.

▲ *Due to the positioning of their claws, cats are unable to climb down a tree head first.*

▲ *Kittens love playing and it is a good natural practice for perfecting hunting skills and timing.*

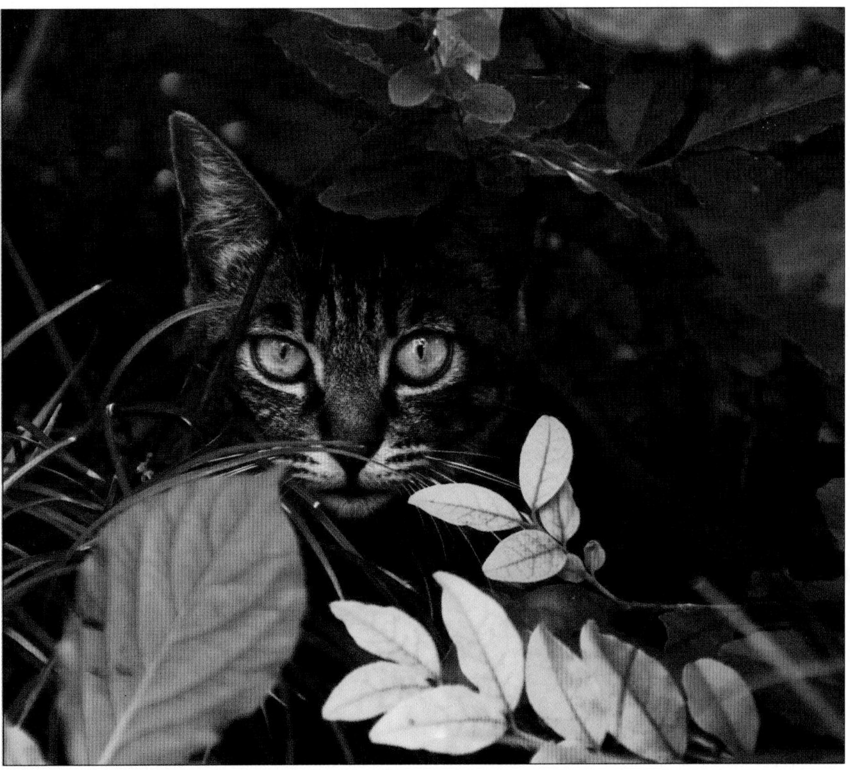

► *Stalking is part of a cat's learned hunting ability. They learn these skills from their mother while still kittens.*

Territorial rights

The cat instinctively carves out a social and hunting territory for itself. This behaviour is most marked in the unneutered (unaltered) male, whose main purpose in life is to pass on his genes to future generations. He may extend his territory to cover an area of as much as 10km (7 miles), maintaining his position in the social hierarchy and priority access to any local females by fighting. His life can be violent and short.

An unneutered female can fight as effectively and as viciously as the tomcat, as she develops and defends her hunting territory. From about four months of age, she periodically attracts all the male cats in the surrounding neighbourhood and will regularly become pregnant.

▲ *A male Burmese goes hunting: it could roam as far as 10km (7 miles) in search of food and female company if it is not neutered.*

▼ *Two cats demonstrate their affection for each other by rubbing their foreheads together. Other signs of friendship may include licking each other or brushing whiskers.*

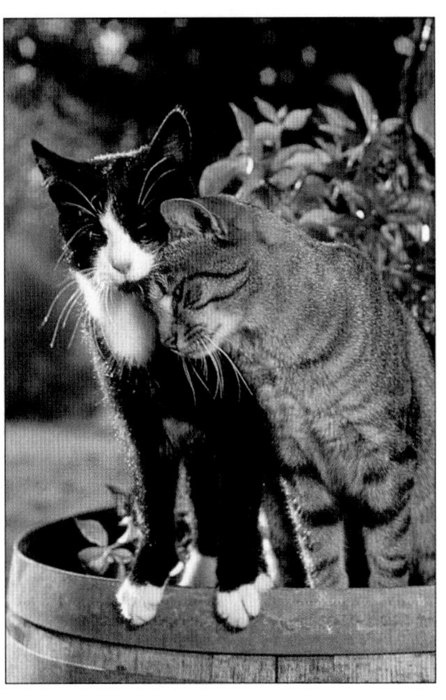

DOMESTIC IMPLICATIONS

For the domestic neutered (altered) cat, its own home and garden are the focal points of its territory. An unneutered cat will extend the area and challenge the neighbourhood cats. Kittens that are brought up together usually co-exist happily unless there are too many cats in the household, which could result in some territorial marking. If an adult cat is introduced into a home where there are cats already, care and sometimes expert guidance is needed. Among neutered cats, territorial rights may be resolved by some violent vocals, body language, and the establishment of non-violent dominance. If the cats are unneutered, it is a different story.

SPRAYING

The cat marks the boundaries of its patch with a spray of concentrated, very strong-smelling urine. It will also do this if it feels threatened or

▲ *A cat sprays to mark the boundaries of what it considers to be its territory. If the cat – whether male or female – has been neutered, the smell is thankfully unlikely to be obvious to humans.*

insecure, for example, if strange visitors or animals come into the house. The most common and the most pungent spraying comes from unneutered males, but unneutered (entire) females spray, especially when they are on heat. Neutered cats also spray, but the odour is less offensive.

In extreme situations, the marking may involve dropping faeces away from litter trays. This is not simply dirty behaviour, but dysfunctional, and the causes must be established. A cat that constantly re-marks its territory is trying to reassure itself that it is worth something. The wise owner checks with the vet for medical advice. Home treatment of attention and affection may solve the problem. If the behaviour continues, you may be referred to an animal behaviourist.

Neutering dramatically reduces a cat's urge to exert territorial rights. Territory becomes confined to an area around the home (although this will still be robustly defended).

▸ *A kitten begins to explore outside, ready to take its place among the local community and hierarchy of cats.*

In a neutered, or castrated, male, the means of producing the hormones that fuel sex drive – the testes – are removed. Castration takes place ideally from four months of age. It is done under general anaesthetic. No stitches are needed, recovery is complete within 24 hours, and there is no discernible traumatic effect on the cat. Long-term, however, the animal's territorial, sexual and hunting behaviours are modified. A female is neutered or spayed by the removal of her ovaries and uterus, or womb, so that she cannot become pregnant. She no longer comes on heat or attracts all the male cats in the area. The operation is ideally carried out from four to five months of age. Once the cat has recovered from the anaesthetic, she is usually fine. Longer-term she may become more friendly and placid than previously. Desexed animals do tend to convert their food more efficiently, and may be less active. If they start to put on weight, some attention to their diet may be necessary.

▲ *Son, aged six months, is keen on keeping close to his mother. The dominant, unneutered female, however, is not always this complacent, and often asserts her independence.*

▼ *Two neutered Burmese, who have known each other since kittenhood, are happy to share their limited territory of house and garden amicably.*

The hunting instinct

The most powerful of all instincts is that of survival. To survive, a cat must eat and so the hunting instinct, that of being able to catch and kill food, is very important. Feral cats rely on their ability to hunt for their very survival. Older or sick members of a feral community will not survive if this ability is impaired. It takes a lot of effort to be able to hunt successfully and this gives meaning to the evolutionary theory of the 'survival of the fittest'.

It is interesting to note that feral cats that are fortunate to be well fed by humans will continue to hunt even though they cannot be hungry. It is untrue that a hungry cat is a better hunter. Some farmers used to believe that if they didn't give their cats much to eat the cats would be more likely to clear the buildings of rats and mice.

Most domestic cats kept as pets do not have to hunt to eat but will continue this activity for fun. This can be seen when watching litters of kittens who will stalk and pounce on items even though they have never seen a prey and are getting all their nutritional requirements from their mother. Kittens will start to stalk objects, and littermates, at around three weeks old and the hunting instinct is well developed by the time they are five weeks of age.

Mothers teach their kittens how to kill prey. In the wild she will bring dead prey back to the nest so that the young learn to identify different quarry

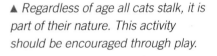

▲ *Regardless of age all cats stalk, it is part of their nature. This activity should be encouraged through play.*

▲ *All cat claws are curved. The ones on the front feet are sharper than those on the back.*

▼ *Cats crouch prior to pouncing upon their prey. They use this time to assess their target.*

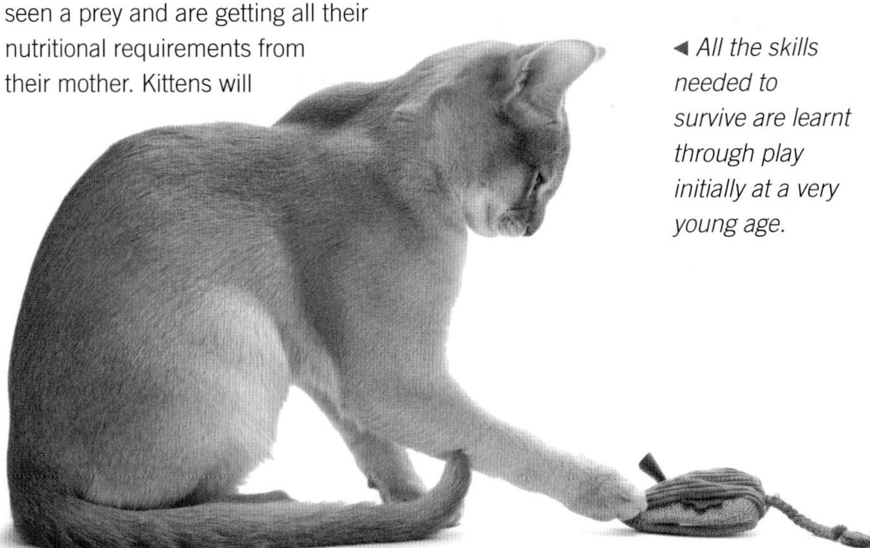

◄ *All the skills needed to survive are learnt through play initially at a very young age.*

by its scent. When the kittens are a little older she will bring back live prey and allow individual members of her litter to make the kill. The more successful the mother is at hunting, the better the hunting abilities of the young. Those with a mother who is a poor hunter, or one that doesn't have the opportunity, can still become proficient hunters. It may take longer to learn and they might not have the special skills that a good predator mother would pass on to them.

Cats kill their prey by biting through the neck and severing the spinal cord. Owners often wonder why cats play with their prey rather than performing a straight kill. This is a case of self-preservation. By throwing or batting the victim about they are likely to injure or disorientate it and so diminish its ability to bite back. A cat has a short face and must put its head close to the victim to deliver a fatal neck bite. If the prey attempts to defend itself the cat risks a potentially dangerous wound to the face or eyes. This can have severe consequences for a feral cat. Cats also use this tactic to tire their prey out so that when they let go of the victim in order to administer the fatal bite it can no longer run away.

Some cats will bring home live prey as gifts for their owners. As felines consider hunting the greatest of fun, they might think that their owner would appreciate the chance to practice their hunting skills too. This is considered the most likely explanation. This behaviour is common in neutered females who have never had kittens to teach hunting techniques to. Other cats prefer to make their own kills within the home. It is thought that this is because the cat is on its home territory and so feels more confident of being able to recapture the victim if it escapes. In both cases, owners will agree that these are the less agreeable aspects of having a cat as a pet.

If watching a bird through a closed window, cats often tense their bodies and make a distinctive sound. This noise is made by chattering the teeth together while admitting a rattling sound in the throat. The sound is very different to a 'chirrup'. This is termed as a 'vacuum reaction'. It is thought that the cat becomes so engrossed in the bird outside that they actually think they are going to kill it. The action of the teeth is the same as required to administer a fatal bite to the neck.

▲ *A good vantage point is advantageous for spotting prey and offers protection to the hunter.*

▲ *Scratching on trees or fences leaves a visible sign, marking territories be it home or in a hunting area.*

▼ *Despite no longer having to hunt for food the domestic cat still enjoys the thrill of the chase.*

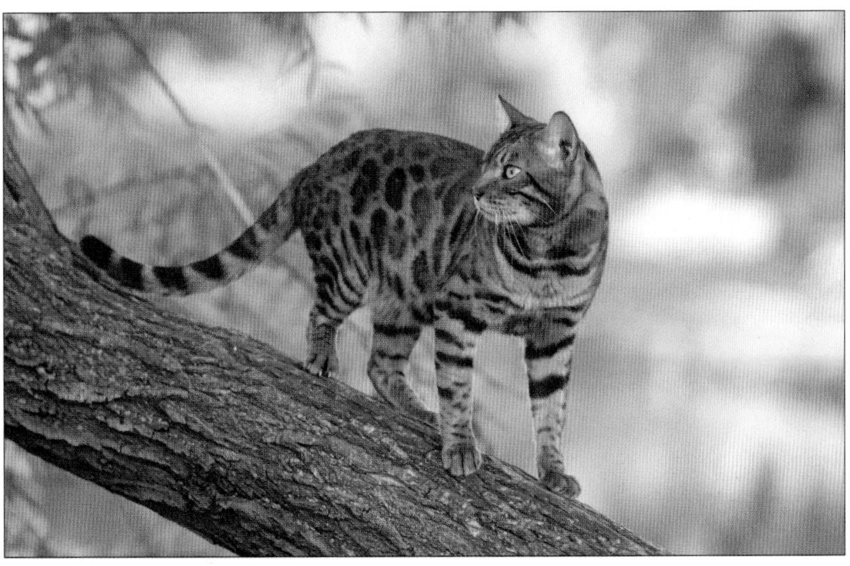

Behavioural problems

It is sometimes difficult to recognize symptoms of stress in the solitary, individualistic feline. Some breeds are more nervous than others. Highly strung Orientals, for example, can react very badly to strange situations, and even the first visit to a cattery may change the personality. Stolid domestic shorthairs may be equally upset, but are more likely to react aggressively – by hissing, scratching and biting. Cats probably show stress to a greater extent than dogs, but the first signs are sometimes too subtle for us to spot.

SYMPTOMS OF STRESS

When feeling vulnerable, a cat withdraws into itself, and cold aloofness is one of the first clues to its condition. A cat about to go into battle tries to appear as large as possible, but in distress it tries to become mouse-sized. Fur is flattened, the tail is curled round and the cat crouches. If the situation continues, the cat starts to shake. Salivation, vomiting and defecation can also be signs of nervousness and tension.

A cat may react actively or passively when it is frightened. Typical, active signs are pupil dilation, arching back, piloerection (the hair stands on end) and hissing. A cat may react to any attempts at reassurance with further aggression.

Passive symptoms of fear are more subtle and harder to detect. The cat may hide or try to appear smaller, placing the ears back and becoming immobile. A timid cat will start at the slightest movement or unexpected noise. This may be because it was abused as a kitten, or simply because it lacked proper socialization. If you breed, it is important to socialize your kittens to prepare them for everyday household life and noise.

DEALING WITH FEAR

Mild fear may be overcome by the owner. A timid cat needs a safe, quiet place to retreat to, such as a covered bed. Avoid forcing your attentions on the cat – wait for it to approach you. Always move slowly, speak to it softly and evenly and keep strangers or strange situations at bay until it has become more confident.

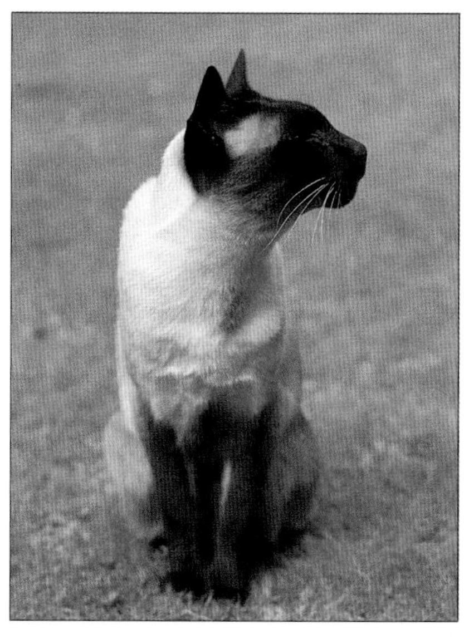

▲ *The areas between a cat's eyes and ears are often more sparsely covered with fur than elsewhere. On this cat, however, the extreme baldness may be a sign of stress and be due to excess rubbing.*

► *An aggressive cat seeing off an unwanted visitor. Neutering makes a cat more placid.*

◄ *A timid cat crouches or hides when feeling threatened by the slightest noise or an unexpected situation.*

▲ *A kitten in listening mode. It is important to talk encouragingly to your pet when it has behaved well, and never shout at it or hit it. A firm, quiet 'no' and a tap on the nose should be sufficient to stop any mischief.*

▲ *Scratching is fun for the kitten, but does not do the soft furnishings much good. Provision of a scratching post and a little training should solve the problem.*

It is important to identify the cause of a cat's fear so that you can deal with it. This may not always be easy, unless it is obvious – a one-off visit to the vet, for example. There may be an ongoing situation, such as mild teasing behaviour by a child, or persistent noise or confinement. Once the cause is established, it must be removed and the cat's confidence regained.

It may be that you can persuade the cat to overcome its fears. Cats have a highly developed flight response and when faced with any threatening situation, such as being trapped in a carrier, their immediate reaction is to try to get away. You may be able to control this with soothing words or by gradually making the cat realize it needn't be afraid by exposing it little and often to the situation.

After an initial shock reaction, cats often settle down in catteries or veterinary hospitals after about 48 hours. If they are handled, however gently, during that time, they may associate the handling with the initial fear and bridle every time anyone approaches to feed them. Left alone, they usually calm down and soon start to make overtures to the very people that they hated the day before.

▼ *Play with your indoor cat as often as you can to ensure it gets enough exercise and attention, or its boredom could turn to destructive tendencies.*

DEALING WITH AGGRESSION

If a cat that is normally calm and well-behaved suddenly starts to scratch and bite, it may be ill, bored or frightened, and the underlying cause should be addressed. It is important to train a kitten from the beginning that aggressive behaviour is unacceptable, even in play. A firm no, immediate cessation of play, and a light tap on the nose whenever it bites or scratches should correct this behaviour. Do remember that a cat likes its independence, and if you impose your attentions on it when it does not want them – for example, if it is asleep – it may react instinctively by attacking you.

Training and learned behaviour

Switched-on, intelligent cats will soon learn to manipulate doting owners. They can also be trained to produce predictable repeatable behaviour. The degree of training depends very much on the amount of time the owner has to spend with the cat. A kitten's play is, in fact, its instinctive means of acquiring hunting and survival skills. Although many hunting actions are instinctive, they are also learned from other cats. Solitary, hand-reared kittens do not learn to hunt.

Each kitten is an individual with a unique temperament and balance of skills. In encouraging and extending a kitten's play, you can observe the strengths and weaknesses in its temperament and skills repertoire. Observing and enhancing natural traits is the secret behind the methods of successful animal trainers. All cats show skill at balancing and spacial awareness, but some are much better than others. A kitten may pick up a piece of crumpled paper and bring it to its owner to be thrown again. You can encourage repetition of this trick with a tasty titbit and pretty soon you will be boasting about your amazing 'retriever' cat!

You can train your cat to conform to certain household standards, using spoken commands which the cat is well able to understand and respond to.

◀ *A Bi-colour Ragdoll kitten has retrieved a toy. It may take it back to its owner for it to be thrown again.*

ESTABLISHING COMMUNICATION

The first step in training is to establish communication between cat and human, and a kitten should be given a name as soon as possible. If an adult cat joins the household, it is advisable to retain its existing name even if you dislike it. If you use the cat's name repeatedly when you are attracting its attention, it will soon learn to respond. From there it is easy for the cat to learn certain command words.

◀ *Each kitten is an individual with its own strengths, weaknesses and special skills. This kitten's speciality seems to be acrobatics.*

▶ *Kittens and young cats enjoy playing hide-and-seek – as long as they are found quickly, congratulated and cuddled.*

◀ *The intelligent cat helps itself to a treat.*

▶ *To dissuade a cat from nibbling your houseplants, provide it with its own pot of cat mint. You could also try wiping the leaves of plants you want to protect with a solution of lemon juice and water.*

▶ *Here's a positive response to an owner's call. From the look of expectancy and the line of the tail, it is probably supper time.*

Repetition of the verbal message, spoken firmly in a low voice, and never shouted, is the key. Avoid shouting, for this can traumatize a cat and lead to behavioural problems.

SAVING THE FURNITURE

A cat scratches a tree – or your furniture – to sharpen its claws, to mark its territory, or just for the satisfying feeling. If you want to conserve your furniture, therefore, provide your cat with a scratching post, and, as an extra incentive, rub some catnip into it. Whenever the cat begins to assault the curtains or the best sofa, say no, gently but firmly, take it to the scratching post, and place its paws on the post. If the cat uses the post, give it some praise and a stroke.

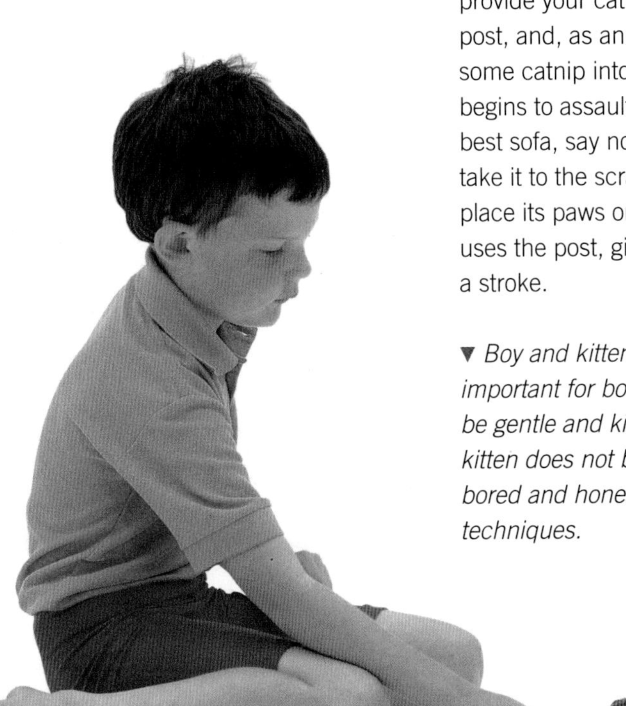

▼ *Boy and kitten play together. This is important for both – the child learns to be gentle and kind to animals. The kitten does not become lonely or bored and hones its hunting techniques.*

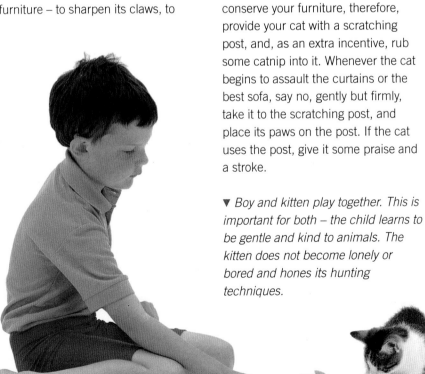

USING THE CAT FLAP

Practice and encouragement is also the key to training a cat to use a cat flap. Make sure the door is at a comfortable height for your cat and that the flap swings easily. Place some tempting food on the far side of the door and gently push the cat through. Then open the flap slightly and call the cat back. Repeat this process a few times and the cat will soon learn to operate the flap itself.

▼ *A cat enjoying the companionship of its young owner. Although independent, most cats are social animals and prefer to have company.*

Teaching your cat simple tricks

Contrary to popular belief it is possible to train cats to do a variety of tricks. Unlike dogs, who generally work for praise, cats need a higher incentive. Food is the key to cat training. Training treats need to be something that your cat really loves, not just their normal biscuit kibble. Try cubes of cooked chicken, small flakes of tuna, prawns or even little dollops of meat-based baby food. Retailers stock a range of premium treats that might appeal to your pet. To keep a cat interested while training alternate the treats that your cat enjoys so that every morsel is a surprise.

Patience and repetition are basic requirements when training any feline. All training sessions should be short, only lasting a few minutes, and be repeated several times a day. Reward for any required behaviour but never punish if your cat fails to perform the requested trick. Only conduct a training session if your cat appears interested; if not it is better to wait and try later on in the day.

▲ *Rewards do not have to be edible; try using toys, cuddles or even a belly rub and see which one works best.*

CLICKER TRAINING

The use of a clicker training aid can be useful. Clickers are small boxes that 'click' when pushed. Every time the cat performs the correct behaviour 'click' and reward with a treat. In time the cat will realise the click means that they have done the right thing and you won't have to use so many treats. Some cats object to the sound of a clicker as it can be over-loud. If this is the case, or you don't have a clicker, try using a pen that clicks the writing nib in and out instead. These are readily available in most homes and have a softer sound. Don't vocally label a trick until the cat has learnt it.

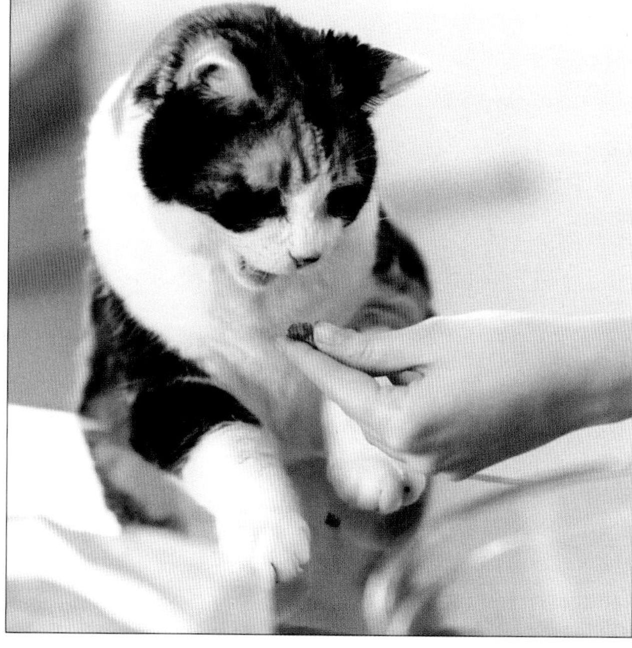

◀ *Take a natural behaviour, name it (for example 'sit pretty'), and reward every time you see it.*

▲ *If your cat is prone to obesity cut treats in half and restrict the amount given for rewards.*

If you ask a cat to 'sit' it will have no idea what you want it to do. It is far better to 'click' and reward the cat when it is sitting. Once the cat has learnt to sit every time treats are about you can then start to introduce a word command.

The best trick to start with is 'come'. Try rattling some treats in your cat's food bowl and call its name. When your pet starts to move towards you click and reward. Let the cat wander away when it has eaten its treat and then repeat the exercise. When the cat comes to you every time you rattle the bowl, even when it is sleeping in the sun, introduce the verbal command and remove the bowl lure. From there it is easy to introduce the 'sit'. When you call your cat only click and reward when it naturally sits in front of you. If you have patience your cat will quickly learn to do this required task. When the cat will sit every time asked, try click and rewarding for a new trick, such as a 'high five' action. Most cats do this when trying to pat you on the leg to gain your attention. This in turn can lead to teaching your cat to beg when both front feet or off the ground.

Don't confuse your cat by trying to teach more than one trick at a time. Only move on to a new exercise when your cat will perform the previous most times that it is asked. Take things slowly and if your cat appears confused you may have rushed the training. Go back a step, reward for required behaviour and then gently try again.

A whole range of tricks can be taught that lead from one to another. It is possible to teach your cat to shake a paw, wave, close doors, retrieve, lie down, stand tall on their hind legs, go over small jumps, run through a tunnel, pat a target, jump through a hoop, give kisses and even play the piano. Detailed instructions for teaching a wide range of tricks can be found on the internet.

Trick training is beneficial to owner and cat alike, regardless of the age of either. It should be considered as a special period to spend time together and increase the feline/human bond. Any cat can learn a new skill but their personality and temperament will decide how quickly, if at all, they take to the task. Be patient!

TEACHING YOUR CAT TO RECALL

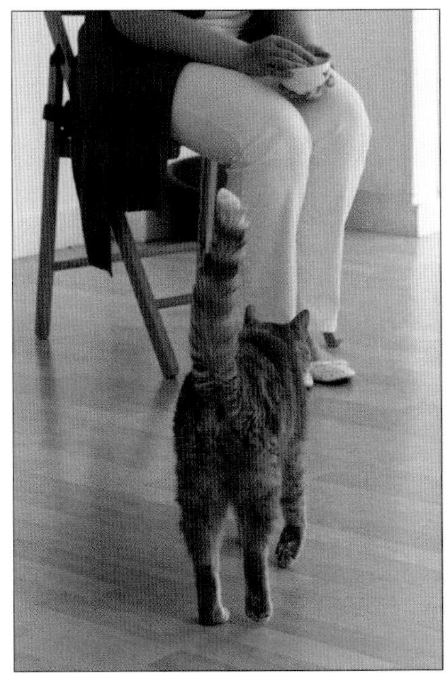

1 Settle down somewhere comfortable and call your cat. Praise him or her as he or she walks towards you.

2 Continue praising him or her, adding in your chosen command, until he or she reaches your side.

3 Reward and wait until he or she wanders off again. Repeat the exercise several times daily.

CHOOSING THE RIGHT CAT

Many households are entirely suitable for a cat, or even a companionable pair of cats, but it is important to consider the effects a cat will have on the household. Although they are known for their independence of character, cats do need care and attention. A normal, healthy cat may live for fourteen years or more, and you need to consider whether you can stand such a long-term responsibility and commitment. Cats may all be roughly the same size and shape, but they vary a great deal in temperament, interests and needs. Before you buy a cat, it is wise to look at your lifestyle and home, and consider the type of cat that will happily fit in with it.

◂ *Before choosing, evaluate the relationship you would like with your cat. Are you looking for a cuddly, placid companion or an active playful pet? These are important considerations.*

Why choose a cat?

The cat's adaptability and independence make it a very practical pet for the modern working household. Cats do not have to be taken for walks; they self-clean and self-exercise. Some can happily adjust to a life spent totally indoors in a high-rise apartment. Depending on their character (and breed type if they are purebred), they can also learn to live with other domestic pets. For many people, though, it is the beauty of the cat that is so alluring. A cat on watch at a window, on the prowl or playing in the garden, or simply as a soothing, sleeping presence, is a graceful and rewarding, easy-care asset to the home and family.

▲ *Cat and bird, as well as dog and cat, are legendary enemies, but it need not be so. Cats can be persuaded to live harmoniously with other domestic pets.*

▼ *A pair of farm kittens look irresistible. They may grow up to be much-loved pets, but will probably also earn their keep as valuable mousers.*

THE RIGHT CAT

The choice of cat depends very much on personal preference for a particular type of cat, for long or short fur, or a particular coat colour and pattern. A major determining factor is how much you want to spend. At the top end of the price scale are cats whose parents and grandparents can be traced through long pedigrees back to the late 1800s. At the other end of the scale are unplanned litters of non-pedigreed cats which may be picked up for free. In between are cross-breeds – a random or deliberate result of a mating between different breeds, or the unplanned mating of one pedigreed partner with a non-pedigree. At a fraction of the cost of a true pedigree, you could have a cat with the aristocratic qualities of its purebred mother and the resilient health of its father, or vice versa.

Size is not an issue. Unlike dogs, domestic cats do not vary greatly in

▼ *A purebred cat with a pedigree will cost considerably more to acquire than a non-pedigreed animal, and caring for it may be a lot more time-consuming.*

► *A stray cat can be adopted for free but they need particularly careful medical attention.*

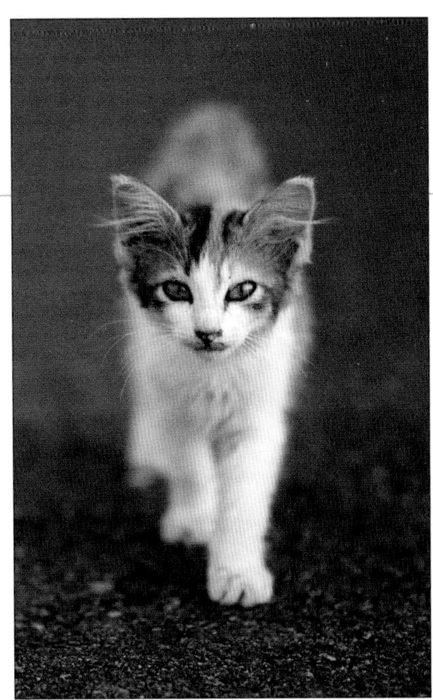

size – there is no feline equivalent of the Great Dane or the tiny Chihuahua. Living-space restrictions do not generally present a problem as cats are very adaptable, wherever they live. Allowances need to be made for some active breeds, but most cats can settle into quite a small apartment as happily as into a large house.

THE PEDIGREE OPTION

Buying a purebred dog from a reputable breeder has long been accepted. However, it is only comparatively recently that interest in pedigreed cats has become established. Until about 30 years ago, there was a scarcity of breeders and, with the exception of Blue Persian and Siamese breeds, pedigreed cats were not readily available. This situation has been radically redressed by the cat fancy (the world of pedigreed cats) being much more active in its publicity. The showing and breeding of cats with a known ancestry has become a popular hobby – both at shows and online – making a much greater range of breeds available.

A key advantage of buying a pedigreed kitten from a reputable breeder is that there are safeguards woven into the transaction.

OFF THE STREETS

Cats that have been abandoned by their owners, or that have been born on the streets, carve a life for themselves as strays. They revert to a feral (wild) state, form colonies with other cats, and breed prolifically. It is perfectly possible to adopt a stray or feral cat you have found on the streets. One might even adopt you. However, they have been exposed to a host of infections and diseases, so thorough medical examination and inoculation is particularly important. You will also need to spend more time with a stray to help it bond with you and adjust to a settled way of life.

▼ *The non-pedigree from a known background is inexpensive and likely to be healthy and of good character.*

Longhair or shorthair?

Having a longhaired cat requires you to set aside some time every day to groom it, to keep the coat free from tangles and matting. At the other extreme, the almost hairless Sphynx cat needs extra care as it is very susceptible to temperature change and skin problems.

If you are living in a hot, humid climate, a longhaired cat (even if it sheds its cold-weather coat) is not a wise choice unless it is to live in an air-conditioned home. The coat of a Sphynx does not adapt at all to climatic changes, and the cat would need to be kept in a centrally heated environment in cold winters.

If you are allergic to cats, it will probably make no difference whether you have a longhair or a shorthair. Most human allergies to cats are due to the proteins in the scurf (dander) or in the dried saliva covering the hair.

► *A sleek Oriental Shorthair with an easy-care coat will need extra grooming from its owner only if it is being prepared for a show – or for pleasure.*

► *The fur of the Devon Rex cat is fine and wavy and can be so delicate in places that it is broken just by the cat's own grooming. Grooming should be with a very soft bristled brush.*

▲ *This Persian cat has a splendid long coat that requires a lot of attention. If it lived in a hot climate, however, it would not develop such a full 'show' coat.*

▼ *The Maine Coon Cat is a breed with a semi-longhaired coat, which will not need as much extra care as the long fur of a Persian cat.*

Fur types
Longhair: Soft guardhairs up to 12.5cm (5in) long
Semi-longhair: Soft guardhairs varying between 5cm (2in) and 10cm (4in) long
Shorthair: Maximum about 5cm (2in) long
Hairless: Suede-like coat with no guardhairs
Curly hair: Short, soft, often delicate fur with rippled effect
Wirehair: Short, bristly coat

Body types
Cobby: Short-legged, stocky body; round, flattish face with small ears, such as the Persian
Muscular: Sturdy, medium to compact build; medium-length legs and tail; round face, medium ears, such as the American Shorthair
Oriental: Long, lithe body; long, slender legs and tail; wedge-shaped face; large, pointed ears, such as the Siamese

Gender and age

▲ *A kitten will adapt to your lifestyle more readily than an older cat, simply because it has not yet fully developed its mature character.*

If cats are neutered (altered), there is little difference in behavioural terms between a male and a female. However, a neutered male may be a little more indolent than a female. If you already have a cat in your home, it may be worth going for the opposite sex in your new cat. The established resident is more likely to defend its territory against a cat of the same sex. Once sexual urges have been quelled by the neutering process, cats are likely to exhibit their true breed characteristics more strongly. The Siamese cat's attachment to its owner is accentuated, for example, and the Persian becomes even more placid.

Male cats are generally larger than females. On average, a full-grown, neutered male cat tends to be a little heavier than an entire male, with an average weight of between 5–7.5kg (10–15lb). Females are usually about 1kg (2.2lb) lighter. The largest pedigreed variety is the Maine Coon Cat from the north-eastern United States. Male Maine Coons have been known to reach about 10–12.5kg (20–25lb) in weight. The smallest, or most dainty breed is the Singapura (the 'drain cat' of Singapore) at about 2.7kg (6lb), but breeders take care to make certain that their cats fall within the minimum weight range to ensure successful breeding.

▲ *Male cats are usually bigger than their female equivalents, although if they have been neutered (altered), they may be a little more indolent.*

CHOOSING AN ADULT CAT

It can be easier to give a new home to an older cat than to a kitten. This is especially so if the cat is obtained from a major welfare source which has carried out rigorous health checks. (With a kitten from a private home, the onus of the initial health checks is usually left to you.) An older animal will be more settled in its ways and certainly have an established temperament. A poor temperament due to the cat coming from an environment where it was unhappy, can improve with changed circumstances, but you do not have the fresh start you would have with a kitten. Male cats that have only recently been neutered (altered) may carry some battle scars from their fighting days, but this is a purely aesthetic consideration.

◄ *Although the Singapura may have evolved into one of the smallest breeds because of its tough background on the streets of Singapore, it is a sturdy animal.*

▼ *Deciding to take in an adult cat that you have found in a cat home may save the animal from being humanely put to sleep, and it will soon learn to be content in its new environment.*

Where to find a healthy kitten

It is essential to choose a healthy kitten. One picked up from the street should be approached with caution.

Despite the pro-neutering campaigns of welfare agencies, unneutered (unaltered) cats do roam freely. This, together with the rapid maturation of the cat, makes it possible for a four-month-old cat to become pregnant, resulting in the next generation. Such kittens may not be physically strong, they may have been separated from their mother too soon, and are unlikely to have had any veterinary attention or inoculations. Diseases such as feline influenza and feline enteritis can strike a very young kitten and kill rapidly. In addition, feline immunodeficient diseases (feline AIDS) may be present.

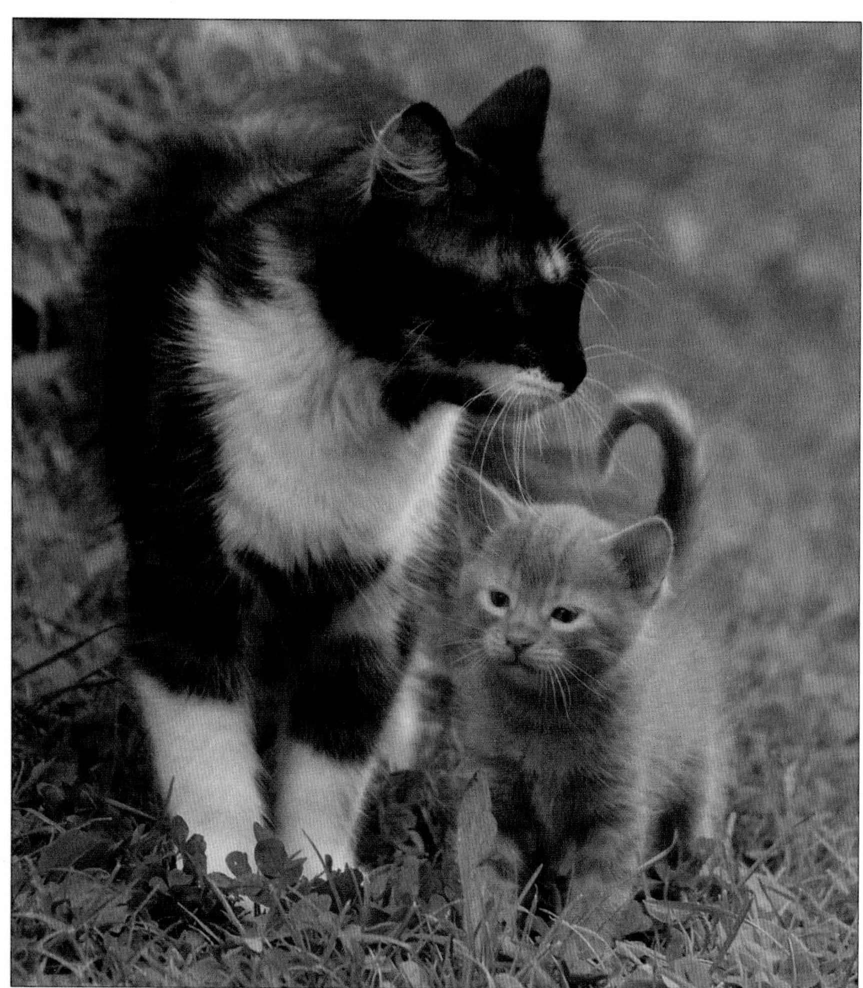

▲ *An attentive mother watches over her kitten. A kitten's strength is largely dependent on the physical wellbeing of his or her mother and her ability to rear the kitten successfully until weaned.*

ACCEPTABLE FREE GIFTS

Some owners allow their cats to have one litter before neutering, and then offer the kittens 'free to a good home'. They may ask searching questions about your ability to look after the kittens well. Take this in good grace, for these are people who want the best for their kittens.

◄ *A kitten is hand-fed using a syringe and a special formula milk, as the mother has either died or is unable to take care of her litter.*

► *The weight of the hand-reared kitten is checked daily. It needs to gain about 9g (⅓oz) a day, and to be kept constantly warm.*

▶ *The last kitten left in a pet shop pen may look appealing, but think carefully before you buy. Will it have picked up parasites from other animals in the shop? Did it have the right medical checks and inoculations before it was put up for sale?*

CAT SHELTER

If you want to give a home to an unwanted cat or kitten, go to a welfare agency or humane society. There are several big, well-known organizations as well as many smaller charities that cater for homeless or unwanted cats.

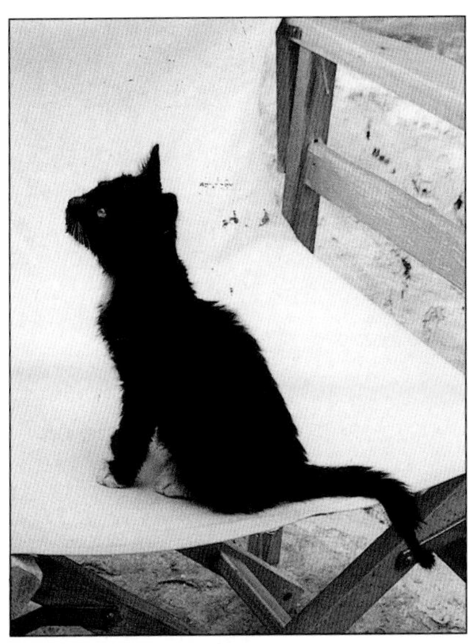

◀ *A tiny stray kitten may not be very strong or healthy as it was probably abandoned by its mother too soon – and the mother herself is unlikely to have been in top condition.*

Cats are not usually released to a new owner until they have been given a veterinary check, but the organization may not have had the time or resources for full investigations. This is particularly the case with feline immunodeficiency disease or feline Aids, the test for which is quite expensive. However, coats are routinely checked for parasites and fungal conditions, and the usual vaccinations are often given.

The main welfare organizations usually do investigate thoroughly, including blood-tests to ensure feline Aids and leukaemia are not present. In addition, once an animal has been chosen, they visit the home of the prospective new owner to ensure that it is suitable. Such attention to detail means that they may charge for the kitten, which may make the potential owner think twice before buying. But whatever the cost, it will certainly be less than the uncertain cost of bringing a stray in dubious condition to peak fitness.

Some pet shops offer kittens for sale only after the necessary veterinary checks and inoculations have been done. However, for the kitten, the stress of leaving its mother, being in the shop, and then being sold on to yet another new environment within a very short time can set them back developmentally. By law in the United Kingdom, kittens must not be sold under six weeks of age. In the United States laws vary about how early kittens can be sold, so check your state's laws. If the kittens appear tiny, it is wise not to purchase.

Where to find a pedigreed cat

Breeders can be found through local newspapers, on social media, as well as various cat breed forums who can advise and inform. Cattery websites are also in abundance and will give you an idea of what is available in your region. Some unscrupulous breeders produce kittens of the most popular breeds purely for profit. They may show little concern for either the future welfare of the offspring, or for the breed as a whole.

A far better idea is to ask at your local veterinary surgery or clinic for information on those in the area who specialize in various breeds. Often, if one breeder has no kittens available at the time you want one, he or she will recommend another. Some breeders operate on a large scale and have big catteries, while others are 'front parlour' breeders, who may be interested in breeding from just one pet queen. Either can be a good source; the best way to find out about them is by recommendation via a vet or a local breed club. It is also valuable to visit cat shows well before you actually buy. Here you will find enthusiastic owners and breeders who will explain the advantages and disadvantages of their favourite breeds and let you know of available stock. Find out about cat shows from one of the specialist cat magazines.

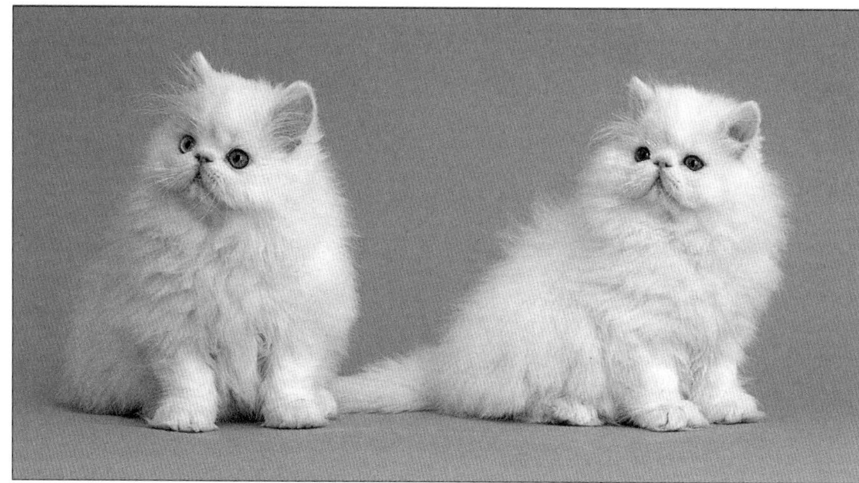

▲ *The charms of a pedigreed kitten are displayed by these two White Persians.*

▼ *The Supreme Show is where you can see the best examples of all the pedigreed breeds in the United Kingdom. There are cat shows in most countries at breed club, local and national levels.*

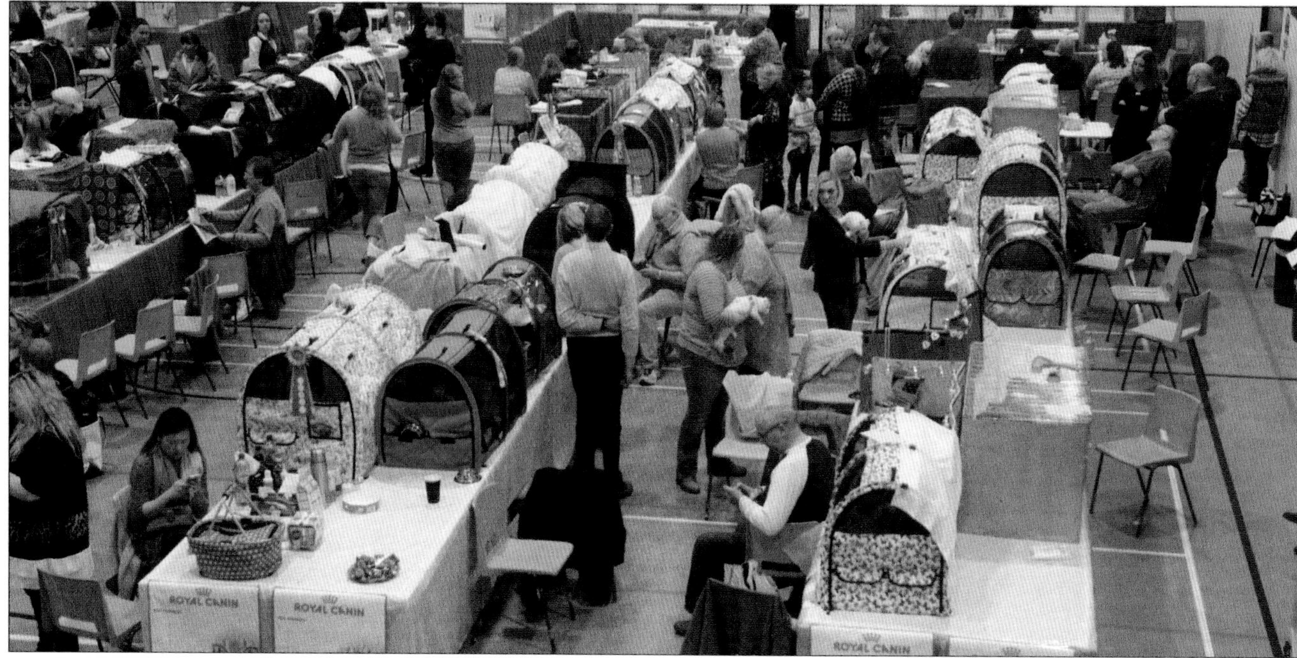

Visiting the breeder

Some breeders house their animals in an outside cattery, others within their homes. A reputable breeder will not hesitate to allow a prospective owner to visit. The advantage of the house-reared litter is that the kittens are socialized earlier. They have greater contact with day-to-day noise, humans and perhaps other animals such as dogs. On the other hand, the disinfection and restricted contact routine of a first-rate cattery reduces the risk of disease and infection. Kittens from a good cattery will be handled and socialized, but this process cannot be as complete as if they were raised within the home. Beware of the unscrupulous cattery owner rearing kittens solely for financial gain. Conditions can often be substandard.

Usually, you need to make an appointment to see and select from a litter of kittens, but it is also possible to book a kitten in advance of delivery if you are drawn to a particular cat. By visiting the breeder, you can assess the general environment and conditions in which the kittens have been brought up in the first few vital weeks of their lives. If you ask the right questions and see the rest of the litter, the mother, and possibly the father, you will be able to build up a complete picture of the kitten's heritage – its breeding line; how long its relatives have lived; how big it is likely to grow; what it will look like as an adult. In addition, you can lay the foundations of an ongoing relationship with the breeder, who, if reputable, will be able to advise and help in the future.

A pedigreed kitten will not usually leave its breeder's home until it is twelve to fourteen weeks old. By this time it should be properly house-trained, inoculated and used to being handled. If it has been brought up in a family environment, it may already be happy with dogs and children. But if it has not been in an ideal environment, it may have difficulties bonding with a new owner. In this case (and with a non-pedigreed kitten only) it may adapt more easily if it is taken away at seven or eight weeks.

A kitten ready for handing over to a new owner should have been gently weaned and introduced to a suitable diet of fresh, canned and dry foods. It should have been registered with one or more of the many registering bodies worldwide, and the registration documents and pedigree should be ready to take away. There may also be a health insurance policy that lasts approximately six weeks – enough time to let the new kitten settle into its new home.

The cost of a pedigreed kitten depends very much on the breed; seek guidelines from the individual breed clubs. It is possible to spend a great deal of money on rare, new varieties while the well-established, popular varieties are less expensive. Kittens that are of show quality are priced more highly than those of lesser quality.

▼ *Kittens being prepared to leave their breeders for a new home. If they have become used to a friendly family environment from birth, they should settle down quickly.*

Selecting a healthy animal

A kitten from a responsible breeder will have had trips to the vet for inoculations against cat flu, feline infectious enteritis, and possibly chlamydia and feline leukaemia. It will have been wormed and its coat will be free from parasites (such as fleas) and fungal lesions (ringworm).

The queen passes on natural immunity to the diseases to which she is herself immune, through colostrum (first milk) during the kitten's first few days of life. This immunity is effective until the kitten is six to ten weeks of age, when it must be replaced by the artificially acquired immunity provided by inoculations. Before the age of eight or nine weeks, it is best not to interfere with the immunity acquired from the mother.

It is not advisable to take the kitten home before inoculations start if you have other cats. They might be carriers of feline diseases to which the mother of the kitten is not immune and against which, therefore, the kitten has no protection. The certificate from the vet confirming first or complete vaccination carries with it the important implication that the cat is in good health – otherwise the inoculation would not have been administered (see pages 172–73).

▲ *You may be tempted to buy both of these kittens. They have grown up together so are likely to be friendly and will enjoy playing together. Make sure both are neutered, however.*

▼ *At nine weeks old these non-pedigreed kittens could be taken from their birth home. However, some cat associations recommend they are left until 12 weeks, after the first vaccination course has finished.*

WHAT TO LOOK FOR

The prospective owner can make his or her own immediate checks when selecting a kitten. If you are able to view the entire litter, look for the individuals with evenness of growth and solidity of muscle tone. Male kittens may already be showing a larger skeletal frame than the females. The kittens will be heavy for their size, and their spines should be well-fleshed and not feel ridged and bony.

If you see the litter shortly after feeding, the kittens will probably be sleepy, but if they are inclined to play,

▲ *This Chocolate Silver Tabby Ocicat not only has fine tabby markings, but his clear, bright eyes suggest he is in peak health.*

you can assess sociability. Frightened, unsociable kittens rush to hide and show fear and displeasure with trembling, bad language or claws – or maybe all three at once! The sociable but sleepy kitten purrs and almost certainly demands that its tummy is tickled. The playful kitten in good health has stamina and a spring in its step. It is alert and may already be displaying intelligence and leadership in play. Rather than you doing the choosing, a particular kitten may choose you, inviting you to play with it, and possibly ending up going to sleep on your lap.

The kitten's nose leather should be naturally slightly warm and a little damp. It should not be hot and dry, or have any discoloured discharge from the nostrils. Breathing should be deep and natural with no rasping or snorting. Eyes should be clean and bright with no discharge, tears, staining or redness. The mouth should show nice light-pink gums with no furring to the tongue or ulceration. Ears should be clean and free of wax.

COAT INDICATORS

Clean kitten fur has a lively feel with a warm, naturally wholesome scent, with no evidence of parasites, rough patches or lesions. The most common ectoparasite is the flea, which leaves gritty, granular droppings. Typical sites for these droppings are just above the base of the tail, between the shoulder blades, under the chin and in the armpits. Excessive infestation of fleas may cause a lack of liveliness, and also indicate that the animal may be worm-infested.

Signs of worm infestation are commonly a staring, harsh coat and a bloated abdomen. In severe cases, the kitten may show signs of anaemia and diarrhoea. Check under the tail for staining or signs of soreness, which indicate diarrhoea.

CHECKING AN ADULT CAT

The health check for the older cat is much the same. You need to check that male cats have been neutered (altered). If this has happened recently, they may show some battle scars, but this will only affect their appearance. The most likely place for wear and tear to show is in the mouth. Teeth may be missing or broken, and the gums may show signs of disease, but this can be treated by your vet, who may advise home dental care.

Whatever the age of the kitten or older cat you are thinking of buying, however sweet and charming it is, if you have any doubts about its health, and especially if you have other cats, do not take it home with you.

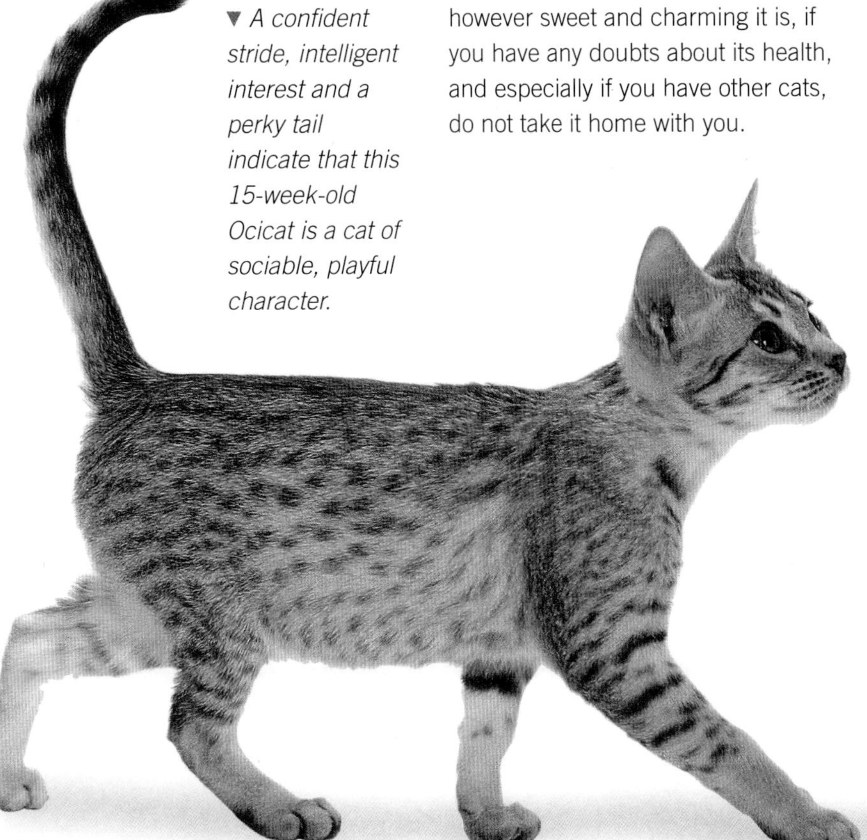

▼ *A confident stride, intelligent interest and a perky tail indicate that this 15-week-old Ocicat is a cat of sociable, playful character.*

CREATING THE RIGHT ENVIRONMENT

The domestic life is one in which a pet cat can feel secure in the knowledge of where the next meal is coming from. If you also provide an exciting and stimulating environment in which it can rest comfortably and where there are opportunities to climb and play, your cat will be a well-adjusted and rewarding companion. The financial outlay of buying the right equipment for your cat may seem high, but it is the first step in ensuring it leads a contented life. Buying the best you can afford is wise as quality products will last longer and not need replacing as often. Check that more expensive items such as self-cleaning litter trays, trackers and electronic equipment have satisfactory guarantees before parting with your money. Excellent buys can be found online as well as in your local pet store.

◄ *When preparing a safe and secure home for your cat, remember the most important thing to provide is love, and there is no price on that.*

Settling in

Acquiring a cat should not be decided on a whim but with an awareness of the animal's continuing needs throughout its life in your home. Thoughtful preparation and planning before a new cat arrives is essential if the transition between old home and new is to be stress-free for both you and your pet. A cat needs time and space in which to adjust, and will settle down more easily, too, if all the right equipment is there when it first arrives.

FORWARD PLANNING

This will be a new and strange environment for your cat, so before you collect it, check its diet with the breeder or cattery so that you know what it likes to eat and drink and can have some food ready.

The journey itself may be the first time in a kitten's short life that it has no other feline company. Even an older cat can be disorientated. While travelling, talk to the animal in a calm voice. Do not be tempted to let it out of its carrier (in a car, for example) unless you have a companion with you who can restrain it.

▲ *The first sortie in the new home. The cage should be kept to hand so that the kittens can be put back in it until they become used to their new environment, and any other animals in the home can be surveyed from the safety of the pen.*

▼ *A young ginger cat has settled happily in the cat basket. A favourite blanket brought with it from its first home is an additional comfort.*

▼ *A Siamese half-breed kitten explores the new home. It is important to let kittens explore in their own time, but supervision is advisable in case they become stuck or locked in a cupboard.*

Equipment checklist

Not all the following are essential; those that are, are in heavy type.

- **Bed and bedding**
- **Litter and litter tray**
- **2 food bowls**
- **Water bowl**
- **Carrier**
- Collar
- Harness and lead
- Identity tag
- Cat flap

THE ARRIVAL

A new arrival is a novelty and family and friends will want to be introduced, to stroke and play with the cat, especially if it is a kitten. This exciting time makes particular demands on children who, without realizing the implications, may treat the new animal

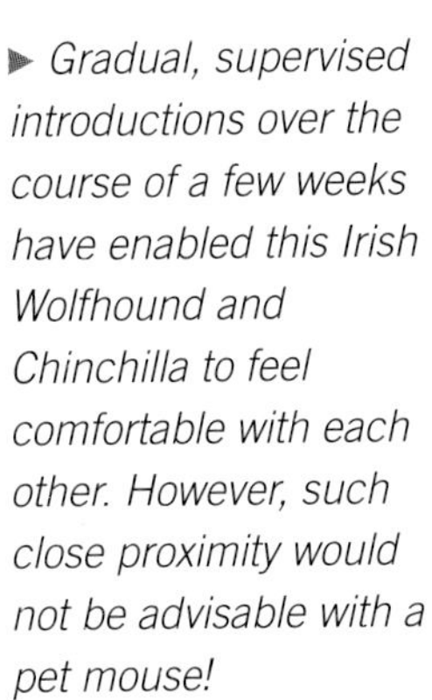

▶ *Gradual, supervised introductions over the course of a few weeks have enabled this Irish Wolfhound and Chinchilla to feel comfortable with each other. However, such close proximity would not be advisable with a pet mouse!*

like a toy. However, try to make sure there are not many people around when the new arrival is introduced. It is tempting to rush straight into the living room and let the cat out of the carrier. Instead, take it immediately to where its litter tray, sleeping space, food and water bowls are going to be permanently positioned. Such items are part of a familiar routine, which will be comforting. A drink and a little food may be all that is wanted.

EXTENDING TERRITORY

A kitten will want to explore and take in all the sensory experiences of this new environment. It must be allowed to do this in its own time, and if that means that it wants to scurry about under a kitchen cupboard, out of sight, so be it. Eventually it will emerge and continue its exploration. Allow the kitten to do this at leisure. However, supervision is wise, in case it becomes locked in a cupboard or stuck on a high shelf. Handle the cat calmly and gently. Over-enthusiastic handling can be very disorientating and may bring out the defence mechanisms. Being bitten or scratched does not endear anyone to a new pet, but from the kitten's point of view it was probably justified. By all means stroke the cat as it passes and talk to it. The reassurance of the human voice helps bridge the gap between old and new homes. When a new cat is tired, it will probably find its bed on its own and it should be left to sleep undisturbed. Cats and kittens sleep more than any other mammal on a daily basis and, for a kitten, adequate sleep maintains and encourages the assimilation of food and enhances regular growth.

If you already have another cat or a dog, confine the new arrival to a small area at first – or even a cage – so that it can get used to where its food, water and litter are in peace, and the animals can adjust to one another in their own time. A cage in the kitchen or living room will provide security for the new arrival and quickly allow it to adjust to any other animals in the household and vice versa.

If you have a baby in the house, it is a good idea to put a cat net over the pram or cot. A cat is unlikely to harm the baby, but could be attracted to a warm, sleeping body and may want to curl up alongside it.

▼ *Kittens will quickly seek out the most comfortable places to relax; if you do not want them in your bed, you need to keep the door shut!*

Handling and holding your cat

If you watch a mother cat, you will see how she picks up a tiny kitten by taking hold of the loose skin at the back of the neck and gently lifting. The kitten then demonstrates one of its inborn reflexes, which is to curl up into an apparently lifeless ball. It will not move until its mother puts it down. This loose skin, which becomes far less apparent as the kitten grows, is the scruff or nape. The action of picking up a cat in such a way is called scruffing. While it is possible to lift your cat in this way, scruffing should normally only be considered if absolutely necessary – if instant control is required, for example, when the cat is at the veterinary surgery. For less flexible adult cats, it can be an unnerving experience, particularly as they freeze when scruffed.

It is far better to pick up your kitten or cat by placing one hand under the chest, supporting the backside with the other hand and then lifting. In this way the animal feels completely secure, with no limbs left dangling. This total support technique is essential if you are holding the cat for any length of time. As you and your cat become more confident, you can try different holds. Avoid tucking the cat under your arm with its body, back legs and tail dangling like a ragdoll. This leaves most of its weight unsupported and puts a great strain on the internal organs. Many cats do not like being held for too long, and should be gently let down if they start to wriggle.

It is important not to throw or drop your cat to the ground if it starts to

◀ *An established resident cat has soon become accustomed to a new arrival, and the two now provide extra warmth for each other.*

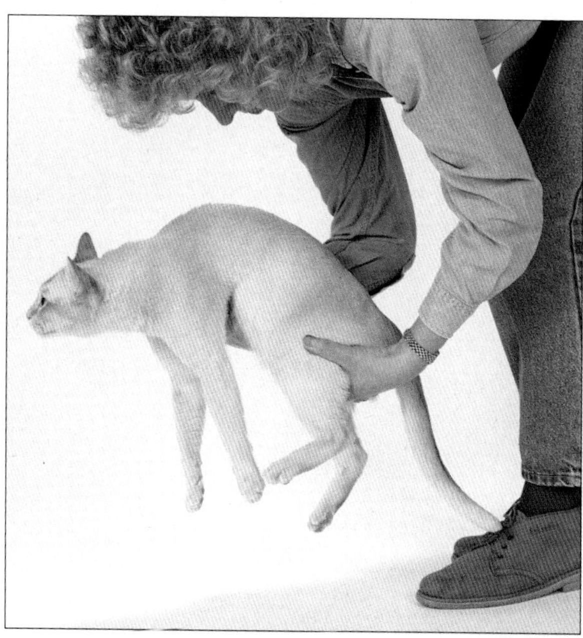

◀ *Avoid surprising the cat when you are about to lift it. When it is relaxed, support the top of the hind legs with one hand and the chest with the other.*

▶ *When holding a cat, keep the back end and legs supported. If the cat starts to wriggle, let it down gently; never force it to be held against its will, unless it is necessary.*

◄ *Avoid having your face too close to a nervous cat when you pick it up and don't clasp it tightly to your body.*

struggle as it may lose its balance and land awkwardly. Slowly lower it down so that all four feet are on the floor before releasing it. This is not possible if your cat decides to jump. Be prepared for this, don't try to grab at it, and step away quietly so not to cause additional distress.

Children need to be taught how to correctly handle cats as they are inclined to grasp and pull at them. Depending on their age it may be best to instruct very young children that the cat should not be picked up at all but just gently stroked while on the floor. As little ones love cuddling cats, providing your pet is placid, the cat can be placed on the lap while the child is sitting down. Tell them that they must not hug the cat too tightly. All children must be supervised while holding or playing with a cat.

There is controversy as to whether a cat should be approached from the front or the side prior to picking it up. Advocates for approaching from the front consider this best as the cat can clearly see you coming and guess at your intent. Those that prefer the side approach think that approaching from the front can be viewed as threatening. Never approach a cat from the rear as this will definitely startle even the most relaxed cat.

Cats that don't like being picked up often have had a frightening experience that makes them nervous. Alternatively, they may not have had much contact with humans when they were kittens. Take time to build up trust and increase the bond between owner and feline. Stroke them first and talk quietly so they are not taken by surprise. Try gently holding a paw for just a few seconds and then reward with treats. Teach your pet that having all the parts of its body handled is pleasant before you attempt to pick it up. This may take weeks or even months but is worth the effort.

◄ *Talk gently to the cat to reassure it and don't hold it for too long until it gets used to the experience.*

► *This cat is now totally relaxed while being held and is clearly enjoying the experience, and tummy rubs.*

Beds and bedding

During the initial settling-in period, a new kitten or cat should be able to settle down within easy reach of both litter tray and water. A simple cardboard box placed in a draught-proof spot with an old pillow and blanket is ideal. Then, if there are accidents, or if the cat's bedding becomes parasite-infested, everything can be burnt and little is lost.

Acrylic bedding is widely available, hygienic and easily laundered. Woollen materials, particularly if knitted, are not suitable as claws may become caught. Some cats seem also to be addicted to sucking wool and chewing soft materials and this can cause congestion in the throat or digestive system.

Once the new arrival has settled in, you may want to provide a permanent bed. This can be made of wicker, moulded plastic or padded fabric, but it must be easy to wash and disinfect. Any bedding should be changed regularly. Very soon a collection of cushion beds, old jumpers, carpet-covered houses and other oddities will be adopted. Place these strategically where the cat likes to sleep at different times of the day.

▲ *A cat is not fussy about the design of its bed. The advantage of a cardboard box is that if it becomes soiled or worn out, it can be easily replaced.*

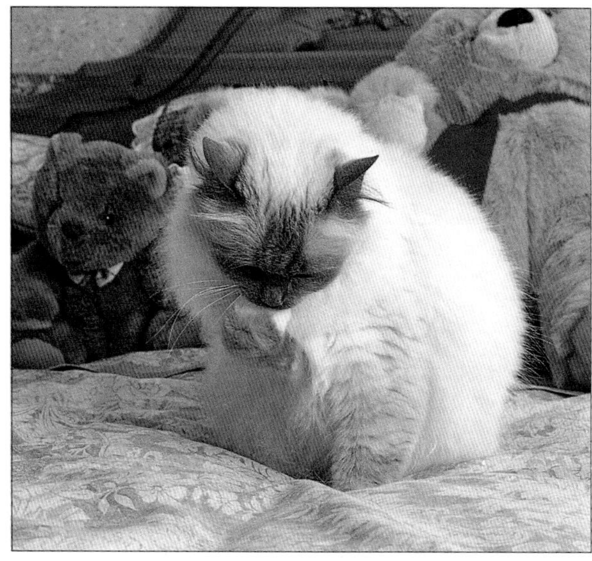

◄ *The owner's bed is often a favourite spot, especially if it has comfortable quilts and cushions.*

◄ *There is now such a range of pet beds available that you can choose one to match your decor. Whether you go for an enclosed, draughtproof and portable model or an open version, the easy-to-wash factor is the most important consideration.*

▲ *The material can be removed from the metal frame of a radiator bed and is generally machine-washable.*

▼ *Wicker beds are lovely to look at but be aware it may end up as a glorified scratching post.*

Cats prefer to sleep in a warm place. When the sun is streaming through the window this includes the windowsill. Flat pad beds are available that fit right across the length of the sill. These are washable and large enough for all the cats in a multi-cat household to find a place in the sun.

Radiator beds are similar to small hammocks, usually made from a synthetic fleece material. They are on a removable metal frame that hooks on to the top of a radiator. This type of bed provides a warm, snug sleeping place that is off the floor.

Electrically heated beds are available, which are ideal if your cat sleeps in a colder area of the house. They have a heater element, with a thermostat, that fits under a protective cover. A soft pad or blanket can be placed on top. If you decide to buy a heated bed check that it is made by a company that conforms to the required safety standards. It needs chew-resistant cables, be waterproof and have a temperature control.

Cat furniture, in the way of bunkbeds, sofas and chairs, appeal more to the owner than the cat. They might provide the cat with some comfort but seem to be bought mainly because they look cute or match the existing home decoration. If you decide to buy one, check that it is well-made and that there is no way your pet can get its head stuck between any of the wooden struts.

Cup-style beds, sometimes called cat caves, are a relatively new design. The cat enters from a hole in the top of a circular sleeping area. These beds appeal to most cats as they provide an element of privacy. Additionally, the cat sleeps in a natural curled position and this, plus the shape of the bed, means that body heat is retained.

Before washing any pet bedding, vacuum it first to remove excess pet hair and dirt. Ensure detergent is pet-safe and that you have read the washing instructions on the item. Always wash pet bedding separately.

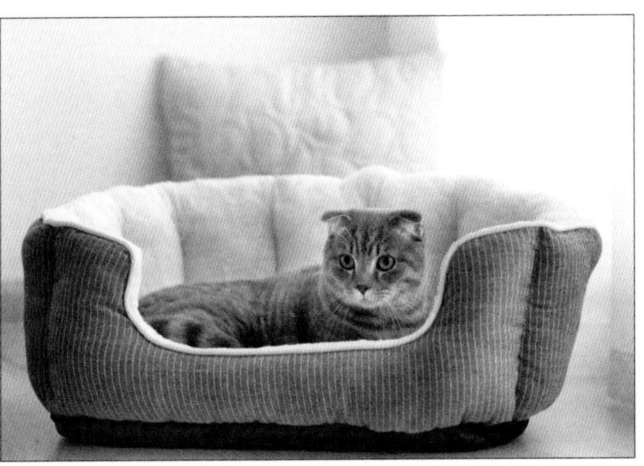

◀ *Cheap imported synthetic beds may contain harmful toxic chemicals. Buy from reputable companies.*

▶ *Patterns to make your own beds are available online to download.*

Litter and litter tray

A kitten or cat needs access to a litter tray if it is not able to go outside when it wants to. The tray may become redundant once a kitten is fully immunized and has learnt to use its cat flap into the garden, although it is preferable to encourage your cat to stay in at night. Even when very young, kittens are inherently clean and will not soil their bed. If a cage or crate is being used during the settling-in period, it should be large enough to contain a litter tray.

There is a wide range of products available, from basic plastic trays to covered models with entrance flaps and filters to minimize odour. The key point about litter trays is that they must be easy to clean, and tough enough to withstand frequent washing and disinfecting. They should also be in a position that can be cleaned easily.Toxoplasmosis is an infection that can be shed in a cat's faeces without the cat showing any signs of disease. It is, however, a hazard to humans, especially pregnant women. Disposal of faeces less than 24 hours after passing and regular cleaning of litter trays with plenty of water and detergent is effective in the control of toxoplasmosis. Some household products contain ingredients, which, although fine for use in the home, can be toxic to cats. The staff at your vet's should be able to advise on these.

► The most important consideration when buying a litter tray is that it should be easy to clean. Use a scoop to remove faeces independently, rather than changing all the litter in the tray every time.

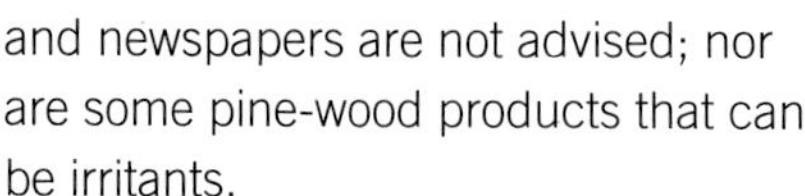

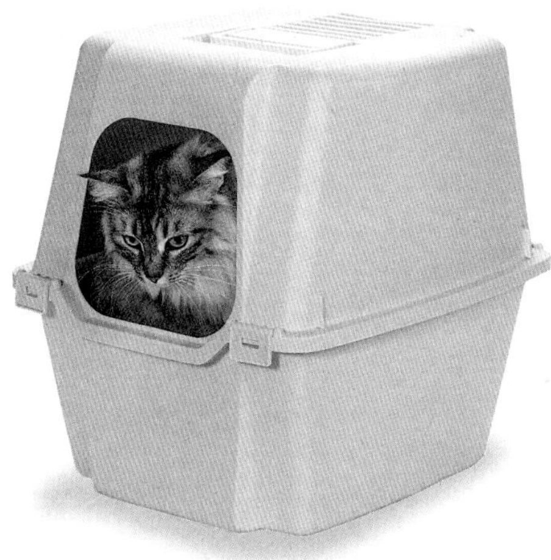

▲ The ultimate litter tray is not only draughtproof and private for the coy cat, but helps contain odours.

LITTER OPTIONS

The various litter products available should be acceptable to the cat, reduce odour and absorb urine. It should also be easy for the cat to scrape the litter over any faeces deposited, which it does instinctively. Sawdust, woodshavings, cinders, ash and newspapers are not advised; nor are some pine-wood products that can be irritants.

There are two types of clay-based litter, clumping and non-clumping. Clumping clay is made from bentonite. This is an absorbent litter that forms a 'clump' in the spot that the cat urinates, making it very easy to remove the soiled portion. Unfortunately, it is heavy to carry, non-biodegradable and dusty. Non-clumping clay litter is cheaper but harder to remove the soiled area and therefore needs changing more regularly.

Silica gel crystal litter is highly absorbent and dust free. It is an expensive option but controls odour efficiently. If ingested in large amounts, or over a prolonged period of time, this litter can cause a cat to vomit.

▼ Left to right: Clay, wood and paper-based litters: some are highly absorbent, others are superfine and form clumps when wet.

◄ *Re-usable rubber or disposable latex gloves should always be worn when cleaning litter trays.*

► *After cleaning a litter tray, avoid touching your face until you have thoroughly washed your hands.*

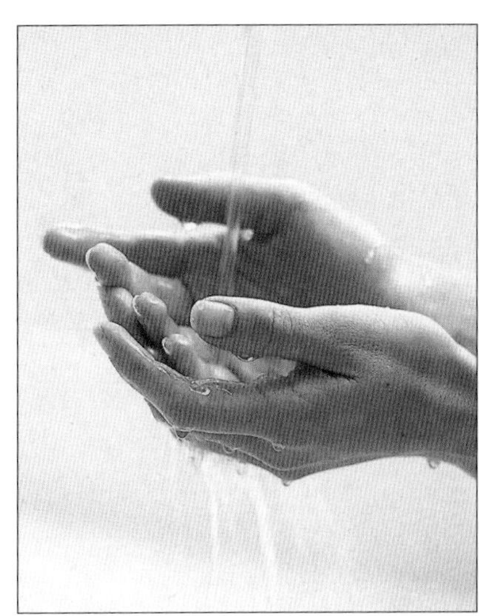

Soiled non-biodegradable litter should be double-bagged, ensuring bags are tied tightly, before placing in the rubbish bin or trash can. This will prevent the smell and harmful bacteria escaping. Never leave dirty litter where it can cause cross contamination to other cats.

A biodegradable litter is made using crushed walnut shell. This is dark brown in colour, is highly absorbent, clumps and has good odour control. Recently a biodegradable litter made from grass has also come onto the market. This is a fine-grained substance that also clumps and controls odour well. Both of these litters are made of 100% natural plant material and soiled material can be used as a mulch in the flower garden provided faeces have been removed first. Never place around vegetable plants, fruiting trees and bushes or areas that children may play in.

Litter should not be flushed down the toilet. Clay and silica types will rapidly clog up waste pipes resulting in expensive bills to unblock the drains. Some biodegradable types are marked as 'flushable' but when soiled may contain the bacteria *Toxoplasma gondii*. This is the cause of toxoplasmosis. It can't be killed by normal waste treatment plants and so could contaminate the water supply.

Some countries have legislation regarding the disposal of cat litter. There are regions where animal waste is not allowed to be mixed with other domestic rubbish and is collected separately. Always check with your local environmental officer to see if restrictions apply in your area.

▼ *Cat litter can get everywhere. Have a dustpan and brush handy to avoid it getting trodden on.*

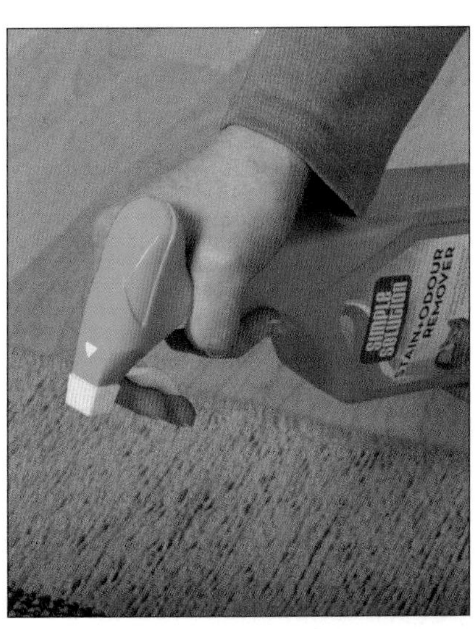

▲ *Cat-safe deodorizing sprays are available and remove any traces of unpleasant odours.*

Carriers

It is essential to buy, rather than borrow, a cat carrier. You will need it not only to bring the cat or kitten home, but also for visits to the veterinary surgery – and anywhere else for that matter. Any visit to the vet will quickly reveal that very many owners have great faith in their pets' ability not to escape! They arrive with all sorts of contraptions for carrying their cats; sometimes with nothing at all to restrain an animal which may be in pain, very frightened and invariably highly stressed.

SIZE CONSIDERATIONS

Do not be seduced into buying a sweet, kitten-sized carrier; consider the future and purchase accordingly. That cute little fur-ball is going to turn into a considerably larger adult. A carrier of around 30cm x 30cm x 55cm (12in x 12in x 22in) should last into the cat's adulthood. For an extra-large male, it might be wise to go to the next size up. Cats prefer to be in a fairly snug environment if they are experiencing a rare and disturbing event such as travelling, but they do need to be able to turn around and stretch out a little. They also like to be able to see out so that they feel a little less trapped.

► *A top-loading wicker basket which could double as the cat's permanent bed.*

▼ *Large cat carriers provide plenty of room for your cat and can double up as pens for the settling-in period. They are, however, awkward to carry.*

If the journey is going to be a long one (over an hour or two), have a carrier that can take a small litter tray as well as clip-on water and food bowls. However, if you are likely to have to carry the cat very far, for example, when attending shows, remember the larger the carrier, the more awkward it is to carry. Strained shoulders and backs are not uncommon among exhibitors.

WHAT IS AVAILABLE

Basic cardboard carriers, preferably coated with plastic, are bought flatpacked, and, when assembled, are suitable for transporting a sick and possibly infectious animal, as they are inexpensive and can be burnt after

▼ *An easy-to-clean plastic container that might cause loading and unloading difficulties.*

▼ *A collapsible cardboard carrier that can be dispensed with after being used to carry an infectious animal.*

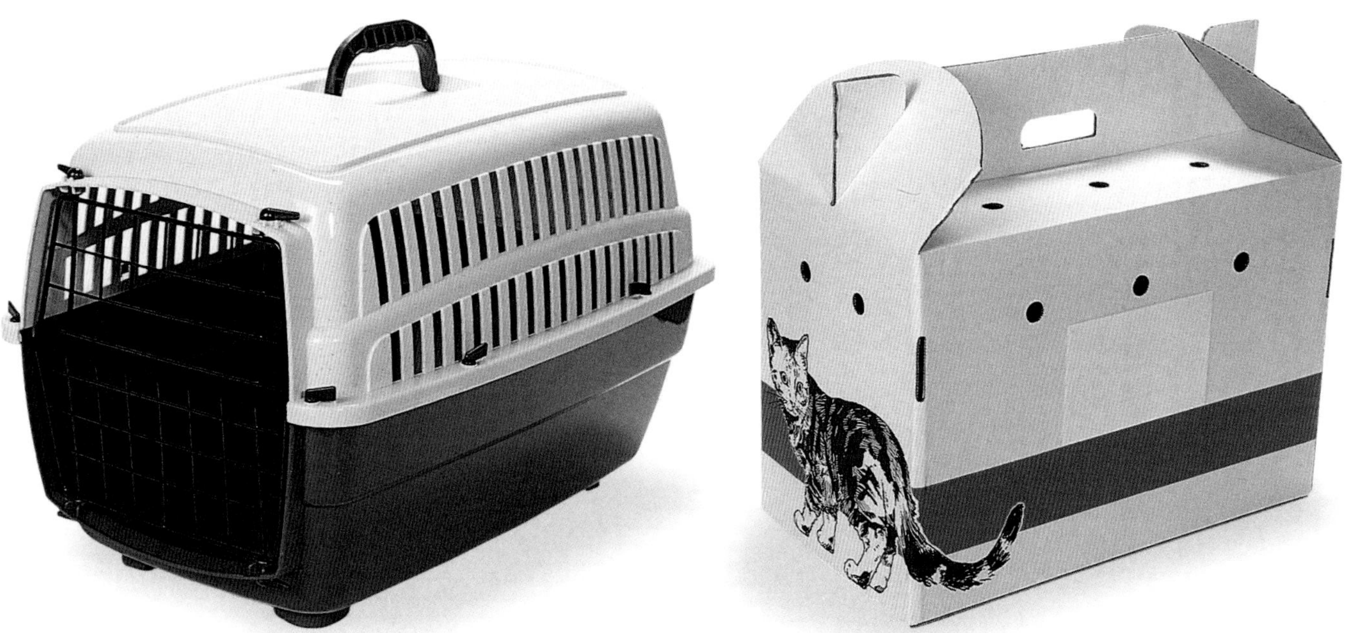

use. However, they are not suitable for more regular use as they cannot be cleaned and disinfected effectively, and are not durable. Traditionalists choose wickerwork baskets, which come in various shapes, and usually have leather straps and a handle. These are attractive and could double as the cat's permanent sleeping quarters – at least the cat would be calmer if travelling in its own bed.

Openwork wire baskets, especially with the wire covered with white plastic, have veterinary approval because they are so easy to disinfect and the cat is easily visible. The top opening is secured by a separate rod pushed through rigid loops. Moulded plastic carriers with strategically placed ventilation holes are available in a great range of designs, are easy to dismantle for thorough cleaning, and reassembling is no problem either. Clear moulded plastic (Perspex) carriers with airholes are a less worthwhile investment as the plastic tends to crack and degrade over time. If carried in sunlight, its occupant can quickly overheat.

The most practical designs are those with top access; they are less stressful both for cat and handler. The cat can be grasped from above and removed without a struggle. With a front-loading carrier, the often frightened animal has to be recovered from the back of a tunnel. It can also be difficult to put the cat back inside.

▼ *If you want your cat carrier to look distinctive or decorative, you could paint it with an appropriate design.*

Collars, harnesses and leads

A collar is not necessarily merely decorative. A tag may be attached to it so that the cat can be identified if it gets lost or injured. An identity tag may be a simple engraved disc or a screw-topped cylinder containing a roll of paper with the cat's name, owner's address and telephone number, and sometimes the vet's emergency number. Magnetic tags that allow your cat exclusive entry to its cat flap can also be fitted on collars.

Most collars come with a bell which rings when the cat moves and may reduce the death toll among garden birds and other potential hunting targets. Some collars are impregnated with an anti-flea substance, but keep a careful check on your cat when you first put one on it, as they can cause an allergic reaction. Signs of irritation around the neck or eyes are the main indications of allergy. A flea collar should never be combined with any other form of flea control.

Collars have two main disadvantages. If worn continuously, as they should be if they are carrying any form of identification, they will damage the fur

▼ *A soft collar with a bell attached will help you find your cat, and will drastically reduce its hunting successes by warning birds of its presence.*

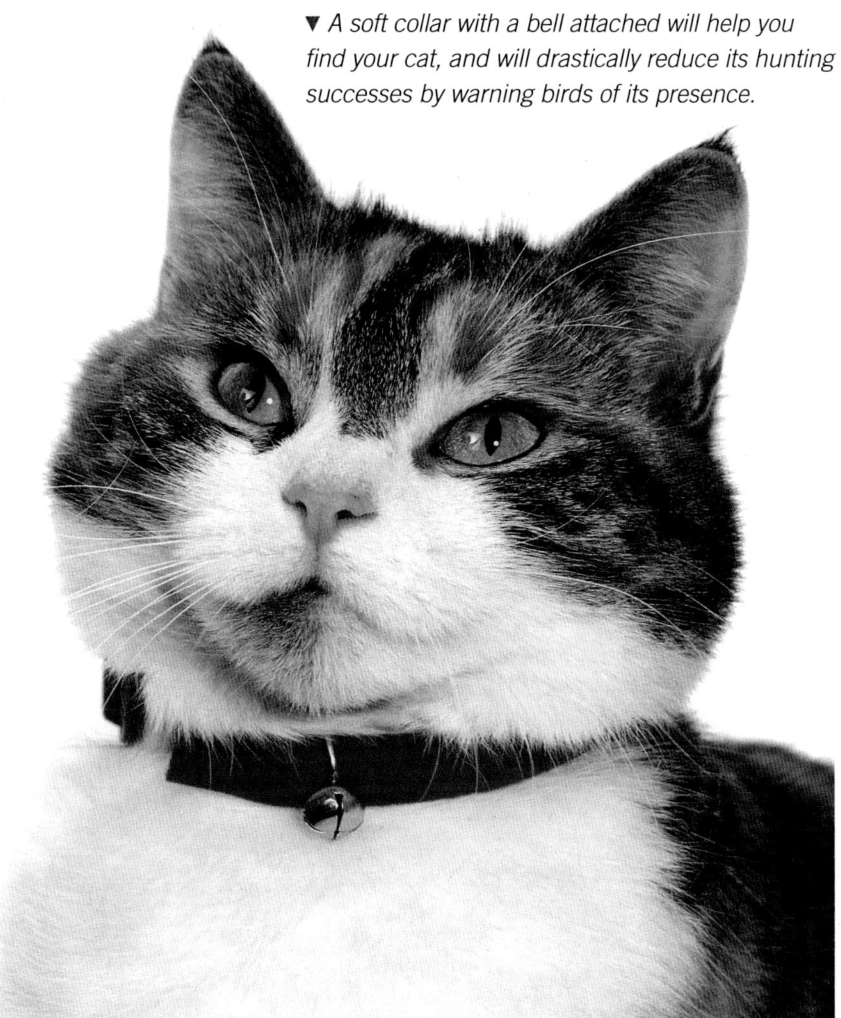

▼ *A soft, padded flea collar with a bell and an elastic section. Flea collars should only be used on cats over six months old. They may cause an allergic reaction in some cats.*

▼ *A soft leather collar with the all-important elastic section. Any collar you buy should have this, for if the collar is caught the elastic will stretch, allowing the cat to escape unharmed.*

▼ *Fabric collars, which can be cut to size without fraying, are useful for kittens and small cats. They are cheap enough to be changed regularly, or even to have a selection of colours.*

▶ *Magnetic tags double as a means of identity and a 'key' to enable the wearer to go through its cat flap.*

◀ *Identity tags can be simple metal discs engraved with the owner's name and telephone number, or an information-packed barrel containing the owner's address and the vet's address and emergency telephone number.*

around the neck, especially that of longhaired cats. This can be unsightly and is considered unacceptable by many exhibitors; although most show judges realize the reason for any marks around the neck, they may still penalize the cat. Secondly, there is always the fear that the collar can become caught when the cat is hunting in trees or shrubs. However, if it is made of soft leather, suede, or soft fabric and has an elasticated insert, this will stretch if the collar catches, and the cat will be able to free itself. The collar should always be adjusted so that it will slip over the cat's head in an emergency, but not loose enough to allow the front leg to slip through and the collar to lodge under the armpit, which could cause injury.

GOING FOR A WALK

Cat leads are only necessary if you intend to take your cat for walks or if you are taking it to a strange house and need to keep it under control. Some cats actively enjoy this, particularly Siamese. It is not unusual to see this breed travelling on public transport on a lead. However, most cats are naturally resistant to wearing any such controlling apparatus and will fight against it, especially if they become frightened. To take them on a bus or train on a lead rather than in a carrier is foolhardy under any circumstances. If the cat panics, it could either become tangled and hurt itself, or escape. If a lead is worn on a suitable outing, it should be no more than 1m (3ft) long, and have a fitted harness rather than a collar for attachment. This not only allows more control and comfort, but is more secure. Cats are great escapologists, however, and even the most carefully fitted harness may prove insecure.

Introduce your cat to a harness and lead as early as possible. Put the harness on first by itself, and just for a short time each day. After you have done this for a few days, attach the lead for a short time, several days running, but just leave it trailing. When the cat seems relaxed about the lead, try walking it, first indoors for brief spells, then in the garden, and then in a street where the cat can get used to traffic and people, but do not overdo it!

▶ *Some oriental cats appear to enjoy going for walks, but they need to be familiarized with a collar or harness and lead from an early age.*

Feeding equipment

If you already have perfectly suitable dishes, special purchases may not be necessary. The most practical choices are made of hard plastic, ceramic or stainless steel. All equipment should be easy to clean and disinfect. Discard cracked or chipped ceramic bowls, as germs may be harboured in the cracks. Once any container, new or old, has been allotted to the cat, it should not be used for anything else. Many people feed their cats in the kitchen; if there are dogs around, it is also likely that the cat is fed on a working surface. In either case it is especially important to maintain strict standards of hygiene to guard against the risk of toxoplasmosis (see box). The feeding area must be easy to clean and disinfect regularly. This is also important for the cat because it has a highly developed sense of smell and will reject food that has become tainted and hardened. For the same reasons, put down fresh water at least once a day. A closed-off eating area is advisable if you have crawling babies or toddlers.

For the busy owner whose lifestyle makes feeding the cat at regular times uncertain, automatic food bowls with timer switches are available. The cover automatically lifts to reveal food at pre-set times. A water bowl is kept

▶ *Clockwise from top left: The cutlery for serving the cat should be exclusively for this purpose; plastic lids to cover unfinished cans prevent the food from drying up and the smell from spreading; a metal bowl; an automatic feeder; a plastic combined water and food bowl; a simple plastic bowl.*

Toxoplasmosis

Toxoplasmosis affects many animals but cats are the only ones that shed the parasite in their faeces. This only happens for a short time after the cat has become infected and the faeces are only infectious after 24 hours or more. In most cases there are no visible signs of disease or illness in the cat. The infection is carried in the cat's faeces and in 24–48 hours can pass on to humans.

Unless their immune system is not functioning properly, humans contracting the infection are unlikely to become ill, but if a pregnant woman is infected, there is a 40 per cent chance that her baby will also be infected. Of these infected babies, 15 per cent may spontaneously abort or acquire some abnormality.

- Wear gloves when gardening in an area frequented by cats.
- Cover children's play areas, such as sand-pits, when not in use.
- Empty litter trays on a daily basis and clean regularly with plenty of water and detergent.
- Use a separate set of feeding equipment for the cat and do not use it for humans; clean regularly with cat-safe detergent.

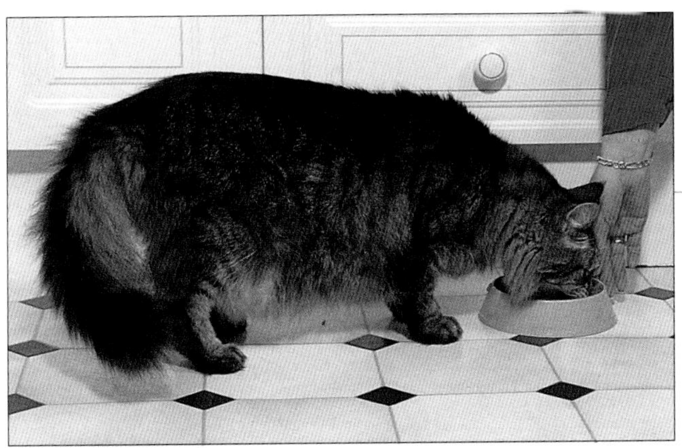

▲ *It is more hygienic to put your cat's food on the floor rather than on a working surface where food is prepared for humans.*

▲ *Non-slip feeding mats are available and should be regularly wiped clean or washed. Cats hate the smell of stale food.*

topped up with water from a reservoir, but you do need to remember to change the reservoir frequently.

A feeding mat is a simple but handy piece of equipment. It acts as a placemat on which the food or water bowl is placed. Many have anti-slip bumps that stop dishes sliding about. Some even have raised lips so that any spillages are contained. They are very durable and generally made from soft silicone. Before buying check that it is labelled as non-toxic and non-allergenic. Mats are easily cleaned either by wiping with a damp cloth or immersing in a water and detergent solution. Various retailers sell mats that are dishwasher proof too.

Opened cans of cat food should never be stored uncovered. Plastic lids are available but make sure that they will fit the size of can that you use before buying. Dry food will stay fresher longer if decanted from cardboard packaging and stored in an airtight container. Wash lids and storage containers regularly. Cats dislike the smell of citrus. Avoid cleaning products containing, or scented with, citrus as the residual odour may put your cat off its food.

The last decade has seen the emergence of some very high-tech cat-feeding equipment. Puzzle or maze feeders do not allow the cat to put its head into the bowl. Instead each morsel of food has to be extracted using a paw. These feeders allow the cat to eat in a more natural manner, that of little and often, and provide the cat with entertainment. Both can be used for wet or dry food but are time-consuming to clean when using wet diets.

Owners of multi-cat households have never been sure how much each cat is eating, as pets will often choose to share bowls. This can be problematic when nutrition needs to monitored, for example when caring for obese felines or those that are poor eaters. It is now possible to buy bowls that are covered with clear Perspex lids which will only open when activated by an individual cat's microchip. This ensures that each cat eats from the correct bowl and that you are not feeding every stray cat that comes to visit.

◄ *The lid of this electronic feeder only lifts and allows access to the food when the set time is reached.*

▼ *Teardrop-shaped bowls make it harder for the cat to get at all the food without using its paws.*

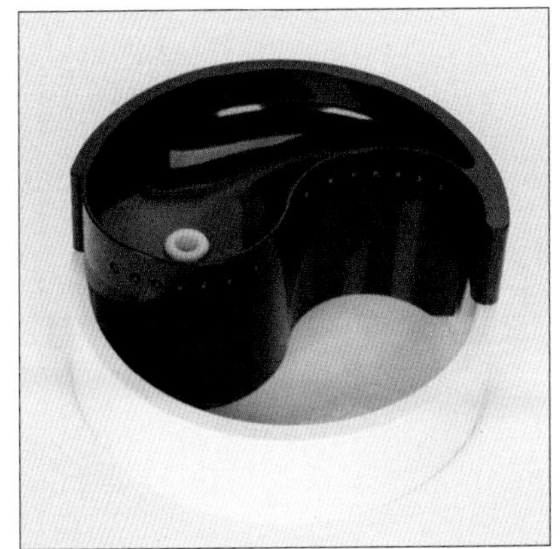

Extras and toys

Play for a young cat is just as essential for its wellbeing as it is for a human child. It is particularly important for the owner to play with the cat if it is the only one in the household. Through play, muscles are exercised and conditioned, the brain is kept alert and the eyes bright. And if the owner joins in the play, it strengthens the bond between the feline and its adopted human family.

At the very least your cat should have a scratching post, which it can be encouraged to use instead of the furniture and soft furnishings. A cat will naturally use surfaces such as the bark of a tree to sharpen and control the length of its claws – they are its main means of defence, and also provide grip when climbing. You can make an indoor scratching post yourself by binding a stout fence post with heavy-duty sisal string or cotton rope, and attaching it to a suitable base. A strip of old carpet is an alternative, but this is not as effective for the cat, as it frays quickly, creates a great deal of fluff, and needs to be renewed regularly. If you do not mind your cat equipment taking over the home, feline climbing frames of varying size and complexity are readily available. Some are over 2m (6ft) high, with circular supports covered in sisal rope, carpet-covered perches, houses and barrels. They are likely to be found at cat shows, online or through advertisements in specialist cat magazines and larger pet stores.

▲ *Being ten months old does not mean that this youngster has grown out of shredding curtains for fun.*

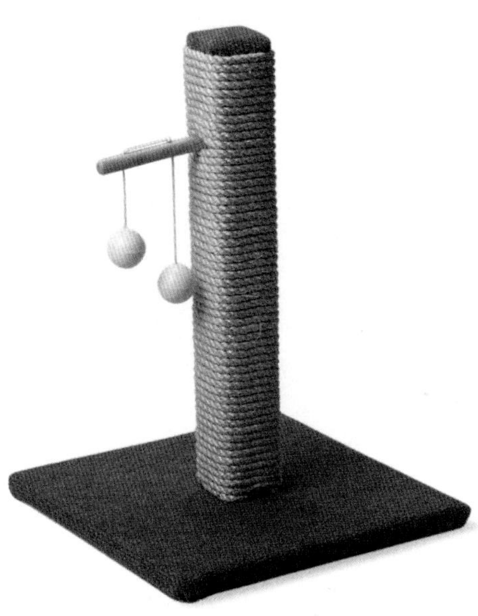

◄ *A young cat needs something to scratch. Instead of the commercial type, shown here, sisal rope bound around the upright of a bookcase or banister would be just as effective.*

PLAY WITH A PURPOSE

A cat's play is orientated to the hunting process. When a cat swoops after a leaf in autumn, that leaf is an imaginary bird. The ping-pong ball just

► *Kittens enjoy playing with someone, especially if they are an only cat; they will soon become bored playing on their own with a ball.*

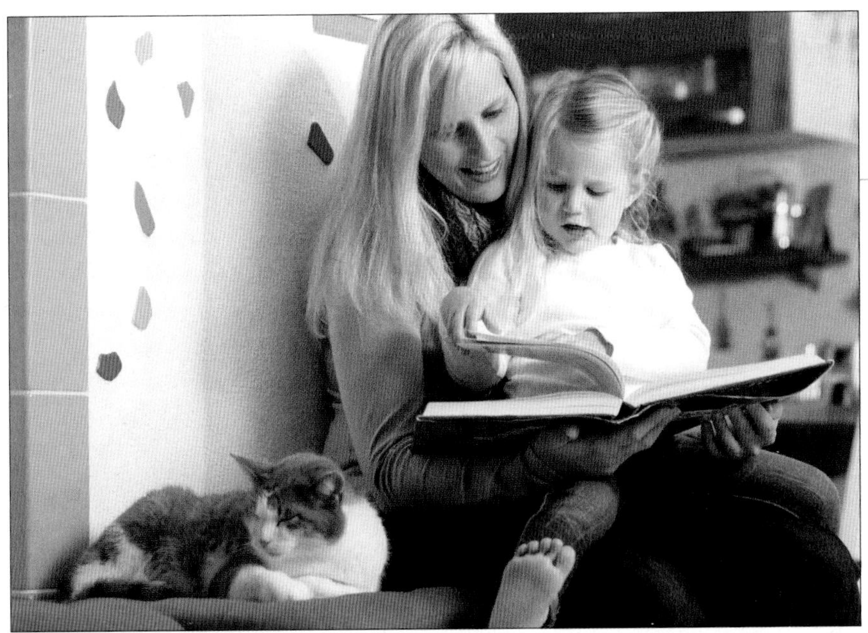

◀ Children must be taught that a resting or sleeping cat does not want to play and should not be disturbed.

▲ Cats are nature's most efficient predators: a fabric mouse filled with delectable catnip may not last long in the grip of this young Ocicat.

visible behind a chair leg is a mouse to be stalked, pounced upon and batted around. The screwed-up paper hurled into the air, caught and thrown away to be chased and sent flying again, is being hunted. Even in an apparently sterile environment, a cat will find a scrap of paper, a lost button, or a shadow to play with. However, do be careful of everyday household objects like the odd button or needle and thread. Swallowed thread can do even more damage than a needle as it cheesewires its way through the bowel.

Do check that any cat toys you buy are reasonably solid. Some plastic materials that are safe for children can be toxic to cats. All that is needed is to be found in the home: paper scrunched into a ball and thrown by the owner for retrieval up and down the stairs; a paper 'butterfly' tied to a piece of string and dragged around for the cat to chase, or suspended from the back of a chair to bat. Some cats are particularly fond of hide-and-seek. For group play, nothing is better than the great game of the ping-pong ball rolled around the carpet between family members and friends, and pursued by your cat.

► A clockwork mouse is a poor substitute for the real thing, as it has to be wound up, but it is less messy for the owner.

▼ You will probably need a continual supply of balls as they are constantly being batted out of sight.

▼ Here's a soft, friendly chap to dig your claws into. Let's hope the bear's eyes are well secured so that the kitten does not swallow them.

Additional extras and toys

Toys on a cord attached to a stick are very popular with felines. People playing with the cat can move the toy in unpredictable directions which holds the interest for a long time. Not only is this fun but also great exercise for your pet. These toys have the added benefit of reducing accidental scratches to the human because of the distance between the hand and plaything. This makes them a safer option for a child. These toys must be placed out of reach except when play is supervized.

A range of toys offer the cat a reward when they play with them. The reward is often in the form of a treat. Cats have to use their brains to work out how to achieve the edible delicacy. These are ideal if the cat is left alone for periods of time as they will entertain for hours and require no human interaction. Reward toys vary in difficulty, so start with a simple one and work upwards as your cat learns to use its intelligence.

Examine all toys carefully to see that they are safe. A toy should never be small enough to swallow. Likewise check that no small parts, such as glued eyes or noses, are likely to fall off, or be chewed off, and then ingested. Inspect labels on plush toys detailing the material used as a filling before buying. Those containing polystyrene beads, wool, beans or crushed nut shells should be left on the shelf. Battery-operated toys are exciting but should only be used during supervized play. The batteries must be removed when not in use.

▲ *Cat play towers keep your cat active. This one incorporates a scratching post as well as a hiding place.*

◄ *Check each playtime that the toys are securely attached to the wand and not likely to become detached.*

► *Take care when playing with this toy, the cat may accidentally claw your hand.*

◄ *Cat tunnels encourage the natural behaviours of running, hiding and pouncing. Cats find them great fun.*

Old toys that no longer hold interest can be rejuvenated by placing in an airtight box with a handful of dried catnip. The toy will absorb the scent after a couple of days and will become the best thing ever. Strangely, kittens are not enchanted by this scent until they are at least six months old so delay buying catnip-filled toys until they are old enough to enjoy them.

Cat massage stations are sturdy, low, floor-standing constructions made from materials in a variety of textures. Areas are designed for chewing, helping to keep teeth clean. Other parts encourage the cat to rub against and so receive a 'massage'. Several

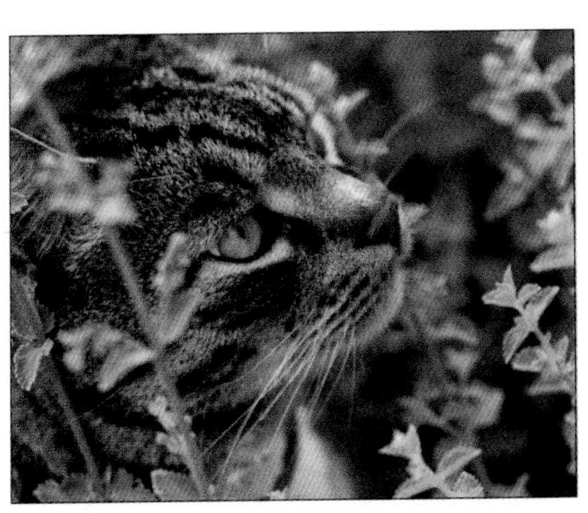

▲ *Both catnip and cat mint can easily be grown in a pot or seed tray and brought indoors as required.*

▲ *Regularly check the cat tree to see that there are no loose cords that might entangle or even hang your pet.*

even include brushes for your pet to roll on to remove dead hair. Some cats get a great deal of enjoyment from these toys while others have no interest at all.

There are many extras available for the cat owner to buy. Those that involve modern technology are rapidly becoming very popular. Laser light toys are generally floor-standing cones with a red laser beam at the top. They work on batteries and once switched on will shine the light beam in random patterns. Cats and kittens love chasing the beam, which of course is impossible to catch. Most have a timer and will turn off automatically.

Although not a necessity, cat trackers provide additional peace of mind. They work by transmitting GPS information from the cat's collar to the owner's smartphone or laptop. Top-of-the-range collars are able to send other data including temperature, pulse, respiration and activity rates. The collars are lightweight, have elastic safety inserts and are splash-proof. Owners can see the whereabouts of their cat at all times. They are an expensive outlay coupled with a monthly charge but, providing the collar isn't lost, remove all the worry experienced when a cat is missing. This technology would be particularly valued by owners of outdoor cats.

Interactive Wi-Fi cameras allow owners of indoor cats to watch what their pet is doing in their absence. Again this technology is linked to a laptop, tablet or smartphone. Advanced camera cubes not only send constant videos of the cat back to a receiver but enable the owner to interact with their pet from a distance. Some transmit voices so that you can speak to the cat whenever you like. Others enable you to play with your pet by operating a beam of light, remotely, for the cat to chase.

▼ *Laser light toys are one of the most popular toys and provide hours of fun for both cat and owner.*

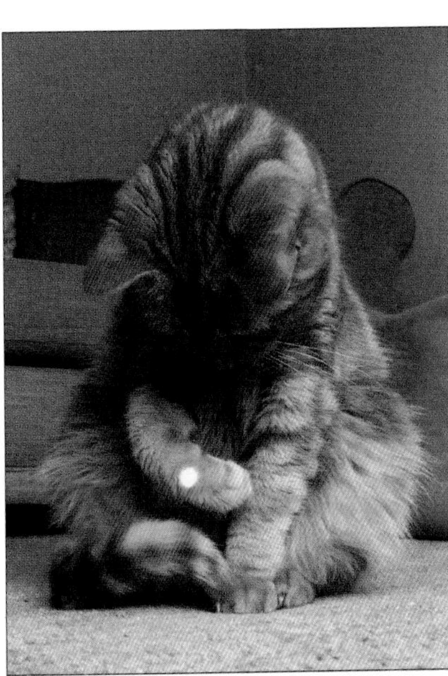

▼ *Securely tied feathers, ribbon or material scraps firmly attached to a cord make a fun home-made toy.*

CATS AT HOME AND AWAY

An inquisitive cat is capable of getting into all sorts of trouble if it is both bored and given the opportunity. A cursory glance round the home and garden may well reveal dangers that can be easily rectified.

If you need to use a boarding cattery do not leave finding one to the last minute. Visit several before you make your choice and then reserve a place as far in advance as possible. The best catteries are booked very quickly in peak travel periods. When travelling with your pet it is your sole responsibility to ensure that all conditions and regulations are adhered to and that necessary paperwork has been correctly completed. It is also the owner's duty to see that the cat is made as comfortable as possible and, as far as possible, that all its needs are met.

◄ *A cat instinctively knows its physical limits; it can also, through learned behaviour and training, avoid potentially dangerous situations. The wise owner strikes a balance between giving the cat the freedom it needs, being aware of the dangers it could face, and protecting it from them.*

Access to the outside world

It always used to be common practice to put the house cat out at night, so that it could carry out its rodent extermination duties, and to avoid mess in the house. Effective rodent control and the availability of litter trays have made this unnecessary. Now how much freedom a cat has is more likely to be dependent upon human work patterns. However, unless you have pedigreed cats which you keep for exhibition and show, or your living space necessitates an indoor lifestyle, you can allow your pet various degrees of access to the outside world, either during daytime or at night.

Some cats automatically confine their territories to the back garden. Others may develop an awareness of the traffic in their area, and avoid rush hours, for example. However, it is difficult to be sure of their abilities, and even quiet streets can be dangerous because of the occasional, unexpected vehicle. For these reasons, and the risks of territorial fighting and exposure to infection, it is worth exercising some form of control over your cat's freedom to roam.

CAT FLAPS

Cat flaps are cat-sized windows that are fitted about 15cm (6in) from the base of a door. The most practical design is one that is gravity-loaded so that the door automatically closes after entry or exit, and with a clear plastic window so that the cat can look through it before venturing outside.

Flaps are a boon to the indoor/outdoor cat that is not afraid of operating the flap and whose owners are not always home to obey the cat's every whim. They allow both cat and owner a degree of independence from each other. The main disadvantage of cat flaps, particularly when there is no such feline control, is that neighbours or feral cats will soon learn to use them, particularly if delicious food is known to be available on the other side of the flap. This could lead to disease or infection being brought into the home, or territorial fights, or both. One way of overcoming this is to have an electronically operated flap that allows entry only to cats wearing the appropriate collar and gadgetry – usually in the form of a magnetic tag that doubles as an identity tag. Some cat flaps also now work with the cat's microchip and will only open for the right microchip.

Alternatively, you can allow your cat limited freedom, and, for example, lock the flap at night when you are unable to keep an eye on unwanted visitors. It is useful to buy a flap that can be locked to prevent your cat from going out at certain times, or other cats from coming in. Your cat will soon become used to whatever routine you set.

When you introduce your cat to the cat flap, encourage it with your voice and show it how the door works. Put the cat on one side and call from the other. After a few tries, it will know exactly what to do. However, it is not unusual for some cats to refuse to use a flap – particularly if the flap was introduced after the cat. The same goes for flaps on covered litter trays.

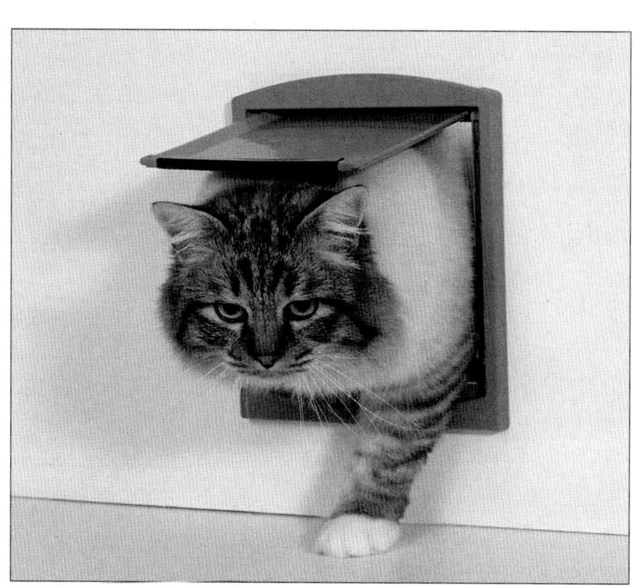

◄ *A cat will soon learn to use its cat flap with confidence. The flap swings shut when the cat has passed through.*

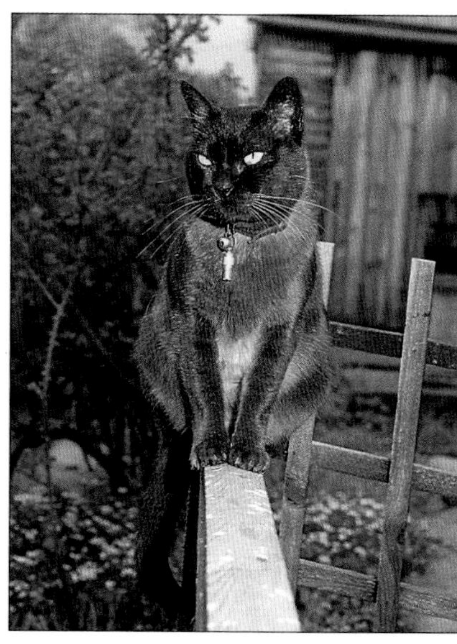

► *A Brown Burmese selects a high vantage point from which to survey the surrounding territory.*

► *A tomcat prepares for his nocturnal prowl. Many of the small rodents that cats hunt are active as night falls, and this also seems to be a prime time to look for a mate.*

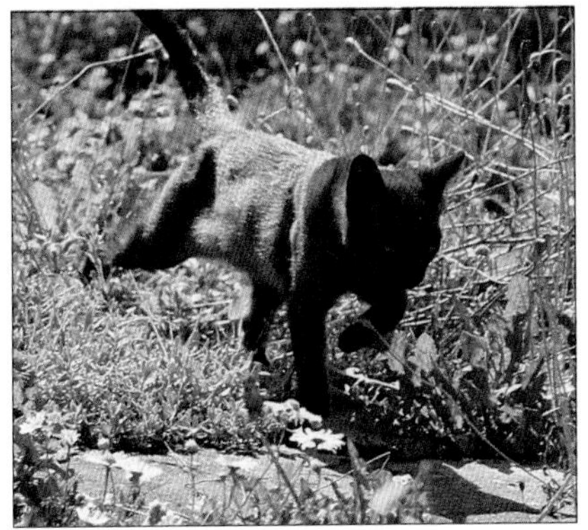

▲ *A lithe hunter like this Brown Burmese will be a joy to watch in your garden.*

OUTDOOR CONFINEMENT

Indoor living can be supplemented by a safe secure outdoor area. Suitable areas of a garden can be fenced in with wire or plastic mesh like a fruit cage, or a purpose-built shed or pen can be provided. Climbing plants can be trained to cover the sides to soften the appearance, but take advice on which plants to choose – some are poisonous to cats (see pp 100–01).

A pen can be constructed in the garden or as an extension to the house (with access via a cat flap). It should be sturdy in structure with wire or plastic mesh stretched between a solid wood frame, and roofed. Features could include a covered shelter and an outdoor play area with logs, shelves and playthings to keep the cats amused. Such pens are commercially available. In extreme cases, or with very small areas, whole gardens are secured around the perimeter to prevent cats from escaping or other cats from getting in. You can make a framework of stout posts to a height of say 3m (9ft) and attach wire netting between them. If the netting is loosely fitted the cat will not be able to climb up it and there will be no need to roof in the top. The base of the wire should be buried or well secured.

► *Cats are often attracted to the shelter and warmth offered by parked cars, so always check beneath your car before you drive away. Knock on the bonnet or hood too as cats can also sit on top of the engine.*

▼ *Cats enjoy fresh air and sunshine from the safety of an outside pen.*

In the garden

To watch a cat move and play in a garden is a source of delight, but there are dangers. Cats can swim, but are not generally renowned for their ability in this area, and there are cases of accidental drowning each year. The simple solution in the case of a garden pond, stream or swimming pool, is to cover the water with very fine mesh or to erect a barrier to make the area inaccessible to the cat.

Cats do have a wonderful righting ability which enables them to almost invariably land on their feet when falling from a height. However, vets regularly see cats that have been badly injured as a result of falls. If a cat lands on an unyielding surface, it is likely to injure itself if the fall is more than 3–4m (9–12ft), which is equivalent in height to the first storey of a house. The same applies if they fall out of trees. The most common problem with cats climbing is that they become absorbed in either hunting or exploring and end up on a branch too small to turn around on and escape. This is invariably when the rescue services have to be called in. Discourage habitual climbers by placing wire netting around the base of favourite or particularly dangerous trees. However, be aware that the determined feline may just look for another tree.

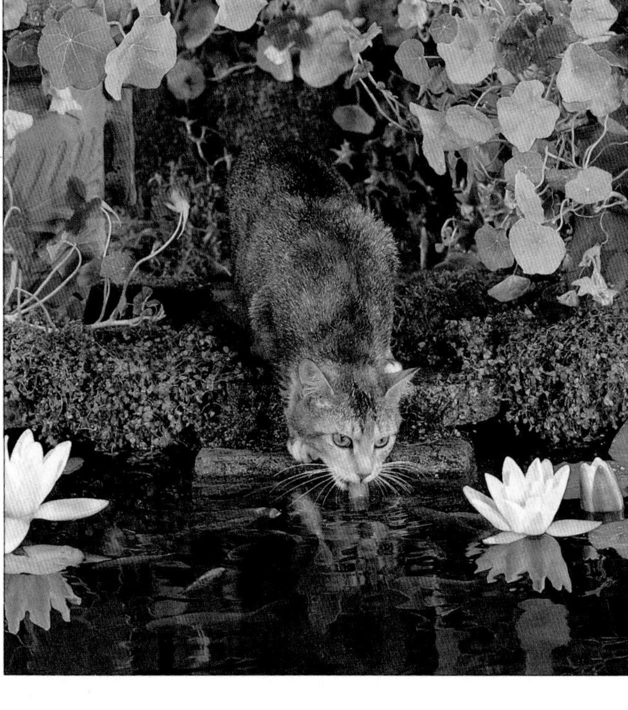

► *Thirst, reflections and goldfish are all good reasons for cats to be interested in water. They are not renowned for their swimming skills, however, and a net over the garden pond is worth considering.*

▼ *When maturity and wisdom have taken the place of adventure and curiosity, a garden can be a great place for sunning and relaxation.*

▼ *Another sticky situation for an exploratory kitten. At this stage of their development, adventurous kittens should be supervized.*

▲ *A broken pane of glass in the garden shed spells danger for this cat. If it attempts an escape through the hole, it could cut itself badly. Carry out all repairs promptly.*

▲ *This kitten is in danger. Curiosity has led it to explore beyond its limits to a narrow perch where its leg could become stuck, or from which it could fall.*

TRAPPED

Apart from harbouring dangerous substances, garden sheds and garages can become prisons from which there is no escape. A brief period of captivity will not do a cat too much harm. A cat can survive for 10–14 days without food and almost as long without water, provided the ambient temperature is not too high, but the resulting dehydration and starvation may have serious consequences for the proper functioning of kidneys and liver. Such a physically challenged cat is then prey to secondary infections it would normally easily shake off. If you have not seen your cat for a while, check in cellars, cupboards, tool sheds and garages, in case it is trapped. Before you go away, make sure your cat is there, and that a neighbour (or the person looking after the cat) has access to the house, and any sheds or garages.

Insurance

Compare the cover and terms of several companies that specialize in animal insurance before you make your decision. The owner of a valuable cat may want to insure against loss, death or theft, in order to reclaim the cat's value. More general policies cushion the owner against the cost of veterinary bills in the event of accident or emergency, injury or disease, but do not cover initial injections, neutering or standard booster inoculations. The annual premium depends upon the level of cover selected and upon the insured animal's medical history.

Deciding whether or not to insure is a matter of balancing what can be a fairly steep monthly or annual premium against your ability to pay any sudden, costly vet's bill. The alternative, as with any insurance cover, is to have your own contingency account to cover emergency expenses.

Cat breeders sometimes issue basic health insurance cover notes with kittens. Cover starts from the date of sale and is usually valid for six weeks. After that, the new owner can continue with the same policy or seek another one.

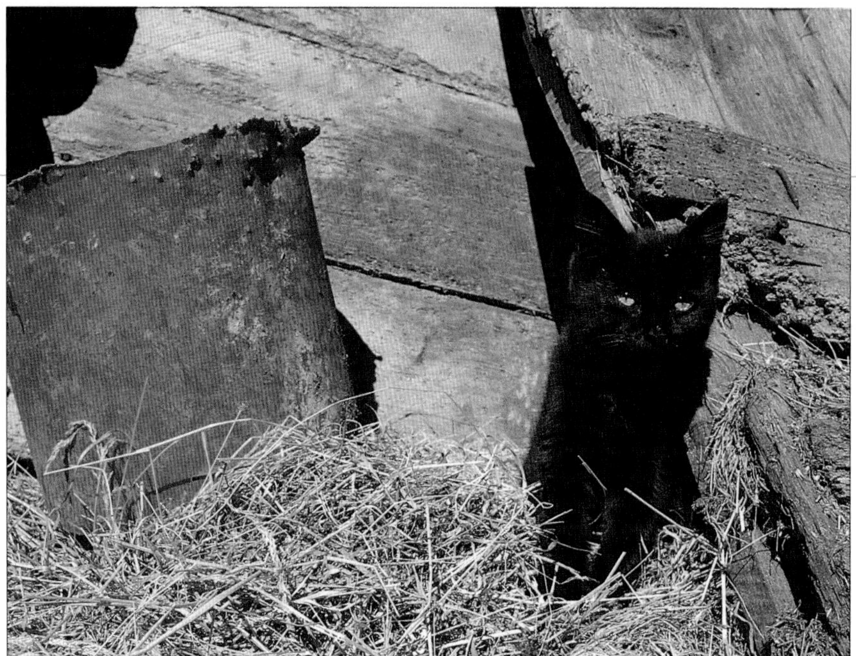

◄ *A farm kitten has found a sunny spot to sit in. Let's hope there are no nitrates or rat poison lying around!*

THE RISK OF POISONING

A cat enjoys exploring and takes an interest in dark, small places where danger can lurk in the form of toxic substances. A cat can be poisoned by eating or drinking poison, by indirect absorption from eating a poisoned animal, or, more commonly, by licking poison deposited on the fur or paw pads. These substances can also be absorbed through the skin itself, particularly through the paw pads.

It is vital to keep household cleaning agents in cupboards with cat-proof doors, and antifreezes and weedkillers safely locked away in garages and tool sheds. Always read the labels of such products carefully; if there are warnings of the danger of the contents to children, they are likely to be bad for your cat too. Although a cat is not likely to choose to drink a bottle of paint-stripper, it could knock over a bottle containing some. If a toxic substance is spilled on a surface where a cat is likely to tread, mop it up thoroughly. If you are decorating, keep the cat out of the room. Even the smell of modern decorating materials can affect some cats.

Some of the preparations used to keep garden pests at bay are particularly lethal, as they are spread

▼ *This terracotta pot looks safe enough – as long as it does not topple over, and there are no dangerous substances left inside.*

▼ *A cat has taken over the greenhouse. Tomato plants are toxic to cats, so the plants and all potentially dangerous substances were removed before the cat moved in.*

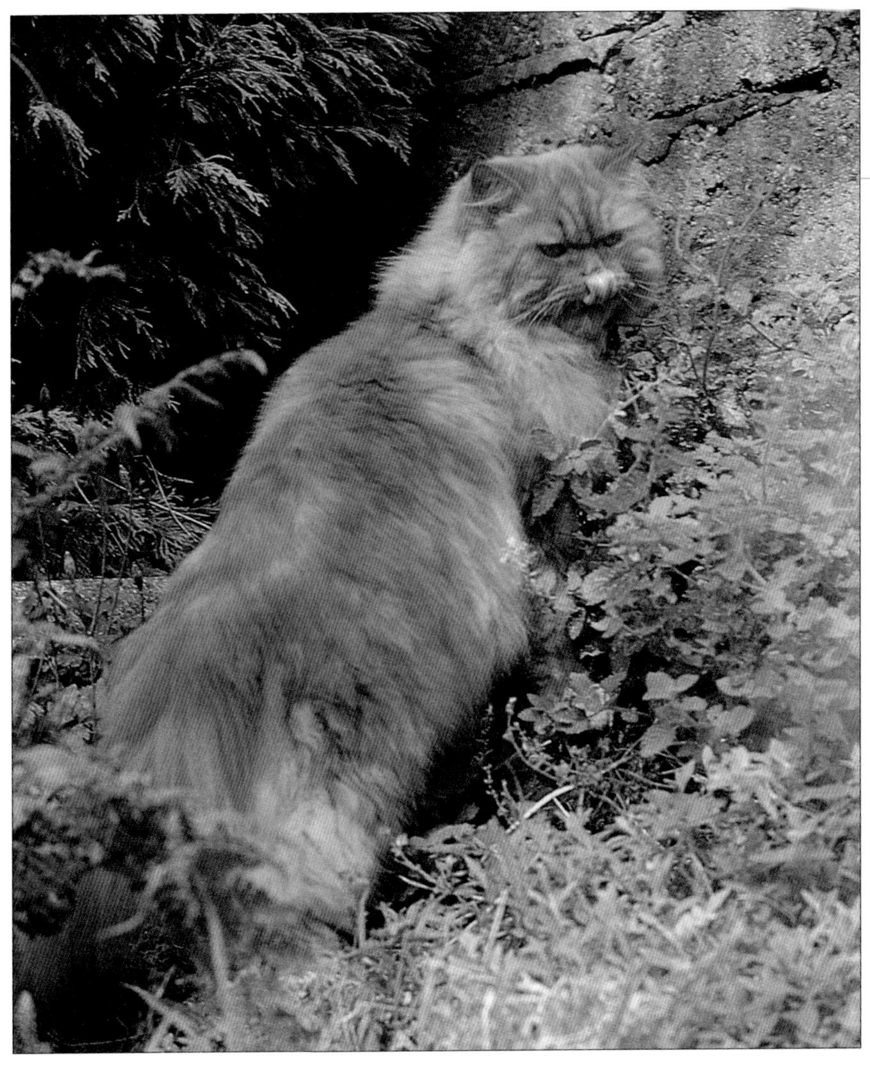

However, indirect poisoning could possibly occur if the cat were to eat a bird or a small rodent that had fed on such a plant. Cats do eat grass and other herbage to provide minerals and vitamins, and to act as emetics to get rid of fur balls, for example. Outdoor cats are free to choose their own greenstuff and, because of their normally fastidious nature, seldom make mistakes by taking a mouthful of a toxic plant. Seeds of grasses that are beneficial to cats are marketed, and can be grown indoors. If you do have an indiscriminate plant chewer, avoid having plants that could be dangerous in the house and garden. A garden centre should be able to advise on what these are (see pages 100–01).

▼ *The mouse that this young cat is playing with could carry toxins picked up at an earlier point in the food chain.*

▲ *A robust ginger non-pedigree is seeking out some greenstuff to supplement his diet. Most cats instinctively avoid potentially poisonous plants.*

around the garden. Your cat might eat the bird that ate the slug that took the slug pellet, or it just might lick its pads on to which a slug pellet has adhered. So check the contents of weedkillers, slug bait or growth enhancers and opt for the environmentally friendly varieties. Even these may carry a warning regarding domestic pets, and some cats have particular reactions to a few substances that are safe for the majority, so keep alert.

Cats usually instinctively avoid the plants which are poisonous to them.

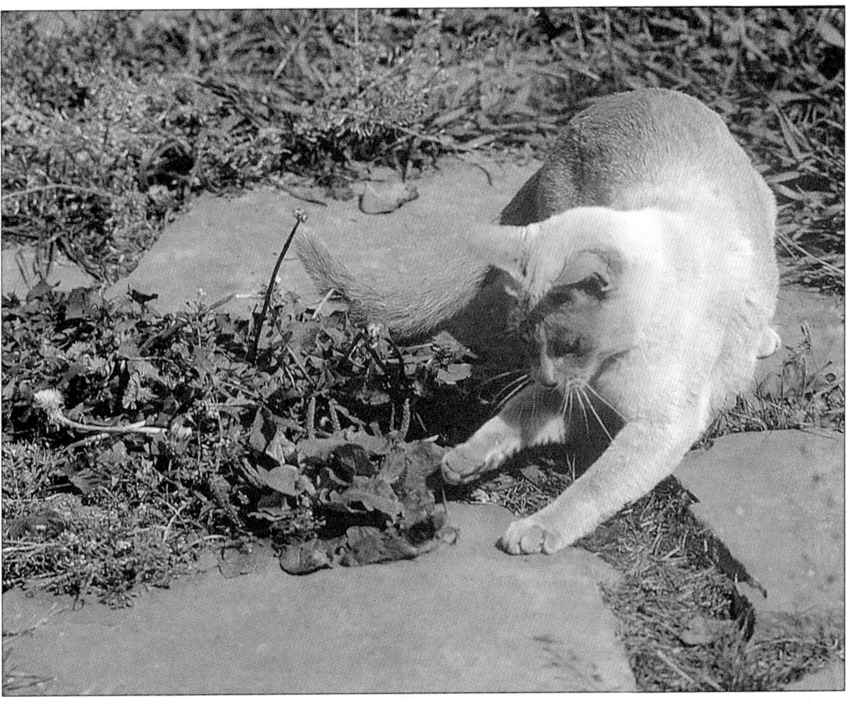

Poisonous garden plants

Garden plants that adversely affect cats fall into two categories, those that form an ingestion hazard and those that are a contact hazard.

Ingestion hazard plants may cause digestive upset or discomfort if eaten. A smaller number are extremely toxic and can cause severe poisoning, or even death. Although cats with access to a garden will not often chew plants, this is not always so, especially in the case of kittens or younger cats.

It is often hard to tell if your cat has ingested hazardous plant material unless you catch the cat in the act, see chewed foliage or find plant material in their vomit. If you suspect this might be the case seek immediate veterinary treatment. It is important to take a sample of the plant, including flowers or berries if available, to the vet with you. If your cat has vomited it would be helpful to the vet if you collect and take some of the vomit too.

Owners need to think outside the box when assessing the danger of hazardous plants. Most of us are aware that yew trees, for example, constitute a danger if ingested and would correctly think it extremely unlikely that a cat would chomp on a yew. But consider the fact that the yew needles (leaves) fall to the ground, the cat rolls on the earth and gets the needles in its coat. Being fastidious they then groom themselves and ingest the needles. Things are not always as clear cut as they may first appear.

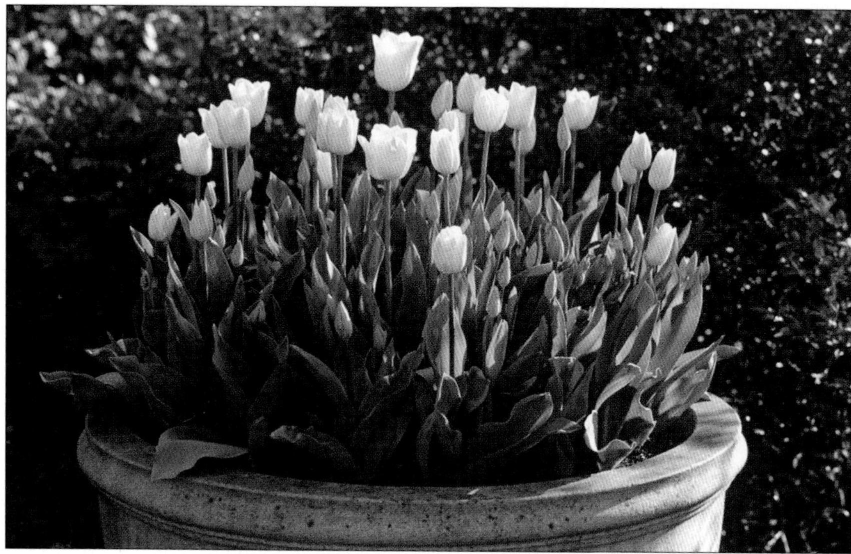

▲ *The bulbs are the most toxic parts of tulips but any part of the plant can be harmful to your cat.*

Contact hazard plants are those where the sap, pollen or hair-like structures on the leaves or stem are an irritant. These plants can cause burning sensations, blistering,

▼ *Seek immediate veterinary assistance if you think your cat has eaten any part of a daffodil or narcissus.*

▼ *Potato toxicity can be fatal: do not allow your cat to eat raw potatoes or uncooked potato peelings.*

▲ *Symptoms of ivy poisoning include muscle weakness, breathing difficulties, diarrhoea, vomiting and fever.*

▲ *Foxgloves are a cottage garden plant. They are highly toxic to cats, in severe cases leading to cardiac failure.*

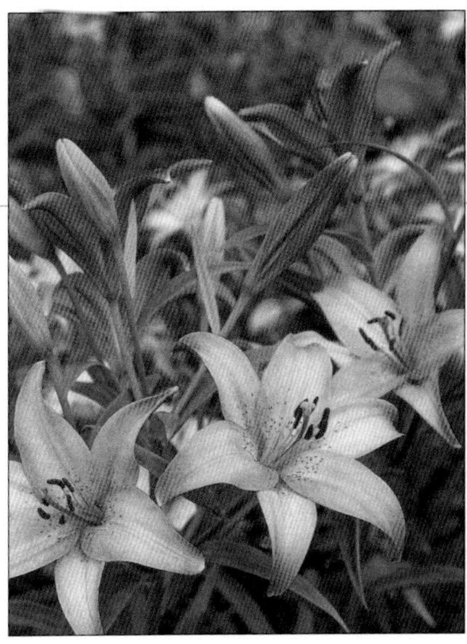

▲ *All types of lily are extremely toxic to cats, dogs and humans. Consider if the floral glory is worth the risk.*

swelling, allergic reactions, skin discolouration or redness. Swelling, especially around the mouth, eyes or face, can induce breathing difficulties, and in a few cases can cause death.

If you suspect your cat has been in contact with an irritant plant, remove any plant material from the skin and coat, taking care not to rub any into the skin. If necessary, wash the cat with warm water. Seek prompt veterinary attention, taking a sample of the plant with you.

Cats wandering in the garden are extremely likely to brush against contact hazardous plants and problems can be exacerbated by self-grooming and ingesting the irritant. So, in the case of the cat, these two groups of hazardous plants can overlap.

If planning a new garden or adding plants to an existing garden it is better to be safe and avoid any form of toxic plant material. Lists of plants that are toxic to cats are readily available from the internet or from good reference books. Established plants within your garden should be identified and risk assessed.

Plants, shrubs and trees are not the only vegetable material in the garden that could prove to be toxic. Some fungi are poisonous and best removed when visible. Cyanobacteria (also known as blue-green algae) is found in ponds, lakes and brackish water and is toxic to pets, livestock and humans alike. Avoid allowing any animals drinking from water that appears to have a blue-green 'bloom' across the top. The 'bloom' appears in the summer months and is a particular problem in parts of the USA.

Toxid common garden plants

Below are common garden plants that are toxic to cats. This is, by no means, a comprehensive list. Many garden and house plants overlap and cat owners are advised to read the pages on poisonous house plants as well (see pages 112–13).

Aconite (leaves, flowers and roots)
Autumn Crocus (all parts)
Azaleas and Rhododendrons (all parts)
Boxwood (all parts)
Clematis (all parts)
Common Privet (foliage and berries)
Daffodil (all parts)
Foxgloves (all parts)
Gladiola (bulbs)
Hydrangea (all parts)
Ivy (leaves and berries)
Juniper (needles, stems and berries)
Larkspur (all parts)
Lilies (all species – all parts)
Macadamia Nut (all parts)
Marigold (new leaves and stems)
Nightshade (berries)
Oak (buds, young shoots, sprouts and acorns)
Oleander (all parts)
Peony (foliage and flowers)
Potato (sprouts, vines and unripe tubers)
Snapdragon (foliage and flowers)
Sweet Pea (all parts)
Tulip (bulbs)
Verbena (foliage and flowers)
Virginia Creeper (sap)
Yellow Jasmine (all parts)
Yew (needles, seeds and bark)

Wildlife and the outdoor cat

The cat is a born hunter and this can cause some issues, both emotional and environmental. Feral cats kill to eat but a well-fed domestic cat kills because it is instinctive.

It is estimated by the Mammal Society that domestic cats in the UK catch up to 100 million prey items per year. In the United States lowest figures estimate around 7.6 billion assorted birds, mammals, amphibians and reptiles are killed annually by combined domestic, feral and wild species of cat.

The RSPB estimates that cats kill 27 million birds in Great Britain each year (these are the birds that are known to have been killed) but state that there is still no scientific research proving that predation by pet cats has any impact on bird populations in the UK. Evidence suggests that cats take weak or sick birds that were unlikely to survive. Blue tits are the second most commonly killed birds but, despite the large upsurge in domestic cats, their numbers have increased by 18 per cent between 1970 and 2017.

There are always exceptions to the rule, the most notable being that of the Stephens Island wren *Xenicus lyalli*. Once found throughout New Zealand, its last refuge was Stephens island in Cook Strait. The whole population was wiped out, over a hundred years ago, by a cat called Tibbles that belonged to the lighthouse keeper.

Birds are most vulnerable when feeding, so simple precautions such as not putting bird food on the ground can do much to improve their safety.

▲ *Although cats are more likely to kill small rodents than birds, they are opportunists and will stake out bird feeding stations.*

► *In theory a bell on a collar may alert wildlife but it is amazing how quickly cats learn to move without ringing the bell.*

▼ *Bird nesting boxes and feeders should be positioned in places that a cat cannot climb up to.*

▲ *Chipmunks, ground and flying squirrels and gophers are all easy prey for cats in North America.*

▶ *This skilled hunter will remain totally still until it judges the time is right to make the fatal pounce.*

Bird tables and feeding stations can be made cat-proof by fixing a cone or upturned can to the post so the cat is unable to climb on them. Using a metal pole to support the table is ideal as the cat will find this more difficult to climb up. Planting thorny or spikey plants beneath the table will stop the cat sitting underneath and give some protection to ground feeding birds eating spilled food.

Nest boxes should be positioned where the cat cannot reach or climb up to them. It is important to site the boxes in a place where the cat can't sit near, as this might prevent the nesting bird returning to its eggs or young.

Birds are most active in gardens an hour after dawn and an hour before dusk. Cats could be fed indoors during these times thus leaving the garden free for the birds.

Putting a collar, with a bell attached, on the cat helps to prevent it catching birds and mammals alike. This is endorsed by the International Cat Care (formerly the Feline Advisory Bureau). The collar must be correctly fitted with room to place two fingers between the cat's neck and collar. Collars should either have an elastic insert or a safety 'snap' mechanism to prevent the cat getting hooked up and unable to free itself. It is possible to purchase collars equipped with electronic sonic devices that work in the same way as a warning bell.

Soft neoprene bibs are available that can be attached to the collar and hang loosely over the cat's chest. They work by interfering with the precise movement coordination required to catch prey. They look ungainly but the majority of cats are relaxed about wearing them within a couple of days. Statistics show that wearing a cat bib reduces the likelihood of the cat catching a bird by 81 per cent and catching mammals by 45 per cent. Cat bibs also interfere with the cat's ability to catch or kill reptiles and amphibians too.

The most common mammals caught by cats belong to the mouse, shrew and vole families. But there are occasions when the feline predator will tackle a larger prey. This can sometimes result in the cat sustaining an injury. Although most bite wounds are caused by cat to cat conflict, racoon, possum or rat bites are not unheard of. Whatever mammal inflicted the bite, all wounds should be assessed by the vet as this type of injury can quickly become infected without proper care.

Cats will hunt snakes and appear to be unafraid of them. Many snakes are non-venomous but, for example, in the area around Perth, Australia, 30–40 cases of cats receiving bites from venomous snakes are reported annually. If you suspect your cat has been bitten by any snake take it rapidly to the nearest vet where it can receive urgent treatment if required.

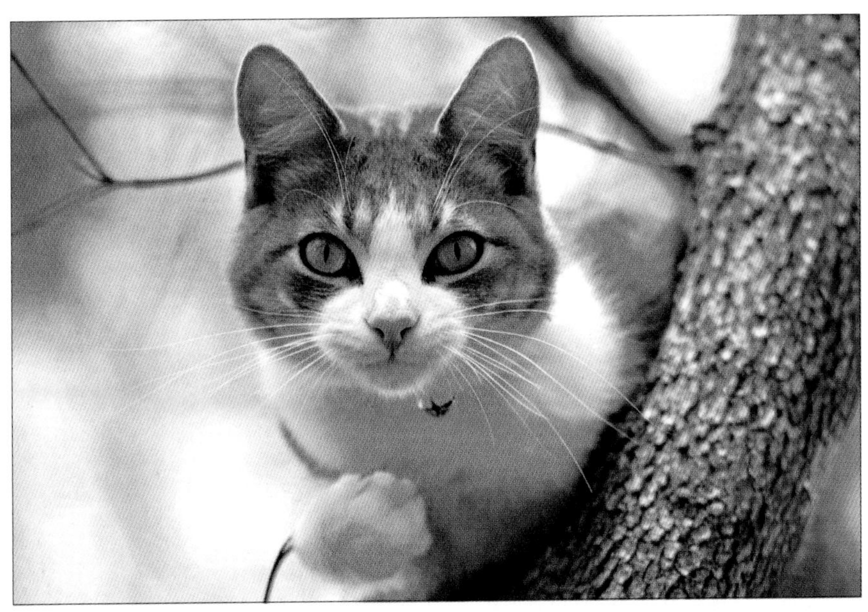

◀ *Ever watchful, this cat is just waiting to practice its hunting skills.*

Homing instinct

► *The homing instinct is not as strong in kittens who may not trust their internal compass and become confused.*

The 'homing instinct' is the term used to describe the ability that some species have to be able to navigate from a distant point back home. Most people are aware that pigeons have this natural skill and fly long distances from a release point back to their loft. It is thought that birds are able to do this by following the earth's magnetic field lines, and using the position of stars and the sun. They may also use visual clues such as rocks, mountains, rivers and seas.

Cats have two types of homing instinct, the ability to find their way home and also the ability to track down their owners when they have been separated.

Scientific tests have been conducted to prove that many cats are able to navigate their way home from a start point that they have never been to before. Theories abound as to how they do this but no one is sure of the answer. It has been found that cats allowed outdoors are better at this than cats confined indoors. Studies show that cats are more able to find their way home if the distance they have to travel to return is less than 12km (7.5 miles). The homing instinct also appears to wane over time. This is why it is so important, if moving home, to keep your cat shut in for at least two weeks. There is much anecdotal evidence of this type of cat-homing instinct. Tigger, a persistent three-legged cat living in the USA, after a house move, returned to his old home over 75 times, completing a trip of almost two miles each journey.

The ability of a cat to find its owner when it has been left behind is called 'psi-trailing'. Again scientists are as yet unable say how cats, and dogs, are able to do this. A French cat belonging to a soldier travelled 120km (75 miles) across the Vosges mountains to re-join its owner when the soldier had to move military barracks. Animal ethologist and Nobel Prizewinner Nikko Tinbergen considered these abilities 'was by processes not yet known to us'.

◄ *If a cat gets lost place its litter tray outside. It is believed that it can smell it from a mile away.*

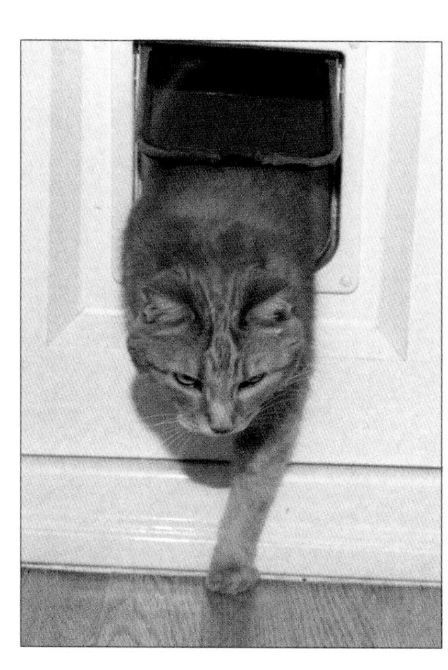

► *Indoor cats who have escaped outside are unlikely to go far but may not understand the concept of a cat flap on return.*

Controlling a cat's territory

If you live in an apartment block or in a busy urban environment, or your cat is frail or a valuable pedigree, it is perfectly feasible – and acceptable to most cats – to keep it indoors all the time. In some parts of the United States, vets actively recommend this for cats in urban environments. Because of the balanced pet foods now available, modern cats do not need to go out to supplement their diet by hunting. Outdoor exercise is also unnecessary, as long as the owner provides toys and plays with the cat.

Although cats are nocturnal by nature, it is really unwise to allow much-loved pets to stay out at night. Train them to stay in from an early age and make sure there is always a clean litter tray available. This training also ensures that they are equally happy if kept indoors for long periods.

The outdoor cat's tendency to roam and exposure to the dangers of traffic, fighting and infection from other cats, can be reduced at a snip – that is, by being neutered (altered). The sex-drive of a calling queen or an active tomcat will override any considerations for road safety. The unneutered male cat can hunt over an area of about 11km (7 miles). His desexed counterparts will probably exercise territorial rights over maybe 200m (240 yards) at most.

The making of an indoor cat

The consultant of this book, a breeder of Maine Coon Cats, does not let his cats out until they are well over six months old – two-to-three months after they have been neutered. The cats are trained to litter trays and so, when they are eventually let out, it is not long before they rush back in to use their usual toilet facilities.

Because they are neutered, their hunting and roaming instinct is greatly curtailed and they seldom stray beyond their familiar garden.

► A ginger kitten has taken over the best armchair. An indoor cat needs plenty of toys and active input from its owner if it is not to become bored and substitute the upholstery for a tree.

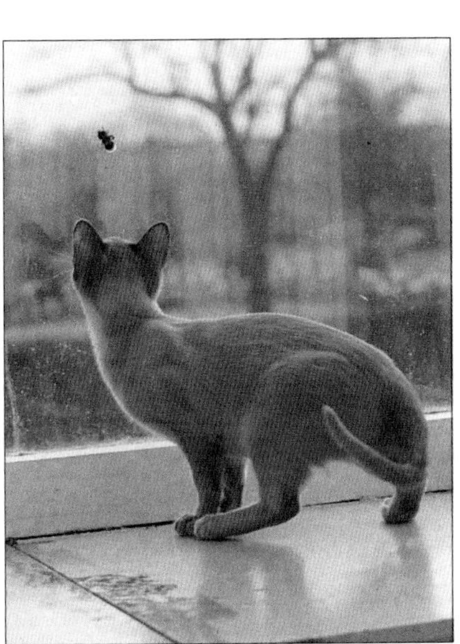

◄ A Burmese is attracted to the outside world. Some cats are freedom-loving and do not like being kept indoors.

► A Persian has the comfort-loving temperament suited to an indoor life, and its long coat is easier to care for inside.

Looking for a missing cat

Discovering that a cat is missing is every owner's worst nightmare. Try not to panic and enlist the help of friends and neighbours to assist you in the search for your pet. Cats seldom get lost unless they have recently been moved to the neighbourhood and are trying to find their way back to their old home. Even then most, amazingly, can accomplish this task.

Firstly, check your home carefully. Cats love to hide and often ignore owner's entreaties to respond to their name if they are settled in a comfortable and private place. Search every cupboard, even those you do not think that you have opened. Under beds and in the bottom of wardrobes are favourite hiding places. Look in, and behind, electrical appliances such as washing machines, tumble dryers, cookers, fridges and the heating boiler. If your house has a cellar or attic look there too. If you haven't located your cat next search the garden and in particularly the garage and shed. Check these buildings carefully as the cat may be hiding behind boxes or other objects. When you have established that your cat is not on your property it is time to broaden the search.

▼ *Cats frequently get shut in sheds or garages. Ask all neighbours if they, or you, can check outdoor buildings.*

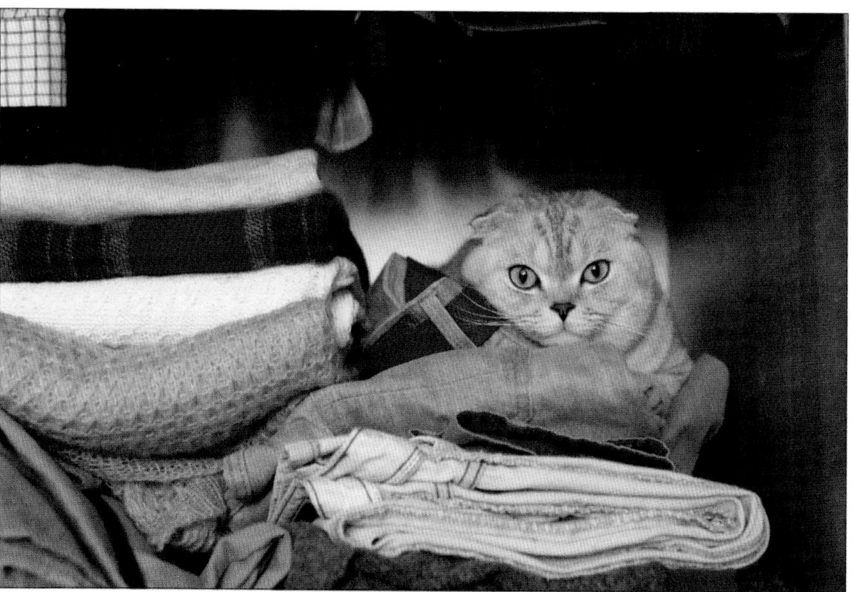

▲ *Wardrobes, airing cupboards (hot presses) and drawers are all places a cat might accidentally get shut in.*

Before you leave your house make sure that the cat flap is open, or that the cat can enter the house in its normal manner, should it return during your absence. Begin by asking neighbours to check gardens, sheds and garages. If you are not sure that they will, or can, do this ask if you can check yourself. Also look under parked cars in the roadway nearby. Cats love to watch the world go by from the perceived safety of a stationary vehicle.

If the above produces negative results alert the company that stores the details of your cat's microchip and report your cat as missing. You will need the microchip number when you make this call. At the same time call local vets and animal sanctuaries and give them your cat's description and your contact details. Most people who find a cat that they consider either

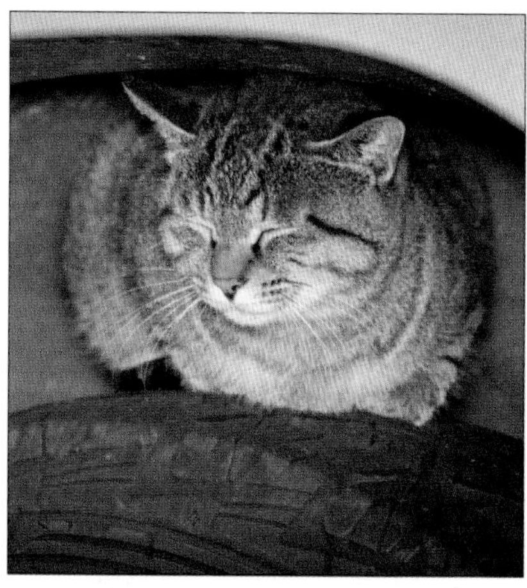

▲ *Cars have an irresistible appeal. An open window, door or tailgate offer an invitation to a warm sleeping place.*

▼ *If you should find a stray cat that neighbours do not recognize take it to a local vet to see if it is chipped.*

injured or a stray will take it to a vet where it will be scanned for a microchip.

Using the most recent photo, make posters reporting your cat lost and give a contact number for any information. If you are unable to make up posters yourself there is bound to be someone among your friends and neighbours who can. If possible, laminate the posters so that they can withstand the weather. Fix the posters on lamp posts and fences in your neighbourhood. Ask people living close by if they will put one in their window, or on their garden gate. Local pubs, shops, hairdressers, vets and doctor's surgeries are also good places to put a poster as they have a large footfall.

Social media is an excellent tool to use when trying to find a missing cat. Both Twitter and Facebook have produced exceptional results reuniting lost animals with their owners. Post a photo and a request to people to look in their sheds and garages. Also ask that they share the posting with their friends. Genuine groups and forums can be found who will be able to offer support and advice. Avoid those that ask for money to instigate a search. Sadly, there will always be those who trade on people's distress. The internet will provide you with websites of organizations, such as CatAware, The National Pet Register and Animal Search UK that help in the search for lost pets free of charge.

If your cat is insured check the policy as many include financial assistance if your pet is lost. This could be used to produce professional posters, although homemade ones work just as well. You may be able to claim for the cost of placing an advert in the local newspaper. Local radio stations will often put out an appeal for a lost pet free of charge. If one presenter turns you down don't be afraid to ask another as programme schedules vary.

Take heart in the fact that many 'missing' cats turn up of their own accord several days later and can't understand what all the fuss is about.

▼ *Circulate 'missing' posters throughout the neighbourhood, at vets, doctors, local shop and schools.*

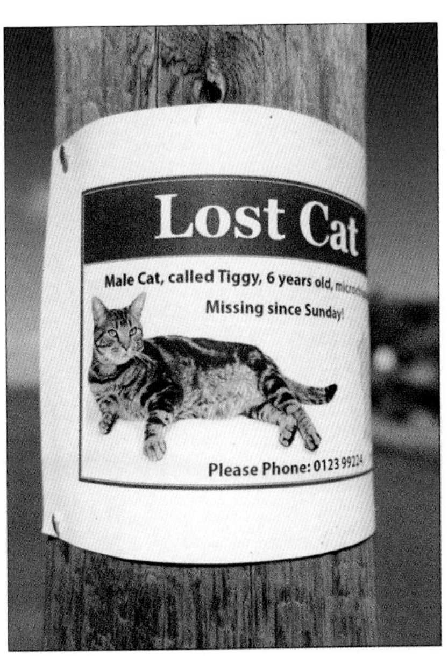

▼ *If your cat is handed into a shelter or vet you may have to provide proof of ownership before they can return home.*

Dangers in the home

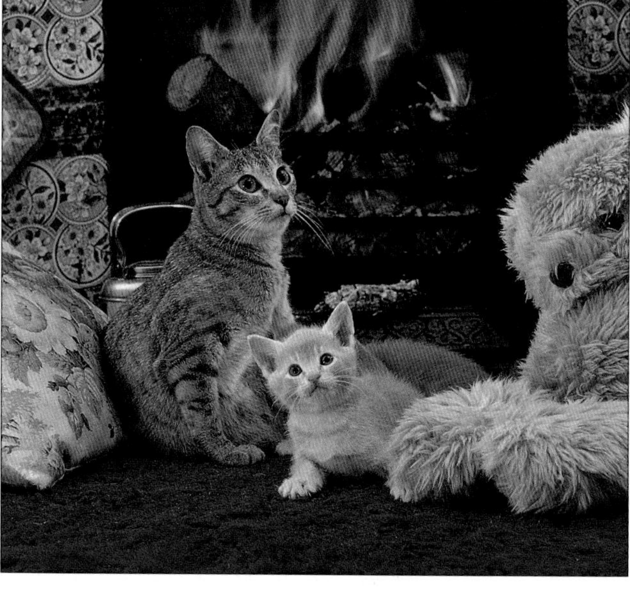

► *A very cosy scene for mother and kitten – however, open fires should always be kept guarded unless you are in the room to keep an eye on your cat.*

There are dangers even for the cat that is kept indoors all the time. Those who live in high-rise buildings should erect netting across open windows and around balconies. The defences can be camouflaged by plants. Even within the house, cats should be allowed access to heights only if they are considered safe. A specific danger area is a staircase with openwork bannisters from which a kitten could launch itself into space – not necessarily landing on its feet. Kittens should always be supervized as they explore.

The warmth, the smells and the movement of washing and drying machines attract a cat's attention. Always make sure that the appliance's doors are kept closed when not in use. Before you turn the machine on, check that there is no cat curled inside. The smell of food in a fridge is also enticing. At least if it were to be inadvertently incarcerated, a cat would survive there for some time, as long as there was sufficient air available. It would not, however, survive for long in a freezer. Fifteen minutes would probably be long enough to cause irreversible hypothermia.

▼ *The washing machine has just been turned off and is still warm, making it a possible spot to curl up in for an undisturbed sleep.*

PLAYING WITH FIRE

Burns and scalds sustained by cats exploring the source of interesting food smells are not unusual and are sometimes very severe. Cats have been known to dance across the hot rings of an electric cooker, badly damaging their paws. Electric cables are potential playthings, so make sure no wires are loose or exposed, and if you spot your cat chewing them, conceal the cables beneath a carpet, or cover them with a cat-proof material such as thick rubber or plastic tubing.

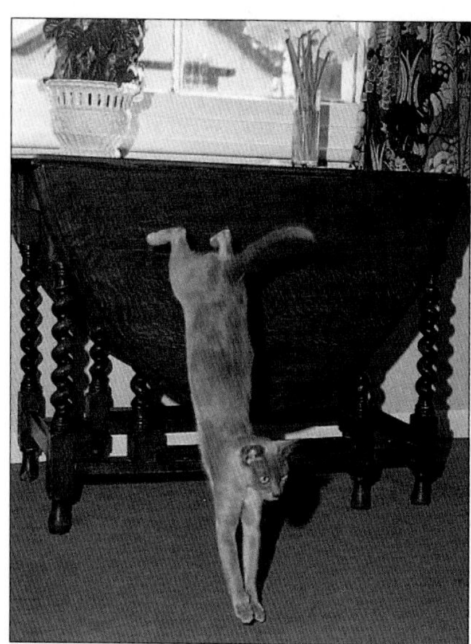

A cat will nose around drawers and boxes packed with interesting oddments – but here too, are potential dangers such as pins and paper clips. Tasty, pingy elastic bands may be fun to pick at and chew, but could cause choking and suffocation, and the same goes for lengths of wool or cotton, or plastic film. Cats are also attracted to olives, the stones of which are just the right size to become stuck in a feline throat. Open fireplaces should always be guarded, even when a fire is not lit, for cats like climbing up chimneys and may become stuck or break a limb, or at the very least emerge soot-covered. Electric and gas fires can be equally dangerous. One cat owner was faced with a fire in her living room and some very frightened kittens, after the combined weight of

◄ *The deliberate leap from the table is well within this cat's capability, but a kitten could hurt itself if it fell or jumped from such a height.*

▶ *Prevention is better than cure. Invest in a specific cat-proof bin with a close-fitting lid and a sliding catch.*

the litter of kittens toppled a highly flammable chair against the bars of a gas fire.

REFUSE DANGER

The rubbish bin or trash can is another source of potential danger. The scent of waste food makes it very attractive to the inquisitive cat. But raiding the bin for a tasty snack can prove very dangerous indeed. Raw meat or fish scraps may contain disease causing bacteria, for example *E. coli*, or parasites such as *Toxoplasma gondii*. Ingesting either could make your cat very ill and in the case of a young kitten even prove fatal. Tinfoil, polystyrene food containers and the string or netting used to shape meat joints are all choking hazards. If eaten, these items often cause intestinal blockages requiring surgery. Empty cans are enticing to lick out and empty plastic bags fun to play with, but both can cause suffocation if they get wedged on the cat's head. Ensure all bins have well-fitting lids.

OTHER DANGERS

The bathroom is another danger point. A number of kittens are drowned annually in unattended baths or sinks full of water, and even in the toilet. Some cat owners are amused by the fact that their cat drinks from the toilet bowl but this habit should be actively discouraged by closing the lid. Toilet cleaners, especially those that are activated by every flush, leave a poisonous residue. Dental floss and all medication should be stored out of reach, preferably in a closed cupboard.

Cats, especially kittens, delight in climbing up window blinds or curtains. Sadly, they can easily hang themselves on the blind slats or looped cords. Cutting the cords so that they no longer form a loop is a sensible precaution. Potpourri and tobacco products, including nicotine gum and patches, all contain substances that are toxic or fatal to cats.

Reclining chairs, rocking chairs and folding or sofa beds can trap and even kill feline pets if they are used without checking that your cat is nowhere near.

Cat owners should take time to assess their home and its dangers. Not only could this save your cat's life but will change a hazardous habitat into a cosy, comfortable and safe retreat for your pet.

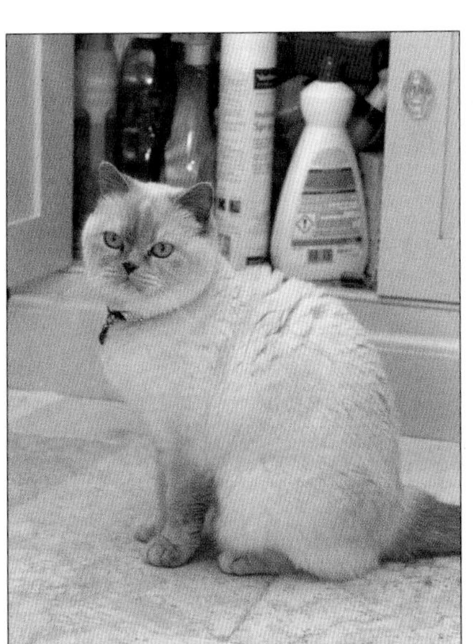

◀ *Many cleaning agents contain the detergent benzalkonium chloride, which is a toxic irritant to cats.*

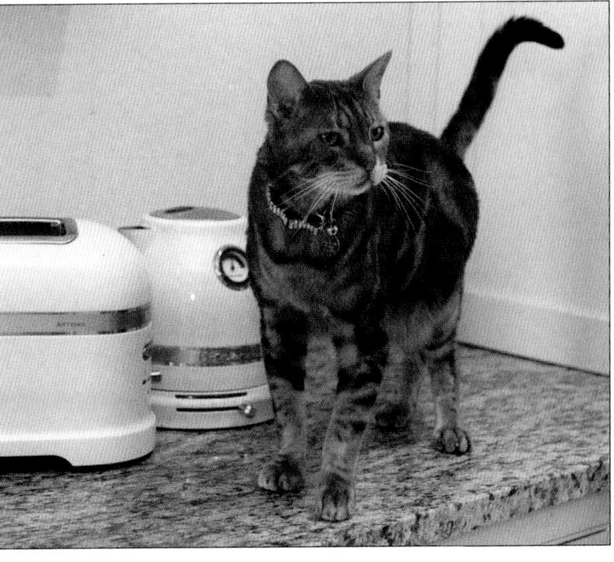

▶ *If your cat is prone to chewing it would be wise to wrap exposed wires in rubber covers.*

Enriching the indoor cat's life

Living indoors is not a natural environment for a cat, in fact it is a bit like existing in a zoo. But some circumstances dictate that it might be the best, and safest, situation. If the owner makes this choice, then they are totally responsible for providing the cat with everything it needs to lead as natural a life as possible. Although, in general, indoor cats live longer than those with access to the outdoors, without the right environment they are not necessarily as happy. Those that are not stimulated are more likely to suffer from stress-related issues such as self-mutilation or excessive grooming.

▲ *These two are enjoying the sun from safe and protected high vantage points in an outdoor run.*

A PLACE OF ITS OWN

Cats need to be able to climb and scratch; this is a normal behaviour for felines. Cat trees fulfil this requirement and can be purchased or made. There are many different styles for sale and plans for homemade structures are available on the internet. Choose one that is as tall as the environment will encompass. Ensure that the base is sturdy so it won't topple over and the ledges are strong enough for the cat to walk or rest on. U-shaped perches are better than flat ones as cats like to feel something against their backs. Many incorporate a scratching post, but if not, a separate scratching area will be required. Cat walkways and ladders are also available, enabling your cat to satisfy their love of high places. Only minimal DIY skills are needed to construct your own from a disused bookcase.

A private place for your pet is essential. It should be somewhere your cat feels safe and secure and can retreat to whenever they wish. This can be as simple as placing a comfortable bed on the windowsill, a fluffy blanket on a chair or even a cardboard box containing bedding

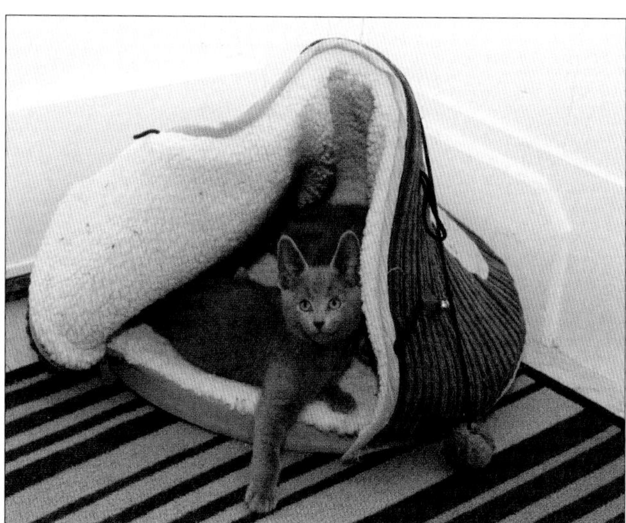

◄ *Cats love to play hide and seek, lurking behind the curtains, in a box or in a soft nesting bed.*

► *Make time each day to play with your cat. Active exercise is important and fun.*

▶ *Placing some of your cat's favourite treats around the house will encourage a rewarding hunting game.*

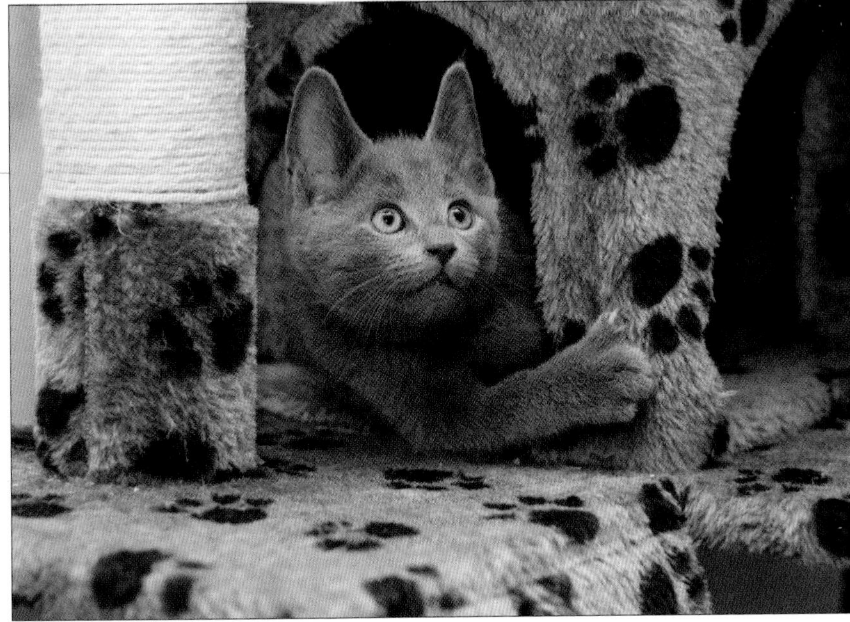

hidden behind the sofa. If you have a multi-cat household each cat will need to be provided with its own safe place.

ENTERTAINMENT AND EXERCISE

Keeping your cat entertained is essential, especially if your pet is left alone for periods of time. Looking through a window is an absorbing occupation for every cat. Ensure they have a clear space to sit, removing anything breakable from the windowsill. Hanging a bird feeder outside will give a cat lots to watch with the added bonus of providing food for the birds. An aquarium, providing it has a well-fitting lid, is equally captivating. It's possible to buy specially produced DVDs for your cat to watch. These play on a continuous loop, and feature birds, fish and small mammals. It is proven that cats enjoy music, especially classical pieces, so a softly playing radio will be appreciated.

Exercise is an important element in a cat's life. Indoor cats can become very sedentary or bored if they have nothing to do. Puzzle feeders will keep your pet occupied for hours and encourage exercise. The principle behind these feeders is that the cat has to manipulate them to release small morsels of food or a treat. They are available from most pet retail outlets and work equally as well with dry or wet food. A homemade version can be made by cutting holes in a pizza box which contains some cat food. The cat will then have to work hard to fish the food out with its paw. This is an especially entertaining game as the box will slide about on the floor making the task much more difficult.

Enclosures can be purchased that attach to the house and can be accessed via a window. These allow cats to have a taste of the outdoors in perfect safety. But they can be costly and beyond the budget of many owners. If this is the case, then try bringing a small piece of the outdoors into the home. Pots of live, growing cat grass give felines something to nibble on and catnip plants, cultivated in a shallow tray, make an excellent area for a cat to roll in.

Food and water stations, litter trays, toys and company, either feline or human, are vital requisites for the indoor cat. All of these are covered elsewhere in this book.

◀ *Cats enjoy nibbling on young blades of grass. Pot some up in a tray and bring it indoors.*

▶ *Providing your cat with a suitable robust scratching post will save your furniture from damage.*

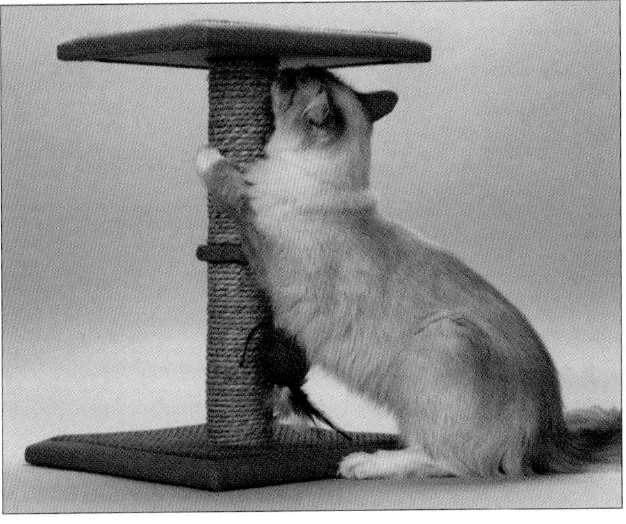

Poisonous indoor plants

Plants and flowers look glorious in the home, but extreme care must be taken if you own a cat. Indoor cats are far more likely to ingest or brush against them than their outdoor counterparts. This is especially true with kittens or younger felines. Because indoor life is more restrictive anything new requires investigating, chewing and rubbing up against and even rolling on. In these situations, the saying 'curiosity killed the cat' is, sadly, often spot-on.

It is perfectly possible to make your home a safe place for your cat and enjoy flowers and pot plants provided simple precautions are taken.

Wherever possible place plant life in an area that is inaccessible to your cat. A window box display will brighten any room but because it is outside the window the indoor cat cannot access it. Within the home, wall sconces are ideal for bouquets and plants alike. Small, high wall shelves will serve the same purpose providing the cat can't jump up on to them. Hanging pots, baskets or glass terrariums from the ceiling, out of reach from your pet, are another option as long as they are securely fixed.

Be aware of common indoor plants and cut flowers that are especially toxic and do not bring them into the home. All species of the lily fall into this category. Their leaves, flowers and bulbs are poisonous to cats, dogs and humans alike. Ingesting any part of this plant can be, and often is, fatal. Amaryllis bulbs are often given as gifts but are also part of the lily family.

Many spring flowers, such as daffodils, hyacinths and tulips, are toxic to cats. Primroses are sold in pots or baskets to be enjoyed within the home. If ingested by a cat, they will cause vomiting and digestive irritation. The toxic substance in this pretty plant is unknown.

In the summer it is tempting to cut flowers from the garden and arrange them in vases indoors. Although many blooms are harmless, there are numerous species that are not. This list includes familiar varieties such as dahlia, sweet peas, carnations, gladiola and chrysanthemum. Asparagus fern and baby's breath are regularly included in bouquets – both

▲ *Although a typical Christmas gift, poinsettia sap is toxic and contains chemicals similar to detergents.*

▲ *It is the bulb of a hyacinth that is especially toxic to cats. If ingested, it can lead to death.*

▼ *All species of primroses and the primula family are irritants to cats, dogs and horses, as well as humans.*

▶ *If giving cut flowers to a cat lover, for safety's sake, check the bouquet does not contain lilies or irises.*

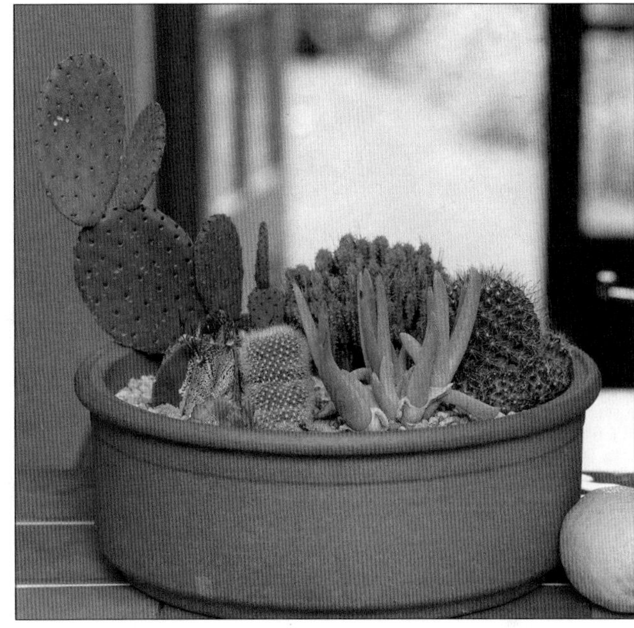

▶ *Sharp cactus spines and fuzzy hair can be particularly problematic for cats.*

will induce vomiting and diarrhoea in your pet, if eaten.

Unfortunately, all the traditional festive greenery that we bring into our home at Yuletide is toxic to cats and dogs alike. Holly berries and leaves cause stomach disorders, lethargy and drooling, and if enough is ingested can be fatal. If any part of mistletoe is eaten your cat may suffer from cardiovascular, gastrointestinal or neurological issues and could die. The leaves of a Christmas cactus contain an irritant while the poinsettia, although not deadly, causes oral irritation and vomiting.

Flowering pot plants to avoid include azalea, cyclamen, begonia and bird of paradise. The first two can be fatal if enough plant material is eaten. Foliage plants such as *Caladium* (Mother-in-law's tongue), *Ceriman* (Swiss Cheese Plant) and *Dieffenbachia* (Dumb Cane) are all toxic. Symptoms of poisoning by any of these include oral irritation, intense burning of the mouth, lips and tongue, difficulty in swallowing, vomiting and excessive drooling.

Cat owners should never be embarrassed to politely refuse a floral gift that they think might be hazardous. Unfortunately, few people realise the harm that a bunch of flowers or a pot plant could do to an inquisitive animal. A gentle explanation of the toxicity of the gift will not offend but may inform.

▼ *If eaten, amaryllis can cause loss of appetite, stomach pain, vomiting, diarrhoea, lethargy and tremors.*

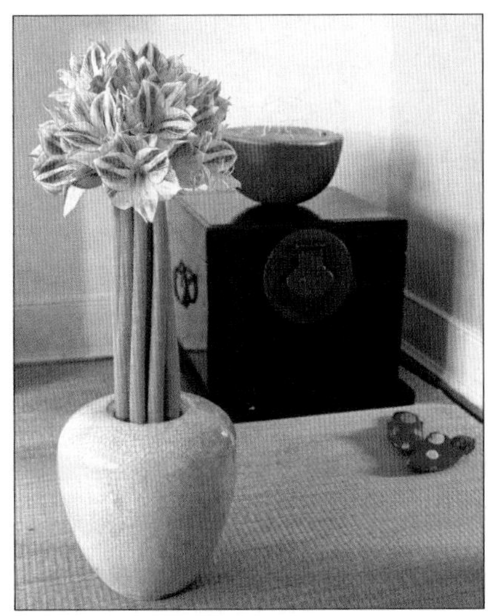

Cacti are non-toxic but some pose an additional danger to cats. The spines can puncture or even embed in the skin. This may not immediately be apparent and only become noticeable when the wound becomes infected. Cats are very partial to chewing cacti, so wounds are often found in the mouth or facial area.

It is impossible to list all the indoor plants that are harmful to cats here but excellent and informative sites are available. Many have pictures for easy plant identification. It is wise to consult one of these sites or a good reference book prior to buying flowers or houseplants. When in a garden centre be wary of advice given at point of sale as it may not be correct. Check all plants out for yourself, it is always 'better to be safe than sorry'.

Going away

Most cats are probably happier to stay in their own homes when owners are away, and there are organizations that will arrange for people to move in and care for your pets. However, this service can be expensive if only one animal is involved. Most people arrange for friends, neighbours, or relatives to live in or to come in regularly to feed and check on the cat. This can sometimes present problems as cats are great individualists, and even if they appear friendly with the sitter when the owners are present they may adopt a different view when the owners have left. In such a situation, a cat might become stressed and stray. It is wise to have a few practice runs and leave the cat for a few days before risking a two-week break. There is usually no problem with indoor cats, or with outdoor cats that are able to continue coming and going via a cat flap. However, this can be an added worry for the carer, who may prefer the cat flap to be securely locked during the owner's absence. Cats used to freedom might be very keen to escape if suddenly confined in this way. Do make sure, before you leave, that the person who is to look after your cat knows where the cat is and has the keys to all the places to which the cat might have access – the house, the garage, plus any outhouses. Always leave your contact telephone number, and the address and telephone number of your vet, including the emergency service. Discuss responsibilities before you go to ensure that what needs to be done is absolutely clear. Leave written instructions if necessary.

▲ *Food, water and a clean litter tray are not all a cat wants when its owners are away. Cuddles and games are also important if your cat is not to feel lonely.*

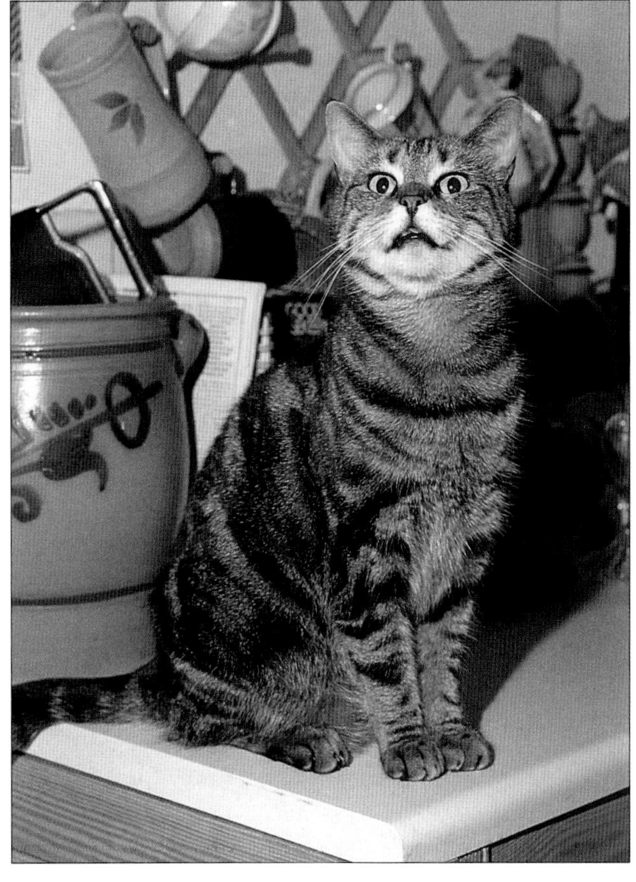

◄ *Being home alone while the owners are away does not present too much of a problem for this cat. It has the freedom of the house, a cat flap for outside access, and a reliable neighbour to call in and feed it.*

BOARDING OUT

If you decide not to have someone looking after your cat at home, ask your vet for approved local catteries (many veterinary practices have boarding facilities of their own), or ask friends for first-hand recommendations. Do make arrangements well in advance of your departure, as the best boarding catteries may be booked up for months ahead. It is a good idea to visit the cattery before booking to see if the environment and atmosphere will suit your cat. Most prefer you to make an appointment beforehand. There are also questions a boarding

▲ *If your cat is on a veterinary diet or medication make sure you take adequate supplies to the cattery.*

▲ *On your preliminary visit to a cattery you could check other residents to see if they look contented.*

cattery owner will ask of you, most importantly whether the cat is in good health and has up-to-date vaccination status. The cattery should have details of your vet's name, address and telephone number, and your own contact address and telephone numbers while you are away. You will be asked for details of special dietary requirements for your cat, a supply of any medication they are on, and you will need to sign a consent form regarding appropriate treatment in the case of illness, and your acceptance of any necessary veterinary bills.

▼ *Check there is enough sneezing distance between one pen and another, just in case one inmate develops an infection.*

Boarding cattery checkpoints

Points to check on your preliminary visit to a cattery:

- Are there individual runs?
- Are the runs and houses inside or outside, and are they are adequately heated?
- Are the pens sheltered, clean and safely out of the reach of dogs if they are taken in too?
- Are the beds and bedding disposed of or thoroughly disinfected for each new resident?
- Are the feeding bowls sterilized between residents?
- Do the staff seem happy, bright and animal-loving? Do they have any qualifications?
- Is there plenty for your cat to watch?
- Do the runs have appropriate sneeze gaps between them? Are the partitions impervious?
- Are there climbing posts permanently available?
- How often are the cats visited during the day?
- Are the kitchens clean?
- Is there access to a vet at all times?

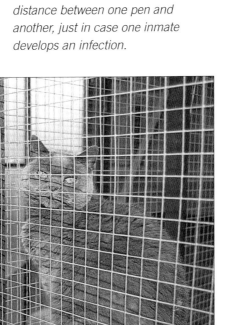

Travelling tips

If you anticipate regular travelling with your cat – to shows, for example – it is worth introducing travelling at an early age. Any length of journey can be very stressful for a cat, and you should try to create as secure an environment as possible within the carrier. Some cats – especially Siamese – can complain loudly throughout a journey if they are distressed because they feel trapped. This can be very distracting for the driver. A vet can administer a tranquillizer, but this should be avoided if possible. Because of the stress factor, it is not advisable to subject a pregnant cat, or a nursing mother and young kittens, to travelling.

If there is no room for a litter tray, lay some form of absorbent padding – absorbent kitchen paper, or a baby's nappy or diaper – on the base. Avoid newsprint, especially if you have a light-coloured cat whose fur might stain. Spread one of the cat's usual sleeping blankets or towels on top, and add a favourite toy.

◀ *A pedigreed cat is going off to a show. As it is travelling alone with the driver, the carrier will have to be firmly secured on the back seat of the car.*

Seasoned cat show travellers suggest that the cat carrier should be placed as far away from the engine as possible, away from engine noise, and from direct blasts of dry air from heaters and fans. Some carriers have a specially designed cover to keep out light and draughts. Otherwise, on cold days, you can cover the carrier with a blanket or towel. However, do make sure there are sufficient gaps for ventilation. In the early days of cat shows, owners would send their prize animals by train in such carefully sealed baskets that on some unfortunate occasions the cats arrived dead from suffocation.

▼ *A Seal Point Siamese emerges from its lightproof and draughtproof container.*

BOOK AHEAD

Before booking a bus or coach journey, always contact the company you intend to travel with well in advance to check their regulations on the transportation of animals. Different rules can apply from company to company and it may not be possible for your cat to travel with you, if at all. In the United States, for instance, the Greyhound bus line does not permit pets. You will almost certainly have to pay a fare for your pet. Few companies consider them as hand baggage.

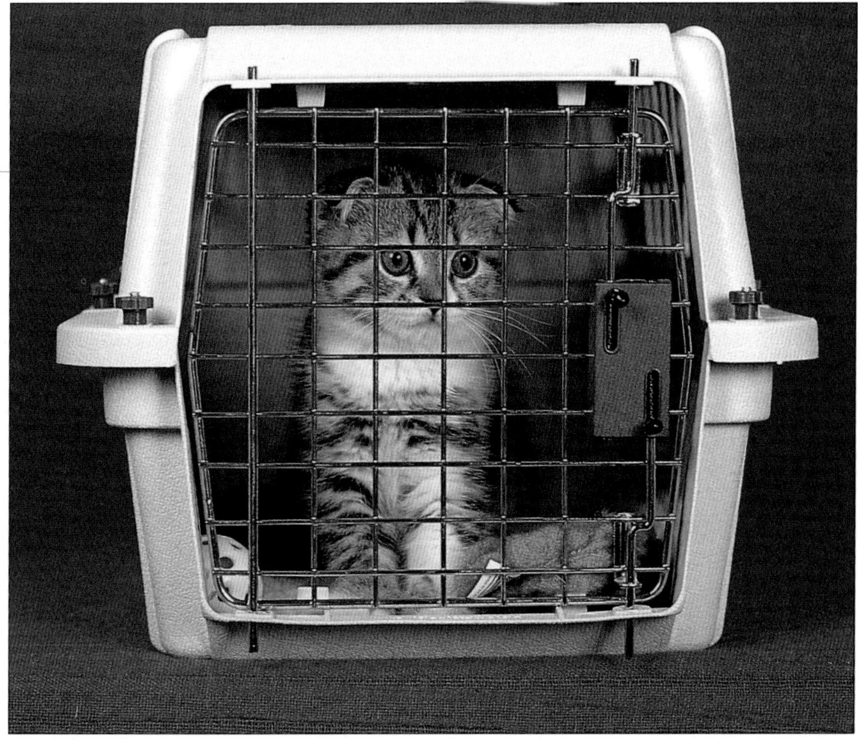

▲ *A sturdy carrier suitable for an air journey has a ridge around it to guard against the ventilation holes becoming blocked.*

AIR TRAVEL

Commercial airlines have well-established regulations for the transportation of pets. These conform to International Air Transport Association (IATA) regulations. It is vital to contact the airline offices at least a month in advance of the travel date to ascertain requirements. You may be required to buy a carrier that has to be ordered by mail from a specialist supplier. In any event, the carrier should be of a strong, rigid material, stable and well-ventilated. There needs to be a handle for ease of carrying, and a door that can be locked to guard against anyone opening it. A label carrying the owner's name and address, together with instructions for any feeding or watering that might be necessary, should be securely attached. If the journey is to be a long one, and the carrier is not big enough for a litter tray, line the base with plenty of absorbent towelling or a disposable nappy.

Some airlines allow a cat in its carrier to stay with its owner in the passenger section. Usually, though, your cat will be housed with other animals booked on the flight in a special area of the hold which provides an environment with heat, light and air-conditioning, according to current IATA regulations. Regardless of whether you are travelling by plane or overland, ensure your cat is wearing a collar with your contact details on it. It is worth investing in two collars, one containing your home details and the other with your destination details. Remember that mobile or cell numbers have different country codes, and it will be necessary to change your cat's collar and ID accordingly.

We all rely on our mobile phones to store numbers and I am sure that you have logged in the number of your vet at home and also the number of a vet local to your destination. Sadly, phones get broken, lost or even stolen. The simple precaution of writing these vital contact details on a piece of paper as well will save time in the event of an emergency. If your cat is microchipped, write down the chip number and company contact details too.

▼ *Some countries require that cats are microchipped before allowing entry. Check whether this ruling applies to your destination country in good time.*

Changing countries

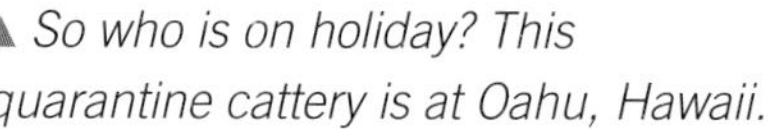

▲ *So who is on holiday? This quarantine cattery is at Oahu, Hawaii.*

It is not only top breeders who export their highly prized pedigreed cats and kittens to countries around the world. Retirement, career changes or even health considerations can prompt cat owners to move from one country to another, and if it is for any significant length of time, the cat goes too!

Arranging exportation first involves contact with the local animal health offices of the relevant government department – the Department for Environment, Food & Rural Affairs (DEFRA) in the United Kingdom, or the Department of Agriculture in the United States. This should be done as soon as possible and will provide essential information. You will need an export licence, and it is advisable to apply for this about four to six weeks in advance. This is due to the fact that vaccination against specific diseases is mandatory for a number of importing countries and has to be administered at a specific minimum time before import is allowed. Many countries receiving cats from the United Kingdom will insist upon the rabies vaccine having been administered at least 28 days prior to import.

With a few exceptions your cat can travel from one EU country to another or from a non EU country to a EU country if it has been microchipped, vaccinated against rabies, treated for tapeworm, has a valid EU Pet Passport or EU Health Certificate.

If travelling from the United Kingdom, an Animal Health Certificate and/or an Export Health Certificate replaces a pet passport unless (in some circumstances) your cat has been issued a Pet Passport in a EU country or Northern Ireland.

Documentation required for animals entering the UK is dependent on the

◄ *A cat in quarantine should have a private shelf and plenty of room in which to run around.*

country of origin. Owners are strongly advised to seek clarification from their vet on this subject.

Generally, there are no restrictions to bringing domestic cats into the USA. A rabies certificate is not required but the cat will be subjected to a veterinary check to ensure it is free from disease. Both Hawaii and Guam do have quarantine requirements, however.

Importing to Australia requires that an import permit is in place before arrival. The application for this can take 20–25 days to process. If travelling to South Africa, cats have to clear through either Cape Town or Johannesburg. Provided the import documentation, which is quite complicated, is correct the animal can move straight to its new home. If an error is found the cat will be placed in quarantine until the fault is rectified.

Owners wishing to import or export cats are advised to check up-to-date regulations as these can change at short notice. They should also be aware that airways impose rules for travel by plane which can be more exacting then those required to enter a country. These vary from company to company.

▲ *A show cat is not subjected to the strict quarantine regulations still imposed in Britain, as long as certain requirements are met.*

IMPORT OF SHOW CATS

The British regulations have relaxed a little for animals intended for 'trade' – which means show cats are included but not ordinary household pets. Such animals can be imported into Britain without undergoing quarantine, provided that stringent pre-entry requirements are met. These include vaccination against rabies, blood-testing to assess immunity, implantation of an identity microchip, and importation from a registered holder on whose premises the cat has either been born or been continuously resident for the previous six months.

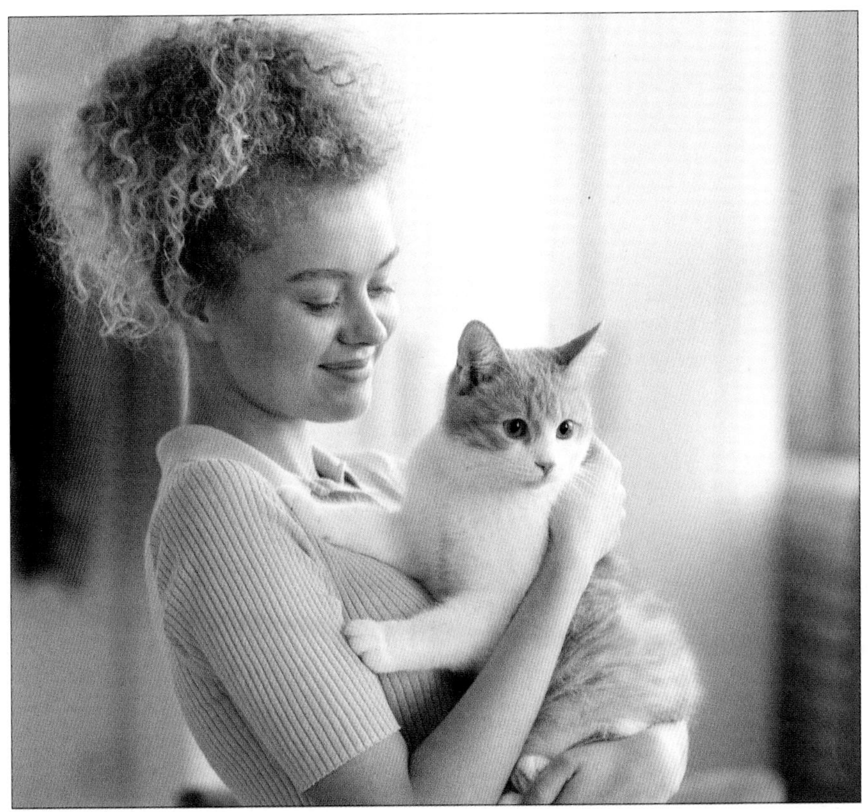

◄ *When your cat arrives in its new home, it will need a great deal of attention and to be kept indoors for a while.*

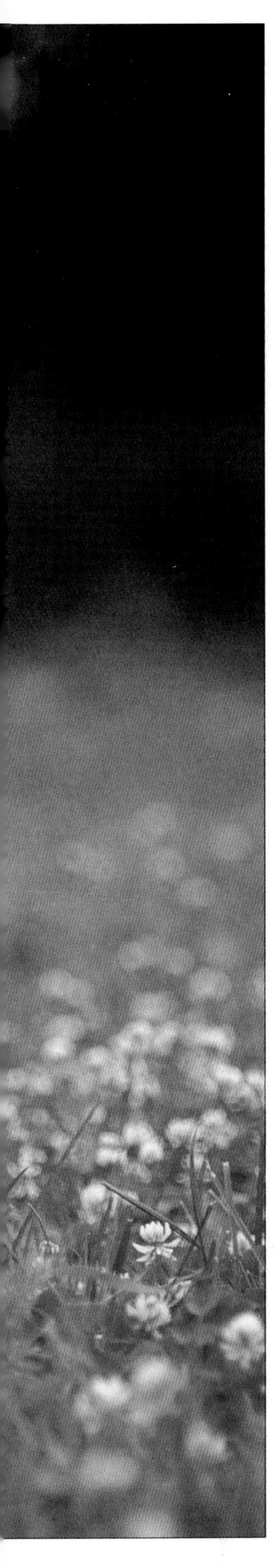

CARING FOR YOUR CAT

Responsibility for a cat's welfare rests with the owner. This includes nutrition, grooming, veterinary attention, first aid and pain relief. All cats should be registered with a veterinary practice before they become ill and inoculations kept up-to-date. There is a vast array of cat foods now on the market and it is important to ensure your pet is getting all the vitamins and minerals he or she needs at each stage of their development. Longhaired cats require daily grooming regardless of whether they are destined for the show circuit. Even shorthaired cats will need some attention paying to their coat and this fact alone should influence the decision on what type of cat is best for your circumstances. All cat owners should be aware of the signs of good and ill health and be able to spot the tell-tale signs of something being amiss with their pet. First aid cannot be considered a substitute for veterinary attention, but can be vital in stabilizing a sick or injured cat prior to transporting it to a veterinary clinic.

◄ *A happy cat looks good, has a healthy appetite, a zest for life and will spend most of the day doing whatever it is that it likes doing best.*

Good health in cats

Cats are graceful, elegant and independent animals and, treated correctly, they make wonderful pets. As mammals, their life cycle closely mirrors our own.

A new-born cat begins its life as a kitten, in which state it is totally dependent upon its mother. After a few weeks, it is weaned and begins to learn how to socialize and how to keep itself clean. This period is followed by a short adolescent stage, during which time social training is completed, and the young cat learns how to hunt for itself. Mature adulthood follows, and the cat becomes old and eventually dies. The average lifespan of a cat is 16 years.

A cat has the same basic requirements throughout its life. These will be influenced by its age and the type of lifestyle that it is allowed to lead. Kittens and young cats are more lively than older ones and need more opportunities for play and exercise. Consequently, a fit, active, young cat needs more food than an elderly one. Generally speaking, older cats are more sedentary, and may need special diets which cater for specific health conditions.

Cats are all more or less the same shape and size, regardless of their breeding group. Distinguishing features tend to be the length of fur, fur colour and patterning, and the shape, size and colour of the eyes.

Whether pedigree or non-pedigree, and regardless of distinguishing features, fit, healthy cats share certain characteristics. Their coats are in good condition and do not smell. Their eyes are bright and their faces are alert and clean and are not stained by tear-spillage and other discharges. Their ears and nostrils are clean, without any discharge or smell. A healthy cat moves with ease and grace and does not limp. It is able to exercise under normal conditions, without coughing or showing signs of distress, for a period of time commensurate with its age. Like us, cats may tire more quickly as they grow older, but they should still move easily and without pain, and they should be able to enjoy all that life offers.

Emotional health should not be disregarded, it goes hand in hand with physical health with each influencing the other. Cats deprived of opportunities to conduct their natural behaviour

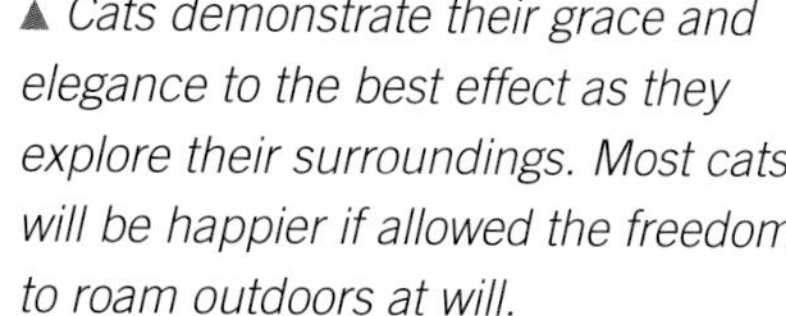

▲ *Cats demonstrate their grace and elegance to the best effect as they explore their surroundings. Most cats will be happier if allowed the freedom to roam outdoors at will.*

▶ *The natural curiosity of the cat is displayed in young cats which hunt and play with more unusual objects found around the home.*

▶ *Spending time playing with a cat or tickling its tummy is of enormous benefit to pet and owner and will strengthen the bond between them.*

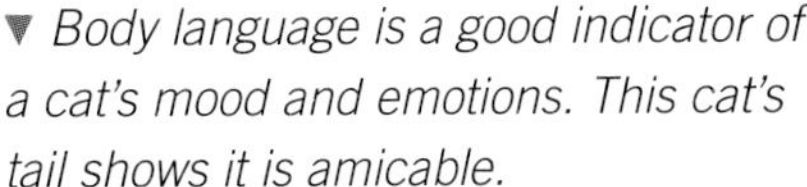

▼ *Body language is a good indicator of a cat's mood and emotions. This cat's tail shows it is amicable.*

often exhibit signs of stress. All animals are equipped with physiological systems to be able to cope with short periods of anxiety. This forms the basis of the flight or fight theory. In most instances, the cat living naturally, can either remove itself or defend itself from the source of unease. This is not always the case for the domestic pet.

Long-term stress will have a direct impact on health and can alter a cat's behaviour. Signs of chronic stress vary and can be difficult to detect as they usually develop over a period of time. It is easy to miss the first indications that all is not well in your cat's perceived world. A cat may show one or several symptoms including lack of appetite, over-eating, hiding, aggression, extreme vigilance, feigned sleep, over-grooming or coat plucking, displacement behaviour, increased vocalization and inappropriate urination and defecation. Clearly none of these actions are symbolic of good mental health.

A happy and content cat will be curious and enthusiastic. In their home surroundings, they will walk with head lifted and tail held high, often quivering at the tip. When alert the eyes will be wide open and ears erect. They may trill or chortle a greeting. Purring is an indication of contentment, but this is not always the reason for a purr. Relaxed resting cats will often lay with their paws tucked under the chest. Eyes appear sleepy and half closed. A cat that lays on its back with its legs in the air does not feel stressed or threatened in any way. Cats that enjoy sitting on a lap may show their happiness by kneading or paddling with their paws.

Playfulness is a good indication of lack of stress. Kittens will play for hours but this activity will decrease as the cat ages. A senior cat will still enjoy a short game providing the toy offers sufficient excitement and hunting appeal.

▶ *Cats signal trust by exposing their stomachs. This activity is not necessarily an invitation for a belly rub.*

Exercise for cat health

A fit cat is a healthy cat. Exercise plays an important part in your pet's overall health and wellbeing. A cat needs the chance to run, pounce and climb freely. This stretches and strengthens its muscles, keeps its heart in good order, and maintains its lively and acute sensitivity.

Free-roaming cats have the chance to exercise, but many are lazy and do not make best use of the opportunity, often preferring to sun themselves in a warm spot rather than run about. It can also be difficult for an owner to get the balance right between freedom and safety, as many cats are killed or injured in road traffic accidents every year. It is possible to train some cats to walk on a collar and lead, but this is not ideal as a cat also needs some more dynamic form of movement.

In the wild, queens start to wean their young at about four weeks. They will bring in stunned, live prey for their kittens, who start to practise hunting skills at this age. Wild kittens will learn to kill mice from about five weeks. Most socializing skills are learnt at 7–12 weeks. If you have a kitten it will need lots of active play and attention. Kittens should not play for more than 15 minutes at any one time, but they need three short periods of playtime each day. Games that teach hunting skills are obviously the best, and are also more likely to get a response from the kitten. A small ball can be used as 'prey', but roll it past or away from the kitten, rather than towards it, so that it can chase it. An irregularly shaped ball, or a bias-weighted one that will roll irregularly, will bring more realism and interest to the game. Fishing-type toys are now made for cats, and these, too, are generally popular and bring variation to the game. Catnip toys can be bought or made for the kitten to play with. Like any child's toy, these should be checked for safety before they are given to the cat: look for small parts which could detach and get swallowed or cause injury.

▼ Obesity restricts the physical activity of a cat and will seriously reduce its desire to play.

At six months, the kitten's training in hunting and social skills will be complete. However, it is important to carry on playing with your cat throughout its life. Playing together helps to stabilize and reinforce the relationship between you and your cat. It will also bring a variety of experience into the cat's daily life, as well as being fun for both of you.

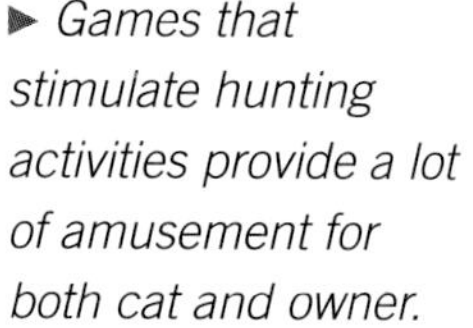

► Games that stimulate hunting activities provide a lot of amusement for both cat and owner.

If your cat is a house cat, it is essential that it has enough scope for daily play and exercise indoors. Tower and tree-like objects are useful as they bring the play into three rather than two dimensions. They help to teach the cat co-ordination and strengthen muscles. Sophisticated modular climbing frames are available which can be changed around from time to time to provide a change of scene for the cat. They usually incorporate ledges, boxes to hide or rest in, and a carpeted or rope-covered scratching-post for sharpening claws. The physical action of climbing will wear the claws and lessen the cat's need to scratch at furniture. Climbing frames are particularly useful for cats that are kept indoors all the time. If the cat does not have one of these, a scratching post at least 1m (3ft) high will be needed.

► When your cat has caught its 'prey', it should be allowed to play with it as a reward.

▲ *It is harder to motivate an indoor cat to exercise. Cat towers, or cat trees, provide great entertainment.*

► *The outdoor cat will spend time exploring their territory as well as engaging in hunting activities.*

For breeding stock kept in outside runs, large branches and tree trunks should be provided to give the cat a chance of vertical movements as well as ground-level exercise. A wide variety of hanging and moveable toys should be available, which should be changed regularly to prevent boredom.

Try to make your home safe for your cat. Upper windows and high balconies should be made cat-proof. Cats have incredible balance, but they do fall from such places. This is not usually from a lack of balance but, more likely, from chasing insects or from sleeping on a narrow ledge and rolling over the wrong way. Cats have remarkable righting reflexes and always seem to land on their feet, but if they fall from a great height, the impact can be enough to break legs.

Dogs are so simple to exercise compared to a cat. You only need to pick up their lead and they are ready for the off. Cats often have to be enticed to move from a sunny window sill or comfy bed and give their muscles a work-out. However, exercise is vital to maintain health and it can be difficult to ensure that cats take sufficient. This is especially true for indoor, older or solitary cats. Two cats tend to play together even in their more senior years.

There are a number of fun ways that owners can offer occasions to exercise. Cat trees or towers stretch muscles as the cat climbs or jumps to different levels. This can be encouraged by leaving small treats at various points on the tower. Do this several times a day to keep the cat interested, but remember to adjust their daily food ration if using a large number of treats. Scratching posts also provide opportunities for a good work-out.

Provide a wide range of toys to prevent boredom. Laser lights and fishing toys are extremely popular and enable your pet to practice leaps and turns. Both could be trailed over a sofa or armchair to add interest and challenge to the game. Puzzle toys vary in difficulty, some have adjustable levels, and make the cat work, both physically and mentally, for a reward. Ping pong balls are an old favourite and are great for chasing and batting with a paw. Placing one in a large cardboard box increases the fun as the cat tries to hook it out and the ball ricochets off the walls. This is great entertainment for the cat and will delight the owner while they watch their pet's antics.

Not all cats like catnip but most find the substance exciting. Placing soft toys in a sealed box containing a sprinkling of this herb for a couple of hours will enhance them. Brush off any loose catnip before giving the toy back to the cat.

Providing exercise opportunities for a cat enables the owner to increase the bond with their pet and it is great fun too (see also pages 88–91).

◄ *A simple toy gives this kitten a good work-out as well as mental stimulation and a good deal of fun.*

NUTRITION AND FEEDING

If you give your cat a well-balanced diet, it will radiate good health. The massive array of cat feed on the shelves of the pet store or supermarket can be bewildering. Closer examination of the products will reveal that many are age-specific: kitten, adult or senior. Then there are those specifically manufactured for the needs of an indoor or outdoor cat. After that, flavours and different textures abound. Purchasing a quality food is a good investment but only if your cat will eat it. The wise shopper buys a small quantity when trying a new product to avoid a cupboard full of food that their cat finds unpalatable. Veterinary-prescribed feline nutrition is available from the vet's surgery or specialized websites. Ensure you never run low of these premium products as they may need to be ordered and a substitute could cause medical or gastric upset.

◄ *A healthy cat has a healthy appetite. Lack of interest in food could signify the start of an underlying veterinary or behavioural problem.*

Eating habits

The cat is a carnivore which means that its natural diet consists of the prey which it eats. The cat's teeth and whole dietary adaptation are geared towards the consumption and digestion of entire insects, small rodents, birds, amphibians and fish. While cats do eat some plant matter, they have specific requirements for certain nutrients that can only be found in animal tissues. For this reason, meat must form at least part of a cat's diet. For an owner to try to impose a vegetarian diet would be cruel.

Nutrients are the part of the food that provide energy or raw materials from which the cat builds or replaces its tissues. Unless they are provided in the correct quantity and balance, the cat will not be able to maintain a normal, active life. Nutritional requirements vary at different stages of the cat's life cycle, which is why commercial cat foods are now available for kittens, adults and senior cats. The belief that feeding a cat well makes it less likely to bring its prey into the house, or that keeping the cat

▲ *A cat stalks its prey, a pastime it enjoys and does instinctively rather than being driven by pangs of hunger.*

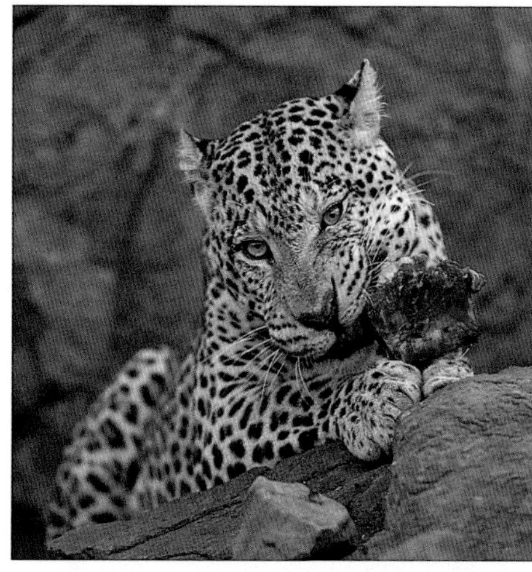

► *A leopard with its natural prey. Even a domestic cat will appreciate the occasional raw bone.*

▼ *Abandoned kittens enjoy a balanced diet and security at a cat welfare home.*

▶ *When feeding feral cats, it is better to use several smaller feeding dishes rather than a single larger tray.*

hungry will make it become a better mouser, is ill-founded. A cat does not need the incentive of hunger to hunt; the healthier it is, the more successful it will be as a hunter.

The natural way for a cat to eat in the wild is to have a quantity of small meals each day. They are solitary feeders who work on an 'eat as they catch and kill' basis. The lion is alone in being the only member of the cat family that hunts and eats as a pack.

Once we bring a cat into our home we expect it to conform to our preferred method of feeding it. This is seldom the best way for the cat. A few minor adjustments on our part and a better understanding of the cat's natural behaviour can greatly enhance your cat's feeding enjoyment.

In the wild, a cat will eat shortly after it has killed. This means that the meat it is eating is warm. Yet in the home we store opened, canned cat meat in the fridge and expect the cat to eat chilled food. This is easily remedied by leaving the food to come to room temperature or warming it up before it is offered to the cat. Food can be warmed in the microwave or by the addition of a little hot water. The ideal temperature for cat food is around 38°C (101°F), which is roughly the same as their body temperature.

As solitary feeders, cats in a multi-cat household should each have their own individual feeding area. This might also mean an area free from human company too. Owners often marvel at a cat that will pick up a mouthful of food, move it away from the bowl and place it on the floor before eating. This is nothing fancy, just the cat looking for a more private place to eat.

Small numerous meals are best, but in our busy lives this is often not possible. Leaving a shallow bowl of biscuits for the cat to pick at during the day is one way of overcoming this problem. Owners could also consider scatter or puzzle feeders. These are interactive feeders where the cat has to work with its paws to obtain each piece of food. Most of these feeders work equally well with wet or dry food.

◀ *A queen will feed her kittens on demand. She will require additional rations to avoid weight loss.*

▶ *Even well-fed cats are opportunists.*

Routine

Feed an adult cat once or twice a day. Serve the food in the same place at around the same time each day. A mixture of canned and dry food is a good idea, for variety, and so that the cat uses its jaws and teeth on the dry food. For the correct quantity, follow the manufacturers' recommendations on the can or packet. An adult 4kg (8lb) cat generally needs around 400g (14oz) of canned food per day or about 50g (2oz) of dry food, depending on its lifestyle. Cats with freedom to roam will need more than an indoor cat, and more may be required during cold weather. Avoid giving snacks between meals. If your cat asks persistently for more, check the quantities are within the above range, but do not feed on a demand basis. If concerned, ask your vet's advice. Overeating and obesity do occur in cats, although to a lesser extent than with dogs. Do not leave food, especially canned food, lying around for long. It dries, begins to smell, attracts flies, and generally offends the cat's acute senses of smell and taste. Clear away any uneaten food immediately, and wash specially designated utensils and bowls thoroughly. Feeding your cat titbits from the table is not recommended. Cats readily form anti-social habits, and pester you at meal-times.

◄ *A meal served at room temperature is eaten with gusto. Cold food straight from the refrigerator may be rejected.*

► *A cat takes its meal on a windowsill, so that the house dog does not steal its food.*

▼ *A Siamese can persistently ask for more food in a very loud voice. Some indoor/outdoor cats do need more food in cold weather, or simply because they are more active than indoor cats.*

A balanced diet

Within its diet the cat requires a balance of proteins, carbohydrates, fats, vitamins, minerals and water. If you give your pet meals at regular times, and offer a variety of fresh and commercial cat foods following the guidelines below, it should get all that it needs without the addition of any dietary supplements such as vitamin pills. Read the labels of commercial cat foods to check the nutritional contents.

PROTEINS FOR STRENGTH

Proteins are made up of amino acids which are the building blocks of the body. They are not only used for growth and repair, but they can be metabolized to provide energy. The amount of protein in a cat's diet depends on its age. As cats become less active with age, they need a less protein-rich diet. In addition, their livers and kidneys have reduced efficiency and are less able to flush out the toxic by-products produced from the body's breakdown of proteins. A kitten, however, because it is growing and building up its muscle mass, needs around 50 per cent of protein in its diet, compared with over 30 per cent for a young adult. These levels are around 20 per cent more than those required by a dog of comparable age. The cat's digestive system processes proteins so efficiently that only five per cent of total protein absorbed is lost through waste products. Regular ingestion of protein must occur or the cat loses weight and condition. In the wild, feral cats acquire the essential amino acids through a variety of captured animals. Protein-rich foods are meat, fish, eggs, milk and cheese. Today, all nutritional needs are covered in the commercially available, scientifically formulated cat foods.

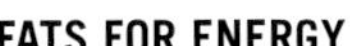

FATS FOR ENERGY

Fats are the second major source of energy for cats and should form a minimum of nine per cent of the dry matter of the diet. The cat can digest up to 95 per cent of the fat it consumes; any excess is stored beneath the skin to provide insulation and protection for the internal organs. However, an imbalance between intake and fat used up through normal exercise can lead to an excess of fatty deposits and obesity. Fat is broken down in the body into fatty acids,

▲ *Cats enjoy a varied diet and are not averse to raiding the owner's food supplies to achieve it.*

▼ *A pair of Singapura kittens clearly have sufficient animal fats and tissue in their diet to provide them with an abundance of energy.*

▼ *Natural instinct is the driving force for a cat to hunt, not hunger. Feeding your cat a healthy and adequate diet will not stop it hunting, and could improve hunting performance.*

◀ *Night vision can be helped by vitamin A. This should be provided by a balanced diet that includes some liver, for example.*

▶ *The teeth of the wild cat and its domestic descendants are geared to killing and eating small animals. A vegetarian diet would not be appropriate for your cat.*

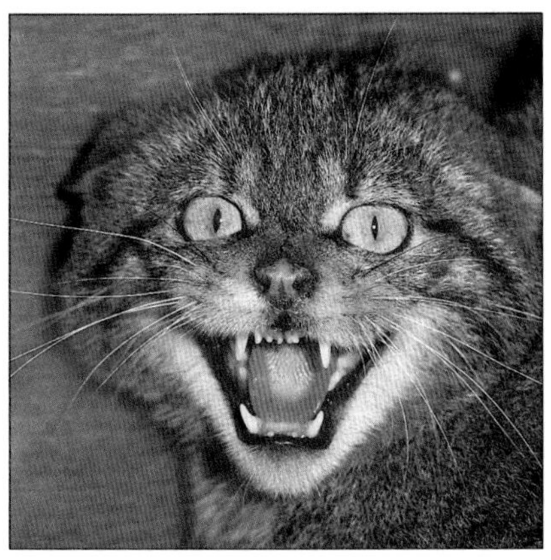

which are important in the formation and maintenance of cell membranes throughout the body. Some fatty acids are essential to the cat's diet, and are almost entirely absent from vegetable foods. They come from animal fat and tissue. In addition, fat also provides fat-soluble vitamins to the cat, including vitamins A, D, E and K.

CARBOHYDRATES FOR BULK

Carbohydrates are the major energy source for most animals, but the cat can, in fact, survive without them. The cat's main natural food sources, birds and mice, are relatively low in carbohydrates, apart from what is found in the stomachs of the prey. However, carbohydrates are a considerably cheaper energy source than protein-rich meat and fish, and a percentage of them are therefore usually incorporated into most commercial cat foods.

Carbohydrates can provide a beneficial boost of readily-available energy at times of growth, pregnancy, nursing or stress. They are also a useful source of fibre, which although not digested by the cat, provides bulk in the faeces. A wild cat would obtain fibre from the fur, feathers or stomach contents of its prey, but the domestic cat obtains it from most commercial cat foods in the form of cellulose or plant fibre.

Carbohydrates should not make up more than 40 per cent of the diet.

MINERALS AND VITAMINS

Proteins, fats and carbohydrates are macronutrients, whereas vitamins and minerals are micronutrients – they are required in only small quantities. A cat synthesizes vitamin C for itself, and therefore needs no extra. Vitamins A, D, E and K work together to refine the bodily functions, and they should all be present in a healthy, balanced diet, together with the vitamins of the B complex. An excess of vitamins can be harmful. Cats fed exclusively on liver, for example (which they love because of the high fat content), may be getting an overdose of vitamin A which is stored in the liver. This can lead to serious arthritic problems involving the legs and spine, even in young cats.

◀ *A determined attempt to reach the treats at the bottom of the jar is likely to end in success. It is wise to keep cat-friendly food in sealed containers in cat-proof cupboards if you do not want your pet to help itself at will.*

▼ *Keep wet canned food and dry biscuits in separate bowls or compartments.*

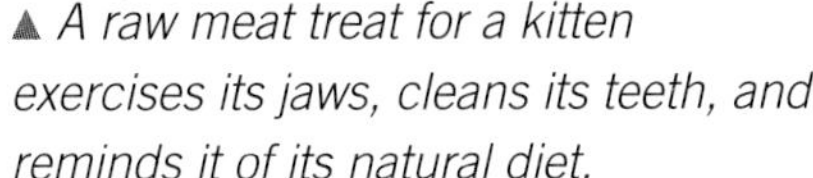

▲ *A raw meat treat for a kitten exercises its jaws, cleans its teeth, and reminds it of its natural diet.*

Minerals need to be available in the correct amounts which, in turn, have to be correct in relation to each other. The daily requirements even of macro minerals (which include phosphorus, calcium, sodium, potassium and magnesium) are measured in milligrams (one thousandth of a gram). Trace or micro minerals are also necessary, but daily requirements are measured in micrograms (a millionth of a gram). A cat that has a regular and balanced diet is unlikely to suffer from mineral deficiency, and supplements should not be necessary. Calcium and phosphorus, for example, are both present in milk, and are very important for the growing kitten. Kittens fed on an all-meat diet and deprived of adequate supplies of milk will develop serious bone abnormalities because they are receiving too much phosphorus, and not enough calcium. For many years, Siamese breeders weaned their kittens on to a meat and water diet in the belief that milk caused diarrhoea. As a result, bone problems often occurred.

▲ *Greek feral cats fend for themselves on the harbourside, their diet of fish supplemented by scraps thrown by tourists from the tavernas.*

FOOD SOURCES

You can supplement your cat's canned or dry commercial food for the sake of variety. It is obviously more time-consuming to prepare special meals, but leftovers and scraps can introduce different tastes and textures with minimal effort and preparation. It is essential, however, to have an idea of the benefits and drawbacks of certain foods, and the danger of an unbalanced diet, such as too much liver and vitamin A. If you want to feed your pet exclusively on home-prepared foods, it is advisable to discuss this with your vet, particularly with regard to types, variety and amounts.

FRESH MEAT

A house cat may traditionally have lived off table scraps and odd bits of meat and fish thrown out for it by the cook – which probably provided perfectly good nutritional levels. The feral cat will eat a small rodent in its entirety, including bones, innards and muscle and will benefit from the nutrients these contain.

If you want to feed your cat on raw meat, this must be supplemented with

► *A pedigreed cat not interested in its food could be ill or simply not hungry. It may also be bored with the same meal served up yet again and be yearning for variety.*

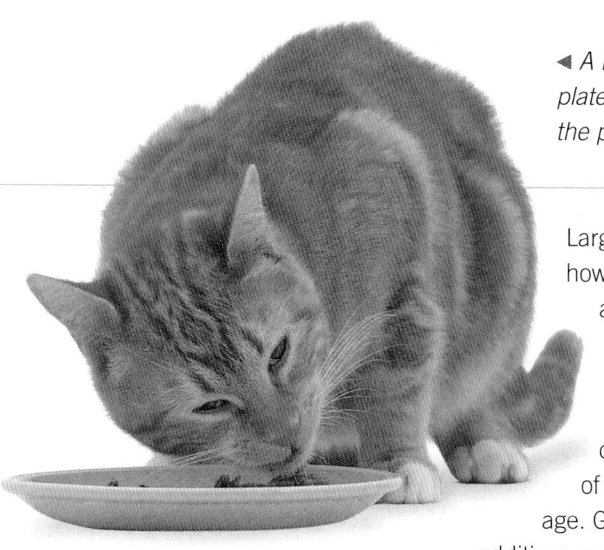

◄ *A Red Tabby tucks into a meal served up on a plate. It is important, for reasons of hygiene, that the plate is reserved especially for him.*

other foods, such as pasta and vegetables for carbohydrates, minerals and fibre, that will provide the equivalent nutritional content of the bones and intestines of the naturally caught rodent.

The best meat, irrespective of type, has a valuable protein content of about 20 per cent. It is best served raw or lightly cooked as many of the vitamins can be destroyed, and the proteins denatured in the cooking process. Protein decreases and fat content increases as the cuts of meat become cheaper. Fat is not a problem, as the cat is well able to digest it and convert it into energy.

Poultry can be served, giblets and all, but make sure the bones are removed, as they become brittle with cooking and could be dangerous.

Large pork or lamb bones, however, can provide a cat and kittens with hours of gnawing pleasure and also help to develop jaw strength, keep the teeth clean, and reduce the risk of dental problems in old age. Generally, avoid meats with additives and high salt content such as ham, bacon and sausages. Offal, such as liver and heart, is rich in minerals such as iron, but is also rich in vitamin A, too much of which can cause serious arthritis.

FISH

Uncooked fish has a protein level of over ten per cent, while fish roes have a high protein level of 20–25 per cent. Raw fish should only be a rare treat, however, as it contains an enzyme that destroys some essential B vitamins. This could result in a variety of symptoms affecting the nervous and gastro-intestinal systems and skin. Oily fish, such as mackerel, herring or sardines, is highly nutritious and is also higher in fat, making it a better choice than white fish. A weekly meal of oily fish may help a cat to cope with the fur balls that collect in its stomach, as well as providing valuable fat-soluble vitamins.

VEGETABLES

Cats on a diet of commercial cat food do not need vegetables. Sometimes they eat grass, which is considered to be a natural emetic and possibly a source of minerals and vitamins. Vegetables are often included in commercial or home-prepared foods as a cheap source of protein and fibre.

DAIRY PRODUCTS

Milk has a useful fat and protein content, as well as lactose (milk sugar), all of which can be beneficial during periods of growth, pregnancy, lactation or stress. Cheese and milk also provide useful minerals such as calcium and phosphorus, but are not part of the cat's natural diet, and should be an occasional treat. Too much can cause diarrhoea, particularly in an older cat. Eggs, mashed or scrambled, are full of protein and vitamin A, but should never be fed raw as they contain an enzyme that can also destroy some essential B vitamins.

▼ *Oily fish, such as pilchards or sardines, are nutritionally better for the cat than white fish.*

► *Most cats are lactose intolerant. Their digestive system cannot process cow's milk. A small amount of goat's milk could be given as a rare treat.*

Prepared cat food

▲ *Meat is meat to these two cats; acceptable food has been found, and it will save a great deal of time and bother for their owner if they have the same thing all the time. Some cats appear to demand variety, but it is not essential for good health.*

Over the last few decades, there has been a tremendous revolution in feline feeding methods. Today there are commercial foods available that cater for all stages of a cat's life. These are available in dry, semi-moist or canned forms, and, in addition, there are deep-frozen foods which come the closest to fresh meat or fish. If the commercial foods are manufactured by reputable, well-known brand names, you can be sure that the contents displayed on the wrapper are balanced. If they are marketed as complete foods the only necessary addition is drinking water. No vitamins, minerals, or other supplements are necessary.

However, cost does increase with quality, and the most expensive varieties are those that are scientifically researched and geared to the dietary needs of cats in each of the three major stages of development: kitten, active adulthood and old age.

Do check the labels for additives (preferably minimal), ingredients and breakdown of nutrient content. Bear in mind, however, that while the average protein content of a can of food may be only 6–12 per cent, this is usually the total content per 100g (3.5oz) of food, rather than being calculated on a dry-weight basis. About ten per cent protein in canned food is equivalent to over 40 per cent dry weight, and is therefore acceptable.

If your cat is fed an exclusively dry diet, provide a bowl of fresh water and change it at least once a day.

THE IMPORTANCE OF WATER

Water is vital for many functions within the body. A cat can survive for 10–14 days without food, but a total lack of water can result in death within days. The daily intake depends very much upon factors such as the moisture content of the food and the climate or temperature. Cats are not great drinkers, and many will hardly seem to drink at all, as they obtain most of their needs from their food. Fresh meat and canned food are made up of about 75 per cent water, whereas dry food contains only about ten per cent. Because of the domestic cat's evolution from desert dweller (the African wild cat), the kidneys are extremely efficient at conserving water. However, fresh water should be always available, especially if your cat eats dry or semi-moist food.

▼ *Dry food (ten per cent moisture) can be kept longer when opened and left longer in the bowl than wet food, without becoming tainted.*

▼ *Semi-moist cat food has a moisture content of 40–50 per cent, and so the cat will require less supplementary water than with a dry-food diet.*

▼ *Canned food (75–85 per cent water) dries and spoils if not eaten immediately. Supplementary biscuits provide exercise for the jaw.*

Cat treats

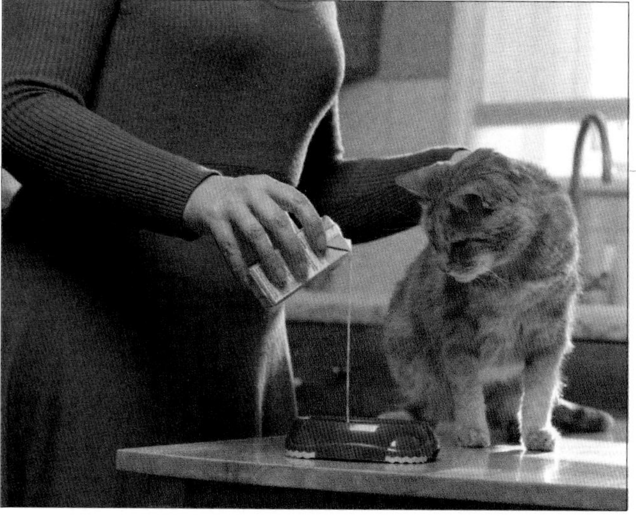

◀ *Lactose in milk can cause stomach upset. Special 'cat milk' has a dramatically reduced lactose content.*

Cat treats should be given as an edible supplement and not as the main diet. If the average cat owner is asked why they buy treats, the most likely answer would be because they enjoy spoiling their cat. This is a fair reply but treats can be used in a number of other beneficial ways and still allow the owner the pleasure of buying a special purchase for their pet.

Treats provide variety in taste and texture to the daily diet. It is important to keep a cat on a consistent and quality diet to avoid stomach upsets, but the occasional treat should not cause a problem.

Treats can be a useful aid to training. The most common use is the rattling of the treat or biscuit box to teach the cat to come inside when called. If you want to teach the cat a new command or to reinforce a positive behaviour, a treat will act as a welcome reward. Always give your cat the chance to respond and reward with a tasty morsel for the action that you require.

▼ *Treats can be used as a teaching aid, to reward behaviour or given just for the fun of pleasing your cat.*

Specially designed treats are used for dental care. These can be bought either from your vet or most pet retail outlets. Firm and fairly hard treats will assist in cleaning teeth by removing plaque and tartar. Some freshen breath too. These often contain rosemary extract and chlorophyll.

If a cat has had an injury or operation and is reluctant to eat, soft flavoursome treats may be a good starting point. It is important not to substitute them for the normal diet, but the odd one may encourage the cat to eat. They can also be crumbled on top of a small portion of the normal ration to make it more tempting. If your cat doesn't quickly regain its normal appetite seek veterinary advice.

Some treats promote good feline health. Hairball remedy treats are available though shouldn't take the place of regular grooming but only used as a supplementary preventive. Treats containing glucosamine and chondroitin can help to maintain healthy joints. These are an excellent choice if your elderly cat suffers from arthritis or stiffness.

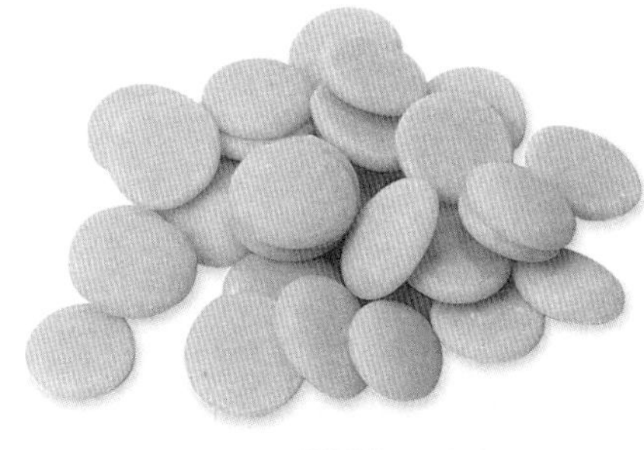

▶ *Commercially available snacks, such as these biscuits and milk-flavoured drops, should be given in ones and twos, as an occasional treat, not in bowlfuls as a main meal.*

Homemade cat treats

▼ Recipes are available for no-bake cat treats. Even children could help make these.

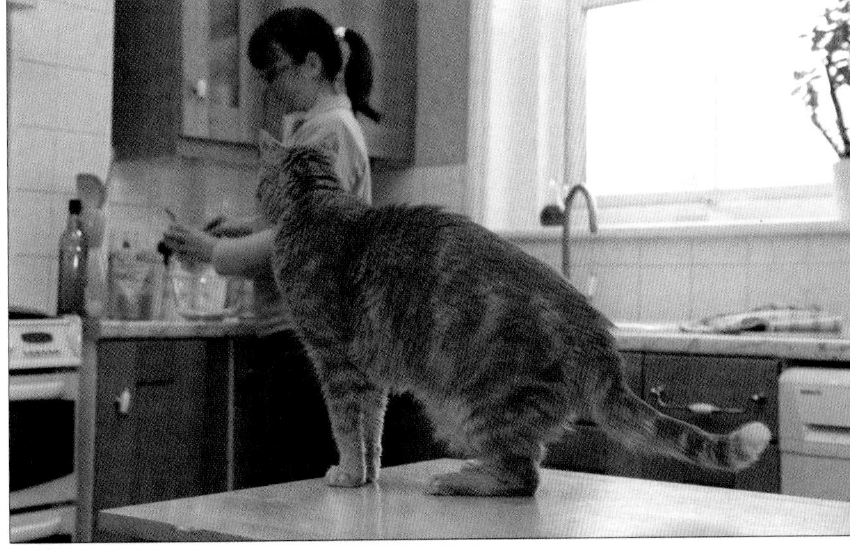

Making homemade treats is an inexpensive way of ensuring that the tid-bits you give your feline friend contain natural ingredients and are not packed full of additives and preservatives. Many shop-bought treats contain cheap fillers and artificial colourings that you may want to avoid too.

All cats have individual food preferences and recipes can easily be adapted to cater to their taste. It is important, when making homemade treats, not to use too much grain- or cereal-based products as these, in large quantities, are not good for cats.

HOMEMADE TUNA TREATS

1 small can of drained tuna in spring water (with no added salt)
1 large egg
115g/4oz/1 cup oat flour (if you can't buy oat flour it can be made by grinding culinary oats in a clean coffee grinder)
15ml/l tbsp olive oil
15ml/l tbsp dried catnip

Preheat the oven to 180°C/ 350°F/ Gas 4. Line a baking tray with baking parchment or greaseproof paper. Place all the ingredients into the bowl of a food processor and blend until smooth, thick and pliable. Add a little more oat flour if the mixture is very sticky. Divide the dough into small balls, each containing about half a teaspoon of mixture. Mark a cross on each ball. Place on the baking sheet and cook in the top half of the oven for 10–12 minutes until slightly browned and firm on the top. Cool completely and store in an airtight container in the fridge for up to seven days.

CHEESE SQUARES

75g/3oz grated Cheddar cheese
115g/4oz/1 cup wholemeal (whole-wheat) flour
60ml/4tbsp plain yogurt or sour cream
30g/2 tbsp cornmeal
45g/3 tbsp grated Parmesan cheese
5g/1 tsp chopped fresh parsley

Preheat oven to 180°C/ 350°F/Gas 4 and line a baking tray with baking parchment or greaseproof paper. Mix the ingredients together and knead to form a dough. Add a little water if the mixture is too dry. Roll out to 5mm (¼in) thick and cut into 2.5cm (1in) squares. Place onto the prepared tray and cook for 25 minutes. Cool and when cold store in an airtight jar.

▼ Care should be taken when cooking or storing homemade treats to avoid any food-born illness.

◄ Home-made treats can be made in a size to suit your pet. Smaller treats are better for overweight cats.

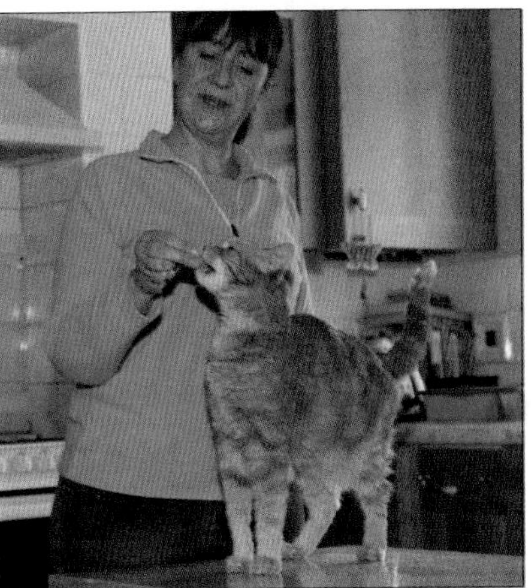

Special dietary needs

A great deal of research has gone into specialized diets for specific conditions such as heart disease, digestive disorders, lower urinary tract disease, and obesity. If you think your cat needs a special diet, seek the advice of your vet. Most of the diets are only available on prescription.

THE ELDERLY CAT

In young and adult life, cats need protein for growth, to replace worn-out tissues and also as a significant energy source. As cats grow old, they become less active, vital organs deteriorate, and their need for protein is reduced. In general terms, a cat is deemed to be elderly at around 11 years of age.

▼ *An elderly cat's diet should supply easily-assimilated protein in the right quantities to sustain energy but not overload the system.*

► *It may take six months or more of carefully controlled dieting to return this obese cat to a normal weight. Weight reduction in cats is more difficult than in humans or dogs.*

If you maintain the cat on the same diet it had when it was young and active, there will be an excess of protein. This throws strain on the kidneys and liver, as the protein has to be broken down and eliminated from the body. If the kidneys are not fully functioning due to age, the body tries to maintain the status quo by increasing thirst, and the cat starts to urinate more. This flushes out some of the toxic products, but at the same time removes some essential vitamins and minerals.

Elderly cats in general require a protein level that is reduced from 40 per cent dry weight to about 30 per cent. There needs to be a corresponding increase in fat levels to ensure that sufficient non-harmful energy is available, but not in quantities that might cause obesity. Carbohydrates (such as starches and sugars) should be avoided, as these are more difficult for the elderly cat to digest and can cause diarrhoea and other problems. Sometimes weight loss is noted in an elderly cat even though its appetite has not diminished, or may even have increased. In such circumstances, consult your vet, as this may be due to

▼ *Perhaps its owner has left stale water in the cat's bowl. In any event, the movement of the drips makes this a far more exciting way to drink.*

▼ *An active adult cat needs – and can assimilate – a higher level of protein in its diet to fuel its lifestyle than an elderly cat.*

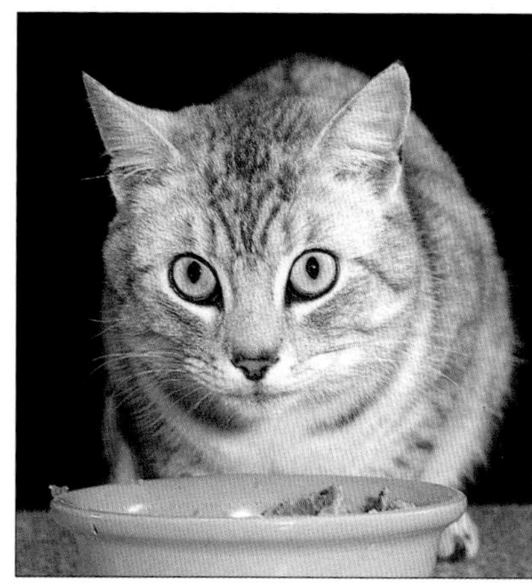

▼ *The advances in feline nutrition can be seen in the increase in life span of the average pet.*

a condition such as hyperthyroidism, which can be treated.

FOOD ALLERGIES

Food intolderance, food allergies or food sensitivity are all terms used to describe a condition where a food component, usually a protein, causes an adverse reaction to the cat. Often a cat can eat a food for years before it develops an allergy, but once this occurs it may remain for life. This can happen at any age. Some breeds, such as the Siamese, appear to be more prone to this condition. Allergies may first present after gastric inflammation, surgery or disease when the cat's physical system is under stress.

The most common symptoms of a food-based problem are skin irritation, vomiting or digestive upset. Other more diverse symptoms may include chronic ear problems, coughing, wheezing, flatulence, hair loss and inflamed skin. In the case of any of the above, see your vet first as these are also symptoms of other serious conditions that need immediate veterinary attention.

If your vet decides that a food allergy may be the source of your cat's problems then dietary elimination trials are important to find which food or foods are the culprit. Frequently it is a protein source with the most common items being beef, lamb, soy, fish, wheat gluten or milk products. It is essential during a dietary trial to withdraw all treats, table scraps and tasty little snacks as well as the normal diet. Your vet will guide you through this step-by-step procedure. This normally involves feeding food items that your cat has not eaten before for a period of approximately 12 weeks. Special diets are available to use through this process and are often labelled as 'limited antigen' or 'hydrolyzed protein' diets.

Unfortunately, there isn't any evidence that blood tests can diagnose food allergies so there is no alternative to food elimination trials if this condition is suspected.

Once the irritant food component has been isolated a special diet will be required. This could be prescribed by your vet or you may be able to make up a homemade diet. If using a homemade diet, it is important to ensure the food contains all the nutritional items vital for the health of your cat.

▼ *Today there is a very wide range of prescribed foods available, which should only be used on veterinary advice.*

► *If the special diet does not tempt the patient to eat, try warming it to blood heat.*

◀ *A nursing queen provides everything for her kittens, including the perfect diet, for at least the first three weeks.*

▼ *This Brown Burmese kitten has lost its mother, but is not fazed by having to join a litter of bull terrier puppies for lunch.*

MOTHERHOOD

The first sign of a cat's pregnancy will probably not be a noticeable increase in abdominal size but a demand for more food. If the queen is in good condition at the time of mating, she should not need extra food until about the last third of the pregnancy (seven to nine weeks). By this time the foetuses will be growing in the womb and space is at a premium, so the cat needs frequent small meals, up to four times daily. The total quantity should only be increased by about one third. Quality, nourishing food of low bulk is of special importance at this time.

To maintain the amount of milk needed for her kittens, a nursing queen will certainly at least double her normal food intake. Food should be of high quality and low bulk – in other words, as much energy and nutrients packed into as small a volume as possible. These requirements are most easily met by some of the special high-energy diets specially devised for nursing queens. Alternatively, kitten food can be used.

THE KITTENS

Kittens suckle from their mother exclusively for the first three or four weeks of their lives. As they become more aware of their surroundings they may start to nibble at their mother's food, a sure sign they are ready for weaning. The queen will happily continue to nurse her litter to some extent well into their third month of life. However, by the time they are about eight weeks old, the greater part of the kittens' diet will usually be provided by the owner. There is a fine line between allowing the kittens to

◀ *These 12-week-old kittens are likely to be demanding three meals a day.*

▲ *Unweaned kittens requiring supplementary feeding need a balanced nutritional product to thrive.*

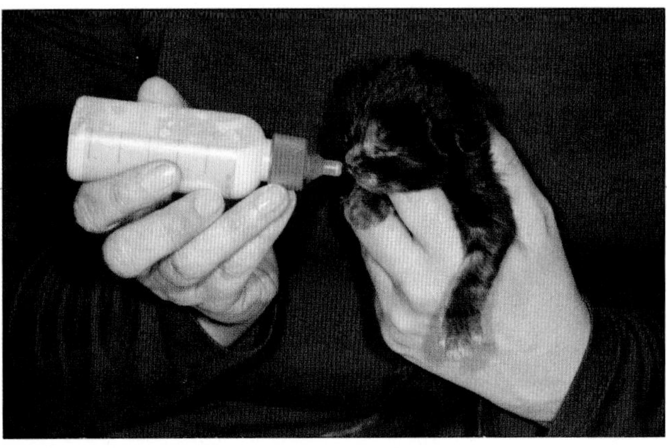

► *Feed newborns every two hours; they have tiny stomachs and high nutritional requirements.*

gorge themselves, which may cause digestive problems, and giving them enough to maintain healthy growth. The weaning process should be gradual, and the kittens fed little and often, with small quantities of high-protein food well chopped so as to be easily consumable. The easiest method of weaning is to use one of the readily available, well-established kitten foods, either in the dry or canned versions.

During the actual weaning process, canned foods are probably preferable, as the kittens may be attracted by the meaty smell. However, the dry foods are just as nutritious and have proven success. Do plan feeding times carefully so that mother and kittens may eat the extra meals in peace, away from other animals or disturbance in the household.

At about eight weeks old, kittens should be fed little and often. If you are feeding dry kitten food (which can be left out for longer than canned food), you can try providing it on a continuous basis for the kitten to nibble as required. Such a routine should be avoided, however, if your kitten shows a tendency to be overweight. Four or more meals a day for the kittens is normal, and can be gradually reduced to about three meals by the age of three to four months, and two meals at six months.

THE YOUNG ADULT

The feeding regime can gradually be reduced to one main meal as the kitten reaches adulthood at nine to twelve months of age. However, young, active cats will become very hungry if they have to wait 24 hours between meals. Many owners therefore offer a snack in the morning, with the main meal at night. If this is done, it is important to ensure that the main meal is reduced in quantity by the equivalent of the earlier snack, so that too many calories do not lead to weight problems. Most breeds of cat reach their adult size at about a year of age, although some of the longhaired breeds continue to develop until they are about four years old.

If you do have a slow-maturing cat, it is essential to ensure that adequate food of high quality is available throughout the growth period. A routine of two or three meals a day with a dry-weight protein value of over 30 per cent should continue over the growth period in order to maintain peak development.

▼ *A Persian kitten matures over four years and frequent, nutritious meals need to be given during this time.*

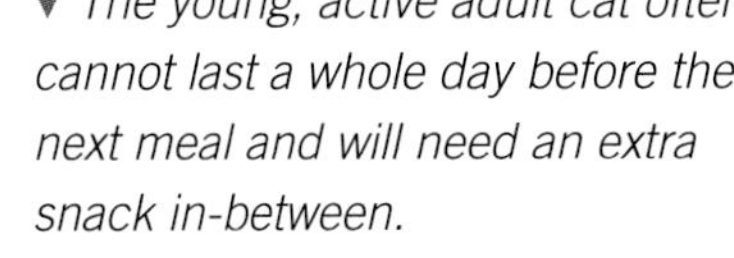

▼ *The young, active adult cat often cannot last a whole day before the next meal and will need an extra snack in-between.*

Homemade diets

► *All homemade diets should be nutritionally balanced. Table scraps are not suitable.*

With today's pressure on time and resources, it is likely that most cat owners will rely on commercially produced food for their pet. It is perfectly acceptable to feed a fit cat on nothing but commercial diets. The foods are scientifically prepared to meet the cat's nutritional requirements in terms of carbohydrates, proteins, fats, vitamins and minerals.

The quality of commercial diets may not be as high as we would like, however. The use of meat stuffs unfit for human consumption is banned in the United Kingdom, but not in many countries. Animal protein can include reclaimed protein from parts of an animal that a human would not willingly eat, and many manufacturers add meat 'flavouring' to improve the taste of their product.

A BALANCED APPROACH

Every cat's diet must contain protein from meat or fish, amino acids like taurine and arginine, fatty acids, vitamins and minerals. These requirements can all be sourced from natural foodstuffs but it is a case of getting the balance right.

Owners may consider a good home-prepared diet is preferable to a commercial one, as you are more able to give the cat the kind of diet it would get in the wild. Unfortunately, this can prove to be costly and rather time-consuming. The ideal diet would consist of something like 80 per cent raw chicken wings and 20 per cent liquidized green vegetables and overripe fruit. Offal can be used to replace some of the chicken, but liver should never make up more than 10 per cent of the diet. Fish can also be substituted for part of the meat ration, but it should always be lightly cooked and deboned. Cooking fish is important as it destroys the enzyme thiaminase, which can deactivate the cat's own vitamin B1, thiamine. Eggs, too, can be added, but these should be cooked, as egg white can interfere with the absorption of biotin, another part of the vitamin B complex. Small amounts of carbohydrates such as rice or corn can be added but aren't really necessary. They do, however, provide additional energy and can reduce the cost of the homemade diet.

Arginine is essential in a cat's diet. Arginine is an amino acid; it forms the protein ornithine which is vital as it works to 'mop up' ammonia resulting from the breakdown of proteins. Feeding trials have shown that a diet deficient in arginine can result in symptoms of ammonia toxicity, such as drooling, vomiting, lethargy and even convulsions within hours of eating the meal. Feeding a diet low in

◄ *Most homemade diets are soft and may need to be supplemented with dry biscuits to increase your cat's chewing action.*

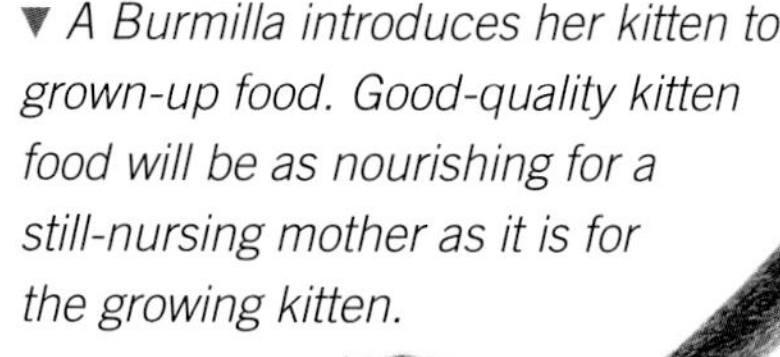

▼ *A Burmilla introduces her kitten to grown-up food. Good-quality kitten food will be as nourishing for a still-nursing mother as it is for the growing kitten.*

▶ *Your cat will appreciate it if you make small batches of treats each time so that they are temptingly fresh and not stale-smelling.*

▲ *Before embarking on a homemade food regime for your cat, talk to your vet about the food that you intend to make and they will advise if supplements are needed.*

this amino acid can prove fatal. Arginine is found in turkey, chicken, beef, peas, seafood including fish, and dairy products. As with taurine, levels are reduced if the meat is cooked.

Cats also require taurine in their diet. This is a sulphur-containing amino acid. It can be found naturally in fish, sea algae, seaweed, krill, dark chicken meat, beef, lamb and egg. It is also present in Brewer's yeast which is easy to add to a homemade diet.

USEFUL ADDITIONS

Vegetables, in limited quantities, can be added to the homemade diet. The best to offer are lettuce, spinach, broccoli florets, green beans, courgettes (zucchini), peas and carrots. All these vegetables should be cooked and very finely diced or puréed. The addition of liquidized watercress and parsley, which are both high in vitamins and minerals, can be included in the vegetable part of the diet. Do not include garlic, onion, avocados, mushrooms or tomatoes as these are either toxic to the cat or difficult to digest.

2.5ml (½ tsp) Cod Liver Oil and Evening Primrose Oil, given twice-weekly, will help maintain levels of fat-soluble vitamins and essential fatty acids, especially arachidonic acid. Seaweed, available from health food stores in either powder or tablet form, is an excellent source of vitamins, minerals and amino acids.

Owners wishing to use any homemade diet are strongly advised to seek veterinary advice and approval, once they have formulated their recipe, and prior to feeding it to their pet. Show your vet the written recipe, including all weights and measures, so that they can assess that the diet will be correctly balanced, fulfils all the cat's nutritional requirements and is safe and healthy to use.

▶ *The addition of a sprinkle of dried green herbs can enchance the flavour of a homemade diet.*

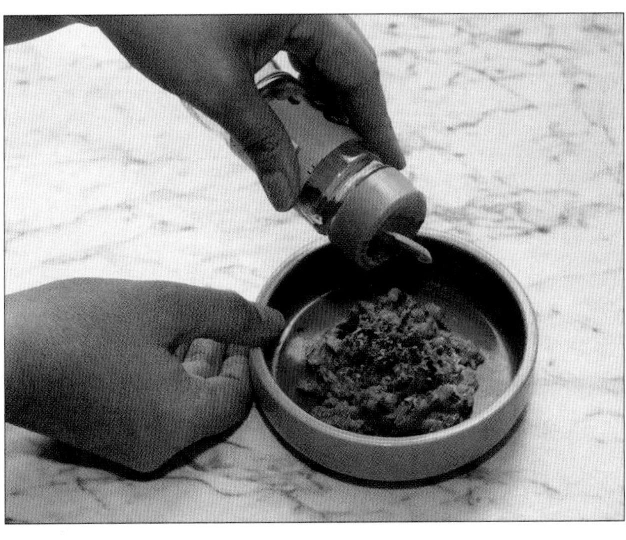

Obesity in cats

It is estimated that between 37–52 per cent of domestic cats worldwide are obese. Different breeds are different sizes, so there is no set weight for an 'average' cat. Obesity can have a detrimental effect on a cat's health and shorten its lifespan. Overweight cats are at a greater risk of acquiring diabetes, osteoarthritis, lower urinary tract problems and constipation. Excessive body fat also negatively affects the major organs of the body, the digestive tract, bones and joints and can restrict breathing capability. Over-feeding is a true example of 'killing with kindness'.

The only way to assess if a cat is the correct weight is to evaluate its body shape. As a rough guide, the following will help determine if a cat is overweight. When the cat is in a standing position look at it from above. A 'waist' should be visible behind the ribs and in front of the hips. Viewed from the side this area, called the abdominal tuck, will be smaller in diameter than the chest if the cat is a healthy weight. When a hand is run over the side of the cat the ribs should be easily felt without having to apply pressure or having to push down with the fingers. In a feline of correct body mass, the bones at the base of the tail can be felt without difficulty. The spine and hips will also feel fairly bony but not to the extreme of being pronounced. Many cats develop a sagging bit of flesh that hangs down between the back legs. This is called a primordial pouch and is a form of protection from bites during cat fights. Although, when viewed from the side, it can look like a sagging belly it is not an indicator of obesity unless it is filled with fat.

If, after examination, you conclude that your cat may be overweight steps need to be taken to rectify the problem.

▲ *This chunky chap is probably suffering some form of joint pain from carrying so much excess weight.*

▼ *Cats do not understand obesity, but humans do. It is the owner's responsibility to help resolve the issue.*

▼ *If a cat is uncooperative on the scales weigh yourself holding your pet and then deduct your own weight.*

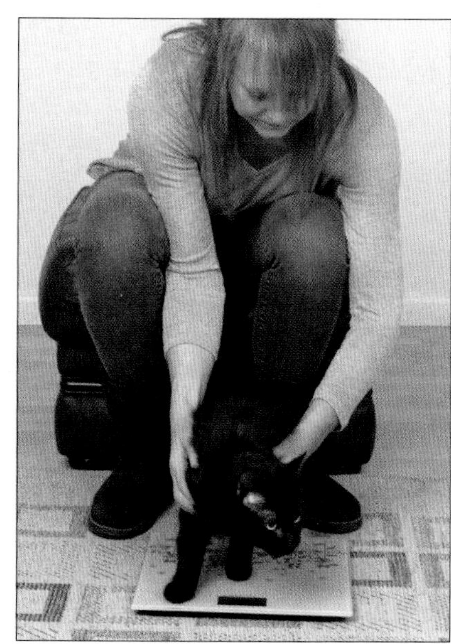

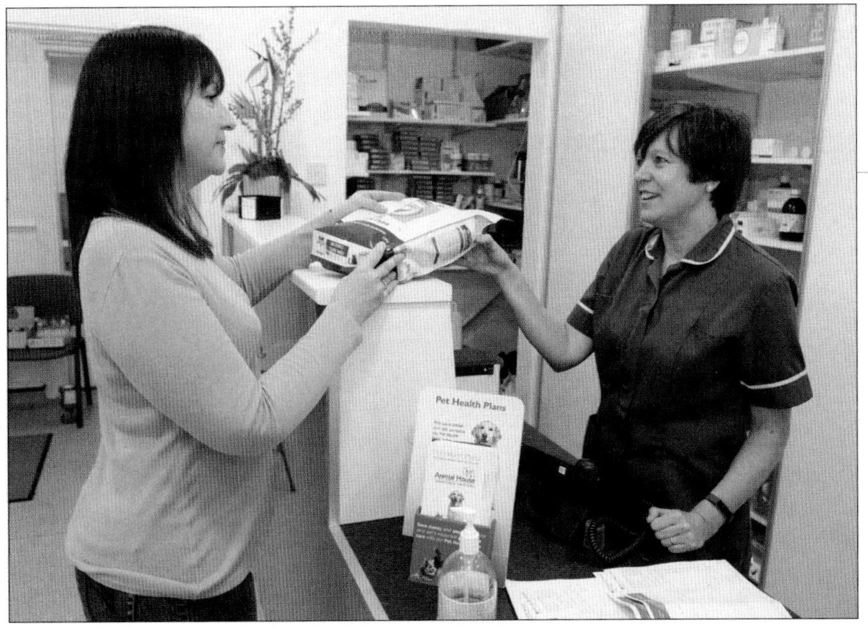

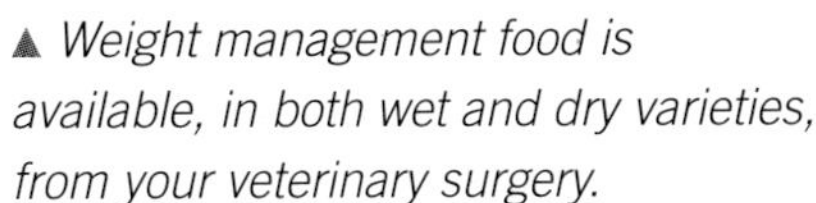
▲ *Weight management food is available, in both wet and dry varieties, from your veterinary surgery.*

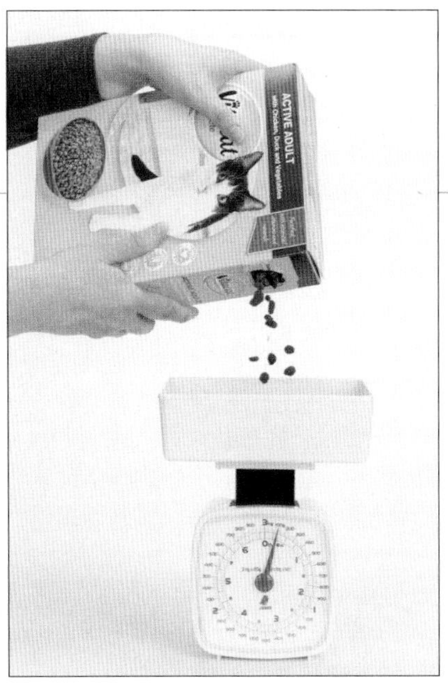

▲ *Most people never weigh out their cat's food as per the manufacturer's guidelines and so, unknowingly, vastly over-feed their pet.*

A visit to the vet will confirm if the cat is obese, give an accurate current weight and a preferred goal weight. The vet will also check that there is no adverse medical reason for the obesity. Although there are diseases that may have a weight gain as part of the symptoms, the most common cause of obesity is too much food and too little exercise.

If it is agreed that your cat needs to lose a few of those extra pounds, then the first step is to look at its diet. Cut done on the volume of food offered and split the daily ration into several small meals. That way your cat will not feel hungry or deprived. Low calorie or obesity diets are available and may be the answer if you don't want to cut down on the volume of food offered. If your cat is already on food that has been recommended by your vet check if it is advisable to change food before doing so. In either case, food should be changed gradually over a period of a week to avoid stomach upset. Treats, and cat milk, are generally high in calories and these should be restricted or withheld until the cat has reached the goal weight. Part of your cat's daily food ration can be reserved for treating instead.

The next step to a healthy weight is to increase the daily exercise that your cat takes. Most indoor cats have insufficient exercise as they do not have the opportunity to hunt. Playing with your cat is a great way to increase fitness but older felines can be hard to motivate. Try to dedicate a few minutes a day to encouraging play with an interesting toy. Puzzle feeders make the cat work for its dinner and are ideal for young and old alike.

Weight loss should be gradual. Never embark on a crash diet, this is not very kind and would be harmful to your pet's health. Check the cat's weight every two weeks. This can be done by standing on the bathroom scales while holding your pet and then deducting your own weight. Once the optimum body mass is reached adjust the cat's diet so that it stays at a steady, healthy weight.

► *All cats love boxes. Instead of just a sleeping place, a little imagination can turn one into an exciting toy.*

GROOMING

Cats are fastidious animals and devote a large part of their waking hours to grooming themselves. A little extra help from their human friends is required by longhaired and semi-longhaired cats. Even for shorthairs, the grooming process is important. It can be a pleasurable, bonding and rewarding experience for both cat and owner. Extra grooming also contributes to general health, as it stimulates the blood vessels just below the skin and improves muscle tone.

Grooming gives the owner an opportunity to thoroughly examine the cat for cuts, abrasions, lumps and parasites that may not be apparent in normal handling. It is also an excellent opportunity to assess weight and muscle condition. Show cats need to be presented in the peak of perfection necessitating careful and fastidious grooming and bathing. This can be time-consuming but is a vital part of this competitive pastime. Cats need to be trained to allow this amount of handling.

◄ *Self-grooming or mutual grooming (allogrooming) is an important part of natural cat behaviour. Over-grooming by your pet could indicate that it is stressed.*

The cat's coat and skin

Skin acts as a protective barrier to the hazards of the environment and helps to regulate temperature. It is the largest organ in the cat's body. Depending on the size, breed and age of the cat it forms 12–24 per cent of the body weight. Without skin, a cat would have no sense of touch or protection from the outside world.

There are three main layers of skin. The epidermis, from the Greek word epi meaning 'over', is the top layer. New cells are made at the base of the epidermis and move upwards in a process called keratinization. Eventually they form a layer of dead cells on the surface of the skin. This layer keeps in water, fluids, salts and nutrients. It also provides a defence against infection and hazardous substances. Healthy skin cells are essential for the production of melanin, which is a skin and hair pigment that helps protect against sunburn. Melanin is responsible for influencing skin, hair and eye colour. It is a complex polymer derived from the amino acid tyrosine.

Under the epidermis is a layer called the dermis. This contains a network of blood vessels that supply the epidermis with required nutrients and regulates skin and body temperature. This layer is where sensory nerves and hair follicles are found. The sensory nerves respond to heat, cold, pain, itch and touch. The dermis contains immune cells that defend against any infection that may pass through the epidermis. It also produces collagen and elastin which give support and elasticity to the skin.

The bottom layer of the skin is called the subcutis. It is comprised of muscles and subcutaneous fat. Subcutaneous fat acts as insulation and as a shock absorber, assisting with the provision of energy and holding fluids and electrolytes. The muscle that produces a 'twitch' is located just below the skin.

Hair, claws, sweat and oil glands grow out of the epidermis and dermis. When a kitten is born it has simple hair follicles, one hair growing from each follicle. As the kitten develops these will turn into compound follicles with a central hair surrounded by 3–15 smaller secondary hairs all produced from one pore. There can be up to 130,000 hairs per square inch in a cat's coat. Hair is formed from keratin, which is a protein structure. Each hair is made up of a root situated in the skin and a shaft that is visible above the skin. Hair protects the skin from ultraviolet light and physical damage. Additionally, it regulates heat. In cold weather the

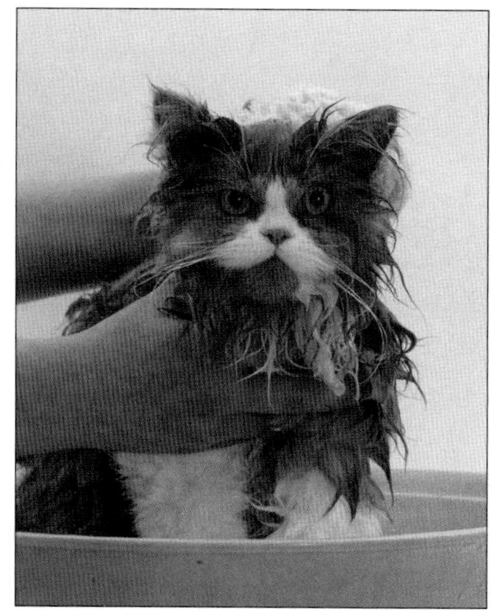

▲ *If the coat gets wet it no longer acts as insulation and body temperature will drop rapidly.*

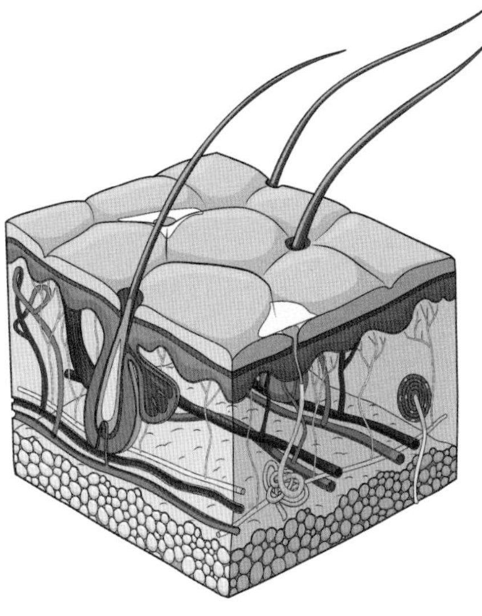

▲ *In this cross section the three layers of skin (epidermis, dermis and subcutis) can clearly be seen.*

▼ *Cats are very fastidious, trying hard to avoid soiling their paws with urine, faeces and other nasty substances.*

◀ *On average, the hair length of a shorthaired cat, such as this Korat, is less than 4cm/1.5 in.*

▶ *Longhaired cats, like Persians, can have fur up to 12.5cm/5 in long and shed their coat constantly.*

coat acts like a duvet, trapping air that is warmed to body temperature. This is why cats that come from colder climates often have longer and finer hair as this is more efficient at conserving heat. Breeds from warmer areas generally have shorter, thicker hairs with less secondary hair to facilitate free movement of cooling air. Felines do have sweat glands on their feet but these play a very minor role in heat regulation. Cats normally shed hair twice a year in response to changes in temperature and sunlight hours. Nutrition, disease, hormones, medication and environment all affect the growth of hair.

Oil is produced by sebaceous glands into the hair follicles and onto the skin. Large numbers of these glands are found at the base of the tail, on the rump, base of the neck, under the chin and near the paws. This oil has two main uses. Firstly, it stops the skin from drying out, so remaining pliable, and gives coat hair its sheen. Secondly the oil forms part of a cat's scent-marking system. By rubbing against an object a cat will leave a trace of sebum fatty acid and pheromone behind, thus marking their territory.

A dull coat or dry skin are indicators that all is not well with your cat. This may be due to a wide range of complaints. Some conditions can be easily rectified while others may be long term or life-threatening. Unless the cause is obvious, for example fleas, it can be difficult and time-consuming to diagnose the underlying problem. Both internal and external disease plus environmental factors and poor nutrition can affect coat quality and condition. Concerned owners should seek veterinary advice promptly.

▶ *This Norwegian Forest cat is a semi-longhair and as such lacks the dense undercoat seen on a Persian.*

Grooming the natural way

The cat is well-equipped to groom itself: tongue, teeth, paws and claws are all pressed into service. The cat's tongue has a rough surface which, combined with saliva, helps to remove grit and sticky substances from the fur. Even though cats are very flexible, there are areas they cannot reach directly with the tongue – so the front paws are licked and used rather like a face flannel. As the coat dries, the cat nibbles the fur back into place with its small incisor teeth and removes any foreign matter that the washing process failed to dislodge.

The back claws act almost like a wide-toothed comb and remove larger objects from the coat. The front paws stimulate slight oily secretions from glands around the head, and transfer them to other parts of the body during grooming. The cat is preening its coat with its own perfume, which can then be used to mark territory.

CHANGING COATS

In the natural state, the cat sheds its coat once a year, usually in spring. However, the process is dependent on light and temperature. In warm, artificially heated and illuminated homes, indoor cats tend to shed throughout the year. It does not happen in one vast shedding of fur, but in discreet areas across the body so that hair loss is hardly noticed – except on the owner's carpets, furnishings and clothes.

When self-grooming at any time of the year, the cat dislodges loose fur, some of which is swallowed. This gradually builds up into a fur ball or hairball which can eventually solidify into a pellet in the cat's intestine. Most cats automatically bring up a small fur ball every few days or so, but sometimes one can become stuck, causing loss of appetite and a rundown condition. In extreme cases, a vet may need to operate to remove the obstruction. The fur ball problem can strike at any time, although longhaired cats are most at risk. The occasional meal of oily fish may help ease the passage of the ingested hair. A healthy, well-balanced cat will spend

▲ *A fluffy silver and white kitten shows her remarkable flexibility as she grooms her hind leg. Careful grooming is particularly important with long fur, to remove any matting that could lead to a skin infection.*

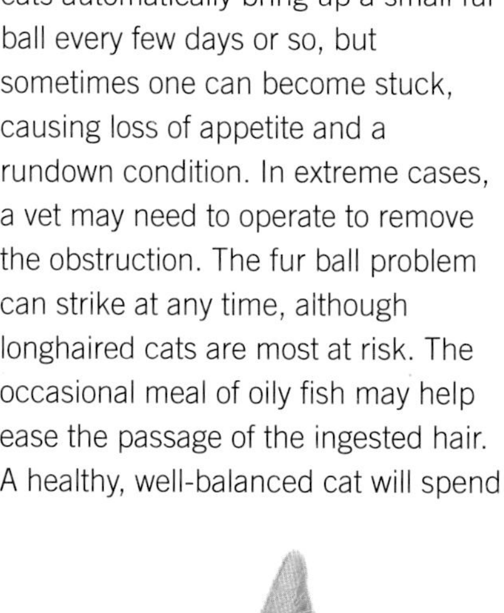

▼ *A Silver Tabby licks a front paw so that it can then use it rather like a face cloth to wipe its face.*

▼ *The grooming process is completely absorbing for these two kittens. As well as being necessary, grooming is an activity that cats enjoy.*

► *If cats mutually groom it means that they have socially bonded and enjoy each other's company.*

▲ *Cats try hard to keep their ears clean and rarely need human intervention unless an infection arises.*

50 per cent of its waking hours grooming itself. Cats are clean animals, but personal hygiene is only one reason for this activity.

Self-grooming is an important aspect in regulating body temperature. By licking the coat with their tongue, they are able to distribute the oil produced by the sebaceous glands evenly around the body. This oil helps to waterproof the hair and assists the coat to lie smoothly. A sleek, well-maintained coat is better able to retain heat. Cats groom themselves for the opposite reason too, that of cooling down. As the saliva applied to the coat (via the tongue) evaporates, it assists in a cooling process and helps to regulating body temperature.

By cleaning, cats are protecting themselves from predators who may be attracted by the smell of food and even the scent of the cat itself.

The act of grooming stimulates blood flow in the skin. The cat's bristle-like tongue is able to stimulate circulation. Improved circulation and blood flow are important for healthy skin and good hair growth.

It is thought that cat's saliva contains enzymes that turns into a natural antibiotic. Licking or washing a wound is the cat's way of guarding against infection. Unfortunately, at times, they can be over-zealous and make the situation worse by not allowing the wound to scab over. The rasping tongue can also cause inflammation to the surrounding skin. Any wound that becomes inflamed or does not show signs of rapid healing needs veterinary attention and advice. The cat may need to be restrained from trying to heal itself.

Shared grooming between cats is a social activity. It is a way of showing trust and friendship and involves the exchange of saliva. It is not unusual to see two cats in one household grooming each other. For the cats this is a pleasant activity. It is interesting to note that when your cat licks you that they are including you in their trusted group. So your cat really is giving you a kiss because they love you.

▼ *Cats principally roll on grass to scent mark, but also seem to enjoy a massage and dust bath.*

Grooming with human aid

► *A longhaired cat is lying down on a towel specially reserved for its grooming. Having a waste (trash) bin nearby is also a wise move.*

A feral cat in good physical condition usually keeps itself reasonably well-groomed. Domestication and selective breeding have resulted in changes to the cat's coat, such as longer hair, that sometimes require more maintenance than the cat is able to provide for itself. Assistance is then needed from the owner. Older cats, too, may lose the motivation and energy to groom themselves and welcome extra help.

You can remove some of the loose dead hairs which accumulate just by stroking a cat. The polishing action gives the coat a beautiful sheen. Some experienced owners claim that the best time to groom a cat is just after washing the dishes, for if your hands are very slightly damp, stroking is even more effective. Thin rubber gloves have a similar effect in removing loose hair.

EQUIPMENT

The grooming equipment you need depends on the type of coat your cat has. You will also gradually discover what works best for your pet. If you have a pedigreed cat, ask the breeder's advice. First-hand experience, especially from a breeder who keeps show cats, can save time and money.

Start regular grooming as a part of a kitten's routine as soon as it comes into your household. An older cat may need some encouragement to submit to the experience, but will probably soon enjoy it immensely, if you are gentle. Choose a quiet time in the cat's observed routine, make sure all you need is accessible and settle the cat on a towel on your lap. It is pointless trying to restrain a cat that just wants to play; scratches are far less likely if the cat is relaxed.

Equipment required to groom a cat will depend on the coat length, the tolerance of the cat and the time and

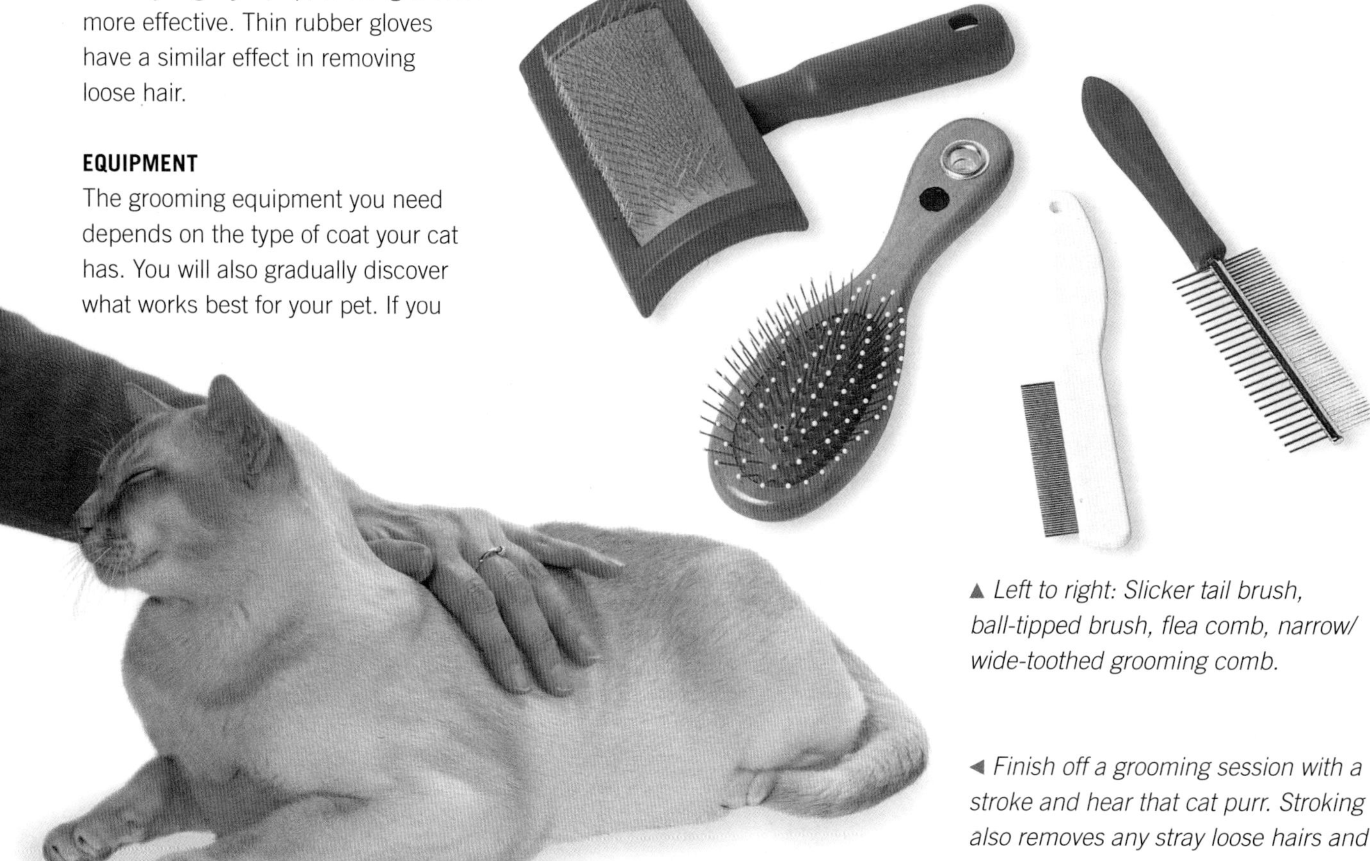

▲ *Left to right: Slicker tail brush, ball-tipped brush, flea comb, narrow/wide-toothed grooming comb.*

◄ *Finish off a grooming session with a stroke and hear that cat purr. Stroking also removes any stray loose hairs and gives a final polish.*

▶ *There is a range of de-shedding combs and brushes. They can be purchased at various outlets.*

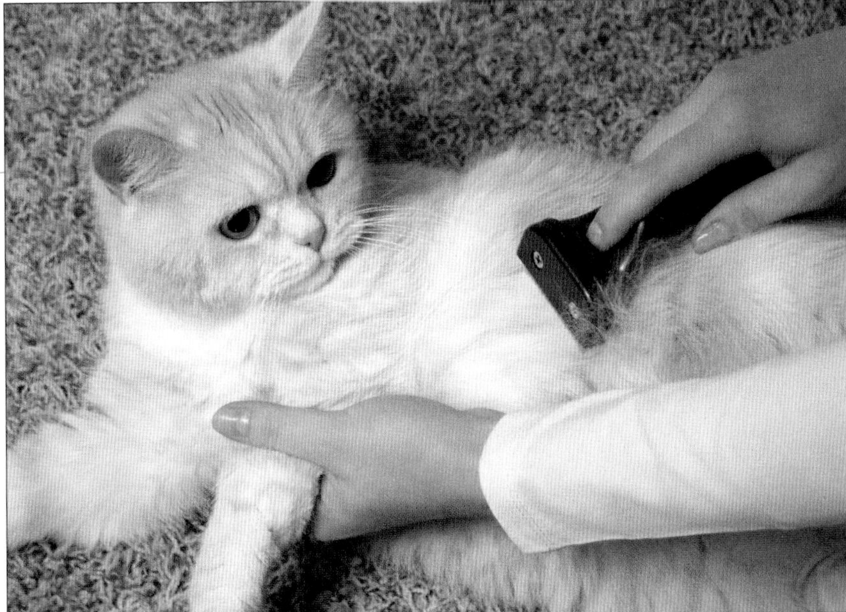

▲ *Use extreme caution and care when cleaning your cat's eyes and the surrounding area.*

expense the owner wishes to invest. Basic brushes and combs are illustrated here, but many other options are available.

Hand-sized rubber pads with thick bobbles, similar to a horse's soft rubber curry comb, are an excellent choice for removing loose and dead coathairs in shorthair cats. They are dual action and will also massage and stimulate the skin during the grooming process. Furthermore, they have the added benefit of being very effective at lifting hair from human clothing too. The Furminator is a very useful tool for de-shedding coat on longhaired cats. It is a fairly expensive item costing up to £30.00 ($40) each. Vets recommend them as they reduce the risk of hair balls because they will remove up to 90 per cent of dead coat in one grooming session. They come in a shorthair variety as well but, as this type of coat is easier to deal with, owners may feel that it doesn't justify the cost.

Once again modern technology has entered the feline world with the introduction of electrical grooming tools. These come in two varieties, those that are standalone grooming equipment and those that are an attachment to a vacuum cleaner. Both types work on the principle of sucking dead hair and debris from the cat's coat. They are effective at this job but don't massage and stimulate the skin in the same way that hand grooming does. Some cats love them while others will not tolerate them at all. If you think they might be something you would like to try, see if you can borrow one before buying so that you can judge your cat's reaction first. Never under any circumstances use a vacuum cleaner attachment pipe on your cat as the suction is too powerful and can cause serious injury.

Whatever equipment you choose to use the most important aspect of grooming is that it is a pleasant and relaxing experience for you and your cat alike.

◀ *Flea combs have the teeth set very close together so they trap the fleas and lift them from the cat's coat.*

▶ *Comb daily to remove fleas and their eggs. Dip the comb into a dish of water with detergent to kill the fleas.*

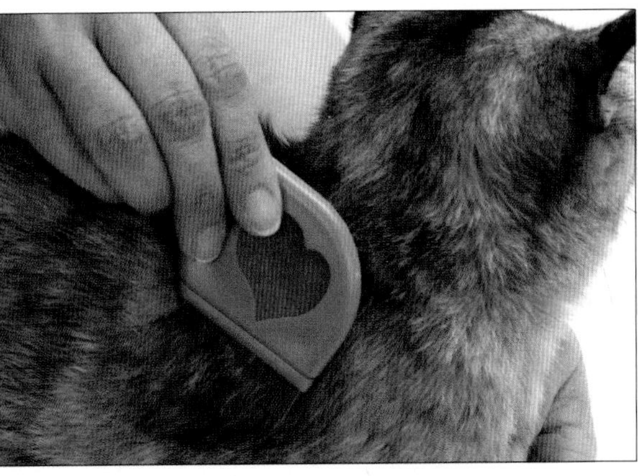

Grooming a shorthaired cat

Supplementing the self-grooming of a shorthaired cat is really only absolutely necessary if you are showing. But an extra groom, say twice weekly, does help keep loose, dead hairs under control and off the furniture. It is also a good opportunity to check for fleas, or the onset of any ear or dental problems. In addition, the activity is pleasurable for both cat and owner. The process is, of course, far simpler than for a longhaired cat. Grooming aids can include a metal comb with round-tipped teeth, a soft, natural-bristled brush to settle the fur, a brush with stiffer bristles (a rubber brush is essential for Rex cats, as it does not scratch the skin), and a polishing cloth of silk or chamois leather.

Start the grooming session by gently stroking the cat to relax it. Use the stiff brush first, brushing very gently along the lie of the fur, to loosen the dead hairs and dirt. Brush the whole body, but be especially gentle in delicate parts around the ears, armpits and groin, and under the belly and tail. Next, use the metal comb to extract the dead hairs. It may set up some

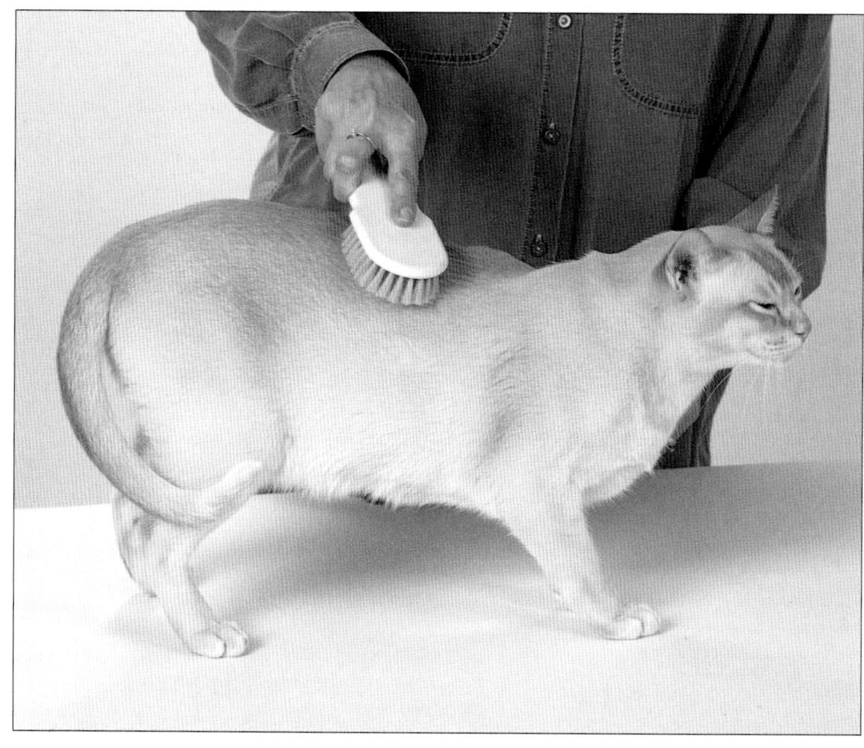

▲ *A soft-bristled brush settles the fur after any static triggered by the use of a metal comb.*

Checklist

- Towel
- Rubber-bristled brush
- Wide-toothed metal comb
- Natural, soft-bristled brush
- Flea comb
- Chamois leather or velvet glove
- Cotton wool
- Ear cleaner
- Eye wipes

▼ *Left and right: When grooming is finished, it's time to rest and watch a friend finish off his tail. Cats often groom together if they have the opportunity; it is an important social activity.*

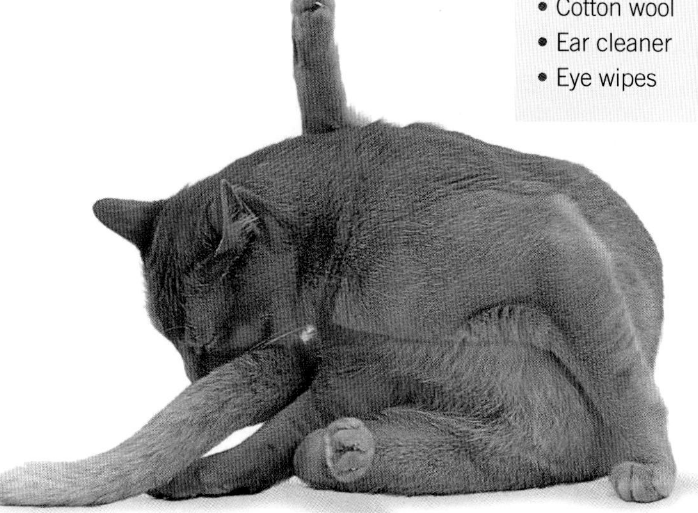

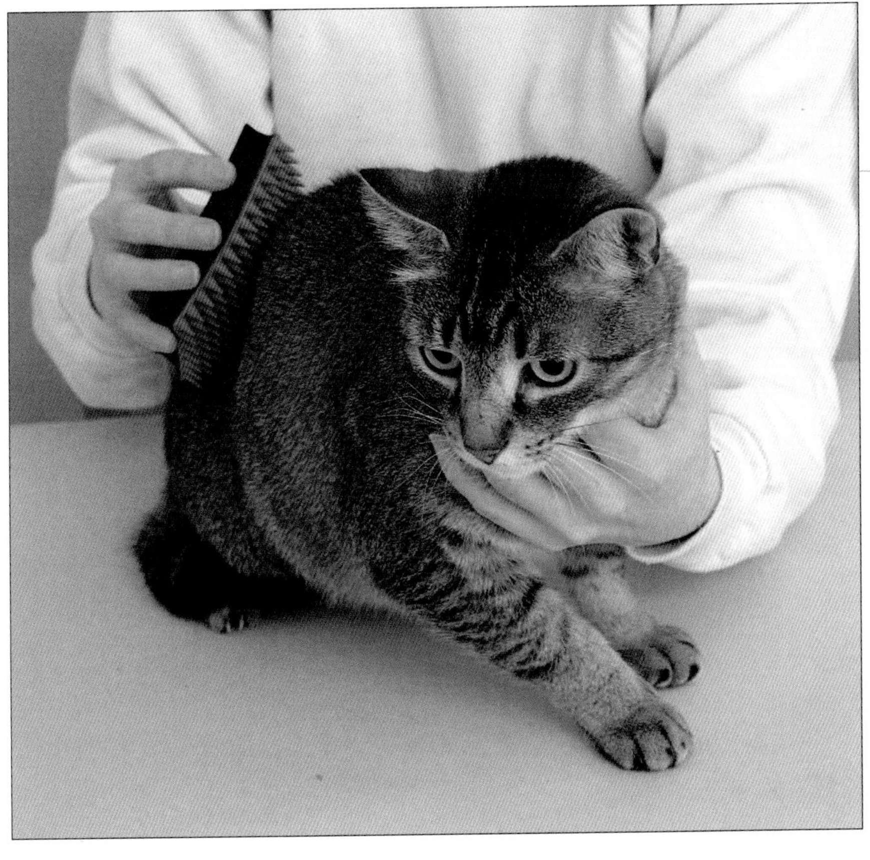

◄ *A rubber brush is not only gentler on the shorthair's skin, but the cat seems to relish the feel of it, too. It removes not only dead hair but dandruff as well.*

static in the coat, causing fur to clump together or the guardhairs to develop a wispy life of their own. This will be corrected with the soft-bristled brush, and a final polish with the chamois leather, velvet or silk.

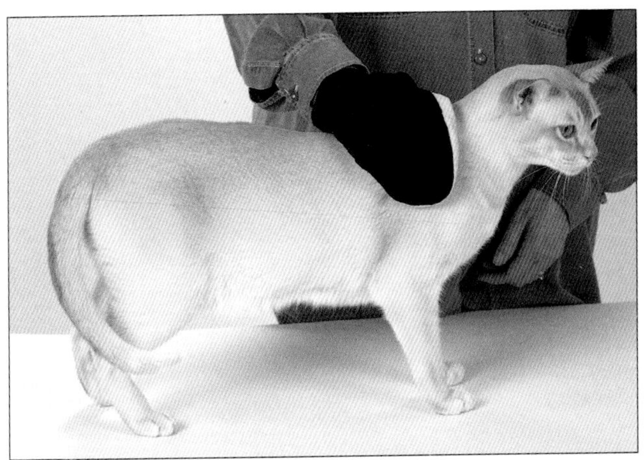

► *A final sheen is encouraged on a shorthair's coat by stroking it with a chamois leather or velvet glove. A silk scarf would also do the job.*

A DRY SHAMPOO

It is rarely necessary to wash a shorthaired cat unless it is a pale-coloured exhibition cat, or unless the cat has become greasy – from sitting under a car, for example. Some exhibitors give their shorthairs a bran bath to remove excess grease, dirt and dandruff. Warm a good five or six handfuls of natural bran flakes in the oven to a comfortable hand-hot temperature. Rub these over the cat, avoiding the face and inner ears, working the hands thoroughly through the coat; then simply brush it all out with a soft brush. A coat that is predominantly dark will take on a shine immediately; pastel blues and creams may take a couple of days before their texture and shine reach the peak of perfection.

All the grooming in the world will not have the desired effect if your cat is lacking vital vitamins and minerals. This can be particularly noticeable on a shorthaired cat.

◄ *A contented and very sleek Red Burmese following a full grooming session.*

Grooming a longhaired cat

Longhaired cats, whether they are Persians or semi-longhairs – the so-called self-grooming breeds such as the Maine Coon Cat or Norwegian Forest Cat – all need considerable grooming help from the owner. This is true whether the animal is purebred or not. Longhaired cats pick up dirt and debris in their coats, and they need help to keep the fur clean and free from tangles. This must be done daily. If not, the hair matts, particularly in the armpits and groin, and can become uncomfortable. A severely matted coat is unyielding and prevents the cat from moving with ease. Any movement results in individual hairs being pulled. The build-up of fur leads to deterioration in the general condition of the coat and a much greater likelihood of fur balls or hairballs.

Grooming procedures are more elaborate than for the shorthairs. Start with the wide-toothed comb with blunt teeth to ease out tangles and debris. Try the comb on yourself before you try it out on the cat. If it does not feel sharp on your head, it should be fine for the cat. To deal with obstinate knots and tangles, sprinkle them with unscented talcum powder and ease them free with your hands. A sprinkle of talcum powder also helps pick up excess grease and dirt. It should be brushed out thoroughly at the brushing stage. Make partings in the

CORRECT GROOMING SEQUENCE

1 Use the comb gently to ease out any tangles, knots and twigs. Sprinkle with unscented talcum powder once a week. Do the underbelly and legs first.

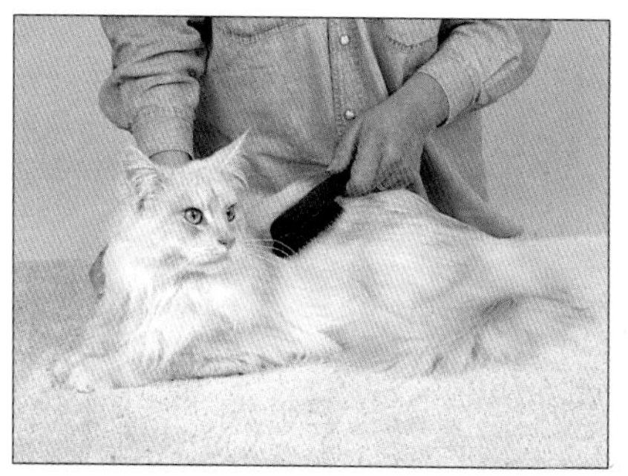

2 Brush the body fur firmly in sections against the lie of the fur towards the cat's head. Brush thoroughly to remove talcum powder, if you have used it.

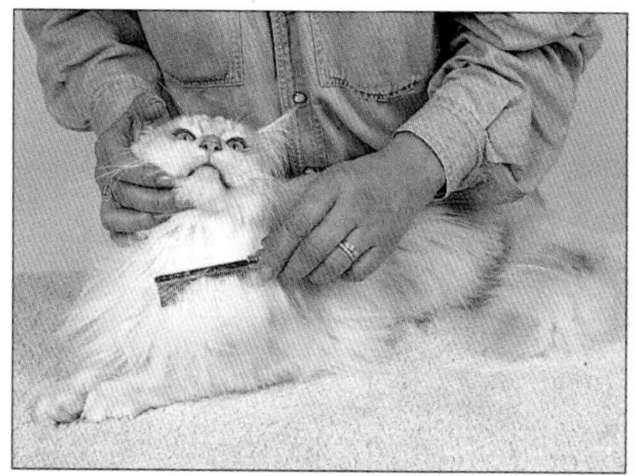

3 Use the fine comb for the neck fur. For Persians, the fur should be combed upwards to form a ruff beneath the chin.

Checklist for shampoo and groom

- Towels
- Wide-toothed metal comb
- Fine comb
- Natural-bristled brush
- Unscented talcum powder
- Feline or baby shampoo
- Shower attachment
- Hairdryer

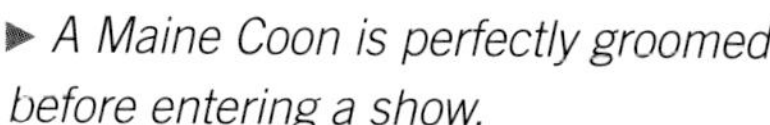

► *A Maine Coon is perfectly groomed before entering a show.*

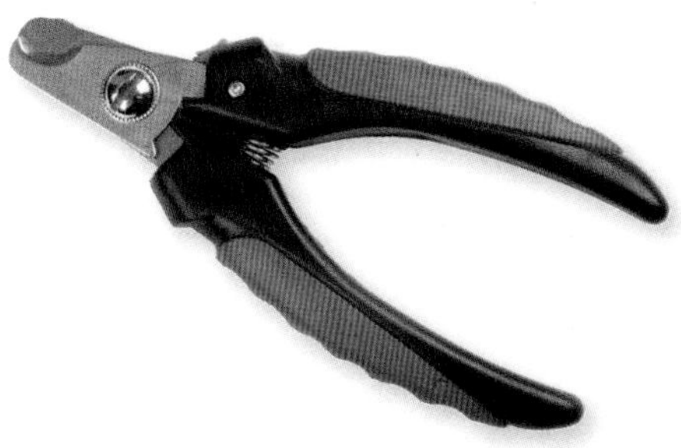

▲ *Some types of claw clippers have a safety guard to prevent cutting off too much of the claw.*

▶ *Over-long claws can cause a cat to get caught up on carpets, and similar fabrics, to equal distress of cat and owner.*

tail, and brush each parted section sideways. Finish with a well-earned stroke in all the right directions.

Unfortunately, not all cats are so tolerant towards grooming. To a certain extent, owners can get away without having a rigorous grooming routine if they own a short-coated pet. This is certainly not the case with a long-coated feline. A neglected coat quickly gets out of control. Knots and small matts 'felt', forming a solid pad of hair that lies close to the skin. This causes discomfort and pulls on the skin when the cat moves. In extreme cases they can cause sores and even restrict movement.

There are many reasons why a longhaired cat may become unkempt. But by far the most common reason is that they will not allow combing and brushing. This is generally because they don't trust or have previously had a frightening or painful experience.

Allowing grooming is essential if your cat is longhaired. Owners need to convince the cat that it is a pleasant experience for them. If your cat is uncooperative, try playing with it first so that it is tired and relaxed. With the cat on your lap, engage in a stroking session so the cat feels comfortable. Gently begin by combing the fur on its back with a de-shedding comb. These have alternate long and short teeth and don't pull as much as conventional combs. Avoid matted areas initially. Comb for as long as the cat will allow but do not restrict it if it wishes to move away. Praise after each session with a treat or physical touch. As the cat learns to trust you, each grooming period should last longer.

To avoid discomfort, matts that can't be teased apart should be cut away. This is a difficult procedure and extreme care must be taken. If owners have any doubts regarding their capability performing this task it may be best to engage the services of a professional groomer. In extreme cases the whole of the longhaired coat may have to be clipped off. Generally, the coat will regrow back as normal. Occasionally clipping can alter the texture of the hair but this is a small price to pay for the comfort and health of your cat.

▼ *Pump-action spray conditioners and anti-tangle serums for the cat can be purchased online and from pet shops.*

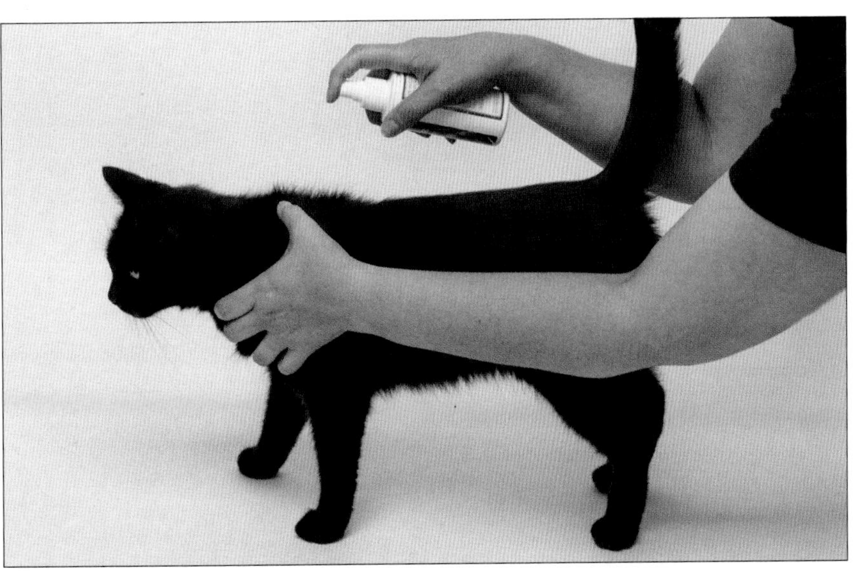

Attention to detail

EYES

The discharges that accumulate in the corners of the eyes can be removed carefully with your finger. Short-faced cats are prone to show tear stains beneath the eyes, which can be cleaned with a special preparation available from pet stores or your local vet's surgery.

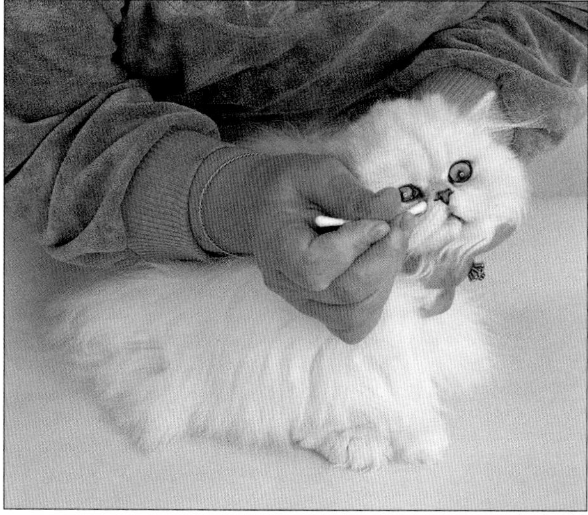

◄▼ *Daily cleansing of the area around the eyes is particularly necessary with Persian cats. This kitten is being introduced to the idea at an early age. A cotton wool bud (swab) dampened with tepid water is used, and the area is gently wiped with absorbent tissue.*

MOUTH AND NOSE

A dark brown or black tarry secretion on the cat's chin indicates an excess production of sebum from the hair follicles, which is used in scent marking. A similar condition, known as stud tail, can occur around the base of the tail. Veterinary treatment is usually necessary. Recurrence may be prevented by cleansing with special anti-bacterial shampoo from your vet.

TEETH AND GUMS

Keeping your cat's teeth clean reduces the risk of gum disease which has escalated with the advent of modern cat foods. If tartar can be kept under control, the risk is reduced. Some vets give cats a general check-up once or twice a year, and if necessary, perform a scale and polish under general anaesthetic. The alternative is for the owner to clean the cat's teeth once or twice a week. Special toothbrushes that fit over your finger and cat food-flavoured toothpastes make the job easier, but do not necessarily guarantee success. Just before feeding time, you could try wrapping a piece of fabric sticking plaster around the index finger. Smear this with a little wet cat food, and gently try to rub against the teeth while holding the head.

◄ *A cat is more inclined to allow its teeth to be cleaned if the toothpaste is flavoured with chicken, fish or meat.*

▼ *The owner cleans tartar from the outside surfaces of the kitten's teeth. The cat's rough tongue will take care of any tartar build-up on the inside surfaces of the teeth.*

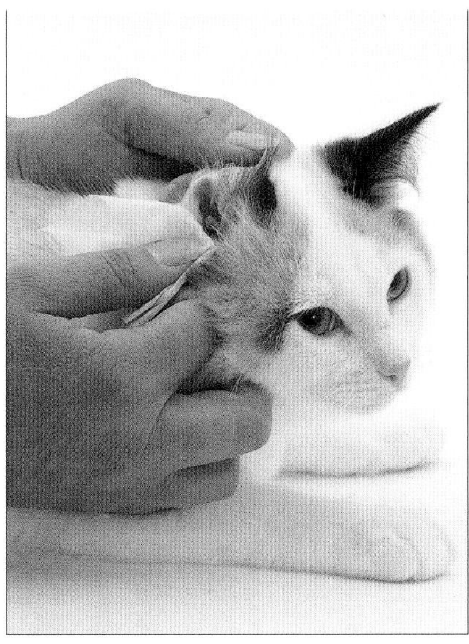

▲ *A shorthair has its ears checked as part of its grooming routine. A slight build-up of wax means a gentle wipe with absorbent tissue.*

► *A Burmese-cross is having its nails trimmed with a nail clipper custom-made for cats. Clippers designed for human nails may split cats' claws. Only the very edges are trimmed. If you are at all uncertain about your skills, it is wise to ask the vet to do this job.*

EARS

If ears appear soiled on the inside, wipe them out gently with a soft absorbent tissue on your finger, dampened with olive oil, liquid paraffin or ear cleaner from the pet shop. Never clean further than you can see, and do not use cotton wool buds (swabs). An abundance of dark brown, dry waxy material may indicate mites, in which case veterinary treatment is necessary.

CLAWS

Some Siamese cats and their derivatives, such as Balinese, Oriental Shorthairs and Oriental Longhairs, are unable to retract their claws completely and are therefore ill at ease on hard, uncarpeted floors. Elderly cats of any breed may have similar problems: the nails continue to grow and, because older cats take less exercise, are not worn down. Due to stiffness, they are not fully retracted either. Trimming the nails will help. Outdoor cats should have only their front claws clipped, so that they are not completely disarmed if they meet an enemy, and will be able to climb should a rapid escape be necessary.

If claw clipping is necessary, ask the vet to do it, for a mistake could be dangerous. On light-coloured claws, a dark blood vessel can be seen. Cutting this (called 'cutting to the quick') causes copious bleeding and pain.

Declawing, or onychectomy, is considered an unnecessary mutilation in the United Kingdom. It is widely practised in the United States, and is often carried out at about the same time as sterilization. It is a major operation that removes the cat's main means of self-defence, and should be reserved for indoor cats.

▼ *A thorough self-groom for this cat will help keep fleas and parasites at bay, and in warm weather, help it keep cool. The saliva takes the place of sweat in humans, evaporating and cooling the cat.*

Shampoo and style

Washing a cat is time-consuming, but essential if you are to show your cat. Unless the idea is introduced during kittenhood, a cat may object to being bathed, so it is helpful to have two pairs of human hands.

Make sure the room is warm, free of draughts, and escape-proof. A large, flat-based kitchen sink is ideal. Allow plenty of clear space around the sink, with a stock of dry towels nearby, and one on the draining board. Have all you need at hand before you start.

Most cats have never had a bath in their life and are none the worse for missing this experience. They are very clean animals and, unlike dogs, seldom smell. But there are circumstances when bathing is required.

Exhibition felines need regular cleaning to keep their coats in tip-top condition. Some breeders will bathe them while others prefer to use a 'bran

WASHING A CAT

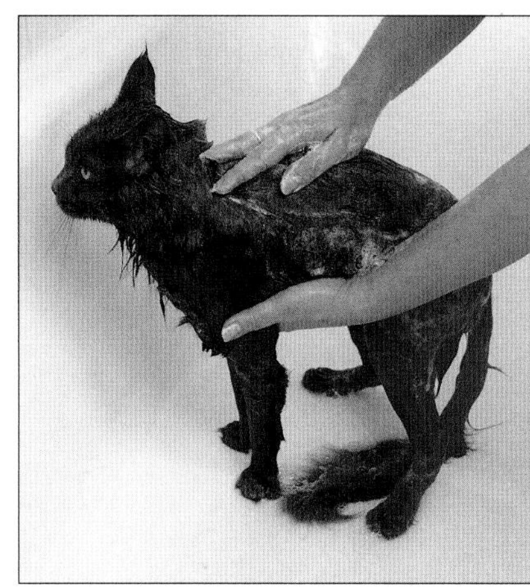

1 Fill the sink with warm water to about 5cm (2in). Talk soothingly to the cat all the time. Using a shower attachment, test the water first, then wet the fur thoroughly. Apply a little shampoo and work into a lather. Make sure no shampoo goes near the cat's eyes, nose or mouth.

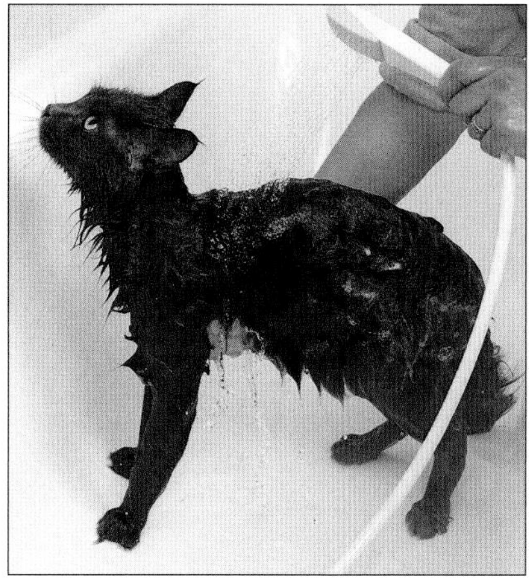

2 Rinse thoroughly and repeat the shampooing process. If you are using conditioner, put a drop on the back and work it through the coat with the wide-toothed comb. Rinse thoroughly and then squeeze down the whole body, legs and tail to remove excess moisture.

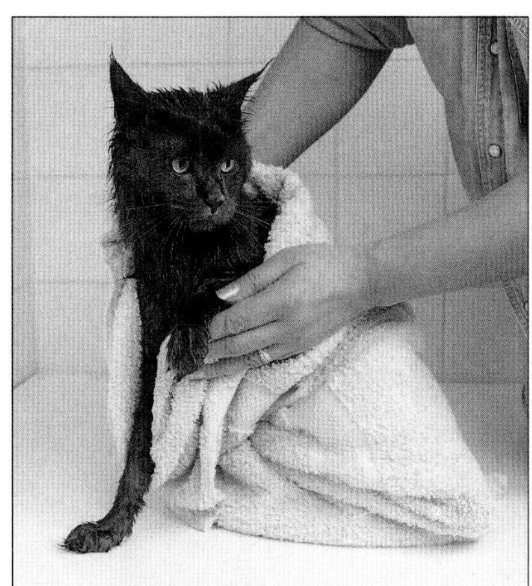

3 Lift the cat from the sink and wrap it immediately in a towel. Rub gently to absorb most of the water. You may need several towels!

4 Set the hairdryer on low. Do not direct the airstream too close. Lift and comb the fur as you dry (this is easier if the dryer is on a stand), and stop when the fur is still slightly damp and tacky. If your cat objects to a hairdryer, do not persist, but resort to towels, brushes and patience.

5 Use the soft-bristled brush against the lie of the coat, lifting and brushing as you go. Separate any knots with the fingers. Pay particular attention to the flow of the tail plume. Make sure the leg fur is well separated, and that the fur on the underparts does not become curly. On Persians, work up the dramatic ruff of fur around the neck.

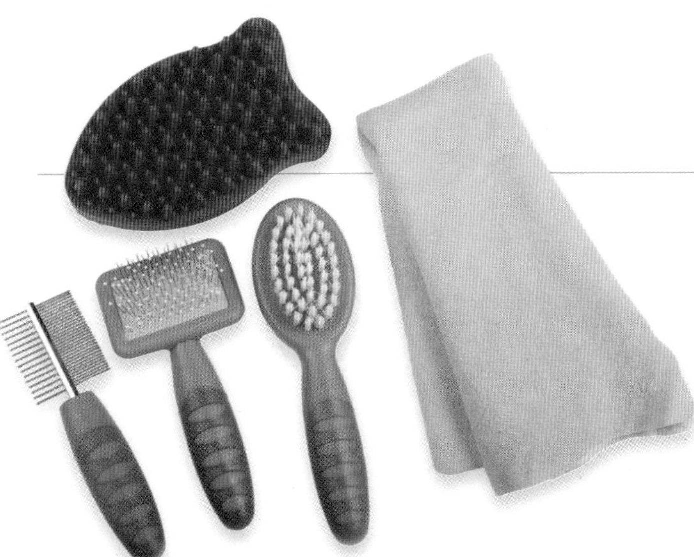

◀ *Lay out ready all the equipment that you think you might need prior to putting your cat in the bath.*

◀ *Most cats are fearful of aerosol sprays. Look for pump action products if you require a finishing spray.*

bath' or dry shampoo. A bran bath is less traumatic than using water and only requires one pair of hands. All that is required is a cup full of bran heated to body temperature. Place the cat in the sink and massage the bran into the coat. Leave it in the coat for 10–15 minutes and comb out. This will remove oil and dirt from the coat.

Some cats are poor at personal hygiene and don't wash themselves. Their coat will quickly become sticky and attract dirt and debris. Washing the coat is the only way to rectify this. Longhaired cats, in particular, may get faeces stuck around the anus area which will need to be soaked or bathed off. The same may occur with a cat that has had a bout of diarrhoea.

Cats that have come into contact with a toxic element – oil, petrol or paint – will need careful and thorough bathing. They should not be allowed to wash themselves, as the substance will then be ingested, increasing the danger. These cases are best treated by a vet as they may need a specialist cleansing agent and careful monitoring.

The Sphynx, Don Sphynx and other hairless breeds require regular bathing. Like all cats they produce sebum but as they have no hair it is not distributed onto the coat. Therefore they are prone to oily skin which encourages a bacterial build-up, leading to infection and feline acne. The oil must be washed away, and the skin cleansed by bathing every 7–14 days. Their skin should be cleaned using a suitable shampoo and a sponge, flannel or exfoliating glove. It is important to ensure all skin folds are thoroughly cleaned as well as the head, feet and tail.

▼ *After bathing, keep your cat in a warm room until it is completely dry. Time to reward with a treat?*

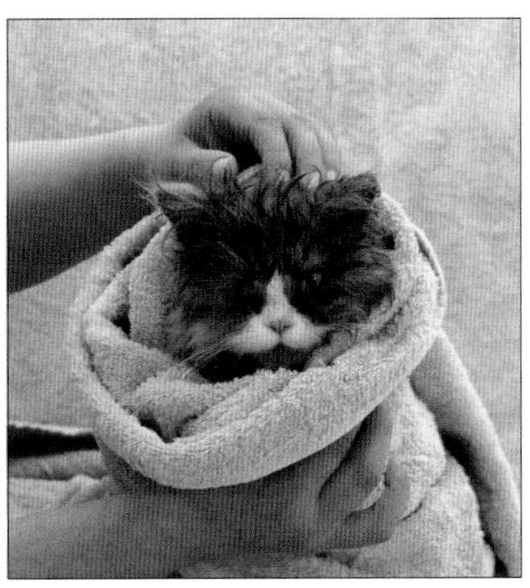

▲ *Your cat will appreciate being wrapped in a pre-warmed, soft towel after their bath.*

Finishing touches and products

Finishing touches and using the correct product will produce a content and beautifully groomed cat.

Longhaired cats, especially those with a Persian-type coat, will benefit from the careful trimming of hair around the anus. This will prevent faeces getting stuck in their fur. Not only will the cat be more comfortable but, importantly, it will prevent bacterial infections and unpleasant smells. This trimming can be extended to the inside of the back legs if desired.

There are specialist feline products that will remove tear stains over a period of time. These marks are more noticeable on cats that have a pale coat colour around their eyes. Before use ensure there is no veterinary reason why the eyes are running.

Tubs of ear wipes are a worthwhile investment. They are quick to use and easy to keep on hand.

All shampoos must be specially designed for cats. Never use human shampoo; cats do not have the same pH balance, so these products will be skin-drying and too aggressive. The pet shampoo that you choose should not contain petrochemicals, parabens, sodium laurel sulphate or artificial dye. Check the contents before you buy. A range of shampoos is available for different coloured coats. They don't contain dye but work with natural colour enhancers and light refractors. Foaming waterless shampoos are convenient if bathing isn't possible or time is short.

◄▼ *Only use products specifically manufactured for cats and always check that they do not contain any toxic ingredients.*

▼ *Microfibre towels are very soft and absorb five times more moisture than a normal cotton towel.*

Microfibre towels are invaluable. They are highly absorbent and much more efficient than household towels. They are available from most pet stores and online.

A healthy cat should have a shiny coat but sometimes nature needs a helping hand. A range of conditioners are available to use on cats. Some are applied to a wet coat and rinsed out, others are brushed into a dry coat and left. Dull, damaged or longhaired coats profit from their use and become much more manageable. Avoid any that have any citrus ingredients as cats dislike this scent.

Anti-tangle sprays can be bought but the best way to control matted hair is to establish a good grooming routine. Anti-static sprays are useful to introduce into the routine if producing a cat for the show ring.

Using a professional groomer

Many people will never need the services of a professional groomer, either because their pet's coat requires little attention or they have a good, established routine. Others find a specialist pet beautician invaluable.

There are three types of grooming service to choose from, saloon, mobile or home visits. Each have advantages and disadvantages.

Pet grooming salons mostly cater for a range of domestic pets. Enquire if they have a 'cat only' day to reduce stress caused by barking dogs. Avoid those who expect animals to be checked in during the morning and can't be collected until the close of business. When choosing a grooming saloon or pet spa ask to see the working area. The premises should be clean, calm and secure. Make sure you have a firm appointment and ask how long they will require your cat. Ensure you know exactly what you are paying for and if there are extras that will occur an additional fee.

Mobile groomers have a vehicle, kitted out with a grooming area and facilities for bathing, that they will drive to your home. Generally, they are more expensive than saloon grooming but money will be saved on travel expenses. Prior to making an appointment ask to see their insurance policy as some work with no cover.

Home groomers visit and groom within your home. If you wish your pet to be bathed, they will use your facilities. They are unlikely to have a portable cage dryer. Again, ask to see an insurance policy prior to making an appointment.

▸ *A good grooming shop is clean and tidy with friendly and helpful staff who welcome you and your cat.*

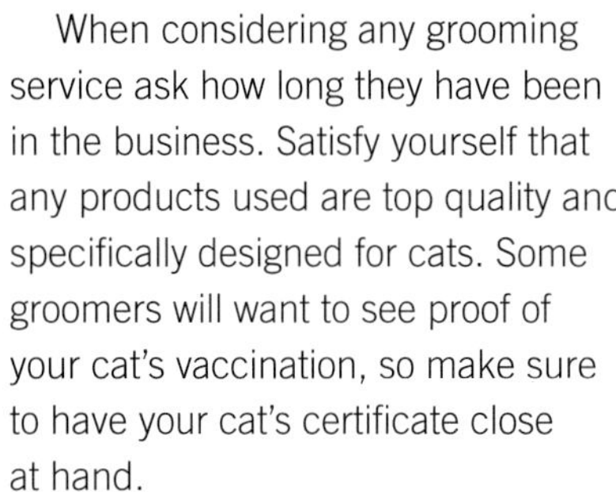

When considering any grooming service ask how long they have been in the business. Satisfy yourself that any products used are top quality and specifically designed for cats. Some groomers will want to see proof of your cat's vaccination, so make sure to have your cat's certificate close at hand.

The best groomer to choose is the one recommended by fellow cat lovers. Qualifications are important but a kind attitude and friendly personality are imperative.

▾ *Prior to leaving your cat carrier with the groomer, attach a label to it so they know who it belongs to.*

▾ *A groomer will carefully examine each cat and may need to use electric clippers to remove difficult matts.*

▾ *All cats like being clean, not just pedigrees, although some do not enjoy the bathing and grooming process.*

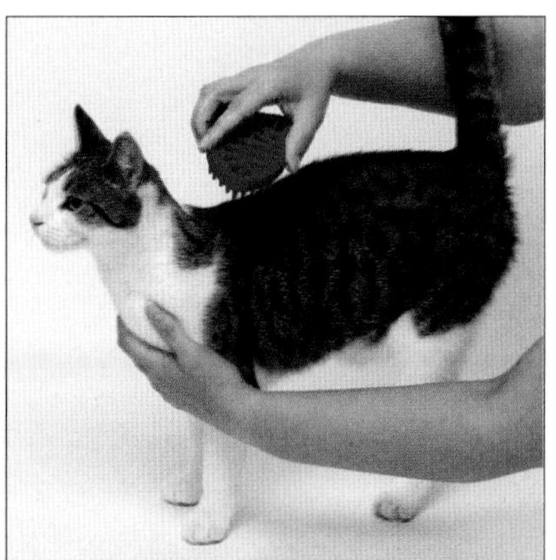

GENERAL CARE

A cat is a survivor, and if it is injured, will often keep going regardless, making it difficult to spot if anything is wrong. Getting to know your cat's character, giving it regular checks, and understanding a little about the strengths and weaknesses of its body will help alert you to the first signs of illness or injury. Vigilance and care will keep the vet's bills down, too. If an emergency arises, knowing how to deal with it may save your cat's life and increase its chances of a full recovery. Simple preparation, such as having the vet's number keyed into your phone and being able to quickly access a first-aid kit, can, quite literally, be a life-saver.

◄ *Veterinary insurance gives peace of mind if your cat falls ill. Vet's bills quickly mount up.*

How to tell if your cat is sick

The cat's coat is a barometer of health. It reflects the quality of its diet and general condition, and should be gleaming and free from dandruff. The healthy cat's eyes are bright and clear with no discharge, redness or blinking. The tissue around them is pale pink in colour rather than red and inflamed. Nose leather is cool and slightly moist from the cat's tear ducts, and licking also keeps the nostrils moist.

Often, it is only by knowing your cat and understanding how it normally behaves, looks and reacts within its usual environment that you can tell if anything is wrong. You are the mirror of your cat's health, so do not be afraid to mention anything abnormal that you have noticed, no matter how small. The vet may only see your cat once a year and does not know its normal character or behaviour. Particular points to look out for are changes in eating or drinking habits.

SIGNS THAT SOMETHING IS WRONG

The first sign that your cat is not well may be a change in its behaviour or appearance that may only be perceptible to you. If a normally friendly cat shows signs of aggression, or an outgoing animal suddenly becomes withdrawn, timid and shy, look for other signs of illness. Lack of response to being called may be due to fever or temporary deafness caused by ear mite infestation. A dull, ungroomed look to the coat with abnormally raised fur (this is called a 'starey' coat) is a general indication of ill health.

If you still have cause for concern, check the cat's stools: they should be firm and without extreme or pungent odour. If you have an outdoor cat, confine it if possible and provide a litter tray, so that you can make this important check.

Where cats have access to dustbins, diarrhoea may be caused by a stomach upset resulting from eating contaminated food, but could be a sign of something more serious, especially if it is persistent. Constipation, causing the cat to strain, can also be a problem, especially if there is any blood in the stools.

When to call the vet

If your cat is displaying any of the following symptoms, call the vet immediately:

- Blood in vomit, urine or faeces
- Excessive thirst
- Swollen and tender abdomen
- High temperature
- Vomiting and diarrhoea together
- Bleeding from penis or vulva
- Straining when it tries to pass urine
- Shallow, laboured breathing
- After a road accident

▲ *An alert expression, pricked-up ears and a glossy coat suggest that this cat has a balanced diet and a healthy, contented life.*

◄ *A Red Tabby is interested in the life going on around it, as every healthy cat should be.*

▼ *A cat playing is in character – if it were suddenly to become uninterested in playing and listless, this would be a sign to the owner of possible ill health.*

▶ *As part of the regular care routine, make a random check in the fur by parting it until you can see the skin.*

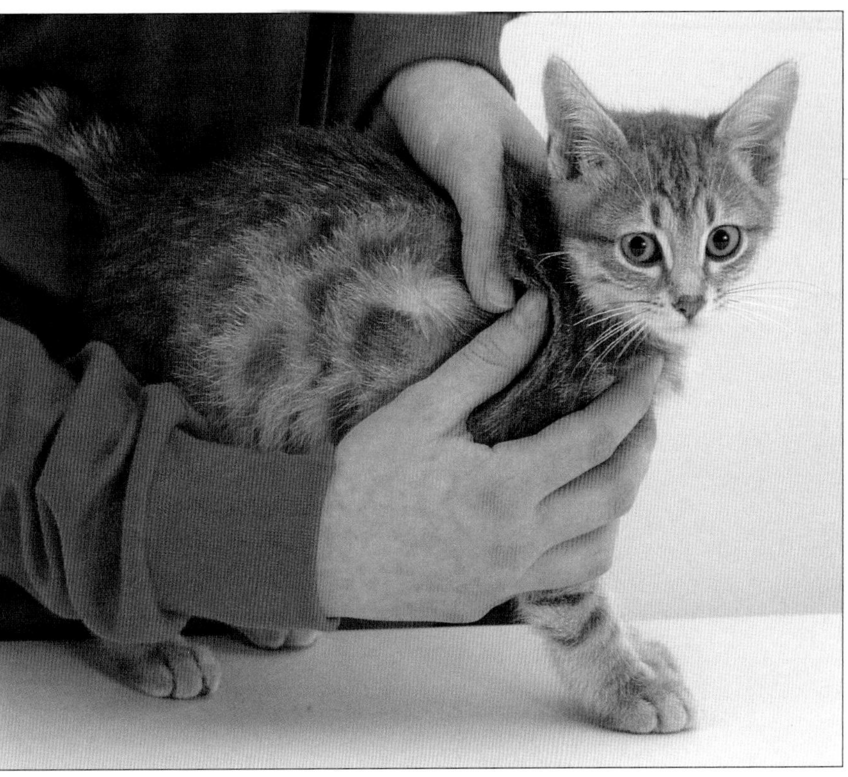

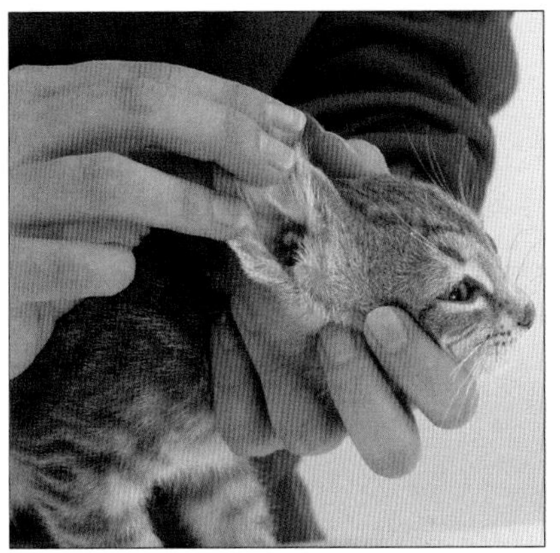

▲ *An owner gently holds back the ear to check that there are no scratches on the pinna (the inner lining of the outer ear). Also check for dark, waxy deposits.*

If the third eyelid – the haw or nictitating (blinking) membrane – is visible, it indicates an infection or possibly that there is a foreign body in the eye. Any signs of redness or inflammation or excessive and persistent, thick, yellowish discharge are cause for concern. If either pupil appears dilated or does not react to bright light, this needs very prompt veterinary attention.

Clear wax in the ears is normal, but a dark brown waxy deposit may indicate ear mites that need veterinary treatment. Look out for seeds, such as grass seeds, too. A seed may lodge in the ear and enter the ear canal, making the cat shake and scratch its ear. The wall of the ear canal and flap (pinna) is extremely delicate and vulnerable to damage in fighting situations. A puncture to the pinna often results in a haematoma (a large blood blister) that could become infected if not treated. If the ears are very hot, the cat may be running a temperature, but before rushing to the vet, check this is not due to your cat lying in the sun or next to a radiator!

SICKNESS

Light vomiting is very often no cause for alarm. It may be due to the cat having bolted down its food too fast, a reaction to something it has caught and eaten, to grass that it has chewed to clear its system out, or a

▶ *As in humans and other animals, the state of a cat's eyes can indicate problems elsewhere in the body. This cat's eyes are those of a radiantly healthy animal.*

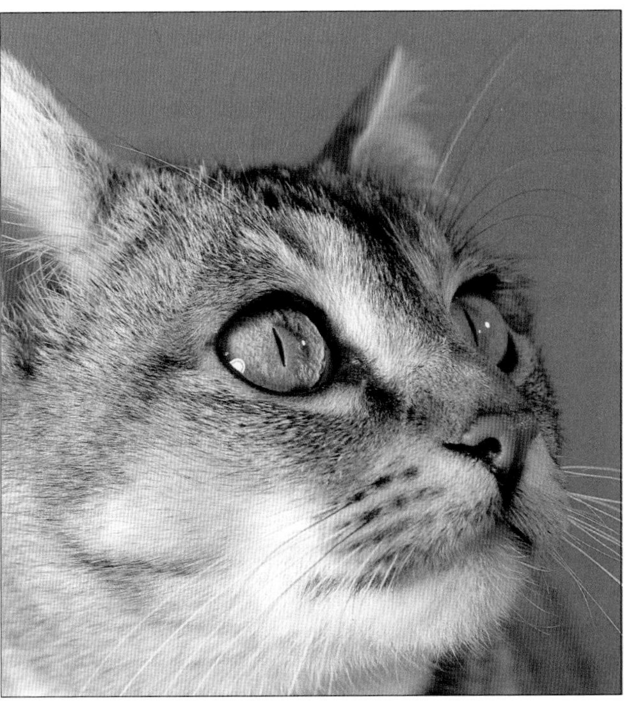

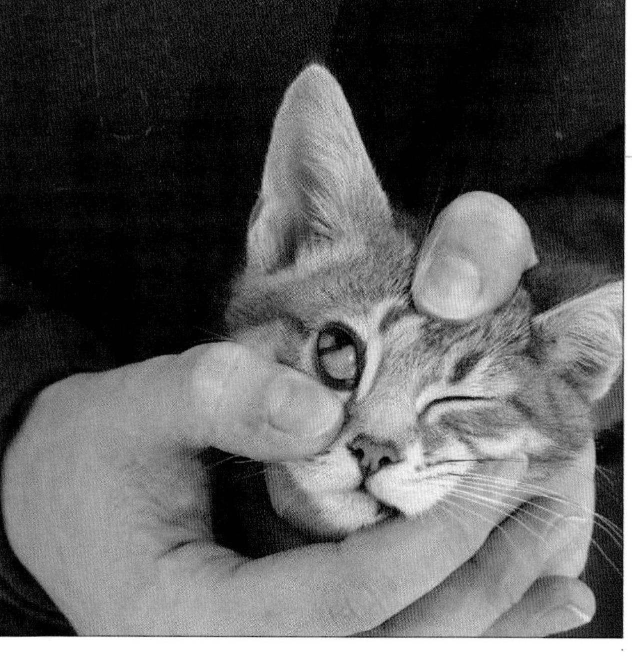

◄ *It is important to check the cat's third eyelid, or nictitating membrane. If this shows on its own, it suggests there is something wrong. The cat may have an infection or a foreign body in its eye.*

physiological response to remove hairballs. Persistent vomiting, however, especially if it contains any blood, is significant, and is reason enough to check with the vet.

OTHER INDICATIONS

A good indication that the cat has a raised temperature is if the ears feel hot. A rectal thermometer is needed in order to take a precise temperature reading, which should be 38–38.5°C (100.5–101.5°F). Unless you have been shown how to do this properly (see page 177), it is best left to a professional.

Key pulse points in a cat are located under the forearms (armpits) and back legs (groin). The pulse rate may vary between 120 and 170, depending on how active the cat has been recently. The average is 150.

The caring and wise owner checks the pet regularly to make sure it is in top condition. Early signs of conditions such as mite infestation or fleas will prevent more serious problems developing later. The check-up can be at a time when you are relaxing with your cat, or if it is one that needs regular grooming, as an integral part of the grooming routine. If a cat does show any signs of ill-health or discomfort, you can go through the checking points described on the previous pages. Then, if you do take it to the vet, you can give a report on anything unusual you have noticed.

One good reason for grooming your cat regularly, even if it is a shorthair, is that you will be quickly alerted to any lumps, or signs of attack by fleas, ticks, mites or lice. If the grooming process rakes out some grit-like dirt, check further. Comb the cat over moistened absorbent paper. If the grit leaves a red stain, these are the blood-gorged faeces of fleas. If not, the cat has been rolling in the garden.

Small, raised grey or whitish lumps indicate ticks. These can irritate the cat considerably as the tick's head is buried deep into the skin, leaving only the body visible. They should be removed as soon as possible but great care has to be taken to ensure that the head is removed as, if left behind, an abscess or sore can develop.

Check that ears are clean and free of dark waxy deposits and seeds. Even minor scratches need to be kept clean to prevent infection. Check for broken or discoloured teeth, swollen gums and bad breath, and make sure there are no lumps (enlarged glands) around the neck.

The claws of an indoor cat need to be checked regularly in case they need clipping and to prevent them from ingrowing. Also check for any soreness or wounds on the pads.

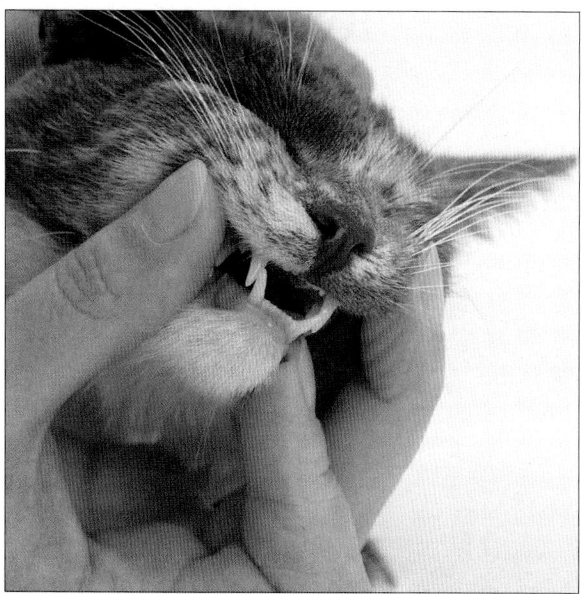

◄ *Modern cat food does not give a cat's teeth the exercise and cleaning power that would come from hunted food. It is therefore important to check your cat's teeth regularly.*

A quiet place for your cat

All cats require a quiet and safe place to retreat to. They use this place for a variety of reasons. The most common being an escape from the hurly burly of everyday life, somewhere to curl up and have a snooze without fear of disturbance from their human family or feline companions. This is completely natural behaviour.

Generally, cats will choose these places for themselves, looking for somewhere warm and dark where they feel protected. Common sites include cardboard boxes, bags and suitcases, cupboards and wardrobes, under beds or furniture, behind electrical appliances or floor-length curtains, under potted plants or shrubs in the garden and even in the kitchen sink. Unfortunately, they don't always choose wisely and may decide to settle down in an unsafe place. These include the tumble dryer or microwave, warm ashes in an unlit wood burner, heating ducts, dishwashers, washing machines and inside reclining furniture.

Because your cat may not make a sensible choice it is prudent to provide a safe, quiet place and encourage your cat to use it. Choose a place that is dark, warm and draught-free, for example behind the sofa. Provide a semi-enclosed container, an igloo-style bed is ideal but some cats prefer a simple cardboard box. Make it warm and snug by adding clean, soft and comfortable bedding. A little encouragement to use this space can be offered, but ideally the cat should find it itself. After all, your cat needs to consider the area as their secret hiding den.

It was always assumed that a cat would take itself off, and hide away, when it thought it was going to die. This is not strictly true as cats have no concept of their own death. What they do understand is that if they are unwell or in pain they are more vulnerable to attack from predators. For this reason, they will hide away. Therefore, it is important to monitor the amount of time that the cat uses the quiet place. If a cat spends more time than usual in its hiding place this can be an indication that the cat is unwell. In this case veterinary advice should be sought.

▲ *This pet has chosen an unsafe hiding area. Someone could put washing in without noticing the occupant.*

▼ *This is an ideal safe and snug place for any cat. Clean boxes of all kinds make lovely warm beds.*

▼ *Sleeping in the sun, but able to keep an eye on the wildlife at the same time.*

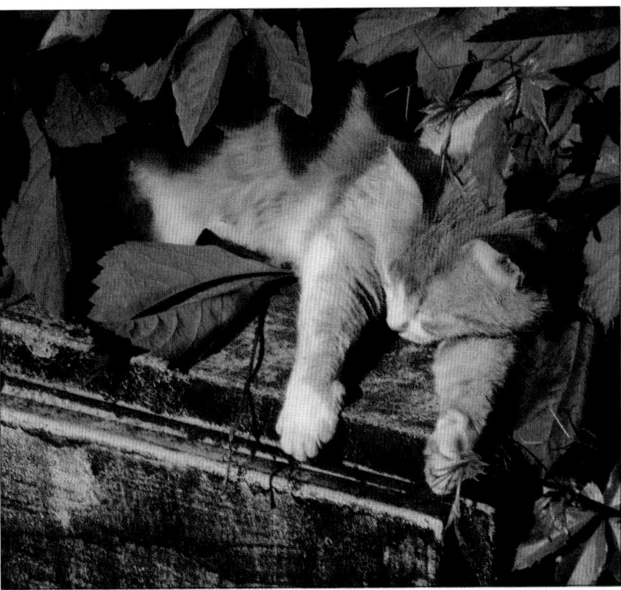

Choosing a vet

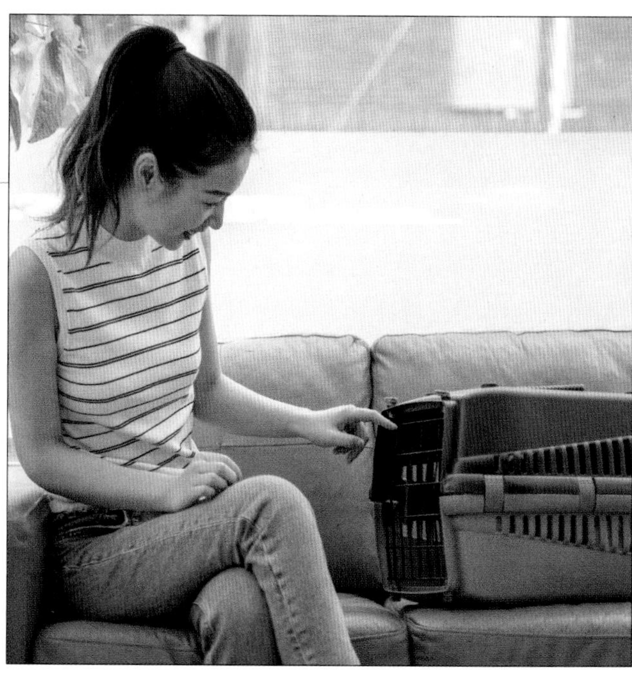

▶ *It is safer to take your cat to the vet's surgery in a travel carrier in case there are other animals waiting in the room with you.*

Do not wait until an emergency arises before you look for a vet. It is wise to have made arrangements before you bring a new animal home. If you found the kitten locally, ask the sanctuary, home or breeder. You may be able to continue with the vet a kitten has already visited for its initial check-ups and inoculations. If the kitten is from a different area, ask friends in the neighbourhood who already own cats, or a local cat club for recommendations (addresses and telephone numbers are available from The Governing Council of the Cat Fancy in the United Kingdom, the Cat Fanciers' Association in the United States and equivalent organizations in most other countries).

WHICH VET?

Selecting the right vet for your pet is just as important as finding the right doctor for your family – but there is one great difference. While doctors only deal with one species – the human one – vets have to cope with a wide range of different animals, from hamsters to cows. They are unlikely to be specialized in all fields, and not all will be up-to-date with feline ailments. This may be a problem if you live in a rural area, as veterinary practices may be geared to large animals such as cattle and horses. In urban areas, most surgeries are small-animal practices, devoted to the care of cats, dogs and other small domestic pets.

If you have time contact a number of different practices; telephone first if you wish to visit. Ask for a list of fees for consultation, and the cost of care items such as inoculations, blood tests, flea and worming products.

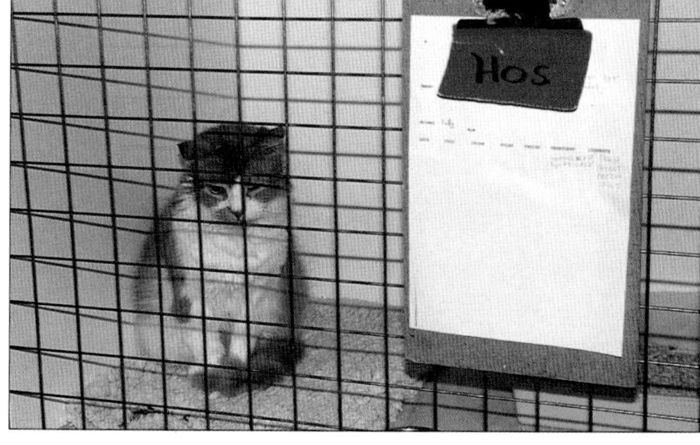

◀ *A cat has its annual check. This is an opportunity for comments on general condition, any booster inoculations and restocking of worming and flea treatments.*

▲ *If your pet is to have an anaesthetic, the vet may advise taking it in the night before. In this way, the surgery can control food intake and the cat has time to settle down.*

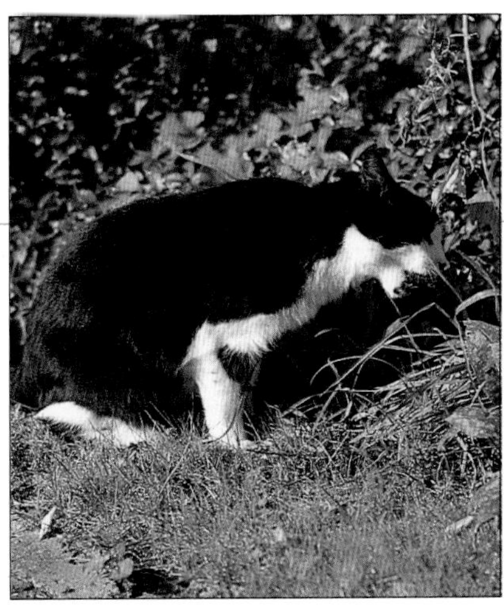

▶ A cat eats grass as a natural emetic – it may help to clear the system of obstructions, such as hairballs, and provide extra vitamins.

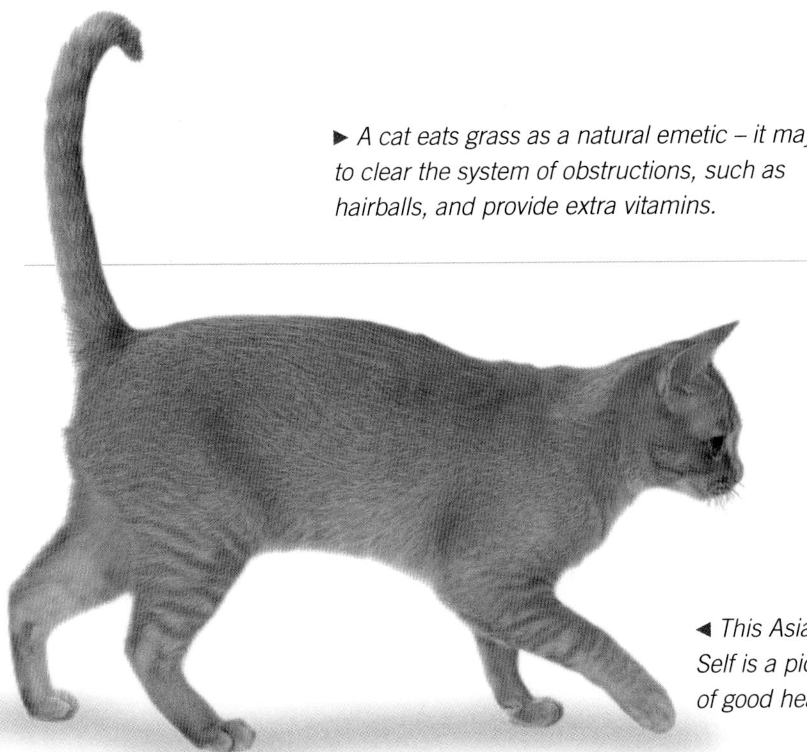

◀ *This Asian Red Self is a picture of good health.*

QUESTIONS TO ASK

Before you go, consider what you want from the vet. If you have a neutered (altered) cat that rarely goes out, you will probably have to visit the vet only once a year for the booster inoculations, so enquire about policy for routine check-ups. If your plan is to show or breed from your cat, you will need to think more seriously about locating a vet who is perhaps interested in breeding, and knowledgeable about pedigreed breeds and showing. This is usually easier in a city than in a rural region.

Once you have found a practice that is cat-friendly, it is worth going through a mental checklist of what you need to know.

Check opening hours. Is an appointment needed, or does the practice run on an open-surgery basis whereby you turn up unannounced between specified hours? Both can operate well in an efficient practice, but if you are working, you may need a combination of both options for maximum flexibility. You will also need to make sure that there are weekend and occasional evening surgeries.

Check that there are arrangements for emergencies around the clock. If so, will your cat be treated by one of the practice vets or a separate emergency staff? This may be significant if you have a pedigreed animal that requires special attention. Also, what is the policy regarding home visits? This may be important if you are intending to breed from your cat, in case you need help at the birth.

Is the practice a veterinary hospital or does it specialize in feline medicine and surgery?

If it is a member of a national advisory organization (such as International Cat Care in Britain) it will be well up-to-date with all the latest health care information.

Ask about the attitude towards alternative or complementary treatments, such as homoeopathy, chiropractice and acupuncture. Look for a positive, holistic approach, as the benefits of these treatments, especially for older cats, can be substantial.

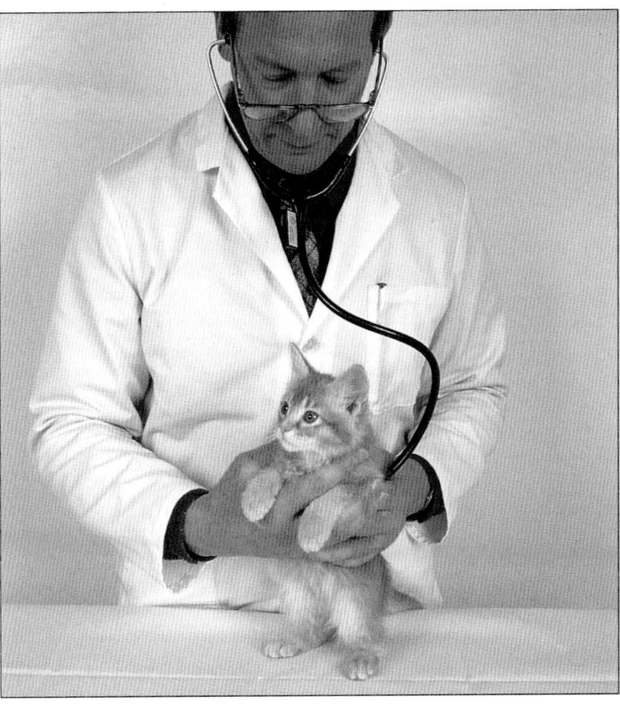

▶ *A kitten has its first check at about nine weeks. This will coincide with the first inoculations and, with pedigreed animals, will probably take place before they leave the home where they were bred.*

Standard treatments

However hardy your cat is, it runs the risk of being struck down by a killer virus infection unless it is inoculated and boosted on a regular basis. If a cat contracts one of the diseases for which preventative vaccines are available, it is very serious, for there is no treatment that can be guaranteed to save it. All a vet can do is to treat the symptoms and minimize suffering, and hope that your pet's natural immunity will fight the illness.

INOCULATIONS

In the first few days of its life, a kitten's resistance is boosted by the antibody-rich colostrum that is the mother's first milk. Although this is replaced by normal milk after the first few days, this also contains some antibodies so, as long as the kittens are feeding, the mother's immunity will pass down to them through the milk. As soon as weaning starts, this natural protection diminishes. From now on, immunity has to be built up actively by the kitten and will no longer be acquired passively from the queen. Active immunity can be built up by exposure to infections or, more safely and securely, by inoculations. Taking your cat to the vet to be inoculated is a vital part of routine care. Inoculations are given at 9–12 weeks; the kitten is then kept in for a week or two to prevent exposure to infection while the aquired immunity from the vaccine becomes effective. Inoculations subsequently need to be boosted every year. Some kittens or adult cats may feel a little under par for a few days after first inoculations or the annual booster, but it is rare for there to be any major problems.

▲ *A two-week-old kitten is still gaining some immunity from infection through its mother's milk – as long as the mother herself has been kept fully up-to-date with her inoculations.*

► *Six-week-old kittens may be introduced to new social experiences, but three weeks before their first vaccination, they must not be exposed to other cats in the outside world.*

▲ *A stray cat with its single-kitten litter. The mother's tough and probably deprived lifestyle may have limited her ability to produce a bigger litter.*

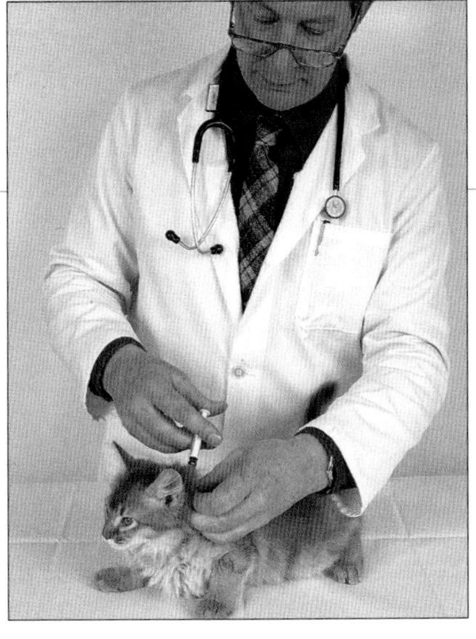

▲ *A kitten receives its first vaccination at six to nine weeks of age. It will have to be kept indoors for another two to three weeks after it has received its second vaccination.*

FREEDOM FROM WORRY

Over the past 30 years, there have been enormous steps forward in the prevention and cure of feline ailments. The diseases that used to pose the greatest risk to pedigreed and non-pedigreed felines alike, are no longer a problem if the regular, recommended inoculation programme is followed.

WHICH INOCULATIONS?

Recommendations regarding vaccinations vary in different countries. In the United States, for instance, where, in urban areas, owners are often advised to keep their cats indoors, both cat flu viruses, feline infectious enteritis (FIE) and rabies are considered the core inoculations. Those against chlamydia, feline leukaemia virus (FeLV) and feline infectious peritonitis (FIP) are often considered necessary only for cats likely to be exposed to risk in the outside world. However, bear in mind that your cat could escape and come into contact with one of the diseases you decided not to inoculate against. Take your vet's advice.

The most serious infections are: cat flu (viral rhinitis), which encompasses two viruses that affect the cat's upper respiratory tract; feline infectious enteritis; chlamydia; and feline leukaemia virus. Rabies should be added to the list in countries where the disease is known to exist. Although these are not the only viruses to affect the cat, these are the major viral conditions that have wrought havoc in the past among domestic cats. Effective vaccines against cat flu and feline enteritis have been around for several years. A vaccine to treat the leukaemia virus is a more recent addition. At the time of writing, in the United Kingdom, where rabies does not exist, the vaccine can only be administered by authorized vets to cats that are going to countries where the disease exists.

What to do when

- 9 weeks: first vaccination
- 12 weeks: second vaccination and discuss with the veterinary surgeon a timed programme for administering flea and worm treatments
- 16 weeks: spaying for females
- 4–6 months: neutering (altering) for males
- Every year: booster vaccinations and check-up

GENERAL CHECK-UP

The vet will only inoculate your cat if it is in good health, so do not take it if it is below par for any reason. At the same time as the annual booster vaccinations, ask the vet to give your cat a check-up – to look at ears, teeth, gums and general condition. With luck, this will be the only time the vet sees your cat. You can also stock up with treatments for worms and fleas.

▼ *A Chocolate Silver Ocicat kitten at 15 weeks old has had all its vaccinations, and is independent of its mother.*

Neutering (Altering)

Neutering, altering or desexing not only prevents reproduction but also the inconvenience of the female cat coming into heat (oestrus) or calling. In the female cat this is called spaying. For the male, the operation, castration, reduces the tendency to spray and also the odour of the male cat's urine.

Although you may be nervous about putting your pet through this procedure there are very many benefits to it being done. The operation has the effect of modifying behaviour associated with sexual desire and establishing and marking territory (see *Behaviour and Intelligence* pages 44–59). The result is that the desexed cat is usually more stable and affectionate, and bonds more easily with the family. Recent work in Britain and the United States has shown that the operation in either sex can be carried out earlier than was previously thought with no ill effects. Some rescue organizations now desex kittens before they are homed at 8–12 weeks, but the majority of vets prefer to carry out the operation when the kitten is older, at four to six months. As both operations are carried out under a general anaesthetic, no food or water can be taken for about 12 hours beforehand. The operation cannot be reversed in either sex.

▼ *Burmillas are generally known for their good nature, but any aggressive tendencies will be further modified by the desexing process.*

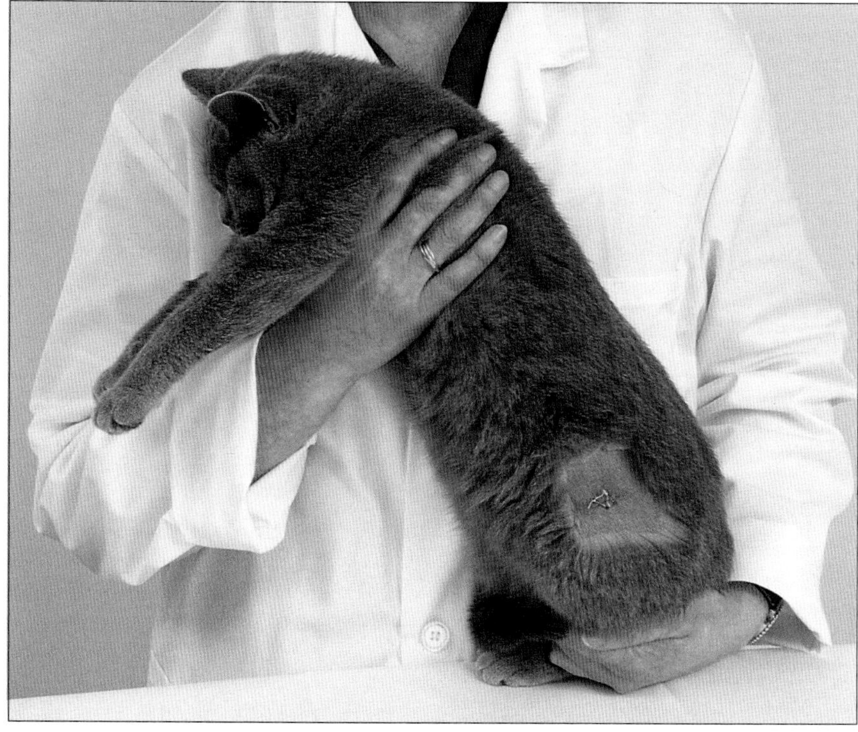

▲ *A recently spayed female shows the shaved area where the incision was made. There is a slight possibility that the fur may grow back a different colour in this area.*

CASTRATION

The operation involves the removal, under general anaesthetic, of the cat's testes. Tiny incisions are involved and usually no stitches are necessary. Within 24 hours the cat is usually back to normal. Both kittens and adult cats can be castrated. If you consider giving a home to a stray tom, castration will ensure that he settles quickly, is less aggressive, less territorial and less likely to roam. This also means that he is less likely to pick up infections and be involved in traffic accidents.

SPAYING

Female cats do not miss motherhood, and gain security, as they no longer have the urge to roam when coming into heat or calling, and are no longer targeted by unneutered (unaltered) male cats. Spaying or altering the female cat is more complicated than

► *Kittens born to an unneutered female are the cat owners' responsibility whether the litter was planned or acccidental.*

in the male. The cat's ovaries (where the eggs are produced) and womb (uterus) are removed to prevent her coming into heat. She should not be on heat at the time of the operation. A small area of fur is shaved on the abdomen and an incision made, which has to be stitched afterwards. The spayed female cat is usually back to normal quickly but will need care, warmth and light meals until the stitches are taken out by the vet.

Other than population control, there are some valid health reasons for neutering your cat. In the case of a male, the decrease in territorial defence and aggression not only means that he is less likely to fight, but also that he is less likely to be the target of other male cats. Cat bites cause deep puncture wounds that are not always visible until they have become infected. These wounds are a leading factor in transmission of feline leukaemia (FeLV) and feline immuno-deficiency virus (FIV) among un-neutered males. Both can be transmitted by saliva and each can have fatal consequences. Additionally, the risk of testicular diseases is eliminated in castrated cats.

Un-spayed females are at risk of pyometra. This is an accumulation of pus within the uterus due to physiological, hormonal and anatomical changes that happen after a female has finished her heat cycle, coupled with a secondary bacterial infection. This condition is potentially life threatening and requires immediate veterinary attention. Unfortunately, it can be difficult for owners to detect the symptoms of pyometra until after it is too late for veterinary intervention. Although there a few incidences of a neutered cat suffering from this condition, the risk is significantly reduced after spaying. Neutering a female cat will also greatly diminish the occurrence of mammary tumours. Spaying a cat before her first estrous cycle reduces the chance of cervical cancer and eliminates all risk of ovarian cancer.

There are environmental benefits of neutering too. A male that is not constantly seeking a female, or a female that is not feeding kittens, doesn't need so much food or feel as hungry. Therefore, they are less likely to hunt to top up their nutritional requirements, so leaving their local area a safer place for wildlife.

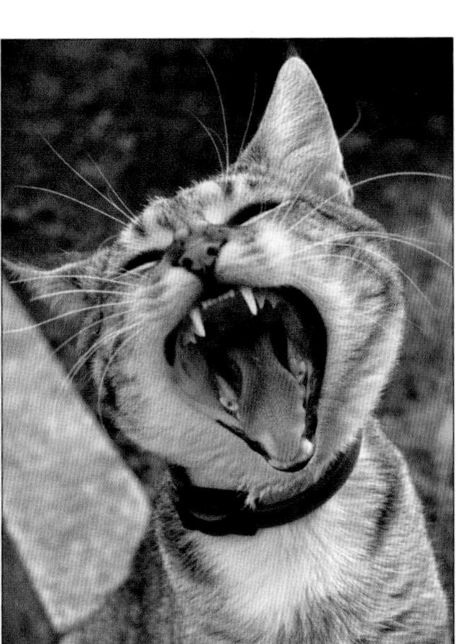

◄ *Females constantly calling for a mate, or males serenading, can make for an extremely noisy neighbourhood.*

► *Generally a kitten's testes descend into the scrotum while still in the womb or within the first six weeks of life.*

Microchipping

Currently, unlike dogs, it is not a legal requirement to microchip a cat, although many animal charities are calling for it to become law. It is compulsory in some countries for animals that are going to travel abroad, or enter a foreign country, to be microchipped as part of the identification, vaccination and health check process.

A microchip is about the size of a grain of rice and contains a unique digital number. These numbers can be read with a scanner. Each number is stored in a database along with the details of the relevant pet's owner. These details include the pet's name, owner's name, address and contact details. It is also possible to list any major health conditions that an animal may have and vital necessary medication recorded too. The cost of recording details on the database is generally included in the cost of the microchip procedure. An additional cost may occur if the details have to be changed, for example change of address due to a house move.

Microchipping can be done either by a vet or a specially trained person. The chip is inserted under the skin between the shoulder blades of the cat using a needle. This procedure will momently 'sting', like any injection with a fairly large needle. Any discomfort is very short-lived. Chipping is normally done when a kitten is 10–12 weeks old. Some breeders chip all kittens routinely prior to them going to a new home.

The main benefit of microchipping is the part they play in helping to reunite an owner with a lost pet. Most animal shelters have a scanner which they will pass over every stray cat. If a chip is detected, the digital code will lead to the owner's contact details. Sadly only two per cent of unchipped cats in rescue are ever reunited with their owners.

The cost of chipping varies, those done by a vet generally being the most expensive, although there are some very reasonable packages when combined with recommended vaccinations. Many animal charities offer low cost, or free, microchipping. It is worth checking prices in your area.

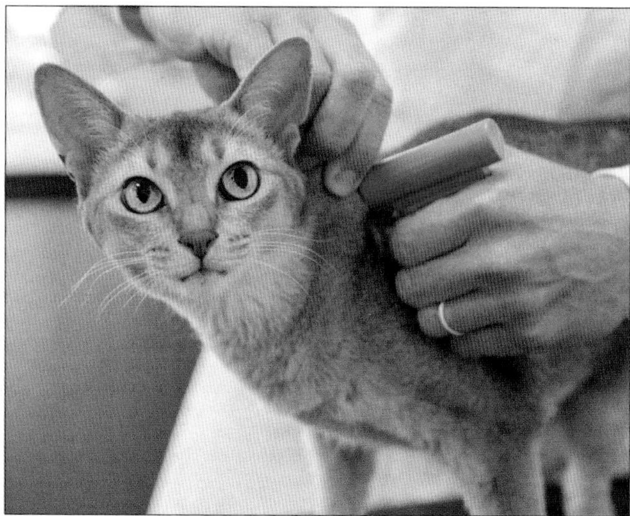

◄ ▲ *Once inserted, the microchip has an average operational lifespan of 20 years. It is rare for them to fail.*

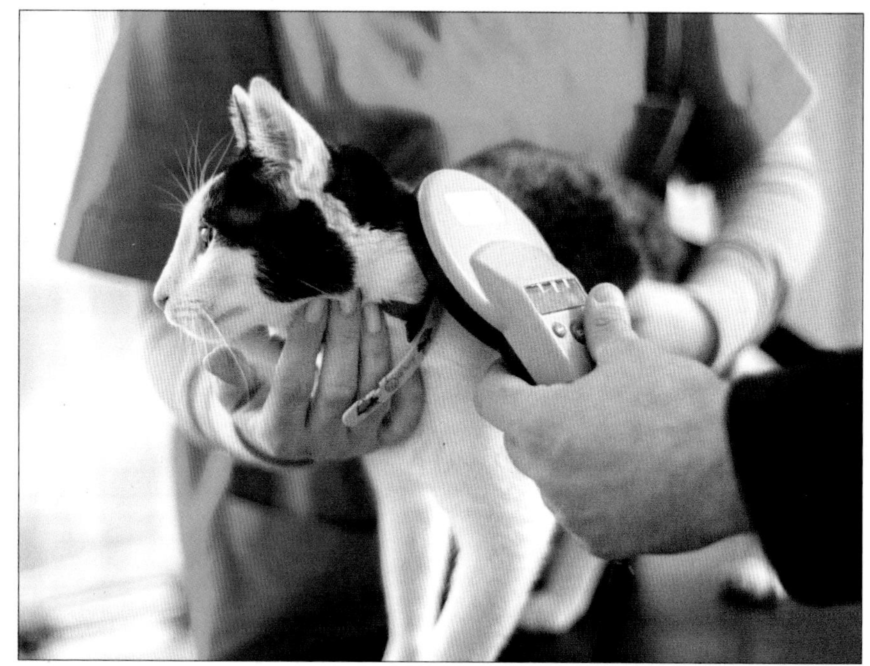

▼ *The scanner is passed slowly over the shoulder area until the chip is detected and a 'bleep' heard.*

Checking temperature and pulse

The adage that healthy cats and dogs have cold wet noses isn't strictly true. An estimate of temperature can be roughly judged by feeling how hot the ears are, but the only accurate way of telling if a cat has a fever is to take its temperature with a thermometer. Using an in-ear thermometer is not recommended; it is best to purchase a digital rectal thermometer. These give a quicker reading and are safer than a mercury one. The cat's thermometer should be clearly labelled so that it is not used by members of the human household. Signs that a cat may have a fever include lethargy, loss of appetite, changes in behaviour and vomiting.

Taking a cat's temperature is easier with two people, one to hold and one to insert the thermometer. It is possible to do this alone if the cat is of a calm nature. If the owner can't manage this, and has no one to help, a trip to the vet is required if there is cause for concern.

Prior to checking the temperature restrain the cat by wrapping it in a towel or blanket leaving the head and tail exposed. Alternatively, thick leather gloves can be worn and the cat restrained by holding the loose skin on the back of the neck (scruffing).

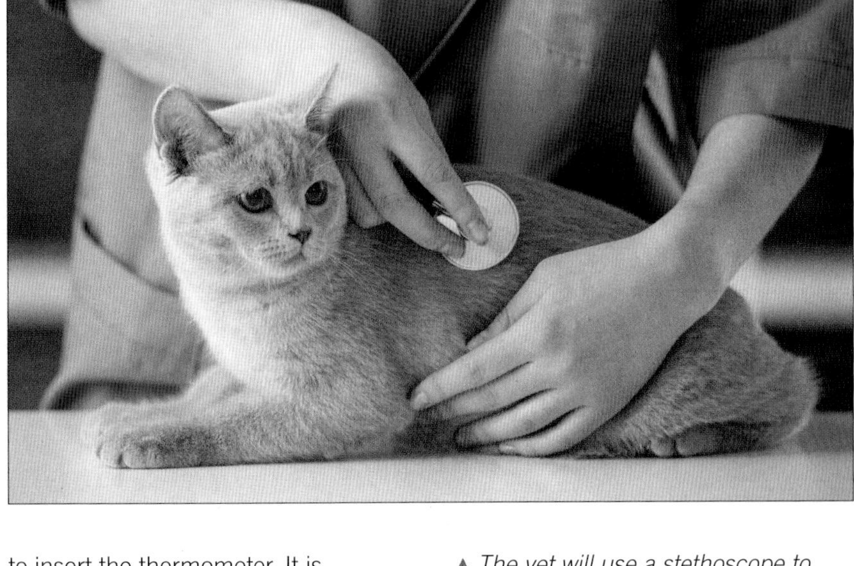

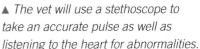

▲ *The vet will use a stethoscope to take an accurate pulse as well as listening to the heart for abnormalities.*

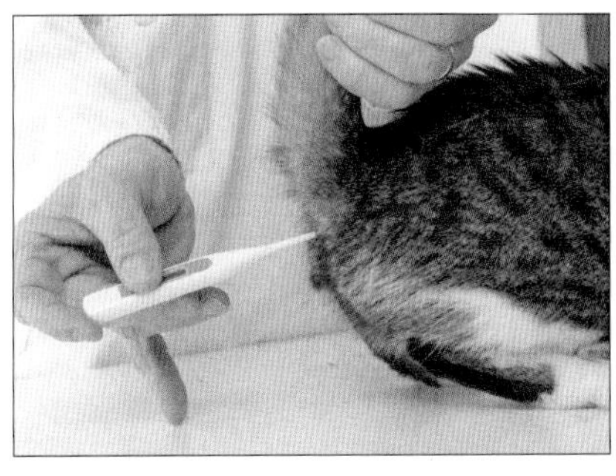

▲ *KY jelly or Vaseline are both suitable to use as lubricants when taking a rectal temperature reading.*

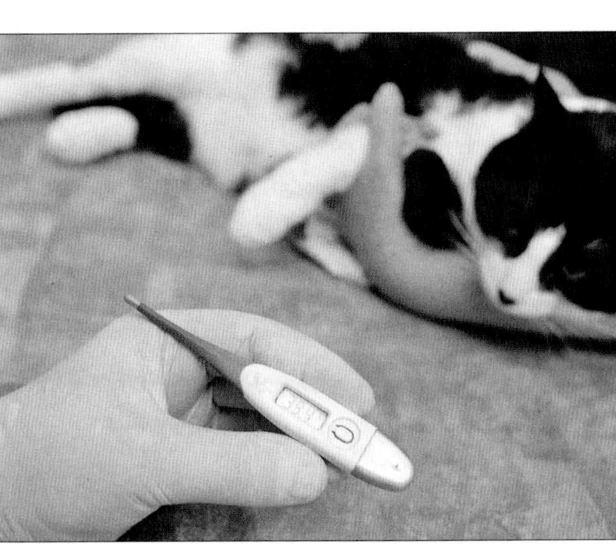

► *After any use, wash the thermometer with warm soapy water or medical rubbing alcohol.*

Lubricate the end of the thermometer with a proprietary water-soluble lubricant. Turn the digital thermometer on and wait for the bleep noise that indicates it is ready to use. Lift the cat's tail and gently insert approximately 2.5cm (1in) into the rectum. The thermometer will bleep again when it has registered the reading. Remove it at this point. Clean the instrument after use. The normal temperature range is 37.8–39.2°C (100.4–102.5°F). Any deviation from this range requires immediate veterinary attention.

To check a cat's pulse, wait until the cat is relaxed and press the two forefingers inside the upper hind leg where the large femoral artery lies. It can be difficult to do this if the cat is obese. Count each pulse over a 15-second period and multiply by four. This will give the pulse rate by minute. The normal range of an adult resting cat is 160–180 per minute.

How long will your cat live?

From about the age of ten to twelve years, a cat may begin to show signs of growing old. This may not be immediately apparent as the slowing down process is very gradual. Internal organs may not work as well as they once did and joints may become that little bit stiffer. Over time the cat seems to restrict its activities, is far less playful and becomes a creature of sedentary habits. Particular health conditions such as diabetes or arthritis require constant supervision and medical intervention.

The oldest cat recorded was a cat called Crème Puff who died aged 38 years and 3 days. She is listed in the 2010 edition of *Guinness World Records*. Crème Puff belonged to Jake Perry from Austin, Texas. Interestingly, Jake Perry also owned a cat called Grandpa Rex Allen who was the previous record holder. The breeding of both these cats is not listed but it is known that they were unrelated. Their grand ages are very unusual. The average age span for a cat is between 14–16 years with a few reaching 20. It is easier to record the accurate age of a pedigree cat as they are normally registered with the exact date of birth and registration number.

When you first get a 12-week-old kitten, it is very likely that its lifespan will be between ten and fifteen years. This could mean that the cat will become a companion to your children as well as to yourself. A longer life is not unusual, in which case it may well live to see your grandchildren as well. To borrow from the dog world, a cat is for life, not just for Christmas. This has to be thoroughly understood before a kitten joins the household.

▲ *A Blue Bi-colour Persian father seems to contemplate the continuation of his pedigreed line with one of his kittens.*

▼ *The start of a long relationship: this kitten will probably live long enough to be a companion for this owner throughout her childhood and teenage years.*

FACTORS INFLUENCING LONGEVITY

Neutered (altered) cats have a slightly longer lifespan than those which remain unneutered. This is particularly true of male cats. An unneutered (unaltered) tom will fight to defend territory and the resulting injuries and infections may shorten his life. Females lead a much quieter life, and a career spent having kittens, in an environment in which her condition is well-maintained, appears to have little effect on the female's longevity.

Apart from differing nutritional requirements at various stages of its life, a cat's physical responses slow down as it gets older and joints become stiff. This not only has the effect of reducing suppleness and

► *Kittens that receive poor nutrition while growing may develop long-term health problems.*

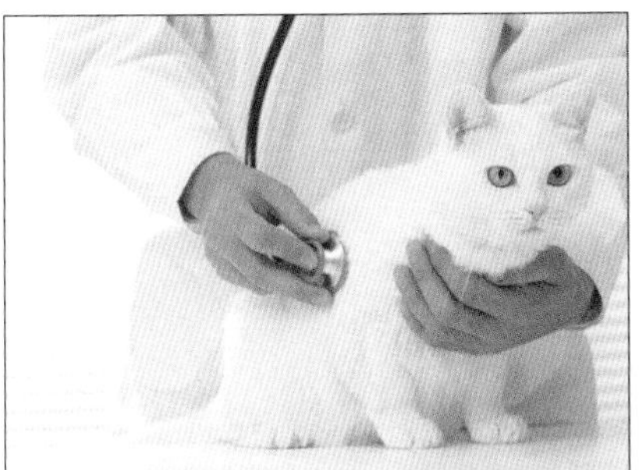

▲ *Adequate exercise and correct body weight are essential for good health and longevity.*

agility, but has implications for the daily care of the cat such as grooming.

Other factors can influence the lifespan of a cat, the main one being if they are indoor or outdoor cats. Cats living indoors have a much more sheltered and protected life than those allowed outside for sustained periods of time. They do not have to cope with predators, the risk of being hit by a car, being shut in a building, or receiving injuries from another territorial cat. Neither are they subjected to extremes of temperature, ingesting poison or having to hunt for their food. Outdoor cats are more susceptible to contracting life-threatening diseases such as Feline Immunodeficiency Virus and Feline Leukaemia. The average life expectancy for a feral cat, or one that has been dumped by its owner, is only 4–6 years, which clearly illustrates this point.

The breed of cat is another influencing factor. It is generally recognized that non-pedigree or mixed pedigree cats live longer than their pedigree cousins. This is thought to be due to the diversity of genetic make-up that reduces the risk of inherited genes that may cause adverse health implications. This does not mean that a well-bred pedigree cat cannot live a long life too. Many breeds are known for their longevity including Siamese, Burmese, Sphynx and Maine Coon.

Ensuring vaccinations are up-to-date and taking the cat for regular routine health checks play an important part in improving life expectancy. Many problems can be detected by a vet at an early stage and prompt attention can prevent them becoming life-threatening. Dental health is also an important aspect as the inability to ingest the correct nutritional requirements will dramatically reduce lifespan.

Living in a stress-free and loving environment helps to prolong life too. A contented cat is less likely to be as distressed by the natural changes that occur in the aging process. Caring owners quickly observe changes in behaviour that may indicate the early onset of a problem and either resolve the issue themselves or seek veterinary assistance. This is particularly true in the case of senility, which could have catastrophic consequences to a cat allowed outside.

► *Cats that have comfy lives are less environmentally stressed and so tend to live longer.*

Care of the elderly cat

Cats over the age of 11 years are considered seniors. As the body ages, changes will occur and this can cause difficulties. The most common is the onset of arthritis, with 90 per cent of cats over the age of 12 showing some sign of this condition. Much can be done to ensure that the older cat still enjoys an active and happy life.

The single most important thing an owner can do for an elderly cat is to have regular check-ups with their vet. This can be combined with vaccination booster appointments. At these sessions, the vet will have an opportunity to assess the health of the cat and the owner can discuss any worries that they might have. Early veterinarian intervention can prevent or alleviate any age-related health problems. Maintaining body weight is essential and your cat's diet may need to be changed accordingly.

▼ *Note down your cat's weight every time so that you have an accurate record of any gains or losses.*

▲ *Raising the height of a food bowl reduces stress on muscles, joints and bones, as well as aiding digestion.*

WEIGHT MONITORING

Weight loss can be an indicator of an underlying veterinary problem. This may be as simple as a dental issue, or a more serious condition such as the onset of renal disease. If you suspect weight loss, pop along to the vet so that they can evaluate your cat's body condition. If they are concerned and can find no obvious reason for the loss they may suggest blood or urine analysis. Excessive weight gain, or obesity, can make life difficult for a cat with arthritic joints. Senior diets are available that are designed to stabilize weight while providing all the nutritional requirements for the older cat. Many contain additional ingredients that can help to elevate the symptoms associated with arthritis.

Arthritic joints will affect activity levels. Many older cats stop using vertical scratching posts as this action causes pain. Horizontal scratch mats should be offered as an alternative and keep a careful eye on the claws so that they can be trimmed before they become over-grown. As a cat ages, it tends not to retract its claws as much because muscle tone decreases. Over-long claws can catch on the carpet, making movement difficult and even frightening. Similarly tiles and laminated floors may be too slippery to get a good grip, when walking, if

▼ *Mash food with a teaspoon of warm water so that it is soft, tempting and easy to eat.*

▲ *Electric heat pads provide warmth and comfort. Ensure the cable is armour-plated to avoid chewing.*

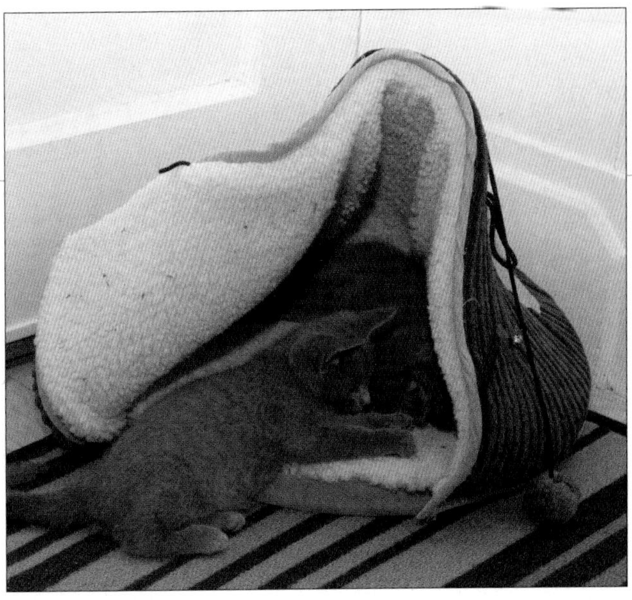

▲ *Older cats appreciate draughtproof beds that they can snuggle into and keep their backs warm.*

muscle tone is reduced. Encourage your cat to play – they may no longer feel like chasing a LED light, but most will still find a few strategically placed cardboard boxes fun to climb in and out of. If your cat enjoys them, puzzle feeders provide additional low level activity. Stiff, painful joints can alter the routine that your cat has established over years. Jumping on to the windowsill to watch birds in the garden may become impossible. Simple devices, such as placing a low box or stool under the window so it can be reached in two small bounds instead of one giant leap will enable an old cat to continue with this pastime.

CREATURE COMFORTS

Consideration should be given to your cat's bed. Question if it is warm and soft enough now that your pet spends longer sleeping. Igloo or pod beds are ideal as they keep out draughts and provide a place of privacy. Additional bedding can be placed inside if required. Equally, cat litter trays may need to be changed. Covered trays can become difficult to enter while a shallow open tray can be accessed from any direction with little effort. If your cat has a condition that causes increased thirst, and therefore increased urination, the depth of litter in the tray needs to be increased too.

Food and water bowls should be in an area that is easily accessed and placed on a surface that is not too slippery. Check your cat's teeth regularly as dental problems are common in the older cat. As the senses decrease, food with a stronger odour may encourage those with a diminished appetite.

Continuing grooming sessions is important as older cats lose flexibility and can no longer reach all parts of their body. Not only does this remove shedding hair and cleans the coat but allows for checks for lumps and bumps.

▼ *Regardless of age all cats love to sit in the sun. They use sunlight to help make up the drop in body temperature when they sleep.*

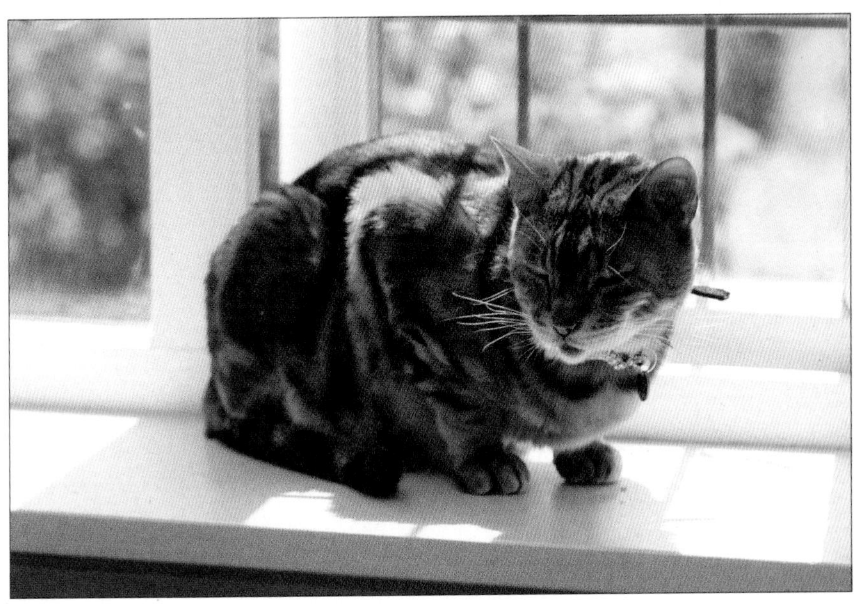

The death of your cat

Like the seasons, the cycle of birth, life and death follows a natural and unbreakable cycle that will always be completed. It is a widely held view that the essential life source of any living being, human or animal, continues to exist beyond physical death, perhaps rejoining the one invisible, universal source of all living things.

Whatever is the case, eventually the responsibility will fall upon you to see that your cat has as peaceful a transition from life to death as possible. The most desirable scenario is that when death approaches, your cat will die quietly in its sleep, or that you will be on hand to comfort it. Often, however, dying is a slow and painful process and you may be forced to make the difficult decision of whether or not to have your pet put to sleep.

Most owners find the decision concerning euthanasia a very difficult one and often seek the advice of the vet. Almost any vet would take the view that the relationship between cat and owner is a two-way contract. You have cared for your cat and made its life as full and satisfying as possible. In return the cat has rewarded you with the pleasure of its company. If the work of nursing your dying pet is proving stressful and starts to have an adverse effect on your health, or if the animal is suffering terribly, then having it put to sleep should be considered. Although vets are qualified to judge when the pain is too great for the cat to bear, they cannot know how you are feeling, or how your life is being affected. Ultimately it is up to you to decide when the partnership should finish: you will usually know when that time has come.

Holistic care can be of great assistance even at this difficult time. Both you and the cat can benefit from the Bach Flower remedy *Walnut,* which can help to relieve the stress and cope with the change brought about by major life transitions. Homeopathic *Arsen. alb.* given in rising potencies, helps to dispel the fear of dying that the cat may

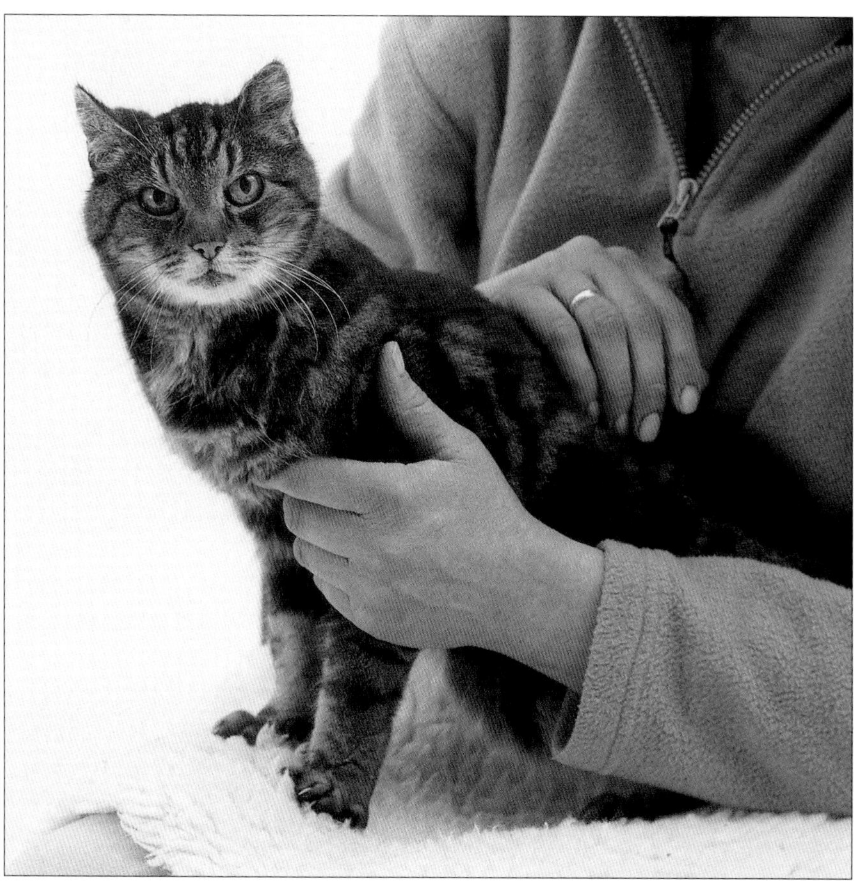

▲ *Your cat should have a long, happy life and a dignified death.*

▼ *The Bach Flower remedy Walnut can help both you and your cat during the last few days of its life.*

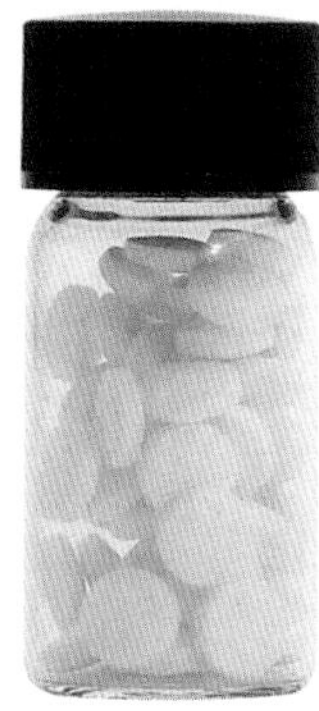

► *The homeopathic remedies Ignatia or Natrum mur. will help you through the grief that accompanies the loss of a great friend.*

▼ *Sadly, cats do not live as long as humans. Grieve when the final goodbye is said but delight in the love you both shared.*

experience towards the end of a long terminal illness. For grief, *Ignatia* is a good remedy for you to take: it will help the grieving process and allow you to adjust to the loss of your cat. If the grief seems never-ending, *Natrum mur.* can help you finally come to terms with the death of your pet. For further information on using Bach Flower remedies and homeopathy see pages 456–459.

If you have reached the decision that it might be time to let your cat go a little preparation can make the situation a little more bearable. Uncertainty is an awful feeling. If you are not sure what choice to make talk all the options over with the vet. You don't have to attend the surgery to have this conversation. You could arrange to talk to the vet on the phone.

▼ *The decision for euthanasia is taken to avoid further suffering. Do not feel guilty or that you are to blame.*

It is always hard to balance your grief with the welfare of your pet, but most owners know when it is time to let go.

If you are making an appointment with the vet for euthanasia ask for a quiet time. Many surgeries reserve appointments at the end of consulting hours for this purpose. When making the appointment discuss payment, can you pay in advance or will they bill you, either option means that you can walk straight out and not have to queue at the reception at a very distressing time.

If the decision for euthanasia has come as a shock during a consultation, you can ask for a little private time with your pet so that you can say goodbye. All vets understand this need for a few last moments together, so do not feel embarrassed to ask if this is something you feel would be helpful.

You can either stay with your pet during the final moments or choose not to be present. This is entirely up to you and you should pick the option that is best for you. Either way your cat will receive nothing but kindness from the veterinary professional as it slips away into a dreamless sleep.

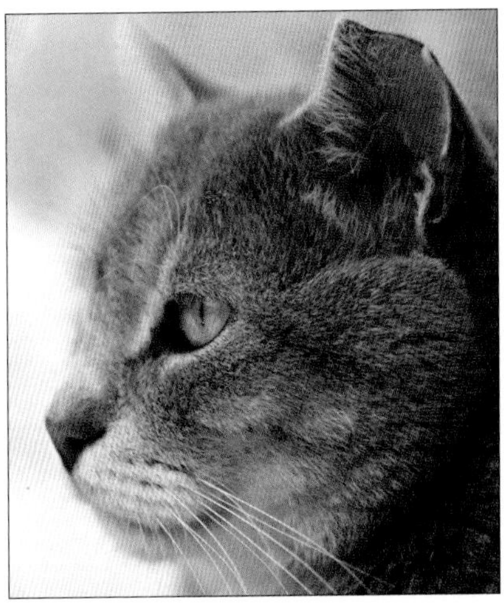

Allowing your cat to be free from pain and distress is the greatest gift that you can give. It is the ultimate act of love.

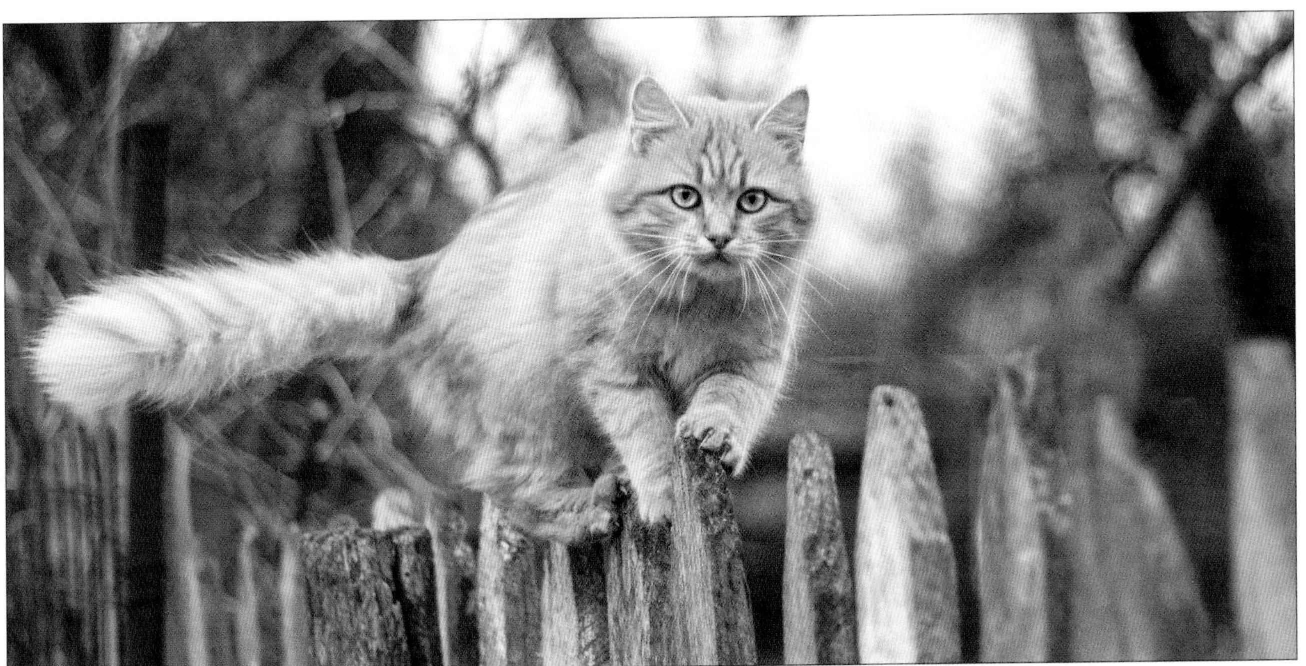

Choices after death

Whether we lose a cat after a tragic accident or to the gradual progression of old age, the moment of death always comes as a shock. This is made even worse by the fact that straight away we must make decisions.

Firstly, there is the decision of what to do with the mortal remains of our much-loved companion. Your vet, or a specialist company, can make arrangements for cremation, either individual or communal, if this is what you wish. At this time money is the furthest thing from a bereaved owner's mind but some options, such as individual cremation, can be very costly. Your vet will be able to furnish you with prices to enable you to make the best choice. In individual cremation, the ashes are returned and can be kept or scattered in a place that your cat loved. This could be in a sunny spot in the garden or under a favourite shrub. Many owners prefer to bury their cat's body in the garden but check that this is not legally prohibited in your area. Pet cemeteries exist and are often the choice of people who worry about what might happen to a pet's grave if they must move home. Details of these can be obtained from the internet.

Deciding when and what to tell children is always difficult. It is not a good idea to tell a child that a pet has gone to live in the country or a similar tale. The child may feel betrayed by the cat's desertion or not understand why it hasn't come back home. Most children are more robust than we give them credit for and can cope with death. Involving them in some way, for example getting them to choose a plant to put in the garden in memory of their feline friend, is helpful.

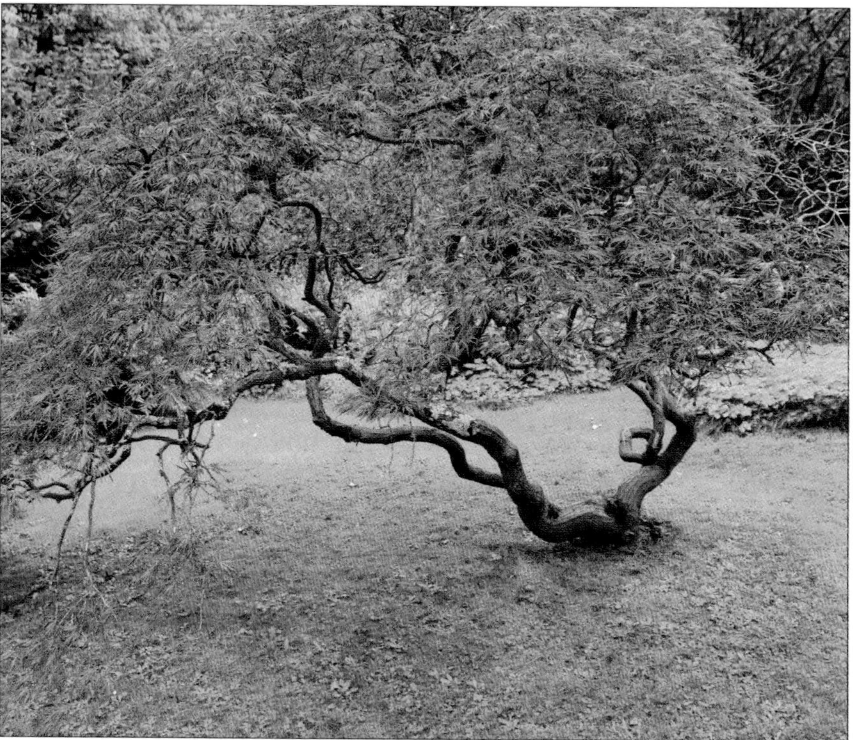

▲ *Burying your cat under a tree ensures that the grave will not be disturbed. A memorial plaque could be fixed to the trunk.*

▼ *Take time to mourn privately as well as with the family. Be kind to yourself. Grief is exhausting.*

Preparing some sort of memorial for your cat can assist in coming to terms with your feelings of grief and loss. This could take the form of a funeral or planting a tree in memory of your feline friend. Other possibilities include making up a photo album or scrapbook so that you can look back and see all the happy times that you spent together. Some people choose to give a donation to an animal charity. This could be for a specific item of your choice, such as payment for veterinary treatment or a comfy bed for a long-term resident in the shelter.

Coping with personal grief is hard when all around life continues as normal. Sadly, many people, including

▼ *Choosing and planting a living memorial, such as a tree, is an activity all the family can be involved in.*

▼ *A more natural setting for a pet burial could consist of a simple planting of a perennial herb, such as lavender, and a neat pile of stones to mark the site.*

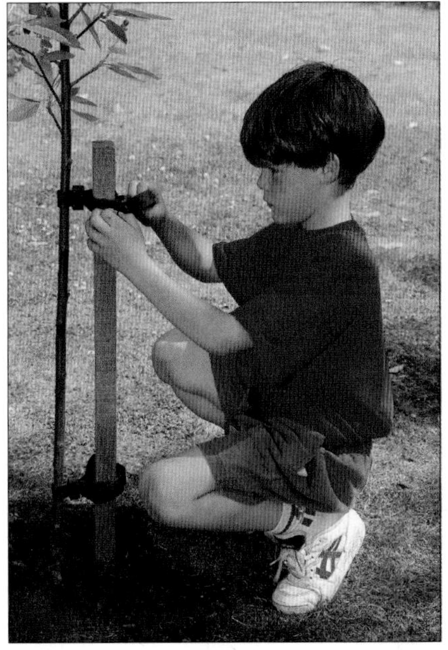

some employers, are dismissive of the pain caused by the loss of a pet. If this is the case don't feel distressed by the fact that they may not consider your grief is appropriate. It is a sad fact that not all family members or friends will be able to comprehend your personal feelings. In this event look elsewhere for the empathy and support that you need. Free pet bereavement counselling is available from national animal charities and it does help to talk to someone who understands how you feel. There are also forums on social media where people in similar situations get together and help each other through the bereavement process. Grief can be crippling and, if persistent, may lead to depression and isolation. Don't be embarrassed to seek medical help if you feel that you are not coping. Most doctors understand that the loss of a pet is a traumatic experience and will be able to help.

If you have other cats they could exhibit behavioural changes after the death of a feline companion. This can occur even if they did not appear to like each other. It is important that you keep to their normal routine as this will help them feel settled and more secure.

After the death of a cat you may feel you are not ready to go through the heartache of losing another cat again or you may feel that you can't bear to be without a cat. Either way this is your choice, don't let anyone push you into a rushed decision.

▼ *You could find a plant as a memorial with the same name as your pet, for example, the rose Bobbie James.*

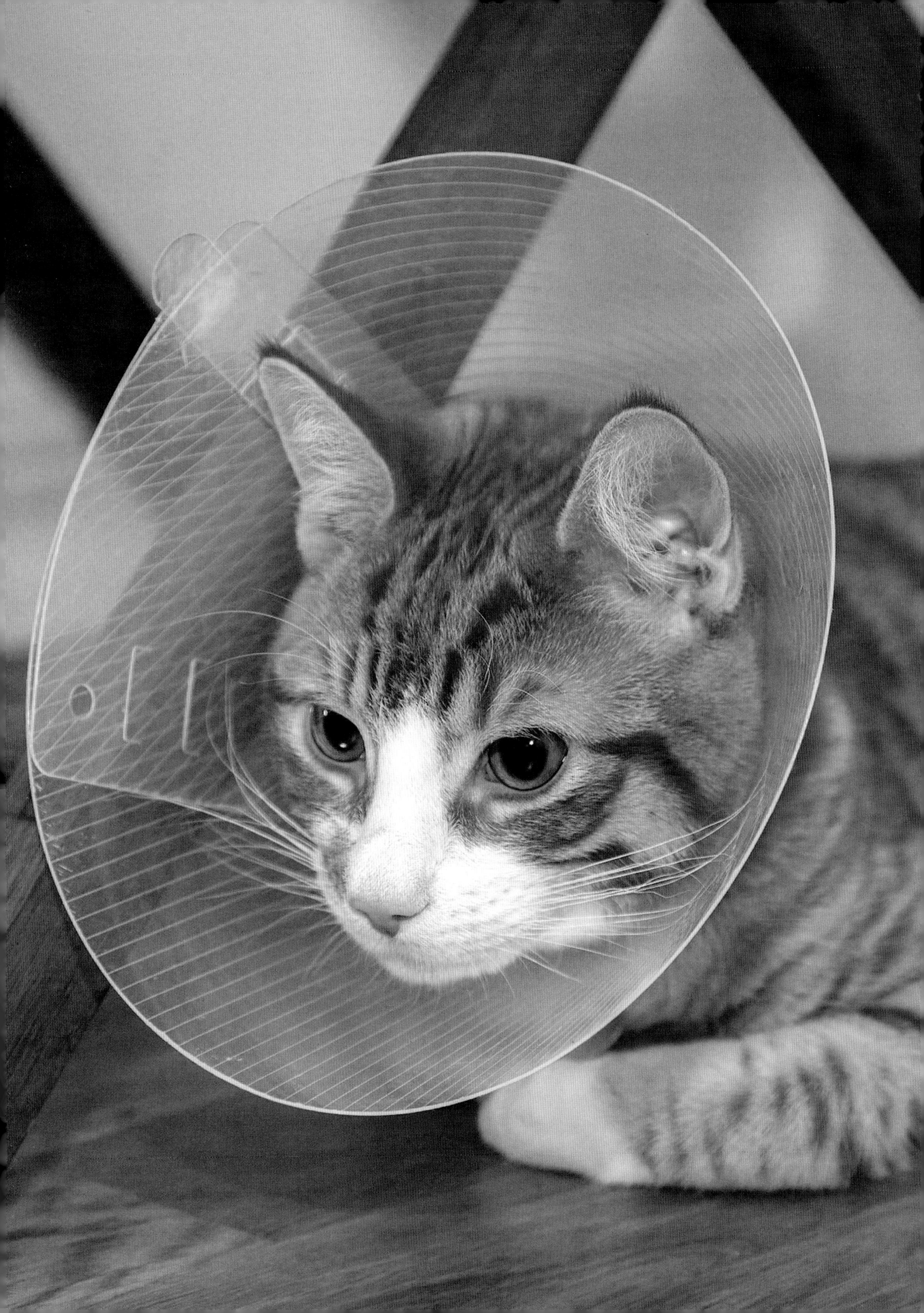

INJURIES AND AILMENTS

Cats traditionally live longer than dogs. Twenty years is not unusual. If you provide a balanced diet, the correct inoculations and regular check-ups, there is no reason why your cat should not live a long and happy life. However, illness or injury can strike at any time, so it is important to keep an eye open for any unusual behaviour in your pet that might indicate all is not well. In most cases of injury or disease, you will need to call the vet, but much can also be done at home in the way of first aid and general nursing. It is worth investing in a suitable feline first-aid kit, a human one will not be suitable. Items can be bought separately, alternatively your vet or breeder will be able to recommend where to order a complete kit.

◄ *Plastic hoods, inflatable rings and fabric bibs all fasten round the neck and are designed to prevent the cat licking a wound.*

Home nursing

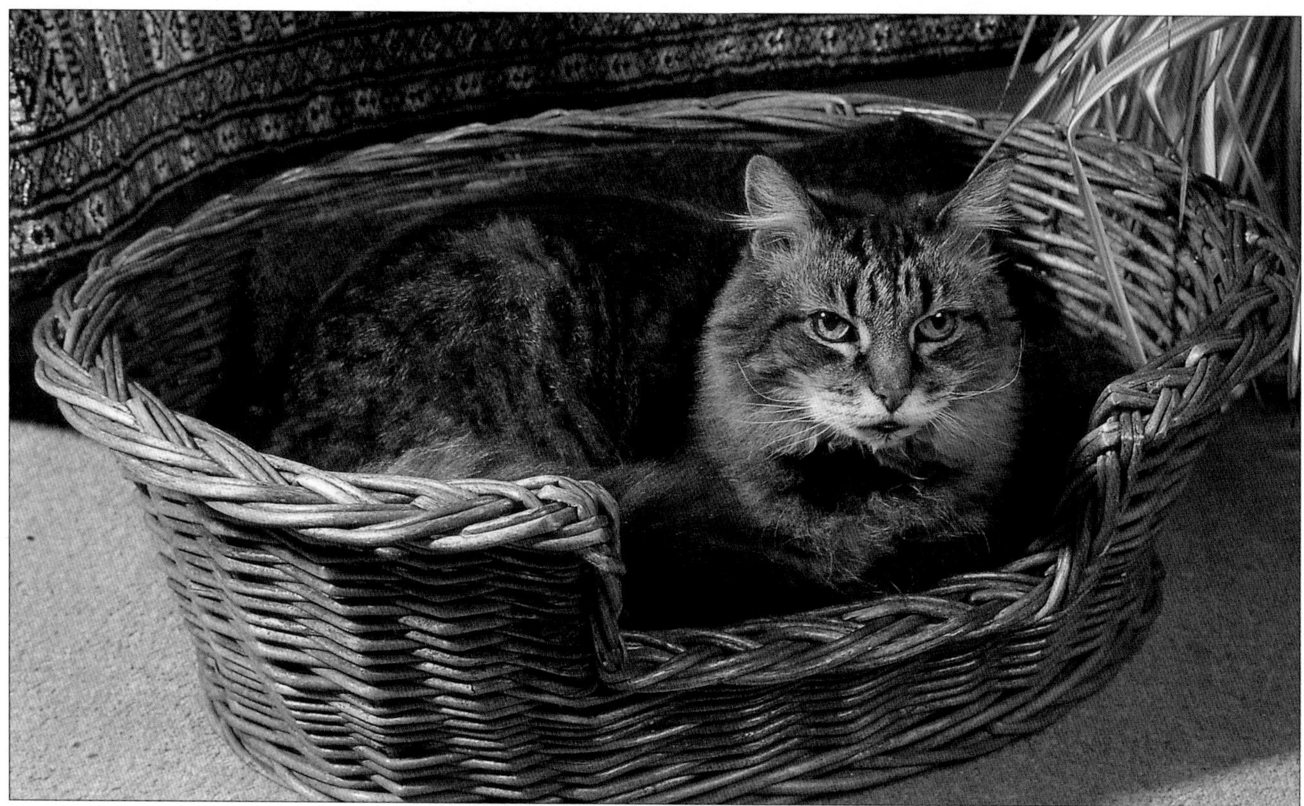

▲ *A warm, comfortable bed and plenty of tender loving care are essential when nursing a sick cat.*

A sick cat should be confined in an area that is warm and free from draughts, quiet and capable of being easily cleaned and disinfected. The first two requirements are relatively easy to fulfil, whereas the third could cause some problems. Many modern homes are carpeted throughout which makes disinfecting difficult. If there is not a separate utility room with a floor that is easily cleaned, you should consider buying a large, plastic travelling carrier which comes apart so that every part can be thoroughly cleaned.

Use a disinfectant agent recommended by your vet – it is most important to avoid any substances containing coal-tar, wood-tar, phenol, cresol and chloroxylenols. These agents are fine for use with people but can be lethal for cats. If a condition is seriously infectious to other cats, you should set aside some old clothes and shoes to wear when handling the sick cat, and wash thoroughly afterwards. Always dispose of any used bandages or applicators promptly. Thoroughly clean up any vomit or faeces without delay and disinfect the area carefully.

BEDSIDE MANNER

You can help your cat's recovery tremendously with care, love and attention. Spend time talking quietly, maintaining appropriate physical contact without being overwhelming, and ensuring that its bodily needs are catered for. The cat may not be able to do anything for itself and, therefore, feeding, watering, grooming and assisting with toilet procedures become your responsibility. While this is very time-consuming, the bond you have already achieved with your cat will grow even stronger. The veterinary technicians will help if you need advice on the various techniques involved with the grooming, feeding and toileting of a sick cat.

ADMINISTERING MEDICINES

Your vet will always give advice and instruction on how much and how often you should administer any medication your cat needs for treatment. Medicinal preparations come in several forms – liquids, pills, capsules, drops and lotions. The secret of administering any of these successfully and with least disturbance to the animal is to have confidence in your ability to do so. However, some cats will object tooth and claw to having any foreign object forced into their mouths. If this is the case with your cat, you will need to ask someone to assist you and, if necessary, wrap the cat securely in a towel to help immobilize it.

► *Special syringes, available from your veterinary practice and some pet shops, will help you administer medicines.*

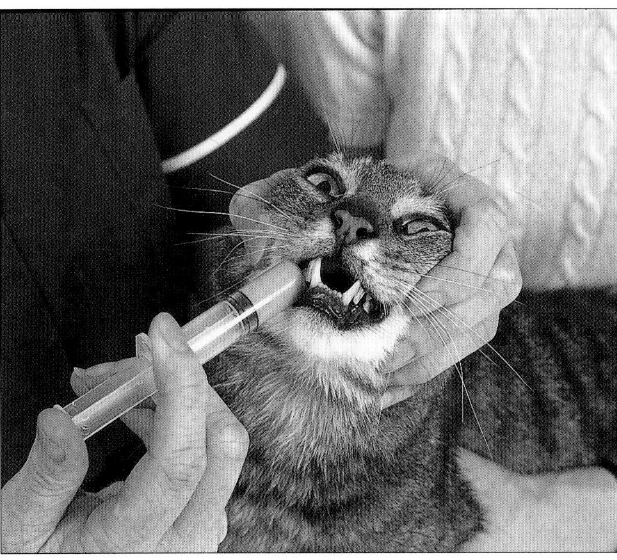

Liquid medicines can be given using a plastic syringe obtainable from your vet or from most pet shops. After use it should be cleaned thoroughly and then stored for future use in a sterilizing agent such as one of those used for baby feeding equipment. Draw up the amount for one dose into the syringe. Holding the cat's head firmly, gently insert the syringe between the lips, at the side of the mouth. Push the plunger gently so that the cat receives the dose slowly and gradually, allowing it time to swallow. This reduces the risk of any liquid going into the lungs, which could cause pneumonia to set in rapidly in the case of a sick cat. Pill poppers which look like elongated syringes are available if you have difficulty opening your cat's mouth. The pill is placed into the popper and a plunger pushes the pill to the back of the cat's tongue. Direct the instrument towards the palate rather than pressing on the tongue. Hold the cat's mouth closed and stroke its throat until it has swallowed.

Most preparations designed to be dropped into the eyes or ears are supplied with a dropper or a dropping nozzle. If not, droppers can be purchased from most chemists or drugstores. Always carefully read the directions about how and when to apply the medication, before using.

The membranes of the eyes and ears are very delicate and it is most important for the cat to be held securely. Another pair of hands makes the job much easier.

With eye drops, one drop is usually sufficient. For ear drops, hold the pinna (ear flap) firmly to open the canal, and place two or three drops into the ear, then massage gently. Ear drops are usually oily and overdoing the drops results in a greasy head.

ADMINISTERING TABLETS

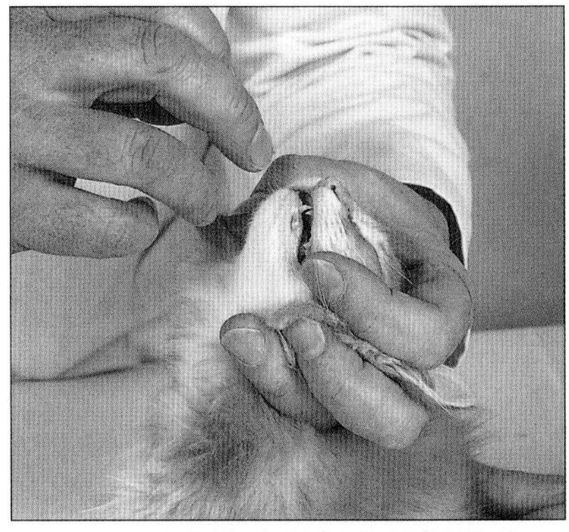

1 Hold the cat's head firmly, with your fingers on either side of the jaw, and gently pull the head back until the jaws open.

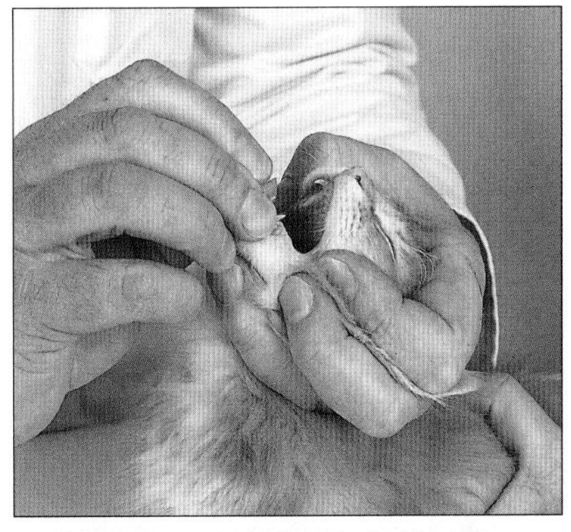

2 Talking quietly and encouragingly to your cat throughout the process, drop the pill or capsule at the back of the cat's tongue.

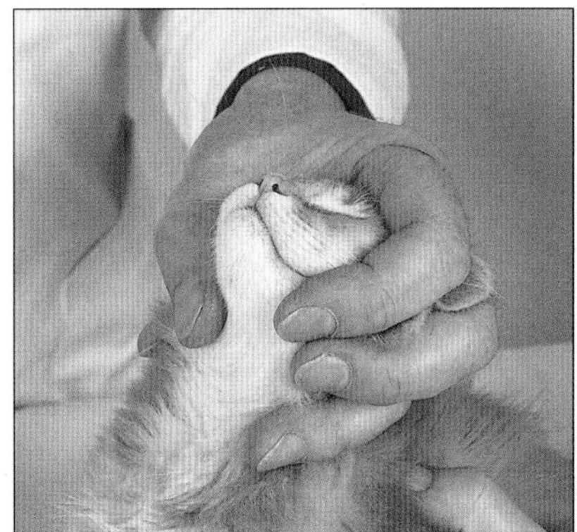

3 Hold the mouth closed and massage the throat until a swallowing action shows that the pill or capsule has been ingested.

Disinfectants and cleaning

Routine cleaning of the home or cattery is essential for good feline health. Caution should be taken over the choice of cleaning agent as many are toxic to cats.

The best, and safest, method of cleaning floors and hard surfaces is steam cleaning. A domestic steam cleaner is adequate in most situations. It is not necessary to add any cleaning agents to the water source unless advised by a vet. Heat is a very effective way of killing a wide range of pathogens. Pathogens are micro-organisms that cause disease. This is a collective term that includes viruses, bacteria, fungi and protozoa.

Prior to any form of cleansing, remove the cat from the area. A weak dilution of bleach and water is an effective cleaner but the area must be rinsed with clean water after use. A small amount of white vinegar added to water makes a safe cleaner for work tops. If choosing to clean with a more traditional method of water and detergent, check that the product is non-ionic or anionic and not cationic. This information should be displayed on the label. The latter is more likely to be hazardous and an irritant. Diluted washing-up liquid is a safer option than a household surface or floor cleaner. Concentrated toilet cleaner is particularly hazardous. Always shut the lid on the toilet bowl after use.

When using disinfectant always read the label and follow the instructions regarding dilution. Don't allow cats access to the area cleaned until all surfaces are dry. Store these products in an area the cat cannot access and mop up any spills, or residue on the outside of containers. If using disinfectant outside, the same rules apply. Areas that become wet with rainfall can be toxic for several days after application. Keep the cat in until the area is dry again.

Disinfectant is not the same as antiseptic. Disinfectants destroy pathogens on non-living objects and should never be applied to living matter. Antiseptics are used on living tissue to kill infections on or within the tissue; they are not a cleaning agent.

◀ *When spot cleaning, paper towels are a great way to rapidly dry the treated surface.*

▼ *Only ever use cleaning products that are suitable for use around cats. If in doubt, don't buy it.*

▲ *After use, both the mop and the bucket should be cleaned with warm soapy water.*

▶ *Odour removal products are available. Alternatively cleaning with equal parts of vinegar and water will work just as well.*

Home first-aid kit

Wise owners prepare a pet first-aid kit before there is need. Items should be stored in an airtight container that is clearly marked so that it can be easily distinguished from the human first-aid kit. It is a good idea to fix the phone number of your vet inside the lid. This can save valuable time in an emergency. It is also worth adding the telephone number of at least one pet carrier in case public transport is not running or the car is out of action. These numbers might be needed if you have to take the cat to the veterinary surgery in an emergency. Store the container in a safe dry place, making sure that all responsible members of the household know where it is kept.

Periodically check the use-by date of all the products in the kit and replace as necessary. Dispose of any items that become dirty or damp. Sterilize and dry scissors and tweezers after each use. Clean the digital thermometer carefully each time that you use it and replace it back in its protective sleeve.

It is a good idea to keep a torch near the first-aid kit. Lots of accidents happen at night and a good light is essential when assessing the situation. Check the battery life every couple of months. A freshly laundered towel stored in a plastic bag to keep it clean is another essential item. This may be needed to place the cat on, either to move it or to wrap it in.

The first-aid kit

- Sterile pads and dressings
- Bandages: 2.5cm and 5cm (1in and 2in) widths
- Cotton ear buds (swabs)
- Adhesive medical tape for fixing bandages
- Styptic stick or powder
- Stretch fabric adhesive strapping
- Lint padding or cotton wool roll
- Cotton wool balls (uncoloured)
- Antiseptic wipes, cream and lotion (as recommended by your vet)
- Small, blunt-ended scissors
- Tweezers
- Nail clippers
- Vet wrap bandage
- Ear cleaner
- Liquid paraffin
- Kaolin mixture
- Antihistamine cream
- Digital rectal thermometer
- Water-based lubricant
- Eye dropper
- 5ml (1tsp) plastic syringe
- Sterilizing agent
- Elizabethan (medical) collar
- Surgical gloves
- Suitable carrier or box

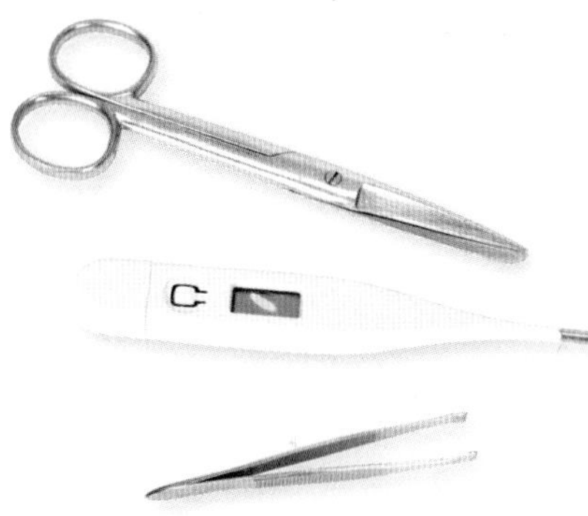

▲ *It is important that items are stored in a dry place. Check scissors and tweezers annually for rust.*

▼ *Surprisingly, some bandages and gauze pads have a use-by date. Dispose of and replace as required.*

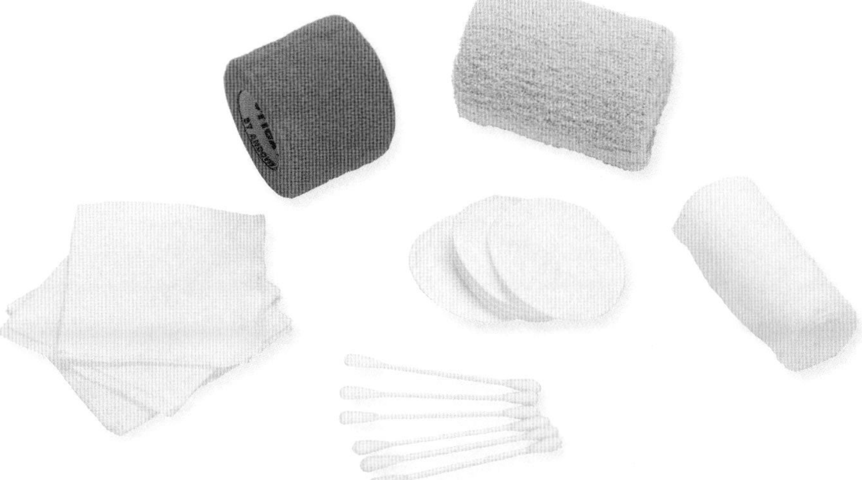

▼ *Wound cream is particularly useful if the cat will not tolerate frequent inspection and cleaning of the injury site. Check all products are safe for cats.*

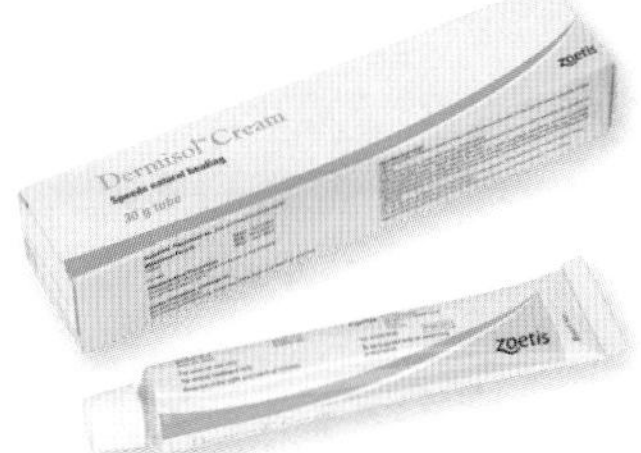

Accident and injury

Emergency treatment is often required for accidents within the home. Do not assume that a cat or kitten will automatically know its physical limits or be able to tell, for example, which plants are poisonous. It might well be able to fall from any angle and regain its footing, but only within certain heights. A cat falling from a balcony is just as likely to sustain serious damage as any other animal. Cats can be as vulnerable to accidents as children, and you should keep a constant eye on safety in your home.

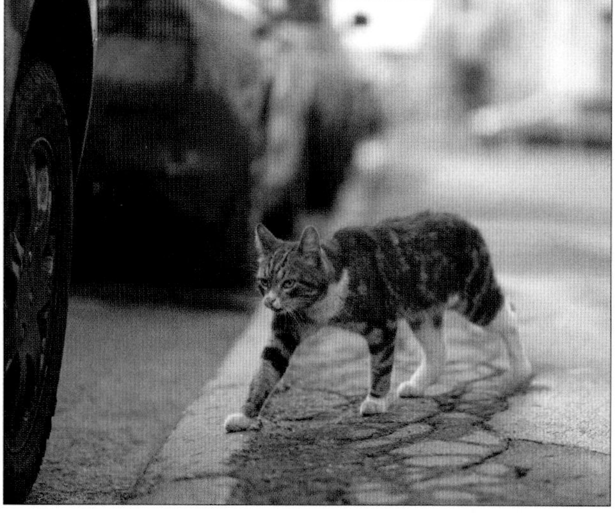

◄ *Traffic accidents are, sadly, all too common. Cats will sleep under cars; sound the horn before you move away.*

EMERGENCY CARE

It is valuable to know what on-the-spot treatment you can give before the cat receives veterinary attention. In extreme situations, this could make the difference between life and death. A cat that is very frightened or in pain may instinctively withdraw, and scratch and bite if handled. If this happens, talk calmly and keep the cat as warm, comfortable and confined as possible until professional help is available. As with any emergency, the first rule is not to panic and the second is to rely on your common sense. However inexperienced, you will learn by careful observation to recognize the real emergency. Prompt first aid may be all that is needed, but if you are in the least doubt about the seriousness of any condition, seek professional help immediately. All veterinary practices have to offer a 24-hour emergency service. Phone the surgery number first to check for any special emergency arrangements, or at least to give the surgery advance warning of your imminent arrival.

A cardboard box is a good carrier in an emergency; if an injured cat is placed on a board serving as a stretcher, it could easily fall off. Keep the cat warm by covering with a blanket and call the vet immediately. Try not to panic and handle the cat as gently as possible.

▼ *An injured cat will often run to hide in a sheltered place such as under garden shrubs and hedges.*

▼ *A cat is so intent on stalking a moving leaf or insect that it may end up on a branch that cannot support its weight and fall.*

▼ *'Tablet poppers' are a brilliant invention. They 'pop' the tablet into the cat's mouth quickly and easily.*

▼ *No animal likes wearing an Elizabethan (medical) collar, but given time they will get used to it.*

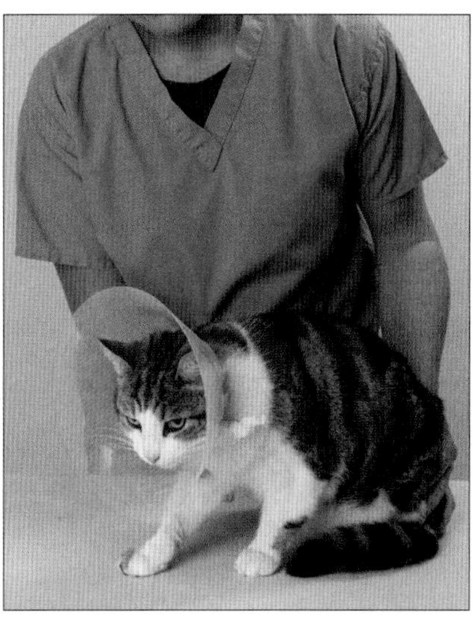

When to worry

- Obvious or suspected injury from a fall (usually 4m/12ft, or more), or from a road traffic accident
- Obvious fractures or dislocations
- Profuse bleeding
- Choking or respiratory distress
- Severe burn or scalding
- Collapse or a fit lasting more than a few seconds
- Injuries to or foreign body in the eye
- Persistent vomiting

Before leaving home for the vet, check that you have your purse or wallet with you. Although vets have a duty of care regarding animals in pain, it can be very distressing worrying if they will only treat your cat if you can pay immediately. If you have time, take some clean bedding with you so that soiled items can be replaced for the journey home.

▼ *Untreated eye injuries could lead to blindness. Always consult your vet.*

If possible, get someone to travel with you so that one can drive and the other can keep an eye on the cat. Talk gently to the cat on the journey but refrain from poking and prodding to see if it is ok. Drive carefully to avoid the cat being thrown around and switch off the car radio.

ROADSIDE ACCIDENT

Accidents and injuries affect stray cats as well as much-loved pets. The most common accident is the result of being hit by a car. Unlike dogs, there is no legal obligation to report hitting a cat with a vehicle. Sadly, many drivers just continue with their journey leaving the injured animal by the side of the road. If you hit a cat when driving, or see the result of this situation, there are things that you can do.

First, ensure your own safety while on the road and, if driving, park your car where it will not form a hazard. Approach the cat slowly, making sure you don't startle it. Assess the situation visually. If you consider that the cat needs veterinary attention you have several options. You can either attempt to take the cat to the nearest vet yourself, contact an animal charity such as the RSPCA for assistance, or ask at nearby houses if they know who the cat belongs to. If the cat runs away, note the direction of travel and contact an animal rescue charity who may be able to send a welfare officer to try to find it.

If you decide to take the injured stray feline to the vet, you will not normally accrue veterinary charges. The vet will first scan the cat to see if it is microchipped and then contact the owner. If no microchip is found they will provide pain relief; this may be euthanasia if that is the most appropriate action. If treatment could be provided and result in a satisfactory outcome, they will generally contact an animal rescue charity who will pay for treatment and arrange ongoing care.

In the unfortunate situation of finding a dead cat, if you feel able, take the body to a vet so that they can scan for a microchip and advise the owner. Alternatively, contact an animal rescue shelter who may be able to collect and scan the body.

Taking immediate action

What should you do in an emergency? If the cat is in a situation where further injury could occur, move the animal carefully. Depending on the position of the injuries, try to grasp the cat gently by the scruff and support its weight with the other hand. Put it in a suitable box or carrier. If the cat is unconscious, take precautions against choking by clearing any blood or vomit from the mouth and pulling the tongue forward. The head should be below the body level when the cat is lying down so that any fluids can run out.

If there is severe bleeding try to stem it by putting a pressure bandage (like a tight bandage) over the wound. This works well in areas such as the limbs. Otherwise, try applying finger pressure to the wound.

▼ *Although cats can swim – and Turkish Van cats like this one are supposed to have a particular love of water – they will drown if enough water enters the lungs.*

▲ *A cat that roams freely may have a more active and varied life, but it also runs a greater risk of accident and injury than the indoor pet.*

CHOKING

If a cat is fighting for air and gasping for breath, wrap it in a blanket or towel to immobilize it, and try to look in the mouth to see if there is any obstruction. While someone is calling the vet, you could try to dislocate the object by shining a small torch down the gullet and pulling the object out with a pair of tweezers. Take care you are not bitten. If a sharp object has been swallowed the problem should be dealt with by a vet. If the cat swallows a length of string or thread, do not pull it out. Leave it or tie the exposed end to an improvised collar so that it is not lost on the way to the vet.

FOREIGN BODIES

If grit, seeds or other objects become lodged in a cat's eyes or ears, you may be able to use ear or eye drops to float them out. Do not use tweezers in these areas. A cotton bud (swab) can sometimes be used gently to remove foreign bodies in the eye.

If potentially dangerous substances such as oil, paint or chemicals are spilt on a cat's coat, wash them off immediately with a dilute solution of mild detergent or soap and water. Patches of fur that are badly soiled should be cut off carefully and the area washed with soap and water.

HEART ATTACK

There has been a recent increase in the number of cats, especially pedigreed cats, who collapse and die of a condition called cardiomyopathy, of which there are various types. An apparently healthy cat may suddenly keel over and die. This condition is thought to run in families, but the mode of inheritance is unclear and is the subject of much research worldwide. Sometimes, in mild cases, massaging the chest between finger and thumb does help.

ELECTRIC SHOCK

A cat can sustain an electric shock as a result of chewing through electrical flexes and cords. Switch off the electricity immediately to prevent further shock. The vet's advice should be sought as severe burns to the gums and lips can result.

How to resuscitate a cat

There is no point in being squeamish if the cat's life is to be saved. A feline kiss of life is difficult to administer and will require coming into intimate oral contact with either the cat's nostrils or mouth. The instinct to save life is very strong so, for most owners, this aspect of resuscitation will not pose a problem.

1 Clear the airways of any vomit or blood and check that the tongue is pulled forward. Hold the cat's head gently backwards and blow into the nostrils. If the nostrils are restricted in some way, pinch the cat's mouth open with your fingers pressing both cheeks to create a restricted opening, take a deep breath and blow into the mouth. Do not overdo it, as a cat's lungs are very much smaller than a person's.

2 Between each breath, gently massage the chest to allow the air to trickle out, and maintain a rubbing motion on the cat's chest to try to stimulate heartbeat. Keep on with the mouth-to-mouth process until the cat can breath regularly by itself. It may be that this form of resuscitation does not work, in which case heart massage is the last option.

3 Heart massage may damage the cat. A delicate rubbing motion will just not stimulate the heart into beating so, with the cat on its side, preferably supported on a blanket or towel, press downwards firmly on the chest just behind the front leg, about once a second. In some cases, ribs have been broken in elderly animals, but the cat has survived. If this does not work, at least you know that you have done everything possible.

RESUSCITATION SITUATIONS

A completely collapsed cat which may appear dead can sometimes be resuscitated if you act swiftly. The condition most frequently occurs with a newly born kitten. It is very simple to assess if there is still a heartbeat by feeling for a pulse in the armpit. If no pulse is found it does not necessarily mean that brain death has occurred and you may still be able to resuscitate the animal by gently massaging the chest between finger and thumb and holding the head down.

DROWNING

It takes very little liquid to cause drowning. All that is required is enough for the lungs to be filled so that oxygen is unable to enter the bloodstream. Patting the cat's back may be all that is needed to expel the water from the lungs, but more often drastic measures have to be employed such as swinging the cat by the hind legs in an attempt to get the liquid out. Then resuscitation can begin (see box above).

▼ *An Elizabethan (medical) collar is attached around the neck to prevent a cat from reaching back or down to lick a wound or medical dressing. The cat's owner then has to take on all grooming responsibilities.*

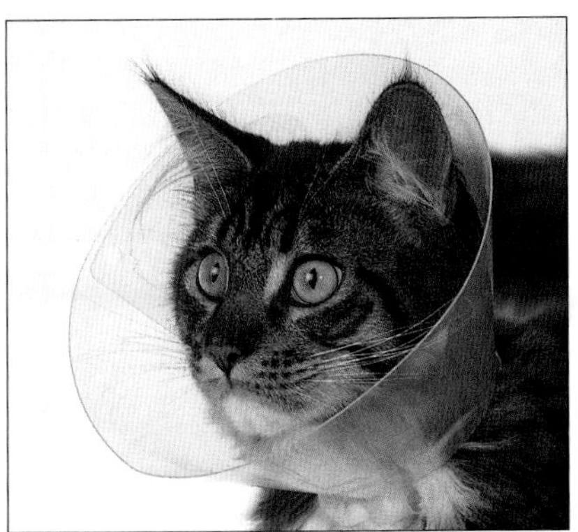

ANIMAL BITES

The cat that roams freely outside is much more likely to come into contact with other animals than the house-bound feline. Fights over territorial rights around the home are likely. The bite of any animal, including other cats, dogs, rodents and snakes, can be dangerous, as many bacteria are carried in the mouth.

It may not be immediately obvious that your cat has been bitten. Usually a cat that has been hurt will find a quiet, secluded spot to lick its wounds, quite literally. This is the cat's own first aid, as its saliva contains a natural antiseptic. You may not discover a hidden bite until you actually touch the site of the wound and the cat reacts. Keep the cat warm and comfortable and seek advice. Delay could mean that the cat will develop infection which will make treatment more complicated and therefore more traumatic for the cat. Wounds will need regular cleaning and bathing with a suitable antiseptic.

ABSCESSES

Any untreated puncture wound is liable to become infected and result in an abscess, which is a large, pus-filled swelling. Without treatment, the abscess may eventually burst, with a real risk of septicaemia (blood poisoning) due to toxins from the untreated abscess entering the bloodstream. The original puncture wounds soon heal, so the correct

To apply a tourniquet

1 Place a loop of soft, narrow fabric, such as a stocking or a tie, around the limb, on the heart side of the wound site.

2 Insert a pen, pencil, piece of cutlery or thin, strong stick between the skin and the fabric loop.

3 Twist the fabric until it is tight enough to cut off the blood supply below it.

4 Loosen the tourniquet for a few moments every two or three minutes and then re-tighten.

5 If there is any swelling, apply a cold compress by wrapping a few ice cubes in a plastic bag and wrapped in a cloth, or (an athlete's tip) use a packet of frozen peas.

6 Gently wash the affected spot with a recommended antiseptic, diluted to the manufacturer's instruction

7 Any bleeding should stop. If it does not, the tourniquet is not tight enough.

8 Try to bandage the wound and take the cat to the vet as soon as possible. The wound may need stitching.

treatment will involve a trip to the vet so that the abscess can be lanced, allowing it to drain properly.

Septicaemia is serious, as it is with people. The onset is rapid and within hours a cat can be running a very high temperature. This may be followed by fits, sickness, a rapid fall of temperature to sub-normal level, collapse and death.

The greatest cause of an abscess is a bite or claw puncture from another cat. Such wounds are invariably sustained during a fight, so the most common abscess sites are around the head and neck, paws, and at the base of the tail.

SNAKE BITES

Many snake bites can be poisonous and may be followed by swelling around the wound, progressive lethargy and hyperventilation which may be accompanied by fits, followed by collapse and coma.

Once the wound site has been identified, try to apply a tourniquet above the punctures as quickly as possible (see box above). The most likely site of a bite is on the leg, near the paws, in which case the tourniquet should be applied to the upper leg. If the wound is around the face or neck, then there is little that can be done.

When applying a tourniquet to a snake bite, the aim is to prevent the venom entering the bloodstream. However, remember that the application of a tourniquet cuts off the blood supply to the limb. The tourniquet should therefore be slackened every two to three minutes to ensure that the tissues are kept alive, even if this results in releasing a limited amount of the venom into the bloodstream. If this is not done, there is a possibility of such severe tissue damage that the limb would have to be amputated.

STINGS

It is the cat's nature to chase and pounce on insects regardless of any danger. A single wasp sting is not too alarming but remember the wasp is able to sting repeatedly. Although a cat moves fast, a wasp tangled in the cat's

IMMOBILIZING A CAT THAT IS FRIGHTENED OR IN PAIN

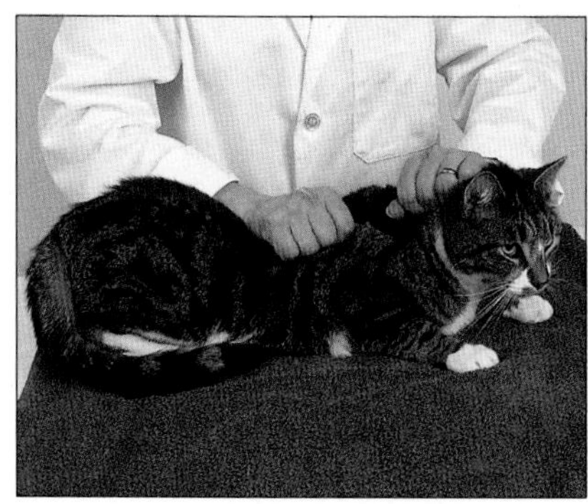

1 Place the towel on a table and the cat on the towel. Place one hand firmly on the cat's neck to control its head. Press the other firmly on the cat's back so that it lies down.

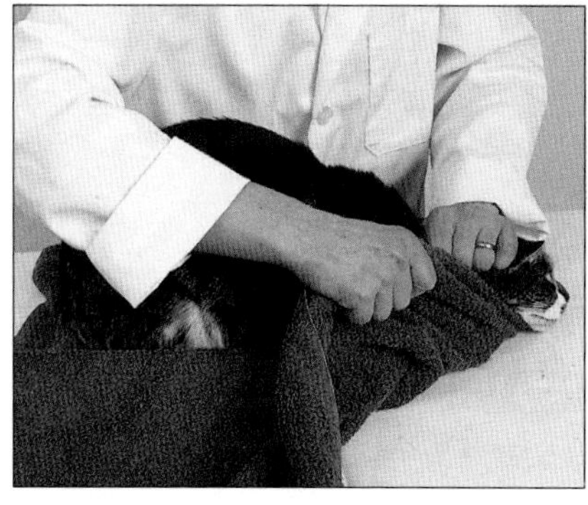

2 Keep one hand firmly on the cat's neck so that the head is under control throughout. With the other hand, bring the towel over the cat's neck, legs and body so that the legs are restrained.

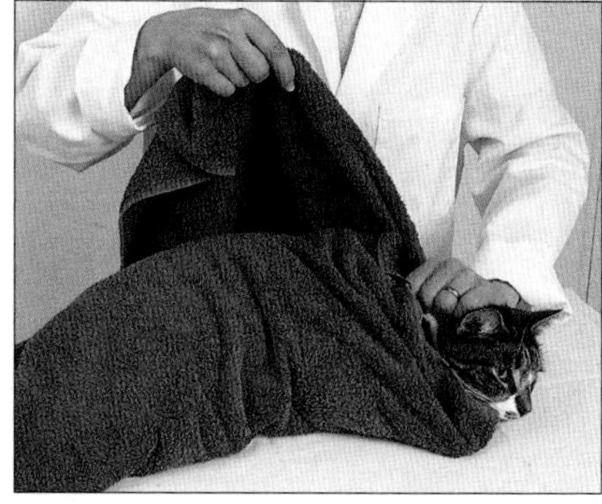

3 Still keeping a firm but gentle hold on the neck, tuck the towel underneath the cat's body. Do not forget to talk to your pet in a calm voice all the time you are doing this.

▶ *A vet feels a cat's leg for any breakages in the bone or internal swellings that might suggest a sprain or arthritis, to find the cause of a limp.*

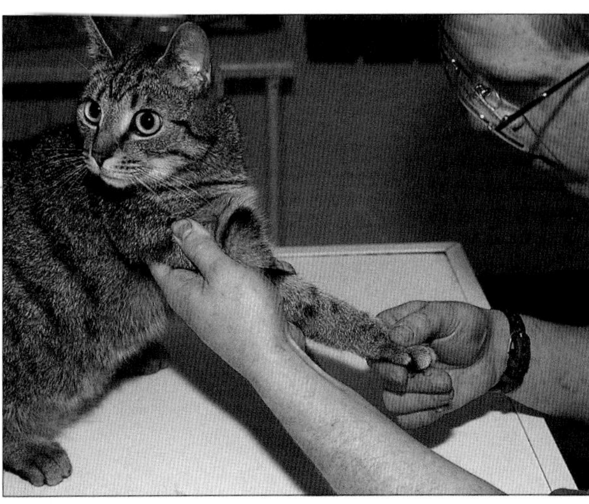

◀ *If your cat is limping, the first action is to examine the paw for any foreign body, such as glass or a thorn, which may be lodged there.*

fur can sting a number of times before it can be brushed off. In contrast, the bee leaves the sting behind in the cat. The bee sacrifices itself when it stings, and the full quota of bee venom is left behind. Stings can occur in the mouth or throat if the insect is swallowed. This will cause swelling, and breathing and swallowing might be restricted. If external this is unpleasant and painful; internally, it can be dangerous.

The cat may show an alarming allergic reaction to a sting. If the swelling has been caused by a bee sting, the actual sting remnant may be visible. This must be removed, if possible, with tweezers. Whether the sting is internal or external, the cat should have veterinary attention without delay.

As a first-aid measure, external stings by bees or wasps may be treated with a commercially available antihistamine cream or lotion. If this is not immediately available, simple home remedies can be used. Bee stings can be treated with alkaline substances such as bicarbonate of soda, whereas wasp stings respond to the application of an acid such as vinegar. The cat should not be allowed to lick at any of these substances.

▼ *Give a cat a toy to play with in the garden, and with a bit of luck, this may distract it from pursuing the local wildlife.*

POISONING

Cats are great wanderers and they may well walk through any range of toxic materials. Transferred to the mouth through washing, such substances can easily cause poisoning, and burning to contact areas. Thorough washing of paws with a mild shampoo followed by thorough rinsing will alleviate some of the pain before the vet is involved. Vomiting, lassitude, apparent blindness, convulsions and collapse are all signs of poisoning. If such symptoms occur, seek veterinary aid immediately.

It is inadvisable to try to find a way of easing the animal's suffering yourself beyond keeping the cat warm and quiet. Take a sample of the substance if you know what it is, or note the name, so that an antidote may be found quickly if available. Your vet will have access to the national poison hotline. In some countries, where stray animals are a nuisance, cats and dogs are sometimes deliberately poisoned by those who consider them pests.

If your cat returns home covered in motor oil, it is important to remove the oil from the coat immediately, as it

▼ *A vital nerve was severed in this cat's foreleg. The cause was barely visible – a tiny puncture in the skin, perhaps from a barbed wire fence or an animal bite. There was no improvement after a month, and the leg was amputated, but the cat continued to lead an active outdoor life.*

could poison the cat's digestive system and result in kidney damage. Use a mild household detergent in lots of warm water, and seek veterinary advice if in difficulty.

STRAINS AND LIMPS

The cat may limp and resort to excessive washing of the injured spot. If you suspect something is amiss, first examine the paw carefully to see if there is a splinter or thorn in it, and remove it with tweezers if possible. Disinfect the area and keep your eye on the cat. Confine the cat indoors, and if there is no improvement, ask the vet to have a look at it.

If the problem is a strain, a cat by its very nature will not rest of its own accord, and its continued physical activity could not only aggravate the strain further but also prevent it from healing.

SCRAPES AND BRUISES

Bruises are much less easy to detect than cuts, though you will suspect their presence if the cat becomes unusually unhappy about your touching the spot where the bruise is rooted. Similar signs are apparent if an abscess is developing on the site. As with human bruises, some come to the surface of the skin reasonably rapidly, whereas deep-seated bruising can take days to work its way out. Seek professional advice if in doubt.

Bruises and contusions respond very well to the application of *Hamamelis virginiana* (witch-hazel). Although such a remedy can be taken orally in very limited doses, it is better to prevent the cat from licking off any application by putting a medical collar around the neck.

BURNS

Cats attracted by cooking smells may leap on to unguarded cooking areas and even into ovens, and may be scalded by spilled hot liquid. A cat may also receive appalling burns, externally and internally, if it comes into contact with any of the lethal chemicals to be found in the house and garden.

Once the skin is burned, the body institutes its own first-aid regime. Body fluids are rushed to the affected area, and a blister forms protecting the underlying tissue. Do not burst the blister as the fluid in it helps to prevent infection. You can bathe the burn with ice-cold water until all heat has been taken out of the damaged area. Call the vet.

You can also apply a sterile, dry dressing loosely over the burn to keep out infection. Do not apply greasy substances – this would be like putting butter into a hot frying pan.

BANDAGING

Cats are not keen on being bandaged and will spend time trying to remove the offending item as soon as your back is turned. They will do this by scratching or biting at the dressing. If your cat has to have a bandage applied, an Elizabethan collar is the most effective way of preventing them from doing this.

If they do manage to remove the bandage it can be re-dressed by your vet or you can try to replace it. This is much easier if you have someone to hold the cat, leaving you with both hands free to apply the bandage. Bandaging different parts of the cat's anatomy requires different techniques but the basics remain the same. Before you start on the task ensure that you have all the items that you are likely to need close to hand. Open any packaging prior to starting. Never apply bandages too tightly as this can cut off the circulation. When in place check the bandage twice daily to see that it is still in the correct position, that there is no swelling, reddening or chaffing above or below it. It is important that it remains dry. A cat

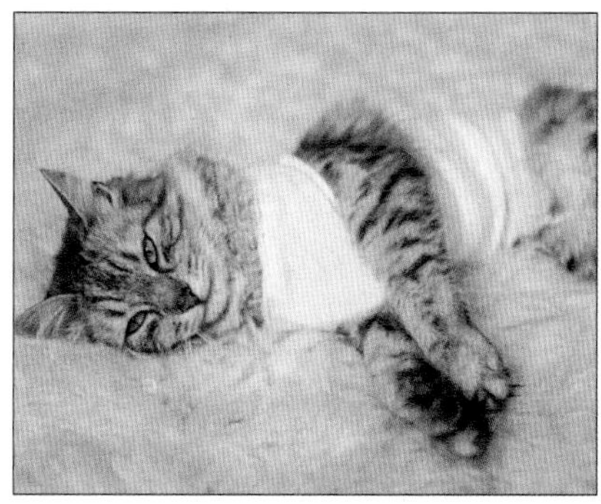

▲ *Cat veterinary body suits or an old child's tee-shirt worn over the top of the dressing will help to prevent it getting dirty*

▼ *It is critically important that dressings do not get wet. Use an anti-lick spray and change bandages daily.*

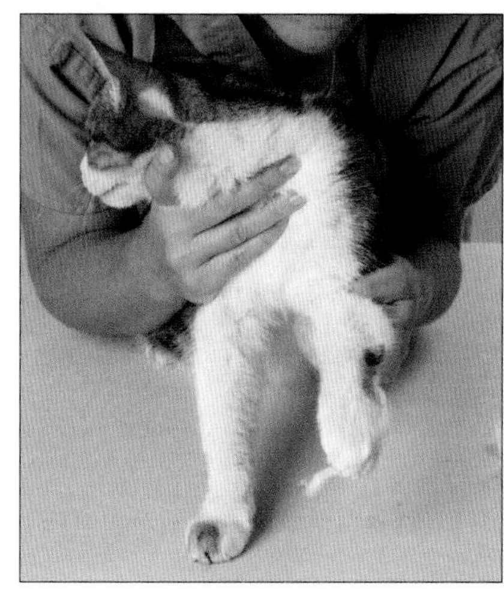

▶ *It is always easier to have someone hold the cat, leaving both hands free to apply the dressing.*

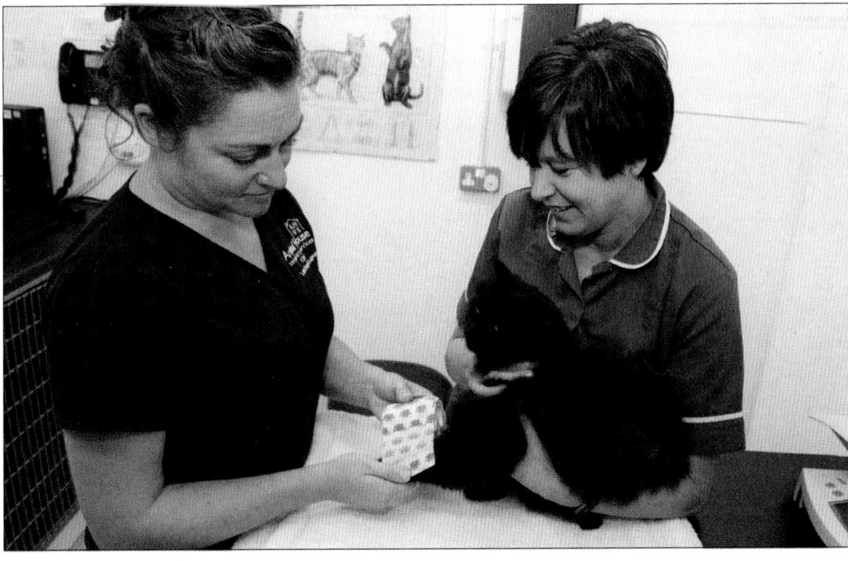

with a bandage, on any part of its body, should be confined indoors.

If you have to bandage the torso, this is best done if the cat is standing, but cats are seldom as cooperative as we would like. Roll the bandage over the dressing to be secured and around the body, overlapping each time by one third. Use as many bandages as needed to complete the task. When the area has been covered twice, take the bandage between the front legs and back over the shoulder and around the body again. Do this on both sides making a type of harness. This will prevent the torso bandage from sliding backwards. The 'harness' can be padded with cotton wool to make it more comfortable. Check the harness and torso bandage is not too tight. You should be able to slide the tip of your index finger easily between the bandage and the cat's body.

BANDAGING A LEG

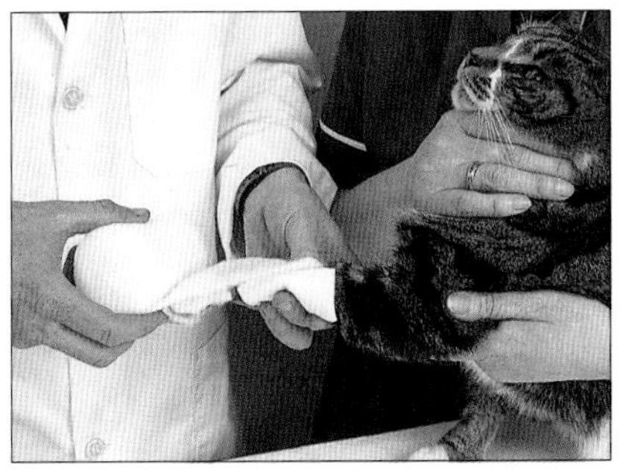

1 One person should hold the cat, and the other apply the dressing. Place lint over the injured area and hold it in place with your hand.

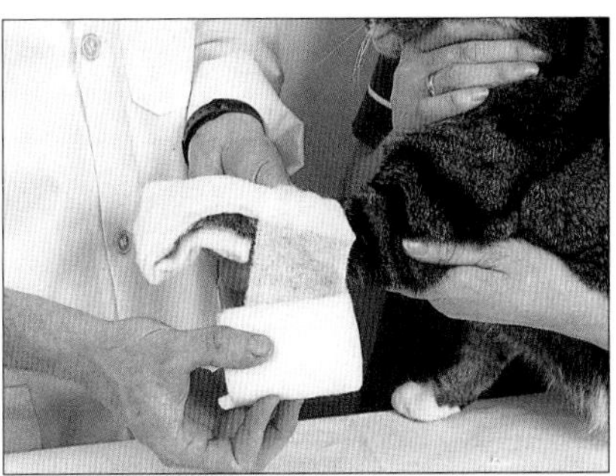

2 Use the bandage to bind the lint into position by taking it down over the paw and back up again; then wind it around the leg.

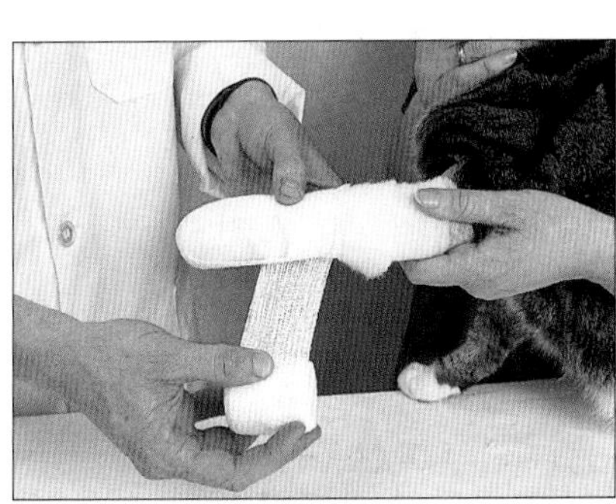

3 Continue winding the bandage firmly (but not so tight that the blood supply is cut off) and evenly around the entire length of the leg.

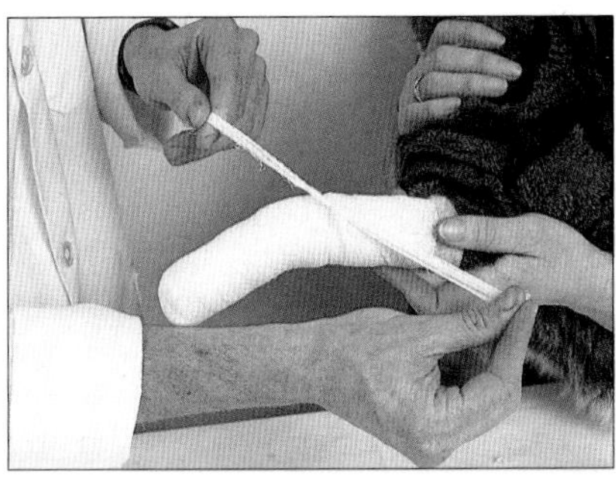

4 Split the end of the bandage leaving two ends long enough to take back around the leg in opposite directions. Tie the two ends together.

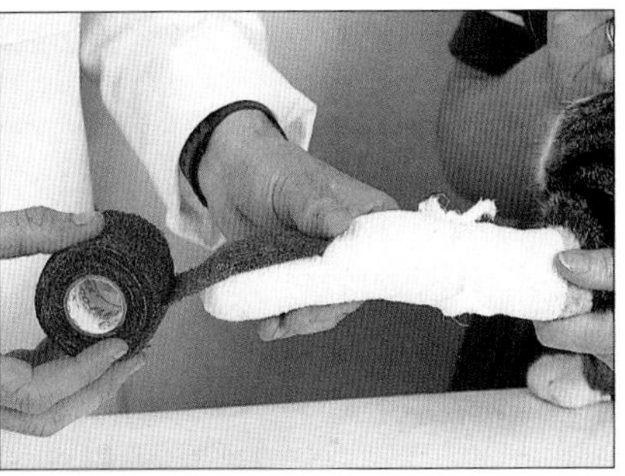

5 Tape adhesive bandage over the end of the paw and back up again as before. Wind around the entire length of the leg.

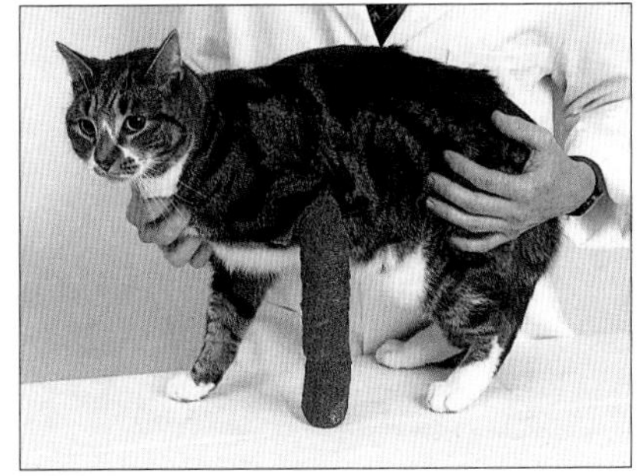

6 Keep the cat indoors while the dressing is on. Change the dressing regularly as advised by the vet, or when it becomes grubby or loose.

Special care after surgery

Caring for your cat after surgery starts before you bring it home from the vets. Begin by preparing a quiet, warm and comfortable place for the cat to rest. A spare bedroom is ideal as the cat must, initially, be confined. The door can be shut to prevent the cat escaping and has the advantage of restricting boisterous children or curious adults from entering. Move the cat's bed into the room ensuring that it is clean or lined with fresh bedding. The patient also needs a cat litter tray and a bowl of fresh water. To avoid anyone opening the door and letting the cat out a 'do not enter' notice can be fixed to the door. You may have to feed a light diet for the first twenty-four hours so prepare a little boiled fish or chicken. Remember to serve meals at room temperature and not straight out of the fridge.

On arrival at the vet's surgery, listen carefully to any instructions. Many vets discharge animals with a care sheet advising on exercise, medication and feeding to refer to at home.

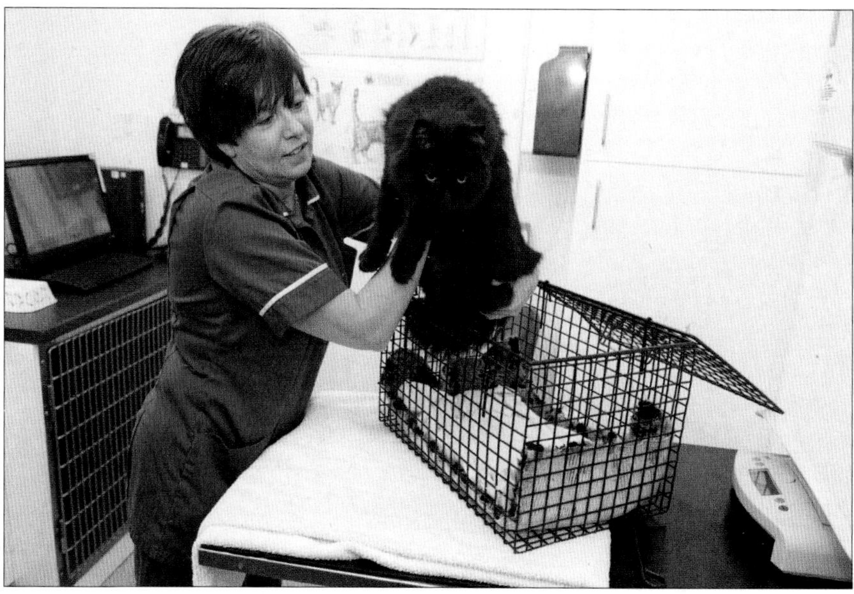

▲ *It is much easier to gently get a cat out of a top opening carrier as opposed to a side-opening one.*

AT HOME

Most animals feel groggy and are a bit wobbly after anaesthetic. Your pet may seem tired and sleep more than normal for a day or two. Clearly, after surgery, the cat should not be let out into the garden until it is quite recovered from the operation. Cats have a tendency to hide up if they feel unwell and this could have disastrous consequences. Even if your cat appears desperate to go outdoors, confine it until the vet says it can have its liberty.

◄ *On collection take your cat straight home to a quiet room away from other pets and boisterous children.*

► *A familiar bed will be appreciated. Allow the cat to recover in its own time, checking progress regularly.*

▼ *Never put disinfectant, creams or any ointments on a wound site unless directed by your vet.*

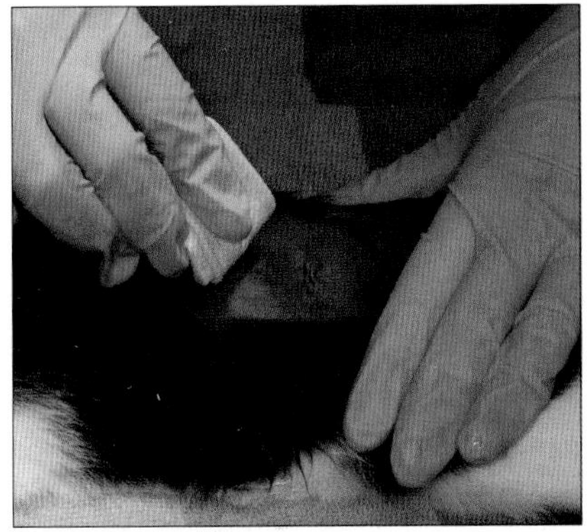

▼ *Stitched incisions should look clean with normal skin colour and edges of the wound touching each other.*

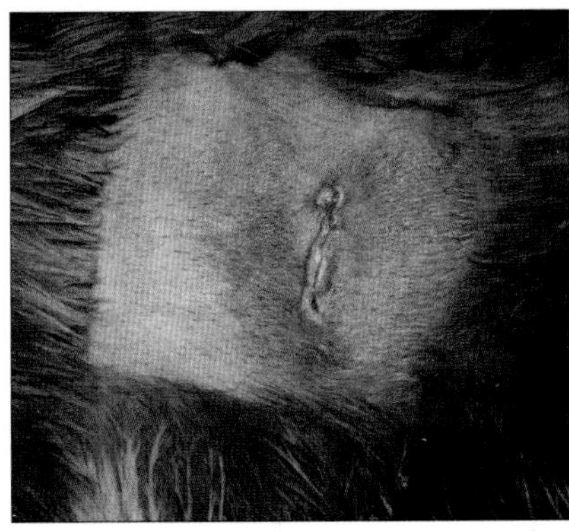

Often the cat will return from surgery wearing an Elizabethan (medical) collar. This can be distressing for the cat but it will get used to it. A day or two of discomfort is much better than having to have a wound re-stitched. Check that the cat can eat and drink with the collar on. If it doesn't appear to be able to, try changing the size of the bowl. It is easier for the cat if the Elizabethan collar fits right over the bowl. If your cat can't cope with a rigid plastic collar, softer or fabric versions are available. Your vet will be able to supply, or order, one for you. Cats appear to find these more comfortable but they are harder to clean.

GIVING MEDICATION

Anaesthetic, and some medication, can cause stomach upset, so keep meals tasty but bland and feed little and often. If your pet still has loose stools or diarrhoea the day after surgery advise the vet. Correct administration of medication is important; follow the instructions that you are given carefully. Pain control is a vital part of recovery; a stressed body is slower to heal. Cats are very good at hiding pain so never assume that painkillers are no longer required. Continue with the medication as advised by your vet. Antibiotics may also be prescribed. It is important that the full course of these are given. If you cannot give, or get the cat to take, any medication, talk to a member of the veterinary staff who will be able to give you some helpful tips or even prescribe an alternative medicine.

Check the operation site at least twice a day. The cat should not be able to lick or scratch this area as they may dislodge the stitches or staples. Your feline friend will naturally want to clean the wound area but this can do more harm than good. The incision should look clean and dry. Call your vet for advice if you see any reddening, swelling or discharge. Bandages or dressings should not be allowed to become damp. If either becomes loose, too tight, discoloured or seems smelly, return to the vet to have it changed.

Stiches or staples are usually removed about ten days after the operation. Some operations call for internal stitches. These are dissolvable and will not require removing, although the cat will still require a check-up appointment. At any post operation appointment, the vet will check on the incision and the cat's general health. They will advise you on any ongoing care or medication and if a follow-up consultation is required.

▼ *Cats might be tempted to eat by offering a little warm minced chicken or steamed white fish.*

Viral infections

Viruses need a host body to provide the energy they need to reproduce. Not all viruses cause disease. In the cat, pathogenic (disease-producing) viruses are responsible for such serious conditions as feline enteritis, cat flu and rabies. Some viruses, such as the one responsible for enteritis, are stable and resilient, surviving for long periods, while others, such as the flu virus, are readily destroyed by common disinfectants. Some viruses produce acute disease very quickly, while others have a long incubation period, such as the feline immunodeficiency virus (FIV).

Ailments described in this section

Even though you are able to protect your cat from many serious viral infections by means of vaccination, it is not yet universally common veterinary practice to inoculate against rabies or feline infectious peritonitis. Both vaccines are available worldwide but not necessarily universally licensed. In the United Kingdom, for example, the rabies virus is only used on animals intended for export. You should check carefully before travelling with your pet to confirm whether they will need to be vaccinated against rabies. The viral diseases that are effectively protected against by vaccination include feline enteritis and the flu viruses.

Infections are not necessarily the same as disease. Disease is any impairment of the normal functioning of the animal, and is usually, but not always, caused by infection. For example, cats will become infected with feline coronavirus, but may not show any signs of disease or illness at all. Infections are not always contagious, that is, they need not spread to other animals by contact.

CHLAMYDIA

Chlamydial organisms fall midway between viruses and bacteria (which, unlike viruses, are self-contained cells and do not need a host body) and are responsible for a disease of the upper respiratory tract in the cat, with symptoms very similar to those of cat flu. Minor outbreaks cause one or both eyes to become inflamed and to show an unpleasant discharge. More severe attacks also cause nasal discharge and a subsequent loss of smell and appetite. Chlamydia organisms are susceptible to similar antibiotics to which bacteria are sensitive. A vaccine has been available since 1991, and though the majority of cases are observed in households with pedigreed breeding stock, it is also known in the wider cat population.

INFLUENZA (VIRAL RHINITIS)

This is a distressing illness affecting the upper respiratory tract, which is caused by two main viruses, Feline calicivirus (FCV) and Feline herpesvirus (FHV). Both viruses cause coughing and sneezing. Discharge from the nose and the eyes cause the cat great distress, and a rasping soreness in the throat discourages eating or drinking. Feline calicivirus often causes serious ulceration of nose, mouth and tongue. Feline herpesvirus may cause the nose, windpipe and lungs to become seriously inflamed, resulting in a lot of coughing and sneezing. The cat that is

▼ *The acute conjunctivitis and corneal opacity in one of this Blue Tonkinese kitten's eyes are symptoms of chlamydia, a respiratory disease.*

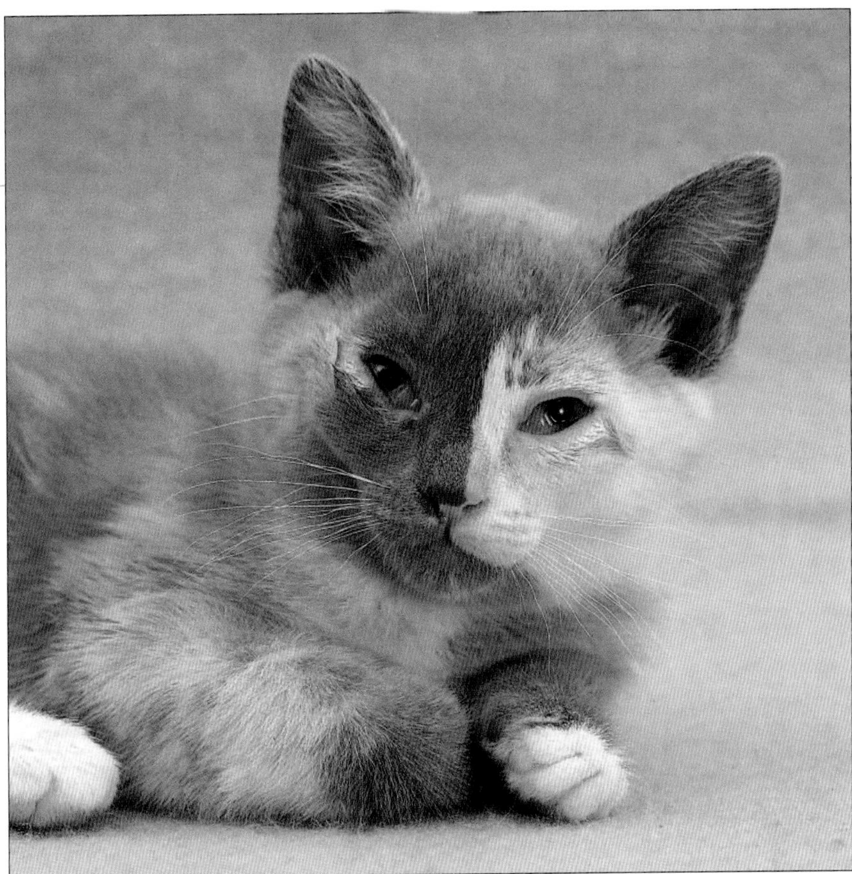

▲ *A Lilac Cream Burmese-cross kitten has severe conjunctivitis – a symptom of feline flu.*

kept warm and comfortable and is encouraged to eat and drink stands the greatest chance of survival. Antibiotics reduce the risk of secondary infections but do not attack the primary viruses. Effective vaccination against cat flu is the best preventative course.

FELINE INFECTIOUS ENTERITIS (FIE)

This disease, a cat version of the distemper that infects dogs, is also known as feline panleukopaenia and feline parvovirus. The first symptom of this sometimes astonishingly rapid killer virus is usually a very high fever. The virus attacks rapidly dividing cells, particularly in the bowel. Symptoms may include unusually depressed behaviour, loss of appetite, vomiting, and a desire to drink but an inability to do so. Diarrhoea is not always present. Rapid dehydration sets in followed by coma and death. The rapidity of the disease, after its short incubation period, can mean that death occurs two or three days after vomiting starts or even within 24 hours. The disease is highly infectious. Treatment is supportive: keep the cat warm and free from draughts, and administer rehydration therapy as advised by your vet.

FELINE LEUKAEMIA VIRUS (FeLV)

This virus first came to the notice of breeders of pedigreed cats in the early 1970s. Originally there were fears that it could be a health hazard to humans, particularly children. This is most certainly not the case – the virus cannot be transmitted except to another cat. To begin with, it was thought that particular pedigreed breeds were more prone to the disease than other cats, but this has not been proven. All cats may be similarly and as rapidly affected when they come into contact with the virus. It was found that a larger percentage of the normal domestic cat population was affected than expected, and many of these cats lived into old age. This made a nonsense of early veterinary advice that cats with feline leukaemia virus should be euthanased immediately.

Some cats do succumb rapidly to other serious and untreatable infections as the virus wreaks havoc with the cat's immune system, while others are less affected. If one cat is affected within a multi-cat household, it should be removed, as the virus is easily transmitted through saliva or blood. The infected animal could be moved to a single-cat household where it may live out its life without infecting others. Testing for the virus is through a blood sample. It is possible for a cat to test positive and then, two weeks later, to show a negative result, only having had a passing contact with the virus. For some years, a vaccine countering this disease has been available in the United States, and since 1992, FeLV licences have been available in the United Kingdom.

Most breeders have all their animals, whether elderly, neutered (altered) or young breeding cats, regularly tested to show that they are FeLV-negative. Females are only mated to males which also regularly test negative, so that the kittens are automatically negative too. They can then be protected by vaccination. Many breeders leave this to the new owners. If there are other cats in your home, it should be done immediately. If the kitten is the only pet, inoculation may be left until it is a little older.

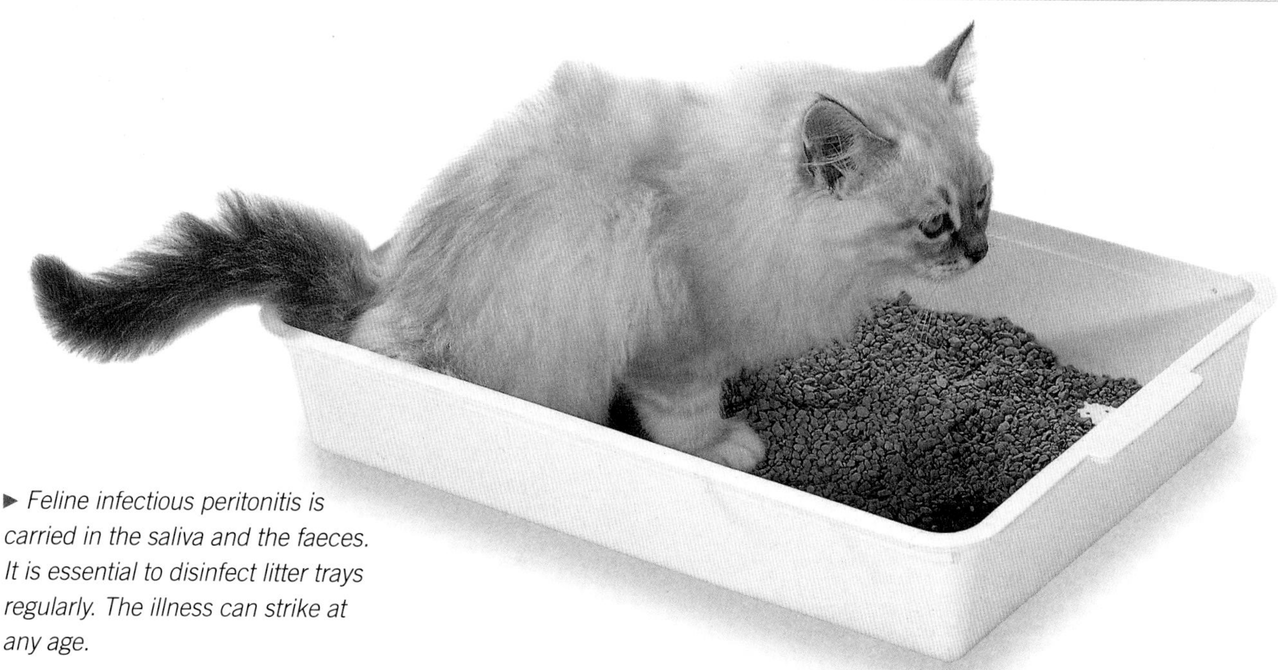

► *Feline infectious peritonitis is carried in the saliva and the faeces. It is essential to disinfect litter trays regularly. The illness can strike at any age.*

FELINE IMMUNODEFICIENCY VIRUS (FIV)

This is a similar virus to the human immunodeficiency virus (HIV) which may lead eventually to acquired immunodeficiency syndrome (AIDS). The feline version cannot be passed on to a human being, and HIV cannot be passed on to a cat.

FIV progressively breaks down the cat's immune system. This leads to the cat becoming increasingly vulnerable to infections. Despite periods of apparently normal health, the cat slowly succumbs to minor illnesses which become untreatable. No vaccination exists at present.

FELINE INFECTIOUS PERITONITIS (FIP)

The virus that causes this disease is found in many cats and normally only occasionally causes a transient diarrhoea. However, in about 10 per cent of infected cats, the virus leaves the intestines, invades the blood vessels and causes a severe inflammation – which is feline infectious peritonitis. The membrane which lines the abdominal cavity is called the peritoneum, and once the blood vessels of this have become infected and inflamed, treatment is extremely difficult, and often unsuccessful. As yet no definitive pattern to the progression of illness has emerged. The disease can be triggered in almost all age groups; even young kittens are susceptible.

▼ *A cat is spending a night in the vet's pens before surgery in the morning.*

Wet FIP is the most common form of the disease. Onset is usually rapid. Just 24 hours after appearing lively, playful, of good appetite and with normal litter-tray motions, a wet FIP sufferer will be lethargic, will not want to eat very much and will have sickness and diarrhoea. The coat is often staring and dull, but the most dramatic sign is the grossly distended fluid-filled abdomen. There is no cure. Euthanasia is the only option.

Dry FIP is a less common form of the disease and is often difficult to diagnose. The signs are similar to those of other illnesses. Terminally, the cat may have jaundice and show symptoms akin to cat flu, disorientation, blindness due to haemorrhages in the eyes and, finally, fits.

The presence of the virus is detected by antibody tests. Cats which show none are designated 'nil titre' count. Over 80 per cent of show cats are seropositive, showing they have had some contact with the disease. Some cat breeders advertise their animals as nil (free) status, but most vets regard a low count as being relatively normal. Many cats, even with a very high titre count may seem normal. It is thought that a stressful situation, such as the introduction of a new cat into the household or a long journey, may tip a cat with a pre-existing viral condition into the full-blown illness.

FIP does not seem to be as infectious as was at first thought. The virus is carried in the cat's saliva and the faeces. Litter trays should be disinfected regularly using an agent recommended by your vet. Keeping cats in small, easily managed colonies, observing strict hygiene and, above all, maintaining a stress-free environment should help reduce the possibility of the disease flaring up. The virus is not able to survive very long outside the host and is very susceptible to disinfection agents. Although there is a vaccine for FIP available in some countries it has not been proven to be reliably effective. It is not currently recommended by the American Association of Feline Practitioners Feline Vaccine Advisory Panel.

RABIES

All mammals, including humans, are susceptible to rabies, and the bite of an infected animal is dangerous. Once infected, a cat may show signs of a radical alteration of appetite and voice, with unexpected aggressive behaviour. An inability to drink gives rabies its other name, hydrophobia – fear of water. Other signs follow – foaming at the mouth, swelling of the skull, jaw paralysis and disorientation.

Treatment is possible but must be started promptly after being bitten by a suspected animal. There is very little hope of any infected mammal surviving once the long incubation period of the disease has passed and symptoms have begun to show. Several countries are rabies-free, including the United Kingdom due to rigorous import regulations. Vaccination is available and standard in countries where rabies exists. In Britain it is available, on request, for animals that are likely to travel to another country.

FELINE SPONGIFORM ENCEPHALOPATHY

This disease is caused by a sub-viral protein that is capable of reproducing itself. It is similar to the bovine form (BSE) that has occurred in the United Kingdom, but not elsewhere. The disease seems to be invariably fatal in cats, and is not diagnosable prior to death. It seems to have been transmitted to cats as a result of eating meat from cattle infected with BSE or sheep with scrapie. The cat develops abnormal behaviour, including failure to groom, and often drools with muscle tremors and an abnormal head posture. However, positive diagnosis is only possible on post-mortem examination.

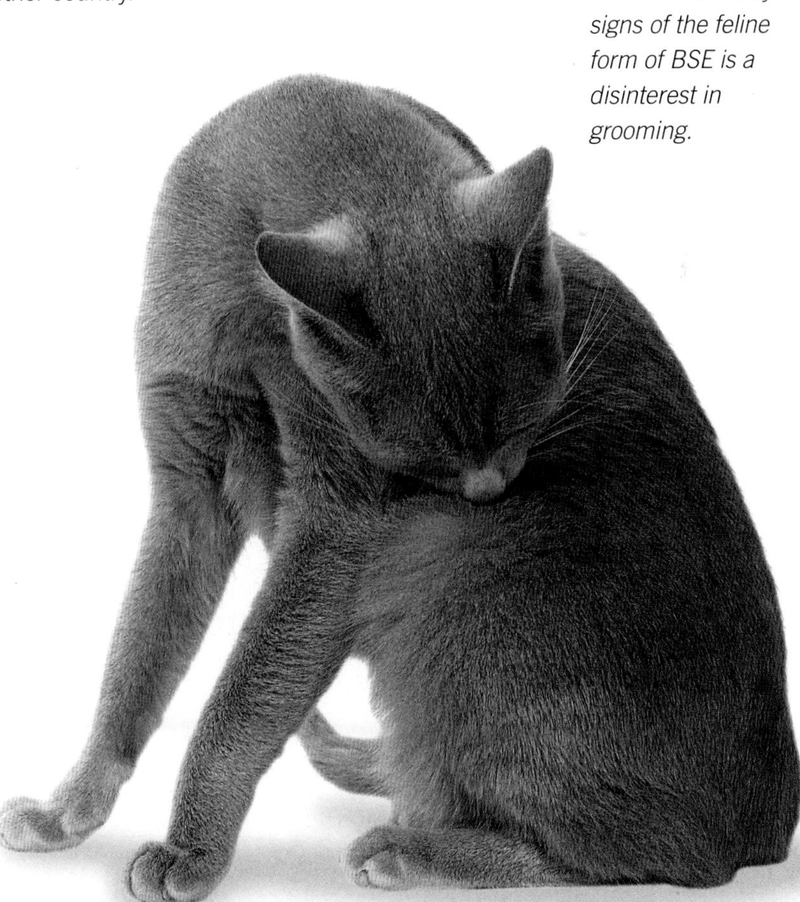

◄ *One of the early signs of the feline form of BSE is a disinterest in grooming.*

Parasites

Being aware of the problems and facts about parasites is the first step in prevention. Routine care of any cat or kitten must include checking that the fur and skin are kept free from parasites.

A parasite is an animal or plant that takes food and protection from a host animal or plant. It survives to the detriment of its host, causing loss of condition, and sometimes death. In some cases, such as ringworm, the parasitic condition of a host cat can be passed on to the humans it lives with.

Preparations to eradicate external parasites such as fleas, ticks, lice, mites and ringworm, as well as internal parasites including worms, are easily available. Ask veterinary advice, follow instructions carefully, and stick to a strict cleaning regime, and parasites should not be a problem.

▲ *A cat is having its regular check for fleas, lice, and ticks. The check-up can be part of a weekly grooming routine.*

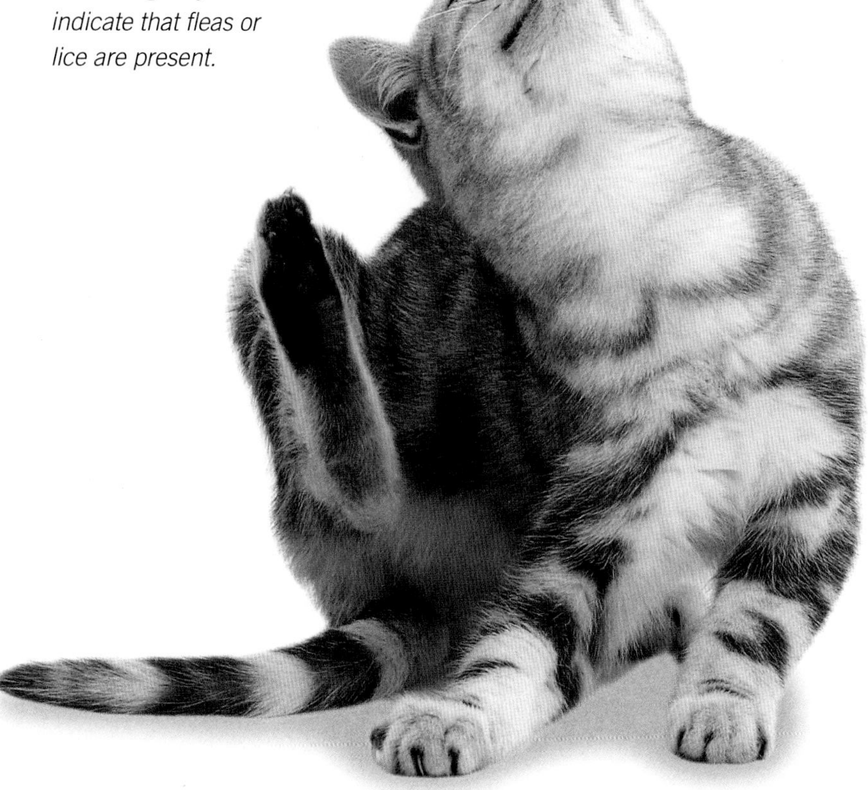

► *Excessive scratching may indicate that fleas or lice are present.*

In the case of indoor cats, regular hoovering of carpets is a must. This warm floor covering is a haven for some parasites and a perfect place for their eggs and larvae.

It is advisable, especially in the first instance, to buy any preparations to combat parasites from the vet. This is especially important when treating kittens and cats with other health issues. In theory over-the-counter preparations should work equally well, but in fact this is often not the case. A recent scientific investigation showed that many of these items, due to resistance to the chemicals used, are only 50 per cent as efficient as those from the vet. So, although these items may be cheaper they do not represent good value for money.

FLEAS

The flea is one of the most common parasitic insects. They are flightless and have laterally compressed bodies that enables them to pass easily through a cat's fur. Mouthparts are adapted so that they can pierce skin and suck out blood. Brownish-red in colour, they measure about 3mm (0.08in) long. They have proportionally long legs, with the hind adapted for jumping. A flea can jump fifty times its body length. The body is covered with scaly plates that can withstand great pressure. It is very difficult to squash a flea. Flea eggs are tiny, white flattened ovals. You would have to have exceptional eyesight to see them. These hatch into larvae, which are worm-like. Larvae feed on faeces, containing dried blood, of adult fleas and other organic matter.

The cat with fleas may scratch obsessively, particularly around the neck, and may groom the base of the spine vigorously and spontaneously. It may also worry at the entire length of the spine. Using the tips of the fingers and nails, groom the cat behind the ears, the neck, spine and base of the tail. If this reveals dark, chocolate-brown grit, put these on a damp tissue. If red leaches from them, they are flea droppings, which are largely made up of dried blood.

In severe infestations or where the cat is actually allergic to substances produced by the flea in its bite, patches of scabby skin may be found with the scabs breaking off to reveal sore-looking, slightly weeping patches. This clears up rapidly with the eradication of the fleas.

Fleas move very fast through the fur of the cat and are difficult to catch even if seen. A cat can be attacked by the cat flea, the dog flea and the human flea. They all lay their eggs in the cat's fur; many will drop out and hatch into larvae in cracks in the floorboards, in the weave of fabrics and in carpets. The larvae develop into fleas that immediately feed from any host that may wander by. A flea can live, with periods of feeding and resting, for up to two years, but two to six months is the norm.

▼ The irritation caused by fleas results in constant scratching that, in severe cases, can interrupt sleep.

▼ Spot-on anti-flea preparations are applied at the base of the neck between the shoulder blades.

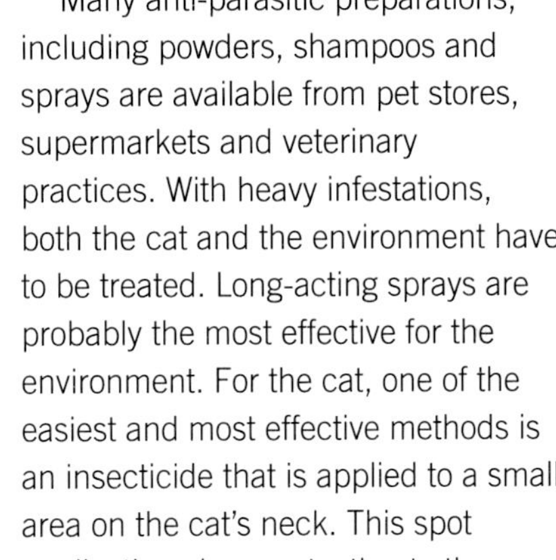

Many anti-parasitic preparations, including powders, shampoos and sprays are available from pet stores, supermarkets and veterinary practices. With heavy infestations, both the cat and the environment have to be treated. Long-acting sprays are probably the most effective for the environment. For the cat, one of the easiest and most effective methods is an insecticide that is applied to a small area on the cat's neck. This spot application gives protection to the whole body for a month.

Modern parasiticides are very safe and some are commercially available that can be applied to even very young kittens. Your vet will be able to advise on the most appropriate products for young cats.

◄ Female fleas lay, on average, 20 eggs a day. They take between 1–12 days to hatch.

► Use the flea comb in the direction of the coat paying attention to the neck, groin, armpits and base of the tail.

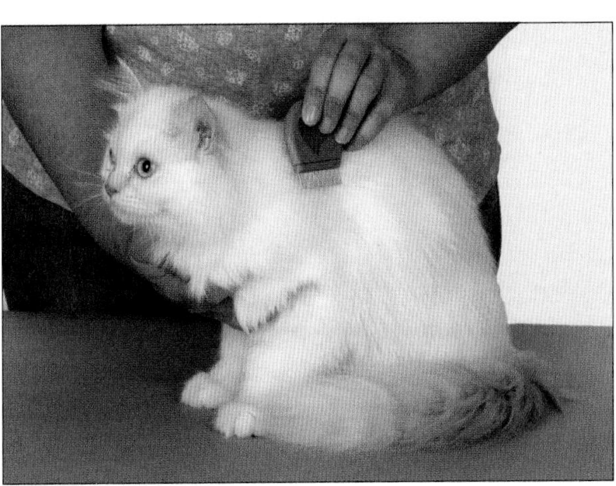

TICKS

Ticks, like fleas, are blood suckers. However, unlike fleas, they live permanently on the cat. This parasite is normally rural in distribution, but the hedgehog tick is common in urban areas. The tick burrows its head into the host animal's skin, and gorges itself on blood. It can sometimes reach the size of a haricot bean, then drop off to complete its life cycle with no further damage to the cat. However, it could move on to other animals in the home. Removal of a tick requires precision, to avoid the head parts remaining buried in the skin. The cat itself may be irritated by the tick's burrowing and knock it off, leaving its head behind. This usually sets up chronic infection followed by an abscess or sore which is difficult to heal. A vet can use substances to relax the tick's hold before removing it. A home equivalent is surgical alcohol (or any form of alcoholic spirit). The whole tick is then carefully removed with tweezers or a custom-made tick remover (available from pet stores).

Tick bites can be responsible for a bacterial disease called Lyme disease. This occurs in the United Kingdom, but is more widespread in the United States. Symptoms include a reluctance to jump followed by acute and recurring lameness, a raised temperature, lethargy and swollen lymph nodes, particularly around the head and limbs. Blood tests confirm the cause, and treatment is a four to six week course of antibiotics. Lyme disease should not occur if ticks are prevented. Most flea preparations also prevent tick infestation.

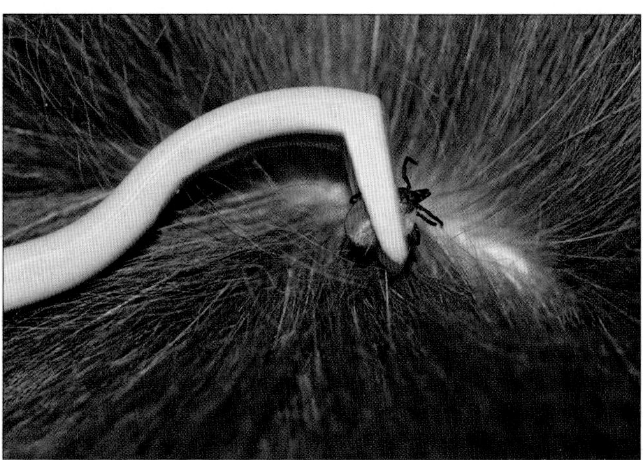

► *There is a real knack of twisting and removing the whole tick. Any portion left in the flesh could cause an infection.*

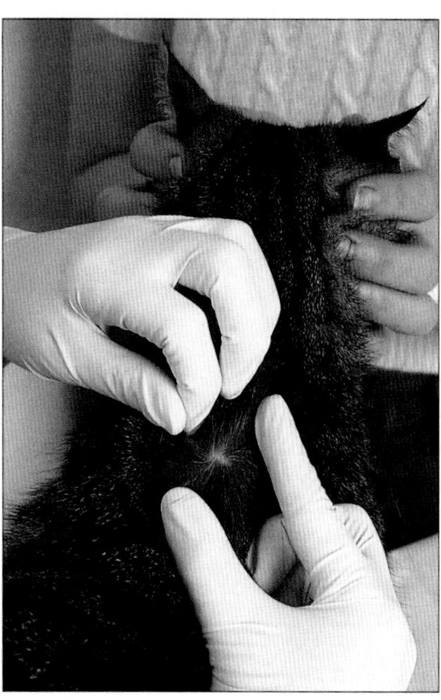

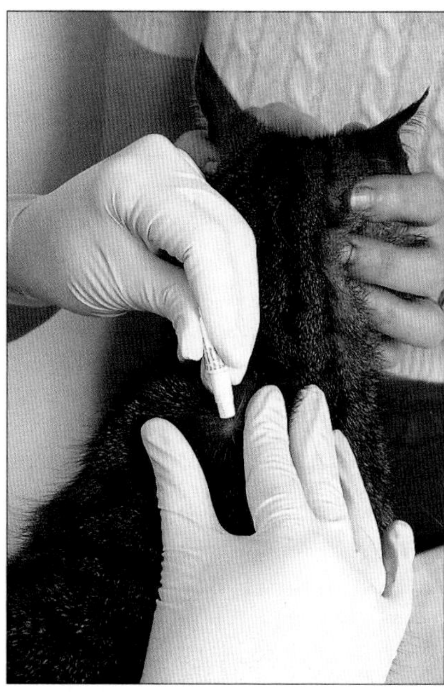

▼ *As a preventative measure against fleas and lice, apply an anti-parasite insecticide once a month. Part the fur on the back of the neck and squeeze on the required amount of medication.*

LICE

Fortunately, lice infestation is uncommon on cats, but poor condition and extremes of age make individuals susceptible. There are three types of louse which are known to occur on cats, one blood-sucking, and two which bite. Telltale signs are some scratching, usually not very excessive, combined with dry skin which shows an unusual increase of scurf or dandruff. The lice may be seen quite easily with the naked eye. The eggs, or nits, are laid directly on the lower third of the hair and seem to be glued in place. Anti-lice preparations are effective.

▼ *Incessant scratching of the head and ears is a sign of ear mites, and could aggravate the problem if not treated quickly.*

MITES

Four groups of mites affect the cat's skin and ears. The harvest mite appears in the autumn (fall). The cat is affected by the larvae which tend to settle in areas where the fur is thin, such as between the toes, on the underbelly, in the groin and around the lips and nose.

The orange larvae are just about visible to the naked eye. They set up irritation which the cat vigorously attacks with teeth and claws, thus creating more irritation. The sores which develop are round, damp and surrounded by scabby skin. Mite infestation is highly contagious and must be treated with insecticidal preparations.

The ear mite is commonly transmitted from cat to cat. Irritation is sometimes severe; the cat shakes its head, holds the ears almost flat, and scratches furiously. This often leads to secondary infections arising from self-inflicted trauma. Evidence of ear mites is a dark brown tarry substance in the ears. Because of the ear's delicacy, it is wise to ask your vet to carry out initial treatment. The owner can then cleanse the ear gently.

▼ *A vet checks for ear mites as part of the routine examination.*

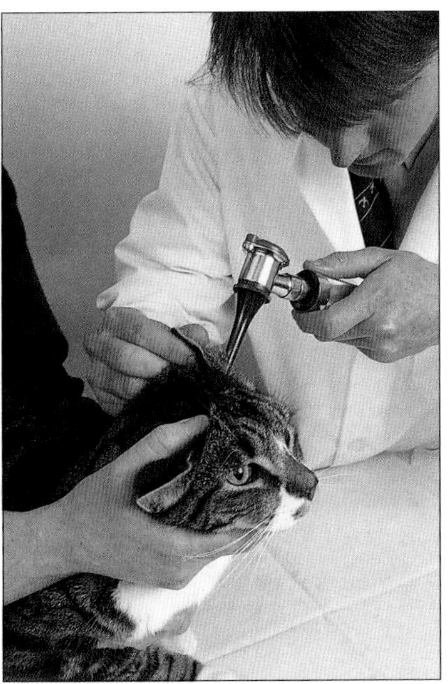

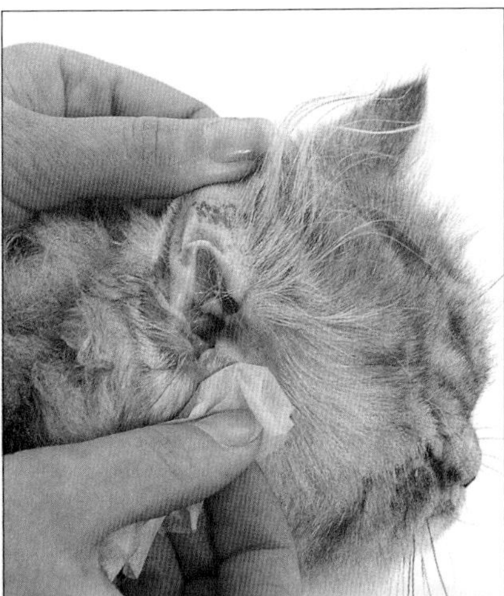

▲ *Regular checking and cleaning at grooming time will keep mite infestations at bay.*

Cheyletiella mites cause a condition known as 'walking dandruff', and are less common. They often seem to cause little irritation to the cat though there may be more scratching and grooming than usual. Excessive dandruff is the usual sign. The mite normally lives on the wild rabbit and can also affect people (rashes appear on chest, stomach and arms). Treatment is with parasiticides – for both cat and human.

One fortunately rare form of mange is caused by a burrowing mite. It is usually found around the head starting at the base of the ear. There is severe irritation, hair loss and general lack of condition. Blood poisoning can occur in severe cases. Antibiotic treatment is necessary for any secondary infections, while the actual skin damage is treated with the use of parasiticidal preparations.

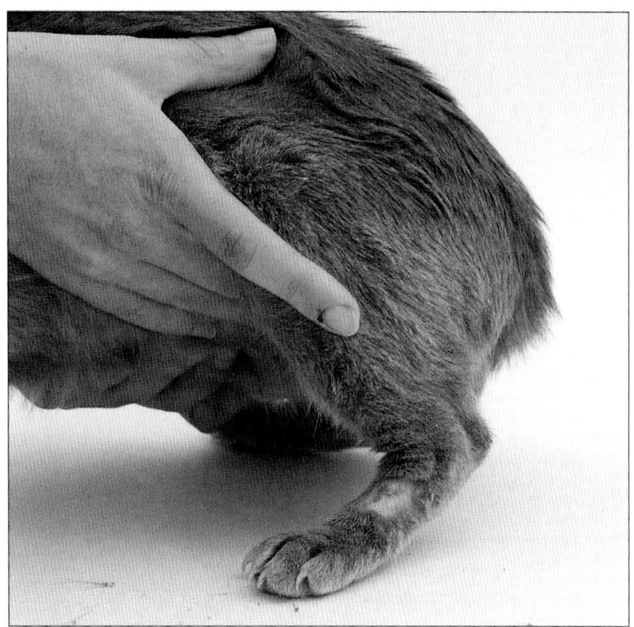

▼ *Thinning and bald patches on the hind leg of a Blue Burmese could be signs of ringworm.*

▼ *The mark on the head of this Lilac Tonkinese kitten is confirmed as ringworm. The kitten, litter mates and mother must now be isolated as this condition is very contagious.*

RINGWORM

Ringworm is caused by a fungus, and can affect humans, especially children. The name comes from the shape of the lesions seen on the skin in humans, which are circular, red, scaly and very itchy. In the cat, particularly the Persian, often all that is seen are tiny pimples and scurf on the skin. (Nevertheless, these cats can still be highly contagious.) At worst, moist, pink sores spread outwards. The fungal parasite lives on the hair and not on the skin, and causes the hair to break off. Ringworm can affect animals that are not in top condition, or that are young, and can be a major problem in longhaired show cats.

Diagnosis is initially by the use of special filtered light (Wood's Light), when about 65 per cent of cases will fluoresce. Laboratory tests are more reliable but take longer. The eradication process is long and tedious. The animals are treated with fungicides, both in the form of baths and external applications, and also tablets. The entire environment, human and animal, has to be carefully cleansed to eradicate all spores. There is no simple answer to the problem. Professional advice on procedure must be taken and, if necessary, the local environmental health department consulted. In the United States and in the United Kingdom, research is aimed at improving diagnostic tests as well as treatments. Considerable headway has been made in the production of a vaccine, but at present only cuts down treatment time.

MAGGOTS

Flies may be attracted to animals by the presence of discharge from wounds, or diarrhoea, and lay their eggs in the fur. Fly strike, as this situation is known, is particularly common in cats in poor condition, such as those in feral colonies. The maggots burrow into the skin and form tunnels which can run for considerable distances. Toxins produced to aid burrowing are absorbed by the cat and cause toxaemia (blood poisoning). If you find maggot infestation on your cat, clean it as thoroughly as possible using soap and water and contact the vet without delay.

BRONCHITIS

Infectious bronchitis is sometimes caused by a parasitic bacterium that lodges in the respiratory tract of animals. The parasite itself does not normally cause disease, but certain strains of the parasite do cause bronchitis. In a dog, this may appear as kennel cough. A cat on the other hand may cough and sneeze, with or without running nose and eyes. Normally, the disease is self-limiting. However, in very young or elderly cats, or those with other debilitating diseases, it can be persistent and troublesome to clear. The organism is sensitive to several antibiotics.

► *Some cats will happily eat up their worming powder if it has been sprinkled over their food.*

WORMS

The cat is affected by a wide range of internal parasitic worms, some of which are regional. Effective worm treatments are available, without prescription, from pet stores and supermarkets. However, experience has shown that these may be difficult to administer with total accuracy. Routine worming treatments – and advice – are best obtained from your vet. Worming preparations which give multiple protection to the cat are now available either as tablets, oral liquid, spot-on or injections. Regular, correctly spaced treatments will keep your cat worm-free. These are often supplied at the same time as the annual booster vaccination, but may need to be given every six months.

ROUNDWORMS, HOOKWORMS AND LUNGWORMS

Roundworms, *Toxocara cati* and the less common hookworm, *Toxoscaris leonima*, cause disease in cats and possible death in kittens. These worms, sometimes called ascarids, swim freely in the intestines. Averagely, they are 8–15cm (3–6in) in length. Cats can become infected by ingesting the eggs in faecal matter or eating the tissue of paratenic hosts such as rodents, birds, earthworms or cockroaches. When ingested the eggs turn to larvae, which can remain dormant in the body or travel through the muscle, lungs and liver before returning to the intestine where they will grow into adult worms and produce eggs. In female cats, pregnancy can cause larvae to come out of dormancy and be passed to kittens across the placenta or through the mother's milk.

Symptoms of large numbers of roundworms include diarrhoea, abdominal discomfort, vomiting, poor appetite and a pot belly appearance. Veterinary diagnosis is made by testing a stool sample for eggs. Treatment involves the administration of a de-wormer at regular intervals as advised by your vet.

The main symptom of hookworm infestation is anaemia, which in a cat is most obvious on its nose leather and gums. The gums appear excessively pale, almost white. There is a general lack of energy and the cat may become very thin.

The intermediate host of the lungworm, *Eucoleus aerophilus,* is the slug or snail, which could be eaten by a cat. However, it is more likely that they will be eaten first by birds or rodents and the infective larvae reach the cat through eating them. Nevertheless, infestation is quite rare. After a complicated journey through the cat's intestine and lymph nodes, the larvae become adult worms, which eventually enter the lungs via the

▼ *Check gums and tongue for any undue paleness that could indicate anaemia and possible hookworm infestation.*

▼ *Worming treatments can be given orally, by professional staff at the vet's surgery, to cats who are reluctant to take tablets of any shape or form.*

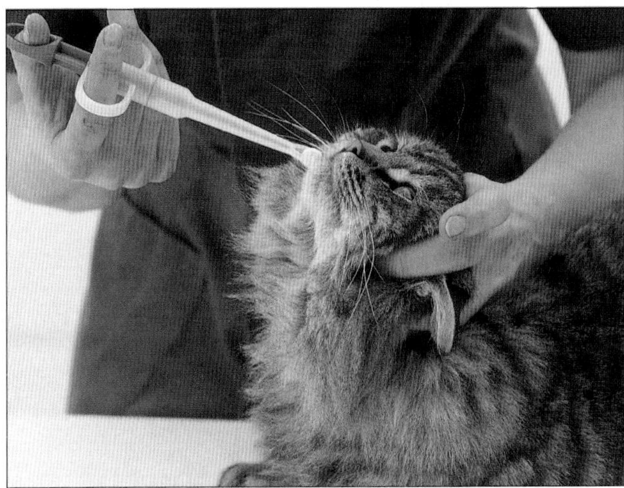

bloodstream. As a result, respiratory symptoms occur, similar to bronchitis or pneumonia.

TAPEWORMS

There are several species of tapeworm that infect cats. A tapeworm looks like a thin, whitish grey piece of ribbon. They are typically found in the small intestine where they hook into the lining of the bowel. They have both male and female parts so can produce eggs on their own. The end of the worm forms an egg sack which breaks off and passes out through the anus. Adult tapeworms are much longer than roundworms and range from 10–71cm (4–28in). Eradication is important, both for the health and wellbeing of the cat and to prevent the transmission to humans.

Tapeworm diagnosis is relatively easy. Segments of tapeworm containing eggs are shed and attach themselves to the fur around the anus. They look like grains of rice. Tapeworms require intermediate hosts and the flea fulfils this role in relation to the most common tapeworm to affect the cat. Flea control for your cat is therefore very important.

Flea larvae eat the secreted tapeworm segments that contain the eggs. The infective stage of the tapeworm is reached as the adult flea preys on the cat for a blood meal. If the cat catches and swallows the flea, as it may do while grooming, the process is completed. The infective stage of the second most common tapeworm to affect cats develops in the livers of small rodents. The infected livers and other intestinal parts will almost certainly be consumed by a cat, if it catches one of these animals.

The way to prevent infestation by tapeworms is to eradicate fleas, and discourage your cat from hunting. Both may be impossible targets, but although tapeworms continue to be a problem, their presence does not seem to affect cats much beyond diarrhoea in the case of very heavy infestation.

▲ *Cats groom themselves several times a day to keep their coats in good order, using their teeth, tongue and paws as tools.*

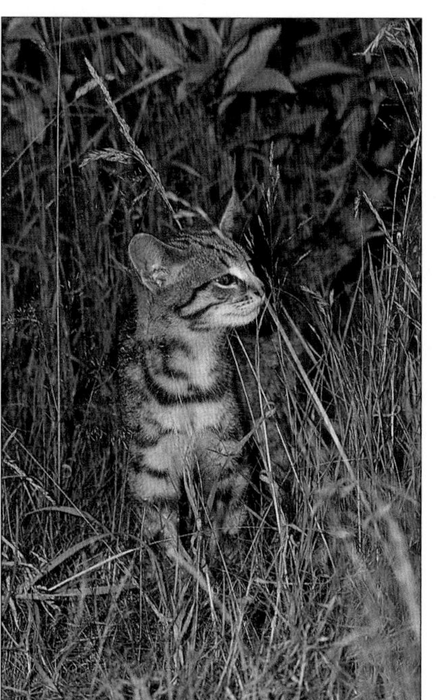

◀ *Even well-fed cats will try to supplement their diet by hunting small rodents or birds. The fitter they are, the greater their chances of success.*

▶ *The abdomen of a cat being palpated; a distended belly may indicate roundworm infestation.*

▼ *Wormers are now available in a tasty treat form that most cats will eat. Alternatively use the liquid form.*

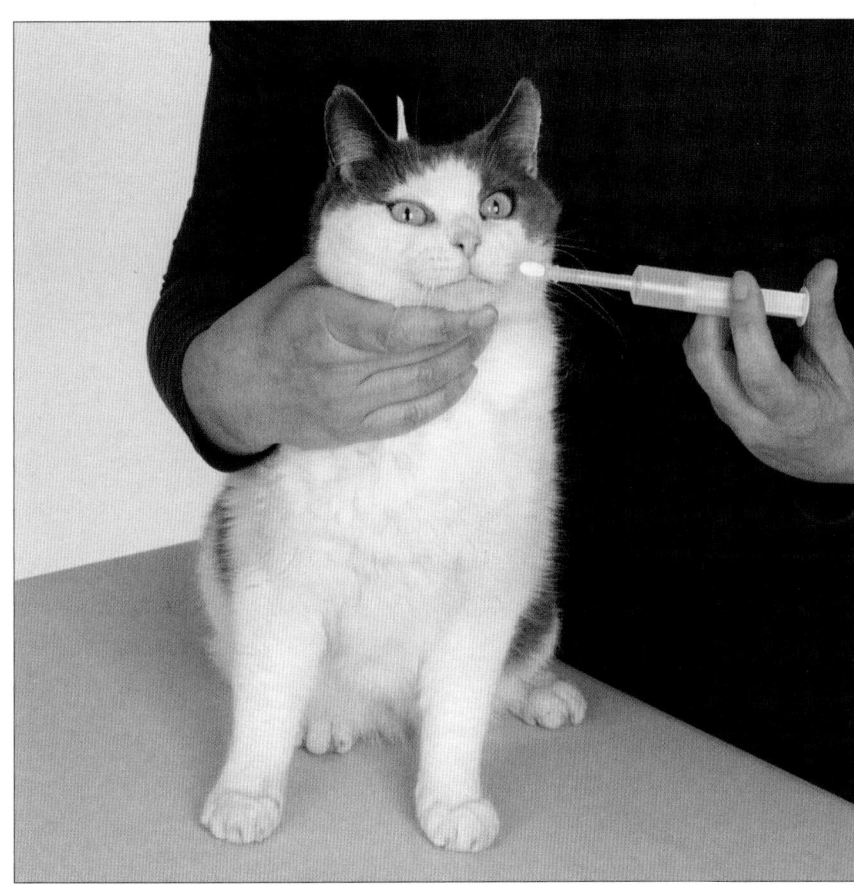

WHIPWORMS AND THREADWORMS

Whipworms infect cats, but are more commonly seen in dogs. Infections of this type are usually seen in parts of Europe and North America. In North America *Trichuris serrata* is found, while in Europe it is *Trichuris campanula*. Eggs are present in animal flesh, the soil, food, water and faeces. Whipworms can exist in an appropriate environment for several years. The adult looks like a whip, being thicker at one end and trailing off to a thin thread at the other. They are 4.5–7.5cm (1.75–3in) long. They infect cats through ingestion. Whipworms infect cats of any age. Once in the host the larvae burrow into the flesh of a cat's colon and feed until they mature to adults.

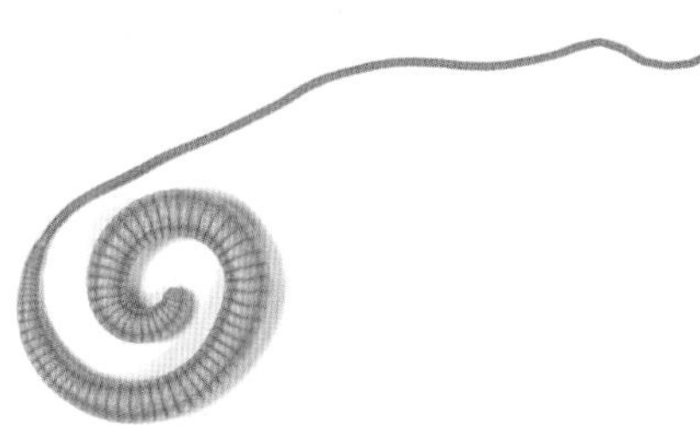

▲ *Whipworm eggs are present in the environment and will remain un-hatched until they are ingested.*

▼ *Diagnosis of threadworm is made by looking at a prepared sample of faeces under a microscope.*

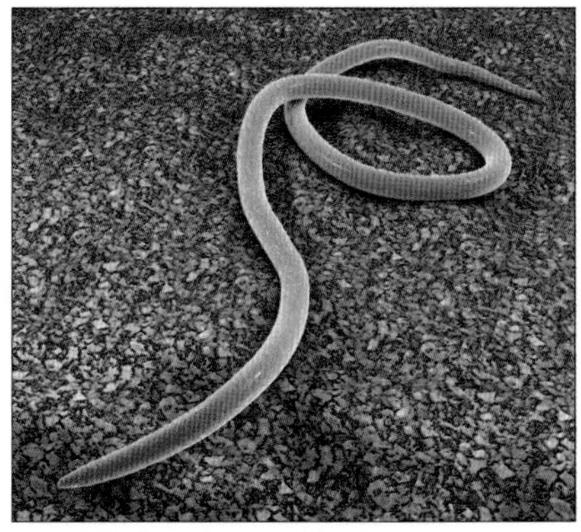

Mild infestations show no symptoms but as the worm load increases weight loss, diarrhoea, dehydration and inflammatory bowel syndrome may become apparent. In severe cases, this could be coupled with bright, red blood in the stool and anaemia. Treatment is through a course of wormers as prescribed by your vet. The prognosis is good but infected cats should be isolated from other pets if possible.

Strongyloides, or threadworms, infect all carnivores and cats are no exception. Different types infect different animals. The name describes this parasite, the adult being approximately 2mm (0.07in) and 0.035mm (0.001in). Amazingly, all threadworms are female, and they are somehow able to fertilize their own eggs. The exact life cycle of these parasites is unknown.

This parasite is more commonly found in India and Australia but may occur in humid areas of the United States. There is a strong connection with animals living in cramped and unsanitary conditions. Symptoms include diarrhoea, blood in faeces and excessive itching. In severe cases, fever and rapid breathing may be seen. Infestation can be fatal in elderly cats or kittens. Treatment is via a wormer as prescribed by your vet and will involve more than one dose.

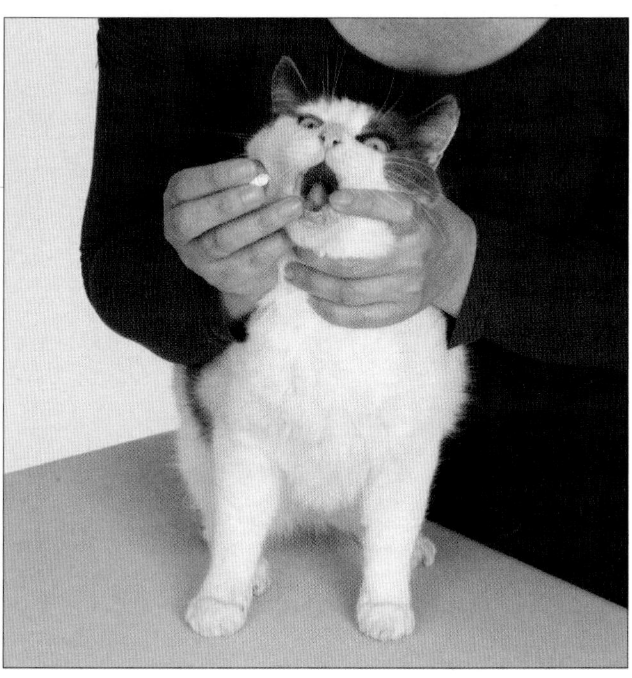

► *To administer a tablet tilt the head upwards, gently pull the jaw down and open the mouth, then put the pill on the back of the tongue.*

HOOKWORMS AND FLUKES

Hookworms are small, thin worms less than 2.5cm (1in) long. They are blood sucking parasites that attach themselves to the small intestines with their mouth parts. They are able to un-attach themselves and move to another site, leaving an ulcerated wound each time. Hookworms are fairly common in cats. Infection is caused by ingestion or by the larvae burrowing through the flesh, typically the feet. This can occur when a cat walks across ground, or uses a litter tray, that is infected by the parasite. Infected cats may have lesions on their feet or between their toes. Hookworms can also be passed from mother to kittens, via her milk.

Symptoms are various and include diarrhoea, constipation or dark, tarry stools. Infected cats look unhealthy, with poor coats and pale linings to the mouth, nose and ears. Appetites are poor. If larvae are in the lungs a cough may be present. Hookworm infestation can be fatal and requires rapid attention. A vet will make a diagnosis by microscopic examination of a stool sample and prescribe medication accordingly.

The cat liver fluke has a complicated life cycle. Infected cat faeces are ingested by snails which are then eaten by lizards, frogs or toads. When the secondary host is eaten by a cat, the life cycle is completed. Liver flukes require a tropical or sub-tropical climate to live so are not seen in colder climes. As the name suggests this parasite lives in the liver, as well as the gallbladder.

Symptoms vary according to the severity of the infection; loss of appetite, dramatic weight loss, jaundice, vomiting, diarrhoea, enlarged liver, distended abdomen, fever and general lack of wellbeing. Diagnosis is made by a liver biopsy. Heavy infestation is a serious condition and may require hospitalization. Treated in time, cats should make a good recovery.

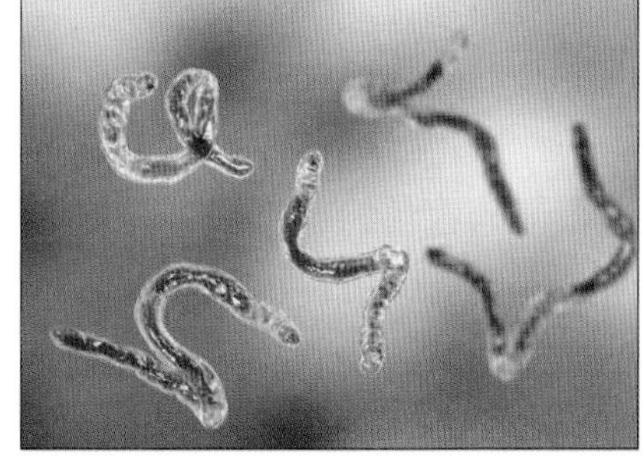

▲ *Hookworms feed on the blood and tissue fluid of their host. They are often less aggressive in cats than dogs.*

◄ *Changes in faecal matter and a general lack of condition may be an indication of worm infestation.*

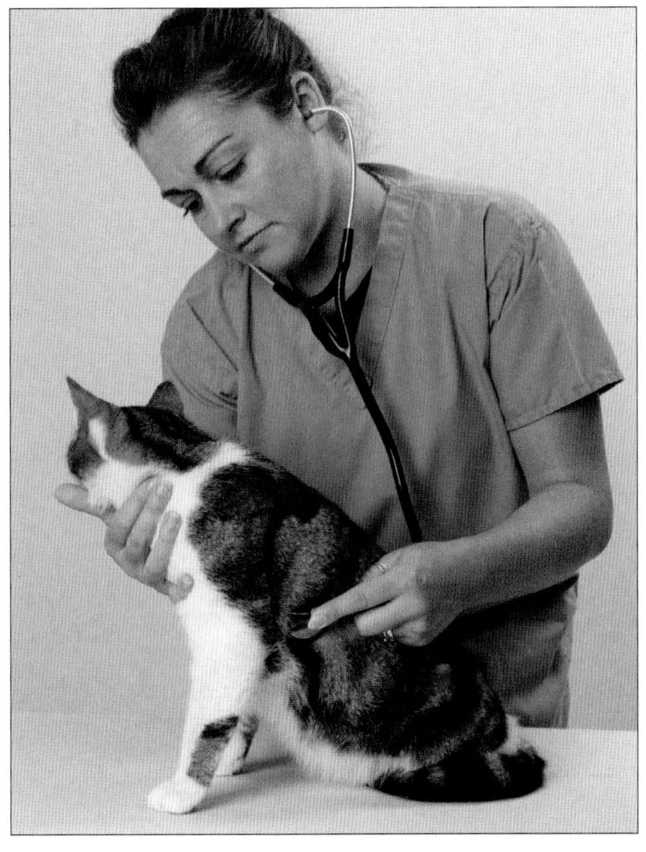

▲ *Vets may use x-rays and ultrasound, along with blood tests, to determine if a cat has heartworm disease.*

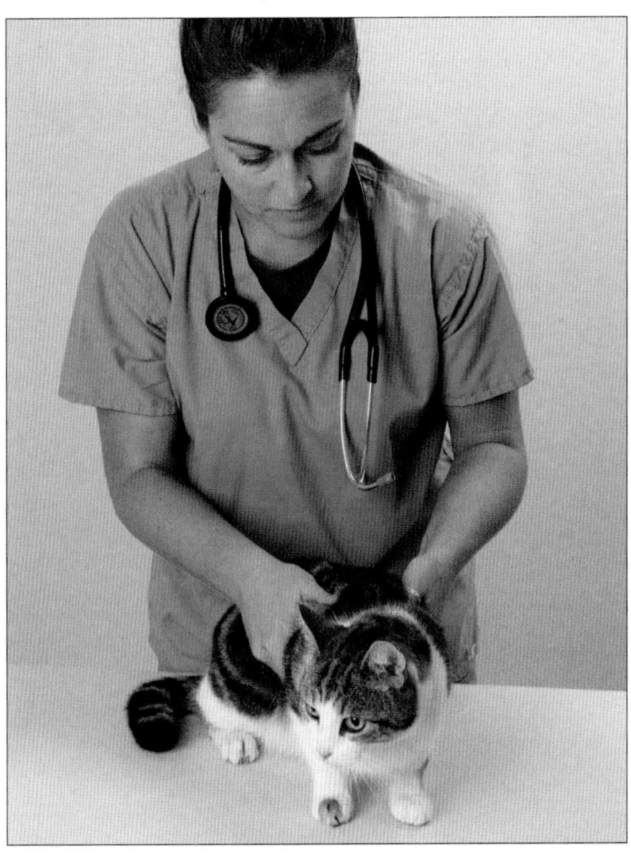

▲ *Due to the small size of their body, a cat with just a few heartworms would be considered heavily infested.*

HEARTWORMS

Heartworm infestation is found in tropical and temperate parts of the world such as South America, Japan, Australia and Southern Europe, as well as all of the USA. Once considered a canine problem, it is now known to affect a greater percentage of cats than previously thought. Wolves, domestic dogs, foxes and coyote are hosts for heartworms, as well as cats and ferrets. The disease is transmitted by mosquito: it is not possible for one animal to infect another directly. Adult heartworms living in a host produce baby worms, (microfilaria) that circulate in the blood. When a mosquito bites a host, they suck up infected blood. The microfilaria matures inside the mosquito, taking 10–14 days to develop into larvae. Then when the mosquito bites another suitable host the larvae are deposited under the skin. It takes up to 6 months to grow to an adult worm that lives in the heart, lungs or associated blood vessels.

Heartworms are creamy white in colour and look rather like spaghetti. They can grow up to 30cm (12in) long. Heartworms living in a cat have a life expectancy of 2–3 years; in a dog this increases to 5–7 years.

Signs of heartworm disease vary from understated to dramatic. Coughing, vomiting, fainting, asthma-like attacks, lack of appetite or weight loss are all indicators but equally could be symptoms of a variety of other clinical problems. Occasionally an apparently healthy cat will just drop dead. Diagnosis is difficult. Indoor cats are not immune from this parasite. At the time of writing there is no viable treatment for heartworm in cats. The de-wormers produced to combat this issue in dogs cannot be used on cats due to significant side effects. There is, however, effective preventative treatment in the form of regular administration of tablets or topical preparations.

◄ *It is hard to stop cats, especially feral ones, from drinking dirty and possibly contaminated water.*

PROTOZOA

Protozoa are microscopic, single-cell organisms. Some are parasites, while others can live on their own. They are not bacteria or fungi but belong to the protozoal kingdom. Toxoplasmosis is the most commonly known disease caused by a protozoan. Giardia infestation is caused by a protozoan of the Giardia species. It is acquired by cats drinking from infected water. The disease is characterized by a cat passing large volumes of foul-smelling, watery stools. This is often coupled with a sudden weight loss. *Giardiasis* responds well to the correct antibiotic and there is now a vaccination against this disease. Cats that have been infected do not gain an immunity and can become re-infected. Careful washing of water containers, preventing cats from drinking from streams and pools, plus thoroughly washing and cleaning indoor environments, will do much to lessen the chance of infection.

There are several types of *Coccidia protozoal.* Transmission is by cat to cat or cat to kitten via the mother's milk. *Coccidiosis* usually targets young kittens but is highly infectious, so adults can be infected too. Sick cats present with mucus-like faeces that may be stained with blood. In severe cases, symptoms include weakness, anaemia, bloody diarrhoea and dehydration. Standard treatment is a combination of antibiotics, a simple, bland diet and increased fluid intake. Hospitalization may be required. Recovered infected cats may become carriers.

Trichomoniasis causes recurrent, chronic diarrhoea that may contain blood and mucus. This disease is commonly, but not exclusively, seen in situations where cats are in close contact, such as catteries. Diagnosis is by faecal examination. Treatment with antibiotics is often unsuccessful. Most infected cats recover of their own accord but this can take many months.

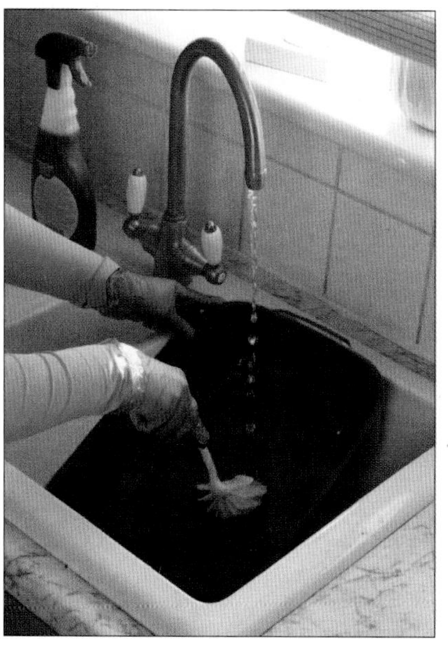

◄ *Good litter tray hygiene is essential to stop cross contamination of internal parasites.*

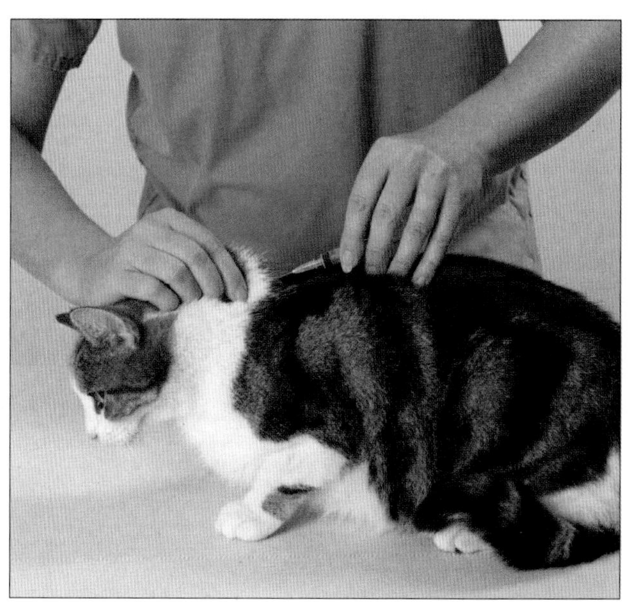

► *Some single-shot antibiotic injections are capable of working for up to 14 days.*

TOXOPLASMOSIS

Toxoplasmosis is caused by microscopic organisms called *Coccidia.* The organisms can infect humans, although symptoms of illness are rarely felt. If a pregnant woman is infected, however, the foetus may be affected, resulting in spontaneous abortion or brain damage to the baby. The disease may not even affect the cat in any recognizable form, although it may cause a chest infection in young cats. In older cats there may be gross loss of condition, digestive disorders and anaemia. Eye problems are not uncommon.

The immature egg of the parasite is passed in the cat's faeces, so that potential contact with any faecal matter when changing and cleaning litter trays must be countered by a rigid routine of hygiene. Oocysts passed by the cat with toxoplasmosis take at least 24 hours to become infective, so litter trays must be changed as soon as possible after use and rubber gloves should always be worn. Small children should be kept away from litter trays at all times. You should also frequently clear away the faeces of any neighbourhood cats that visit your garden and use it as a toileting area.

▼ *Keep an eye open for roving cats using your garden as a toileting area. Your animals may be free of diseases such as toxoplasmosis, but visitors may not be.*

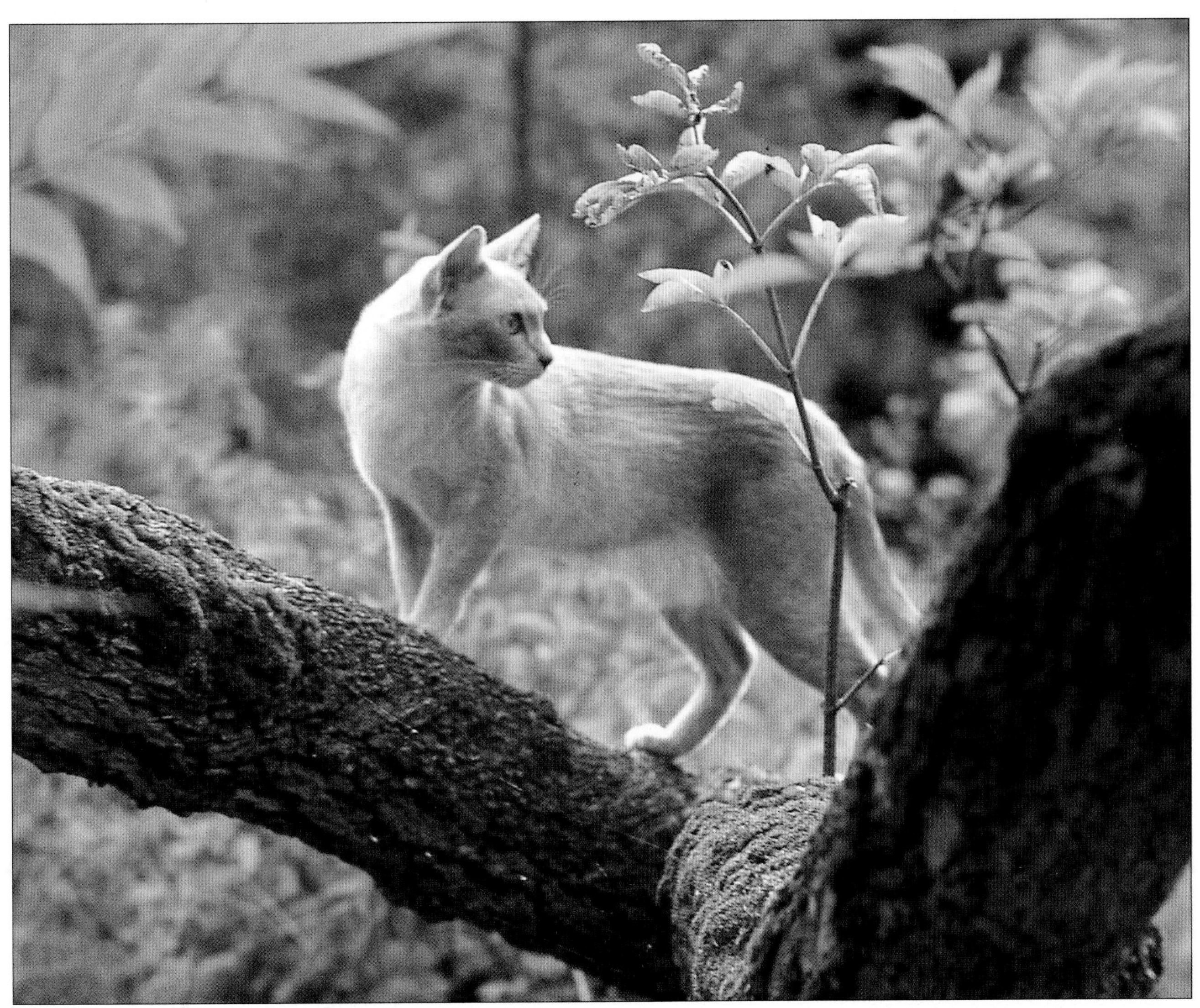

Common bodily ailments

As with all animals, medical issues can arise in different parts of the cat's body.

EYES

Conjunctivitis is relatively common in the cat and can vary from a relatively mild infection often called 'gum eye' by cat breeders to more serious conditions such as that caused by the chlamydia organism.

Gum eye is mostly seen in kittens just after their eyes have opened at about seven to ten days, up until the age of about three weeks. The eyes appear to be firmly glued together with a discharge and this may be due to a mild viral infection. Usually, the mother cat will wash the eyes open, but sometimes you will have to help her. To do this, bathe the kitten's eye(s) with a sterile pad soaked in cold water. Always work from the corner of the eye nearest the nose outwards. Should the gum eye persist over a couple of days, seek your vet's advice.

▼ *A Silver Tabby kitten's runny eyes and nose are probably symptoms of a viral infection.*

EARS

A blood blister called a haematoma can occur on the ear flap (pinna) due to excessive shaking and rubbing caused by irritation. Without skilled treatment, a deformed pinna will result in cauliflower ear.

NOSE

Nasal discharges are usually due to viral infections like cat flu and should be treated by the vet. Certain breeds of cat (Persians, in particular) have restricted nostrils, and the flattening, or foreshortening, of the face causes kinking of the tear duct. The cat will probably always have eye and nasal discharges that have to be constantly attended to by the owner.

Rarely, a cat may show an asthmatic condition, having become allergic to one or more of the thousands of substances it encounters each day. Again, your vet should be able to diagnose and may even pinpoint the allergen. Long-term treatment may be necessary.

CHEST AND LUNGS

Inflammation of the fine membrane that covers the lungs and inside of the chest cavity is called pleurisy. Cats may have fluid in their chests for a number of reasons, ranging from heart failure to injuries. Usually, the fluid is sterile, but it may become infected with certain bacteria, either blood-borne or from a bite or wound. Breathing becomes increasingly difficult, and any sudden exercise results in panting and a wide-eyed, very distressed appearance.

The condition needs urgent veterinary attention, and despite chest drains and antibiotic treatment, sadly many cats do not respond, and die of the condition, which is known as pyothorax.

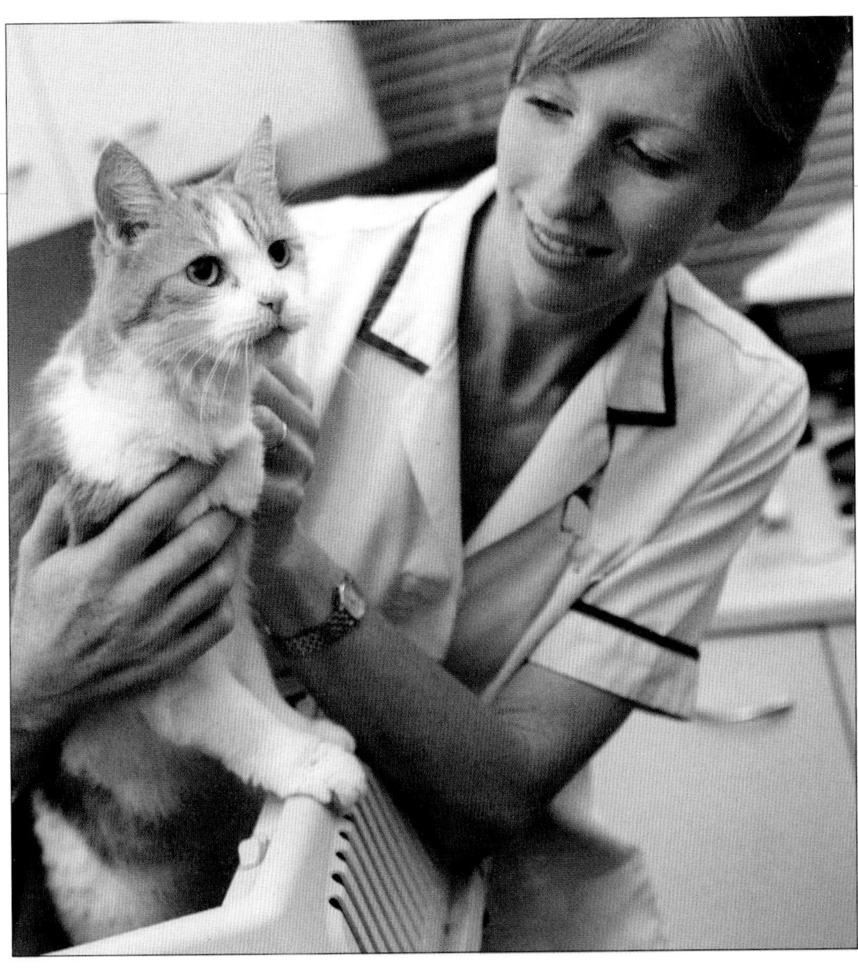

SKIN

Cats can sometimes develop a type of acne, in which blackheads appear on the chin. These are caused by excessive production and secretion of sebum, which lubricates the hair. The pores through which the sebum is released may become blocked. When it occurs on the top of the tail it is known as 'stud tail'. Both conditions should be treated with antibiotics and anti-inflammatory drugs. If your cat has a predisposition for these conditions, keep both areas scrupulously clean to prevent recurrence.

When dandruff strikes, even a shorthaired cat needs to be bathed and a conditioning agent used. If the scurf persists despite your best efforts, there may be something actually wrong with the skin itself.

▼ *Checking mouth, gums and teeth is a vital part of the annual check-up.*

▲ *Some skin problems can be diagnosed by the naked eye.*

▼ *The vet uses an ophthalmoscope to check the cat's eyes.*

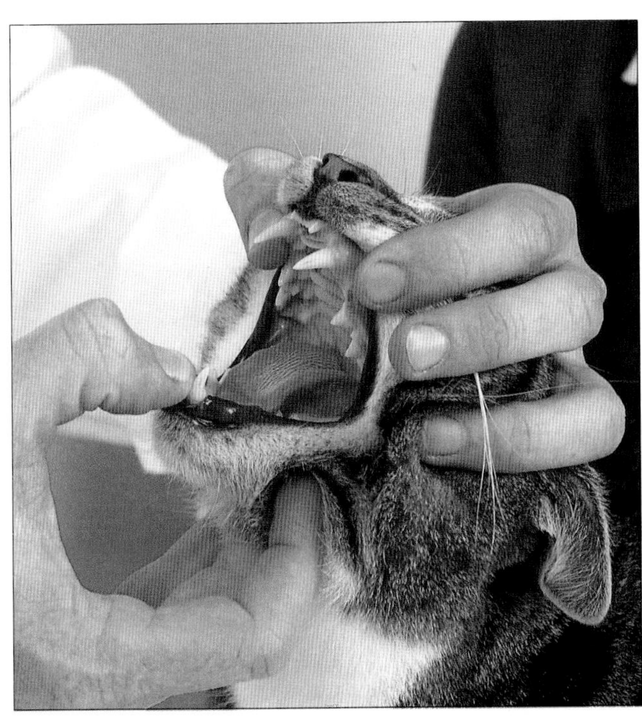

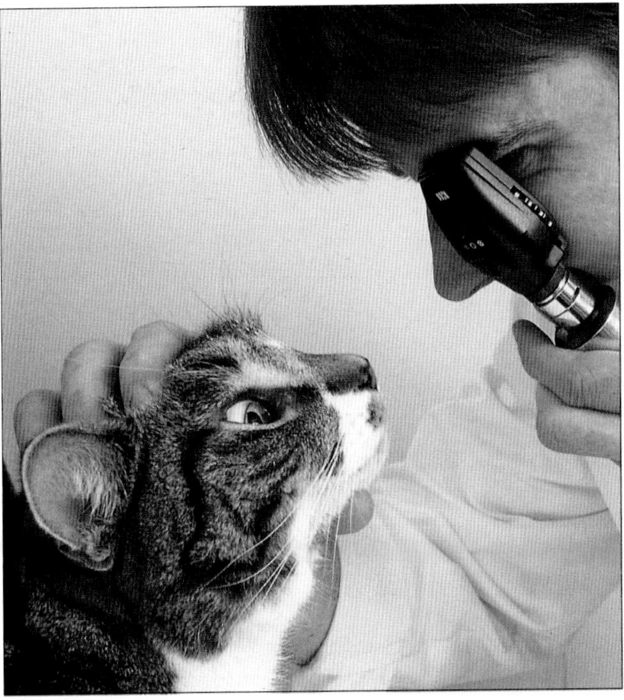

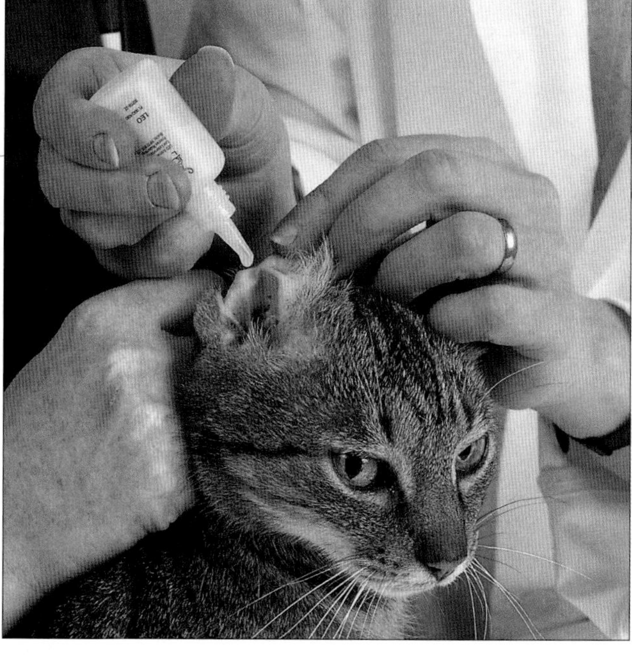

▶ *The vet administers ear drops to a cat with a sore ear. The ears are very delicate, so it is always preferable for the vet to check them initially if you think there is a problem.*

DIGESTIVE SYSTEM

Constipation and diarrhoea often occur during the life of any otherwise healthy cat. There are many reasons why a cat becomes constipated. Fur balls (hairballs) are a usual cause, but sometimes a diet with insufficient bulk or roughage (see the chapter *Nutrition and Feeding* pages 126–145) may be the problem. Introduce some bran or other cereal into the diet, or add a little liquid paraffin to the food. If the condition persists, take the cat to the vet. It may indicate a more serious condition, such as megacolon. If too much liquid paraffin is used, the cat will have diarrhoea.

There are feline preparations on the market, but home-made remedies are often just as effective. These involve a mild diet of bland food which does not upset the system. Try feeding the cat cooked white meat and white fish bulked out with simple boiled rice or pasta. Some cats adore natural yogurt. Another remedy is to sprinkle dehydrated potato granules on the food – it may seem unorthodox, but it usually works.

With both constipation and diarrhoea, the anal glands, which are situated on either side of the anal opening, may become blocked, infected and swell up. Clearing them out can be done at home, but it is not pleasant and does require some skill, so it is probably better left to a professional.

In addition to being uncomfortable, excessive diarrhoea or straining can cause a condition called anal prolapse. This can easily be recognized – a small section of the bowel protrudes through the anal opening. Do not do anything about this yourself; a vet must immediately put this back into its proper place, possibly with a stitch or two to secure it.

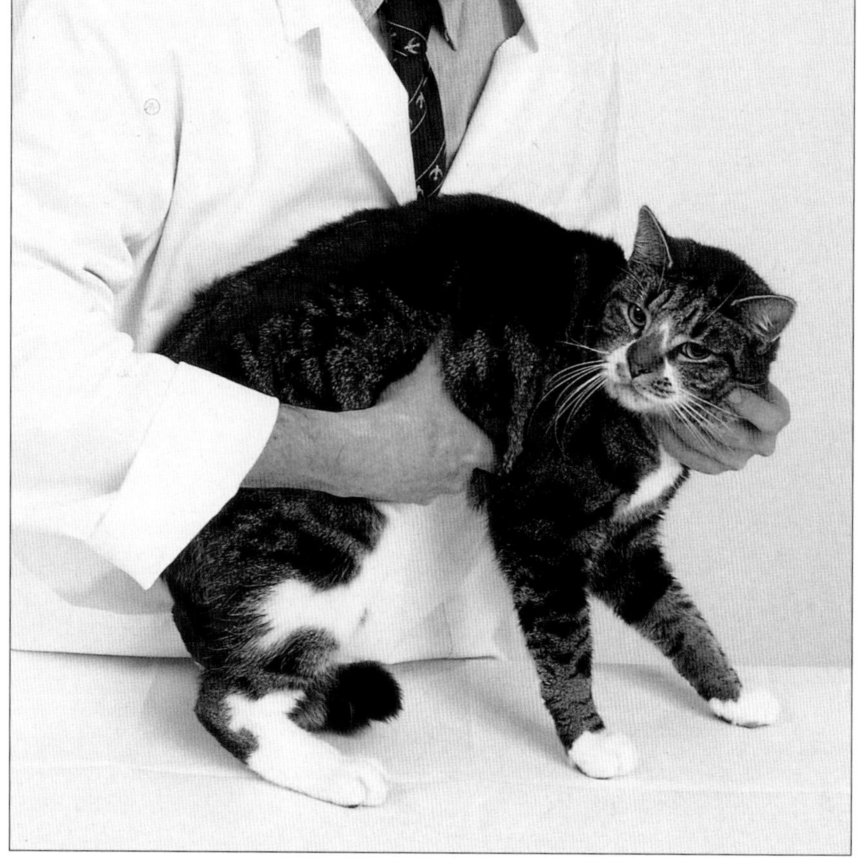

◀ *During a routine examination, the vet palpates the cat's abdomen to make sure that it is neither swollen nor tender, and also the glands around the neck and top of the legs to make sure they are not enlarged.*

Dehydration

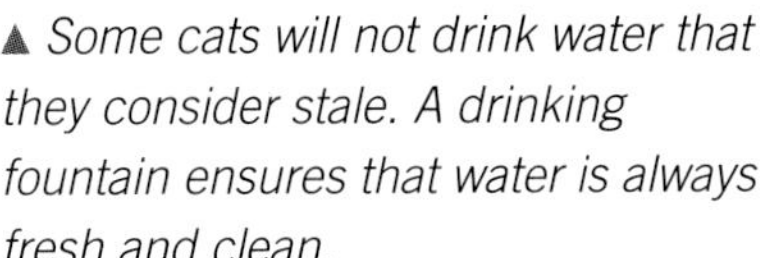

▲ *Some cats will not drink water that they consider stale. A drinking fountain ensures that water is always fresh and clean.*

Dehydration is often associated with serious bouts of diarrhoea but there are numerous other diseases that could contribute to this condition such as kidney disorders, cancer, diabetes, vomiting, fever, trauma and heatstroke. It is seldom a standalone problem unless the cat has been denied access to water or, for some reason, is reluctant to drink from its water bowl. Dehydration occurs in any situation when there is excessive loss of water from the cat's body. Lack of fluid also results in loss of electrolytes such as potassium, sodium and chloride, which are vital for normal body functions.

The classic way to check for dehydration is to gently pinch and pull up a fold of skin at the base of the neck above the shoulders. When the skin is released it should snap back into its normal position. If the skin remains in a 'tent' the cat is severely dehydrated and needs immediate veterinary attention. Other symptoms include elevated heart rate, sunken eyes, panting, listless, poor appetite and tacky or dry gums. In most cases, cats with severe dehydration will be hospitalized and given fluids intravenously. At the same time, the vet will conduct tests to find the underlying cause. Untreated dehydration is a serious concern and can result in organ failure and death.

At home, owners should ensure that there is always plenty of clean drinking water available. This should be changed daily. Many cats prefer drinking fountains to water in a bowl. Sensitive cats may be reluctant to drink from bowls if their whiskers touch the sides of the container. Fluid intake can be increased by adding the juice from a can of salmon or tuna to the water to make it tasty. A small amount of canned cat food mashed and added to the water will have the same effect. Adding ice cubes to water may encourage your cat to drink.

▼ *This image shows how to pull up the cat's skin into a tent to check for dehydration. See above for further information.*

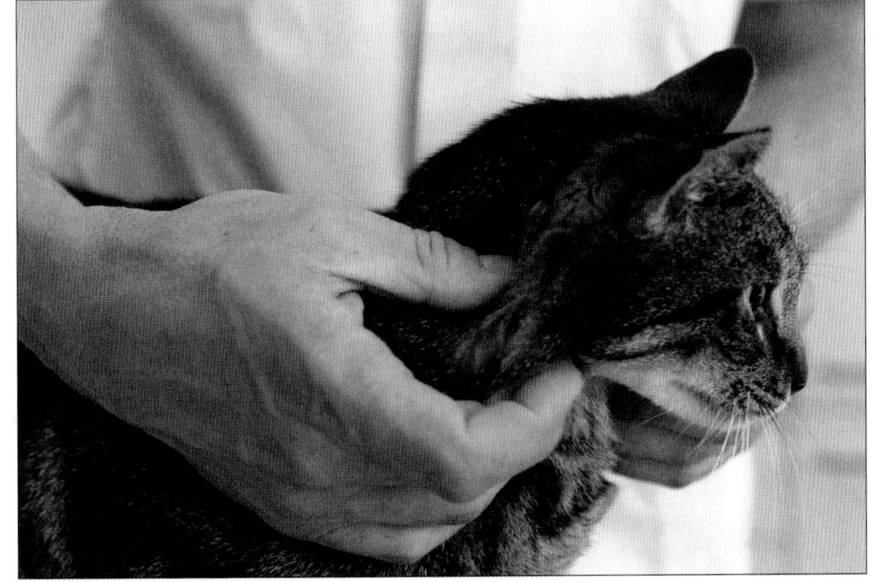

Dental problems

Cats suffer from a diverse range of dental diseases and these are a common reason for seeking veterinary advice and intervention. Dental disorders affect cats of any age but become more severe as the cat ages. It is a shocking fact that 85 per cent of all cats over the age of three years have some form of dental disease. Some cats, and breeds, are genetically more predisposed to developing dental problems as they age.

An accumulation of plaque and tartar causes periodontal disease. This condition is more commonly seen in older cats. Plaque is a film of bacteria that forms over the teeth. It presents as a soft cream, grey or white covering over each tooth. Brushing the cat's teeth daily will remove and prevent accumulation of plaque. If left undisturbed plaque hardens, over time, into tartar. This is clearly visible as a yellow or brown deposit in the tooth. Tartar can't be detached by brushing and needs to be removed by the vet descaling the teeth. This procedure is conducted under anaesthetic. Left untreated, the tartar will continue to build up. This causes inflammation and the ligaments supporting the tooth become diseased. Pus may develop in the infected area. At this stage tooth extraction and antibiotics are the only treatment.

▼ *From a tiny kitten get your cat used to having its teeth examined and brushed, don't wait until it is too late.*

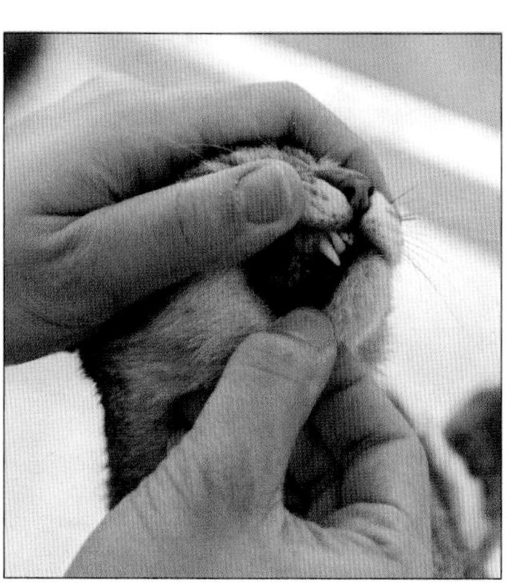

▼ *Visual inspection will reveal red, swollen or bleeding gums, discoloured or loose teeth and visible tartar.*

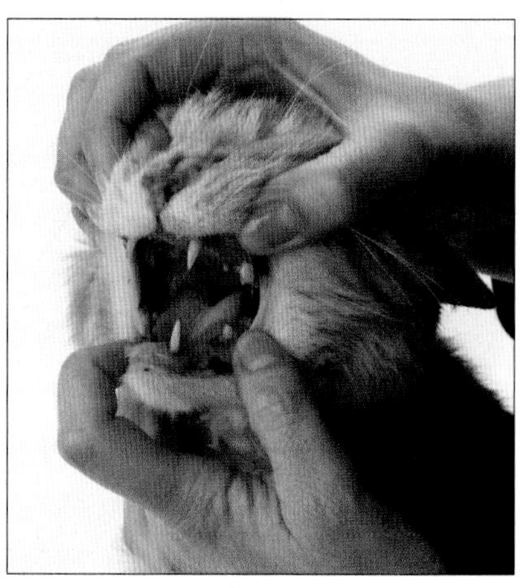

▲ *Prior to any dental treatment you will be given instructions on withholding your pet's food and water. It is vital these instructions are observed.*

GINGIVITIS

Gingivitis is inflammation of the gum, again caused by a build-up of plaque. In the early stage, this condition can be reversed by regular teeth brushing. Untreated, it escalates to a painful condition with similar symptoms to periodontal disease, although the tooth root is unaffected. Gingivitis affects cats of any age including kittens.

Incorrect tooth alignment is caused by congenital abnormalities, retention of 'baby teeth', trauma or over-crowding of the teeth in the mouth. Overcrowding is prevalent in some breeds including Chinchillas, Persians, other very short-nosed breeds, plus British and Exotic Shorthairs. This condition may make eating difficult and plaque will accumulate as teeth are not cleaned by the natural chewing action.

▲ *Bad breath, difficulty in eating, drooling and pawing at the mouth are indicators of a possible dental problem.*

STOMATITIS

Some cats suffer from inflammation of the inside of the mouth. This is called Stomatitis. The exact cause is unknown. One theory is that the cat's immune system reacts too violently to bacteria, or other infections, in the mouth. There is an association with cats that have had FCV or FIV infection but this is not clinically proven. This is an extremely painful condition where inflammation of the gums spreads to other areas of the mouth, particularly the back of the mouth in the glosso-palatine folds. Cats with stomatitis have difficulty in eating, poor appetite, may drool and paw at their mouth, and lose weight. Treatment includes scaling and cleaning teeth plus anti-inflammatory and antibiotic medication. In severe cases, tooth extraction and immunosuppressive drugs may be required, with variable results.

FELINE RESORPTIVE LESIONS

Feline resorptive lesions (FRL) are a very common feline dental problem. FRL is erosion of a tooth at the gum line. A small amount of gum grows out of the eroded tooth to fill the cavity. It is believed that 70 per cent of cats over the age of five have at least one FRL. This condition affects cats of any age. It is hard to identify and is diagnosed by x-ray or probing the teeth. If left unattended the crown of the tooth may snap off leaving the root behind. Affected teeth need to be removed.

The enamel on a cat's tooth is very thin, so fractures or chips to it may expose the dental pulp. This is a painful condition with the added risk of developing an infection. Signs of a tooth fracture are pawing at the mouth, salivation and eating in an odd or one-sided manner. Damaged teeth often have to be removed.

Regular brushing of teeth and feeding an abrasive diet such as crunchy cat biscuits can do much to prevent some of the common cat dental problems. Do not use human toothpaste; specially formulated cleaning pastes are available for cats. Feline mouth rinses are also available. Dental diets or treats containing abrasive and tartar-preventive ingredients can be bought from a range of outlets. It is a good idea to have your cat's teeth checked annually by the vet. This can be combined with yearly vaccination appointments.

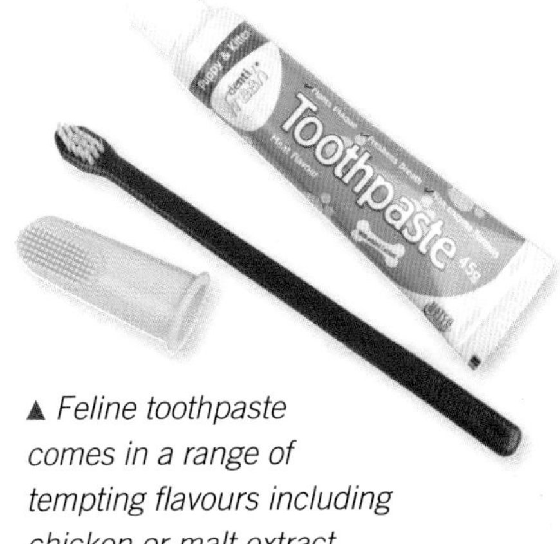

▲ *Feline toothpaste comes in a range of tempting flavours including chicken or malt extract.*

▼ *Initially get your cat used to the brush by just gently touching the teeth and then reward. Ideally clean your cat's teeth once a day.*

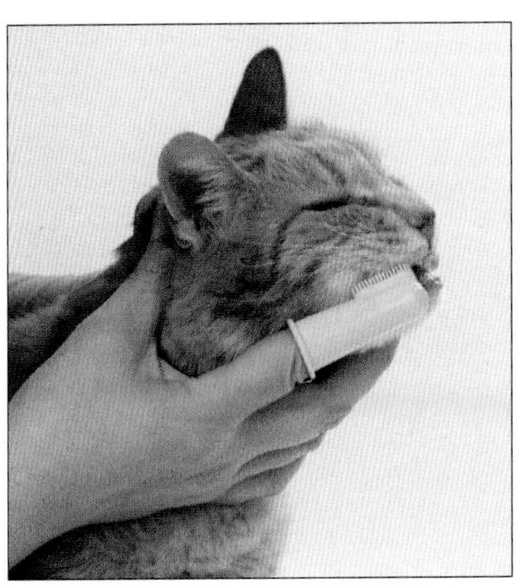

Cats and human health

Diseases that can be transmitted from animals to humans, or vice versa, are called zoonotic diseases. These diseases fall into two broad groups, parasitic (or bacterial) and viral. The risk of contracting a disease from a healthy pet cat is low providing sound hygiene principles are observed. This would include proper cleaning of your, and the cat's, living environment and establishing a good handwashing practice. Toxoplasmosis and rabies are the only two diseases that could have serious, or even fatal, consequences to a healthy human being. The former has already been covered on page 217.

Rabies is a viral infection that affects the brain. It can only be contracted if a rabid animal bites a human. Many countries are regarded as 'rabies free' but in others this disease is still common. All animal bites should be regarded as potentially serious, especially if the animal is unknown or was acting unusually at the time. Washing a wound and surrounding area with hot water and disinfectant as soon as possible after the incident will lessen the infection risk. It is vital that medical attention is immediately sought. Rabies still causes death in people if treatment is delayed. Rabies vaccinations are available to those that routinely come into contact with animals through their work, such as vets, animal wardens, zoo keepers and laboratory technicians.

◄ *Teach children to wash their hands after touching their pet. Never let children handle sick animals.*

Both campylobacter infection and salmonella are bacterial infections that can be passed from infected cats to humans via the cat's faeces. The human symptoms of diarrhoea, stomach cramps and fever are indications of either. Those suffering from campylobacter may also experience vomiting and dehydration, while salmonella sometimes causes acute headaches. Transmission of these diseases is preventable, providing rubber or latex gloves are worn when handling cat faeces and litter trays, trays are kept scrupulously clean and hands are carefully washed after handling your cat. Children

▼ *Dirty litter trays are smelly unpleasant places for both human and cat. Clean them often and well.*

▼ *Play sand pits must always be covered when not in use. To a cat it is just a giant litter tray.*

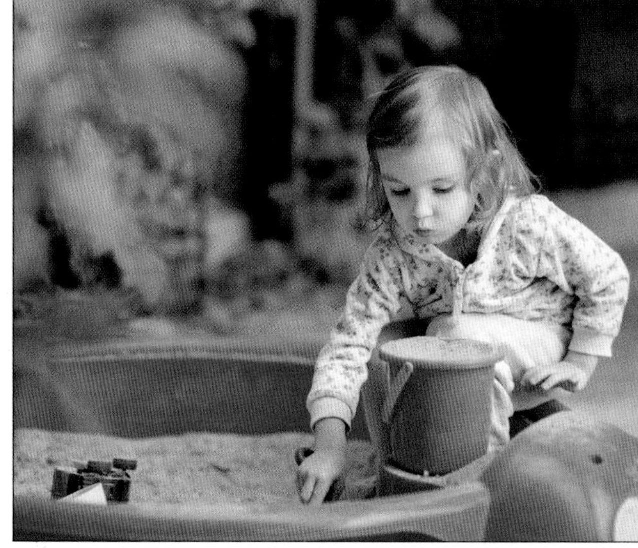

▶ *The health benefits for a senior citizen of cat ownership far outweigh any health risk.*

should be taught to stay away from cat litter trays and their play sandpits must be covered when not in use just in case a visiting cat thinks it is a large outdoor toilet.

Cat fleas will not live on humans but they are not averse to jumping from host to owner and having a quick snack. Bites are seen as clusters of red raised dots on the skin. Some people may develop an allergic reaction to the bite. Try not to scratch the area and treat the bite with an antiseptic lotion or cream. If they are causing intensive discomfort consult a pharmacist about using antihistamine tablets or cream. If your cat and home are regularly treated with a flea prevention treatment this problem will not occur.

Ringworm is a fungus infection that causes circular lesions beneath the skin. It was once, incorrectly, thought to be caused by a parasitic worm, hence the name. It is contracted via direct contact with an infected animal. Children are particularly susceptible. There are several types of ringworm fungus, but the common symptom is a scaly, itchy, raw and painful rash. It can develop anywhere on the body. Treatment involves the use of an antifungal preparation and keeping the infected area clean and dry. Cats showing signs of ringworm should receive immediate treatment and only handled while wearing gloves as the disease easily transmits to humans.

▼ *Flea bites generally, but not exclusively, appear on the feet, ankles and lower part of the legs.*

Humans can be infected by the roundworm (*Toxocara cati*) found in cats. This is a particular problem in developing countries where sanitation is poor. Transmission is by handling infected faeces or drinking water contaminated with cat faeces. Human symptoms vary and include fever, coughing, skin rashes, pneumonia and liver enlargement. Some people are able to rid themselves of this parasite without medical intervention while others require medication in the form of prescribed drugs. Prevention involves regular cat worming, washing and drinking clean water.

Bartonellosis or Cat Scratch Disease is an infection, caused by the bacteria *Bartonella henselae*, in the site of a cat scratch. Cats do not appear to be affected by the disease but in humans it affects the walls of blood vessels. A red, crusty blister forms around the site of the scratch and this may be followed by fever, headache, decreased appetite and enlarged lymph glands. If symptoms are severe medical attention should be sought as antibiotics will need to be prescribed.

▼ *Cat respiratory infections are not contagious to humans. It is unlikely that cats contract colds from humans.*

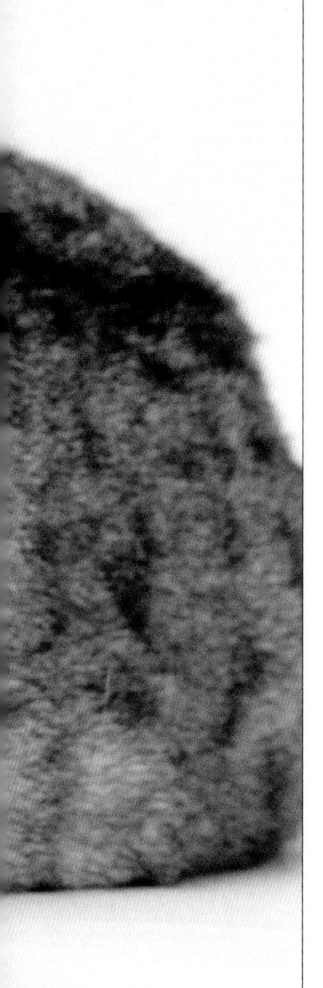

BREEDS, SHOWING AND BREEDING

There are over 120 different breeds of cat and the variety of coat colours, temperament and characteristics of these breeds is enormous. It is vitally important that all potentional purchasers contact responsible breeders to gain in-depth information prior to buying a cat. For the vast majority, having a cat as a companion that shows us love is all that is required, and cat shows are, quite frankly, not everybody's cup of tea. But for those that have the time and patience to train, socialize and prepare their cat to the exacting standard required this is an all-absorbing hobby. Other owners delight in the prospect of breeding a litter of kittens. Hours will be spent poring over pedigrees and studying other cats to come up with the best possible match. Then comes the endless days waiting for the big event. During this time there is much to consider and prepare to ensure the best possible welfare for cat and kittens.

◀ *In ancient Egyptian drawings the sun god Ra is depicted as a spotted tabby cat remarkably similar in colour and shape to this modern-day Egyptian Mau.*

Cat breeds and varieties

Cats have lived with humans throughout most of civilization, but it is only in the last hundred years or so that they have been specifically selected and mated to produce distinct breeds. Unlike dogs, which have evolved over thousands of years and have been bred for almost as long for hunting – with correspondingly wide differences in size, shape and character – domestic cat breeds cover a much narrower range of size and conformation, coat type and other characteristics.

Colourpointed Ragdoll Blue

Lilac Tortie Point Balinese

Chocolate Tabby Persian

Spotted Tabby Oriental Shorthair

WHAT IS A PEDIGREE?

For a cat to be described as a pedigree simply means that its parents have been known and traced back over several generations, and that a written record has been made of this ancestry. A Persian cat of immaculate Persian ancestry could be mated to an equally purebred Siamese. The resulting kittens would be pedigrees, but they would not be classified as a new Persian/Siamese breed until consistent and healthy litters had been produced for a number of generations (the actual number may be three or more, depending on the rules and standards of the registering body). Until breed status is attained, purebred cats can only be shown in an 'any other variety' category, if at all.

How the many breeds are classified varies with individual cat fancies, even those in the same country. Some of the cats featured in this book are considered to be different breeds in some countries, but as colour varieties of the same breed in others. Within the Persian or Siamese breeds are established colours or coat patterns that may have gained official recognition as breeds in their own right, such as the Black Persian or Seal Point Siamese, while the Silver-shaded Burmilla is simply a colour variety of the Burmilla breed. Some breeds or varieties have identical ancestry but have different names or classifications in Britain, continental Europe and the United States – the British Tabby Point Balinese is equivalent to the American Lynx Point Javanese, while the continental Europeans give the name Javanese to the British Angora! Others, such as the Tiffany/Tiffanie have similar names but are unrelated. Attention has been drawn to such anomalies where appropriate. If it all seems rather confusing, do not worry. More important is to look through the following pages to see the wonderful range of cats available. We highlight the essential features and characteristics of each breed or variety, so that you can find the one that appeals to you and that is compatible with your own lifestyle and personality.

Red Birman

Black Tortie Tabby Sphynx

Somali

THE FUR FACTOR

We tend to divide the cat types into Longhair (Persian), Semi-longhair and Shorthair groups, although for judging purposes, longhairs and semi-longhairs are often combined. Longhaired cats of Persian type are more demanding as far as grooming is concerned – their long, soft hair needs to be regularly combed and brushed by the owner. However, all the Persians are placid, dignified animals, very glamorous, and well-suited to a predominantly or wholly indoor life. Most of the shorthaired cats, on the other hand, need little or no help with grooming unless they are going to a show. They tend to be more active and playful by nature than the Persians, and need an owner and lifestyle to match. Semi-longhaired cats cover the middle ground between these two extremes, in that their coats need some attention, but not as much as the longhairs. Their personalities depend on their ancestry. Some are longhaired versions of shorthaired breeds, such as the Somali (a semi-longhaired Abyssinian), which has the energetic and playful characteristics of its Abyssinian parentage. Norwegian Forest and Maine Coon breeds have the cold-weather coats and outdoors personalities of their tough, working domestic ancestors.

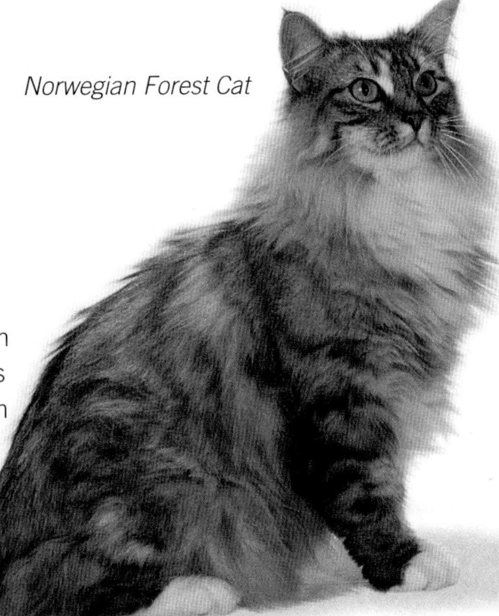

Norwegian Forest Cat

GENE POOL BENEFITS

The great advantage of having a pedigreed and recognized breed is that the outcome of a purebred mating is predictable. Although, depending on the make-up of the ancestral gene pool, there may be colour variations within a litter, the type will be consistent. If you decide to breed from your Maine Coon Cat, you will have Maine Coon kittens. The outcome of a domestic non-pedigreed mating is more of a lottery. The individual breeds and varieties are described according to the ideal standards of perfection set by the various cat fancies. Again, these vary from country to country. An American cat fancy, for example, may prefer a tortoiseshell to have well-defined patches of colour, whereas a European equivalent may like the colours to mingle. Such details are important if you wish to show your cat successfully, and to know what the ideal is may help you select a kitten from a litter. However, many a purebred cat falls short of the official view of perfection, but may still have much of the beauty, grace and temperament of its ancestral heritage.

The Longhaired group

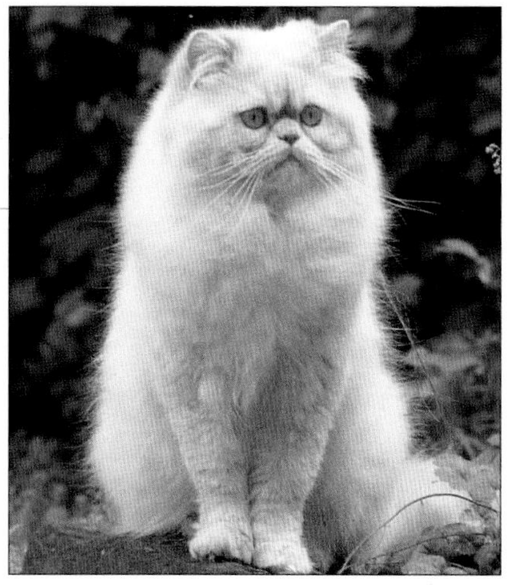

▲ *A Supreme Grand Champion displays all the glamour and distinctive features of the classic longhaired pedigree.*

The fur of longhair cats can be up to ten times longer than that of a shorthair cat. The Persian, and Persian type breeds, fall into this category the world over. There is a discrepancy between a few of the registries as to whether some other breeds are classified as longhaired or semi-longhaired. Not all cats that have the word 'Longhair' in their breed name are longhaired and may be, in fact, semi-longhaired.

Some of the 'longhaired' breeds were probably the result of mating early types of Angora cats from Ankara in Turkey with the original Persian cats from what is now Iran. The longhaired coat has an underlying layer of soft hairs topped by longer, coarser guard hairs. The underlayer provides insolation while the guard hairs offer protection. Cats with long, soft and silky hair are very popular as pets as they are very strokeable and beautiful to look at. Statistics prove that the Persian is the most popular pedigree cat breed overall.

THE MOULT FACTOR

Undoubtedly, longhaired cats are very glamorous but potential owners should be aware that they tend to moult all year round, leaving fur on carpets and furniture. So, this may not be the best choice for the extremely houseproud. Although many longhairs are fastidious about their grooming, they may need extra help from their owners on a daily basis, even if they are not going to be entered for shows. Longhaired cats are more likely to suffer from fur balls or hairballs than their shorthaired cousins. This is unpleasant and messy in the home and can cause a potentially serious obstruction in the cat's digestive tract that may require surgical removal. Therefore, it is important to groom out loose hair. Extensive daily grooming can be difficult for people who suffer from arthritis in the hands or other manual dexterity problems. It is also a time-consuming practice and both these points should be considered when choosing the right breed for you.

A contented, well-cared for longhaired cat, however, will bring a glamorous and dignified feline presence into your life.

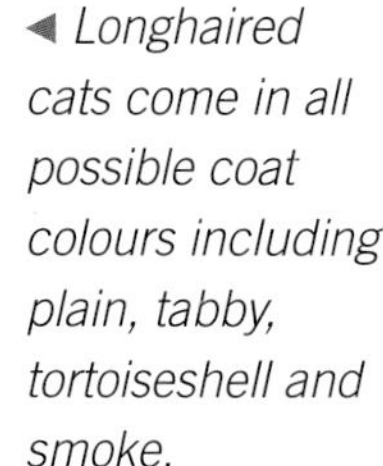

◄ *Longhaired cats come in all possible coat colours including plain, tabby, tortoiseshell and smoke.*

▼ *Longhaired cats acquire their full glorious coat between 9–12 months of age.*

The Semi-longhaired group

The coat of the cats in the Semi-Longhaired group is often as long, in places, as those in the Longhaired group but tends, in most cases, not to be as full or dense. In each semi-longhaired breed, the coat seems to have a distinctive pattern of growth that is like no other. Coats can be rather shorter over the main part of the body but there is a drift of fur on the flanks and 'breeches' on the back legs. This growth pattern is clearly seen in the Maine Coon, for example, where there are the common features of lynx-like ear tufts, inner ear furnishings, and a chest ruff that can reach right down between the front legs. Paws often show tufts between the toes under the paws, and tails are long and plume-like.

Some cats in this group have the word 'Longhair' in their breed name, such as the British Longhair, which in fact is classified as having a semi-longhaired coat. This can cause some confusion with the novice potential cat owner.

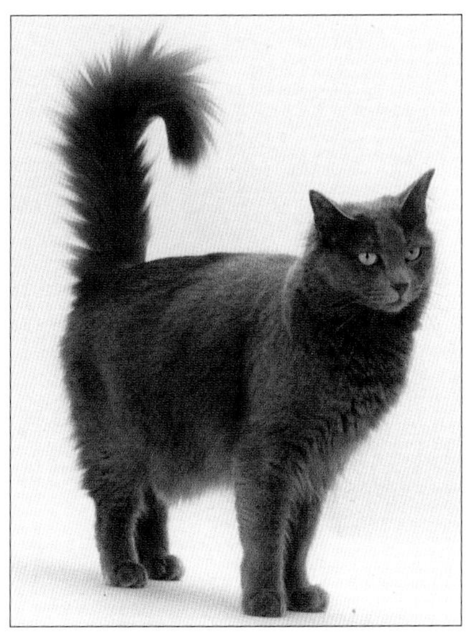

▲ *The Nebelung has a long, shimmering blue coat and is similar in type to the shortcoated Russian Blue.*

◄ *A Turkish Van cat lacks a woolly undercoat but has tufted paws and a full and luxurious tail.*

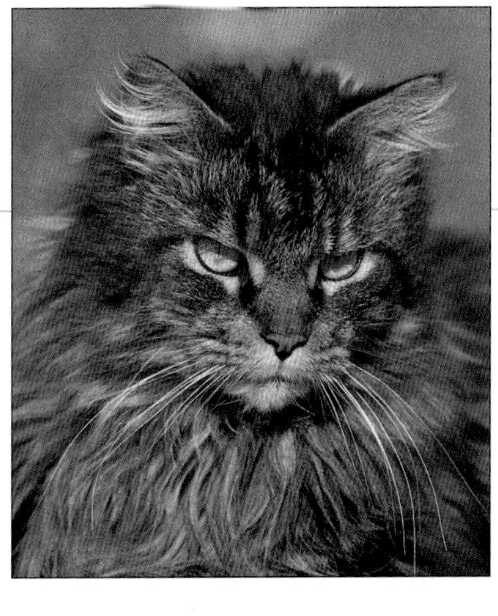

▲ *Some of the semi-longhair breeds have developed coats that provide protection against hard winters; the Maine Coon Cat is one.*

A DIVERSE GROUP

The semi-longhaired group contains some of the largest of the cat breeds. Some semi-longhaired breeds, such as the Norwegian Forest Cat, are of natural ancestral type, while others, such as the Ragdoll and the Somali, are 'manufactured' breeds. Many of these breeds are very active and may not be as placid as the longhaired Persians and Persian types. Regardless, they will still need assistance in keeping their coats neat, tidy and tangle-free. This requires a commitment from the owner to provide time for regular grooming sessions. This can be relaxing and soothing for owner and cat alike. Grooming should start from an early age so that the cat accepts it as a pleasurable experience. As with longhaired cats, this group will shed its coat, leaving a covering of fur on furniture and clothing, thus increasing the amount of sweeping and vacuuming required to keep the house spick and span.

This group contains some very diverse breeds including the stunning Birman, the green-eyed Nebelung and the water-loving Turkish Van. There truly is a breed to appeal to every cat lover.

► *This is a 'mitted' Ragdoll due to the additional white markings on the soft and silky colourpoint coat.*

The Shorthaired group

Most cats, whether pedigree or non-pedigree, are shorthaired like their wild ancestors. Shorthair is not only more practical for a wild hunting cat, but also for the domestic cat and its owner. Domestic shorthairs tend to be more independent and agile than the long or semi-longhairs, and their body shape can be appreciated. Shorthaired pedigree cats have been bred into perfect examples of their type from indigenous domestic types. They fall into two main groups – the sturdy, round-faced American, British and European shorthairs and the long limbed, lean-featured cats of Asia.

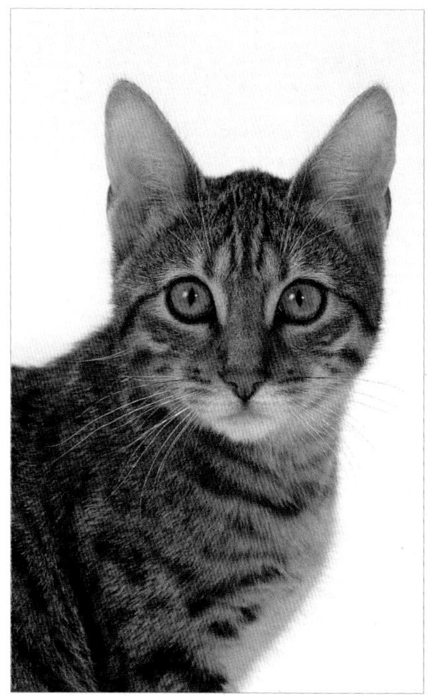

▲ *The Bengal breed was created by crossing selected domestic cats with the Asian Leopard cat.*

▲ *A sleek Oriental Shorthair with an easy-care coat will only need extra grooming if being prepared for a show.*

COAT CARE AND CONDITION

It is a fallacy to say that shorthairs do not shed, they do, but in not such an obvious manner as their longer-coated cousins. They need little or no grooming and, in the main, are able to keep their coats in tip top condition. Some breeds benefit from rubbing over with a silk or velvet cloth, chamois or smoothing with the hand to increase coat gloss or sheen. Shorthaired cats rarely, if ever, with the exception of some show cats, need bathing and even if they do, this is an easier exercise than battling with a long coat. Another advantage of having a shorthaired cat is that wounds are easier to see and treat. There is also less chance of getting fur balls, although these can still occur.

◀ *These beautiful Ocicats were carefully bred to have shorthaired coats that resemble a leopard.*

There are many more shorthaired breeds than longhaired or semi-longhaired, resulting in a greater choice. Short-coated cats come in an amazing range of shapes, sizes and personalities. There is a huge variety of colours and coat patterns, including some of those newer breeds bred to resemble wild cats, such as the Ocicat. No cat is truly hairless, so even the Sphynx, with its short and almost invisible down, falls into this category. Some of the more vocal, elegant and most intelligent cats are found in this group. Many are highly trainable, while some can be quite demanding of human attention. So, if you are looking for a charming, interactive feline companion, without the time constraints of constant grooming, this is the group of cats to choose from.

Hybrids and Mutations

A hybrid cat is one that is a cross between two, or more, other cat breeds. This can happen either 'naturally', where a feral, or domestic cat, breeds with a wild cat, or 'manmade' when humans choose to mate breeds to each other. The latter normally occurs when breeders specifically desire, or wish to improve, a particular trait in a cat. Hybrid cat breeding can be very complex but basically there are three categories: a domestic cat crossed with another breed of domestic cat, a domestic cat crossed with a wild cat, or a wild cat that is crossed with another species of wild cat.

Domestic cat to domestic cat hybrid mixes are readily available, easy to care for and make ideal pets. They could be the result of an accidental mating or the cross may have been carefully planned. Intentional hybrid breeding forms the basis of many well-known and loved breeds, such as the Tonkinese, Havana Brown and Oriental Shorthair Cat. The Bengal, Chausie and Savannah cats are all examples of breeds that have a cross between domestic and wild cats, at some point, in their formation. Normally the mix with a wild cat occurs many generations back in the evolution of the breed, although this is not always the case. Some cat registries do not recognize certain cats of hybrid origin, while others do.

▲ *So-called hairless cats are a natural mutation, but the Sphynx cat was developed through selective breeding.*

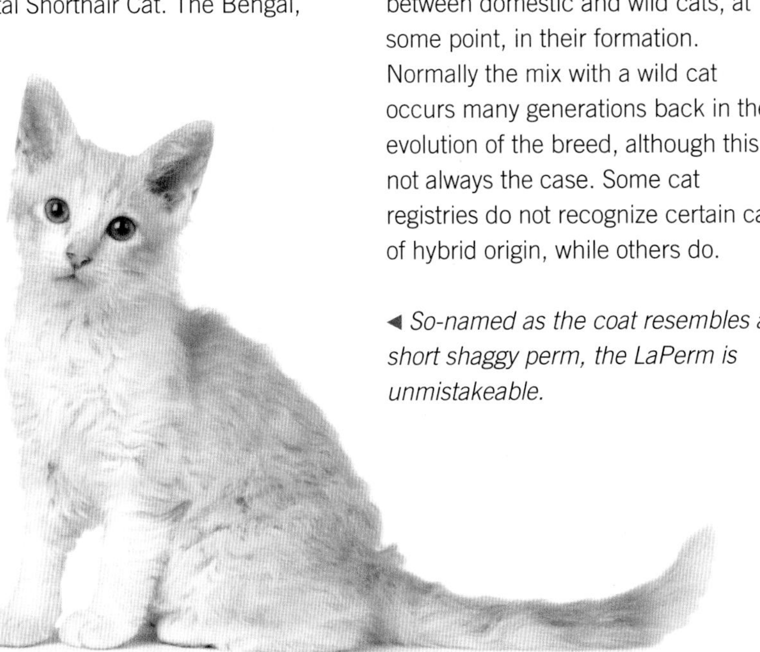

◄ *So-named as the coat resembles a short shaggy perm, the LaPerm is unmistakeable.*

Mutations in cats often occur spontaneously and are the result of a mix of recessive genes. They can alter the anatomy of the cat significantly. The most common mutations in the feline world affect either the tail, legs, feet, coat or ears. Breeders of cats with these traits must consider if they affect the wellbeing of the cat, or cause no disadvantage. Some mutations present lethal problems for the cats and their offspring, while others appear to have no ongoing effect. Not all registries recognize mutated cat breeds, and some organizations work hard to actively ban the breeding of cats with mutations that cause health problems. Careful research, and a chat with your vet, is recommended if considering a cat from this group.

▲ *The Scottish Fold breed has a naturally dominant-gene mutation that affects cartilage throughout the body. This causes the ears to 'fold', giving the cat what is often described as an 'owl-like' appearance.*

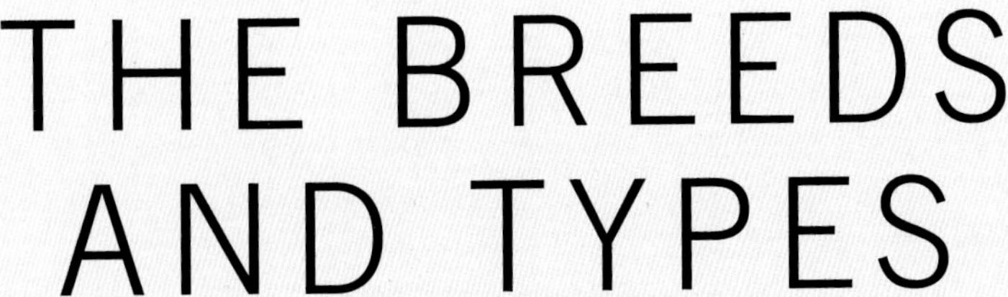

THE BREEDS AND TYPES

All breeds and types of cats can be traced back to one common ancestor, a wild cat from the Felidae family. Initially conformation and coat evolved to suit the area and conditions that each group of cats lived in. All cats evolved to be predatory hunters regardless of where they are from. Archaeological discoveries show that the majority of early domestic cats had striped or spotted coats similar to that of a wild cat. This was important as it had some camouflage properties and was an asset for hunting. Other colour varieties became more commonplace from the medieval times onwards as the cat started to be regarded as a pet and not just a rodent exterminator. Modern cat breeds originated from a desire to breed for specific physical characteristics. This has nothing to do with hunting ability, but for temperament, personality, colour and a form that is pleasing to the eye.

◄ *The beautiful Kurilian Bobtail is a gentle, intelligent cat that would fit into family life very well.*

Abyssinian

Today's pedigree Abyssinian looks like the sacred cats that are depicted in ancient Egyptian tomb paintings. The name comes from the country to the south-east of Egypt that is known as Ethiopia today. The modern Abyssinian is essentially a ticked tabby cat, with tabby markings reduced to a minimum by many years of selective breeding. Some theories suggest that the cat was introduced to the West by British soldiers returning from the region in the 1860s. Another claims the breed has its origins in the small African wild cat *Felis libyca*, an example of which was found in Abyssinia and presented to a Dutch natural history museum between 1833 and 1882. The breed was, in any event, established enough to be exhibited at the early cat shows of the 1800s.

Breed box

Coat: Short, close-lying, fine but not soft; distinctly ticked, resulting in at least four bands of colour – the roots of the fur are the colour of the base hair, and the final band is the ticking colour

Eyes: Wide set, large, expressive, slanting, almond-shaped; amber, hazel or green

Grooming: Easy

Temperament: Intelligent, inquisitive, very energetic, playful, loyal; freedom-loving and enjoy hunting

Hybridization with domestic cats displaying the ticked tabby pattern gradually diluted the exotic blood. A typical ticked tabby has prominent tabby markings on the head, chest, legs and tail, but in the modern Abyssinian, these have been diluted by breeding ticked tabby to ticked tabby. Residual tabby markings may occur around the eyes, as a dark line along the spine to the tip of the tail, or as faint broken necklets and leg bars.

The Abyssinian is a medium-sized, lithe and muscular cat with an arching, elegant neck. Large, cupped ears are set wide apart. The Wild Abyssinian attempts to recreate the look of the early Abyssinian cat when it first came to Europe, but is not yet a recognized breed with any reputable organization. It retains the reduced ticked tabby pattern but has a slightly larger conformation than the usual varieties.

▲ *The Fawn Abyssinian is one of the newer colours that has been developed in the United Kingdom.*

Usual (Ruddy)

The original, or Usual, Abyssinian equates to the brown tabby coat colours. The rich golden-brown base is ticked with black. The nose leather is brick-red and the paw pads are black. In America the colour is known as Ruddy, and is one of the four colours recognized there. The others are Red (the British Sorrel), Blue, and Fawn.

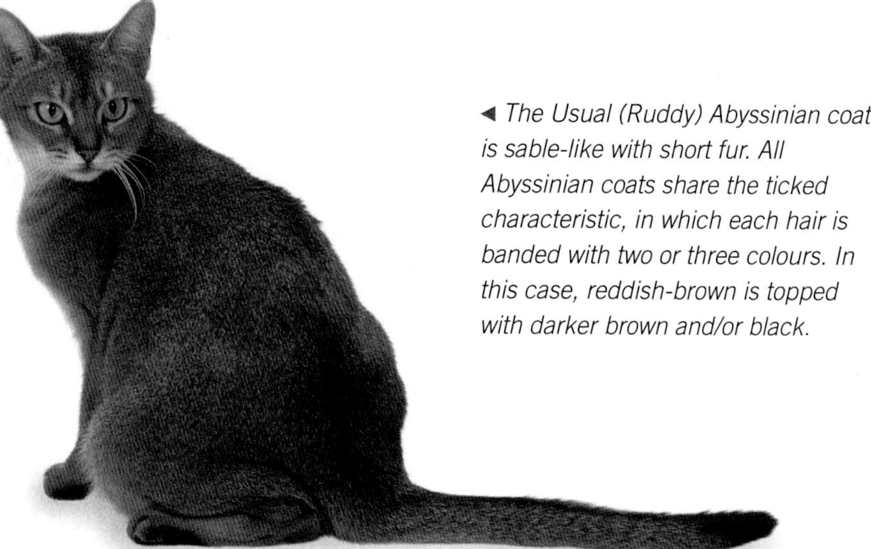

◄ *The Usual (Ruddy) Abyssinian coat is sable-like with short fur. All Abyssinian coats share the ticked characteristic, in which each hair is banded with two or three colours. In this case, reddish-brown is topped with darker brown and/or black.*

Sorrel (Red)

The Sorrel Abyssinian, which was the second colour to be recognized in the modern era, was originally known – and is still known in America – as the Red because of the warm, gingery colour of its coat. The bright apricot base coat is ticked with dark brown. Nose leather and paw pads are pink.

Abyssinian colours and patterns

Usual (Ruddy), Blue, Sorrel (Red), Fawn, Chocolate, Lilac, Red, Cream

Silver: in all above colour variations

Tortoiseshell: Usual, Blue, Fawn, Chocolate and Lilac, and Silver versions of these

◀ *The handsome, muscular physique of the Sorrel is typical of the breed. Abyssinians are lithe enough, but slightly bulkier than Oriental Shorthairs, and their heads are more rounded.*

Fawn

The Fawn Abyssinian is a fairly recent addition to the plain colour range. It has a pale-oatmeal base coat powdered with darker, warm brown ticking. The fur pales to cream at the tips of tail and ears, on the toe tufts and at the back of the paws. Nose leather and paw pads are pink.

▼ *The long bodyline balanced by a firm tail and the slender but powerful legs of this Fawn Abyssinian are typical of the breed as a whole.*

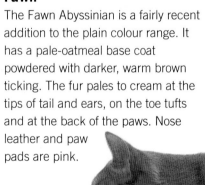

▶

▼ *The demeanour of this Blue, with its lynx-like ears and feral look to the eyes, lends credence to the possibility that Abyssinians may be the wild ancestors of the European domestic cat.*

Blue

Blue Abyssinian kittens occasionally occur in the litters of Usual-coloured parents. This is due to two recessive genes of the type that trigger the dilution pairing up and therefore being able to 'come out' or be expressed. The undercoat is pinkish-beige ticked with slate grey. Nose leather and paw pads are dark pink to mauve-blue.

Lilac

The undercoat of the Lilac variety is pinkish-cream ticked with a slightly deeper hue of soft pinkish-grey. The nose leather and paw pads are mauve-pink, and eyes, as with all Abyssinians, range from amber to hazel or green.

► *A Lilac kitten has a distinct break in the line of its nose, and has the expressive eyes and pricked ears desirable of the breed.*

Silver

The Silver Abyssinian is recognized as an official breed in the United Kingdom and Europe, but not in the United States. The colour variations are Sorrel, Blue, Chocolate, Lilac, Fawn, Red and Cream. All have pinkish to mauve nose leather and paw pads, apart from the Usual, which has a brick-red nose and black paw pads. All variations have a silver base coat ticked with the appropriate colour.

► *One way of judging whether this Silver's tail is long enough for the required pedigree standard is to estimate whether it would reach the cat's shoulders if laid along the back.*

Aegean

The Aegean is a breed that has evolved naturally. They are believed to originate from the Cycladic Islands of Greece, although there is a suggestion that they originally came from Cyprus and travelled to Greece on the boats of fishermen. Because the breed has developed through natural selection they are less likely than some other breeds to suffer from genetic diseases. These cats are a common sight, either as pets or feral, in their home country but not yet recognized by any of the major cat fancy organizations. They are the only native Greek breed. The breed is becoming popular in Northern America, but the majority have been brought back to the USA by holidaymakers visiting Greece.

Breed box
Coat: Semi-Longhaired
Eyes: Almond-shaped eyes either green, blue or yellow in colour
Other features: Lean and muscular; medium-sized
Grooming: Easy; weekly grooming
Temperament: Intelligent, active and communicative

▲ *With its lean and muscular body this cat is every inch the athlete and weights around 3.62kg (8lb).*

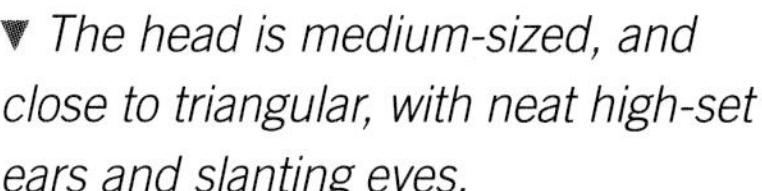

▼ *The head is medium-sized, and close to triangular, with neat high-set ears and slanting eyes.*

Aegean cats are medium in size and have thick tails. Paws are round. Ears are widely spaced with rounded tips and covered with hair. The coat is bi- or tri-coloured, either with or without tabby striping. White is the main colour and should cover from 25–90 per cent of the body. Other colours include red, fawn, blue and black.

This breed is very affectionate and sociable, making them good family pets. They are active, enjoy playing, good with children and are excellent hunters. The Aegean is a talkative cat and quickly learns to use this trait to its advantage when communicating with its owner. A very intelligent cat who is relatively easy to train and enjoys learning how to do tricks. Unusually they love water and are generally happy living on house boats.

◄ *The water-loving Aegean is skilled at fishing and is capable of catching its own supper.*

Alpine Lynx

The Alpine Lynx is an all-white cat that comes from America. This cat shares many similarities to a bobcat and was originally thought to have derived from a mating between a domestic cat and a wild bobcat. Modern DNA evidence disproves this theory and shows that it has completely domestic cat parentage. Due to their coat colouring one of the founding parents must have been a cat carrying the dominant white masking gene. This breed is recognized by the Rare and Exotic Feline Registry (REFR) but by none of the major national or international cat registries. Breeders are seeking recognition of the Alpine Lynx within these registries, but this has not yet occurred.

Alpine Lynx are medium to large in size and have longer hind legs than front legs. Toes are often tufted. The head is large with a square-shaped muzzle and well-defined whisker pads. Eyes may be odd-coloured. Ears can be straight or curled, but in all cases are tufted. The curl can be extreme with the tip touching the back of the ear. The gene for curled ears is dominate. It has a short or absent tail. The tail should not be longer than half way to the ground. The male is larger than the female. Coat length varies and the Alpine Lynx can be either short or longhaired.

This attractive cat has a following in the USA as a pet but is rarely seen in any other country. They are an intelligent and quick-witted breed.

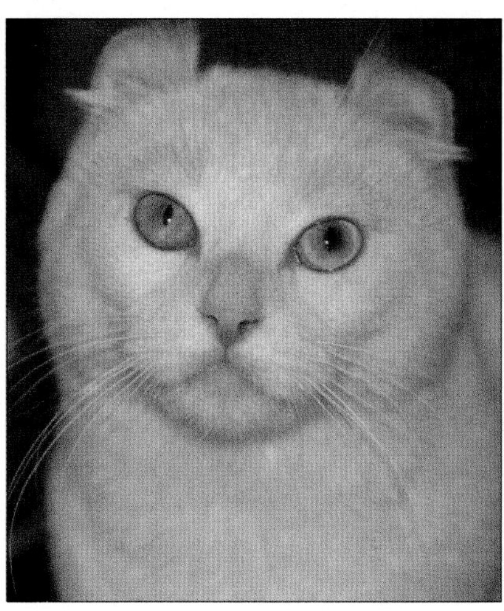

▲ *Heads are large with a well-developed almost square muzzle and very prominent whisker pads.*

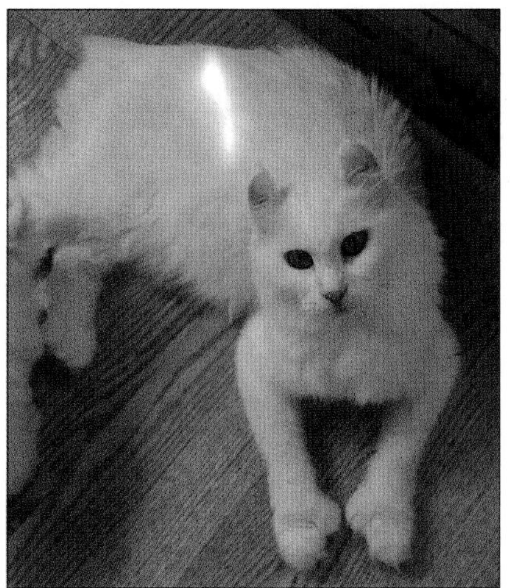

▲ *Ears are smaller than those of the Desert Lynx and are feathered around the edges.*

▼ *This is a powerful cat with well-developed muscles.*

Breed box

Coat: Can be either long or shorthaired

Eyes: Large blue, green or gold set wide apart; sometimes odd-coloured

Other features: Powerful and larger than many domestic cats

Grooming: Dependent on coat length

Temperament: Alert and intelligent

American Bobtail

◀ *A friendly and playful breed with a distinctive short tail as a result of a natural genetic mutation.*

Breed box
Coat: Medium-length double coat with hard outer hairs over a soft undercoat
Eyes: Large almond-shaped and any colour with heavy brows
Other features: This breed has a distinctive wildcat look
Grooming: Moderate, requiring a weekly thorough groom
Temperament: Loving, interactive and intelligent

The American Bobtail is a breed of domestic cat that was developed in the USA in the late 1960s. They have the look of a wild lynx or bobcat but have 100 per cent domesticated parentage, being originally derived from a cross between a short-tailed cat and a Siamese. This breed is rapidly growing in popularity worldwide. It is recognized by many of the international registries although some do not allow it to be shown.

This cat has a broad head with a well-defined muzzle and dramatic cheek bones. Eyes can be any colour and are occasionally odd-coloured. This is a powerful animal with wide shoulders and hips. The legs are strong, with plenty of bone and muscle. Hind legs are longer than the front legs. Feet are rounded and huge, with tufted hair between the toes. Tails are short; they should be at least 2.5cm (1in) long but 15cm (6in) is the preferred length. Any colour or pattern of coat is acceptable.

Often described as dog-like, this breed loves to carry things in its mouth. They are outgoing, affectionate and eager to please. An ideal breed for a family or first-time cat owner, they are vocal and use a range of clicks and chirps to communicate.

American Bobtails appear to have a sense of humour and often act in a clown-like manner. They seem to relish the company of other cats, dogs and children and love having their owners around. A truly delightful character.

▼ *The American Bobtail has a muscular body covered by a coat that is typically shaggy.*

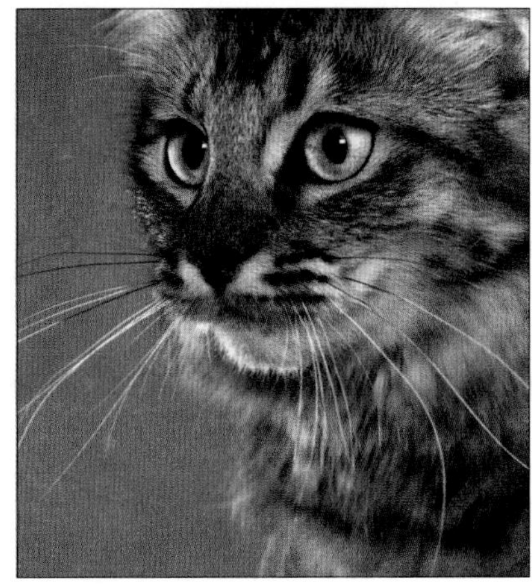

▼ *This breed has a distinctive broad wedge-shaped head and prominent whisker pads.*

American Curl

Early in the 1980s, a stray kitten with strange, backwardly reflexed ears, was discovered in California. Two curly-eared kittens were born to this stray, one shorthaired, the other longhaired. The breed – for this birth heralded the start of the American Curl's rise to fame and fortune – has therefore always had the two coat options. The two kittens were shown at a local show, and the response was electric. It is very rare for the big cat associations to take up a new breed so rapidly, but that is precisely what happened. The American Curl was granted recognition by The International Cat Association in 1985, followed by the Cat Fanciers' Association in 1986.

It is a winsomely charming cat with ears that curve backwards as though windswept, or the cat is listening very carefully to something just behind it.

▲ *Handle the ears of an American Curl very gently; rough handling can result in damage to the cartilage.*

The ears should be wide at the base and open. Otherwise, the breed is medium-sized, well-balanced and well-muscled. The legs are medium-length with round paws, and the tail is flexible and tapering, equal to body length. The American Curl comes in all colours, patterns and colour combinations.

No other anomalies or physical defects have occurred in the breed, and successful outcrossing to other breeds is continuing to ensure that a strong, healthy type is maintained. However, as yet, the breed is not recognized in the United Kingdom, being rejected on the same grounds as the Scottish Fold (see page 352).

► *This smart breed is affectionate and vocal and can live for up to 16 years of age.*

▼ *All American Curls descend from a female black cat called Shuylamith, who had backward-curled ears.*

Breed box

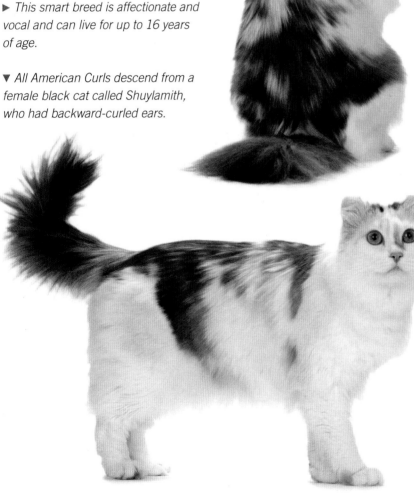

Coat: Long or short; both are silky, lying flat without plushiness

Eyes:Large, walnut-shaped; all colours

Other features: Ears curled back

Grooming: Relatively easy; regular brushing; check ears

Temperament: Eager to please; needs attention

American Polydactyl

Polydactylism is a genetic mutation that causes a cat to be born with extra toes on one or more feet. This gene is dominant so even if only one parent has extra toes, 50–60 per cent of kittens born will also have additional toes. Cats with this feature are commonly found on the East Coast side of North America. The American Polydactyl is bred for these extra toes as well as temperament, health, colour and size. Although many cat fancy clubs don't recognize the breed, it is now recognized by the Rare and Exotic Feline Registry (REFR) as a specific cat breed. This medium-to-large cat can have either a long or short coat in any colour or colour combination. They are broad-chested with strong, powerful bodies. Ears are set wide apart on a broad head with a square chin. Tails can be any length or absent. Cats born with bobtails often have longer hind legs than front legs, and shorter bodies than those with tails. This breed is also called the 'Hemingway Cat' as it was much loved by the eponymous author. After his death his house became a museum and home for his cats. It currently houses around fifty descendants of his cats.

The American Polydactyl is hardy and healthy. Generally, the extra toes don't cause any problems and they are known as good hunters. In times past they were considered lucky by sailors who thought the additional digits helped them to catch more mice. They are active and have a relaxed personality. Their outgoing and affectionate character make them an ideal family pet.

▲ *American Polydactyls can have up to seven toes on a foot with additional digits looking like thumbs.*

▼ *Relatively uncommon outside its country of origin, this cat can adapt to indoor or outdoor living.*

▲ *Polydactyls have, for centuries, been considered good luck charms and so are greatly prized.*

Breed box

Coat: Shorthaired or longhaired; coats are glossy and lay close to the body

Eyes: Round eyes are set at an angle and can be any colour

Other features: Medium-to-large cat characterized by its extra toes

Grooming: Moderate weekly grooming required to remove dead hair

Temperament: Very active and independent

American Shorthair

The American Shorthair should, like the British Shorthair, proudly show its ancestry as a working cat in its power-packed body. It is very similar in appearance to the British version, although the American is rather more lithe with a less rounded face and slightly larger body.

The first Domestic Shorthair (other than Siamese) to be registered as a pedigree cat in the United States was an imported British Shorthair, a Red Tabby. Her owner cross-mated her with a fine American cat, and registered the first Shorthair to be bred in America, a Smoke called Buster Brown, in 1904. It took another 60 years for the breed to become an established pedigree in its own right. The most important feature for a show-standard American Shorthair is its strength and the muscularity of its body.

The American Cat Fancier's Association recognizes most of the various solid, shaded, silver, smoke, tabby, parti-colour, bi-colour and van groupings. However, they are resistant to lilac and chocolate self colours and colourpointeds.

▼ *The Calico Cat is also found in a dilute blue and cream version.*

▲ *The coloured patches on an American Tortoiseshell should be scattered over its body, if for showing.*

American Calico

This is the classic Calico Cat of America, its pretty coat colour named after a popular printed cotton fabric. This cat shows the preferred predominance of white on the underparts. There are also dilute versions of the colour combination available, in which the white feet, legs, undersides, chest and muzzle are combined with even, unbroken patches of blue and cream.

American Tortoiseshell

An American Tortoiseshell Shorthair typically has a black coat patched with unbroken areas of red and cream. A show-standard cat is required to have well-defined patches distributed over its body. There are various shaded and tipped tortoiseshell varieties, too, as well as dilute versions. Eyes may be green or bright gold.

Breed box

Coat: Short, dense, even and firm in texture
Eyes: Large, round, wide-set and slightly slanted; brilliant gold, green; white varieties blue-, gold- or odd-eyed
Other features: Equable nature and sturdy build
Grooming: Easy; regular combing
Temperament: Bold, intelligent, inquisitive, active

American Shaded Silver

The American Shaded Silver, like the lighter-shaded Chinchilla, ideally has the same level of toning on its face and legs. A distinctive feature of the Shaded and Chinchilla varieties of Shorthair is the black outlining around the eyes and nose.

▼ *This Shaded Silver has the rounded head of the breed with well-developed cheeks, and a gently dipping nose.*

American Wirehair

The coat of the American Wirehair – which, as its name suggests, is its most distinguishing feature – is by no means fully rexed, but it is far more crimped, crinkled and bouncy than that of most cats. The origins of the breed go back to a barn in Upper New York State in 1966. A red and white curly-coated male occurred as a spontaneous mutation in an American Shorthair litter. By 1969, a pure-breeding colony had been established, and the breed was given official recognition by the Cat Fanciers' Association in 1978. The breed remains more or less exclusively in the United States, but there was a class for American Wirehairs at a Brussels show in 1996.

It is a medium-to-large cat with a round head, prominent cheekbones and a well-developed muzzle. It comes in all colours and patterns except the colourpointed (Himalayan) series.

▲ *Apart from its curly coat and whiskers, the American Wirehair is very much like its compatriot, the American Shorthair.*

▲ *Even the whiskers, eyebrows and ear fur are springy and wiry in this distinctive breed.*

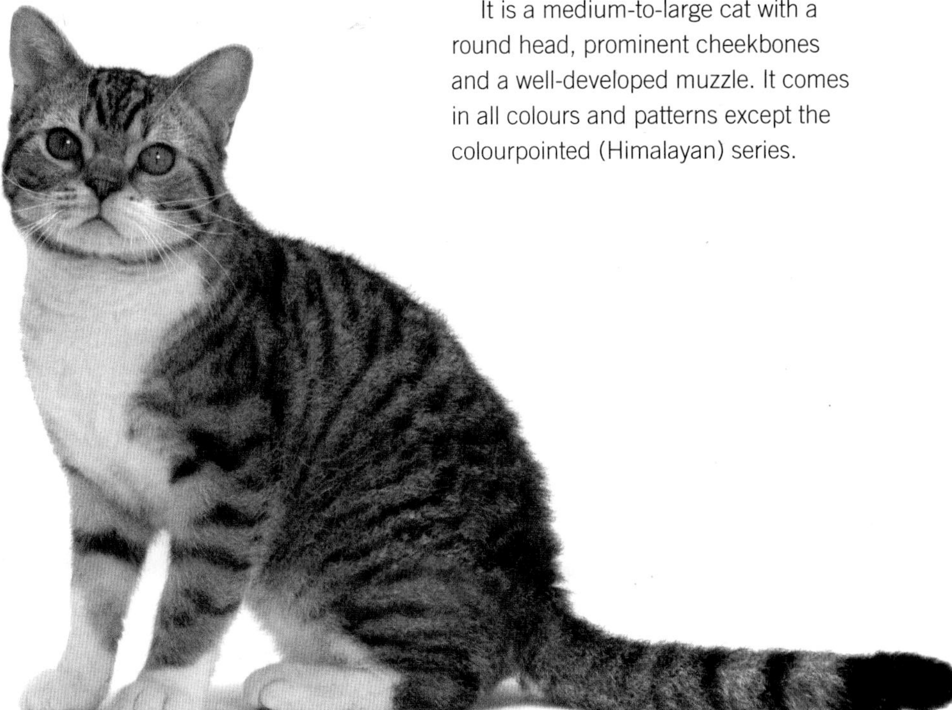

▼ *A cat that has a moderately sturdy build, with females generally being smaller than males.*

Breed box

Coat: Springy, tight, medium in length; individual hairs are crimped, hooked or bent

Eyes: Wide-set, large, round; all colours

Grooming: Minimal with an occasional soft brushing

Temperament: Very positive and inquisitive; they never seem to stop purring

Arabian Mau

This is a natural breed that is perfectly adapted to desert living. It is thought to have originated from the African Wildcat. Domestic cats of similar type to the Arabian Mau are known to have been in existence for over 1,000 years. They are very agile, fast, efficient hunters and can jump high. A breed that copes well with extremes of temperament.

Coats are short and can be red, black and white, brown and tabby, red and white, white or black. This breed is recognized by many cat registries but accepted coat colours vary. The Arabian Mau is medium-sized with a firm muscular body, long legs with oval paws. The tail is medium in length and tapers towards the tip. Eyes can be any colour but are often bright green. Ears are large and set high on the skull. The head appears to be round but is actually longer than broad. Whisker pads are well-defined.

Generally thought of as a quiet cat, the Mau has a high vocal range and sometimes uses its voice to be demanding. Males are often territorial and much larger than females. This cat is very clean and spends time keeping itself neat and tidy. Not necessarily a lap cat, nevertheless they are loyal and affectionate to their owners. They tend to get on well with other animals and are suitable for families with older children. This cat loves its food and is never picky. The Arabian Mau has been allowed to participate in international cat shows since 2009.

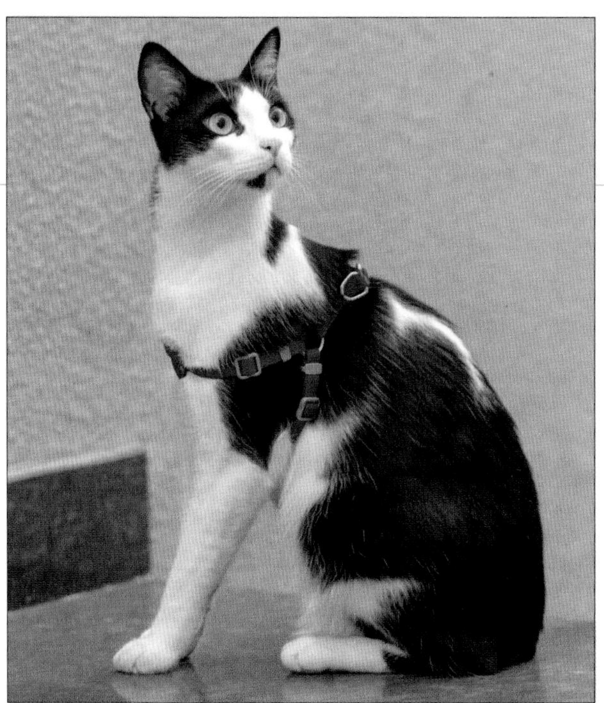

◄ *Robust boned legs are well-muscled and comparatively long. The paws are medium-sized and oval.*

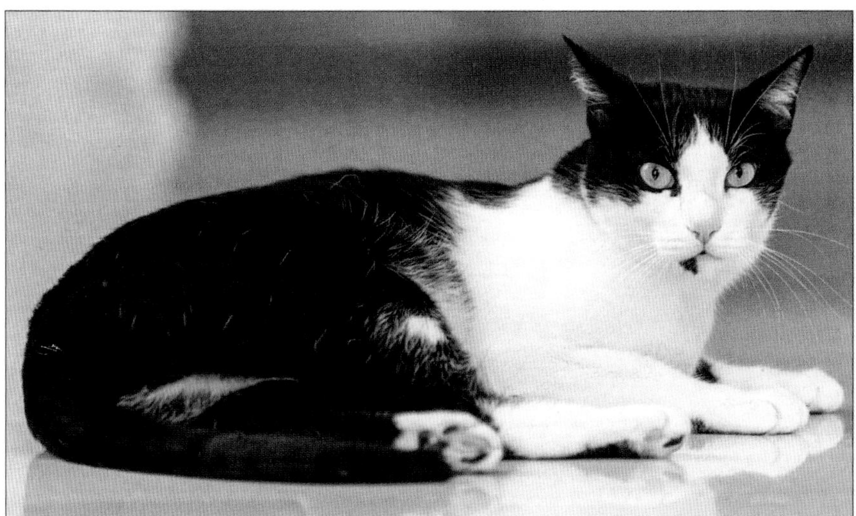

▼ *The Arabian Mau is a highly intelligent cat that requires mental stimulation and enjoys interactive puzzles.*

▼ *This cat does not shed coat or produce as much dander as some other shorthaired breeds.*

Breed box

Coat: Short, firm and glossy in a range of colours

Eyes: Large oval eyes are slightly slanting and can be any colour

Other features: A territorial breed who will patrol the home property

Grooming: Easy; brushing will intensify the gloss of the coat

Temperament: Loving and affectionate

Asian Semi-Longhair

The Asian Semi-Longhair is similar in type to the Asian Shorthair in all aspects, with the exception of its coat. This breed is also known as a Tiffany or Tiffanie. It was developed in the UK in the 1980s. Burmese and Burmillas featured strongly in the early breeding programme and the influence of the Burmilla is visible in this breed. The Asian Semi-Longhaired is recognized by The UK Governing Council of the Cat Fancy but not by any of the USA cat registries.

The head is rounded at the top, tapering slightly to butterfly-wing cheeks and a firm chin. Ears are set wide apart, angled slightly forward, and quite large in relation to the head. Ear tufts are common. The body should have a straight top line from shoulders to hindquarters. This is a medium-sized cat, with males being larger than somewhat dainty females.

Described as vocal, this is not the breed for someone who doesn't want a cat that will join in every conversation and use its voice to express its emotions. They are curious, at times demanding, and can be mischievous. This is a loving cat who becomes very attached to its owner and can be jealous of other cats. Strikingly elegant with its silky, luxurious coat, the Asian Semi-Longhair is a beautiful cat. They are happy to live in the home as they were bred as an indoor cat. Unfortunately, they can be prone to some health problems so regular vet health checks are advised.

▲ *Weighing between 3.6–7.3kg (8–16lb) the Asian Semi-Longair is heavier than it looks.*

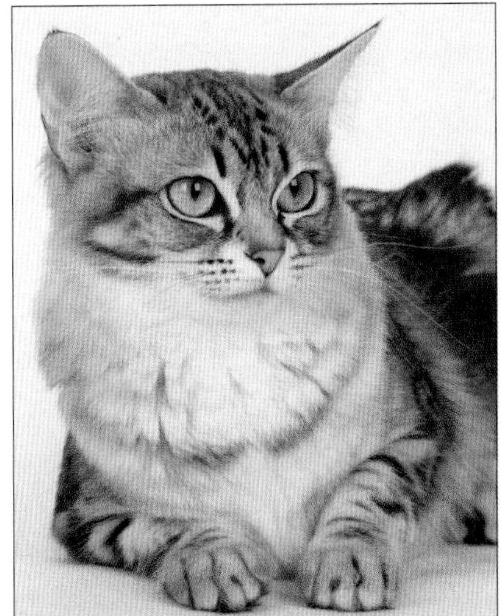

▼ *Ear tips are slightly rounded and ear tufts are a desirable feature. Its gold or green eyes are very attractive.*

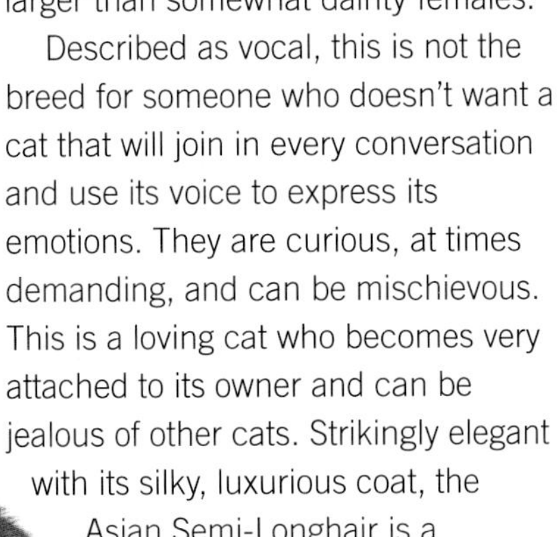

◄ *A stunningly beautiful cat with a luxurious, silky and shiny coat plus a delightful engaging nature.*

Breed box

Coat: All colours and patterns of an Asian Shorthair and Burmese permitted

Eyes: Large, wide-set and slanting gold or green eyes

Other features: Long tail with a woolly plume

Grooming: Needs regular grooming to remove dead hair and debris

Temperament: Playful and loving

Asian Shorthair

The Asian Shorthair is similar to the Burmese in type but not in coat colour or pattern. It is also referred to as the Malayan. The breed was created by Baroness Miranda von Kirchberg in 1981. They can be classified into four distinct groups: the Asian Tabby, the Asian Self, the Burmilla and the Asian Smoke.

Heads are rounded without any flat areas. The body is medium in size, straight-backed and should be compact and muscular with a round, broad chest. The legs are slender and paws oval. The straight tail is medium in length and carried with pride. Eyes and lips are outlined. Females are noticeably smaller than males. Coats come in a wide range of colours and patterns, including tabby, spotted, smoke, ticked and solid colours.

These cats love to explore and play. They will require plenty of toys within the home to keep them occupied during active times. Equally they are very loving and adore being pampered and sitting on laps. Although quite capable of keeping their coats immaculate, grooming sessions are usually greatly enjoyed, as they provide an opportunity to interact with their owners and be spoilt. Grooming has the added benefit of increasing the gloss of the close laying coat. Asian Shorthairs enjoy the company of people, and will even approach strangers for petting if they feel like it. They are best suited to owners who have time to spend with them and can give them the attention that they crave.

► *The body of an Asian Shorthair is elegant and slender with extraordinarily little excess fat.*

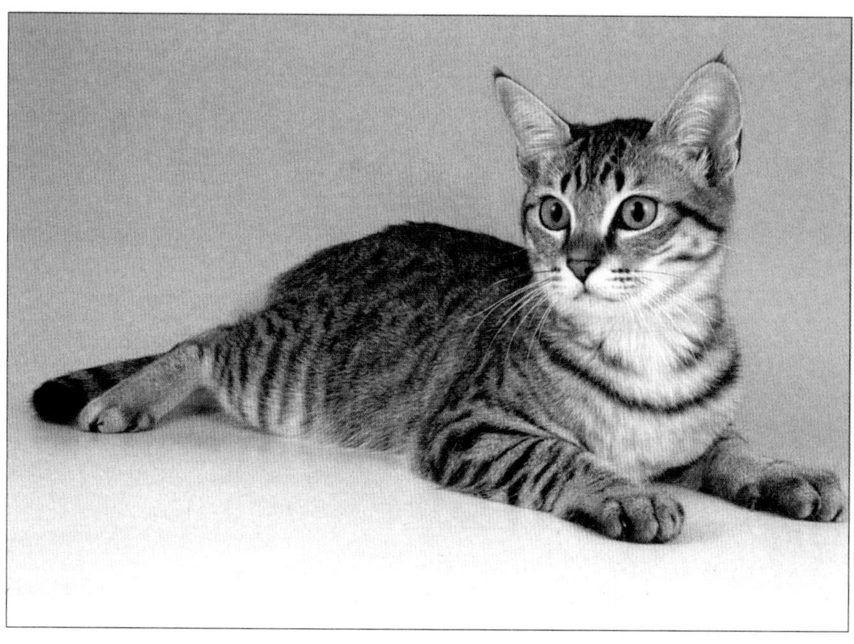

◄ *DNA tests are available for these cats and responsible breeders will only breed from tested parents.*

Breed box

Coat: Fine fur that is satin-like and very glossy

Eyes: Usually yellow in colour; green preferred in Silvers

Other features: Very vocal and will use their voice to gain attention

Grooming: Easy, requiring only the occasional brushing

Temperament: Devoted, strong-willed and inquisitive

Asian Smoke

► *A breed that moves with great elegance with rear legs that are slightly longer than the front ones.*

The Asian Smoke is, as the name suggests, the smoke variety of the Asian group. They were once known as Burmoires. They can be mistaken as an Asian Self, but close examination of the coat will show a silver-white or near-white undercoat. This forms up to half of the hair length in adults. Each hair is silver, while the tip is coloured. Mere suggestions of tabby markings may appear like watered silk on the body, while the head has what are sometimes known as clown marks. These appear as frown lines on the forehead and spectacled eyes.

The British Standard of Points states that members of the Asian group must not resemble a British Shorthair, a Persian or Siamese and that they must have good temperament. This is a healthy group of cats who do not appear to have any health problems specific to the breed. They are relatively long-lived with a life expectancy of 13–15 years.

The Asian Smoke, like all Asian breeds, is a highly intelligent cat that is affectionate and loves showing off. They are superb companions and are suitable for families and elderly alike. This breed adapts well to indoor living.

▲ *With an adaptable nature this cat is happy as an indoor or outdoor cat and will co-exist with other animals.*

Breed box

Coat: Short and plush with a sheen

Eyes: Yellow through to green depending on coat colour

Other features: Matures sexually at a young age

Grooming: Easy; rub with a chamois to produce a high gloss

Temperament: Extrovert and highly intelligent

Asian smoke colours and patterns

Black, Blue, Chocolate, Lilac, Red, Caramel, Apricot, Cream, Black Tortoiseshell, Blue Tortoiseshell, Chocolate Tortoiseshell, Lilac Tortoiseshell, Caramel Tortoiseshell, plus the Burmese versions of all these colours, all with a silvery-white undercoat

▼ *An ideal choice as a family pet, the Asian Smoke is tolerant of children and delighted to play.*

Australian Mist

A relatively new breed, this cat is growing in popularity extremely quickly. It was developed in Australia in the late 1970s by crossing Abyssinian and Burmese cats and adding a mix of domestic shorthairs to produce a spotted coat. Later, a marbled coat was permitted, resulting in the breed name being changed from the Spotted Mist to the Australian Mist in 1998. Recognized as a Championship breed in its country of origin in 1986, it gained recognition by The UK Governing Council of the Cat Fancy in 2011.

The most distinctive feature of the Australian Mist is its coat. There are three colour variants: light base with darker spots or patterning, a light pattern that stands out from the base coat, or ticking over the base coat looking like a misty veil. Rings or bars are present on the legs and tail. The face and neck should have bars or lines of colour. The head is rounded and the body lean and sleek but never angular.

Bred primarily as an indoor cat, the Australian Mist is very sociable and tolerant. It gets on well with children. They generally accept other cats and dogs readily. They have a bit of a reputation as a thief and will steal food if they have the opportunity to do so. It has a tendency to become overweight if the diet is not controlled carefully. This is an ideal companion for an elderly person and is happy to sit on a lap for hours.

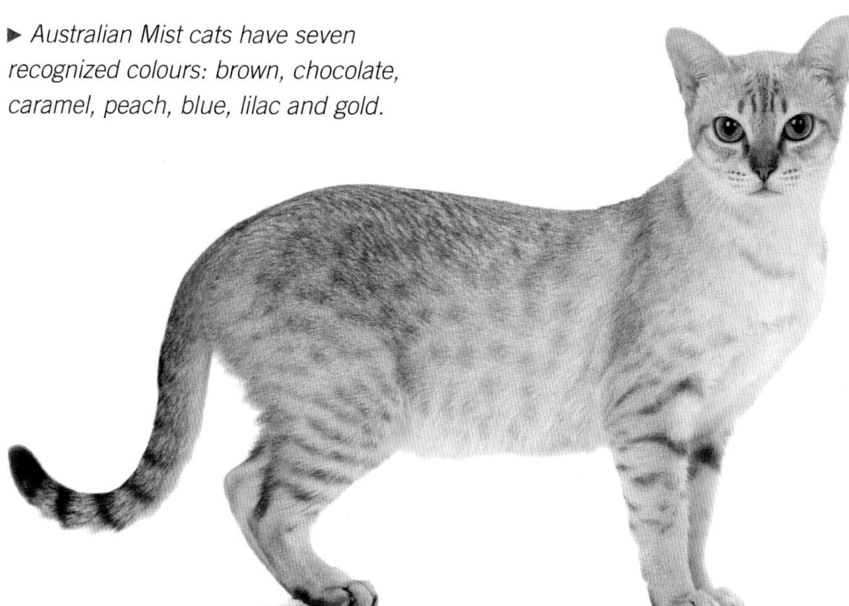

► *Australian Mist cats have seven recognized colours: brown, chocolate, caramel, peach, blue, lilac and gold.*

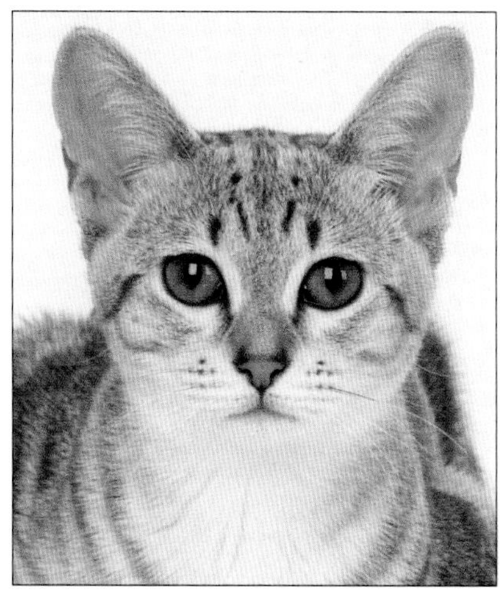

▲ *The first two Australian Mist cats were introduced to the UK by Mary Stuart in February 2007.*

Breed box

Coat: Spotted or marbled shorthaired, single layer coat
Eyes: Large and green with a gentle expression
Other features: Medium-sized with some similarity to Abyssinian and Burmese cats
Grooming: Easy; just brush weekly to remove shedding coat
Temperament: Laid-back and friendly

► *A tolerant breed that accepts handling and can be trained to walk on a harness and lead.*

Balinese

◄ *Vocal, yes, but the Balinese may not be as loud nor as raucous as its Siamese ancestors.*

Imagine a Siamese cat with a long, silky, flowing coat and a feathered tail, and you have an idea of the Balinese. It has the same dazzling sapphire eyes and large, erect ears as the Siamese cat – and comes in the same colour variations. However, the Balinese tends to be a little less noisy than the Siamese.

Its name is probably inspired by the cat's graceful movement that is reminiscent of an Indonesian dancer. The ancestry, however, is certainly Siamese. It is likely that in over 100 years of breeding Siamese cats, the recessive gene for long hair crept in and, in the 1940s, longhaired kittens began to appear in purebred Siamese litters. A Californian breeder decided to take advantage of this tendency, and in the 1950s developed a fully constituted pedigree breed. The new breed was introduced to the United Kingdom and Europe in the 1970s. Soon, some remarkably beautiful animals were being bred.

The fur of the Balinese is shorter than that of many of the other semi-longhairs, and lies smooth over the body. The cat is consequently easier to maintain. It is of medium build, but long-limbed and lithe, with the distinctly wedge-shaped head and long, straight nose of the Siamese. The mask is complete over the face and linked to the ears by traces of the darker colour (except in kittens). In character, the Balinese is bright and very active but loves its comfort.

▼ *Bright clear eyes of intense sapphire blue like those of this Chocolate Point are a scintillating feature of the breed.*

Breed box

Coat: Medium-length silky hair with a plumed tail

Eyes: Almond-shaped, medium-sized

Other features: Can have genetic health problems; ask for health certificate

Grooming: Regular grooming needed to stop the development of hair balls

Temperament: Outgoing and inquisitive

Balinese point colour groups

- Seal, Blue, Chocolate, Lilac (Frost), Red, Cream
- Tabby, Tortoiseshell Tabby
- Seal Tortie, Blue Tortie, Chocolate Tortie, Lilac Tortie

▼ *Balinese cats are found in all the same point colours as the Siamese. This Blue Point shows how the longer fur of the Balinese can have the effect of making a subtler transition between points and main body colour.*

Bambino

The Bambino is a hairless cat that has developed by crossing the Sphynx and Munchkin breeds. It originates from the USA and was granted recognition by The International Cat Association in 2006 as an experimental breed. They are also eligible for registration with the Rare and Exotic Feline Registry. The word 'Bambino' comes from the Italian meaning 'baby'. These cats are also known as Baby Cats. Both names are highly suitable as these cats should look like kittens even when mature adults.

The Bambino has short legs but litters may continue a mix of short-legged and longer-legged kittens. Short-legged cats can suffer from movement restriction. The rear legs are slightly longer than the front. Bodies are medium to long in proportion with deep chests and a rounded abdomen. Heads are rounded wedges with a firm chin. Although termed as hairless, they are actually covered with a very fine down. Whiskers are short and few in number. They have a whip-like tail and some cats grow a puff of hair at the tip. This feature is called a 'lion tail'.

These little cats have huge personalities and are very sociable. They love being cuddled and sitting on laps. The Bambino is very adaptable to change and is ideal for those living in small apartments. They can't cope well with the cold and will require a heated home, especially during the winter months. If you do take your bambino outside you should ensure that they have cat-safe sunscreen on to avoid sunburn. This breed is highly intelligent and trainable. They get on well with children and dogs, making them an ideal family pet.

Breed box

Coat: Hairless with a wrinkled skin

Eyes: Large, round and spaced wide apart

Other features: A dwarf breed that can weigh as little as 2.5kg (5lb)

Grooming: Requires regular bathing to remove build-up of natural oils from skin

Temperament: Affectionate and friendly

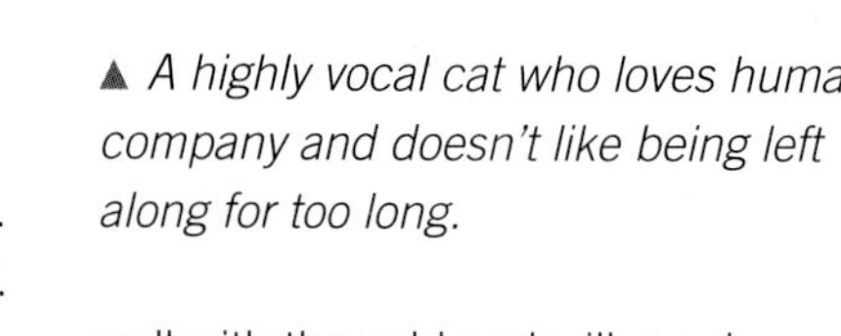

▲ *A highly vocal cat who loves human company and doesn't like being left along for too long.*

▼ *Due to the lack of protective coat, the Bambino will require cat-friendly sunscreen when outside.*

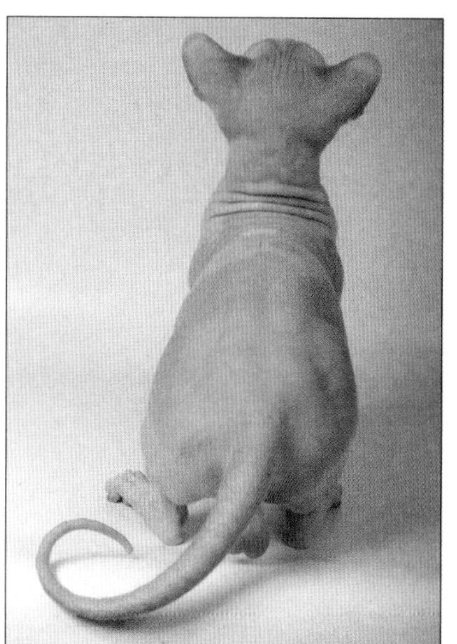

▼ *Surprisingly, considering its short legs, this is an active breed and likes playing with toys.*

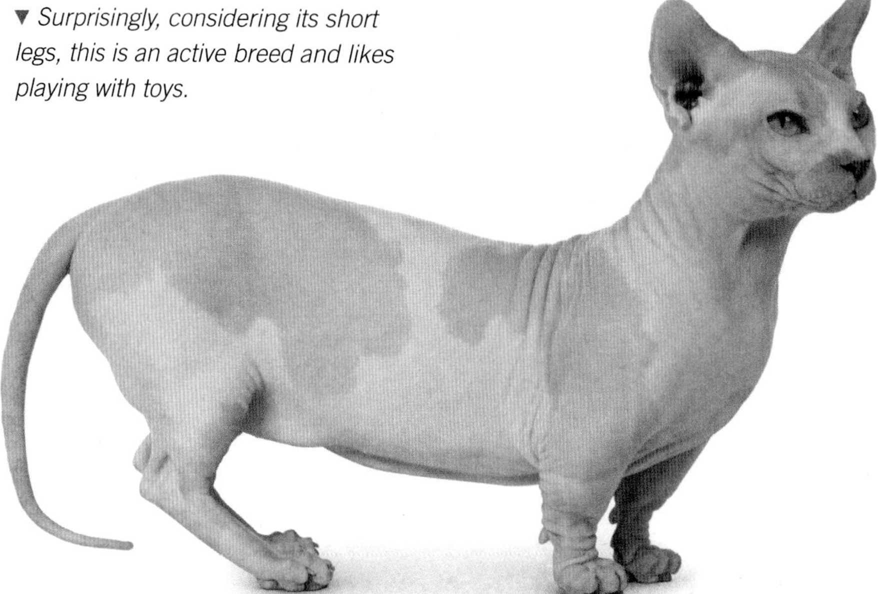

Bengal

The Bengal was developed in an attempt to combine the look of the wild Asian Leopard Cat with the temperament of the domesticated cat. Because this involved crossing domestic cats with the wild cats indigenous to south-east Asia, the breeding programmes have met with some controversy. To gain acceptance, it needs to establish that wild tendencies have been bred out, and that the new breed has the ability to reproduce a consistent type. The first Bengal litters born of wild/domestic parents (known as the F1 generation) tended to produce non-fertile males and only partially fertile females, and in some cases the temperament has been unstable. Most associations, therefore, do not allow these early generations to be shown, and they are often not suitable as pets.

Although the modern breed was pioneered in the desert state of Arizona in the United States during the 1960s, it is not registered as a championship breed by all American cat associations. Most of the American varieties are shades of brown. The Bengal is on its way to gaining provisional status in the United Kingdom, where spotted and marbled variations are being bred. There has been a huge increase in Bengal breeding lines throughout the world, possibly because of the high prices commanded by the kittens.

▲ *The Snow Spotted Bengal is a paler version of the spotted variety. The pale background colour is the result of the recessive Siamese gene, and is complemented by clear blue eyes.*

The concept of hybrids between small wild cat species and domestic varieties is not new. There is a record of a prototype Bengal at the London Zoo sometime before 1889, and at a Dutch cattery during the 1960s.

The modern breed is very striking: it is long, sleek and muscular with beautifully patterned fur. Its coat is its unique feature, quite unlike any other domestic breed, being more akin to the feel of a wild cat's pelt. Smallish, forward-pointing ears extend straight up from the sides of the broadly wedge-shaped head.

▲ *A young Bengal shows off the muscular and athletic body it has inherited from its wild relations, and the spotted tummy so desirable in breeding standards.*

◄ *A Marbled Bengal displays the dramatic coat pattern and long, prowling bodyline.*

Breed box

Coat: Short to medium, very dense, and unusually soft

Eyes: Oval, large, not bold

Grooming: Regular stroking; some brushing

Temperament: Active, playful, loves water

Birman

The Birman falls somewhere between the Siamese and the Persian in its character, build and length of fur, yet it is very much a breed of its own. It also has the distinction of being the sacred cat of Burma (now Myanmar).

All Birmans have colourpointed features – darker coloration on the ears, face, tail and legs. The original Birman was seal-pointed, but there are now blue, lilac, chocolate, and a wide range of tortoiseshell and tabby points. All are now regarded as different breeds, but share the same blue eyes, dark points, white feet, body shape and general temperament.

The Birman body has some of the mass of the Persian's, with thick-set legs and a broad, rounded head. However, the body and legs are longer than those of a Persian, and the face is pointed rather than flat, with a longish, straight nose and relatively large ears.

The unique and most distinctive feature of the Birman is its paw design. Each forepaw ends in a symmetrically shaped, white glove. The show standard is for the white to end in an even line across the paw and not pass beyond the angle of the paw and leg. The white areas on the back paws taper up the back of the leg to finish just below the hock, and are known as gauntlets. These

▲ *The pale coat and coloured points on face, legs and tail are similar to those of a Siamese cat. However, this Blue shows the distinctive white paws that are unique to Birmans.*

Breed box

Coat: Long, silky; full ruff around the neck and slightly curled on the stomach

Eyes: Almost round but not bold; deep, clear blue

Other features: White mittens on forepaws; longer white 'gauntlets' on rear paws

Grooming: Relatively easy with regular brushing and combing

Temperament: Gentle, individualistic, extremely loyal

▶ *The Seal Point original has now been joined by many differently coloured varieties of the Birman, but all have clear sapphire eyes and a sweet facial expression.*

▼ *The mask, tail and legs of Seal Point Birmans take their colour from the rich brown of Burmese soil, according to one legend.*

white finishing touches are the result of a rare recessive genetic trait, although, rather more romantically, there are various legends that explain their origins. One version tells of a raid on a Burmese temple in which the high priest was killed. A white temple cat leapt on to the priest's body, and immediately its fur turned gold in the light radiating from the resident goddess. The cat's eyes reflected the sapphire of the goddess's own eyes, while its legs and tail took on the rich brown of the Burmese soil. The paws that rested on the dead priest, though, remained white, a symbol of purity.

A more recent story reports that in 1919, a pair of seal-pointed Birmans was given to French explorer August Pavie and Englishman Major Gordon Russell. The male died on the journey back to France, but the female survived and bore a litter. This queen may have represented the beginning of controlled breeding of Birmans in France during the 1920s, when Siamese and bi-colour Persians were introduced into the programme. The breed was officially recognized in 1925. Its character reflects the Persian and Siamese input. It is quieter and less active than the Siamese, but not as docile as the Persian. The queens mature earlier than a Persian – at around seven months – and are generally very attentive mothers.

▲ *The Chocolate Tabby Birman, one of the newer colours, shows pale chocolate tabby markings on ears, mask and tail, while the body is light golden beige.*

Birman point colours
- Seal, Blue, Chocolate, Lilac, Red, Cream
- Tortoiseshell points in all colours apart from Red and Cream

▲ *The Red Point Birman has a cream body colour with warm orange points, the trademark white paws, but pink nose and paw pads.*

▼ *A Blue Tortie Tabby Point displays a magnificent coat and tail. A Birman's coat needs some extra grooming, but is less demanding than that of a longhair breed, and rarely becomes matted.*

Bombay

Because there is an Indian black leopard as sleek and black of coat as this particular domestic cat breed, the Bombay cat is named after an Indian city (now Mumbai). The cat's most outstanding features are its gleaming black fur and its large, brilliant golden eyes.

The Bombay was created in the United States in the 1950s in an attempt to breed a pure black Burmese. A Sable (Brown) Burmese was crossed with a Black American Shorthair, and the Bombay was accepted as a championship variety in 1976. A pair of American cats, fittingly named Opium and Bagheera, were exported to France in 1989 to found the European line, and so the type is similar on both sides of the Atlantic.

Not so in the United Kingdom, where Black British Shorthairs were mated with Burmese (although one was later combined with an American Bombay) and ultimately became part of the Asian Group breeding programme. The Bombay is judged in the United Kingdom along the same lines as other Asian self colours. The Bombay on both sides of the Atlantic has a distinct Burmese temperament, is known to purr a great deal, and is a strong and healthy breed. It is a medium-sized cat with a round head that seems large for its body. It has a short snub nose, firm chin and large ears rounded at the tips. Everything about it is black, from the fur that must be jet-black to the tips, to the nose and paw pads.

◄ *With a solid, jet-black coat and deep amber eyes, the Bombay earned the nickname 'the patent-leathered kid with the new penny eyes' in America, its country of origin.*

Breed box

Coat: Short, very close-lying and shiny
Eyes: Large; gold, yellow to green (United Kingdom); gold to copper (United States)
Other features: Patent leather glossiness of coat
Grooming: Little extra grooming is necessary
Temperament: Sedate, affectionate, needs attention

► *The Bombay is a polished, all-black Burmese type.*

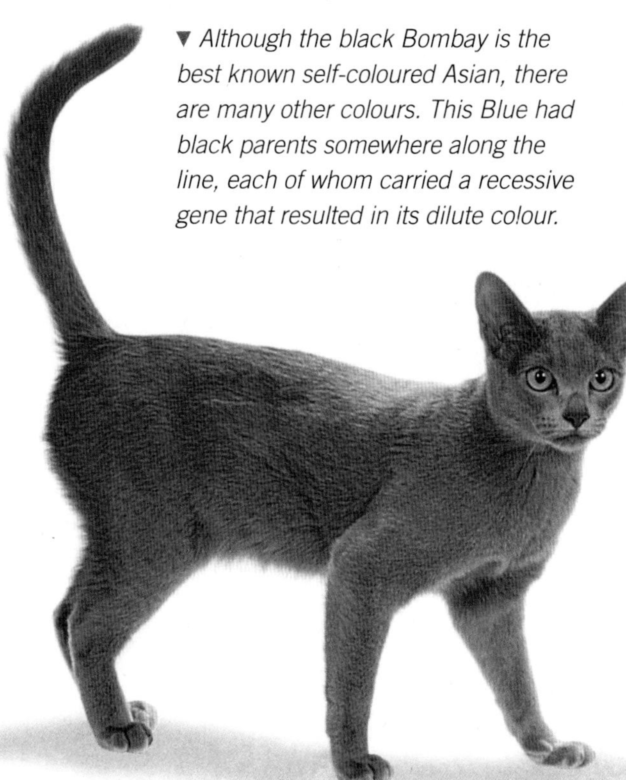

▼ *Although the black Bombay is the best known self-coloured Asian, there are many other colours. This Blue had black parents somewhere along the line, each of whom carried a recessive gene that resulted in its dilute colour.*

Brazilian Shorthair

The Brazilian Shorthair, or Pelo Curto Brasileiro, is the first cat from Brazil to gain recognition. This breed originates from the feral cats still seen on the Brazilian city streets. It is thought that these street cats were originally brought to the country by Portuguese traders, centuries ago, to protect food stores from rodents. They have now been carefully bred to produce the required consistent traits. In 1998 the World Cat Federation gave the Brazilian Shorthair the status of 'Approved Breed'.

This is a medium to large, muscular, well-balanced cat. The body is slender, but less so than that of a Siamese. The tail is medium in length and tapers to the tip. Heads are slightly long, ears rounded at the tip and eyes are almond-shaped. Eye colour is dependent on coat colour. Almost any coat colour or pattern is permissible.

The Brazilian Shorthair forms a strong bond with its owner and can develop behavioural problems if deprived of human company. Members of this breed have been known to move home if they feel that they are not getting enough attention. They are tolerably vocal and will use their voice to demand food or physical contact. These cats are sometimes described as clingy and can be jealous of other cats. Best suited to owners who have plenty of time to spend with them; this is an ideal breed for an elderly person. They are adaptable and equally happy as an outdoor or indoor cat. Playful, mischievous kittens, they settle down as they reach maturity.

▲ *Males have larger heads than females with both sexes having a slightly curved profile and large ears.*

Breed box

Coat: Silky, glossy short hair without an undercoat

Eyes: The space between the eyes should be equal to the size of one eye

Other features: A cat with outstanding agility and elegance

Grooming: Easy; minimum brushing required

Temperament: Active, playful and loyal

▲ *While still uncommon outside Brazil, this breed has been exhibited in Australia, UK, USA, Germany and Japan.*

► *The breed is reputed to have an exceptionally long lifespan with an expectation of living from between 14–20 years.*

British Semi-Longhair/British Longhair

Writing about cat breeds, or types, is fraught with difficulties. The cat registries, worldwide, vary enormously in cat types that they recognize as a breed. A cat can have Championship status in one country and not be recognized, or even frowned upon, in another. To make the situation even more confusing breed names vary from one registry to another. In some cases, a breed is named in one registry but in a different registery the same name can be used for a totally different breed.

This is the situation that affects the British Semi-Longhair/British Longhair. This cat originates from the United Kingdom and is similar in type to the British Shorthair. The only difference is the length of the coat. There are two schools of thought as to how this breed evolved. It is likely that both have had an influence on this cat.

Some consider that a cat found in Britain had two coat variants. It is possible that they had been brought over by the Romans. The shorthaired variety went on, eventually, to become the British Shorthair while the longhaired type was used, with other longhaired breeds, to improve and produce the Persian. This theory is substantiated by looking at Frances Simpson's *Book of the Cat* (1903). The description and diagrams of the Persian, as it was at that time, show some marked similarities to the British Semi-longhair/British Longhair. The Persian has gone on to be a well-known and popular longhaired breed worldwide, while the longhaired British variant fell by the wayside and was considered undesirable.

▲ *British longhairs tend to enjoy food and care needs to be exercised when feeding to avoid obesity.*

Breed box
Coat: Semi-long and very thick
Eyes: Large and expressive
Other features: A large cat that is slightly longer than high
Grooming: Regular daily grooming is essential
Temperament: Calm, independent and somewhat sedentary

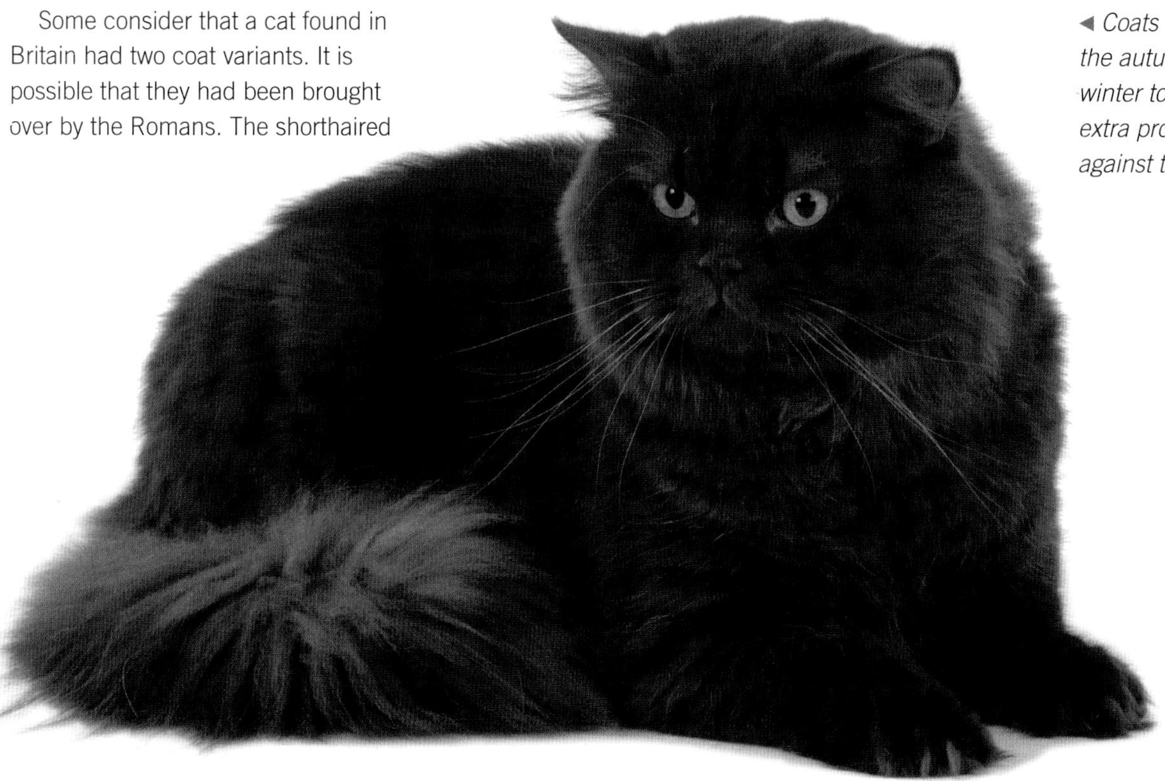

◄ *Coats thicken in the autumn and winter to provide extra protection against the cold.*

Another notion is as follows. Litters of British Shorthairs sometimes produced kittens with longhair. Those with longhair were considered as undesirable. These kittens were not registered but homed as domestic pets. Only cats with the correct coat were bred with. So the longhaired variant faded from popularity.

Somewhat bizarrely, the British Semi-Longhair/Longhair is not yet recognized by The UK Governing Council of the Cat Fancy (GCCF). It is recognized as a breed in its own right in many other parts of the world. There are some breeders who are interested in developing the breed in the UK and they are actively campaigning for breed status. At the moment this cat is in the early stages of recognition in both the GCCF and also the Felis Britannia (the UK branch of the Fédération Internationalé Feline (FIFe). There is no clear idea as to what name will be given to this cat breed, with the British Longhair, the British Semi-Longhair, British Longhair Variant, and the Longhair British all having been suggested.

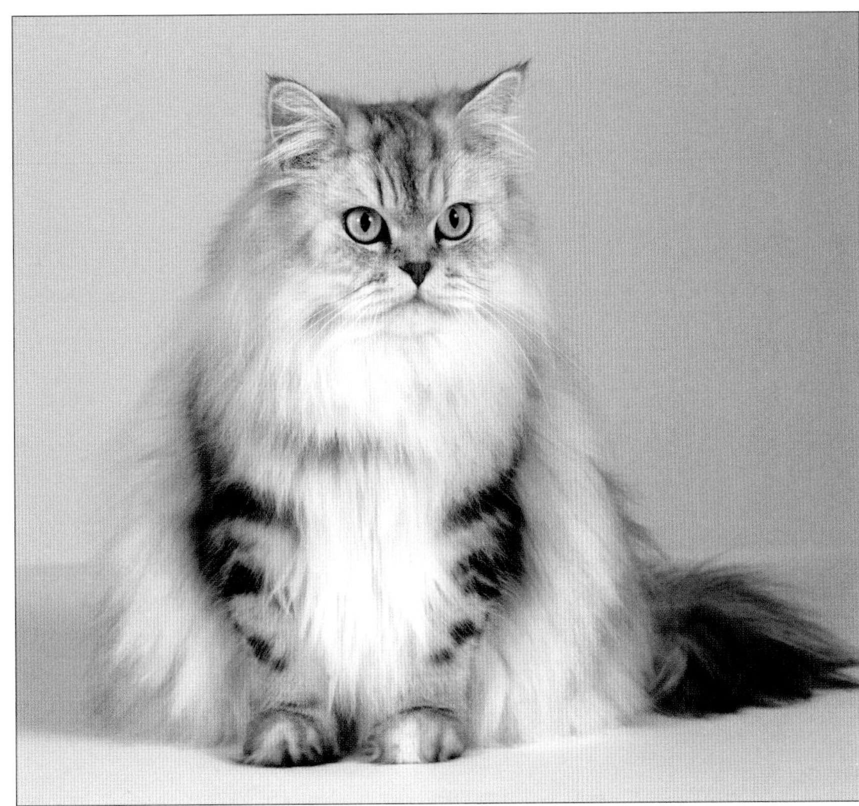

▲ *A lovely breed but not for you if you don't have the ability and time for extensive daily grooming.*

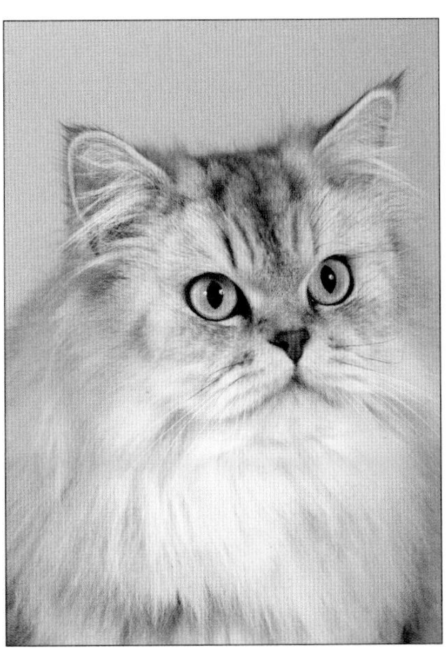

▼ *There are more than 300 coat colour and marking variants, with silver being especially popular.*

This breed has a large following in Europe. In some European countries it is called the Britannica, but in the Netherlands it is known as the Lowlander. FIFe recognizes this cat as a breed but calls it the British Longhaired Variant, the Highlander and the Highlander Straight all in the same standard. This is difficult as the Highlander and the Lowlander are names that have been given to different cat breeds in other countries. Despite the confusion over breed names the British Semi-Longhair/British Longhair is listed as the second most popular long-coated cat in Europe.

In the USA this cat is known as the Lowlander, but is recognized by The International Cat Association as the British Longhair, where it was given Championship status in 2009. It has a strong following in Northern America so it appears that the breed name doesn't really matter to the popularity of a cat.

The only difference between the British Shorthair and the British Semi-Longhair/British Longhair is the coat. In the latter, the coat is of medium length, dense and plush but

▲ *Breeders have different priorities leading to some variations in type in this young breed.*

with the same texture of the British Shorthair. The hair around the neck forms a ruff which frames the face. Coat on the belly can be wavy.

This is a large cat with an average weight of between 8–10kg (18–22lb). The body is compact with a deep chest. The legs are strong and short in proportion to the length of the body. Paws are rounded. The head is a rounded wedge that is slightly wider than long. High cheekbones are clearly defined. The skull appears to be slightly squarer that that of the British Shorthair. Whisker pads are round and prominent. The face has a chubby look and this cat sometimes looks as if it is smiling. Ears are medium-sized, set wide apart, rounded at the top and are tufted on the inside. Almond-shaped eyes slant upwards towards the ears. Eye colour is dependent on coat colour. The tail is thick and well plumed. Males are generally larger than females.

The British Semi-Longhair/British Longhair comes in a wide variety of coat colours and patterns. Colours include cream, blue, black, white, red, chocolate, lilac, fawn and cinnamon. Patterns seen are self, bicolour, tabby, tortoiseshell, colour-point, tipped and smoke. Some of these patterns are not acceptable with all registries. Eye colour varies from amber, gold, and blue through to bright green.

▼ *These cats like, and expect, to be the centre of attention in their household.*

This breed is generally healthy and can live to a very old age. Lifespans of 15–18 years are not unusual. There is some evidence that they suffer more from kidney problems than various other cat breeds. They are not a very active breed and this can lead to obesity if the diet is not strictly controlled. Exercise to promote good muscular tone can be rather challenging. Treat puzzle toys are helpful in this aspect providing the

▲ *It is essential to get kittens used to being groomed from an early age in preparation for adult grooming.*

◄ *The tail of a British Longhair adult or kitten ought to be equivalent to two thirds of the cat's body length. It should be well furnished with dense and fluffy fur.*

treats are taken from their daily ration and not given additionally to their normal meals.

This cat is often described as a 'four feet on the ground' breed and doesn't enjoy being carried. It is playful as a kitten but becomes sedentary when mature. They are often rather lazy and may well prefer to sleep in the sun rather than chase a toy. All in all, a very relaxed, laid-back personality. They are not demanding and are content with their own company although they enjoy being around other animals. This makes them an ideal breed for owners who have to go out to work. An affectionate cat providing it is on its own terms. They are not very vocal and when they do use their voices it is usually softly. The British Semi-Longhair/British

▲ *Feeding dry food formulated to reduce the risk of hairballs is worth considering.*

► *This is an intelligent breed that is capable of performing tricks.*

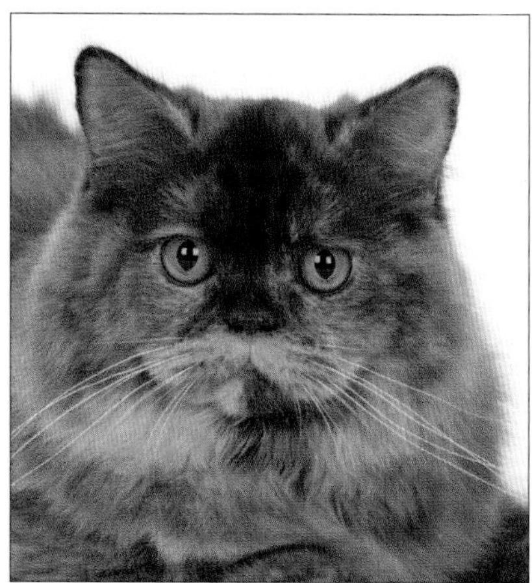

▲ *Large round eyes come in different colours: blue, green, copper or gold, depending on coat colour.*

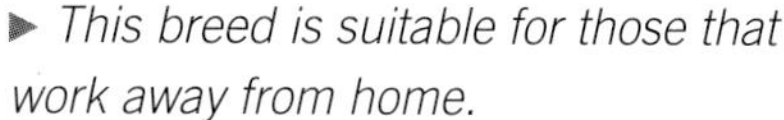

► *This breed is suitable for those that work away from home.*

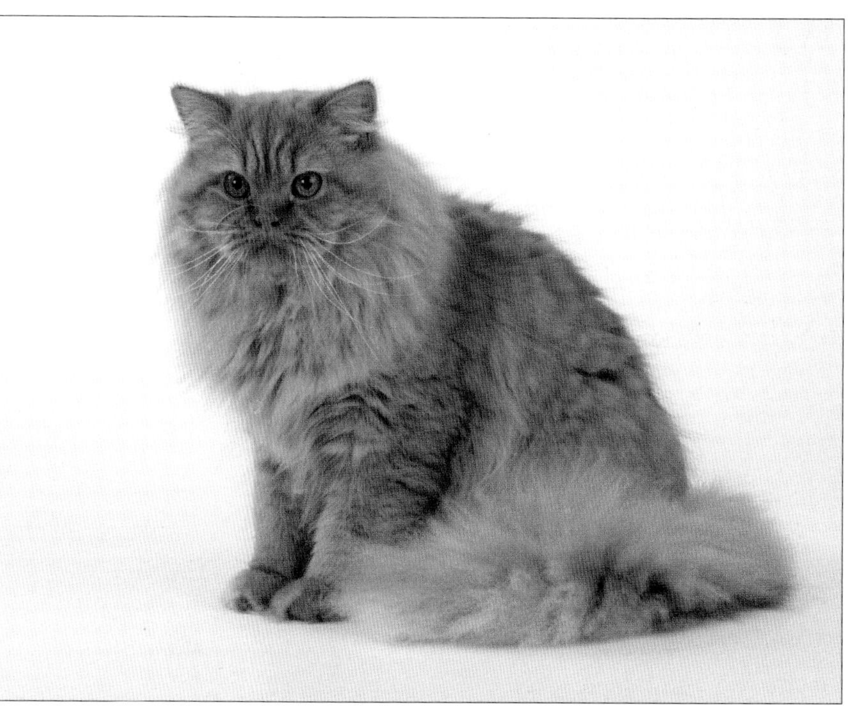

Longhair tolerates children and dogs. Not a classic lap cat, this breed seems to prefer to sit next to you rather than on you. They are equally happy as indoor or outdoor cats but they do seem to enjoy wandering about in the great outdoors. If they are living indoors, due to their thick coat, they can be rather uncomfortable if the central heating is up too high. Not the greatest of predators, chasing a mouse is sometimes just too much of an effort. This is a patient cat that is happy to snooze through the day waiting for their owner to come home.

The dense coat needs regular grooming to keep it tangle-free. The coat thickens during the colder months of autumn and winter, making brushing essential. When the coat is shedding dead hair it needs to be combed out daily to reduce the risk of acquiring hairballs. During periods of high shedding a vacuum cleaner is essential to remove dead hair from soft furnishings and carpets. Bathing will keep the coat in good condition.

This cat is thought, by many breeders and owners alike, to be one of the most beautiful cats in the world and it is easy to see why. It is surprising that it is not better known. Potential purchasers must consider very carefully if they have the time to keep the coat in tip top condition prior to buying a kitten.

Like the Persian and British Shorthair, the British Longhair has a predisposition to develop hypertrophic cardiomyopathy. This is a cardiac disease that causes the heart walls to thicken, decreasing its efficiency. Other symptoms include breathing problems, poor appetite and lethargy.

◄ *Beautiful cats with their teddy bear looks and placid nature, this breed has a lot to recommend it.*

British Shorthair

▲ *Generally enjoying good health, there are a few conditions that the British Shorthair is prone to.*

The national cat of the British Isles, the British Shorthair is the result of selective breeding of the best examples of native street cats. It probably stems originally from the first domestic cats that arrived in Britain with the Roman legions in the first century AD. As a pedigreed variety, the British Shorthair (or the English Cat) was recognized from the very start. The early breeders of British shorthaired cats, were, for some reason, usually male and from the north of England. Now the British Shorthair is the third largest group of registered pedigreed cats in the United Kingdom and popular throughout the world.

It is bred in all the major colour and pattern groups, although to a lesser extent than the American Shorthair, and includes a Siamese pattern. All British Shorthairs have a compact, well-balanced and powerful body. The chest is full and broad; legs are short and strong with large, rounded paws; the tail is thick at the base and rounded at the tip. Of the British, European and American Shorthairs, the British has the most rounded head. The ears are small and set wide apart, the cheeks are round, the chin firm, and the nose short and broad.

The British Shorthair is a streetwise, muscular cat whose characteristic placidity enables it to adapt happily to life indoors. Its intelligent yet phlegmatic nature makes it a solid and dependable feline companion.

◀ *This breed almost died out in WW2. Due to food shortages, it was difficult to find spare food for cats.*

British Black

All the essential characteristics of the British Shorthair type are often seen at their peak in the Black. This is because it was one of the earliest British Shorthair breeds to be selectively bred from the very best of British street cats in the 1800s. It was also one of the first to be shown at the first national cat show in 1871 at Crystal Palace, London.

The top-rate pedigreed Black should have a dense black coat from hair root to tip, with no hint of browning, stray white hairs, patches or tabby markings. This provides a striking backdrop for the large, round, deep copper eyes with absolutely no green. Blacks are often used in breeding programmes to improve the type of other Shorthair breeds, particularly Tortoiseshell and Tortie and White.

◀ *The densely coloured, short fur of the British Black Shorthair is inherited from ancestors reputed to be the familiars of witches. It was the butt of superstition and legend during the Dark Ages and medieval times.*

Breed box

Coat: Short, thick, fine
Eyes: Round; copper, no green
Other features: Round-tipped ears; short nose; big round paws; nose leather and paw pads black
Grooming: Easy; regular combing
Temperament: Companionable, independent, freedom-loving

British White

Pure white condensed into the stocky build of the British Shorthair is the epitome of feline luxury and perfection. British White Shorthairs are universally admired, highly valued, and quite rare, although they have been bred since the 1800s.

There are three varieties with different eye colours. Blue-eyed Whites may rarely be prone to deafness. In trying to breed out this defect by crossing with orange-eyed cats, an odd-eyed variety with one eye of each colour was created. Unfortunately, these cats sometimes suffer deafness in the ear on the blue-eyed side. Orange-eyed varieties are therefore the most commonly seen as pets.

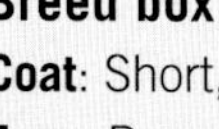

Breed box
Coat: Short, thick, fine
Eyes: Round; clear blue, orange to copper, or one of each
Other features: Round-tipped ears; short nose; big round paws; nose leather and paw pads pink
Grooming: Easy; regular combing
Temperament: Companionable, independent, freedom-loving

◄ *A British White Shorthair with a pristine coat is hard to breed and therefore not very common. A pure white non-pedigree might look very like a pedigreed shorthair, but it is more likely to have green eyes rather than copper, blue, or one of each colour.*

British Cream

The occasional occurrence of a cream-coloured kitten in tortoiseshell litters towards the end of the 1800s provided the motivation to try to produce a Cream pedigree. Some tortoiseshell parentage is necessary to produce the required rich shade of buttermilk, which made it difficult to produce consistently pale coats with no redness or obvious tabby markings. The result was that the breed was not officially recognized until the 1920s and not fully established until the 1950s. Sometimes tabby markings become more pronounced in very hot or very cold weather. The ideal is cream-haired to the roots – with no patches of white.

▼ *British Cream Grand Champion, Miletree Owain Glyndwr, has only the faintest shadow of darker markings, and a gloriously soft-toned coat colour.*

Breed box
Coat: Short, thick, fine
Eyes: Round; deep gold to orange and copper
Other features: Round-tipped ears; short nose; big round paws; nose leather and paw pads pink
Grooming: Easy; regular combing
Temperament: Companionable, independent, freedom-loving

British Blue

The Blue is the most popular of British Shorthair breeds. Kittens often display tabby markings, but these usually disappear after six to eight months. Because the breed is long established, Blues tend to be good examples of the Shorthair type: broad, muscular and good-natured. Occasional injections of black shorthairs and blue longhairs into breeding programmes have preserved the distinctive slate-blue coat.

▲ *A round-cheeked British Blue's hazy blue-grey coat contrasts with big orange eyes.*

Breed box
Coat: Short, thick, fine
Eyes: Round; copper, orange or deep gold
Other features: Round-tipped ears; short nose; big round paws; nose leather and paw pads blue-grey
Grooming: Easy; regular combing
Temperament: Companionable, independent, freedom-loving

British Chocolate

The warm, dark-chocolate coloration comes from the introduction of the chocolate gene from longhaired colourpoints into the British Shorthair breeding programme. The coat can be any shade of rich chocolate but it should be evenly toned, without any white, shading or marking.

▶ *Despite the British Shorthair's reputation for being stolid and reliable, this Chocolate shows the breed's lively intelligence.*

Breed box
Coat: Short, thick, fine
Eyes: Round; deep gold, orange to copper
Other features: Round-tipped ears; short nose; big round paws; nose leather and paw pads brown or pink
Grooming: Easy; regular combing
Temperament: Companionable, independent, freedom-loving

British Lilac

The Lilac, a soft-toned blue-grey with a pinkish sheen to it, is a dilute form of the Chocolate. The gene responsible for the dilution produces hairs in which the pigmentation is collected together in clumps, and microscopic areas of hair have no pigment at all. The dilute colour therefore has less depth and intensity than a pure solid colour. Lilac parents only produce kittens of the same colour, unless they carry cinnamon, so once established, Lilacs are easy to keep on producing.

▶ *The stocky, muscular build that distinguishes the British Shorthair from its European and American counterparts can be clearly seen in this Lilac.*

Breed box
Coat: Short, thick, fine
Eyes: Round; rich gold to orange or copper
Other features: Round-tipped ears; short nose; big round paws; nose leather and paw pads pale grey
Grooming: Easy; regular combing
Temperament: Companionable, independent, freedom-loving

British Bi-colour

There are many bi-coloured cats on the streets of Britain, but the pedigree version must have well-balanced, symmetrical and clearly defined bands of solid colour and white. The coloured areas can be black, blue, red, cream, chocolate or lilac and, in the perfect pedigree, contain no flecks of other colours or any tabby markings. It is also important for the show cat to have the white area covering the nose and lower part of the face, neck and shoulders, chest and forepaws – but over no more than half of the total body area.

◄ The mask over the ears and three-quarters of the face that is such an important feature in the show Bi-colour, suits the rounded features of the British Shorthair very well.

Breed box
Coat: Short, thick, fine
Eyes: Round; gold to orange and copper
Other features: Round-tipped ears; short nose; big round paws; nose leather and paw pads pink
Grooming: Easy; regular combing
Temperament: Companionable, independent, freedom-loving

British Tortie and White

This variation of the Bi-colour has tortoiseshell in place of the solid colour areas. In America, these are Calico Cats, called after the popular printed cotton fabric. The tortoiseshell element can be bright black and red or dilute colours. As with the solid colour and white, the white areas should extend over no more than half of the body. Tortie and Whites are quite difficult to breed to the preferred symmetry for successful showing.

▼ The Tortie and White Shorthair comes in delightful dilute versions such as this softly dappled Blue Tortie and White.

Breed box
Coat: Short, thick, fine
Eyes: Round; orange to copper
Other features: Round-tipped ears; short nose; big round paws; nose leather and paw pads pink and/or black
Grooming: Easy; regular combing
Temperament: Companionable, independent, freedom-loving

► British Shorthairs also come in tortoiseshell without white in mingled shades of red and black, as shown, or the dilute blue-cream shades.

▸ *An alert side profile shows the superb mix of colours in a Tortie Silver Tabby, and the shortish but active tail characteristic of the shorthair.*

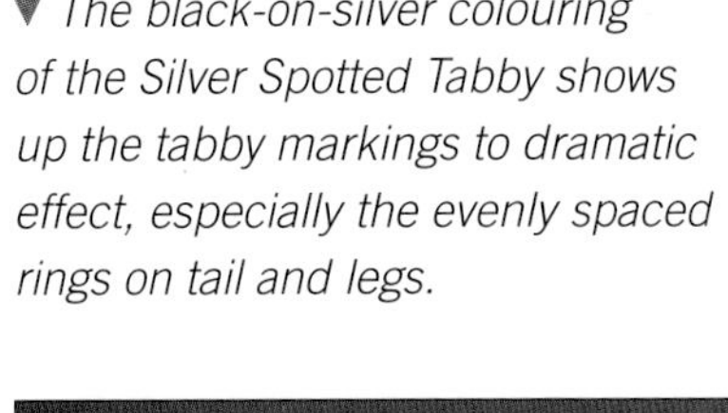

British Tabby

The tabby gene is a forceful one, passed on from the wild species from which the European domestic cat has evolved, and familiar in many a non-pedigree. The tabby markings of a show cat, however, must conform to very exact standards, and most importantly of all, be balanced on both sides of the body. There are three main patterns: the classic tabby, the more markedly striped mackerel, and the spotted. Both have a trio of dark lines running along the spine and distinctive, evenly spaced rings around the neck, tail and legs. The classic, however, has dark spirals of colour on its flanks, a winged shape over the shoulders, and a spotted belly.

Tabby colours range from the thick-cut marmalade variety of red on red, the Brown (the Brown Classic is also described as marbled or blotched) and Silver, to the softer dilutes of Blue and Cream.

▾ *The black-on-silver colouring of the Silver Spotted Tabby shows up the tabby markings to dramatic effect, especially the evenly spaced rings on tail and legs.*

▸ *A Tortie Tabby British Shorthair combines the rich colouring of the Tortoiseshell with the distinctive stripes of the tabby.*

▴ *Note the well-defined facial markings of this Classic Red Tabby – the lines running down from the corners of the eyes, and the M shape on the brows.*

Breed box

Coat: Short, thick, fine
Eyes: Round
Classic Tabby: gold, orange to copper
Silver: green to hazel
Other features: Round-tipped ears; short nose; big round paws; nose leather and paw pads brick-red (and/or black for the Silver Tabby)
Grooming: Easy; regular combing
Temperament: Companionable, independent, freedom-loving

▲ *Classic British build combines with delicate Siamese markings on a British Shorthair Lilac Colourpointed.*

British Colourpointed

Careful outcrossing of British Shorthairs to Colourpoint Persians resulted in the recent development of the British Shorthair Colourpointed. A certain over-indulgence of hair took a bit of ironing out through breeding programmes, but today's British Shorthair Colourpointed has all the right characteristics of type, with a short, dapper fur coat and sturdy build. The cats come in the same versions of colourpointed as the Siamese, including seal, chocolate, lilac, red and cream. The most recent colours to be accepted are cinnamon and fawn points. All versions have big, round, saucer-like blue eyes, set against the colourpointed mask. The colourpointed features – mask, ears, paws and tail – should be clearly defined in good examples of the breed, and any shading in the body colour should tone in with the point colour. Prior to breeding colourpoint cats should be tested for Progressive Retinal Atrophy (PRA).

Breed box

Coat: Short, thick, fine
Eyes: Round; blue
Other features: Round-tipped ears; short nose; big round paws; nose leather and paw pads to tone in with point colour
Grooming: Easy; regular combing
Temperament: Companionable, independent, freedom-loving

British Shorthair colours and patterns

Self colours: White (blue-eyed, orange-eyed, odd-eyed), Black, Chocolate, Lilac, Blue, Cream, Red, Cinnamon and Fawn
Tabby: Silver, Blue Silver, Chocolate Silver, Lilac Silver, Red Silver, Cream Silver, Black Tortie Silver, Blue-Cream Silver, Chocolate Tortie Silver, Lilac-Cream Silver, Brown, Chocolate, Lilac, Blue, Red, Cream, Brown Tortie, Blue-Cream, Chocolate Tortie and Lilac-Cream Patterns – classic, mackerel or spotted
Tortoiseshell: Black Tortie, Chocolate Tortie, Blue-Cream Tortie and Lilac Tortie
Patched: Black Tortie and White, Blue Tortie and White, Chocolate Tortie and White, Lilac Tortie and White, Black and White, Blue and White, Chocolate and White, Lilac and White, Red and White, Cream and White
Tipped: Sparkling white coat with the very tips of the fur dusted with the self and tortoiseshell colours. The Golden Tipped, the non-silver version, has black tipping
Smoke: All self colours (other than white, cinnamon and fawn) and all the tortoiseshell colours
Colourpointed: Colour restricted to the points which can be in all self, tabby, silver tabby, tortoiseshell and smoke colours

► *British Shorthair kitten breeds, from left to right; Tortie, Blue, Black, and Cream Spotted. Potential owners must remember that while they retain the sweet nature of the breed, mature Shorthairs are big, heavy cats.*

British Tipped

Like the Longhaired Persian Chinchilla, the British Tipped Shorthairs have a faint dusting of another colour right at the tips of their predominantly white fur, and at the point of their tails. They also share the classic Chinchilla characteristic of nose and eyes fetchingly outlined in black. The tipping (or chinchillation) – which can be black, blue, red, cream, chocolate, lilac or tortoiseshell colours – is such a mere suggestion that it gives a sense of iridescence when the cat moves. The effect may be concentrated in one or two areas to give a ghost of a patch on the flanks or back, or rings on the legs. An outstanding feature of the Black and Golden-tipped British Shorthairs is their brilliant green eye colour. The Golden-tipped, unlike the other British Tipped, has a rich golden-apricot undercoat with black tipping. The tipped colorations developed as a result of complex interbreeding of cats with Silver genes, that determined the undercoat colour, with Blues and Smokes. The non-agouti version of the tipped effect produces the British Smoke, which appears to be a self or plain-coloured cat until the hair is pushed back to see the startling silver undercoat. British Smokes are also bred in the same wide colour range.

► *The Golden-tipped British Shorthair is in fact gold with black tipping. This kitten has the well-defined eyes that are characteristic of tipped varieties.*

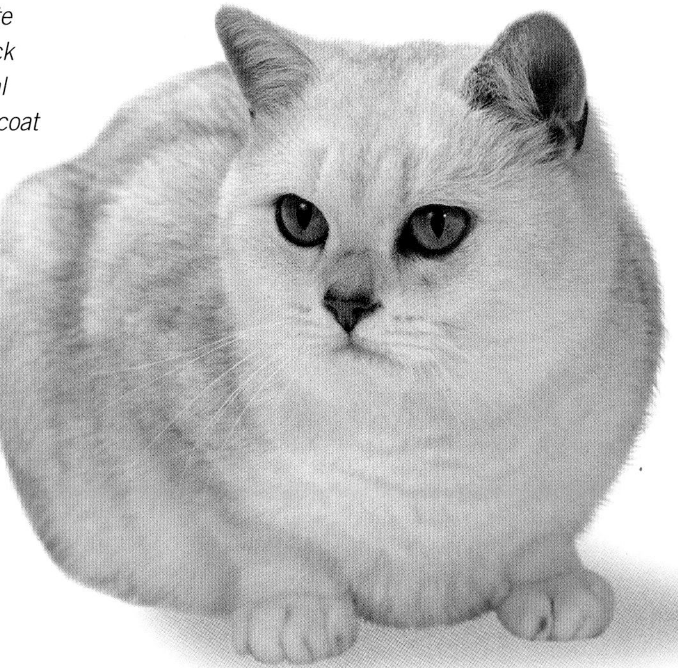

► *Sparkling white dusted with black gives an ethereal shimmer to the coat of this British Black-tipped Shorthair.*

Breed box
Coat: Short, thick, fine
Eyes: Round; copper to gold; green in Black and Golden-tipped
Grooming: Light combing
Temperament: Companionable, freedom-loving

Burmese

The Burmese is believed to have originated from a cat found near the Thai-Burma border in Thailand. The Thai word for these cats 'Thong-daeng' translates to mean 'copper colour', which is a good description of this breed.

In 1930 Dr Joseph Cheesman Thompson, a naval medic, imported a brown female cat from the Thai region to San Francisco with the aim of producing cats of similar type. The female cat was called Wong Mau and she was bred to Tai Mau, a Seal Point Siamese. Wong Mau was then bred back to one of her sons to produce a litter of dark brown kittens. This was the start of the breed Burmese, which in 1936 was granted formal breed recognition by the Cat Fanciers Association (CFA). The breed rapidly became popular and, to produce more kittens, the foundation stock was extensively crossed back to Siamese. This resulted in a change to the original type and a lack of conformity. The problem became so severe that, within ten years of recognizing the breed, the Cat Fanciers Association suspended recognition.

▲ *The top line of the Burmese's eye slants towards the nose, while the lower line is distinctly rounded, giving the breed its unique expression.*

Breed box
Coat: Short, fine and feels like satin
Eyes: Round, expressive and wide apart
Other features: The tail is straight and medium in length
Grooming: Easy; regular brushing will produce a rich sheen
Temperament: People-loving and trusting

American breeders worked hard to produce cats true to type and eventually, in 1954, the Cat Fanciers Association lifted the suspension. Since then the breed stabilized and there has been little change to the breed standard.

At the same time breeders in Britain were also developing this popular breed. Because of a variance in outcrosses the result was a cat of similar type but with some clear differences. This type of Burmese is known as a European or Traditional Burmese. Some breed registries do not classify the two cat types as different breeds while others do.

The Burmese (Contemporary Burmese) is a small- to medium-breed who is surprisingly heavy for its size, 4kg–6kg (8.8lb–13.25lb). This cat is sometimes referred to as 'a brick wrapped in silk'. The body is muscular and stockier than the European Burmese. Legs are long with neat rounded paws. The head differs from its European counterpart being broader with a markedly shorter and flatter muzzle. The coat is shorthaired

◀ *A Brown Burmese shows the breed's tendency to rotundity – unlike its compatriots, the lithe Siamese.*

◄► *The density of a Blue Burmese's fur accentuates strong shoulders and a broad, rounded chest. The Burmese is quite a heavy cat for its size.*

and needs little attention. Originally all copper brown, now four coat colours are permitted, Sable, Blue, Champagne and Platinum. Eyes should be yellow to gold regardless of coat colour.

This is a vocal cat whose voice is not so strident as that of a Siamese. They are very loyal and loving towards their owners. The Burmese needs to interact with their human companion and is certainly not a breed that would be suitable to be left alone for prolonged periods. They are active, kittenish and very intelligent. This breed is dog-like and will follow its owner around the house like a shadow. It is an ideal cat for families and accepts cat-loving dogs. The Burmese is happy as an indoor cat providing it has plenty of attention and a range of toys to entertain it.

▼ *The typical Burmese head is distinctly round, with a short nose and a firm chin, and round-tipped ears spaced well apart. This Lilac shows excellent type.*

► *A Chocolate (Champagne) Burmese shows the typical milky brown colouring that is quite distinct from the richer colouring of the Brown (Sable).*

Burmilla

◄ *A Black Shaded Silver Burmilla is closest in colour to its Chinchilla Silver heritage and has Chinchilla-like kohl-ringed eyes.*

The Burmilla is the longest established and most popular of the Asian Group of cats, and often the starting point for breeding other varieties. It was the originator of the Asian Group of cats in the United Kingdom, derived from a Lilac Burmese queen and a Chinchilla Silver Persian in 1981. The result was a shorthaired Burmese lookalike with the stunning tipping and outlined features of the Chinchilla. The Burmilla is the shaded or tipped representative of the Asian Group. The shaded varieties are more heavily tipped and obviously coloured than the tipped varieties. The undercoat on both variations is the palest possible silver or golden, but tipped at the very ends with one of the standard or Burmese colours. Nose leather and paw pads are brick-red (terracotta), and dark pigmentation around the eyes, nose and lips should be obvious. One of the cat's particularly appealing features is the outlining of nose and eyes in the same colour as the darker tip. The Burmilla consolidates many of the best points of its parents. It is open and sociable like the Burmese but less demanding and noisy; it is stable and dignified like its Persian forebears, but is rather more adventurous and inquisitive.

◄ *A Brown-shaded Silver Burmilla expresses the typical inquisitive nature of its type.*

Breed box

Coat: Short, dense, soft and glossy; slightly longer than Burmese

Eyes: Yellow to green, green preferred in Silvers, gold allowed in Selfs

Other features: Outlined eyes, nose and lips

Grooming: Little extra grooming needed

Temperament: Stable, dignified inquisitive, sociable

Burmilla colours and patterns

Standard: gold base coat

Silver: white base coat; colours less intense

May be shaded or tipped with Black, Blue, Chocolate, Lilac, Red, Caramel, Apricot, Cream, Black Tortoiseshell, Blue Tortoiseshell, Chocolate Tortoiseshell, Lilac Tortoiseshell, Caramel Tortoiseshell, plus the Burmese versions of these colours

► *The Lilac Tortie Burmilla has a white base coat shaded with a mix of frosted pink-grey, and dark and light cream. Nose leather and paw pads are lavender or pink; eyes amber or green.*

◄ *On the forehead of the Burmilla there should be an M-shaped mark – as on this Blue Shaded. There may also be streaks from the outer edges of the eyes and on the cheeks.*

Californian Spangled Cat

As the name suggests, this breed originates from the USA. Although a relatively recent breed it has a fascinating history. Following a conversation with anthropologist Louis Leakey in early 1970s, playwright Paul Arnold Casey was shocked to hear about the barbaric killing of leopards. This slaughter was carried out for sport but also for their fur to make coats and fashion accessories. Casey thought that if he bred a cat that looked like a wild cat, people might take animal conservation more seriously and realise that fur looked better on an animal. Using numerous domestic breeds, the result was a cat that resembled a miniature leopard or ocelot. Numbers of the Californian Spangled Cat, or Spangle, are low as it has been overshadowed by the Bengal and Ocicat. The breed is recognized by The International Cat Association and the American Cat Association.

The lean, long muscular body gives this cat a rather slinky look, similar to that of a hunting wild cat. The short coat is patterned with a spotted tabby. Colours include brown, gold, bronze, silver, red, white, blue, black and charcoal.

Spangles are very athletic and proficient hunters. They love playing with toys, especially those that move. This cat can jump high and will show off by performing acrobatic leaps. Despite the wild look it is affectionate and loyal. They love to be with their owner and can suffer from behavioural issues if deprived from human company. A highly intelligent breed that is easy to train and gets on well with children.

► *Due to the low registered numbers the Californian Spangled Cat, or House Leopard, is unavoidably an expensive purchase.*

▲ *If kept indoors, ample space, a cat tower and a range of toys are absolutely essential for this active and athletic breed.*

Breed box

Coat: Spots are often in round block form but can be triangular or oval

Eyes: Colour varies from deep copper to pale amber

Other features: The tail always has a black tip

Grooming: Easy; low shedding

Temperament: Energetic, curious and social

◄ *The short coat can come in a range of colours including white, silver, black, gold, bronze, brown and blue.*

Ceylon

The Ceylon comes from the country of its name, now called Sri Lanka. It is believed to be a 'natural breed' that has developed on the island. Dr Paolo Pellegatta, an Italian, so liked the cat when he visited Sri Lanka in 1984 that he brought it back to Italy. From there its popularity spread but it is still relatively unknown. It is registered with the World Cat Federation and the Italian Federation of Feline Associations.

This is an elegant cat with a strong, short, muscular body and a broad chest. They are fine-boned and small to medium in size. Hind legs are slightly longer than the front. Paws are rounded. The head is in proportion to the body with a short nose, rounded cheeks and protruding cheekbones. High-set ears are open with rounded tips. Tails are fairly short and thick at the base, tapering to a rounded tip. A distinctive feature is the ticking on the coat. The coat base colour is likened to golden sunlight. Ticking can be black, cream, red, blue or tortoiseshell. Clear lines of colour, or tiger stripes, can be seen on the limbs and around the neck. Some cats have a M-shaped pattern on the forehead.

The Ceylon loves the company of other cats and is possibly not the best choice for a one-cat family. They are playful but also happy to sleep quietly when not much is going on. This is a very sociable trusting cat who is not fazed by strangers.

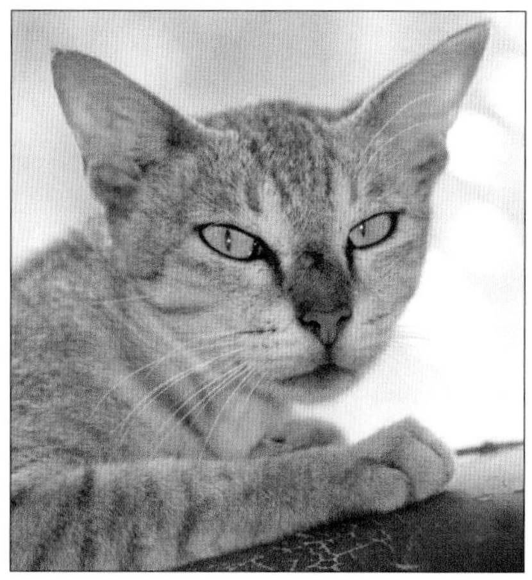

▲ *The Ceylon is also called the Sri Lankan cat. It is a very chatty cat who will verbally express its needs and desires.*

Breed box

Coat: Short, silky, tight to the body with little undercoat

Eyes: Almond-shaped vivid green-yellow eyes

Other features: Has a typically sleepy expression

Grooming: Easy; remove shedding hair when necessary

Temperament: Calm, playful and affectionate

▼ *Adult Ceylon cats weigh between 3.5–6kg (7.75–13.25lb) and can reach up to 35cm (1.2ft) in height.*

▲ *An avid hunter, and if allowed outdoors will track its prey over long distances regardless of any danger to itself.*

Chantilly

◀ *The Chantilly's Asian roots are evident in the large, wide-set, slightly oriental, eyes of this Blue Shaded Silver.*

Depending on the country, the Chantilly is also called the Chantilly-Tiffany, Tiffany/Chantilly or Tiffany. It should not be confused with the Tiffanie which is another breed altogether (see p247). It originates from Northern America. This breed was believed to be extinct in the 1960s until two were offered for sale in an auction. These cats were bred together and their offspring always produced kittens true to type. The breed was recognized by the American Cat Association in the 1970's as 'Foreign-Longhairs', but the breed name was changed as this was considered to be too general.

This cat is slow to mature, not reaching full adulthood until about two years of age. It is a medium-sized cat with a beautiful rich-coloured, silky semi-longhaired coat. Coat colours and patterns vary slightly between registries. In general, blue, black, champagne, platinum, lilac, cinnamon and fawn are all accepted, with a gorgeous chocolate colouring being the most well-known. All cats should have a plumed tail, neck ruff and ear streamers. Females are normally smaller than males.

The Chantilly is an excellent companion but doesn't like being left alone. This is not the breed to choose if the owner works away from home for long periods. They are quite talkative, using quiet trills and chirps. Vocalization is soft and not demanding. They are moderately active, affectionate and will form a strong bond with one person within the household. Mixes happily with children and other pets.

▼ *The Chantilly is found in an enormous range of colours and patterns, as this Brown Smoke suggests.*

Breed box

Coat: Semi-Longhair without undercoat

Eyes: Yellow that intensifies to a deep gold as the cat matures

Other features: White spotting is not allowed

Grooming: Moderate; has a tendency to over self-groom leading to bald patches

Temperament: Sweet tempered and people loving

Chantilly colours and patterns

Self colours: Black, Blue, Chocolate, Lilac, Red, Caramel, Apricot, Cream

Tabby and Tortoiseshell: Black, Cream, Blue, Chocolate, including Silver versions. The Tabby patterns are less defined on the semi-longhair coat than on the Asian shorthaired equivalent

▲ *Although the Chantilly has little or no undercoat, she should still be groomed daily to keep the loose fur out of her coat.*

▼ *A Brown Shaded Silver Chantilly shows excellent shape, with a perfectly straight back from shoulder to hindquarters.*

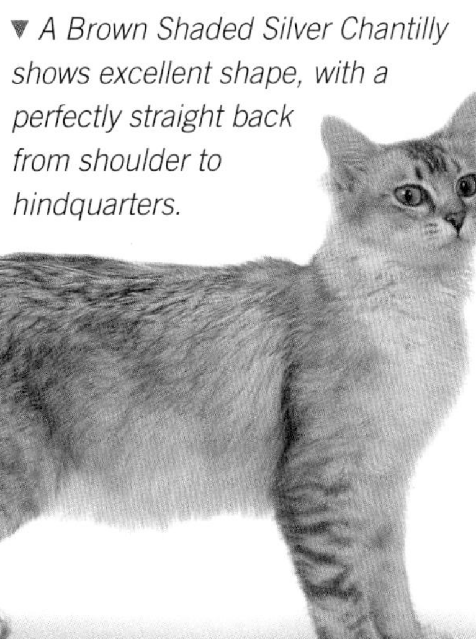

Chartreux

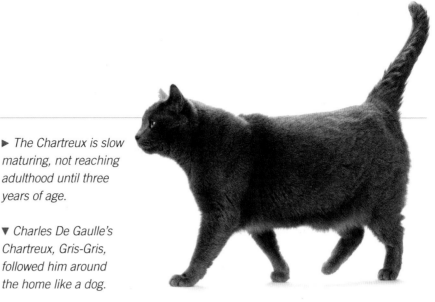

The Chartreux is a stocky bodied cat with slender, agile legs and because of this is often referred to as 'a potato on toothpicks'. Its double coat is shaded blue to grey with the tips of the hairs lightly brushed with silver. Kittens may have a faint imprint of tabby markings and tail rings, called ghost barring, but these disappear as the cat matures. The coat is similar in colour to that of the British Blue Shorthair.

The Chartreux has a robust body, broad shoulders and a deep chest with medium short, fine-boned legs. The head is large with well-developed cheeks and a slight step at eye level. The structure of the head makes the Chartreux look as if it is smiling. The lips should be blue in colour and the nose leather slate-grey. The eyes are rounded, with the outer corners curving upwards. Eye colour is gold or copper, but the copper colour is preferred. Ears are erect, of medium height and width, and set high on the head. This breed matures slowly and can take up to three years to gain a fully adult body. While not a vocal cat, the Chartreux communicates by chirping as opposed to mewing.

There are many legends surrounding the origins of the Chartreux, but what is certain is that this is an ancient breed and was documented in the *Histoire Naturelle* written by Comte de Buffon, published in 1723.

► *The Chartreux is slow maturing, not reaching adulthood until three years of age.*

▼ *Charles De Gaulle's Chartreux, Gris-Gris, followed him around the home like a dog.*

Breed box
Coat: Dense, soft and plush
Eyes: Round, gold or copper
Other features: Stocky body, muscular shoulders, agile legs, smiling expression
Grooming: Easy; weekly comb or brush
Temperament: Loyal, affectionate and very intelligent

Modern breed history is clearer. In the 1920s the two Leger sisters found a colony of these cats on the Brittany island of Belle-Ile and formed a programme of selective breeding, resulting in the breed being approved for exhibit in France in 1931. The Second World War decimated the breed but to keep the bloodlines going in Europe other blue cats, such as the British Shorthair, Russian Blues and Persians, were bred with existing stock. The stock in North America is much purer, as pure breeds, not colour, were used to increase numbers. It achieved Cat Fanciers' Association Championship status in 1987 but is not recognized by The UK General Council of the Cat Fancy because it is too similar to the British Shorthair.

The Chartreux is a wonderful pet which combines excellent hunting abilities with loyalty and adaptability. These cats are very intelligent and can be taught simple tricks. They are generally good with children and other animals and travel well. While they are a robust healthy cat, they can suffer from the congenital disorders of polycystic kidney disease and medial patellar luxation.

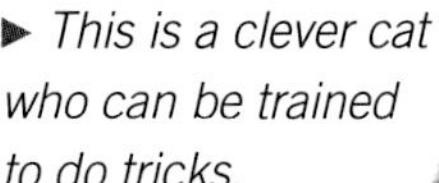

► *This is a clever cat who can be trained to do tricks.*

Chausie

The Chausie has full Championship status with The International Cat Association and is in the process of gaining New Breed recognition in the World Cat Federation. This cat started as a cross between non-domestic jungle cats (*Felis chaus*) and various domestic cat breeds. The breed name is pronounced 'chow see'. It originates from Egypt where there is strong evidence that jungle cats were kept as domestic pets thousands of years ago. Although it appears that breeders had been working to develop this breed for decades, it wasn't until the late 1990s that it started to become properly formulated.

Although appearing to be large, the Chausie weighs less than expected as they have a very athletic build. It is built for running and jumping. Males weigh from 4.08kg–6.80kg (9lb–15lb), females are smaller. It is a rather leggy breed with a tubular body and a deep chest. They have a long sloping forehead and muzzle. Ears are large, upright and often tufted, similar to that of a jungle cat. Tails are slightly shortened. Short-haired coats are brown-ticked tabby, grizzled tabby or black.

This active breed requires both mental and physical stimulation. They enjoy learning tricks, love playing fetch and, if trained, will walk happily on a harness and leash. The Chausie gets on well with children but would prefer to be a one-person cat as long as it is not left alone for long periods. They are fearless cats and for their own sake it may be safer if they are kept as indoor pets.

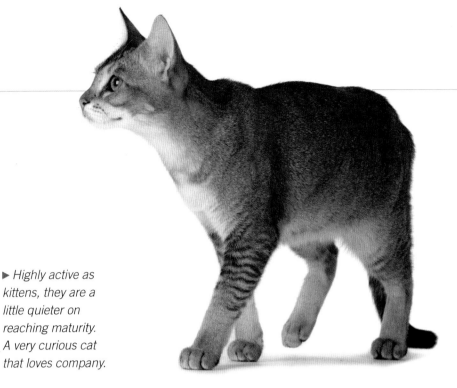

▶ *Highly active as kittens, they are a little quieter on reaching maturity. A very curious cat that loves company.*

▲ *TICA registration certificate codes generally show that these cats are four or more generations beyond jungle cats.*

▶ *The show breed standard only permits solid black, black grizzled tabby and black/ brown ticked tabby coats.*

Breed box

Coat: The grizzled tabby pattern is unique to this breed

Eyes: Golden to yellow or green; semi-oval in shape

Other features: Ears are proportionally large to the head, and whiskers are long

Grooming: Easy; moderate-shedding coat

Temperament: Extremely energetic, highly intelligent and loyal

Cheetoh

The Cheetoh is a new breed devised by crossing a Bengal with an Ocicat. It was accepted by the United Feline Organisation in 2004 and is currently termed as an 'experimental breed' by The International Cat Association. A breeding programme to formulate the Cheetoh was initiated in 2001 with the first kittens being produced in 2003. The criteria were to produce a cat that was wild-looking, but with all the attributes of both the Bengal and Ocicat. Originally from the USA, it is becoming popular in Australia and New Zealand where it is eligible for registration with the Australian National Cats Inc. and Cats Inc. New Zealand.

The Cheetoh is a shorthaired, spotted cat with a chiselled head and prominent ears. They move in a stealthy manner, similar to that of a jungle cat. This is a fairly large cat that has a well-muscled, solid body and a thick neck. Females are smaller and finer-built than males. Coat colours and patterns vary and include brown spotted, silver spotted, cinnamon spotted, brown marbled and blue marbled.

Breed box

Coat: 'Snow' coats are a combination of spotted and marbled patterns
Eyes: Large; colour dependent on coat colour including blue, green and gold
Other features: Front legs are slightly shorter than hind limbs
Grooming: Easy; very little to no shedding
Temperament: Gentle, social and affectionate

▲ *These cats have a high prey drive and if unrestrained will hunt domestic pets such as rabbits and guinea pigs.*

An extremely intelligent cat that has a strong hunting instinct, they are very lovable and enjoy sitting on laps. This is a docile breed that is happy in the company of children. They are described as dog-like and will follow their owners around. Surprisingly, they do not appear to be able to jump as high as some other breeds. Unusually, males show maternal instincts towards kittens and younger cats.

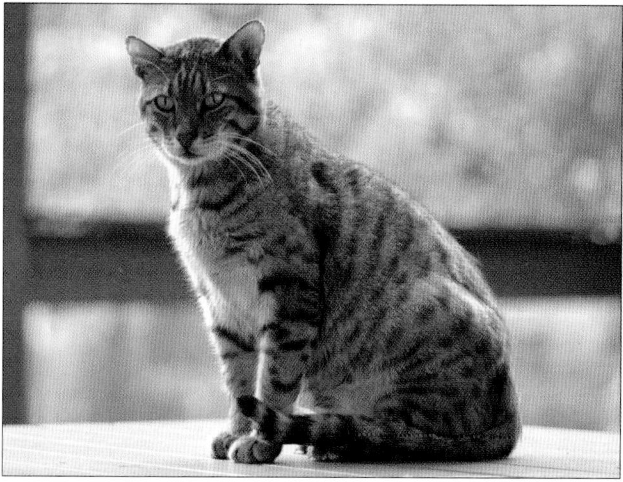

◄ *A wide range of coat colours can be seen including black spotted silver and lynx pointed gold.*

► *The rare, beautiful Cheetoh is one of the largest of the domestic cat breeds.*

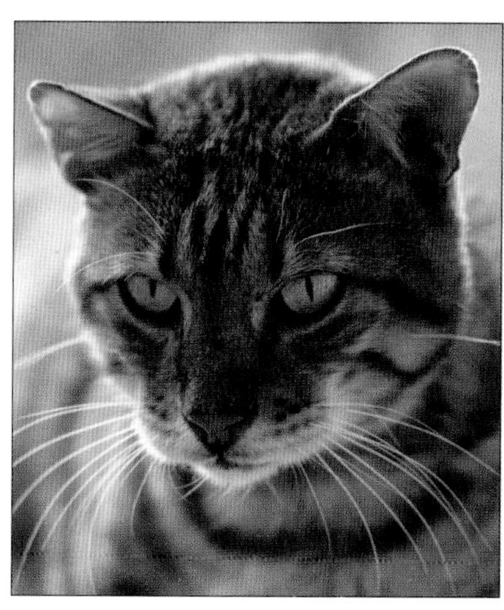

Chinese Li Hau

The Chinese Li Hau is probably one of the earliest known domestic cats. However, it has only recently been recognized within the cat fancy. It is a natural breed, existing for centuries. The name is pronounced 'lee-wah', and it is also known as a Dragon Li and Lu Hau Mao. The more formal Chinese name, Li Hua Mau, roughly translates as 'fox with a flower pattern cat'. It was first exhibited in Beijing under the ruling of the Cat Aficionado Association in 2004. In February 2010, the Chinese Li Hau was accepted by the Cat Fanciers Assocation for showing in the miscellaneous class. This and its rarity have now brought the Li Hau to the attention of the international cat fancy.

▼ *Chinese owners have been known to hold weddings with all the trappings for their Li Hau cats.*

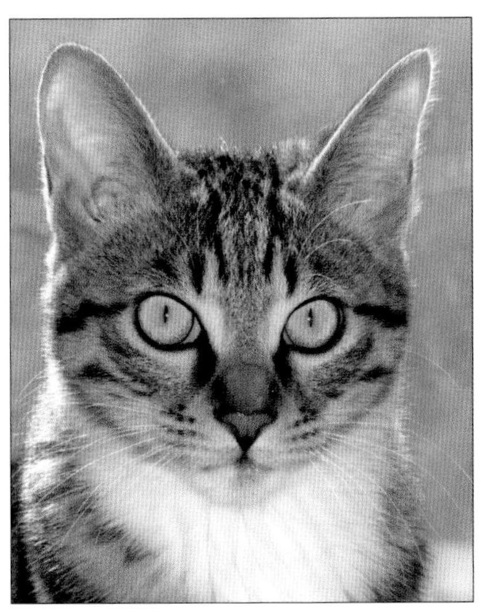

This is a large sturdy cat that retains a somewhat wild look. Its head is broad and diamond-shaped. Medium-sized ears are tufted at the tip. The neck is short and thick. A distinctive black spot at the corner of the mouth makes this cat look as if it is smiling. Legs and tail are banded with black and the tail has a black tip.

This is an extremely agile breed. A folklore story states that this cat is able to leap in the air and turn around twice before landing on its feet. If kept as an indoor cat it will require plenty of climbing equipment. It is a very intelligent breed that enjoys learning tricks and is well-known for its retrieving abilities. The Chinese Li Hau is a very proficient and effective hunter.

▼ *Coats consist of ticked hairs, black at the root, lighter in the middle and brown at the tip.*

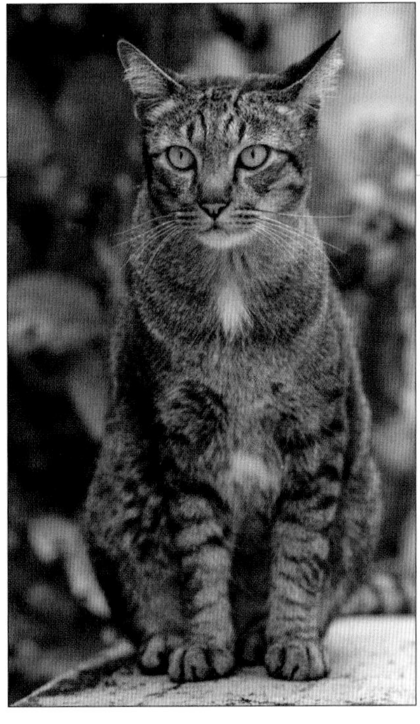

▲ *Part of the Li Hau breed standard states, 'No rat can escape its sharp claw, agile body and strong neck'.*

Breed box

Coat: Short, mackerel brown tabby pattern

Eyes: Luminescent, large, almond-shaped, yellow, brown or green colour

Other features: Takes up to three years to reach maturity

Grooming: Easy; weekly brushing to keep the thick, short coat tidy

Temperament: Affectionate, playful and active

Colourpoint Shorthair

► *This breed oozes elegance with its lean body, wedge-shaped head and large triangular ears.*

Colourpoint Shorthair is the name given by both the Cat Fancier's Association (CFA) and the World Cat Federation to denote a stand-alone breed. They were initially devised by crossing a Siamese with an American Shorthair. This is the same cross that produced the Oriental Shorthair and both breeds are similar in type. In the case of the Colourpoint Shorthair, cats must have the same colouration pattern as a Siamese but in non-traditional colours. The CFA awarded this breed, in all accepted colour variants, Championship status in 1969.

The wedge-shaped head and long, hard bodies are similar to a Siamese. Ears are large and flared. Eyes slant towards the nose. Despite the similarities with a Siamese, the CFA states that if a blindfold person held a Colourpoint Shorthair they would know the difference. Sixteen colours are currently accepted including red, cream, lynx and tortoiseshell points.

Breed box

Coat: Siamese colour points of seal, chocolate, lilac and blue not acceptable

Eyes: Deep vivid blue, almond-shaped

Other features: Bodies are very muscular

Grooming: Easy; remove loose hair and use a chamois to get a smooth finish

Temperament: Affectionate, loyal and sensitive to owner's mood

▼ *These beautiful cats are long-lived and may have a lifespan of up to 15–20 years.*

Some litters of Colourpoint Shorthairs contain kittens with traditional Siamese colouring. These are not suitable for registry or showing but make lovely pets.

This is a talkative breed that communicates with a series of 100 differing sounds. They can be vocally demanding. A very intelligent breed that likes to interact with its owner, they will retrieve and are very trainable. A range of toys will be welcome. Males can be aggressive with other animals and cats. This is a sensitive breed that doesn't adapt well to change and may be wary of strangers. They love warmth and will require a snug, draught-free bed.

▲ *Depending on the registry, the Colourpoint Shorthair is regarded as a distinct breed or a variant of a pre-existing one.*

Cornish Rex

The first recorded Cornish Rex kitten was born in 1950 in Cornwall, England, to a plain-coated tortoiseshell and white female. The kitten was a cream classic tabby with white chest and white belly. Its fur was closely waved. It was mated with its mother, and the resulting litter contained two curly-coated kittens. Because of the close interbreeding of the early Cornish Rexes, the gene pool was restricted and the kittens became weaker. Most of the kittens had to be put down, but one survivor, the son of one of the original kittens, was mated to his daughter before she was exported to the United States. Her lineage was strengthened by outcrossed matings with other breeds, and then back-crossed to rex cats to recreate the recessive curly coat. The breed was officially recognized in 1967.

▼ *The Cornish Rex, with its crisply waved coat, is now available in all colours and patterns, from self colours, to this White and Black Smoke, and all the various colourpoints.*

▲ *The Cornish Rex will require regular bathing due to the lack of coat hairs to absorb oil.*

The Cornish Rex has an elongated wedge of a head that curves gently at the forehead. The muzzle is rounded, the chin strong and the profile straight. The ears are startlingly large. The body is hard and muscular, with long straight legs, and tail fine and tapering. The breed comes in all colours, patterns and colour combinations.

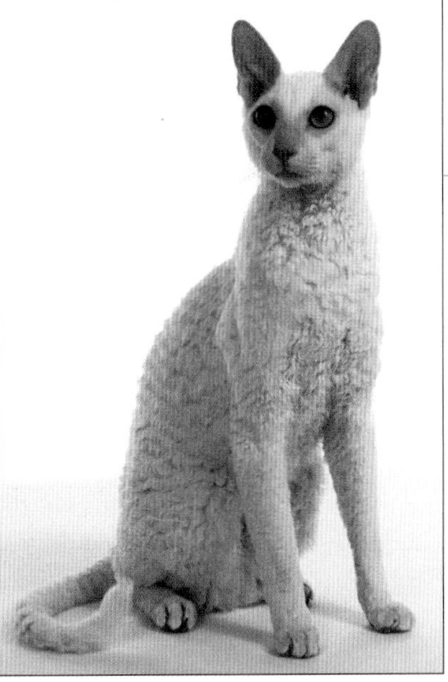

▲ *A loving cat that might demand attention. Really needs a playmate be it human, feline or canine.*

Despite belief to the contrary, the Cornish Rex is not hypoallergenic and will shed its downy coat. This breed loves being the centre of attention and enjoys being handled. They are intelligent and are known for their ability to open doors and cupboards. Although talkative they are not generally strident and vocally demanding. An active breed that retains kitten-like behaviour into old age. Best as an indoor cat as their coat provides insufficient protection from temperature extremes.

Breed box

Coat: Short, plushy, silky; no guardhairs; waves, curls or ripples particularly on back and tail

Eyes: Medium, oval

Other features: Big ears

Grooming: Gentle brushing, using fingers to set waves

Temperament: Intelligent, thoughtful, active

Coupari

▼ *This breed has an extremely sweet expression and makes a gentle, kind and affectionate companion.*

The Coupari differs from the Scottish Fold in the length of its coat. Both breeds share the same origin, that of a white barn cat with unusual ears. This cat produced kittens with both coat types but the longhaired cats were not favoured, as their long coats made them look as if they didn't have any ears. When the standard for the Scottish Fold evolved no mention of the longhaired variant was mentioned. In the 1980s an American breeder started to exhibit a longhaired Scottish Fold and they gained recognition. This breed is called a Coupari by British breeders but in various other registries it is listed as a Scottish Fold Longhair, Longhair Fold and a Highland Fold.

This is a domestic breed that has a dominate-gene mutation that causes the cartilage in the ears to bend forward so that the ears are folded. At birth kittens are born with straight ears but within approximately 21 days the fold starts to show. The Coupari has a round, domed head with a short neck and large, round expressive eyes. This combination makes the cat look rather owl-like.

These are placid cats that become very attached to their owners. They can suffer from anxiety if left alone. Coupari are intelligent but some do have a stubborn streak. They like to keep themselves well-groomed, so it is important to remove shedding hair to avoid the formation of hairballs. This breed is renowned for sleeping on their backs and sitting with legs stretched out and paws on the belly. Couparis can suffer separation anxiety.

Breed box

Coat: Nearly any colour or colour combination, including white, permissible

Eyes: Large, round and expressive

Other features: Full cheeks and a short nose

Grooming: Extensive; brushing required at least three times a week

Temperament: Docile, loving and kind

▼ *The origin of this breed can be traced to the village of Coupar Angus, 21k (13m) Perth, Scotland.*

▼ *The distinctive ears of the Coupari do not fold forward until kittens are three months old.*

Cymric

The Cymric is the longhaired version of the Manx cat. Clear breed standards have been set out by many cat registries. In some the Cymric is regarded as a separate breed and in others as a longhaired variant of the Manx cat. The Cymric (which means of, or from, Wales) was inevitable as far as genetic inheritance is concerned, even though the longhair gene is recessive to the shorthair gene. It was necessary to introduce tailed outcrosses into Manx breeding programmes to strengthen the type.

▼ *Large, full eyes and widely spaced ears plus a dense coat give the head a rounded appearance.*

▲ *The Cymric can look larger than a Manx cat. This is an illusion due to the thick longhaired coat.*

▲ *'Rumpy' cats are most prized among the showing fraternity. Rumpy-raisers have a short knob tail.*

This widened the gene pool and so increased the possibility of the recessive longhair gene finding a match and producing a longhaired version of the Manx cat.

The first recorded Cymric appeared in Canada in the 1960s and the variety gained impetus from that point, mainly in North America. As with the Manx, there is the 'true' rumpy version with a hollow in place of a tail, the stumpy – with a stub of a tail, and the occasional long-tailed version. The rumpy's lack of tail is caused by a mutant gene similar to the one that causes spina bifida in humans, and kittens born to cats with this condition may be stillborn.

▼ *A Blue Cymric – the stumpy version with a short stub of a tail – shows the chunky bodyline of the Manx breed beneath its heavy fur.*

Breed box

Coat: Silky with hard guardhairs; not cottony, uneven in length
Eyes: Large and round; colour in keeping with coat colour
Other features: May have no tail, a stump or a nearly full tail
Grooming: Easy with daily brushing
Temperament: Affectionate, intelligent, extremely loyal; likes to be with its owner

Cyprus Cat

► *The tail of the semi-longhaired variant should be well-plumed as this specimen shows to perfection.*

The Cyprus Cat is a landrace of the domestic cat found in the country of its name. The term 'landrace' describes a species of animal that is traditional and has developed naturally to suit its environment. Most landraces are relatively genetically uniform. This is the case with the Cyprus Cat. These cats were believed to have been originally brought to Cyprus from Egypt or Palestine and evolved to suit their situation. However, recently archaeologists have discovered an ancient cat skeleton in a grave in Cyprus. This cat was buried alongside a human and the remains predate Egyptian cats by 4,000 years. Therefore, there is strong evidence to prove that the reverse actually happened. It is fully recognized by the World Cat Federation, and partially by the World Cat Congress, under the name Aphrodite's Giant. The International Cat Association provisionally recognized the breed, naming it Aphrodite. The Cyprus cat has two coat variants, shorthaired and semi-longhaired. The shorthaired type is found in the hotter coastal areas, while the semi-longhaired cat is more predominate in the cool mountainous regions. It appears that this cat has adapted to suit the climate in which it lives. Both types have a range of coat colours. As it is not yet recognized as a breed in its own right there is no formalized breed standard.

Many Cyprus Cats are feral in the country and can be seen in large populations in major Greek cities. They are particularly good hunters and prey on rodents and snakes. This cat is athletic and energetic and makes a loving domestic pet.

Breed box

Coat: Both semi-longhaired and shorthaired have soft undercoats
Eyes: Almond-shaped with colour dependent on coat colour
Other features: Large muscular bodies, but never cobby
Grooming: Easy-to-moderate dependent on coat type
Temperament: Active and aloof but enjoy being lap cats.

▲ *The breed is known by many names including Cypriot Cat, Saint Nicholas Cat and Saint Helen Cat.*

◄ *In 4th century* AD *it is said that St Helen of Constantinople sent boats of cats to Cyprus to deal with an infestation of snakes.*

Devon Rex

In 1960, another curly-coated cat was discovered in Devon, England, the neighbouring county to the home of the Cornish Rex. A curly-coated feral male had mated with a stray, straight-haired female, and the litter included one curly-coated male. As the curly hair gene is recessive and needs to find a matching one to emerge, the female must have had a compatible gene pool. However, the gene which caused the coat was quite different from that of the Cornish Rex – mating the two breeds resulted in only straight-coated offspring.

The Devon Rex coat is generally less dense than that of the Cornish Rex and, without careful breeding, very sparse coats can result. Physically, the Devon Rex is quite different from the Cornish. It shares the muscular build, slim legs and long, whip-like tail, but it is broad-chested, and has a flat forehead, prominent cheek-bones and a crinkled brow. All coat colours, patterns and colour combinations are allowed.

The Devon Rex enjoys interacting with human companions, is easy to train and will retrieve items. They have dog-like characteristics and will happily follow their owner all around the house and settle on a lap when anyone sits down. It is a vocal breed that uses a series of gentle coos, chirps and trills to communicate. This cat gets on well with children and they will accept dogs and other animals if properly introduced. A delightful breed that remains a kitten at heart throughout its lifetime.

Breed box

Coat: Very short, fine, wavy, soft; can have a rippled effect

Eyes: Wide-set, large and oval; all colours

Grooming: Requires very gentle stroking with a soft mitt rather than a brush

Temperament: Extraordinarily playful; mischievous yet never unkind

▼ *The remarkably large, low-set ears and slightly upturned nose are a feature of this breed.*

▼ *Very intelligent and capable of learning extremely complex tricks with the correct motivation.*

▲ *The Devon Rex is affectionately described as having a pixie-like expression – which reflects its mischievous character.*

► *The facial tactile whiskers are short and curled, often giving the impression that it has none.*

Domestic Cat

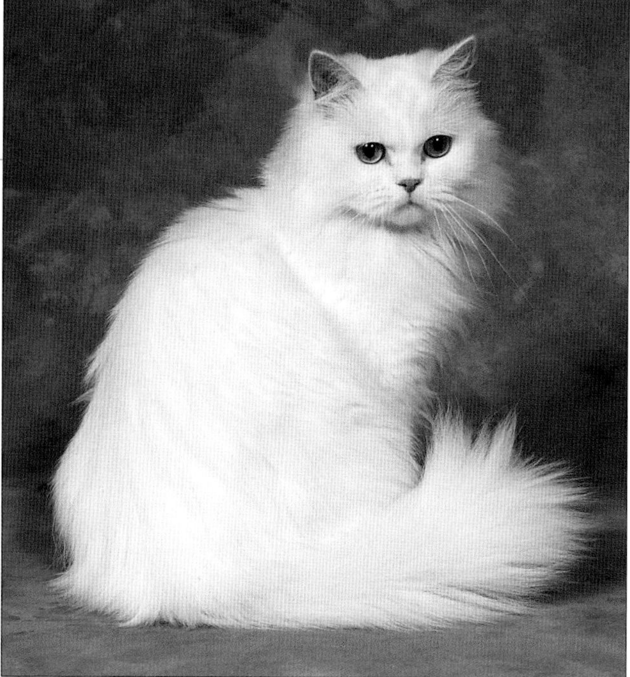

◄ *Would you like a very expensive White Persian or Balinese, or would this extraordinarily pretty non-pedigreed longhaired white do just as well?*

Non-pedigreed cats – also known as household pets, domestic cats or random-bred – are the most common cats kept as pets. Fewer than five per cent of pet cats have a pedigree.

Acquiring a non-pedigree is far easier and cheaper than buying a purebred cat. Rescue organizations and humane societies are overflowing with animals all ready to make ideal companions, and some are as beautiful as their purebred equivalents. It is unlikely that such a cat will cost more than a donation to the society and the cost of vaccinations.

The disadvantage of having a non-pedigreed animal is that you invariably do not know what you are getting, whereas a quality guarantee comes with a pedigree. Because of their mixed ancestry, non-pedigrees are usually intelligent and affectionate, but a bad character gene could slip in.

COMMON HERITAGE

Both pedigreed and pet cats have common ancestors in the domesticated cat. However, the pedigree has evolved as a result of selective breeding, while the pet cat conforms to no special standards except those dictated by evolutionary pressures and the need to survive.

Non-pedigreed cats may have coats of any length and in a range of colours that are usually plain, blotched, striped or patched. Cats of one colour are less common than tabbies, bi-colours and tortoiseshells, and may indicate an unplanned mating with a pedigreed partner. The eyes are usually green or yellow and the majority of non-pedigreed noses are fairly long.

STRAY CATS

Non-neutered (unaltered) mongrel cats roam all over the place, breeding prolifically. The resulting unwanted litters add to a population of feral cats – those that have been born in the wild or that have reverted to the wild state. Some, like those found by the hundred on Greek islands, tread a fine line between wildness and domesticity. Such cats present enormous problems for rescue organizations (if they exist), but have the potential for providing all the qualities looked for in the pet cat. They can be socialized, but the owner has to spend as much time with the cat as possible, particularly during the first few weeks. Medical examination and inoculations are also important.

◄ *If your bank balance cannot stretch to the cost of a Maine Coon Cat, this well-whiskered, soft ginger semi-longhair might suffice.*

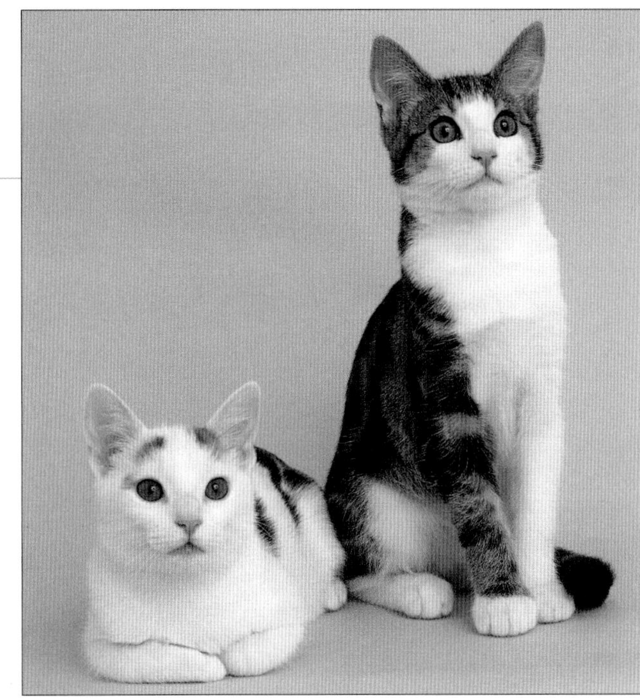

▶ *Any coat length and colour combination is possible in the non-pedigreed range. What these two shorthairs lack in irregular coat pattern they make up for in alertness and pretty, balanced features.*

NEAR MISSES

For something a little more refined, you could go for a cat that only just misses being a pedigree. In one tiny, isolated community, there was only one local unneutered (unaltered) tom – which was clearly the sire of a litter produced by a neighbouring purebred Lilac Point Siamese queen. Four of her kittens were lilac-pointed (albeit with slightly longer, coarser hair than their pedigreed mother), and the fifth looked like a Black Oriental Shorthair. Nonetheless, they were all deemed to be non-pedigree cats. Fortunately for them, they had inherited the best combination of their mother's oriental looks and their father's robust health and character.

Other non-pedigreed cats can have known ancestry too. Farm cats, for example, may have been bred for generations. Some kittens would be selected and kept because they were prettier, more intelligent, or had better mouse-catching potential than others. If the owners had kept a record of these kittens' parentage, they would be beginning to establish a written pedigree. That is how the pedigree system began.

▲ *It looks as if there is a touch of Persian in this short-nosed, cobby ginger, and he seems to have inherited some of the Persian placidity as well.*

SHOW STANDARD PETS

Many cat shows have Non-pedigree or Household Pet classes. There are no set standards of hair length, colour or conformation as there are with the pedigreed breeds. The cats are judged on their general appeal – their friendliness, beauty and condition.

▼ *A well-defined blaze, chest and paws would be desirable in a pedigreed bi-colour, but with this non-pedigree, character would be a more important factor if it were to be entered in a show.*

Domestic Lynx

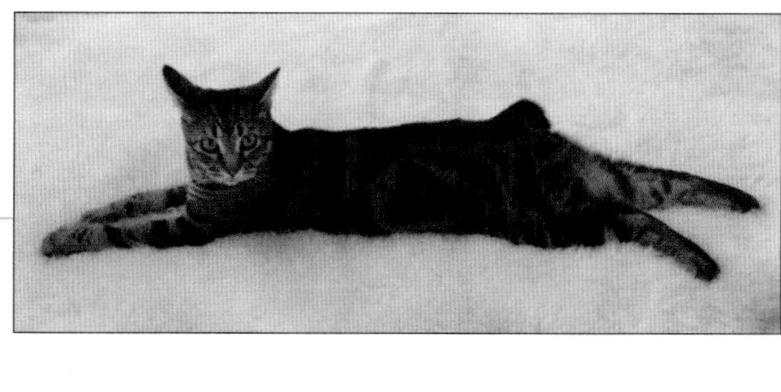

The Domestic Lynx (or Desert Lynx) originates from the USA. This breed is one of a number created by crossing wild cats with domestic cats. In this case, breeders in the 1980s crossed Bobcats and Canadian Lynx with domestic cat breeds. The aim was to produce a cat that looked as similar as possible to its wild ancestors but have the temperament of the domestic cat.

This large rare cat has a triangular-shaped head with a fairly long and broad nose. The chin is strong and jaws are very powerful. Hind legs are slightly longer than the front. Paws are rounded. The tail is short, similar to that of a Lynx. It must be flexible, with a minimum 10cm (4in) length but never hang below the knee. The thick coat has a silky texture and is almost completely waterproof. The neck is covered with a ruff and some Domestic Lynx have a beard. Many colours and patterns of coat are permitted including ticking, spotted and colourpoint. Any white marking is considered a fault. Tails generally have a black tip.

Although Domestic Lynx have a wild appearance they have gentle temperaments. They are affectionate and loving towards their owners. Males can be aggressive to other cats but both sexes normally tolerate dogs. This cat is a very effective hunter. Due to their size they may not suit owners who live in a small apartment. They need to exercise and should be provided with the opportunity to climb.

► Exercise caution and supervise any interactions between this cat and small domestic pets.

► Adult males can weigh up to 7.25kg (16lb). Both sexes have a medium-length body.

◄ Despite its wild look this breed is sociable and playful. They form a loving bond with their owners.

Breed box

Coat: Short to semi-longhair with a longer coat on the belly and thighs

Eyes: Almond-shaped and slightly slanting; all colours permitted

Other features: Massive paws with hair between the pads

Grooming: Moderate; comb through carefully to remove dead hair and debris

Temperament: Gentle, social and trusting

▼ Brown, ebony, silver and blue coats can either be spotted, ticked or clouded markings.

Don Sphynx

The Don Sphynx, also known as a Donskoy, is a 'hairless' breed from Russia. In 1987 a hairless female cat was found in the town of Rostov near the river Don. It was initially thought that she had a skin disease but veterinary checks proved her fit and healthy. They revealed that she was a mutation caused by a dominate gene which could be passed to further generations. She went on to have a litter of kittens who were also hairless. The breed is now recognized by The International Cat Association and the Fédération Internationale Féline. The Don Sphynx is not related to the Sphynx Cat.

▲ *The distinctive Don Spynx has a muscular body, long legs and is medium-sized.*

◄ *This breed is prone to dental problems and gum disease so good dental hygiene is vital.*

Breed box

Coat: Lack of coat and low dander cause less allergies in people

Eyes: Large and almond-shaped

Other features: Heads are wedge-shaped with large and long ears

Grooming: Moderate; the skin needs daily wiping to stop a build-up of oil

Temperament: Active, unique and extremely friendly

Don Sphynx have four distinct hair types. Totally hairless cats are 'Suede', 'Rubber Bald' or 'Nude'; cats that appear bald but feel like chamois are 'Flocked'; while those with fine, thin wiry coats are 'Brush'; and fine, velvet fuzz coats are termed 'Velour'. Generally, all types lose their coat as the cat matures. The breed has long, webbed toes. This gives them a unique ability to pick up and hold objects. Males are significantly larger and more muscular than females.

This breed suffers from changes in temperature. The sun can cause sunburn and they may need clothing to keep them warm in winter. They are more suited to indoor living where temperatures can be controlled. The Don Sphynx is very social and affectionate but needs an owner who is at home for a large part of the day to prevent loneliness. This is a highly intelligent and curious cat that loves attention. There is some concern that the dominant genetic mutation producing hairlessness could cause various health problems.

▼ *Do not be tempted to over- or under-bathe your Don Sphynx as both can cause the skin to be oily.*

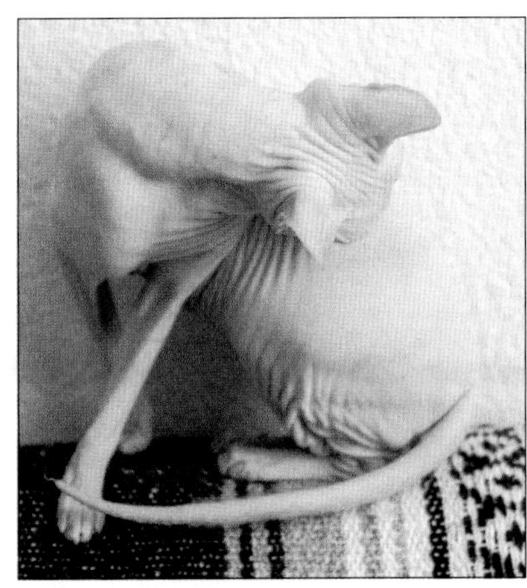

Dwarf Cats

There are a range of dwarf cats, some of which are recognized as breeds in their own right. Others are hybrids and some are listed as experimental breeds with the hope of gaining full breed recognition. Dwarfism in cats is caused by a naturally occurring defective dominate gene. These cats all show symptoms of genetic disorders (osteochondrodysplasia) of the bone and cartilage, the most noticeable being shortened legs. This makes them different to small cat breeds, such as the Singapura. Likewise, they should not be confused with cats described as 'teacup', 'toy' or 'miniature'.

All dwarf cat breeds, variants or types have the Munchkin somewhere in their foundation. The Munchkin is the original dwarf cat and was recognized by The International Cat Association as a breed in 1994. Dwarf cats are popular in America and are starting to be seen in other countries.

There is much controversy surrounding dwarf cat breeds with many registries not recognizing them as legitimate breeds. In some countries breeding cats with this defective gene is banned and they have also been condemned by the European Convention for the Protection of Pet Animals. In addition to short, thickened legs there are other possible health issues associated with these cats. These include brittle bones, heart and lung problems, neurological disorders and mobility restrictions. Dwarf cats are also prone to obesity and must be kept to a carefully controlled diet to avoid additional stress to their limbs.

Potential owners are advised to research carefully prior to purchasing a cat carrying this defective gene.

Social media has done much to promote dwarf cats to the wider public. Some individuals, such as Grumpy Cat and Lil Bub, had a worldwide following and became household names.

► *There are three causes of dwarfism in cats: osteochondrodysplasia, pituitary dwarfism and selective dwarfism.*

◄ *Cats with pituitary dwarfism take longer to grow their adult coat and suffer from dental problems.*

List of some Dwarf Cats

Munchkin	Lambkin
Minskin	Kinkalow
Bambino	Genetta
Dwelf	Elf Cat
Napoleon	Shorty
Skookum	Minuet

▼ *Osteochondrodysplasia dwarfism produces heads that are slightly larger than normal.*

Dwelf

▼ *Short hair is present on the bridge of the nose and on the back and edges of the ears.*

▼ *Both eyebrows and whiskers are short or almost non-existent despite the prominent whisker pads.*

The Dwelf is a small hairless cat that is the result of crosses between Sphynx, American Curl breeds and Munchkin. Each of the foundation breeds contribute a distinctive feature to the Dwelf. They originate from America. The name is devised from the words dwarf; denoting short legs, plus elf; describing its looks. They weigh between 2.7–4.08kg (6lb–9lb), so are half the size of an average cat. Devotees claim that this cat is 'so ugly that it is cute'.

Breed box

Coat: Appear hairless but has an almost invisible down of hair
Eyes: Large, open, slightly slanted and almond-shaped
Other features: Wrinkles on the face, shoulders and legs should be obvious
Grooming: Moderate; requires regular wiping and bathing to stop build-up of oil
Temperament: Playful, affectionate and intelligent

Bodies are stout and, despite its small size, should never look frail. They have a well-rounded abdomen with a just-fed look. The back rises from the shoulders to the tail. Legs are short but proportionally well-boned and muscular. Hind legs are slightly longer than forelegs. The head is somewhat longer than wide, with a flat forehead. Whisker pads are pronounced. Ears are flared at the base, curling inwards with a vertical crimp. The tips curve towards each other, across the top of the head, giving the cat an elfin look.

Dwelf cats retain a kittenish appearance throughout their lives. Like all hairless cats they can suffer in extremes of temperature either with sunburn or hypothermia. Therefore, they are more suitable as indoor cats. Their short legs don't seem to impend their activity and they are able to run and jump, although not as high as the average cat. This cat is suitable for families and those living in small apartments. Children need to be especially gentle when handling these cats as the lack of coat makes them vulnerable to knocks and scrapes.

◄ *As the body is only covered by a fuzz of coat the natural wrinkles in the skin are noticeable.*

► *A fully grown Dwelf cat is approximately half the size and weight of an average domestic cat.*

Egyptian Mau

On ancient Egyptian manuscripts and murals, a cat is depicted that looks very much like the modern breed of Egyptian Mau. The breeder wanted to replicate the cats of the Pharaohs, and founded the breeding line from a native Egyptian breed that seemed to have evolved spontaneously in the Cairo region. The first Egyptian Mau (the name is ancient Egyptian for a sacred domestic cat) kitten was shown in Rome in the 1950s. Its owner emigrated with her cats to America, where the breed was granted recognition by the Cat Fanciers' Association in 1977. It is now available in Silver (charcoal markings on silver), Bronze, and Smoke (black markings on charcoal/silver underlay) varieties. The Bronze, with dark brown to black markings on a warm bronze undercoat, is closest in appearance to the cat depicted on Egyptian murals. Europe did not recognize the breed until 1992. A spotted cat bred from Siamese lines in England during the 1960s was originally called Egyptian Mau, but later became established as the Oriental Spotted Tabby.

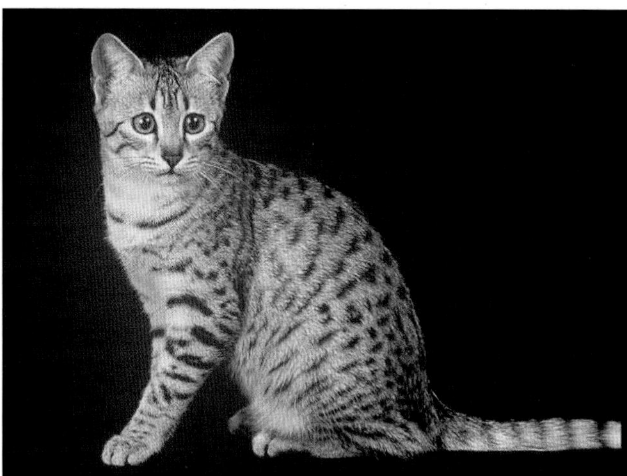

◄ *Spotted cats very similar to this were illustrated in ancient Egyptian manuscripts and murals. The M-shaped mark on its brow is said to echo the pattern on the back of the scarab beetle.*

The Egyptian Mau is a medium-sized, muscular cat, pleasing to the eye, easy to groom, and with an extrovert personality. It tends to bond with just one or two people, and is not averse to learning a trick or two, or to walking on a lead. Its head is slightly oriental in shape, with large, alert ears, although its muzzle is well rounded. The conformation is generally graceful, with hind legs slightly longer than the front legs, and a well-balanced tail.

Despite complete domestication the

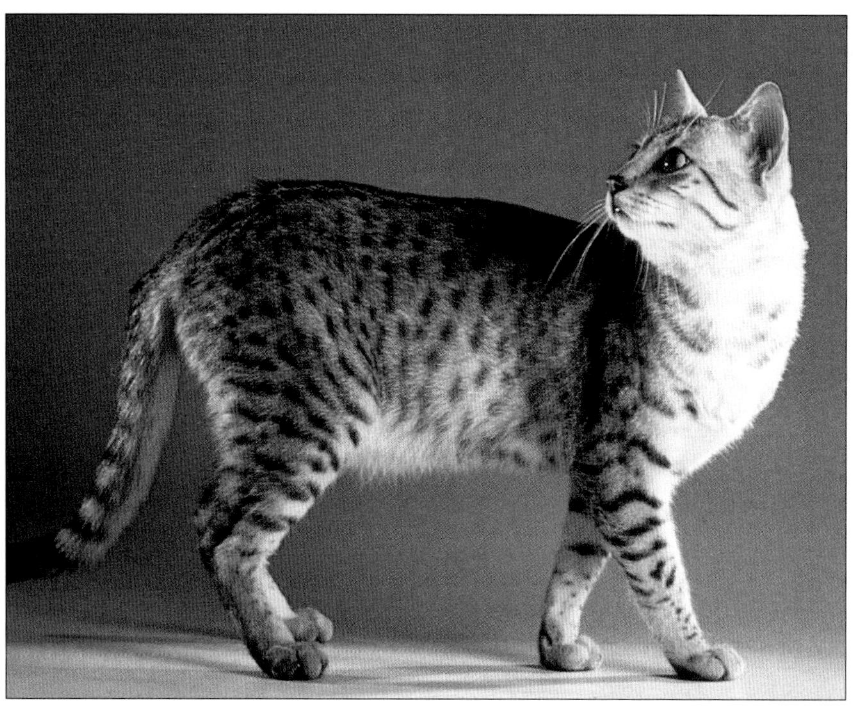

◄ *The well-defined spots are the most important features of the Mau. This Bronze is probably the closest in colour to its Egyptian forebears.*

Breed box

Coat: Medium length, dense, lustrous, silky
Eyes: Large, alert, almond-shaped, slightly slanted; light green
Other features: Spotted coat
Grooming: Easy; regular gentle brushing to remove dead hairs
Temperament: Affectionate, and lively

► *Egyptian Maus have a longer gestation period (approximately 73 days) compared with the average 65–67 days for the majority of domestic cats.*

Egyptian Mau retains a flap of loose skin that runs from the flank to the hind leg knee. This allows the cat more freedom of movement, enabling it to twist freely while jumping. Additional flexibility would have been a great asset, for catching prey or fleeing from a predator, when its ancestors were living feral. The breed also retains the stealth-like gait of a panther. When stationary they should like as if they are on tiptoes, totally balanced and ready to leap. This cat is a true athlete and shows great grace in every move that it makes. They are the fastest of the domestic cat breeds and are capable of reaching speeds of up to 43.5kph (30mph).

In addition to the coat colours previously mentioned, the Egyptian Mau may produce kittens with a dilute coat colour version. These additional colours include blue, blue silver, blue spotted and blue smoke. Dilute Mau's, and those that are black, do not conform to the standard for the breed so are not eligible for showing but make enchanting pets.

This is a moderate to highly active cat and needs the opportunity to exercise. They love climbing. While cats allowed outdoors are able to practise this skill, indoor cats should not be denied the chance to get up high. The Mau loves playing with toys and will stalk and pounce on any moving object. They also seem to get great enjoyment from playing with water and have been known to turn taps on for their own entertainment.

◄ *Egyptian Maus are relatively rare, with less than 300 kittens registered annually with The Governing Council of the Cat Fancy*

▲ *Eyes are very expressive and appear to change from green to turquoise according to mood.*

The Egyptian Mau is a vocal cat that communicates with a unique and wide vocabulary of mews, chirrups, squawks and chortles.

European Burmese

Both the European Burmese and the Burmese share the same foundation ancestor, Wong Mau. This was the name of the first Burmese cat imported from the east to the western world by Dr Thompson in 1930. As she was the only cat of this breed in the USA she had to be mated to a sire of similar type. The chosen cat was a Siamese. Resulting litters proved that Wong Mau also carried a pointed gene. Her kittens were a mix of solid and pointed colours. Only those of solid colouring were used in the future breeding programmes. When the Burmese breed was considered uniform, a few cats were imported to the UK. Again, the lack of breeding stock forced the re-introduction of the Siamese, resulting in the Burmese and European Burmese going in different directions.

It is strange to consider that both breeds had the same ancestor, Wong Mau, but are now completely different, with differing standards. Some cat registries do not recognize the Burmese and the European Burmese as two different breeds but rather as different types. Those that do so, refer to the British version as a European Burmese.

The European Burmese is also known as the British Burmese or the Traditional Burmese. It is an elegant cat, of medium size, with rounded contours. The body is long, slim and muscular but surprisingly weighs heavier than it looks. The back is straight from the shoulders to the base of the tail. Heads are slightly rounded at the top with wide cheeks tapering to a short, blunt wedge. This cat has a strong lower jaw and chin. They have a longer nose than the Burmese. Ears are set well apart, are wide at the base and have rounded tips. Tails are medium length and taper to a rounded tip. Males weigh up to 6.35kg (14lb) and females 3.2–4.5kg (7–10lb).

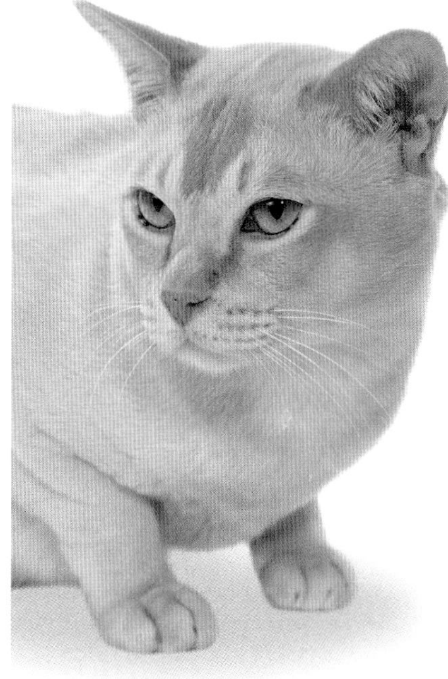

Breed box
Coat: Shorthaired, fine and glossy
Eyes: Slightly curved and slanted toward the nose, yellow to amber in colour
Other features: Legs are long with neat oval paws
Grooming: Easy; weekly brushing will encourage a shine
Temperament: Intelligent, calm and friendly

◄ *You can see the marked kink in the nose of this Red Burmese. This is known as a nose break and is a feature of the breed in general.*

◄ *Basic cream is mingled with pinkish dove grey in the Lilac Tortie. There are also Brown, Blue and Chocolate Torties.*

► *Powderings of colour over mask, paws, tail and legs on the Cream Burmese are like ghostly versions of the points on a Siamese.*

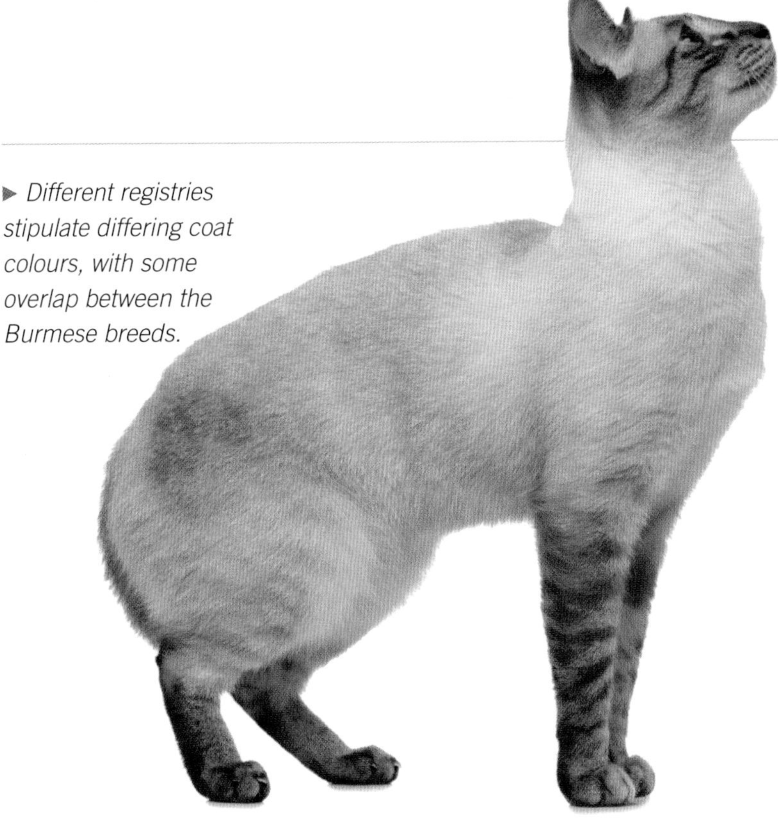

▶ *Different registries stipulate differing coat colours, with some overlap between the Burmese breeds.*

▼ *A wedge-shaped head with long tapering muzzle is typical of the European Burmese.*

This breed has ten coat colours; brown, brown tortoiseshell, chocolate, chocolate tortoiseshell, cream, red, lilac, lilac tortoiseshell, blue and blue tortoiseshell. Any white patches or noticeable white hairs are considered a fault. The shorthaired coat has very little undercoat and lays close to the skin. A high sheen can be produced by smoothing with a chamois cloth or a piece of velvet. Shedding coat should be removed with a rubber pad or brush. Domestic pets will seldom, if ever, need bathing.

This is a highly intelligent breed that takes readily to training. Most are happy to learn a range of tricks including a retrieve. Some even learn how to open doors and cupboards. With time and patience, they can be encouraged to walk on a leash and harness. They are very loyal and loving and although happy to interact with all members of the family will often pick out one person with whom they form a very strong bond. This is not a cat to leave alone for long periods as they thrive on companionship. They are very curious and want to be involved in everything that their owner does. Provide a selection of toys and set aside time to have a daily play session to keep them entertained, both physically and mentally.

◀ *Energetic and dog-like, this people-loving cat will form a strong bond with its owner.*

European Burmese are vocal and have a soft, hoarse and raspy voice. Voices are used to chat as well as to demand. They are prolific purrers. Vets have commented that it is sometimes hard to hear a heartbeat, even with a stethoscope, over their rumbling purr. This is a cat that loves to sit on a lap or to be cuddled. They will expect to share their owner's bed too. This breed is tolerant of other cats and dogs if properly introduced into their lives. Most are good with children and make model family pets. They are also ideal companions for the elderly.

European Shorthair

The smart version of the feral cat of Europe is a little more streamlined than its British and American counterparts. It is probably the closest of the national shorthairs to the wild species. A clear distinction has been made between British and European Shorthairs since 1982.

The European Shorthair is more elegant than the British, with an emphasis on lithe muscularity rather than round cobbiness. In general shape, it is more like the American Shorthair, though it may be rather larger. It is strong, broad-chested and quite deep in the flank, with fairly long, well-boned legs and rounded paws. The tail is in proportion to the body and rounded at the tip, and largish ears are set erect and fairly wide apart.

Unlike the American and British Shorthairs, the European is allowed what is known as open registration in Fédération Internationale Féline shows. This means that as long as it conforms to certain standards and

▲ *The leaner features and longer nose of the European Shorthair compared with its British and American equivalents can be seen in this handsome Tabby.*

▼ *A pair of European Silver Tabbies display the well-defined 'necklaces' and well-spaced leg rings that are characteristic of a good mackerel tabby pattern.*

▼ *This ancient breed originates from Sweden and Finland, with the first cats registered in 1946.*

Breed box

Coat: Dense; crisp texture

Eyes: slanted, gentle expression; all colours

Other features: Territorial, combative towards other cats; prolific breeders

Grooming: Easy; regular brushing

Temperament: Affectionate, brave, lively, independent, freedom-loving (must not be confined indoors)

European Shorthair colours and patterns

Self colours: White (blue-, green- or odd-eyed), Black, Blue, Red, Cream

Tabby: Black, Blue, Red, Cream, Tortie and Blue Tortie Patterns – classic, mackerel, spotted

Tortoiseshell: Black Tortie, Blue Tortie, Red Tortie

Smoke: Black, Blue, Red, Cream, Tortie and Blue Tortie

Bi-colour, Van, Harlequin: solid colour (Black, Blue, Red, Cream, Tortie, Blue Tortie) plus white

Patched: Black Tortie and White, Blue Tortie and White, Black and White, Blue and White, Red and White, Cream and White

characteristic features, and has been assessed and passed by senior judges in Novice classes, any cat may be registered as a foundation pedigree and compete for show titles. Many a worthy European Grand Champion has had its origins in the farmyard! The result of this is that the European Shorthair is particularly adaptable, independent and bright. It also has a remarkably efficient immune system.

The European Shorthair cat is a strong active breed that is adaptable to change within the home, making it an ideal family pet. Most European Shorthairs tolerate dogs well and enjoy the company of other cats. It is an excellent skilled hunter, adept at keeping both house and garden rodent-free. This is a hugely popular breed in Scandinavia.

▲ *A relatively relaxed attitude to breeding programmes means that there is enormous variety of colour and temperament with the European Shorthair pedigree.*

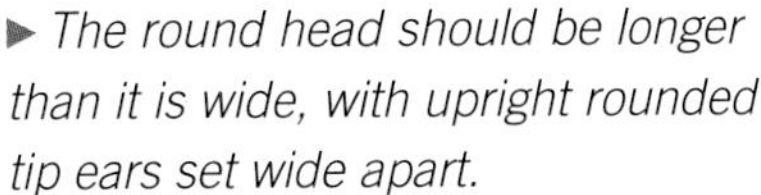

▶ *The round head should be longer than it is wide, with upright rounded tip ears set wide apart.*

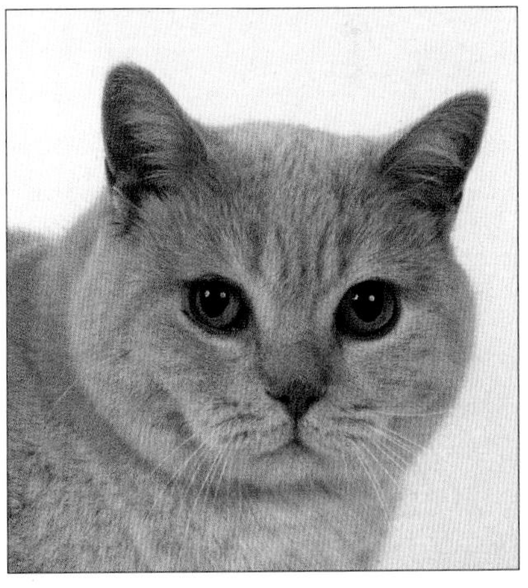

▼ *The European Shorthair is the national cat of Finland.*

Exotic Shorthair

▲ *Eyes complement the rich red of the Red Tabby's coat. Brilliance of eye colour is an important distinction for this breed in general.*

The aim in breeding the Exotic Shorthair (known simply as the Exotic in the United States) was to produce a Persian cat without the long hair to reduce the grooming commitment. These shorthaired cats are judged in the Longhair Persian-type section, which can cause some confusion for newcomers to the showing scene.

In facial make-up and expression, body shape and even character, the Exotic Shorthair has all the characteristics of the Persian breeds, and is even available in the same colours and variations. It is a medium-sized cat with a short body, short, thick legs and large paws. The head is round, with a short nose and small, wide-set, round-tipped ears. Breeders of British Shorthairs maintained a policy for a long time of outcrossing to Persian cats every fourth generation or so. They wanted to encourage massiveness of bone and intensity of eye colour in the existing breed, rather than create a new one. Persian type was not, in fact, very distant from the British Shorthair and was therefore likely to improve it.

American breeders, however, did not have a large gene pool of British Shorthairs. They therefore used the Burmese (which was the one really round-headed cat they did have), and later the American Shorthair. The way in which the American cat fancy had developed the

▲ *Brilliant orbs of gold-copper are startling against the solid density of the Black Exotic Shorthair. The nose leather and paw pads are black.*

▲ *A Silver Tabby shows off her eyes lined in black like a Chinchilla. Her shorter coat, however, appears more darkly tipped and the pattern more obvious than that of the longhaired Shaded Silver.*

◄ *The coat of a Blue-Cream Exotic shows definite, but scattered areas of cream among the subtle shades of soft blue-grey.*

▼ *A Tortoiseshell Colourpointed Exotic demonstrates the distinctive Persian body conformation with the large, round head, full body and shortish tail and legs.*

▲ *Persian facial features combine with the blue eyes of colourpointed varieties in this Tortoiseshell Colourpointed Exotic. The colourpointed range is fully represented in the breed.*

Burmese from its introduction in the early 1930s had ensured that its head shape and eye shape were closer than any other breed to Persian Longhair type. This meant it was only a matter of a few generations of kittens before the Exotic Shorthair was successfully developed in the 1960s. Since 1968, Burmese and British Shorthairs have not been allowed in Exotic breeding programmes in the United States.

It soon became popular, and is now bred in the full range of self colours, bi-colours, tabbies and tortoiseshells, and shaded, tipped and colourpointed varieties. Judging standards are very stringent, with an emphasis on brilliance of eye colour. Any hint of slanted eye shape from the Burmese contribution to its lineage, or a fleck of rogue colour in the iris, is frowned upon. The Exotic Shorthair has the placidity and dignity of the Persian, yet has a playful and affectionate side. It is patient with children, and is contented to be an indoor cat.

Despite being shorthaired, the coat is longer than other shorthaired breeds and requires more attention. It benefits from daily grooming. Try brushing or combing from tail to head, against the pile of the fur to encourage the fur to stand up, brush-like, from the body.

Breed box

Coat: Medium, slightly longer than other shorthairs, but not long enough to flow; dense, plush, soft, full of life; not flat or close-lying

Eyes: Large, round, bright; colour reflects coat colour

Other features: Small, blunt ears, set wide apart and leaning slightly forward

Grooming: Easy; thorough, daily brushing and combing

Temperament: Gentle, affectionate, good-natured, inquisitive, playful

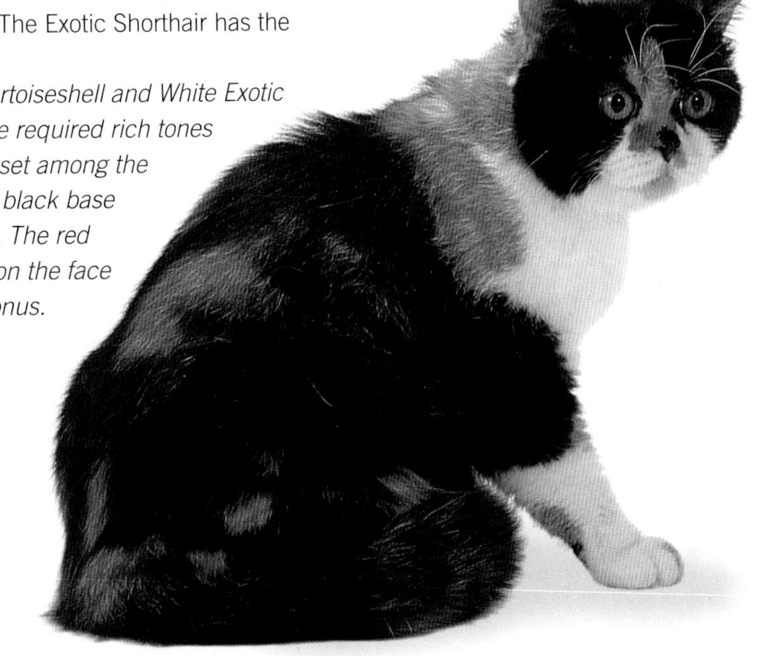

► *A Tortoiseshell and White Exotic has the required rich tones of red set among the dense black base colour. The red blaze on the face is a bonus.*

Foldex

The Foldex, or Exotic Fold, originates from Canada and is recognized by the Canadian Cat Association as a New Breed. Currently this is the only registry that recognizes this breed. It was developed in the 1990s by crossing Scottish Folds with Exotic Shorthairs and Exotic Longhairs to produce a Persian-type cat with folded ears.

Controversy surrounds the Foldex and all cat breeds with folded ears. Skeletal defects are connected with the gene that causes the cartilage abnormality resulting in folded ears. The folding is due to osteochondro-dysplasia, which affects the cartilage throughout the body but in particular the limbs. At its worst, affected cats have grossly shortened, wide and deformed limbs and short, inflexible tails. This results in inflammation, pain and in extreme cases a reluctance or inability to move. Many animal welfare groups are actively campaigning for the cessation of breeding cats with folded ears. Litters contain kittens with straight and folded ears. Initially it was thought healthy stock could

▲ *First registered as a new breed in 2006, the Canadian Cat Association granted the Foldex Championship status in 2010.*

▼ *This is a medium-sized cat with moderate features. They are intelligent and enjoy solving puzzles.*

► *The ears only start to fold in kittens around 21–28 days old. Roughly half of each litter will have straight ears.*

Breed box

Coat: Both longhaired and shorthaired coats permitted
Eyes: Large and round; colour dependent on coat colour
Other features: The nose is shorter than that of the Scottish Fold.
Grooming: Easy or moderate depending on coat type
Temperament: Placid, quiet and loving

be produced if cats with folded ears were bred to those with straight ears. There is now genetic evidence that seems to dispute this theory.

The Foldex has a cobby body with a heavy bone structure. Round heads are set on thick, short necks. This breed has been described as having a face like an owl and the body of a teddy bear. Coats can be any colour or pattern. This is an intelligent, confident cat with a quiet undemanding nature. They adapt well to indoor living.

With its teddy bear looks it is easy to see the appeal of this breed. Foldex enjoy being hugged and cuddled and will happily sit on a lap for hours. The Foldex is a cat that loves to play, and they will physically and mentally benefit from a range of toys as well as human company.

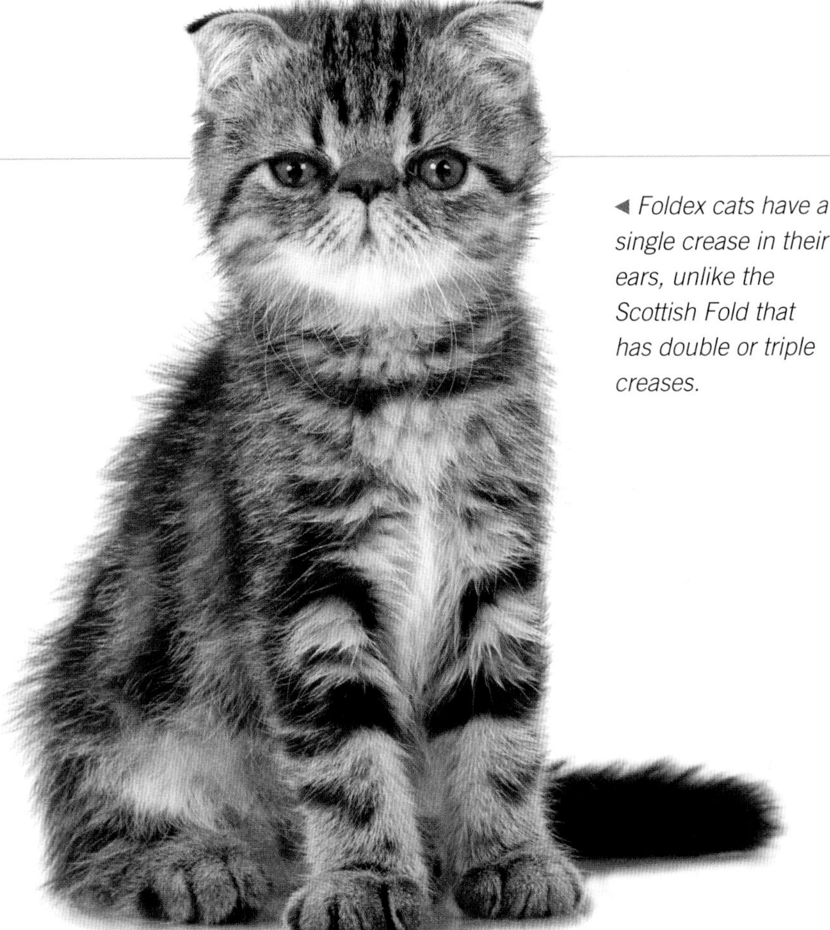

◄ *Foldex cats have a single crease in their ears, unlike the Scottish Fold that has double or triple creases.*

Genetta

The Genetta is a dwarf cat recognized by The International Cat Association as an experimental breed. In 2006 Sharon Kiley, from the USA, decided to breed a cat that resembled an African Genet. A genet is a member of the viverroidea family. Viverrids are small to medium-sized mammals, and although sometimes described as cat-like they are not part of the wild cat family.

The Genetta cat was developed by crossing Munchkin, Savanah, Bengal, Oriental Shorthairs and Domestic Shorthairs. The Munchkin carries a genetic mutation that causes dwarfism and this is passed on to the Genetta. This gene affects bone and cartilage formation; the most notable aspect of the gene being shortened legs.

The Genetta should have short legs and a long body and be 'weasel-like' in appearance. This is a strange anomaly as a weasel does not belong to either the cat or viverrid family. Ideally the tail is longer than the body. The head has a sharp muzzle with rounded ears set high. Coats are black/brown or silver with spotted or marbled markings.

Although the Genetta can run and play, the dwarfism gene inhibits its ability to jump very high. They are playful, energetic and accepting of other cats and dogs. This cat is best suited to an indoor environment. It is a controversial breed. There is some suggestion that Servals and Asian Leopards might be added to the breed mix. Potential purchasers are advised to discuss the possibility of health problems relating to the dwarf gene mutation with their vet prior to considering a kitten.

Breed box

Coat: Shorthaired, thick, soft and low shedding

Eyes: Large and round; colours, green, amber or brown

Other features: Litters of Genetta can contain both long- and short-legged kittens

Grooming: Easy; brush weekly to keep coat in good condition

Temperament: Loving, sociable and intelligent

German Rex

The various Rex breeds are all quite distinct and were discovered and developed quite independently of each other. They are, however, all due to a spontaneously occurring mutant gene. In the late 1950s, in the region then known as East Germany, a female cat living in the basement of Hufeland Hospital had a litter containing two curly coated kittens. This was the foundation of the German Rex breed. Due to the similarities between the Cornish Rex and the German Rex some registries do not classify them as separate breeds. Even in its home country this cat is rare.

The German Rex is a small to medium cat with fine bones. Although they look dainty, this is not a fragile breed. The head is round with a strong chin and large ears. The curly coat is unusual as it doesn't have any guard hairs. A range of colours is permitted including Cream, Platinum, Frost, Fawn, White, Champagne, Lavender, Blue, Black, Brown, Cinnamon, Red, Chestnut, Lavender and Seal. Coats can be solid, bi-coloured, tri-coloured and may be patterned with tabby, tortoiseshell, smoke, ticking or shaded points.

▼ *The foundation queen of all German Rex cats was called Laemmchen. She was curly-haired herself.*

► *German Rex are recognized by the Fédération Internationale Féline and can be found in Germany, England, France and the USA.*

This is an active cat who enjoys human company. It is very loyal, loving and ideal as a family cat. The German Rex loves being handled and petted. It is a very intelligent cat who is highly trainable and capable of learning a wide range of tricks. Grooming is relatively easy but the lack of hair means that natural oils can build up on the skin. Regular bathing therefore will prevent the coat becoming greasy.

Breed box

Coat: Short, silky; curls naturally

Eyes: Blue, green, gold or hazel eyes that look too big for the head

Other features: Whiskers are curled, legs are long and slender

Grooming: Easy; weekly brushing will stimulate the skin

Temperament: Playful, affectionate and athletic

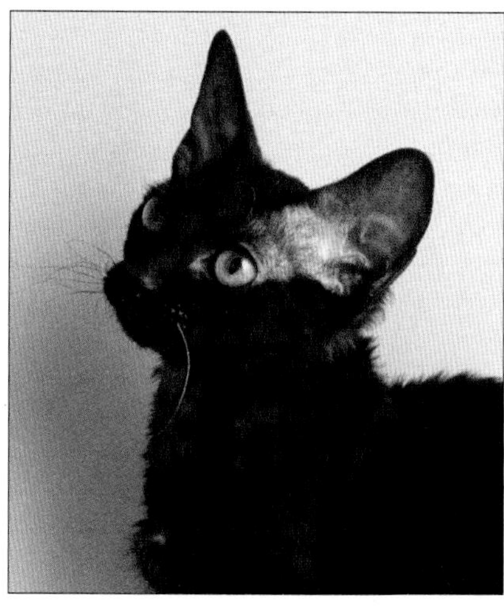

▲ *This rare breed quickly bonds with its owner. It likes to be included in family activities.*

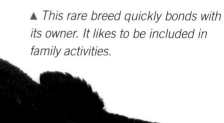

Havana Brown

Despite its name, the Havana Brown originates from the United Kingdom. Documented evidence shows that brown cats were exhibited in Europe in the 1890s. The breed is listed as Havana in Europe and Havana Brown in the USA. One story relates that this cat gained its name because its colour is similar to that of a Havana cigar. The breed is recognized by most cat registries but there is a difference in breed standards.

▲ *The characteristic head narrows to a rounded muzzle with a distinctive stop at the eyes.*

▼ *The Havana Brown uses its paws to communicate more than most other cat breeds.*

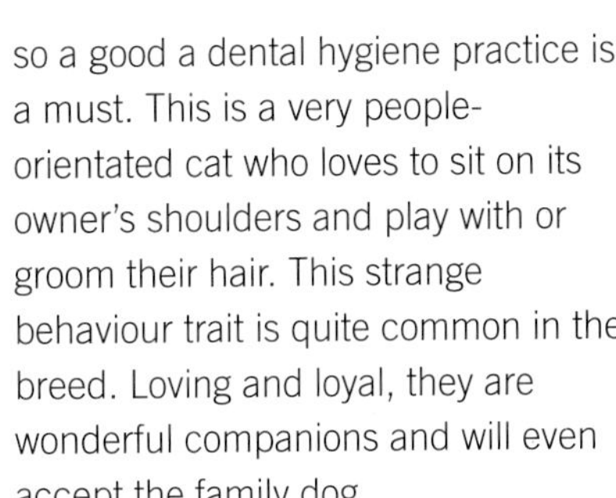

► *Kittens are born with coat markings; these will completely disappear by the time they are one year old.*

These cats were called Swiss Mountain Cats. The breed appeared to disappear during WW2. However, in the 1950s British breeders worked to produce a solid brown cat again. Siamese were crossed with black shorthaired cats. During its formation this breed has had a number of names, including Chestnut Brown Oriental and Chestnut Foreign Shorthair. Coats are a rich chocolate or mahogany colour; the cats themselves are sometimes called 'Brownies'. Paw pads must be pink or rose-coloured and never black or brown. Lilac coats, a pinkish-grey, are also permissible but are not so popular with breeders.

The Havana Brown is a healthy breed with no known genetic issues although it can be prone to gingivitis so a good a dental hygiene practice is a must. This is a very people-orientated cat who loves to sit on its owner's shoulders and play with or groom their hair. This strange behaviour trait is quite common in the breed. Loving and loyal, they are wonderful companions and will even accept the family dog.

Breed box

Coat: Short, smooth and very glossy

Eyes: Emerald green and oval in shape

Other features: Whiskers must match the colour of the coat

Grooming: Easy; brush and wipe with a damp cloth once or twice a week

Temperament: Curious, moderately active and intelligent

Highlander

▶ *TICA divides the breed into two varieties: the Highlander Shorthair and the Highlander being the longhair type.*

The Highlander, with the shorthaired type known as the Highlander Shorthair, was originally called the Highland Lynx. It is recognized by both The International Cat Association (TICA) and the Rare and Exotic Feline Registry. The Highlander has a standard with the former but not with the latter registry. It is a relatively new breed with development starting in 1993 by crossing a variant of the Desert Lynx with a Jungle Curl. The aim was to breed a powerful cat with a wild look. Despite the name there is no wild Lynx in the breeding.

The Highlander has two very distinctive features. Firstly, they have a vertical crimp in the ear, which tips the top of the ear slightly backwards. Secondly, this cat has naturally short tails, often with a kink or curl, and a fat pad at the end. Long tails do sometimes occur. This is a large, heavy cat with a muscular body. They weigh between 5.44kg–10kg (12lb–22lb). It is a slow-maturing breed, taking 3–4 years to reach full maturity. Heads are slightly longer than wide, with a blunt muzzle.

The coat comes in either shorthair or longhair with spotted or marbled markings to resemble a bobcat. Feet are large with prominent knuckles.

The Highlander is a gentle giant. It is very social and adapts well to changes of environment. They enjoy the company of other cats and accept well-behaved dogs. Their intelligence makes them easy to train and they can be taught tricks and to walk on a harness and lead. Breeders state that there is no evidence, so far, that the Highlander has any genetic issues.

Breed box

Coat: Soft long or short hair in a range of colours

Eyes: Slightly flattened oval in shape

Other features: Some Highlanders are polydactyl

Grooming: Easy to moderate depending on coat type

Temperament: Playful, active and confident

▼ *Many Highlanders have polydactyl feet. This trait is not encouraged in breeding stock.*

▲ *The forehead is sloping, and the muzzle blunt with a wide nose. Eyes are set wide apart.*

Himalayan/Colourpoint

The Himalayan or Colourpoint Persian was a result of the pioneers of Colourpoint breeding fusing the Perisan-type longhair with the Himalayan pattern of the Siamese cat. The result was a cat of Persian type with long hair and the restricted coat pattern of the Siamese. The entire catalogue of Persian longhaired cats until this point has been based on a solid colour cat modified by the introduction of the tabby pattern, sex-linked colour, silver or white patching.

The points (mask, legs, feet and tail) are evenly coloured and there is a good contrast between the points and body colour. Light body shading, if present, should be confined to the shoulders and flanks, and should complement the points. The mask covers the entire face. It should not extend over the head, although the mask of a mature male is more extensive than that of a mature female. Kittens are born white and fluffy, the point colours starting to appear in less than a week.

Attempts to transfer the Siamese pattern to Persian type were being made before World War II, but the cats were not shown until 1957 in California, and were only officially incorporated into the Persian breed by the Cat Fanciers' Association in 1984. Breeding lines have since expanded to develop the full range of point colours. The Himalayan or Colourpoint Persian has now outstripped the Blue in the longhair popularity stakes.

▼ *This is a sociable breed that craves attention and can be rather moody if it feels ignored.*

Point colours

Individual organizations recognize point colours that include the Silver series and Red sex-linked Silver series. In Britain, the point colours are represented by four distinct groupings:

Solid point colours: Seal, Blue, Chocolate, Lilac, Red and Cream

Tortie point colours: Seal Tortie, Blue-Cream, Chocolate Tortie and Lilac-Cream

Tabby point colours: Seal Tabby, Blue Tabby, Chocolate Tabby, Lilac Tabby, Red Tabby, and Cream Tabby

Tortie Tabby point colours: Seal Tortie Tabby, Blue-Cream Tabby, Chocolate Tortie Tabby and Lilac-Cream Tabby

In the United States, seven varieties are recognized: Blue Point, Chocolate Point, Seal Point, Flame Point, Lilac Point, Blue-Cream Point, and Tortoiseshell Point

▼ *The Himalayan is more playful and active than a Persian due to its Siamese ancestry.*

Breed box

Coat: Thick, dense, no trace of woolliness; glossy; full frill over shoulders and continuing between front legs

Eyes: Large, round; brilliant blue

Other features: Nose and paw pad colour matches the point colour

Grooming: Demanding; thorough, daily

Temperament: Placid

Japanese Bobtail

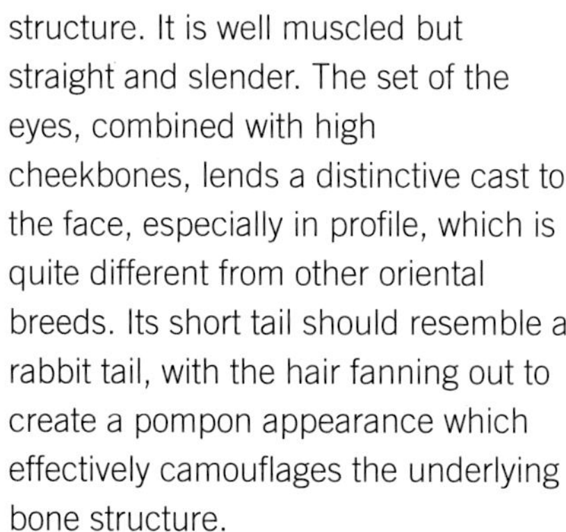

► *While the Japanese Bobtail is accepted in many colours, it is the Tortie and White, which the Japanese call mi-ke (three-colour) that is especially prized.*

There are representations of the Japanese Bobtail on ancient prints and manuscripts dating back some 2,000 years. On the Gotojuki temple in Tokyo, built during the Edo period (1615–1867), is a famous portrayal of a beckoning Bobtail.

Legend has it that a cat in Japan was warming itself in front of a fire when it accidentally set its tail alight. It ran through the city and spread the fire through the fragile wooden houses, which were burnt to ashes. The Emperor of Japan decreed all cats should be punished and ordered their tails to be chopped off. There is a similar story surrounding the origin of Manx cats.

What actually caused this particular gene mutation is a mystery. Unlike the Manx, the mating of two Japanese Bobtails will produce only more Japanese Bobtails.

An American who lived in Japan after World War II returned to the United States with 38 Bobtails to found a breeding line. Provisional status was granted in 1971, and championship status in 1976. Japanese breeders began to develop a long-coated variation in 1954, although the type had unofficially been around for centuries, particularly in the northern regions of Japan. They were represented in ancient Japanese paintings, but had been ignored by the pedigree cat aficionados. The breed was recognized in 1991 by The International Cat Association.

▼ *This breed has a triangular head with a long nose and high cheekbones. Eyes may be odd-coloured.*

The Japanese Bobtail is a medium-sized cat with clean lines and bone structure. It is well muscled but straight and slender. The set of the eyes, combined with high cheekbones, lends a distinctive cast to the face, especially in profile, which is quite different from other oriental breeds. Its short tail should resemble a rabbit tail, with the hair fanning out to create a pompon appearance which effectively camouflages the underlying bone structure.

The cats are now available in most colours and patterns. In Japan, they are thought of as bringing good fortune to a household, especially the van-patterned Tortie and White, known as the mi-ke (three-colours).

◄ *Increase your grooming routine in spring and autumn as the Japanese Bobtail sheds coat then.*

Breed box

Coat: Shorthair: medium in length, soft and silky with no undercoat
Longhair: medium to long, soft and silky with no undercoat; frontal ruff desirable

Eyes: Large, oval; colour reflects coat colour

Other features: Short, moveable tail

Grooming: Easy; regular combing

Temperament: Affectionate, intelligent, inquisitive, needs attention

Javanese

The Cat Fanciers Association has issued a breed standard for the Javanese. Some registries consider this cat a Javanese division of the Balinese or merged with the Himalayan and called Colourpoints. Most other registries agree that this is an oriental type, very similar to the Siamese. Its name is misleading as it has nothing to do with the Indonesian island of Java. The foundation breeds used in the development of the Javanese were Siamese, Balinese and Colourpoints.

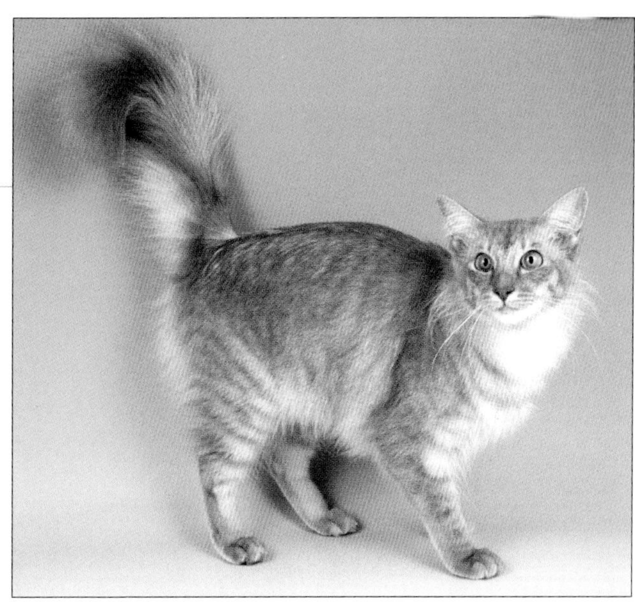

▶ *Body coat is approximately 5cm (2in) with no undercoat. Hair is longer on the chest, tail and breeches.*

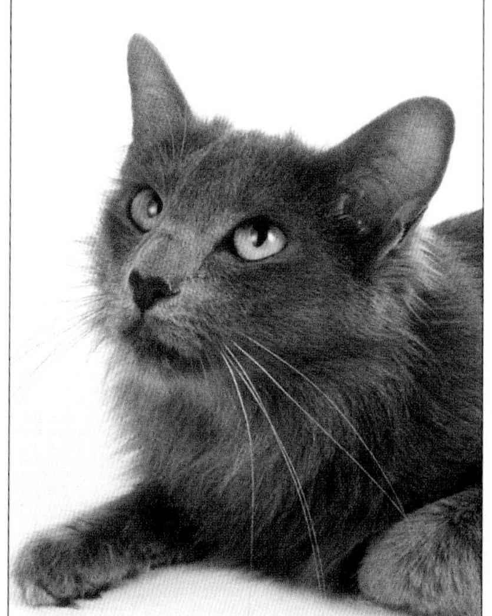

▲ *A cat with many names including Colourpoint Longhair, Colourpoint, Balinese (Javanese Division) and Javi.*

This cat has a fine, silky medium-length coat with a plumed tail. This breed is 'pointed' in the non-traditional colours of lynx, tortoiseshell, flame and smoke. The main body colour is always lighter than the points. It is an elegant cat with a muscular, tubular body. Legs are long and slim with small paws. The Javanese moves in a very dainty manner but is deceptively heavy when lifted. Heads are wedge-shaped with triangular ears.

This breed will follow its owner about and can be demanding. It is a fearless and curious cat and these traits can get it into trouble. Ensure cupboards shut properly and that the home is cat-safe. They love playing and interacting with humans. A range of toys and a scratching post are essential. Javanese love high places and this should be catered for. They are happy to ride on their owner's shoulders and enjoy sitting on laps too. This is an excellent all-round companion cat but will expression its opinion vocally.

Breed box

Coat: The coat should lay close to the body and never be fluffy

Eyes: Oriental, slanted in shape and in proportion to head

Other features: Hair on the tail can grow up to 7.6cm (3in) in length

Grooming: Moderate; regular brushing to remove shedding coat and debris

Temperament: Active, loving and playful

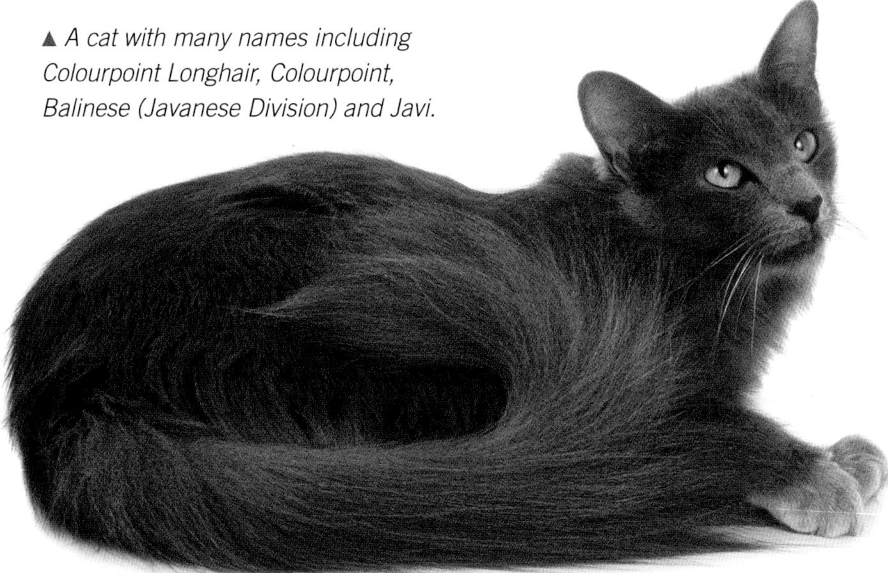

◀ *If a line was drawn across the tips of the ears down to the nose it should clearly form a triangular shape.*

Kashmir

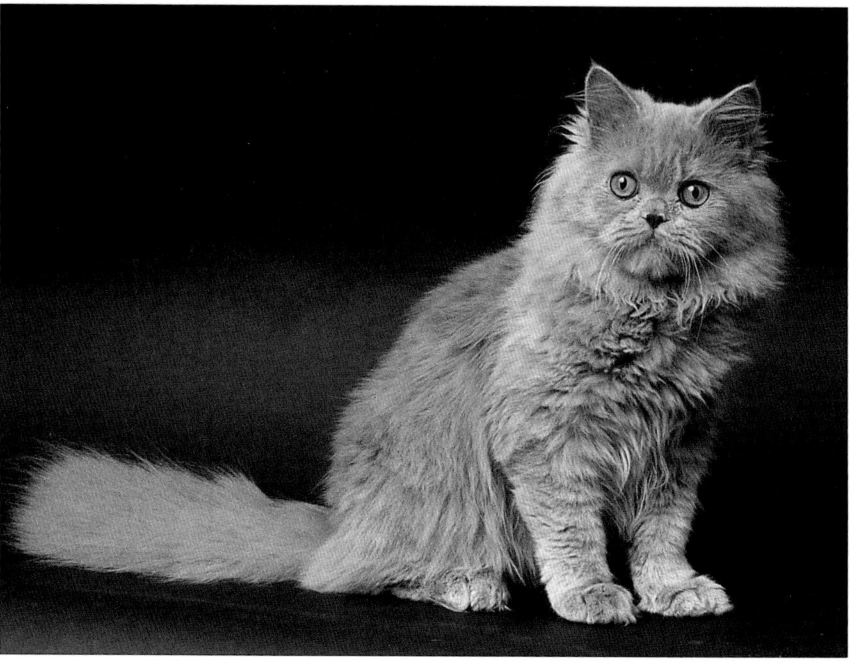

▲ *A Lilac Persian has a coat colour that is even, with no shading.*

The term 'Kashmir' relates to a solid-coloured Himalayan and despite its name this cat has nothing to do with the north-western region of the Indian subcontinent. These cats have lilac, lavender or chocolate coats without points. Some of the cat fancy organizations consider that the Himalayan must have colour points so the Kashmir is disqualified. In the UK Himalayan cats are considered a form of the Persian cat. The Lilac Persian, or Lavender Kashmirm, was, like the Chocolate, an offshoot from the breeding programme for Colourpoint longhairs. It is a dilute form of the Blue with an element of Siamese. This may be the reason why these cats often show an independence of spirit – they are well able to amuse themselves, but quickly bond with their owners.

The perfect pedigree has a thick, silky coat that is warm in tone and

Breed box
Coat: Thick, silky
Eyes: Copper or deep orange; rims lilac
Other features: Nose leather and paw pads lilac
Grooming: Demanding; thorough, daily
Temperament: Placid

Jungle Lynx

Jungle Lynx cats are bred to have the look and characteristics of both the African Jungle Cat (*Felis chaus*) and feral Bobcats (*Lynx rufus*). The original was a hybrid of the two fore-mentioned cats but later generations included a wide mix of domestic cats, while still retaining a wild look. This cat is similar in type to the Chausie but with a stockier body and heavier bone.

Jungle Lynx are tall with long powerful bodies. A range of coat colours and markings occur but leopard patterns are the most desirable. The head is large with a well-developed muzzle and prominent whisker pads. Large feathered ears are set well apart with tufts on the rounded tips. Hind legs are longer than the front legs. Toes may be tufted. Tail length varies from short to the same length of a domestic cat. Coats are generally ebony, silver, bronze, sorrel or chocolate. Cats with a leopard pattern have a dorsal stripe and typical tabby face markings.

This is a very active breed who demands their owner's attention. They are dog-like in behaviour and have the intelligence to learn a number of tricks, including fetch, to sit on command, and walk on a harness and lead. Jungle Lynx have a love of water and will dabble their paws in any that they can find. They have even been known to enjoy taking showers with their owners. This is an active cat who would rather be playing than sleeping. This is a rare breed so it is difficult to find, with kittens commanding a high price.

Breed box
Coat: Long or shorthaired in various colours and patterns
Eyes: Large, set at an angle; colour varying from gold to green.
Other features: Often have extra toes (polydactyl)
Grooming: Easy to moderate, dependent on coat length
Temperament: Athletic, attention-seeking and affectionate

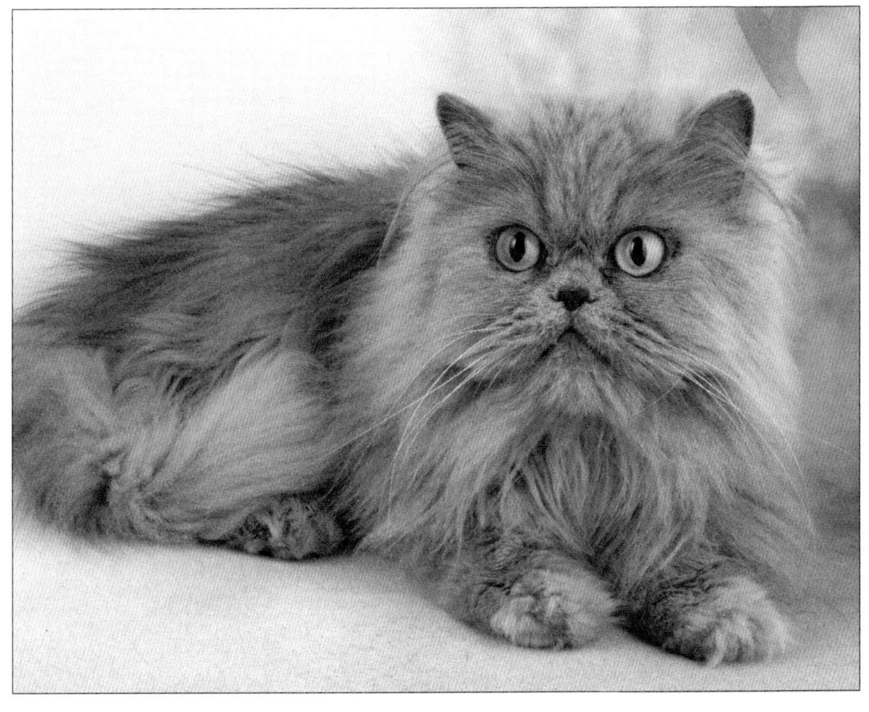

even in colour, with no markings or white hairs. Eyes are copper or deep orange with lilac rims, and the nose leather and paw pads are also lilac. Once the colour Lilac has been produced, Lilac to Lilac matings will only produce Lilac kittens. This applies not only to Persian Lilacs, but to other breeds as well, with the exception of Oriental Shorthair Siamese and British Shorthair breeds.

The Canadian Cat Club consider the Kashmir to be a breed in its own right and have issued a breed standard for breeders and judges. In some other countries dedicated breeders are actively campaigning for this cat to gain breed status.

Some registries do not recognize any form of Kashmir cat and in these cases they are just grouped in the category 'domestic longhaired cats' and not considered a formal breed, or breed colour, at all.

Despite all the confusion, these attractive cats make delightful pets regardless of their breed status, or lack of.

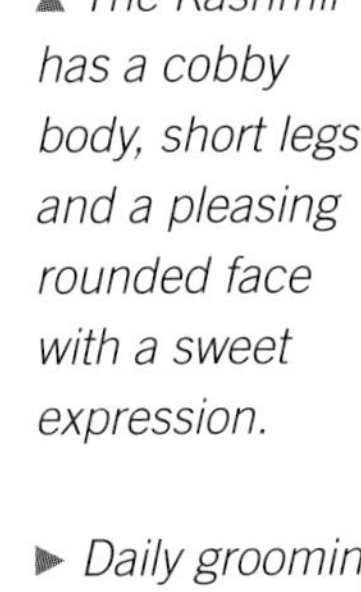

▲ *The Kashmir has a cobby body, short legs and a pleasing rounded face with a sweet expression.*

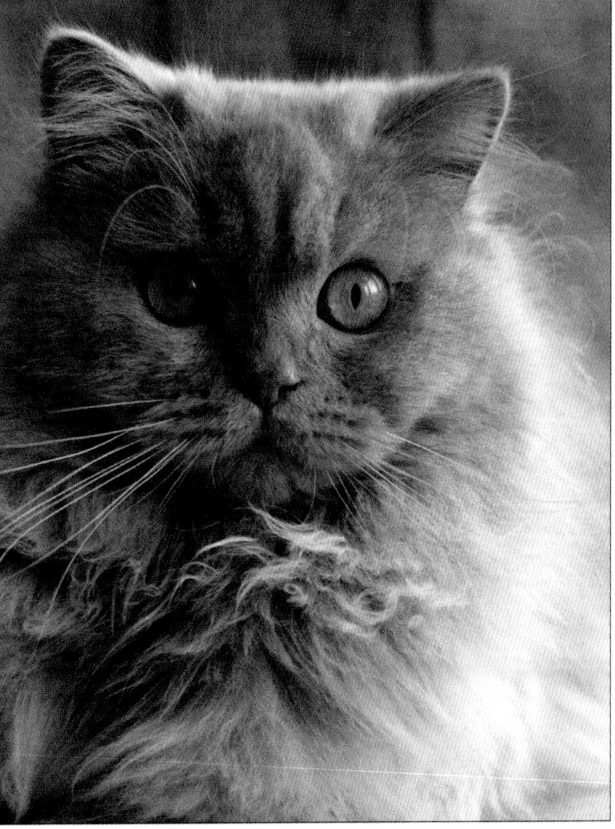

► *Daily grooming of legs and stomach is vital to prevent matting and to remove debris.*

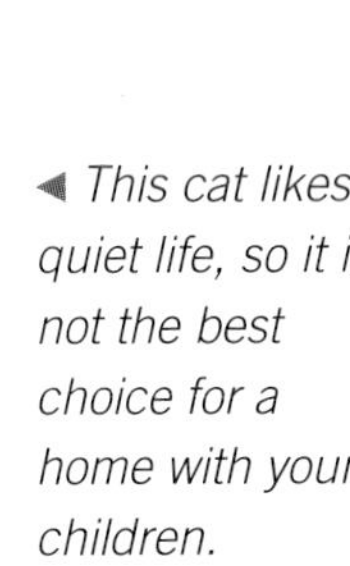

◄ *This cat likes a quiet life, so it is not the best choice for a home with young children.*

Khao Manee

The Khao Manee originates from Thailand and has the distinction of being the most expensive cat breed in the world. It is a rare breed that has been in existence for thousands of years. Mention is made of this cat in the fourteenth-century book of cat poems, the *Tamra Maew*. The breed is also called Khao Mani, Khao Plort (White Gem) and the Diamond Eye Cat. This cat has only recently been introduced to the western world with the first import to the UK arriving in 2009. The Governing Council of the Cat Fancy, the Cat Fanciers' Association and The International Cat Association have all produced a show standard for the Khao Manee and this breed is now globally recognized.

This is a pure white cat who looks oriental in type. It is muscular with a solid body and neck. Both tail and legs are of medium length. Nose leather, lips, skin and paw pads are pink. The most sought-after Khao Manee are those that have odd-coloured eyes. This is unusual as having eyes of differing colour is considered a fault in most animals. Genetics show that it is a completely separate strain to the Siamese and other eastern breeds.

▼ *The 'White Gem' has a less strident voice than a Siamese and devotees praise its attractive purr.*

▲ *In Thailand, this breed is much revered, with some cats believed to have healing powers and bring wealth.*

Breed box

Coat: Short and close-lying

Eyes: Diamond-shaped; blue, yellow, amber or green in colour

Other features: Some kittens have a dark patch on the head but this will disappear

Grooming: Easy; stroking with damp hands will remove dead hair

Temperament: Extrovert, intelligent and affectionate

The Khao Manee is a very vocal breed and will use its voice freely to gain attention. They are very social and love being stroked and sitting on laps. They adapt well to indoor living. This is not a solitary cat and would appreciate another active feline companion.

▼ *Some white cats are prone to deafness in one or both ears. It is not known if Khao Manee are affected.*

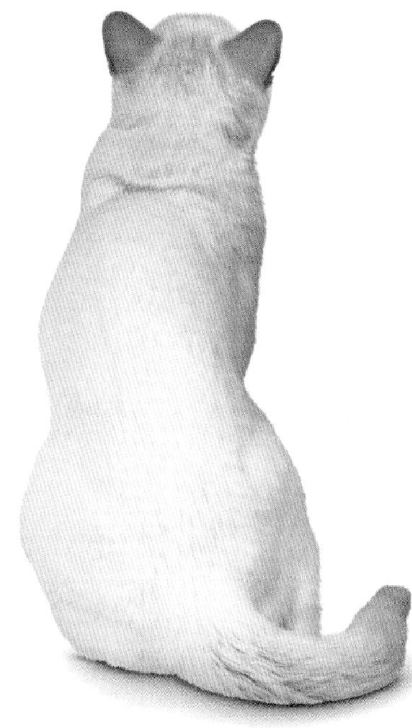

Korat

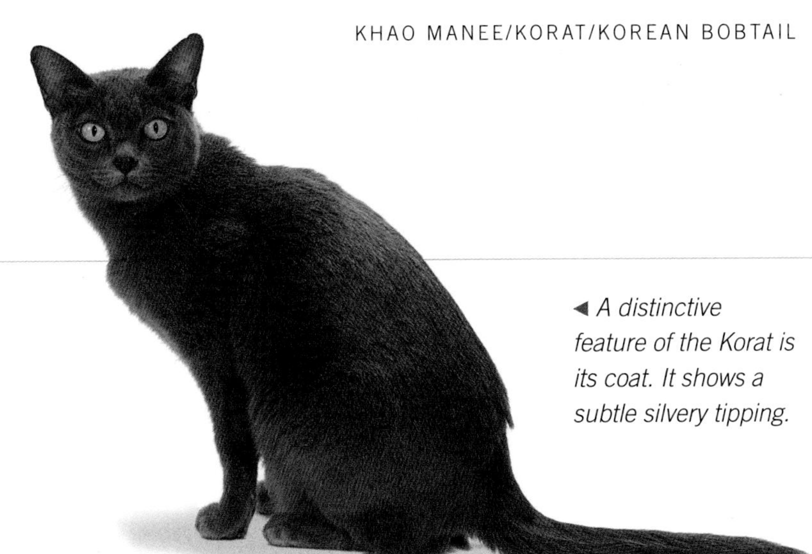

◄ *A distinctive feature of the Korat is its coat. It shows a subtle silvery tipping.*

This popular breed attained championship status in America in 1966. The Korat Cat Fanciers' Association was founded in 1965 with the declaration: 'The Korat is silver-blue from birth to death. It can exist in no other colour. If any other colour should occur it would automatically cease to be a Korat.' Nevertheless, it appeared that the original imports were not as pure as originally thought, and that a recessive dilute gene might result in the occasional lilac, blue point or lilac point kitten. These have been named as the Thai Lilac and Thai Pointed variations.

▲ *The Korat's heart-shaped face is typical; so is the luminous green of its round and prominent eyes.*

The Korat is a medium-sized, lithe and muscular cat, and the females are daintier than the males. The most distinguishing features are the large green eyes set in a heart-shaped face and the silvery sheen of the coat.

Breed box

Coat: Short to medium length; thick, silky; no undercoat

Eyes: Round, large, luminous, prominent; green – colour changes during the course of the cat's early years

Other features: Quietly vocal

Grooming: Easy; regular brushing and combing

Temperament: Loving, very playful

Korean Bobtail

The exact origins of this native breed are shrouded in the mists of time. Modern DNA research advises that the Korean Bobtail may well be the forerunner of the Japanese Bobtail. It is suggested that sailors visiting Japan took cats from Korea with them, which then went on to be part of the ancestry of the latter, now more popular, breed. What is certain is that bobtail cats abound all around Korea both as pets and feral animals. Unfortunately most cats have a very hard time with only a lucky few becoming treasured companions.

Bobtail is the term used to describe a short, stubby tail that is between one third and one half of a normal tail. This is a natural phenomenon caused by a mutation in a gene. The gene is dominant and so is passed on to others of the breed. There are some similarities between the Korean and Japanese Bobtail but the Korean is somewhat stockier with a wider head. The ears are triangular, wide at the base, open and tip slightly forward. The coat is short-haired and dense. A variety of colours and markings occur but bi-colour or tri-colour are most prevalent.

The Korean Bobtail is an excellent mouser – for centuries its ancestors have had to fend for themselves. This cat is rare in the western world but many videos on the internet show them interacting with their owners in a loving and playful manner.

Breed box

Coat: Shorthaired with a thick and dense undercoat

Eyes: Colour dependent on coat coloration

Other features: The tail is usually carried erect

Grooming: Easy to moderate, depending on shedding period

Temperament: Independent, semi-active and affectionate

Kurilian Bobtail

The Kurilian Bobtail has many other names including Kuril Islands Bobtail, Kuril Bobtail, Kurilean, and Curilsk Bobtail. It originates from the Kuril Islands, Sakhalin Island and the Kamchatka peninsula of Russian. This is a very popular breed in Russia, and some parts of Europe, but is fairly rare in North America. Kurilians are recognized by The World Cat Federation, The International Cat Association and the Fédération International Féline.

▶ *The Kurilian loves playing in water. In the wild these cats are outstanding fishermen and hunters.*

Kurilians are substantial, medium to large, stocky cats. The back is slightly arched and back legs are longer than front legs. The head is wide and rectangular in shape. The eyes are described as being walnut-shaped. The ears are triangular and tip slightly forwards. The most distinctive feature of the breed is the short kinked pompom tail. Tails are well coated and should be between two to ten vertebrae. Both lengths of coat are soft and silky and generally non-matting.

This cat is renowned for its hunting and fishing abilities. They are fascinated by water and love playing in it. The Kurilian is a long-lived breed with some cats reaching the grand age of 20 years old. Cats can take up to five years to reach full adult size. Although independent, they form a strong, loving bond with their owners. A breed that is suitable for families and accepting of other cats and cat-friendly dogs.

This cat is rare, in part due to very small litter sizes. Potential purchasers must be prepared to book a kitten well in advance and wait with patience.

Breed box

Coat: Semi-longhair or shorthair, all colours permitted

Eyes: Green, yellow or yellow-green depending on coat colour

Other features: The tail of each Kurilian is unique with differing kinks and length

Grooming: Easy to moderate, depending on coat type

Temperament: Clever, gentle and an excellent hunter

Korn Ja

The Korn Ja is native to Thailand and is one of the seventeen 'lucky' cat breeds featured in the *Thai Smud Khoi* verses. In this manuscript it is called a Korn-Ya-Ja. Very little is known about the origins of this breed except that it has been in existence for centuries and that it is considered as a lucky charm. It is a very beautiful and elegant cat that is rapidly growing in popularity in the western world.

This is a small and finely built cat weighing between 2.72–4.99kg (6–11lb). It has a rather pointed jaw and muzzle. The tail is long, graceful and tapers to a sharp point. Eyes are brilliant yellow and are described as 'the colour of budding yellow flowers'. The vivid eye colour is a prominent feature of the breed. Originally classified as a hairless cat, the modern Korn Ja has a very fine, short coat without undercoat. Generally black in colour but shades of grey do occur.

Best suited to indoor living, the Korn Ja is reputed to have a great fondness for children and will join in with their games. They are very sensitive to their owner's emotions and offer comfort to those that are upset or stressed. Highly sociable and outgoing, this breed loves human company. This is an extremely active cat that loves to play or follow their owner around the home. A large box of cat toys is essential. Will happily accept a well-behaved dog.

Breed box

Coat: Very fine and thin coat with a glossy sheen

Eyes: Startlingly vivid yellow

Other features: The long tail increases agility and balance

Grooming: Moderate; the thin coat requires regular bathing to remove excess oil

Temperament: Highly affectionate and intelligent

LaPerm

The LaPerm is a breed that originates from America. The owner of a farm in Oregon noticed that one of his barn cats had a litter that contained a kitten that appeared to have no coat. By the time the kitten reached eight weeks old, short, soft and curly hair started to appear and at four months it had a full coat of curly hair. The farmer considered this kitten a mutant but after several years the number of curly-coated cats had increased. At this point advice was sought from cat breeders who showed great excitement over these unusual cats. It was discovered that the gene that produced the curls was dominant and carried by both males and females. The farmer decided to call the cats LaPerm and a new breed was born.

► *This rex breed has a rather flat forehead with a straight broad nose set on a wedge-shaped head.*

Breed box

Coat: Each coat is unique and varies from wavy, tight ringlets to corkscrew curls

Eyes: Can be any colour and are almond-shaped, rounded at the bottom

Other features: The head is a modified wedge with full and round whisker pads

Grooming: Moderate; coats change during the cat's life, altering grooming requirements

Temperament: Gentle, loving and intelligent

▲ *Ears are tufted with longer curly hair inside and longer silky hair or 'earmuffs' on the backs.*

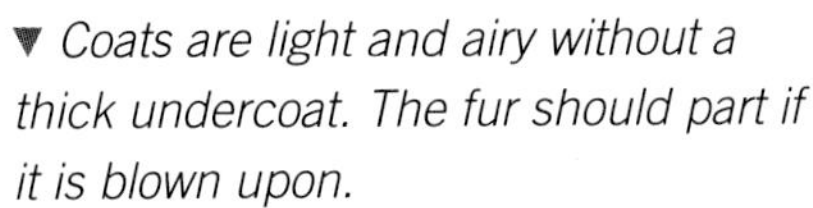

▼ *Coats are light and airy without a thick undercoat. The fur should part if it is blown upon.*

Coats come in every recognized colour and pattern and can be either longhaired or shorthaired. Some kittens are born bald but those that have a coat lose it at around two weeks old. By the time they reach four months the hair has generally grown back and is curly. The hair is soft in texture. Longhaired cats have a curly ruff and plumed tail. Those that are shorthaired often have a parting down the middle and the hair stands away from the body.

This is an affectionate breed that loves to sit on a lap and purr. It is extremely people-orientated and makes a fine family companion. They are also suitable pets for elderly owners. The LaPerm is inquisitive and moderately active.

Lambkin

▲ *Also known as Nanus Rex, this is a stocky breed whose small size is due to a genetic mutation.*

The Lambkin is a dwarf breed that is recognized by The International Cat Association. Development began in the early 1990s by crossing a Munchkin with a Selkirk Rex, resulting in a short-legged cat with a shaggy coat. Originally this was the brainchild of an American breeder called Terri Harris, with other cat breeders following suit. There is controversy over the ethics of this breed with some welfare groups concerned over inherited health issues.

This cat has a small- to medium-sized body with short, thick legs. The chest is broad and rounded. Front legs are shorter than the hind legs. Tails are long and, in long-coated cats, well plumed. Kittens are born with curly coats that gradually straighten and fall out. The coat regrows and body hair is restored by eight to ten months of age. Coats vary, with both shorthaired and longhaired varieties, but ideally they should be curly or crinkly.

Regular grooming is required as many of the breed lack the flexibility to groom themselves due to the length of their body compared to their legs. The dwarf gene that causes the shortened legs can result in a range of health and mobility problems.

The Lambkin forms a strong and loving bond with its owner. They love physical contact and are more than happy to sit on a lap or to be cuddled. This breed will accept other cats, well-mannered dogs and is ideal in a family containing older children. They are best suited as indoor cats and will require a selection of toys to keep them occupied.

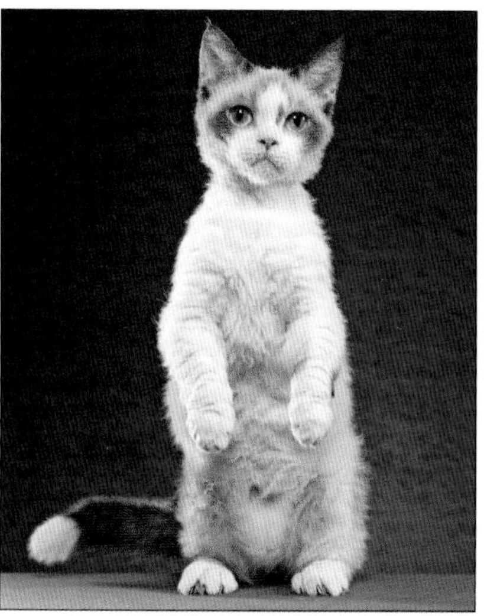

▲ *Avid climbers, these cats will appreciate a robust cat tree and high places to settle in.*

▼ *Tails are long, curved and taper to a rounded tip. Coats come in all standard colours and patterns.*

Breed box

Coat: Soft, kinked, wavy or curly standing away from the body

Eyes: Round in a range of colours

Other features: Faces are round with ears set well apart

Grooming: Moderate to extensive; brush gently as the hair is fragile and can break

Temperament: Playful, social and sweet-natured

Lykoi

► *Kittens are born with full black coats which sheds when they are about five days old.*

This is an American breed that gained Championship status with The International Cat Association in September 2016. At the time of writing it is also classified as an Advanced New Breed in Australia. Lykoi is taken from the Greek word meaning 'wolf' and this cat is also known as the Wolf Cat or the Werewolf Cat. It is said to resemble this mythical creature and breeders strive to promote this aspect with their breeding programmes.

Their wolf-like appearance is mainly due to a natural occurring mutation that affects the coat. Not all follicles have the necessary components to produce hair, making this breed partially hairless. Kittens are born solid-coloured but the adult coat is an equal mix of the birth colour and white, giving them a 'grizzled' look. This is called 'roan'. Although other colours occur, only cats that are black with a roan pattern are eligible to be shown. Unlike a wolf, the coat is soft to touch. The Lykoi is described as 'hound-like' and some cats will even point when something catches their attention.

▲ *This cat is mainly hairless on the chin, nose and muzzle as well as behind the ears and around the eyes.*

Breed box

Coat: Sheds hair and may, on occasions, have periods of baldness

Eyes: Almost round, golden coloured, set in hairless rims

Other features: Sparse coat on the wedge-shaped head gives a werewolf look

Grooming: Regular bathing is needed to stop the coat becoming greasy and dirty

Temperament: Independent, loving and lithe

It is a very loyal breed becoming greatly attached to its owner. They are quite affectionate and demanding. Energetic and bright, the Lykoi can problem-solve and will accept other cats and well-mannered dogs.

Some may consider that it is not the most attractive cat in the world but this is part of their appeal to their followers. Lykoi have a strong prey instinct and will stalk their owners in play. The breed is naturally cautious in new or unusual situations.

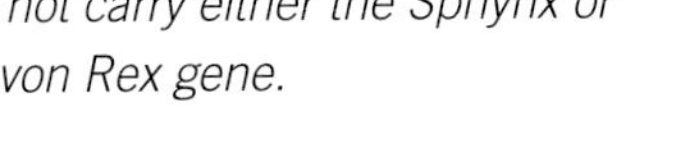

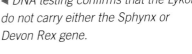

◄ *DNA testing confirms that the Lykoi do not carry either the Sphynx or Devon Rex gene.*

Maine Coon Cat

The Maine Coon Cat is a fine working cat, as well as one of the longest established breeds. As the first part of its name suggests, it comes from Maine, America's most north-easterly state. This is a land of mountains, forests, lakes and inhospitable winters. The Maine Coon Cat is appropriately powerfully built, with an all-weather coat and a reputation for being a wise and skilful hunter.

The second part of its name comes from the long tail and density of fur that have been compared to the similar attributes of the raccoon, an indigenous North American mammal. Like the raccoon, the cat is an exceptional climber. Another theory suggests that the lynx-like tufts on many a Maine Coon's ears are a result of genes inherited from the North American lynx, but this is unlikely. It is more likely that there is a touch of Angora in the breed. Local cats could have bred with Angoras that landed with sailors at the East Coast ports, or, less plausibly, with the cats sent to America by the French queen Marie Antoinette to escape the French Revolution. (The queen did do this, but it is unlikely that her animals founded a new race of cats.) It may simply be that the domestic cats which travelled from Britain to North America with the Pilgrims way back in the 1600s were the true source of Maine Coon Cats, and that the breed's long coat evolved as protection against the severe Maine winters.

The Maine Coon Cat is not only one of the longest established breeds in the world, but also one of the largest.

Breed box

Coat: Thick, dense, waterproof; has an undercoat

Eyes: Full, round with a slightly oblique aperture; all colours (including blue and odd-eyed in white cats)

Other features: Big; good climbers; smallish litters (two or three kittens)

Grooming: Coat rarely gets matted but regular brushing and combing advised

Temperament: Intelligent, calm; freedom-loving (should not be confined indoors)

▲ *A Tortoiseshell Tabby and White has the required large, oval eyes of the breed, a nose of medium length, and a splendid set of whiskers.*

▲ *A Blue Maine Coon Cat shows the ideal head shape and feathered ears typical of the breed. It was once suggested that the ears were inherited from the North American lynx.*

◄ *A black mantle overlays a paler root colour on the Smoke Maine Coon Cat. The fur is generally shorter over the head and shoulders and lengthens down the back and sides.*

▲ *Beneath the thick overcoat of the Maine Coon Cat is a solid, muscular body that has all the necessary power for a working cat.*

It can weigh 9kg (20lb) and more, compared with the average 2.5–5.5kg (5–12lb) cat range. Its history rivals that of many more fashionable breeds, and it now has an international following. The Maine Coon is among the top five most popular cat breeds in the United States. This was not always so.

It was one of the earliest exhibition cats – on show in New York in 1860 and in country shows and fairs in New England. Its early popularity was reversed when there was a craze for the more exotic Persians and Siamese being imported into the United States in the early 1900s. It was not until the 1950s that Maine Coon Cats slowly began to creep back into favour, and it was accepted at championship level in 1976. Now they are found all over the world with the current top American lines taking the highest honours.

Despite its size, the Maine Coon Cat is a gracious animal, with full cheeks and high cheekbones, a square muzzle and a firm chin. Its nose is slightly concave in profile. Ears are large, set high and wide apart. It has a long back, culminating in a very long, bushy tail that tapers at the tip and is carried high and proud. Legs and paws are substantial.

Recently, rexed (curly-coated) kittens have been born to apparently purebred Maine Coon Cats in the United Kingdom, indicating that behind some of the pedigrees, a rexed cat has been knowingly or unwittingly introduced. The variation is not approved of by the clubs and associations monitoring the Maine Coon Cat breed. Every attempt is being made to eliminate the gene.

Maine Coon Cat colours and patterns

Solid: White, Black, Blue, Red, Cream

Tabby and Tortoiseshell: all colours in classic and mackerel patterns, including Silver variations

Also occurs in shaded, smoke, bi-colour, tortoiseshell and white, and van bi-colour. Only one-third white preferred in patched cats

► *A softly coloured Red Silver and White shows paler colouring on chest and paws.*

Manx

A colony of cats became stranded on an island off the west coast of mainland Britain and eventually formed a distinct type. One myth suggests that the tailless Manx cat originated from a mating between a rabbit and a cat; another that the cat was the last to leave Noah's Ark and had its tail chopped in the door. The reality is that the Isle of Man cat community was forced by its confinement into concentrated

Breed box
Coat: Double, well-padded
Eyes: Large, round; colour in keeping with coat colour
Other features: Lack of tail
Grooming: Easy; regular brushing
Temperament: Calm, intelligent, active, loyal; likes to be with its owner

▲ *A residual tail is just visible on the Black Manx, which means that he cannot qualify as a true Manx on the show circuit. He will, however, be valuable for breeding purposes.*

◄ *The strong features typical of the Manx are evident on this Red Spotted Tabby. His cheeks are full, ears are prominent and his nose is broad, straight and of medium length.*

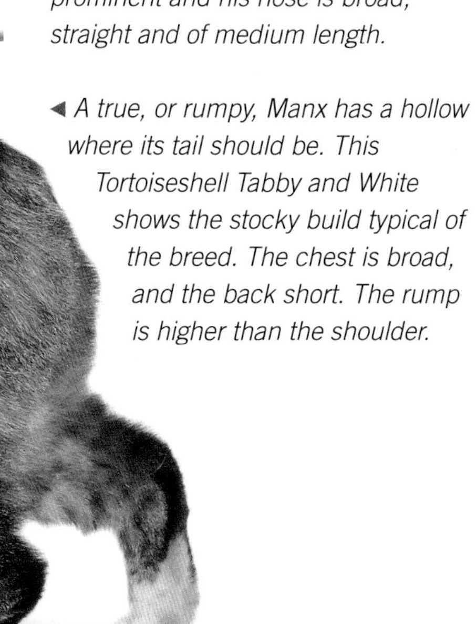

◄ *A true, or rumpy, Manx has a hollow where its tail should be. This Tortoiseshell Tabby and White shows the stocky build typical of the breed. The chest is broad, and the back short. The rump is higher than the shoulder.*

◄ *Manx cats have now been bred in all standard colours and patterns except Himalayan/ Colourpointed. This is a Blue-Cream rumpy, showing the required absolute lack of tail.*

▲ *Note the front legs of this Manx Bi-colour. They are slightly shorter than the long, muscular hind legs which result in a characteristic rabbit-like, loping gait.*

interbreeding. A mutant gene that led to a spinal malformation spread throughout the community and became the norm. The spine was literally curtailed, ending (in what is described as a true or rumpy Manx) in a hollow where a tail should have been. Cats with brief stumps of tails were also born, and these are called stumpies, stubbies or risers. The gene that causes this condition is related to the one that causes spina bifida in humans. If male and female rumpies are mated, some of the foetuses may not develop to full term. Breeders therefore introduce part- or fully-tailed varieties into their breeding programmes. For show purposes, however, it is the taillessness of the rumpy that is accepted as the standard for the breed. It is accepted in all the standard colours and patterns except colourpointed, although Lilac and Chocolate are not recognized by some associations.

Manx cat varieties

Rumpy Shows a hollow where the tail should emerge. This is the Manx cat exhibited at cat shows

Rumpy Riser Has a few fused vertebrae at the end of the spine. These can be seen and definitely felt, which disqualifies the cat from being shown as a Manx. It is, however, used for breeding

Stumpy Has a very short tail that can be moved. The vertebrae are not necessarily fused. This is the form which gives rise to some of the bobtailed cats

Longy Has an almost normal length tail. Often these cats are indistinguishable from the normal domestic feline

Cymric Is a semi-longhaired variety which is a breed in its own right and is described on page 283.

▼ *The occasional tailed Manx is born of Manx parents. He or she will win no prizes, but with the typical bulkiness of the type and a freedom from the spinal defects, is an extremely valuable asset to any Manx breeding programme.*

Mekong Bobtail

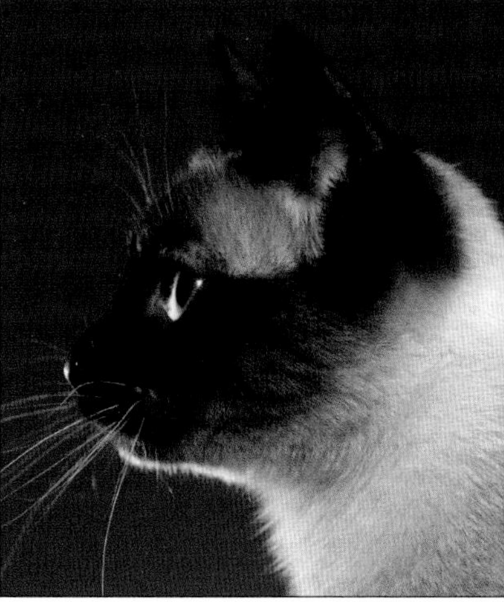

▲ *Mekong Bobtails do not like being left alone for long periods. Loneliness can cause extreme stress.*

The origins of the Mekong Bobtail can be traced back to, at least, the late 18th century. At this time, it is recorded that one was presented by the King of Siam to Nicholas the Second, Tsar of Russia. The breed comes from Thailand but was developed in Russia, and is named after the Mekong river that divides Thailand from the other states of South-East Asia. Legends from this area state that these cats were guardians of temples and bring luck and prosperity to their owners.

Muscular and elegant, this breed has some similarities to the Siamese. The body is rectangular with long legs. Paws are rounded. Coats are short with little undercoat. All coat colours and pointing are permitted except white. As their name suggests they have bobbed or stumpy tails. Tail length varies but is roughly three vertebrae long and often not visible. Each tail is unique with individual twists or kinks. Unusually, claws on the hind feet are not retracted, causing the cat to make a clipping sound when walking.

The Mekong Bobtail is very dog-like and with a little training will walk on a harness and lead, retrieve and learn numerous tricks. They are very vocal but not as harsh in sound as the Siamese cat.

This is a demanding breed that follows its owner around and uses its voice to gain attention. They seldom scratch, preferring to bite if startled or distressed. Nevertheless they make good family pets and are generally relaxed with young children.

Breed box
Coat: Dense, short and glossy
Eyes: Large, oval and often blue
Other features: Medium-sized with a slim and muscular body
Grooming: Easy; brush to remove shedding coat and to increase gloss
Temperament: Inquisitive, athletic and affectionate

▼ *Coats can be any pointed shade or colour provided that there are no white markings.*

▲ *Tails vary from cat to cat but must never be longer than a quarter of the body length.*

Minskin

The Minskin is a small cat developed by initially crossing a Munchkin with a Sphynx. Later Burmese and Devon Rex were introduced to the mix. This relatively new breed was devised in 1998 by Paul McSorley of Boston, USA. The Minskin is recognized by The International Cat Association as a Primary New Breed and as such they are monitoring the breed's progression.

This semi-cobby cat has short legs and a stocky body. The head is round with large ears spaced well apart. The coat is unusual with Kashmir soft fur on the face, ears, legs and feet. The body may be hairless or sparsely haired with a fuzz but the belly must be hairless. All colours are permitted including tortoiseshell and tabby. Colourpoints are very popular. This is a very small breed with adult weights varying between 1.84–2.72kg (4–6lb). As with all dwarf breeds there are some health issues associated with the Minskin. Potential purchasers are advised to research carefully prior to buying.

The Minskin is best suited to indoor living and has a love of high places. Toys and indoor climbing trees are a must to keep this little cat entertained. It is a very friendly breed and extremely people-orientated. This rare cat is moderately vocal and happy to live with other cats, or a dog. An ideal breed for an elderly person as they love to sit on laps and will act as a feline hot water bottle. The Minskin is suitable for families too.

▲ *The breed name Minskin comes from the words miniature and skin. Also known as a Teddy Rex.*

Breed box

Coat: Points are densely furred while body hair is sparse or non-existent

Eyes: Large and round with colour dependant on coat colouring

Other features: Retains a kitten-like appearance throughout life

Grooming: Regular bathing required to remove excess oils

Temperament: Intelligent, affectionate and playful

▼ *This is an indoor cat. The sparse coat means that they need protection from temperature extremes.*

▼ *As with all rare cat breeds, the Minskin is sometimes a target for thieves looking for a fast return.*

Munchkin

The Munchkin has a normal-sized body with short legs. The breed was developed in the latter part of the 1980s. Currently only two registries fully recognize the Munchkin, The International Cat Association (TICA) and The Southern Africa Cat Council. TICA gave the breed Championship status in 2003. The breed is not recognized by The Governing Council of the Cat Fancy, The Cat Fanciers' Association and Fédération International Féline.

The genetic mutation that causes the short legs seen in Munchkins is sometimes referred to as hypochondroplasia or pseudo achondroplasia. This mutation also causes increased evidence of excessive curvature of the spine and hollowed chests which is evident, at times, in this breed. Male Munchkins weigh 3–4kg (6–9lb) and females 1.8–3.6kg (4–8lb). Excessive bowed legs and cow hocks are penalized.

Munchkins are playful and loving. Despite their short legs most are very mobile and love to jump and climb although they may take the scenic route to get from A to B. Toys are a must, with some breeders stating that they are attracted to shiny objects. Best suited to indoor living, Munchkins make great family pets and are happy to live with children, other cats and dogs. This is an intelligent breed that can be trained to undertake a number of tricks.

► *Legs can be slightly bowed. Excessive bowing and cow hocks are severly penalized in the show ring.*

Breed box

Coat: Longhaired and shorthaired coat varieties available in all colours

Eyes: Rounded, with colour depending on coat colour

Other features: Sometimes called the Kangaroo Cat as front legs are shorter than hind

Grooming: Easy to moderate, depending on coat length

Temperament: Outgoing, sociable and intelligent

▲ *These cats will sit up on their hind legs to get a better view of things. Also known as the Sausage Cat.*

▼ *The name Munchkin derives from the small people who lived in Munchkin County in the book,* The Wizard of Oz.

Napoleon

The Napoleon or Minuet Cat is a domestic hybrid formed by crossing a Munchkin with a Persian. A hybrid is a first cross between two differing breeds. Therefore, if you mate a Napoleon to a Napoleon you will not get a Napoleon. This cat is called a Minuet by The International Cat Association and a Napoleon by The Cat Fanciers Federation, which can lead to confusion. The use of the Munchkin in the cross means that litters will contain both long- and short-legged kittens. Viewing a host of sites on the internet it is striking to note that all state that Napoleons have short legs so it is unknown what the long-legged kittens are called!

Taking visible characteristics from both the Munchkin and the Persian, the Napoleon is a true mix. The face resembles that of traditional Persian and is referred to as 'doll-faced' or 'baby doll-faced'. Coats are luxurious, with almost all colours and patterns acceptable including solid, smoke, calico and colourpoint. Napoleons often sit with their fore legs raised in a prairie dog stance and are able to hold this position while they survey their surroundings.

▼ *Sometimes unfairly described as being the feline counterpart to a Corgi or Dachshund.*

▲ *The name Napoleon is a reference to the small stature of Napoleon Bonapart and subsequently, this cat.*

▶ *Unlike that of the Persian, a Napoleon's nose is broad and straight. The face is round.*

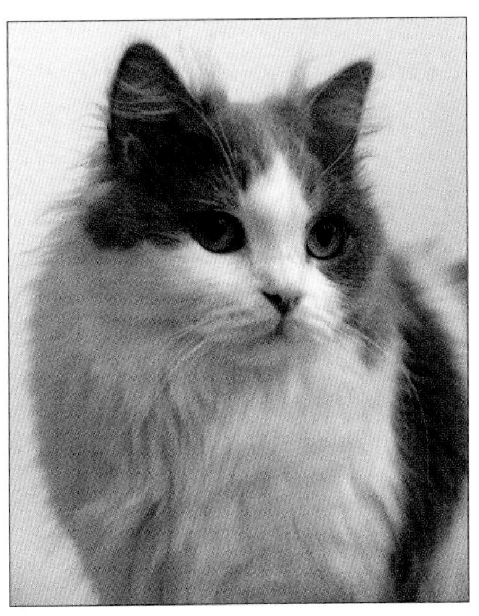

This is a naturally curious cat who loves the company of humans. They are not happy if left alone for long periods of time. Loyal and devoted to their owners, the Napoleon is ideal for those who would like a loving companion. Napoleons enjoy playing and are moderately active. Their non-aggressive character and acceptance of other felines and canines makes them perfect as a family pet.

Breed box

Coat: Dense and plush longhair or shorthair
Eyes: Large and round, with colour depending on coat colour
Other features: Short legs are heavily boned
Grooming: Moderate to extensive; daily brushing and combing is a must
Temperament: Inquisitive, affectionate and playful

Nebelung

The Nebelung is a relatively rare breed originating from the USA. This beautiful cat is gaining a lot of attention and breeders can now be found in parts of Europe, Canada and Russia as well as America. It is also known as a Longhaired Russian Blue. The name Nebelung comes from the German term that roughly translates as 'creature of the mist'. This is a reference to its shimmering silver blue coat that seems to float above the body when the cat is moving.

Similar in type to a Russian Blue, the Nebelung is elegant, muscular and athletic. Heads are a pointed wedge shape set on long, slender necks. The ears are wide at the base and pointed at the tips. Their body is well proportioned, medium-boned but never bulky. Paws are oval and when on the move this cat looks as if it is walking on the balls of its feet. The tail should be at least as long as the body from shoulders to rear end. It is bushy and covered with hair that is longer than that of the body. Both sexes have a ruff around the neck but this is more pronounced in males.

This is a very active breed that requires plenty of physical and mental stimulation. They can be somewhat reserved with strangers but are loyal and loving towards their owners and their family. The Nebelung is very sensitive and doesn't like change. They don't like being left alone for long periods and this can lead to anxiety and other behavioural issues.

▲ *The beautiful blue grey and silver tipped coat can take up to two years to 'come in' completely.*

Breed box

Coat: Soft semi-longhaired double coat that is fine and silky

Eyes: Wide set and vivid green or greenish-yellow in colour

Other features: Tufts of hair are found behind the ears and between the toes

Grooming: Moderate; thorough brushing weekly to avoid matting

Temperament: Lively, mild-mannered and loyal

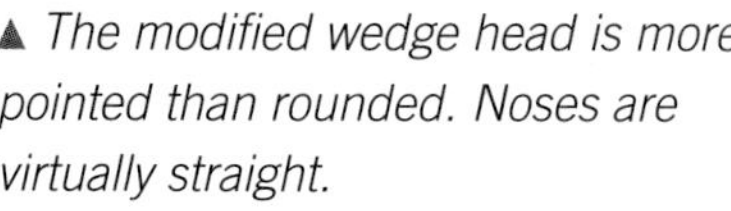

▲ *The modified wedge head is more pointed than rounded. Noses are virtually straight.*

▼ *Forming an extraordinarily strong bond with the person it loves, the Nebelung is reserved with strangers.*

Norwegian Forest Cat

The Norwegian Forest Cat has been described as the 'kissing cousin' of the Maine Coon Cat. The land it comes from certainly has similarities to the forested mountains of Maine. The Norwegian Forest Cat also originated as a natural outdoor working cat, on Scandinavian farms, and its powerful build and skill as a climber and hunter reflect this heritage. Its double-layered coat is heavier during winter, and keeps out both cold and wet. The generous frill and 'shirt front' of fur of the neck and chest may be shed during the summer months.

Although it is a big, strong-legged animal, the Norwegian Forest Cat has a certain elegance. Its head is triangular with a long, straight profile, and ears are pointed, open and erect. Like the Maine Coon Cat, it matures slowly and may not reach full stature until four years of age. All colours are allowed except Chocolate, Lilac and Himalayan/Colourpoint pattern. The Norwegian Forest Cat is one of the semi-longhaired varieties that have developed as a northern hemisphere speciality. Whether it goes as far back as the Vikings – who describe a 'fairy cat' in their legends – is unknown. However, the Vikings travelled not only to the shores of the Mediterranean, and along the rivers of Asia, but also to the east coast of North America. It is entirely feasible that the warrior-traders could have found longhaired Asian cats such as the Angora from Turkey, and taken them back to Scandinavia, and even, perhaps, on to America. The Norwegian Forest Cat may therefore quite possibly share the same rootstock as the Maine Coon Cat, its North American equivalent.

By the 1930s the Norwegian Forest Cat was being taken seriously by pedigreed cat lovers in Norway, and it featured at the foundation of Norway's oldest cat club in 1938. However, it only attained full Championship status from FIFe, Europe's main feline organization, in 1977, and in the United States in 1993.

► *The Norwegian Brown Tabby has the breed's characteristic stance, with a slightly raised rump, and the long, plumed tail raised high.*

▼ *A Blue Bi-colour displays the distinctively long feathering from the ears, and big, slightly obliquely set eyes. There should be extra points for the splendid whiskers.*

Breed box

Coat: Thick; double coat – a woolly undercoat covered by a smooth, water-repellent overcoat; thick ruff

Eyes: Large, round; all colours

Grooming: Relatively easy; occasional brushing and combing

Temperament: Alert, active; loves people; freedom-loving; enjoys rock and tree climbing

Norwegian Forest colours and patterns

Solid: White, Black, Blue, Red, Cream

Tabby and Tortoiseshell: all colours in classic and mackerel patterns, including Silver variations

Also occurs in shaded, smoke, bi-colour, tortoiseshell and white

Ocicat

The Ocicat is one of the glorious accidents in the cat fancy. A breeder from the state of Michigan in the United States set out to create a Ticked Point Siamese. She mated a Siamese with an Abyssinian. One of the offspring was mated back to another Siamese male, and a tabby Point Siamese duly appeared. However, one kitten was ivory-coated with clear golden spots. This was the very first Ocicat, its name inspired by the wild ocelot, because of the similarity in coat colour and pattern. Many breeders used the same breeding formula successfully.

Recognition was granted in the United States in the 1960s, although Championship status was not achieved until 1987. Preliminary recognition in the United Kingdom did not come until 1998. Ocicats are now available in Brown, Blue, Chocolate, Lilac, Cinnamon, and Fawn, as well as the Silver-based versions of these colours. A few authorities also recognize Red, Cream and Tortoiseshell. It is a long-bodied, well-muscled animal, with medium-length legs and a long, tapered tail. It has a round head with a prominent muzzle and large, pointed ears.

Although this breed has a wild look they are in fact very affectionate. The Ocicat is very social and enjoys the company of humans as well as that of other cats and well-mannered dogs. They are intelligent and can be trained to walk on a harness and lead, to

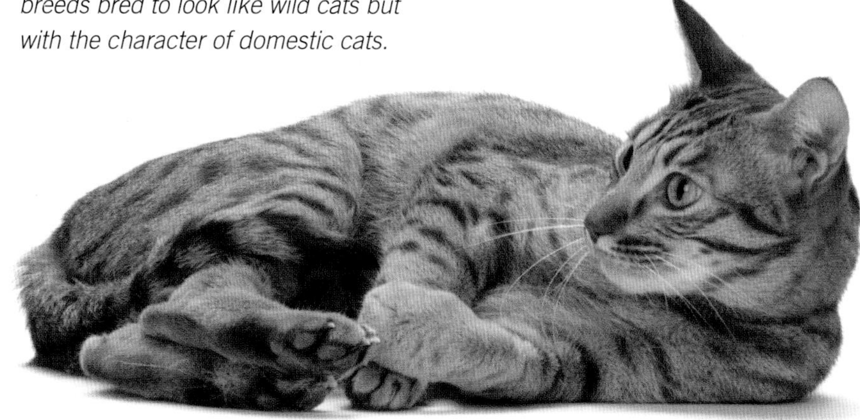

► *The Ocicat was the first of many breeds bred to look like wild cats but with the character of domestic cats.*

▲ *An intelligent cat that can be taught a range of tricks and to walk on a harness and lead.*

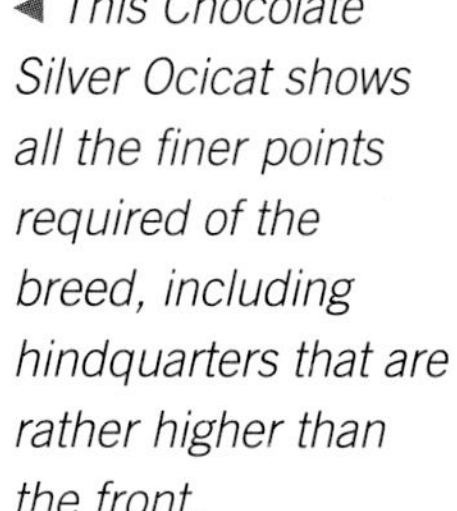

◄ *This Chocolate Silver Ocicat shows all the finer points required of the breed, including hindquarters that are rather higher than the front.*

◀ *There should be a clear 'M' mark on the forehead of Ocicats, but this is less obvious in the dilute colours such as this Lilac.*

▶ *At birth, the Ocicat kitten may have a very indistinct pattern. The spots develop as the cat matures, and this 15-week-old kitten is looking promising.*

retrieve and to meow on command. The Ocicat is a vocal breed and will use its voice to express emotion and to gain attention. They love to be the centre of attention and to be involved in everything their owners are doing. Cats deprived of attention can show signs of stress and resulting behaviour disorders. This breed will accept strangers, children, other cats and well-behaved dogs into its home and seems to revel in company. In fact, the busier the home the more an Ocicat seems to enjoy life.

The Ocicat is very active and needs a range of toys to provide physical and mental exercise. Puzzle or activity toys seem to be made especially for them. They are born athletes and can reach or climb higher than one could possibly imagine.

Recently breeders of the Ocicat in the UK have produced litters with Classic or Aztec patterning. These cats have the 'M' facial markings and unbroken necklaces around the neck and chest. An unbroken line runs down the spine ending with a marking in the shape of a butterfly at the base of the tail. Other lines run parallel to the central line interspersed with butterfly and oyster markings. The tail is ringed with the tip being the same colour as the base coat. Breeders are hoping that cats with this type of marking will be recognized, in the future, as a separate breed to the spotted Ocicat.

Breed box

Coat: Short, thick, smooth and satiny with lustrous sheen
Eyes: Large, slanted, almond-shaped; all colours except blue
Other features: Spotted coat
Grooming: Easy; regular brushing
Temperament: Affectionate, active

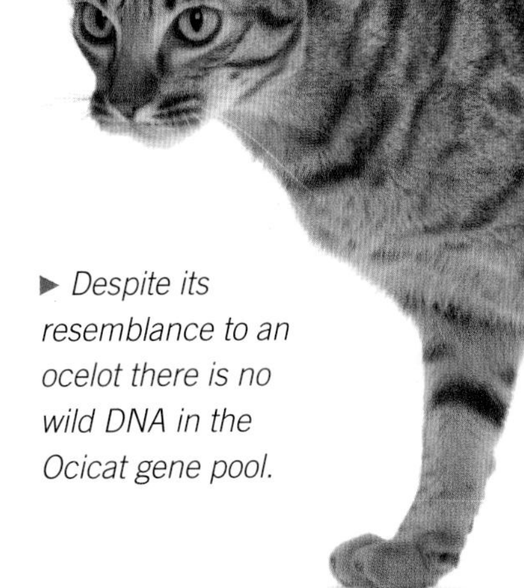

▶ *Despite its resemblance to an ocelot there is no wild DNA in the Ocicat gene pool.*

Ojos Azules

This is a very rare breed that was accepted for registration by The International Cat Association in 1991. A breed standard was produced in January 2004. There are very few of these cats in existence and some controversy surrounds this breed that originated in the USA. Ojos Azules is Spanish for 'blue eyes' and this is an important feature of the breed standard regardless of coat colour or pattern. The gene that causes the eye colouration, in this breed, also causes stillbirth, cranial deformities, white fur and small curled tails. Therefore, blue-eyed Ojos Azules must always be crossed with cats with non-blue eyes to minimize these defects. All litters will contain an equal mix of kittens with blue eyes and those that don't. Due to the low numbers of Ojos Azules it is hard to evaluate the extent or severity of any potential health problems. In some areas breeding these cats has been temporarily suspended while these issues are assessed.

▶ *While markings on muzzle, paws and tail tip are commonly seen, all coat colours are allowed.*

▼ *Unlike many breeds, the gene linked to the vivid blue eyes is not associated to coat colour or pattern.*

Another distinctive feature of the Ojos Azules is the flattened tip to their tails. The tail should be in proportion to the body and not shortened. Heads have a triangular shape with a slightly rounded forehead. All coat colours are permitted and white markings on the paws, muzzle and tail tip are common. This is a medium-sized breed.

Although affectionate with those that they know, the Ojos Azules is reserved around strangers. It is a playful cat but only on its own terms.

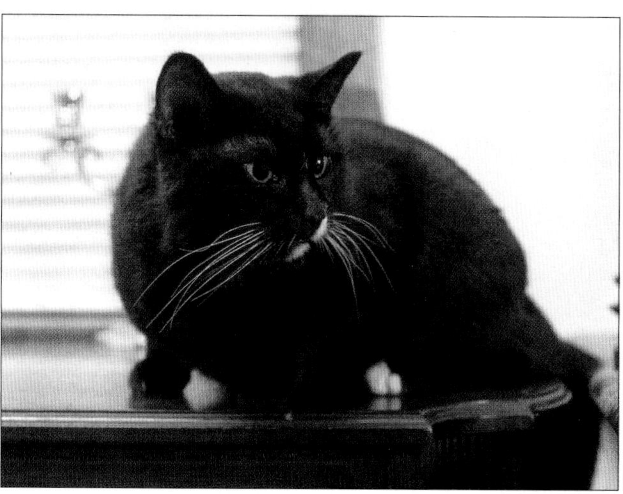

◀ *A medium-sized cat weighing between 4.08–5.5kg (9–12lb) which has an expected life span of 10–12 years.*

Breed box

Coat: Short or longhaired; silky with slight undercoat

Eyes: Large, round and brilliant blue regardless of coat colour

Other features: White-coated, blue-eyed Ojos Azules don't suffer from deafness

Grooming: Easy; the coat requires little attention

Temperament: Active, intelligent and loving

Oregon Rex

The Oregon Rex, coming from the USA, has the dubious claim to fame of being one of the first recognized cat breeds to become extinct. Despite great popularity during the mid-1900s the last surviving purebred cat is reported to have died in 1972. Although they had a typical rex coat, they differed from other rex breeds as this natural mutation was caused by a recessive, as opposed to a dominate, gene. Over the years the Oregon Rex was crossed with other rex breeds until numbers of purebreds had diminished. There doesn't appear to be any reason for this other than popularity of the other rex breeds.

This slender cat had long legs with tiny, rounded paws. Wedge-shaped heads were topped with large, rounded ears set high on the head. This was a small, gracefully built cat. The coat was tightly curled and shorter than that of the Cornish Rex or German Rex. All colours and patterns were permitted. Tails were long, graceful and slim. It does not appear to have had any documented health problems. Lifespans ranged from 12–15 years.

This breed was not advised for first-time cat owners as they could be wilful and difficult to train. They certainly had dominant characters. Although affectionate towards their owners they could not really be described as a lap cats. They were often labelled as being rather arrogant and yet they did not like being left alone for long.

Breed box

Coat: Fine, curly down that lacked guard hairs
Eyes: Oval and medium in size
Other features: Medium-sized elongated bodies
Grooming: Moderate; rex coats were fragile
Temperament: Stubborn, loyal and playful

Oriental Bicolour

Although initial experimental breeding took place during the 1970s and 80s in the UK, the Oriental Bicolour originates from the USA. The founder of the breed is listed as Lindajean Grillo who commenced a breeding programme in 1979. Originally she crossed Bicolour American Shorthairs with Siamese and latterly other breeds were added as outcrosses. Some registries recognize this cat as a breed in its own right while others register them as Oriental Shorthairs.

As the name suggests this breed is of Oriental type with a triangular head, long slender body and a whip-like tail. Ears are large and set well apart. Two types of coat exist. Shorthaired cats have a sleek, glossy coat that lays close to the body. Longhaired varieties have a fine silky coat, without undercoat, and a plumed tail. All the colours normally seen in Orientals and Siamese are permitted but a feature of the Oriental

Breed box

Coat: Silky longhair or shorthair that lays close to the body with no undercoat
Eyes: Large, expressive and almond-shaped
Other features: A very vocal breed
Grooming: Easy to moderate, depending on coat type
Temperament: Energetic, extrovert and intelligent

▶ *The elegant and proportional body is enhanced by a long and slender tail.*

Bicolour is the essential white spotting. White colouring should cover at least a third of the body with more white on the belly and legs than on the back. This white patterning, or splashing as it is also known, is caused by a dominate gene.

This cat is very loving and forms a strong bond with its family. They are very energetic and highly intelligent. Ample physical and mental activity opportunities must be provided to ensure an Oriental Bicolour has a happy and fulfilled life. They make ideal family companions as they are generally very accepting of children, especially if they play with them.

▲ *Eyes are green with the exception of permitted colourpoint varieties who have blue eyes.*

▲ *A vocal cat that will communicate with its human family but hates being left alone for long.*

Oriental Longhair

All of the cats that make up the Oriental group are descended from the Siamese. Some registries group them all together, others place them in sub-groups while some consider them as stand-alone breeds. The Oriental Longhair is known by various other names including Mandarin, British Angora and Foreign Longhair. The breed was given Championship status by The Governing Council of the Cat Fancy in 1977.

The Oriental Longhair is fine-boned but very muscular. They are heavier than they look. The head is wedge-shaped and is triangular when viewed from the side. Ears are large, wide at the base and pointed at the tips, and set wide apart on the head. Despite the word longhair in the name this breed actually has a medium-length coat. A myriad of colour and coat pattern combinations are acceptable. Members of the Oriental group are

► *Heads are similar to those of a Siamese. Ears should be set at a 'ten-to-two' position.*

Breed box
Coat: Silky and flowing with a feathery plumed tail
Eyes: Green, slanted and almond-shaped
Other features: Bodies are long and tubular
Grooming: Moderate as they do not have an undercoat
Temperament: Confident, athletic and intelligent

▲ *This breed is prone to periodontal disease, possibly because of its long slender face.*

▲ *Watch out – Oriental Longhairs have been known to open refrigerator and cupboard doors to help themselves.*

► *A demanding conversationalist, who communicates with a loud and strident mewl.*

sometimes referred to as rainbow cats and it is easy to see why.

This is a very active cat who loves to play the clown and entertain. They are very playful and will join in activities with their family or entertain themselves with a favourite toy. Most enjoy playing fetch and their intelligence makes it relatively easy to teach them a wide range of tricks. The Oriental Longhair is a very vocal cat and will join in all conversations. This is a loving breed that will tolerate changes within the household. Good with children but can be rather dominant around other pets.

Oriental Shorthair

The ancestors of the Oriental Shorthairs are, like the Siamese, from Thailand. They are, in fact, just like Siamese cats but with all-over coat colour and pattern rather than the Siamese colourpoints on face, ears, tail and legs. The eyes of the Orientals are usually green rather than the blue of the Siamese, although in the solid White, they may be blue or orange (though the British standard rejects the orange-eyed). Virtually all colour and pattern variations are represented, except, of course, the colourpoints, making this one of the most diverse of all cat breeds and groups.

In the United Kingdom and Europe, the self colours were originally known as Foreign Shorthairs but the other varieties have always been known as Orientals. Each different colour was given a separate breed category to enable the cats to be entered at shows, as they were excluded from the Siamese classes. In the United States in the 1970s, all the variations were grouped together in the one category

▲ *A Red Oriental can show the tabby markings that come with its red genes, but preferably no white hairs at all. You can see this cat's Siamese heritage in its large ears and long, straight nose.*

Oriental colours and patterns

Foreign White: White with blue eyes (United Kingdom), or orange or blue eyes (United States)

Self colours: Chocolate (Havana), Lilac, Black, Blue, Red, Cream, Apricot, Cinnamon, Caramel, Fawn

Tortoiseshell: As self colours

Oriental Smoke: Any colour with a near-white undercoat

Oriental Shaded: Shaded or tipped with any colour with or without silver

Oriental Tabbies: Spotted, classic or mackerel pattern in all colours with or without silver

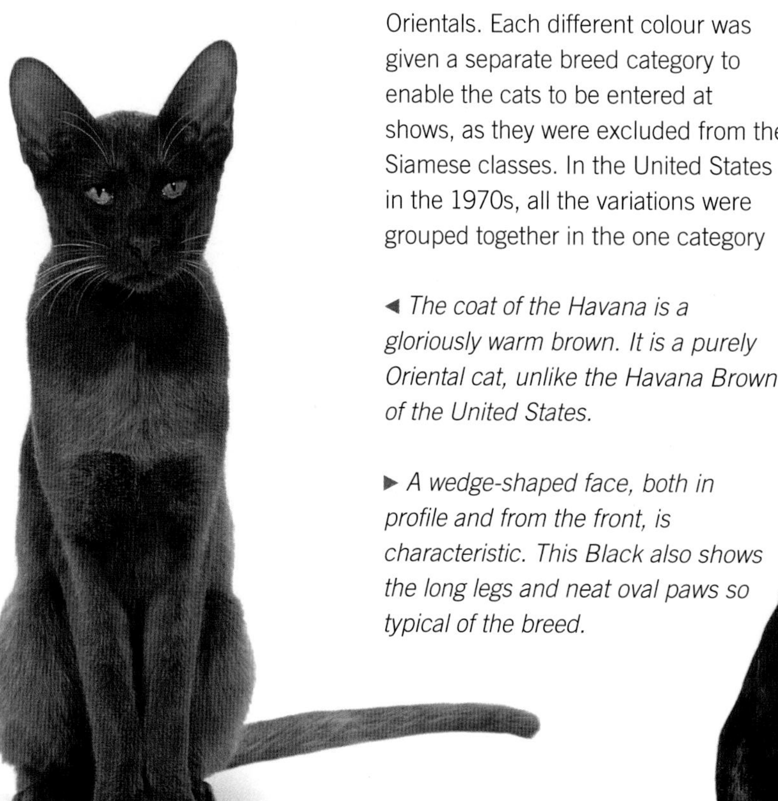

◀ *The coat of the Havana is a gloriously warm brown. It is a purely Oriental cat, unlike the Havana Brown of the United States.*

▶ *A wedge-shaped face, both in profile and from the front, is characteristic. This Black also shows the long legs and neat oval paws so typical of the breed.*

▶ *This cat requires both physical and mental exercise. Laser toys are a great favourite with active breeds.*

Breed box
Coat: Short, soft, fine, lying flat along the body
Eyes: Almond-shaped, slanted; green with no flecks (except Foreign White – brilliant blue)
Other features: Loud voice as in Siamese, large ears, big personality
Grooming: Easy; can be 'polished' with a soft glove
Temperament: Intelligent, lively, inquisitive, active; need company

of Oriental Shorthairs, and this broad term is now universal. However, the British cat fancy still classifies the different colours and patterns as distinct breeds. There are four fundamental sub-divisions: solid colours, shaded, smokes and tabbies.

The Oriental Shorthair type was developed during the 1960s by mating Siamese with indigenous cats such as the British, European and American Shorthairs. They have since only been outcrossed to Siamese, so have a very similar temperament. They enjoy human company generally, and do not like being left alone for too long. In many ways, their response to humans is dog-like – they may run to greet their owners on their return home, and need to be played with. Their athletic physique has also led to canine comparisons – their length of body and the way they move is like the feline version of a whippet, complete with whip-like tail.

Pantherette

This cat joins the ranks of other domestic cats bred to mimic a wild cat. Unlike the spotted and striped breeds such as the Ocicat and the Toyger, the Pantherette is solid black in colour and is devised to resemble a small black panther. Initial breeding was undertaken by Mike and Marie Bloodgood of the Bamboo Cattery, USA. The Bloodgoods have protected the name as a Trademark, which they own. This means that it is illegal for anyone else to use the name Pantherette, even if the cat they have bred looks similar in type. The breed is in its infancy and cats are registered with the International Progressive Cat Breeders Alliance (IPCBA).

There is no panther, of any type, in the breeding of the Pantherette. This hybrid is based on solid-coloured (non-agouti) Bengals with outcrosses to other breeds. The Bengals used as a foundation are solid black and these cats are referred to as Melanistic Bengals. Crosses used have been varied but currently the introduction of the Smoke Mojave Desert Cat is producing impressive results.

As this breed is still being developed it would be impossible to catalogue any lasting behavioural characteristics. Intensive work is being undertaken to ensure that there are no genetic disorders. The intention is to prioritise the production of a healthy cat breed that is panther-like in looks but not in temperament. The Pantherette is being bred to be a striking addition to the domestic cat breeds, not to introduce wild cats into the domestic market.

Breed box
Coat: Black, shorthaired
Eyes: No standard yet produced
Other features: Medium-sized muscular bodies
Grooming: Easy; the occasional brush to remove shedding hair
Temperament: Wild cat looks, with a domestic cat temperament

The Persian Cat

All Persian cats – known officially as Longhair Persian type – have the same basic physical shape and conformation. Their faces are flat with short noses and small ears. Their bodies are broad-chested with sturdy legs and large paws, and they all have a soft, thick fur coat with a distinctive ruff around the neck, and a full, low-slung tail. Persian longhairs come in many different colours and patterns. In some countries the colour variations are considered as varieties of the same breed, but in Britain, each different colour is listed as a separate breed. Longhaired variations of wild species may have spontaneously occurred in colder regions in the heart of Asia, and then gradually become established with subsequent interbreeding. The ancestors of today's Persians were probably stocky, longhaired grey cats brought to Europe from Persia (now Iran) in the 1600s and silken-haired white Angora cats from Turkey (a different type from the modern Angora breed). Today, there are over 60 different colour variations of the Longhair Persian type (see also the Peke-Faced Persian page 339 and the Traditional Persian page 340).

Black

Black Self Persians are thought to be one of the earliest Persian breeds. Today, however, they are not at all common. The show standard insists on a solid, dense coal-black coat, with no hint of rustiness, shading, markings or white hairs. Like many Persians, the Blacks are affectionate and dignified, and have a reputation for being more playful than the White Persian.

► *A fully mature Black Persian.*

Breed box

Coat: Thick, lustrous; full frill at neck and shoulders

Eyes: Copper or deep orange; rims black

Other features: Nose leather and paw pads black

Grooming: Demanding; thorough, daily

Temperament: Placid

White

The White Persian owes its purity of coat colour to the native Angora cat from Turkey. A show standard White Self should be dazzling white and free of marks or shading. Kittens may have coloured hairs on top of the head but these should disappear early on. Whites are meticulous self-groomers, but maintaining an immaculate coat is a major challenge for the owner, too. The fur can yellow, especially around the face, legs and tail. However, white grooming powder is available which both cleans and helps guard against staining. The reward for extra effort is a full-flowing, glacial-white coat emphasizing a magical eye colour.

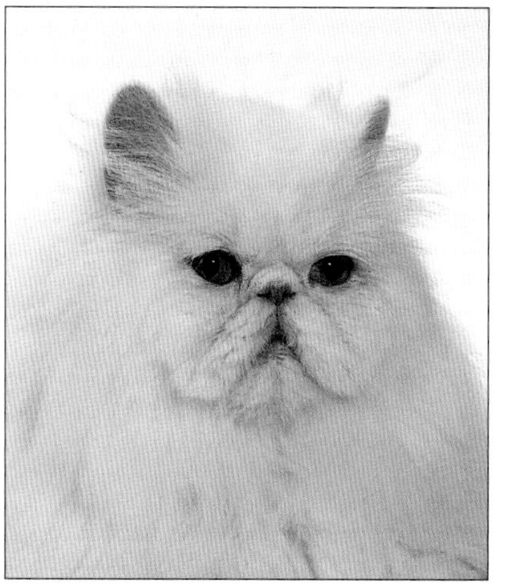

▲ *A White Persian's calm nature make it an ideal indoor cat, although it can also be playful.*

Breed box

Coat: Thick, dense, silky; full frill at neck and shoulders

Eyes: Blue-eyed White: eyes blue with deeper shades of blue preferred; rims pink

Orange-eyed White: Eyes copper or deep orange; rims pink

Odd-eyed White: One eye blue and one eye orange or deep copper; rims pink

Other features: Nose leather and paw pads pink

Grooming: Demanding; thorough, daily

Temperament: Placid

Blue

At the end of the 1800s, Blue Persians became extremely popular as pets of the wealthy, and were specially bred to be sold for high prices. They became particular favourites of European royalty. Queen Victoria of England acquired two Blues, Princess Victoria of Schleswig-Holstein was an enthusiastic breeder, and King Edward VII presented medals for the top prize-winners of the day.

One reason for the Blue's popularity may have been because it was thought to be the nearest in colour to the original Persians brought to Europe by traders in the 1600s. The genetic mutation of the breed we know today may well have arisen on the Mediterranean island of Malta – which is why it is sometimes called the Maltese Blue. The blue-grey colouring is a dilution of black. The blue comes from a lavender sheen which adds a brightness to the pale coat. This is very much in evidence with the show cat, which is ideally an even, medium to pale blue, with no shading, markings or white hairs. A dark, slate-grey coat is considered very undesirable. Because of its long, distinguished history of careful breeding, the Persian Blue is often used as the standard Persian type against which other Persian breeds are compared. For this reason, it is sometimes included in breeding programmes to improve the type of other varieties.

The Blue has a reputation for being a very affectionate and gentle cat that enjoys close human companionship.

▲ *A Blue with a well-earned aristocratic air. Its evenly coloured coat with a lustrous sheen offsets glorious copper-orange eyes.*

Breed box

Coat:Thick, dense, silky; full frill at neck and shoulders
Eyes: Copper or deep orange; rims blue-grey
Other features: Nose leather and paw pads blue-grey
Grooming: Demanding; thorough, daily
Temperament: Placid

Chocolate

There is an element of Siamese in the Chocolate Persian, which may account for a certain sauciness in its nature. The Chocolate Point Siamese was mated with Blue Persian cats to create part of the formula for the Persian Colourpoint. The Chocolate was an offshoot, and gradually, through generations of breeding, it became a recognized variety in its own right. The ideal show cat has a medium to dark, warm and evenly toned coat with no shading, markings or white hairs. Warmth of tone rather than a deep, dark bitter chocolate is very important.

Kittens sometimes show greying, although this often disappears by the time they are six to nine months old. Eyes should be rich copper-orange with no signs of reversion to pale gold or green.

◄ *With their Siamese ancestry, the early Chocolates often had shorter fur than most Persians, but this is no longer the case.*

Breed box

Coat: Thick, silky
Eyes: Copper or deep orange; rims chocolate brown
Other features: Nose leather and paw pads chocolate brown
Grooming: Demanding; thorough, daily
Temperament: Placid

Red

Only a few decades ago, the Red Persian was one of the rarest of all feline varieties. This was largely because of the need to select parents which had had fine mackerel-striped coats as kittens, combined with long fur and intensity of colour. The fiery red coat is much richer than that of the ginger tom. For a show cat, it should be tonally even, with no white hairs. Slight shading on the forehead and legs is acceptable. The sex-linked gene which creates the red cannot mask the tabby markings that Red Persian kittens display in certain lights. It is rare for a Red to be free of these markings until the ground colour has intensified with maturity.

Breed box
Coat: Thick, silky
Eyes: Copper or deep orange; rims deep pink
Other features: Nose leather and paw pads deep pink
Grooming: Demanding; thorough, daily
Temperament: Placid with spark

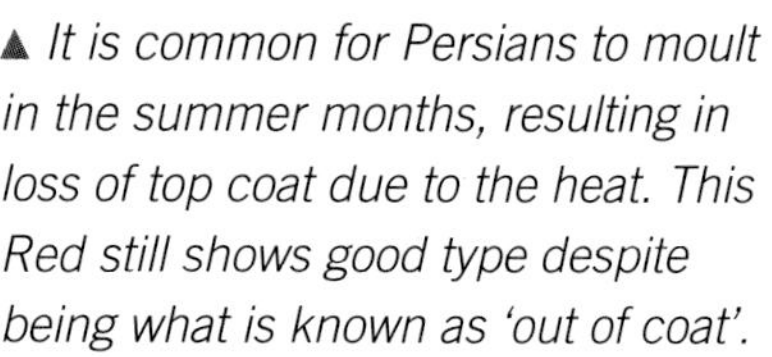

▲ *It is common for Persians to moult in the summer months, resulting in loss of top coat due to the heat. This Red still shows good type despite being what is known as 'out of coat'.*

Cream

The Cream Persian is a dilute Red, with probable input from the white Angoras that were cross-bred with Persians in the 1800s. Then, as now, Blue Persians were not only the most popular variety, but the best examples of type, so breeders of other colours used Blue studs in their programmes. Blues are dilutes of Black Persians, and so dilute genes were released into many breeding programmes, eventually resulting in a whole range of dilute colours.

Early Creams had larger ears and longer noses than their modern descendants, and their eyes were almond-shaped. Today's Cream is the result of over a century of very selective breeding that was initially done in America. The English described these dilute Reds as 'spoiled oranges', and did not regard them as an acceptable colour variation until the 1920s. The ideal Cream has no shading, markings or white hairs. The pale to medium cream coat is even in colour with no white undercoat. As with all Persians the thick coat hides any angles, making the body look very rounded.

▼ *A Cream kitten is particularly precious as some breeders think that this variety has smaller litters than other Longhairs.*

Breed box
Coat: Thick, silky
Eyes: Copper or deep orange; rims pink
Other features: Nose leather and paw pads pink
Grooming: Demanding; thorough, daily
Temperament: Placid

Tortoiseshell

The classic Tortoiseshell colouring is a striking blend of black, red and pale red. The exact configuration of colours is very much influenced by the mix of colour genes carried by the female parent. If the female gene has two red XX chromosomes, the offspring will be red. However, if one of the female's chromosomes carries the red gene and one does not, then the offspring will be a mixture of red and another colour or colours – a Tortoiseshell. Because of the complex genetic make-up necessary to create the Tortoiseshell mix of colours, all variations are usually female. Tortoiseshells, also known as Torties, occur in dilute variations, such as Chocolate Tortie, Blue-Cream and Lilac-Cream. The parentage is reflected in the names.

The object in breeding any Tortoiseshell pedigree is to achieve a perfect balance in the mix of colours. When black and chocolate are intermingled with red, the result can be a brilliant firework display of a coat. Aficionados of these varieties hope that the colours will be well-defined.

Tortoiseshells with red in their make-up are said to inherit the allegedly fiery temperament of the Red Persian, though their fans say they are just full of character. They also tend to be particularly attentive mothers. Tortoiseshell queens are mated with Blacks and Reds for the best chance of producing Tortoiseshell kittens in their litter. The ethereal colour of the dilute Tortoiseshells is said to be complemented by a certain charm and winsomeness of character. Eyes of all Tortoiseshells are large, full and deep copper or orange.

▲ *A Black Tortoiseshell shows off its fine cobby build, with solid, squarish body, short, thick legs and large head. Because Tortoiseshells have been cross-bred with a good mixture of other breeds, they tend to show excellent type.*

► *The Blue-Cream is a subtly coloured Tortoiseshell which arose from crossing a Blue Persian with a Cream. The American and English standards differ. The English like the two colours to merge, while the Americans prefer distinctive bands of blue and cream.*

▼ *This Black Tortoiseshell is differently marked from the one at the top of the page. Tortoiseshells come in several colours, although a mix of red or cream patches on the base coat colour are desirable. No two Tortoiseshells are ever the same.*

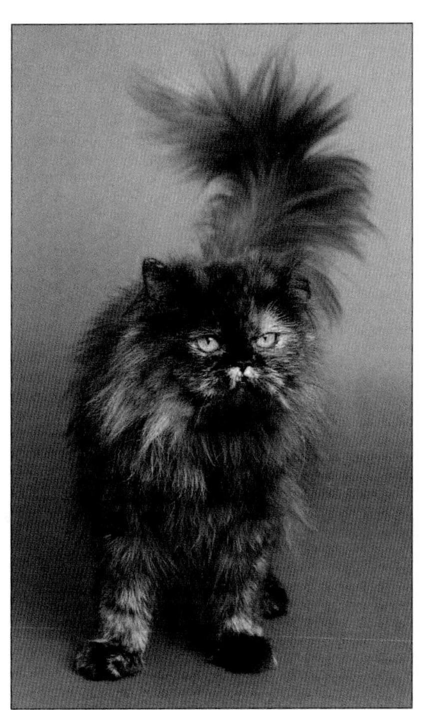

Breed box

Coat: Thick, silky

Eyes: Deep orange or copper

Other features: Nose leather and paw pads pink or black, depending on dominant coat colour

Grooming: Demanding; thorough, daily

Temperament: Placid

◀ Blue Bi-colours are available in all the colours accepted for the Self colours, such as Red, Cream and Chocolate.

Bi-colour

In the early days of pedigree breeding, any longhaired cat with a patch of white was regarded with horror. However, there were so few animals without a white spot that to fill classes at shows, the Bi-colours were allowed to compete. These solid-coloured cats with white undersides, muzzles, chests, legs and feet, were placed along with the Tortoiseshell and Whites, in an 'any other variety' category. The ideal standard is for the white patches to be balanced and even, with a dapper and clearly defined inverted V shape running over the nose.

Breed box
Coat: Thick, dense, silky; full frill at neck and shoulders
Eyes: Deep orange or copper
Grooming: Demanding; thorough, daily, especially the white parts
Temperament: Placid

Tortoiseshell and White

The classic Tortoiseshell's black and red are offset by patches of dazzling white – as long as the cat is frequently groomed. The American standard requires well-defined patches of colour, but in the United Kingdom, any degree of white is acceptable, from some on all four legs, chest and belly, to the van pattern.

► A black Tortie and White displays well-mingled markings.

Breed box
Coat: Particularly long and silky; full frill at neck and shoulders; full, bushy tail
Eyes: Orange or deep copper
Grooming: Demanding; thorough, daily, in particular special care with the white parts
Temperament: Placid

Tabby

Mainstream Tabby colours are Brown, Red and Silver, although other varieties such as Cream, Lilac and Cameo are being introduced. The Brown Tabby is rich, tawny-sable ground with dense black markings. The Red Tabby, with its rich ginger coat and matching eyes, however, remains the most popular variety. Next in line are the Silvers. They have been subject to dispute over correct eye colour for show cats, especially in the United Kingdom. Elsewhere, a looser interpretation of achievable eye colour has meant that Silver Tabby Persians have now been bred to the very best of type characteristics.

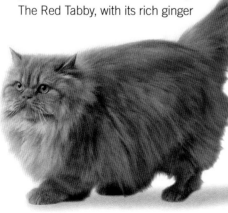

◀ The rich marmalade-coloured coat of the Red Tabby is marked with deep copper – and the eyes are a complementary golden orange.

Breed box
Coat: Thick, silky, often shorter than other longhair varieties
Eyes: Brown and Red: orange or copper with no green rim
Silver: green or hazel
Other features: Brown: nose leather brick-red; paw pads black or brown
Red: nose and paw pads pink
Silver: nose leather red with black outline; paw pads black
Grooming: Demanding; thorough, daily; special care brings out markings
Temperament: Placid

Peke-Faced Persian

The term 'Peke-Faced Persian' both describes a type and a breed. Persian cats that have very flat noses and faces that resemble that of a Pekinese dog are covered by this description. These cats are often referred to as 'extreme' within the Persian cat fancy. Breed standards for the Persian cat vary across the world and in some cases this type is preferred in the show ring.

The Cat Fanciers Association (CFA) lists a recognized breed named a Peke-Faced Persian. This is a solid red-coloured cat, similar in type to a Persian cat but with different head bone structure. The nose is depressed and indented between the eyes. Muzzles are wrinkled and flattened with an additional nose break between the normal nose break and the top dome of the head. Although still eligible for competition in CFA shows, there is a possibility that the breed is now extinct as none have been presented for judging for several decades. The breed box on this page contains details of this cat.

Any cat, be it breed or type, that has a Peke-Face, or extreme facial structure, runs the risk of suffering from health problems. The short nose and wrinkled muzzle can result in breathing and sinus problems. Tear ducts may be obstructed, or too small, causing sore and running eyes. In severe cases, the skin below the eye becomes ulcerated. Queens have a higher than average risk of caesarean section as kittens' round and flattened heads cause them to get stuck in the birth canal.

► *This is a quiet-natured breed that appreciates a calm home life, preferring to be the only pet.*

▼ *Eyes have a tendency to run and will require daily wiping clean to prevent tear stains.*

Breed box

Coat: Typical Persian in length and texture but solid red in colour
Eyes: Large and round; deep copper in colour
Other features: Ears are set slightly higher than a Persian
Grooming: Extreme; requiring thorough daily brushing
Temperament: Placid, quiet and affectionate

► *Peke-Faced cats sometimes have a bad dental bite, which can worsen with age.*

Traditional Persian

▼ *The Traditional Persian has been popular since Victorian times and has graced many royal courts and palaces.*

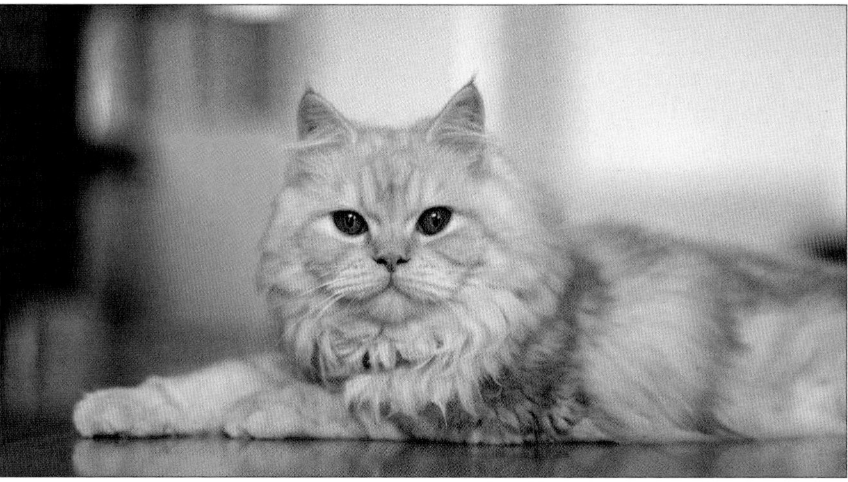

The Traditional Persian is one of many names used to describe the cats that were the forerunners of today's Persian (Modern) cats. Other names used include Doll-faced Persian, Classic Persian, Long-nosed Persian, Old Fashioned Persian, Original Longhair, Traditional Longhair and Old-style Persians. Some registries recognize these cats as separate breeds to Persians. Names used for the breed varies greatly from registry to registry. All Persians originate from Iran and outcrosses have been used to produce the breed types that we are familiar with now.

These cats have a standard, more pointed face than the flatter-faced Persian. The Traditional Persian is less likely to suffer from the health-related issues associated with the Persian, but it is not so popular. Unfortunately, the number of cats that do not carry the gene mutation which causes flattened facial bone structure is decreasing. If this continues, to avoid in-breeding, outcrosses to other breeds may have to be considered if the Traditional Persian, by any name, is to continue.

These cats make lovely calm pets. They are not overly active and are more than happy to sit on a lap. Potential owners need to consider if they have the time to give this cat's coat the attention that it will require to stay knot-free. Shedding coat must be removed to prevent the cat ingesting it when washing itself as this may cause hairballs. A Traditional Persian featured in the James Bond film 'You Only Live Twice', which brought it back to the public eye.

Breed box

Coat: Long, silky and dense
Eyes: Large and round; colour dependent on coat colour
Other features: Similar in type to a Persian in all aspects except head shape
Grooming: Intensive; coat requires daily attention
Temperament: Gentle, friendly and loving

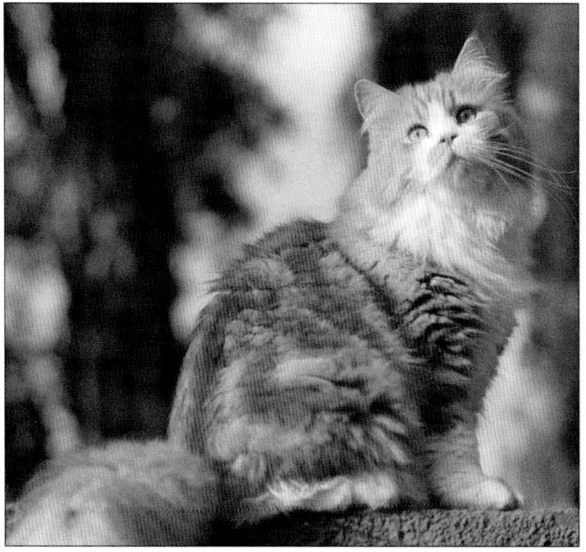

◄ *Both the World Cat Federation and the Southern Africa Cat Council produce breed standards for the Traditional Persian (Traditional Longhair).*

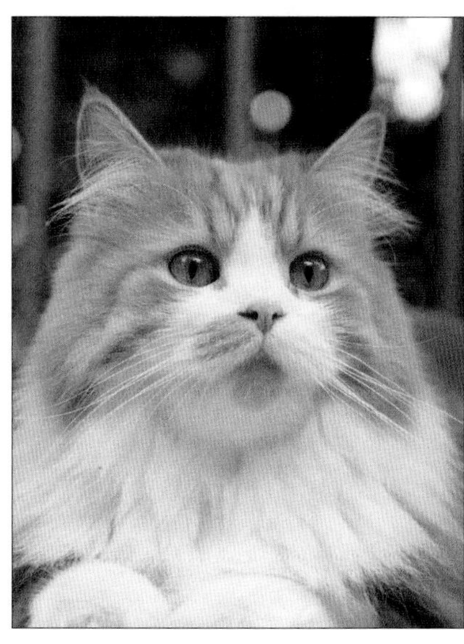

► *A thick neck ruff and dense plume of a tail both contribute to the luxurious look of this long-coated breed.*

Peterbald

In 1994 a Russian cat breeder, Olga Mironova, mated a Don Sphynx to an Oriental Shorthair. The resulting four kittens were the foundation of the Peterbald breed. They are similar in type to an Oriental Shorthair but with a hair-losing gene. This gene is dominate. There is a great variation of coats and litters of kittens will contain a variety of these types.

Heads are triangular-shaped with sharp features and a small chin. Large ears are wide at the base and rounded at the tips. This is a medium-sized cat with a broad chest. Shoulder and rear leg muscles are visible in hairless and flock varieties. The abdomen can appear prominent, but this is only because of the lack of hair covering. Legs are long and dainty. The tail is long and whip-like.

The Peterbald is an extremely friendly and affectionate breed. They need to be protected from the extremes of the weather, suffering from the cold in the winter and susceptible to sunburn in hot summer months. Although suitable as a family pet caution is required when handled by young children as the lack of coat can made them vulnerable to injury. This is a very vocal breed with a loud voice. These cats are not suited to a home where they will be left alone for long periods. The Peterbald loves company and gets on well with other cats and dogs. They are playful, active and huggable.

▲ *Heads have similarities to that of a Siamese, with long muzzles and flat cheekbones.*

Breed box

Coat: Variable from bald, flock, velour, brush (wiry) to 'normal' straight hair

Eyes: Almond-shaped with a slight squint

Other features: Feet are small and oval with long toes

Grooming: Require regular bathing

Temperament: Curious, intelligent and active

▼ *A smart cat that can problem-solve, will follow its owner, and is moderately vocal.*

▼ *The long toes and webbed feet make it possible for the Peterbald to pick up and hold objects.*

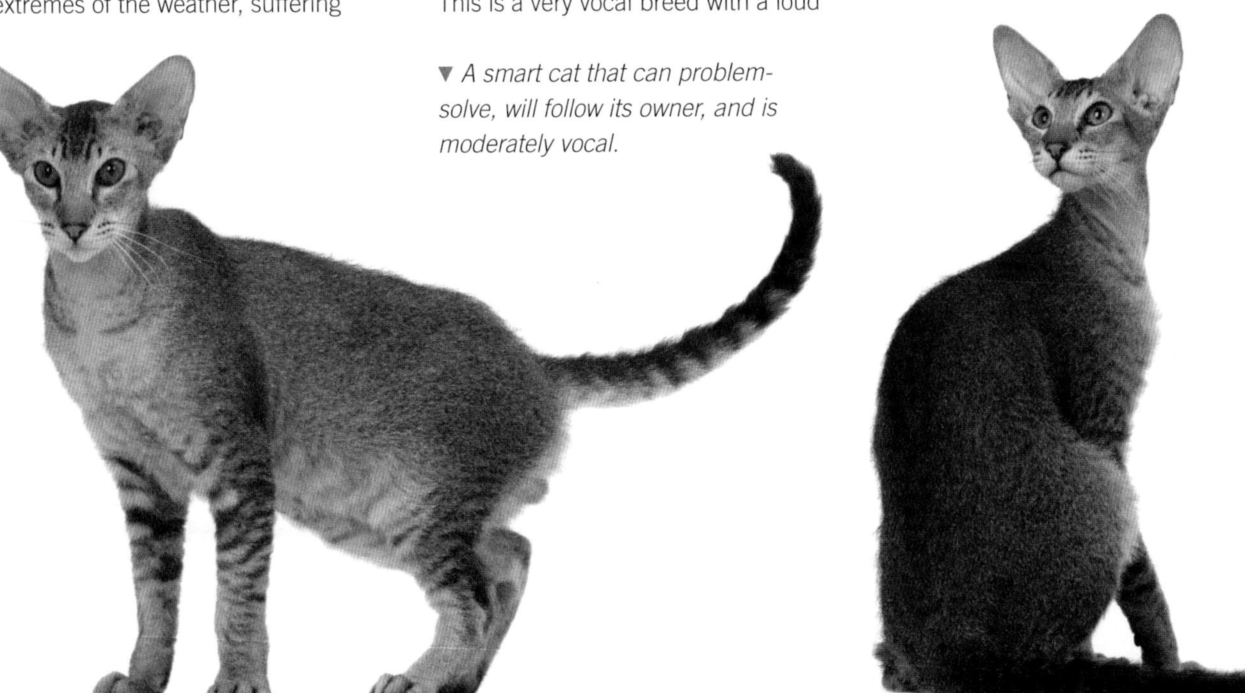

Pixie Bob

► *With its dog-like personality the Pixie Bob likes to join in all activities.*

The Pixie Bob was developed in Washington State, USA by breeder Carol Ann Brewer. She claimed that they were the hybrid progeny of wild bob cats and domestic cats. Recent DNA testing proved that this is not the case. Therefore, Pixie Bobs are considered a wholly domestic breed of cat. The breed is recognized by The International Cat Association (TICA), the American Cat Fanciers Association and the Canadian Cat Association.

Bred to look like a small American bobcat, this breed is very slow to mature taking up to four years to be fully grown. There is some variation in size with most breeders producing cats weighing around 4kg (8lb), while a few prefer larger animals weighing 5kg (11lb) when reaching adulthood. Heads are pear-shaped with a heavy brow. Tails can be either non-existent, two to three inches long, or full length. TICA requires show specimens to have short tails. Coat markings should resemble those of a bobcat but often have a slight red tinge.

The Pixie Bob is a generally healthy, and very intelligent cat. They are easy to train and take to walking on a lead and harness. This breed communicates using a range of growls, chirps and chattering. They seldom meow and some cats never make this sound at all. It is a very friendly breed, sometimes too friendly, as they have been known to follow complete strangers home. It is a great family companion.

Breed box

Coat: Generally shorthaired, although longhaired varieties do exist

Eyes: Triangular that are blue as kittens and green or gold in adults

Other features: White marking under the chin is part of the breed standard

Grooming: Easy to moderate, depending on coat length

Temperament: Bold, sociable and active

Raas

The Raas is an ancient breed originating from the Island of Raas, off the coast of Indonesia. It is a cat of legend. One myth states that these cats have a sixth sense and therefore can only be owned by officials, community leaders and clerics. Another states that if a Raas cat is removed from the island it is bad luck and, if moved in a boat crewed by unmarried people, the boat will sink with loss of life. There is some evidence that the Raas and Korat may have originated from the same landrace.

This is a large cat who, despite its size, has a very elegant and graceful build. Although the skull is round the face has a squarish look. Ears are long, erect and form a point at the tip. Tails are conspicuously long and often turn up slightly at the tip. Shorthaired coats are solid-coloured with a grey, blue or chocolate hue. Occasionally brown coats are seen, but this colour is very rare.

This breed is a born hunter and still has a somewhat wild personality. They may be reserved and even grumpy around humans and it can require considerable patience to form a relationship with a Raas. They will always aim to please themselves and don't seek attention from their owners. Training this moody feline can be difficult. A very active breed that needs space to exercise and toys to satisfy its strong prey instinct.

Breed box

Coat: Soft, smooth shorthaired

Eyes: Dark green, oval in shape

Other features: Tails have a slightly bent edge

Grooming: Easy; occasional brush to remove shedding coat

Temperament: Active, stubborn and intelligent

Ragamuffin

▼ *Once considered a variant of the Ragdoll it was established as a separate breed in 1994.*

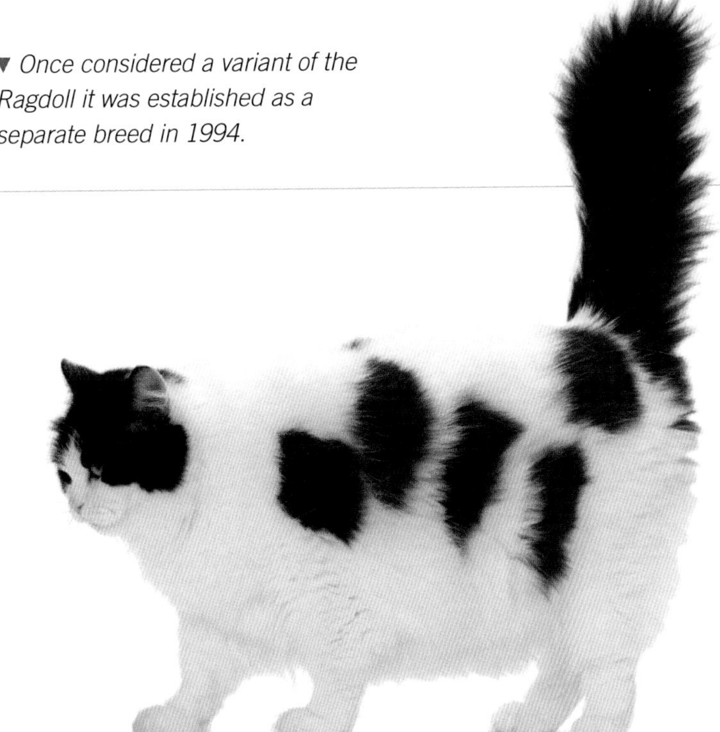

The Ragamuffin started life as a variant of the Ragdoll. Some breeders wanted to introduce new genes and colours into the Ragdoll breed, while others wished the breed to stay the same. The result was the formation of a new breed, the Ragamuffin, using outcrosses of Persians, Himalayans and other longhaired cats. This American breed is recognized by many cat registries including The Cat Fanciers Association, the Cat Fanciers Federation and the American Cat Fanciers Association.

It is a slow maturing breed that doesn't achieve full maturity until four years of age. They are medium to large cats with adult males weighing between 6.35–9.07kg (14–20lb). Bodies are muscular with a broad chest and a short neck. A fleshy pad is often present in the lower abdomen. This breed has a coat that is semi-longhaired and is described as 'having the same texture as a rabbit'. All colours and patterns occur, although some are not permitted at shows. The coat forms a ruff around the neck and chest and is longer on the back of the rear legs forming 'trousers'.

The Ragamuffin enjoys being held and will lie like a baby in its owner's arms. They are very affectionate and don't like being left alone for long periods. Generally, they get on very well with children, making them ideal family pets. This sociable breed also enjoys the company of other cats and well-behaved dogs. Moderately active, they are playful, will fetch toys and can be trained to walk on a well-fitting harness and lead.

▼ *The fur on the face makes the head of a ragamuffin look larger than it actually is.*

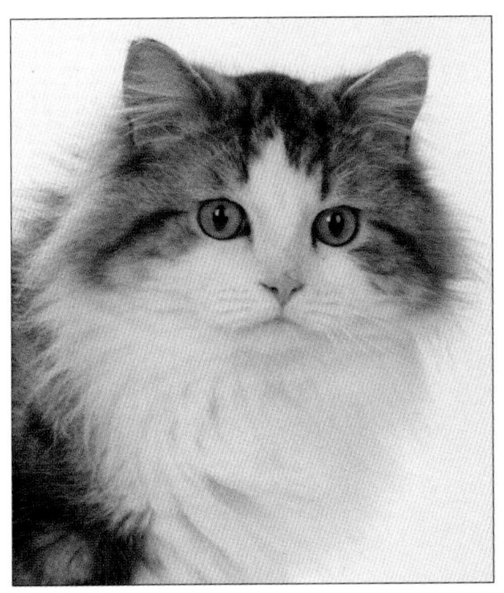

Breed box

Coat: Soft, silky, dense medium-long fur

Eyes: Walnut-shaped and can be any colour

Other features: Ears and pads are furnished with tufts of hair

Grooming: Moderate; weekly brushing needed to remove to remove head hair

Temperament: Docile, puppylike and affectionate

▼ *These cats are renowned for loving their food. Control the diet to avoid overweight issues.*

Ragdoll

When a Ragdoll is picked up it is supposed to go limp – and that is how it came to be named. There is a far-fetched story that the first Ragdoll kittens are said to have inherited this characteristic, together with an apparent resistance to pain, because their white semi-longhair mother, Josephine, had been injured in a road accident. It is more likely that the Ragdoll's docile nature arises from a happy coincidence of character genes. The breed was created in California in 1963. An early alternative name was Cherubim, while some variations are called Ragamuffins. Although the original breeder claimed non-pedigreed parentage, it is likely that Birman and Burmese genes were present somewhere along the line. However, in the majority of cats the dominant white spotting gene creates the look of the Mitted variety, while the one that produces a similar effect in the Birman is recessive.

▲ *A Blue Colourpointed gives a good overall impression of the breed's solid, powerful build. Colourpoints have the traditional pattern of complete coloured mask, ears, legs and tail.*

The Ragdoll is a cat of powerful build, with big, round paws and a long, bushy tail. Its head is broad and wide-cheeked with a slightly retroussé nose and wide eyes of deep sapphire . The three recognized main groupings are Colourpointed, Mitted and Bi-colour. The Mitted has Colour-pointed features contrasting with a pale body, plus white-gloved front feet and rear legs white to the hock or beyond. The Bi-colour is white on the chin, bib, chest and underbody with a triangular blaze over its nose.

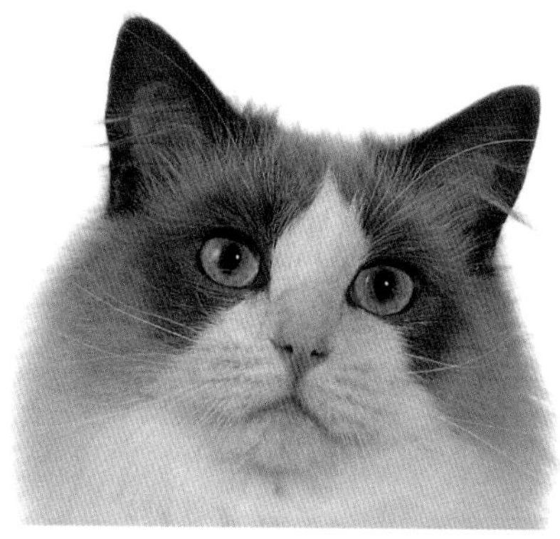

▲ *A triangular nose blaze denotes the true look of the Bi-colour Ragdoll. Bib, chest, underbody and front legs are also white.*

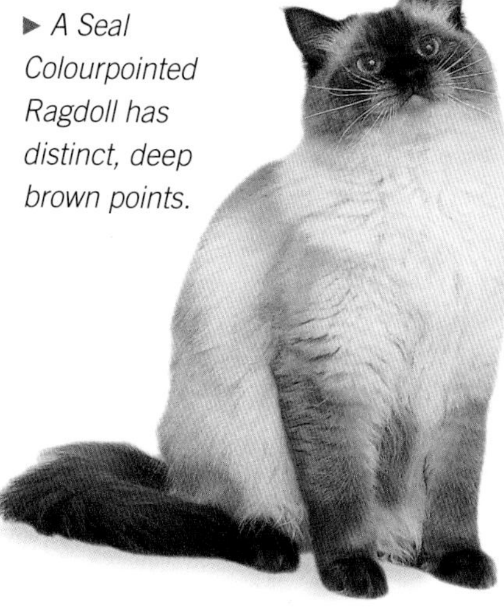

► *A Seal Colourpointed Ragdoll has distinct, deep brown points.*

Breed box

Coat: Dense, silky
Eyes: Small, round, slanted; deep blue
Other features: Goes limp when picked up
Grooming: Easy; daily brushing with soft brush
Temperament: Docile, relaxed, easy to handle; needs calm (so suitable to confine indoors)

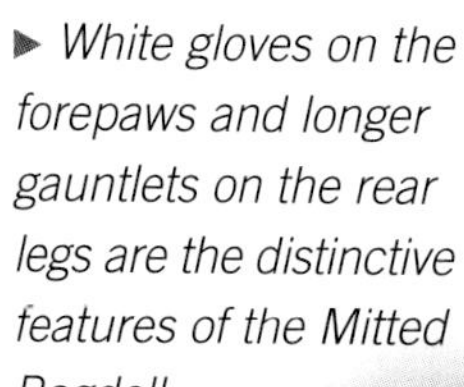

► *White gloves on the forepaws and longer gauntlets on the rear legs are the distinctive features of the Mitted Ragdoll.*

Russian Black/Russian Tabby

The Russian Black and Russian Tabby are derivatives of the more commonly known Russian Blue. The names of these breeds denote a colour specific to the breed. There is no physical conformation difference to that of the Russian Blue. Some cat registries have recognized them as separate breeds since 1971, while others consider them Russian Blue in different colours.

Russian Black and Russian Tabby are generally extremely healthy breeds and it is not unusual for them to reach their mid to late teens. They are medium-sized cats with an athletic and elegant build. The muzzle is prominent with a firm chin. Ears are large and set on top of the head. Each hair in the coat is tipped giving all colours a shimmering look. The Russian Black cat is sometimes described as having a coat like a raven's wing.

These breeds are loyal and friendly but can be somewhat sensitive to their owner's mood. They are gentle and quiet around the home making them ideal as a family pet or a companion for an elderly person. It is rare for them to scratch or bite. Described as dog-like they are happy to retrieve a toy and place it in the hand of their owner. These cats love to play and interact with humans and accept other cats and dogs into the home. All the Russian cat breeds are intelligent and are more than capable of working out how to open cupboards and doors. These inquisitive cats have engaging personalities. They take delight in entertaining their families and enjoy being part of all communal activities.

Breed box

Coat: Shorthaired, soft, plush, dense and silky

Eyes: Almond-shaped and set wide apart

Other features: Facial features make these cats look as if they are smiling

Grooming: Moderate; weekly brushing to remove shedding coat and increase sheen

Temperament: Gentle, affectionate and playful

▼ *Although active, this breed is adaptable. In a suitable environment they cope well with indoor living.*

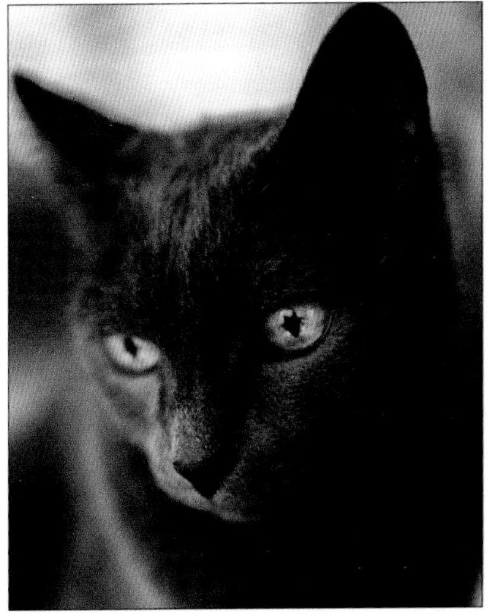

▲ *Along with its dark glossy coat the Russian Black should have a black nose and paw pads.*

▼ *Regardless of colour, the coat of a Russian is dense and should stand out from the skin.*

Russian Blue

As befits a cat that is said to originate from the fringe of the Arctic Circle (and have a possible Norwegian connection, too), the most distinctive feature of today's Russian Blue is its double overcoat.

From the very start of the cat fancy, two types of Blue cat came into competition with each other at shows all over the world. The domestic British Shorthair was one; the other was known as the Blue Foreign. The names suggest a distinct difference in type between the two varieties.

Blue cats were reputed to have reached the West via merchant ships travelling from the port of Archangel in northern Russia, and became known as Archangel cats. Another import was a blue tabby from Norway. There were probably several other blues from other parts of the world that may have helped the true blue breeding programme. The type is also known as the Maltese Blue and the Spanish Blue. By the late 1800s, there were enough Blues bred to be shown at the early cat shows. Unlike the cats of today, though, these early Blues had orange eyes.

Later breeding programmes included the Korat and British Blue Shorthairs. Just before and after World War II, a bid to save the Blue from extinction led to the inclusion of a Blue Point Siamese in one breeding programme, and until fairly recently the occasional Siamese pattern was subsequently found in litters of Russian Blues. Siamese characteristics are now regarded as unacceptable in the breed.

Imports of Blues were brought in from Scandinavia, and many good Russians went to the United States where the standard colour is a little lighter than that required in Europe.

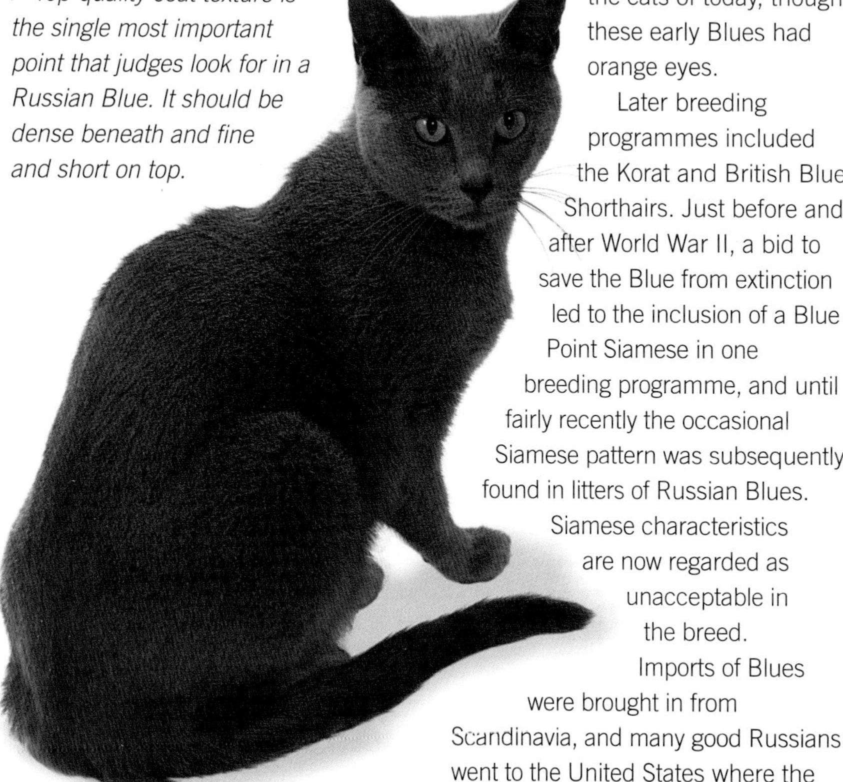

► *Top-quality coat texture is the single most important point that judges look for in a Russian Blue. It should be dense beneath and fine and short on top.*

Breed box

Coat: Plush, heavy, double; brush-like from the body

Eyes: Almond-shaped; green

Other features: Silver sheen to coat as hairs often have transparent tips

Grooming: Easy; gentle, regular brushing so as not to damage the double coat texture

Temperament: Quiet, gentle, affectionate

▲ *The Russian Blue has pronounced whisker pads, wide-set, pointed ears and a face more rounded than that of other foreign shorthairs. These combine to give the cat a gentle expression that reflects its nature.*

There must be no hint of white or tabby markings on the perfect Russian Blue, but there is a silver sheen to its coat, as the slate-blue hairs often have transparent tips. A medium-sized cat, it combines sturdiness with grace. A gentle expression reflects its reputation as a quiet-spoken, affectionate animal.

The solid blue-coloured coat is the crowning glory of this breed. The coat is very plush to the touch due to the undercoat and the fact that each hair grows at a forty-five-degree angle to the skin. This makes the coat stand out from the skin and it is possible to trace shapes and patterns in the coat which will remain until the fur is brushed smooth again. There is some difference in the colour of a Russian Blue with coats varying from a light shimmering silver through to a dark slate-blue.

◀ *The head is wedge-shaped with high, wide cheekbones. Ears are large and flare outwards.*

▶ *With its long, fine legs this breed can often be seen sitting with its front legs crossed.*

The head is a medium wedge shape with a blunt muzzle. Faces tend to appear broad; this is due to the wide set-apart eyes and the dense coat. The moderately large ears are thin-skinned giving them a translucent look. The tips are rounded. Fine boned and muscular bodies give the Russian Blue a lithe and athletic outline. Legs are long and fine-boned with small rounded paws. Paw pads are lavender pink or mauve in colour while nose leather is slate-grey.

This is a breed renowned for its sensitivity to its owner's moods. They seem to be able to pick up on every emotion and act accordingly. Although playful when the fancy takes them they are generally quiet and peaceful within the home. The Russian Blue is a very loyal cat and forms a strong bond with its owner. They can be reserved around strangers. This is a very clean cat who will spend time grooming itself and is also meticulous about using a litter tray. There is a strong hunting instinct retained in the breed so caution is advised if considering introducing pet birds or small mammals into the home. This cat makes an ideal companion for an elderly person.

▶ *A healthy breed that suffers from very few genetic problems. Long-lived, often reaching mid-teens.*

Russian White

The Russian White is a colour derivative of the Russian Blue. Most people do not realise that Russians can come in colours other than the well-known 'blue'. In Australia and New Zealand all cats of this type, regardless of colour, are known as Russians and pure white cats are quite common. Breeding for this colour started in Australia in the late 1960s. Initially a white Siberian cat was mated to a Russian Blue resulting in two white kittens. One of these kittens was kept by breeder Mavis Jones. This cat, White Rose, went on to become the foundation queen of the White Russian. Full registration and eligibility to compete at Championship status was granted in 1975 by the Royal Agriculture Society Cat Club of New South Wales. Today the Russian White breed is fully accepted in Australia, New Zealand and South Africa.

Breed box

Coat: Short, thick, plush double coat

Eyes:Yellow or green, almond-shaped

Other features: The broad, wedge-shaped head is described as 'cobra-like'

Grooming: Moderate; remove shedding coat when necessary

Temperament: Calm, gentle and loyal

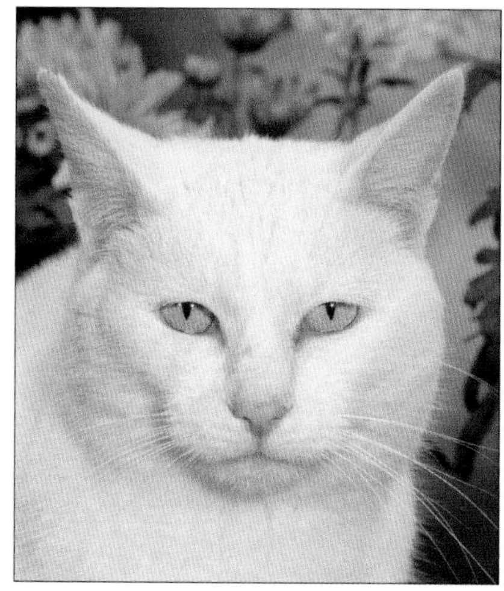

▲ *The nose leather and paw pads of a Russian White cat are pink. White coats should 'sparkle'.*

The Russian White is a striking cat with its yellow or green eyes and plush, lustrous coat that has a sheen that appears to shimmer. In type, this cat is like all the other Russians. They have an elegant build, with long legs and an aristocratic appearance. This is an intelligent breed that is capable of learning a range of tricks. They are very fastidious and may be a little picky over their food.

The Russian White is wary around strangers and can be easily startled by loud noise or unusual activities. Kittens should therefore be exposed to a range of normal household sounds at a young age to improve their confidence.

◄ *Young kittens may have small patches of dark or blue on the head. These should disappear in time.*

Safari

▶ *It is thought that, currently, there are less than a hundred examples of the hybrid Safari cat.*

The Safari cat is a hybrid of a domestic cat and the South American Geoffroy Cat. The Geoffroy is a wild cat similar to an Ocelot or Margay but smaller. They have an unusual hunting method that involves climbing a tree or high place and dropping down onto their prey. There is evidence that Geoffroy have been kept as domestic pets for generations but without constant interaction they will quickly revert back to the wild. Crossing them with domestic cats started at Washington State University, in the late 1970s, to provide animals to use in medical research. Offspring were found to have sweet natures but retained the looks of a wild cat. This sparked interest in some of the cat world. The Safari, although not technically a breed, is a relatively rare cat, but breeders can now be found in the USA and the UK.

These cats are difficult to breed as a domestic cat has 38 chromosomes while a Geoffroy cat only has 36. The resulting Safari Cat has 37 chromosomes. There is some variation in the size of a Safari but generally first crosses (F1) are bigger than a normal domestic cat. This means that they are not suitable for smaller homes and ideally should only be bought by experienced cat owners. They retain a strong hunting instinct and require plenty of opportunities for both mental and physical exercise. Base coat colour varies from silver grey to burnt orange, patterned with darker markings.

▼ *There is no standard for these cats, but they should have an exotic and wild cat look.*

Breed box

Coat: Shorthair, banded legs and tails with spotted or ticked bodies
Eyes: Yellow, walnut-shaped
Other features: An F1 male can weigh as much as 11.3kg (25lb)
Grooming: Easy; little brushing required
Temperament: Very active, powerful and athletic

◀ *This cat needs daily physical and mental stimulation. They love climbing as well as swimming.*

Savannah

The Savannah is a hybrid cross between a domestic cat and a serval. Servals are medium-sized African wild cats with long ears. This breed has now reached F4–F6 generation and is recognized by The International Cat Association (TICA) and the Cat Fanciers Association. In May 2012, TICA accepted the Savannah as a Championship breed.

There is great variation in size depending on sex and generation. F1 males are generally larger but potential purchasers should be aware that a Savannah kitten could possibly grow to the size of a small to medium dog and weigh as much as 11.3kg (25lb).

This breed has a stunningly patterned coat with tear stain markings running from the outer eye corner down the cheek, like that of a cheetah. One of the most striking aspects of the Savannah is its large 'swallow tail' ears that slope backwards and

Breed box

Coat: Shorthaired with a spotted 'wild cat' pattern

Eyes: All eye colours permissible independent of coat colour

Other features: Eyes are set under a hooded brow

Grooming: Easy; the occasional brush to remove shedding coat

Temperament: Active, highly intelligent and affectionate

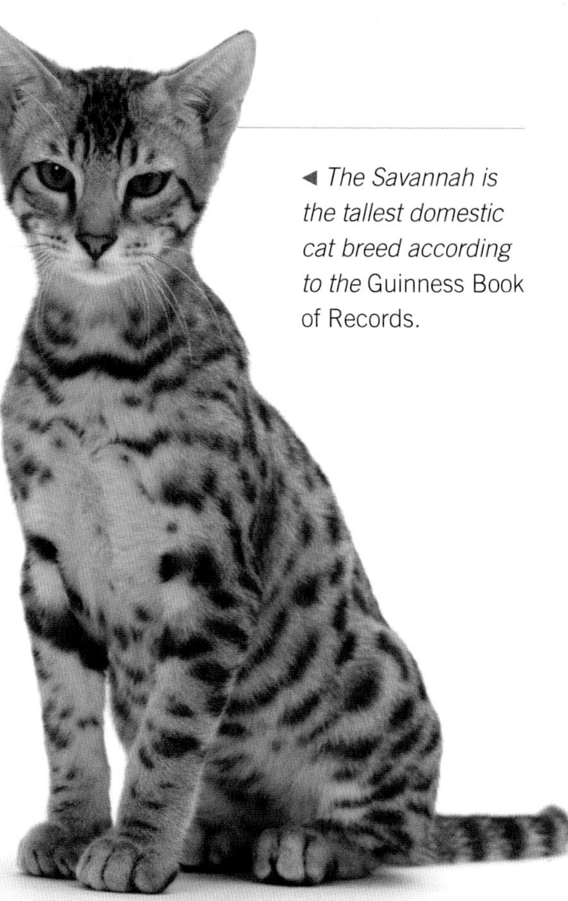

◀ *The Savannah is the tallest domestic cat breed according to the* Guinness Book of Records.

Sam Sawet

This breed originates from Thailand. It is a natural occurring breed, meaning that no other cats have been crossed to form the breed. Along with various cats, including the Siamese and Korat, it is described in the *Tamra Maew*. This is an ancient manuscript containing drawings and poems of cats originating from Thailand. The age of this document is uncertain but thought to be at least 500 years old. Even though this breed has clearly been in existence for hundreds of years, it has only recently found favour outside its native country. Currently, it is not recognized by any cat registry and no standards have been formulated.

Like other oriental cats, the Sam Sawet is slender, lithe and well balanced. The head is wedge-shaped with relatively high and defined cheek bones. This, coupled with a narrow muzzle and no whisker pinch, gives the impression that this cat has a very small mouth. Ears are medium-sized, spaced wide apart and taper to a point at the tip. Coats are commonly tan, brown or black.

The Sam Sawet is increasing in popularity, in part, because it needs very little attention. They do not require grooming as they will keep themselves clean and are considered hypoallergenic, producing a low amount of dander and shedding coat. This makes them ideal for people who are allergic to cat hair. If a potential purchaser is allergic to felines they are advised to spend time around the breed, prior to buying, to ensure that they have no adverse reactions.

Breed box

Coat: Straight and smooth, shorthaired

Eyes: Oval-shaped with outer corners slanting to the ears

Other features: Oval paws have well-defined toes

Grooming: Easy; occasional brushing is all that is required

Temperament: Docile, playful and intelligent

▶ *This cat just loves swimming and climbing up to high places where it will hide.*

▲ *There can be a large size difference between males and smaller females. Life expectancy is up to 20 years.*

▼ *The coat should resemble that of a Serval cat. Accepted colours are black, brown, silver and smoke.*

resemble those of a serval, the African wild cat. It takes approximately three years for this cat to fully mature and reach adult size.

This breed is very dog-like and will follow its owner around. They can be trained to walk on a harness and lead and will retrieve thrown toys. Unusually, the Savannah will wag its tail in greeting. Loyal and affectionate towards their owners, some will hiss at strangers. Socialization of kittens is advised. This cat is not recommended for first-time cat owners. It is a high-priced breed and some countries, such as Australia, have an import ban. They are also banned in the US stages of Hawaii, Georgia and Massachusetts because of their 'hybrid' status. Other areas may have restrictions on ownership. Check the local laws in your area before contemplating buying a Savannah kitten.

An expensive purchase, the Savannah has a bit of a celebrity cult following.

Scottish Fold

▼ *A range of coat patterns including bi-colour, tri-colour, tabby, ticked, spotted, shaded and smoke are acceptable.*

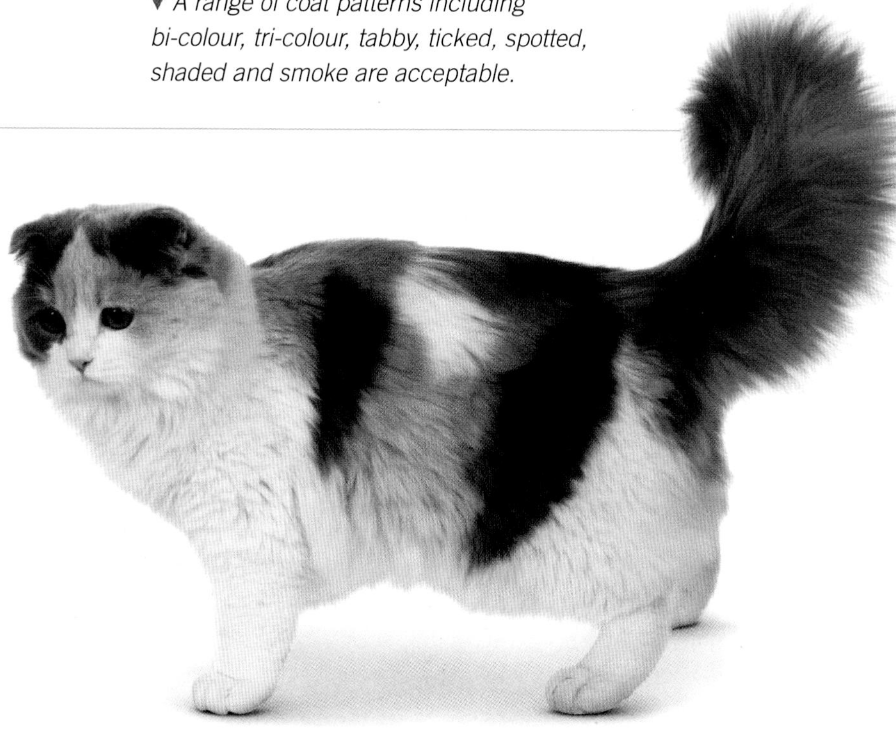

One day in 1961, a Scottish farmer spotted a little white cat with strangely folded ears. A year later, this cat produced other folded-ear kittens. A British Blue Shorthair was introduced into what had become the foundations of the Scottish Fold. However, it was discovered that the gene that caused the folded ears was dominant, and could also cause skeletal problems in some cats. The Governing Council of the Cat Fancy in the United Kingdom, among others, has resisted recognition of the breed because of the risk of a kitten being born with skeletal abnormalities. This may occur even if a Fold is mated with another, proven breed.

The Scottish Fold is found in a wide range of coats and patterns and is a medium-sized cat, which may be short- or longhaired. It has a round head held on a short neck and its nose is short with a gentle curve. Despite short legs, the cat is not inactive.

Currently there is no restriction on the breeding or owning of Scottish Fold in the UK but Scotland is considering bringing in a breeding ban. This cat is prevalent across the USA and pictures of the breed in bizarre poses are often posted on social media, thereby increasing its popularity.

This is a quiet breed that accepts other cats and well-behaved dogs into the household. They generally get on well with children and their laid-back personality make the Scottish Fold suitable for indoor living. This is a cat that is happy to play but likes nothing better than sitting on a lap, making it extremely suitable for an elderly owner.

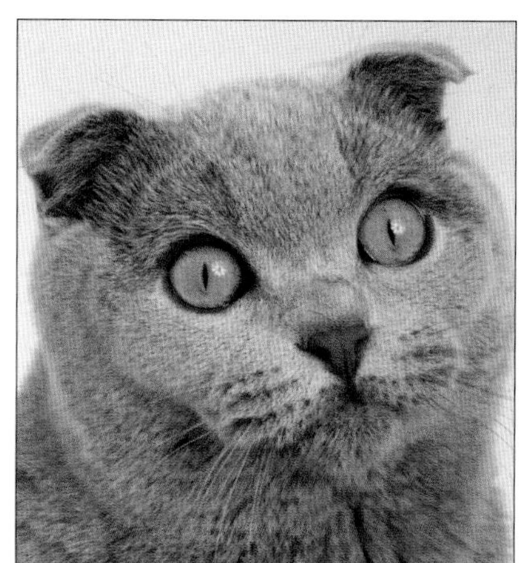

▲ *Blue is the most popular coat colour in this breed.*

Breed box

Coat: Short, dense, plush
Eyes: Wide-set, large, round
Other features: Ears folded forward
Grooming: Relatively easy; regular brushing; check ears
Temperament: A self-assured cat and, because of its British Shorthair and Persian antecedents, generally placid, independent yet very loving

◀ *Originally called Lops or lop-eared after lop-eared rabbits, the Scottish Fold gained its name in 1966.*

Seal Point Rex

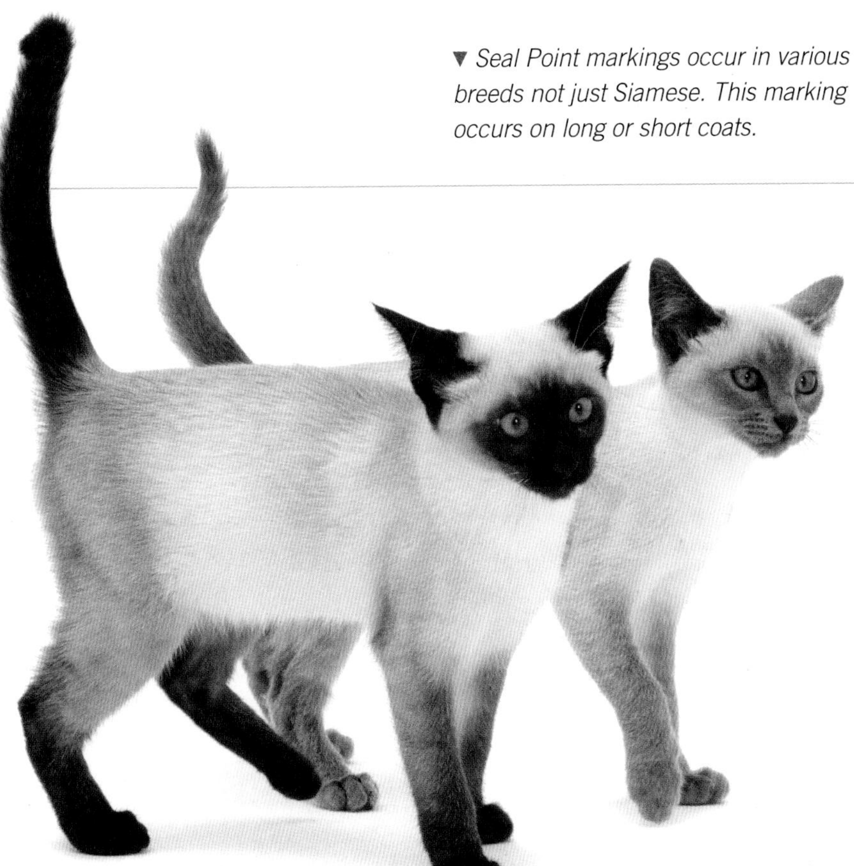

▼ *Seal Point markings occur in various breeds not just Siamese. This marking occurs on long or short coats.*

The term Seal Point Rex describes both a coat type and a colour and not necessarily a stand-alone breed. There can be some confusion over the term for some novice cat owners or those looking at adverts for kittens.

Rex cats are those that have a genetic mutation that causes them to have a distinctive curly or wavy coat. This is a naturally occurring mutation and the standard for some breeds, such as the Devon Rex, Selkirk Rex and the LaPerm, requires this coat type. In breeds where this coat is not standard it is considered an anomaly and therefore not desirable. Rex cats are often described as hypoallergenic but no cat is truly hypoallergenic although they don't shed as much as other cats.

Seal Point describes a coat colour pattern. These cats have a beige or fawn body with dark brown legs, tails, face and ears. In males, the scrotum is also dark brown. This colouring is caused by a mutated enzyme, thermolabile, that is a form of partial albinism. The gene doesn't work at normal body temperature so only affects the body's extremities that are at a lower temperature such as those outlined above. When kittens are born, colourpoints are not evident as the womb is an even body temperature, but develop over time.

Adverts abound for Seal Point Rex but interested parties need to satisfy themselves as to the pedigree and breed of kittens offered.

▼ *It is easy to see the appeal of Seal Point markings when you look at this charming head study.*

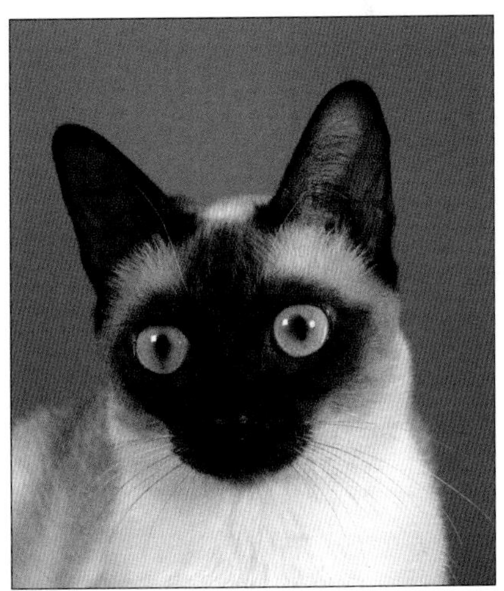

Breed box

Coat: Soft, curly or wavy delicate hair
Eyes: Various shades of blue
Other features: Nose leather and paw pads are brown
Grooming: Moderate; gentle brushing avoiding coat damage and regular bathing
Temperament: Dependent on breed

► *Both Cornish Rex and Devon Rex can be found with seal point markings on their wavy coats.*

Selkirk Rex

A curly-coated tortoiseshell and white kitten was born in a humane society community in Wyoming in the United States in 1987. It was mated to top-quality Persian breeding lines and the offspring crossed back to the distinctive curly-coated Rex line. The resulting Selkirk Rex embraces both long- and shorthaired cats.

The Selkirk Rex Breed Club has stipulated that no outcrosses should be made to other Rex breeds, so that the line retains a strong identity. Only one Selkirk Rex parent is necessary for some rexed kittens to be produced.

The Selkirk Rex has denser fur than other Rex breeds, including guardhairs. The curliness of the coat varies with age, gender, climate and season. Its build is stocky and rectangular, but with a rounded head and wide cheeks. The breed was accepted for registration by the American Cat Fanciers Association in 1992. In the UK, The Selkirk was recognized by the Governing Council of the Cat Fancy in 2003 and given Championship status in 2008.

This breed is an ideal family pet as they are good with children and dogs. This breed adapts to indoor or outdoor living and will settle in quiet or busy households. Affectionate, loyal and placid they are perfect lap cats and will purr their pleasure when interacting with their owners. Their ears can be irritated by the curly hair growing nearby, so check regularly and clean gently when required.

▼ Heads are rounded and have a short muzzle. This breed is also rather charmingly called the Sheep Cat.

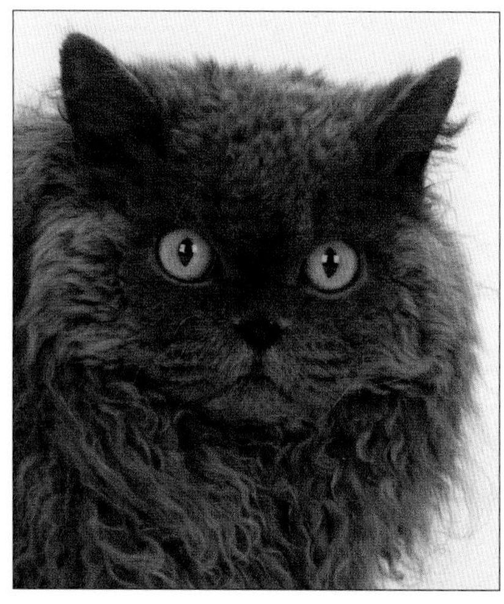

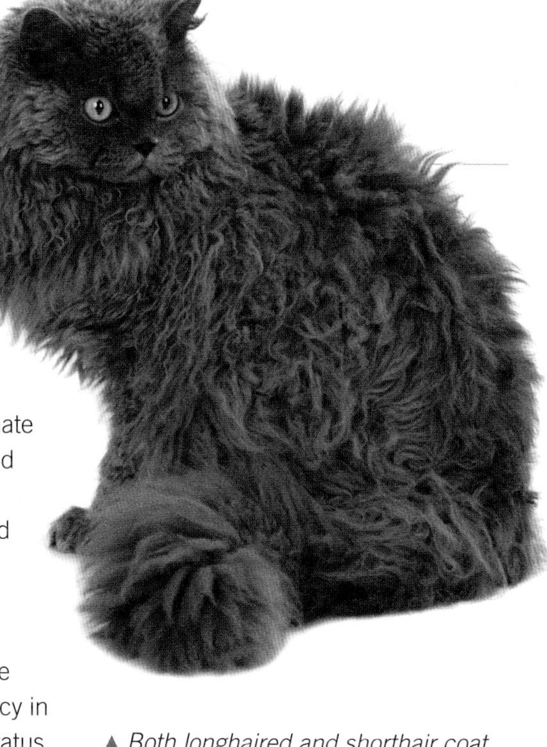

▲ Both longhaired and shorthair coat varieties come in the full range of colours and markings.

Breed box

Coat: Lambswool texture, with curled guard, awn and down hairs; thick and dense

Eyes: Round, full, wide-set; all colours

Other features: Coats can be either shorthaired or longhaired

Grooming: Gentle and regular with a wide-toothed comb

Temperament: Calm, affectionate, playful

▼ The Selkirk Rex is a moderate coat shedder with shedding at its peak in the summer months.

Serengeti Cat

► *Heads are small and triangular. The coat colour is often lighter on the face, throat and belly.*

The Serengeti Cat is bred to look like a serval cat and certainly has a strikingly wild cat appearance. Surprisingly, the breed creator, Karen Sausman of the Californian Kingsmark cattery, did not use serval or any wild cat in the breeds formation. It was primarily created by crossing Bengals with Oriental Shorthair cats. The Serengeti is recognized by The International Cat Association. There is an active pool of breeders in the UK, although the breed is not recognized by The Governing Council of the Cat Fancy. The popularity of this cat is increasing and it can be found in Europe, Russia and Australia.

This cat has very large, wide-based ears that are placed on top of the skull and are rounded at the tips. Ears often have a pattern, like an eye, on the back. The neck is long, as are the legs. They are larger-boned than Orientals but have a similar muscular body. Due to its conformation, the Serengeti appears to be very upright when it is sitting.

Serengeti cats can be reserved initially, and they take their time to form a bond with their owners. Once settled however they are affectionate and will follow their owner about giving credence to the nickname 'Velcro Cat'. Although they get on well with children, this is not a calm breed. This athlete can easily jump 1.65m (5ft) high and will launch itself at its owner if the mood takes it. A very vocal cat who is not afraid to use its voice to gain attention.

Breed box

Coat: Smooth, fine, silky shorthair with spotted pattern or solid black

Eyes: Round, gold to amber or green

Other features: More upright in posture than Orientals

Grooming: Easy; occasional brush to remove loose hair

Temperament: Active, agile and vocal

Serrade Petit

The Serrade Petit originates from France and is a natural breed. Little is known about its history. This cat has only recently come to the attention of the feline fancy and currently is not recognized by any cat registry. Therefore, it can't be registered and a breed standard has not yet been produced.

As the name suggests this is a small cat. Adults weigh between 2.72–4.08kg (6–9lb). The bone structure is delicate, giving the Serrade Petit a fragile look. The head is small with large eyes and big ears. This combination gives the breed a very appealing expression. Legs are medium-length with small, compact and dainty paws. The tail is slender and medium-long. Coats come in a range of colours including white, orange, tan, bi-colour, tri-colour and striped.

The Serrade Petit is best suited to indoor living but requires sufficient space to be able to exercise. Although playful, they appear to have short bursts of activity and then are happy to curl up and sleep in a sunny spot. This is an adaptable breed but may take time to accept having a dog in the house. Due to their small size, they would be more suitable for families with older children. A perfect lap cat that craves human company and should not be left alone for long periods. Vocal, using meows to demand attention and love. This appears to be a healthy breed.

Breed box

Coat: Soft, straight, smooth shorthair

Eyes: Various; no standard in place

Other features: Easy; brush to help remove dead coat when shedding.

Grooming: Coats look coarse but are soft to the touch

Temperament: Laid back, playful and vocal

Seychellois

▶ *A rare breed within the Oriental section that is incredibly similar in conformation to a Siamese.*

The Seychellois is another example of an attempt to create a new, Oriental-type breed. It is a cross between a Tortie and White Persian and Siamese. The long coat of the Persian has not been entirely lost and the variety is recognized (as 'unrecognized colour') by the British Cat Association in both coat lengths. It is fundamentally a cat of slender Oriental build and features, with a white coat splashed with various colours. There are three variations, according to the proportion of white in relation to coloured areas: Septième (Seventh), Huitième (Eighth) and Neuvième (Ninth). All have blue eyes.

The breed is recognized by Fédération Internationale Féline. It has many devotees but is rarely seen outside Europe and the UK.

This vocal cat is very demanding and not for any owner that desires a quiet pet. Their voice is not quite as harsh as a Siamese but is used frequently. They have a reputation for being extrovert, bordering on scatty. The Seychellois loves human company and develops a warm and loving bond with its owner. They are happy to play or sit on a lap in equal measures. This is an intelligent breed that can learn how to open cupboards and doors. This trait, combined with a curious and mischievous nature can sometimes get it into trouble. It is wise to keep accessible cupboards locked.

▼ *A chocolate and white Seychellois shows its Siamese origins in the distinctive point colours.*

▼ *The colour of the eyes of this breed must be a clear and brilliant blue.*

Breed box

Coat: Very short, fine, glossy; also semi-longhair variety
Eyes: Blue
Other features: Colours include white self and tabby colour points
Grooming: Easy
Temperament: Demanding, playful and friendly

The Siamese Cat

▼ *Legend states that this breed was charged with guarding a gold cup. They stared at it for so long their eyes crossed.*

Most pedigree Siamese descend from the same Oriental cats that were originally brought from Thailand. This means that both the Traditional and Modern type share the same genetic fingerprint. As with all cat breeds, the Siamese has a breed 'standard' and the division in type has resulted from the interpretation of this standard by judges and breeders. In the UK, most Siamese show cats are of Modern type. This is not the same worldwide, with different registries favouring one type over another. The International Cat Association recognizes both types, with the Traditional Siamese being renamed as a Thai (see page 370). In some areas, the Traditional Siamese is also known as an Old-Style Siamese.

Although both types could not be mistaken for anything other than a Siamese, there are some subtle differences. The Traditional Siamese has more bone and therefore a heavier skeleton, although the body is still as graceful and sylphlike. The Siamese walks on small, dainty oval paws and swishes a long, thin tail. The head is wedge-shaped but shorter and a little broader than the Modern Siamese. The head is sometimes referred to as an Apple-Head. Eyes are of Oriental type and slant towards the nose.

In temperament, both types are the same. This is a breed of cat that owns its human as opposed to the other way around. They are very vocal and don't hesitate to express an opinion. A very loyal and loving companion.

Seal Point

The original Siamese cat, as described in a 15th-century Thai manuscript, was clearly already well-known at that time. The coat is fawn and the points darken to almost black on the nose and ears. The strong contrast in colour between the points and the pale, even cream of the main area of the coat is important. The dark brown seal points should be restricted to a triangle on the face, the ears, legs and tail. Nose and paw pads are matching dark brown.

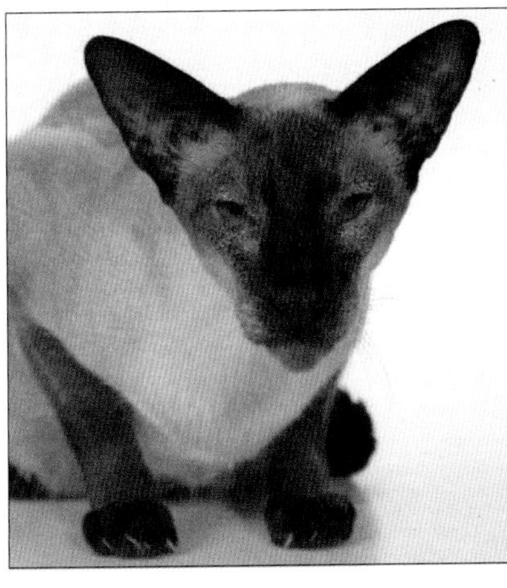

▲ *Illustrations of a cat with dark points like this Modern Seal Point Siamese have been found in a centuries-old manuscript from Thailand.*

◄ *A Seal Point shows off the perfectly balanced lines of the pedigree Siamese, with long neck, long legs and long body following through to the tip of the tail.*

◄ *An alert and enquiring mind is suggested by the attitude of this American Chocolate Point.*

Chocolate Point

Some Seal Points were naturally lighter than others. This characteristic was eventually developed into the Chocolate Point. The brown extremities are a milk-chocolate brown rather than the rich plain chocolate of the Seal Point. The body colour is ivory.

Breed box

Coat: Shorthaired in a wide range of pointed colours

Eyes: Brilliant blue and almond-shaped

Other features: The body is robust but athletic

Grooming: Easy; remove shedding coat with a soft brush

Temperament: Busy, demanding and affectionate

Blue Point

The essence of the Blue Point is a main body colour of icy white with mere hints of the pale bluish-brown of the points. The Blue was one of the early variations of the breed to gain acceptance. It is a dilute form of the Seal.

► *The long, straight Roman nose and startling blue eye colour of the breed are finely demonstrated by this Blue Point.*

Lilac (Frost) Point

As its alternative American name suggests, a main body colour with just a hint of off-white moves into the frosted blue-grey of the points. There is a touch of lavender in the point colour, meeting its match in complementary lavender-pink nose and paw pads. This is the dilute form of the Chocolate.

► *A Lilac Point is carrying on a conversation even while it is being photographed. Siamese are the most vocal and extrovert of cats.*

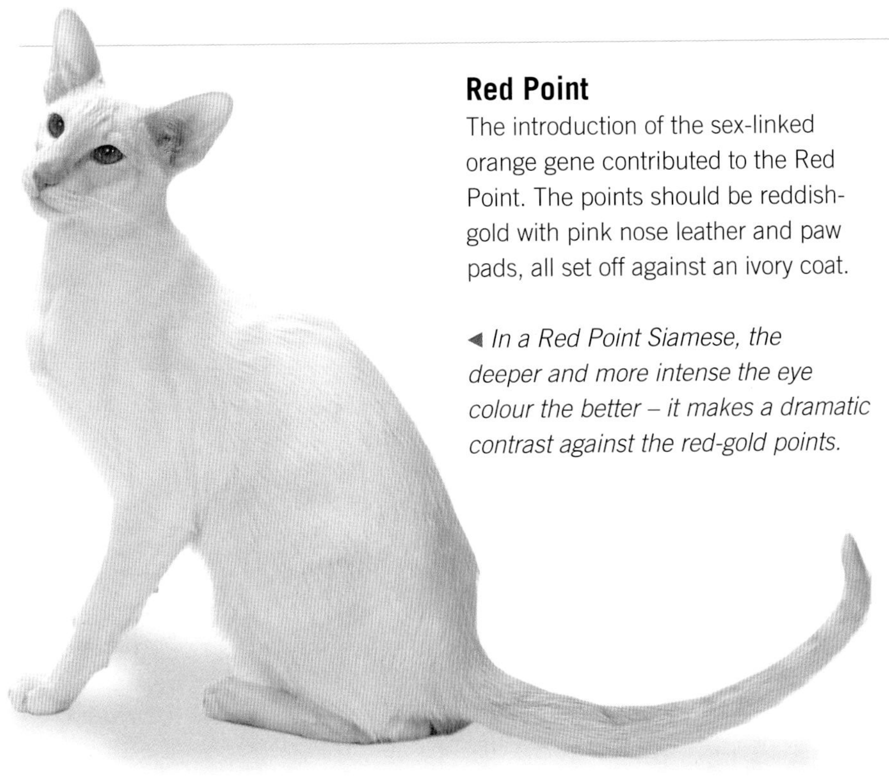

Red Point

The introduction of the sex-linked orange gene contributed to the Red Point. The points should be reddish-gold with pink nose leather and paw pads, all set off against an ivory coat.

◀ *In a Red Point Siamese, the deeper and more intense the eye colour the better – it makes a dramatic contrast against the red-gold points.*

Siamese colour groups

United Kingdom: Seal, Blue, Chocolate, Lilac, Red, Cream, Cinnamon, Fawn, Caramel and Apricot with their Tabby and Tortie combinations

United States: Only Seal, Blue, Chocolate and Lilac (Frost) are recognized. All other colour combinations are available but are grouped in the category of Colourpointed Shorthairs

In some Federations and Associations worldwide, the Siamese is also recognized with Silver-based points, e.g. the Seal Smoke Point

Cream Point

Cream on cream brings an extremely subtle tonal difference. The slightly richer buttermilk points are barely discernible against an ivory coat. Nose and paw pads are pink. The Cream Point is a dilute version of the Red.

▼ *The fur of a Cream Point Siamese shows dense cream points and the palest of cream bodies, against which the eyes are a deep sapphire blue.*

Tabby (Lynx) Point

There are now many variations of Tabby-pointed Siamese. In the United States only the traditional Seal, Blue, Chocolate and Lilac pointed varieties are recognized, so the Tabby joins all other variations under the category of Colourpointed Shorthairs.

In the United Kingdom, Tabby and Tortoiseshell variations are accepted, even in the new colours such as Fawn, Cinnamon and Caramel. This can be confusing to those new to showing.

◄ *This is a Chocolate Tabby Point, showing clearly defined rings on the tail, and a lovely pale, creamy main body colour to contrast with the points.*

Tortie Point

In the United States, the Tortie Point Siamese is bracketed under the more general Colourpointed classification. In the United Kingdom, there are very specific standards. The main requirement is that, as with any of the Siamese, the points are in contrast to the body colour. They should be randomly mottled with various shades of red and cream on whatever the base colour might be. There are Tortie Points in the newer colours, such as Cinnamon, as well as the traditional Seal, Blue and Chocolate.

▼ *A lactating Chocolate Tortie Point queen has all the essential Siamese type characteristics, including a tendency to thrash its tail when bored with the photo session!*

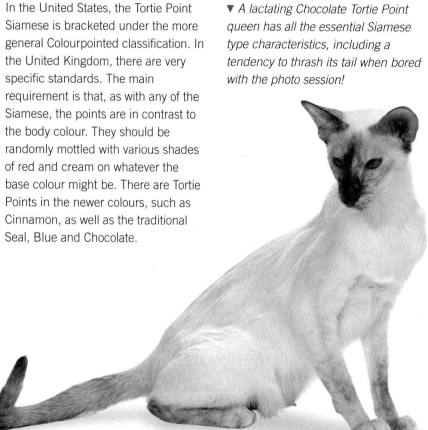

Patched Orientals

Yet another group linked with the Siamese are the Patched Orientals. These are in essence white Siamese cats with distinct patches of colour or tortoiseshell. Such bi-colour and tortoiseshell and white combinations were previously seen before only in Persians and British Shorthairs. Siamese were mated to patched Cornish Rex cats.

Constant back-crossing to Siamese and appropriate Orientals slowly eliminated the Cornish Rex type and increased the amount of white, so that the required balance of white to colour was achieved. Patched Orientals are not recognized by The Governing Council of the Cat Fancy in the United Kingdom or by many overseas organizations.

Siberian

▼ *Siberian cats moult at the end of winter as the day length increases. Summer moults are generally lighter.*

The Siberian cat is a domestic landrace of cat originating from Russia. Although these cats have been around for hundreds of years, breed standards did not appear until the 1980s. The breed is now recognized by many of the feline registries worldwide. Normally referred to as the Siberian or Siberian Cat, it is also called a Siberian Forest Cat, the Moscow Semi-Longhair and, in the case of colourpoint variant, the Neva Masquerade. The breed is believed to be the forerunner and, subsequently, the ancestor of all modern long-haired cats.

There are strong similarities between the Siberian and the Norwegian Forest Cat. The two breeds are closely related. Both are medium to large size. The Siberian is rather barrel-chested, has strong hindquarters and is more substantial than many cat breeds. The hindlegs are longer than the fore, causing the back to arch slightly. Their coat is very dense providing protection against extreme cold. Many colours are permissible including solid, tabby, colourpoint and tortoiseshell.

This strong, powerful cat is very agile and can easily jump up on to high places. They are active and love playing. It is calm in nature and is not fazed by noise or family activity. The Siberian loves attention without being too needy. They make ideal family pets, being both patient and enjoying interaction with children. An intelligent breed that can learn a variety of tricks. It is also a water lover that will play with the contents of its drinking bowl.

Breed box

Coat: The Semi-longhair coat is made up of three layers of hair

Eyes: Large and round

Other features: Foreheads are broad

Grooming: Moderate; despite the dense fur the coat is relatively easy to care for

Temperament: Affectionate, playful and friendly

▲ *This cat has a broad forehead, bold eyes and medium-to-large ears protected by hair.*

◄ *This is an old-established breed that can be seen in Russian paintings dating back centuries.*

Singapura

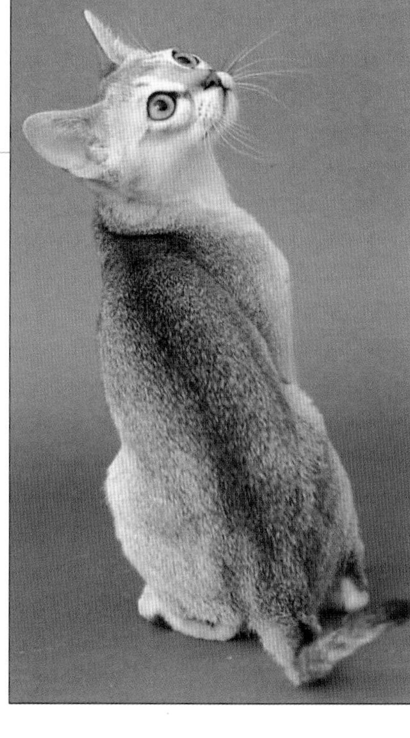

▶ *The Singapura is only available in one colour, a warm ivory overlaid with sepia-brown ticking.*

The Singapura is a small cat, initially reputed to have come from Singapore. There is much controversy as to the actual origin of these cats; this has been a subject of debate for several decades. DNA testing in 2007 showed that there are very few genetic differences between the Burmese and the Singapura, giving credence to the possibility that the latter is not a natural breed. Nevertheless the Singapore Tourist and Promotion Board have decided to use the Singapura as a tourist mascot, renaming it as a Kucinta cat. In Malay, the word 'kucinta' means 'the one I love'.

Breed box
Coat: Shorthair with a ticked tabby pattern
Eyes: Large and almond-shaped in hazel, green or yellow colour
Other features: The tail is slightly shorter than body length and has a blunt tip
Grooming: Easy; polish with a chamois to increase the coat sheen
Temperament: Intelligent, friendly and playful

Despite being one of the world's smallest cats, the Singapura is stocky and muscular. Adult males weigh 2.7–3.6kg (6–8lb) and fully-grown females 2.3–2.7kg (5–6lb). They are slow to develop, not reaching full size until 18–24 months old. Eyes and cupped ears are large and paws are very small. The patterning and colour of the fine coat is all important. Only one colour is accepted, sepia agouti, which is described as 'dark brown ticking on a warm old ivory ground colour'.

A breed best kept indoors as their small size makes them vulnerable to attack by larger cats and dogs. This is a vocal cat that will make its presence known. They are outgoing and extremely curious. The Singapura will appreciate a high perch so that it can look down on its human family. An excellent lap cat that loves attention and human interaction.

▲ *Owl-like eyes are a particular feature of the Singapura, orbs of gold and green fetchingly outlined in black.*

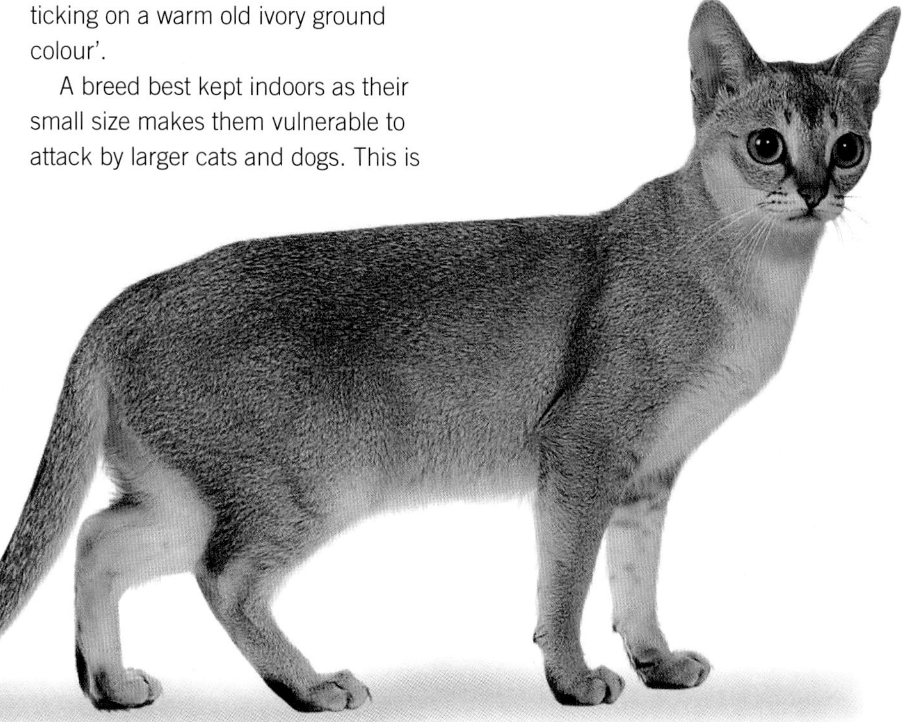

▶ *Small, but perfectly formed, could be an apt description of the Singapura, but the cats are well-muscled and feel much heavier than they look.*

Skookum

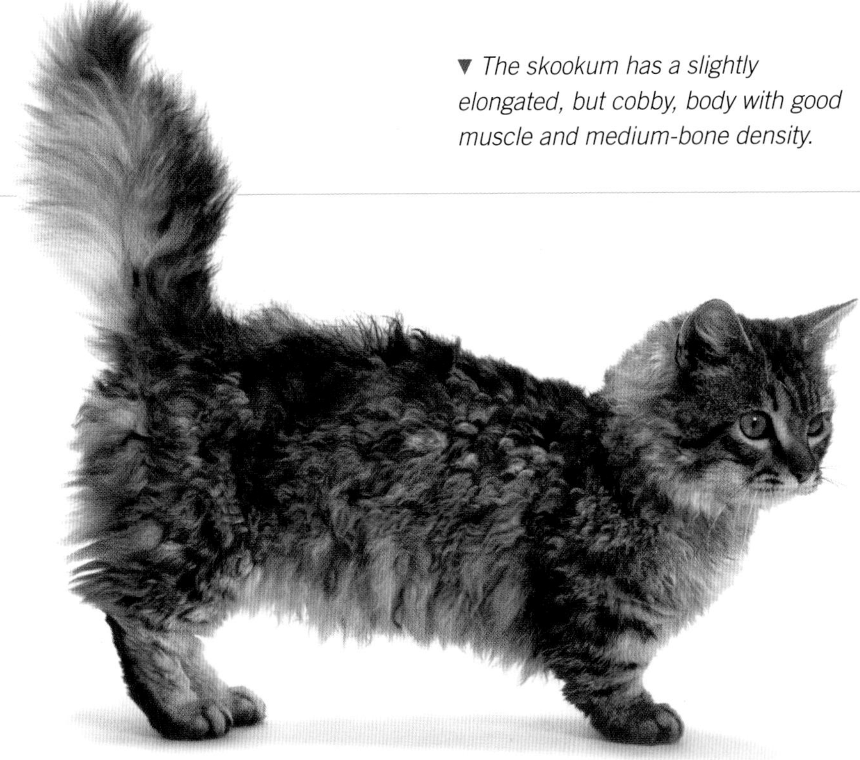

▼ *The skookum has a slightly elongated, but cobby, body with good muscle and medium-bone density.*

The Skookum is a small breed with a curly coat. Early crosses between Munchkins and LaPerms were undertaken by Roy Galusha in the 1990s. Other breeders around the world joined the programme later. The breed is recognized as 'experimental' by The International Cat Association and several of the independent European registries. The national cat registry, The Australian Cat Fancy, allows the Skookum to compete at championship level. The word 'Skookum' comes from the Native American Chinook meaning mighty or powerful.

This small cat weighs between 1.36–3.62kg (3–8lb). Adult males are larger than females. The body is stocky with short legs. Forelegs are shorter than the hindlegs. The head is wedge-shaped with large, pointed ears. Whiskers must show a distinct curl. Tails are long with a rounded tip. The coarse, curled coat comes in a variety of colours including solid, bi-colour and colourpoint.

As with all cats with dwarfism, achondroplasia, there are concerns regarding their long-term health. Advice from The Universities Federation of Animal Welfare states 'because of risks to quality of life, cats with this abnormality should not be used for breeding'. Potential purchasers are advised to discuss any possible health problems with their vet. The Skookum is a lively cat who enjoys play. Despite their small size they can jump quite high. Best suited as an indoor cat, they delight in being lap cats and will cuddle up with their owners, making them ideal companions for the elderly and families with older children.

▲ *In Australia this breed can compete at Championship level in WNCA cat shows.*

► *Coats are light and airy, similar to the LaPerm. Curls, ringlets or waves should spring away from the body.*

Breed box

Coat: Both longhaired and shorthaired variants possible

Eyes: Medium to large, walnut-shaped

Other features: Males are likely to have a tighter curled coat than females

Grooming: Easy; curled coats can be brittle so groom gently with a soft brush

Temperament: Lively, intelligent and affectionate

Snowshoe

Rounded, snow-white paws are a most distinct feature of this cat. The Snowshoe is also a unique combination of the Himalayan, or Siamese point pattern, with white spotting. It was the occasional tendency of Siamese cats to have white feet (which was long perceived as a fault) that inspired the Snowshoe's American breeder into action in the 1960s. The Snowshoe inherited its white spotting, and its bulk, from the American Shorthair. However, the long body, point colour, and bounce in its personality come from its Oriental background. It is a well-balanced and very muscular cat, and when the white is symmetrically marked against the dark points, can be most striking.

The front feet are ideally white only as far as the ankles, while there is a longer gauntlet to the hock on the back legs. The Snowshoe, sometimes known as Silver Laces, is recognized in Seal Point and Blue Point colours.

This is a moderate-shedding breed with a reputation for good general health. They are friendly and affectionate, making the Snowshoe suitable for families. A cat that enjoys playing with water and, unusually, some even relish swimming. They are intelligent and can be trained to walk on a lead and harness, retrieve objects and complete cat agility courses. This cat is generally accepting of other pets, including dogs, within the home. If left alone for any length of time the Snowshoe would appreciate a feline companion. It uses its soft voice to communicate and likes to be the centre of attention.

Breed box
Coat: Medium-short, glossy, close-lying
Eyes: Large, almond-shaped; bright, sparkling blue
Other features: White paws
Grooming: Easy; regular, gentle brushing
Temperament: Siamese bounce with American Shorthair placidity

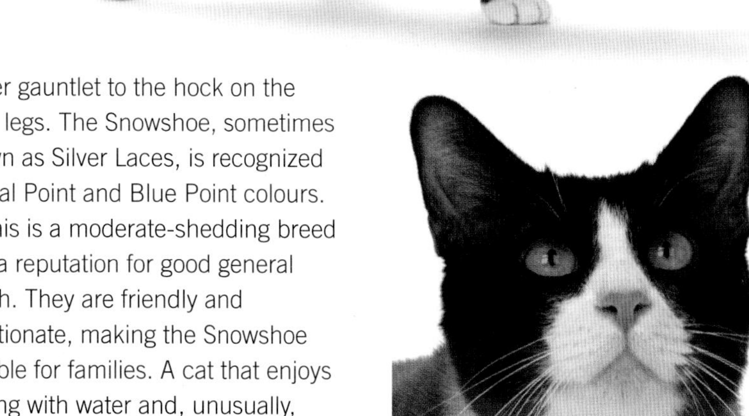

► *Snowshoes can be found in the following colours: Lynx, fawn, chocolate, blue, lilac and seal points.*

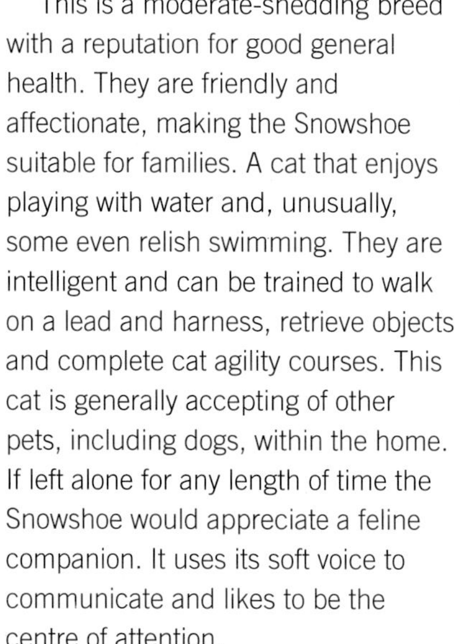

▲ *The triangular or applehead is topped with medium-to-large ears that have rounded tips.*

▼ *Although only moderate-shedding, most Snowshoes love being groomed as it involves time with its owner.*

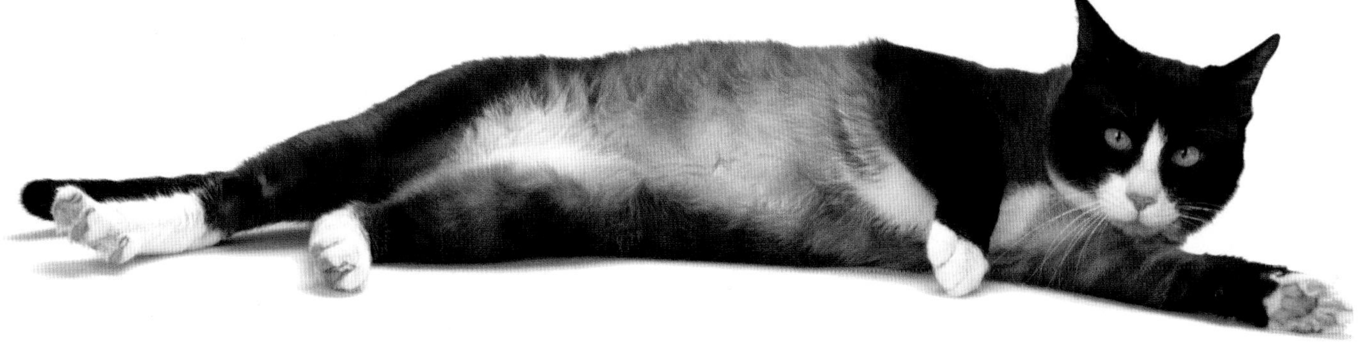

Sokoke

The Sokoke, or Sokoke Forest Cat, is a natural breed of domestic cat derived from a landrace found in the Arabuko-Sokoke Forest Preserve in coastal Kenya. Coconut plantation owner, Jeni Slater, imported the first cats to Europe from her estate in Kenya. These cats formed the foundation of the breed outside their native homeland. The breed was developed and standardized by breeders in Denmark and the USA. The Sokoke is recognized by some major cat registries including the Fédération Internationale Féline and The International Cat Association. The Governing Council of the Cat Fancy (GCCF) and the Canadian Cat Association also recognize the Sokoke.

This is a lean and leggy cat with an athletic build. Heads are relatively small with long ears, not unlike those of some wild cats. Front legs are shorter than the back. The Sokoke has a distinctive tip-toe gait when using its hind legs. The coat is patterned with large patches of brown on a paler ticked base colour. A coat that looks like 'wood grain' is particularly prized.

These cats do not thrive in extreme cold temperatures so are best suited to warmer climes. Life as an indoor cat is recommended as they have a low resistance to common western feline illnesses. For this reason, multi-cat homes and catteries should be avoided if possible. As this is a very active breed that loves to climb, a range of toys and high perches must be provided. The Sokoke is vocal and prefers to follow its owner round the house rather than be a lap cat.

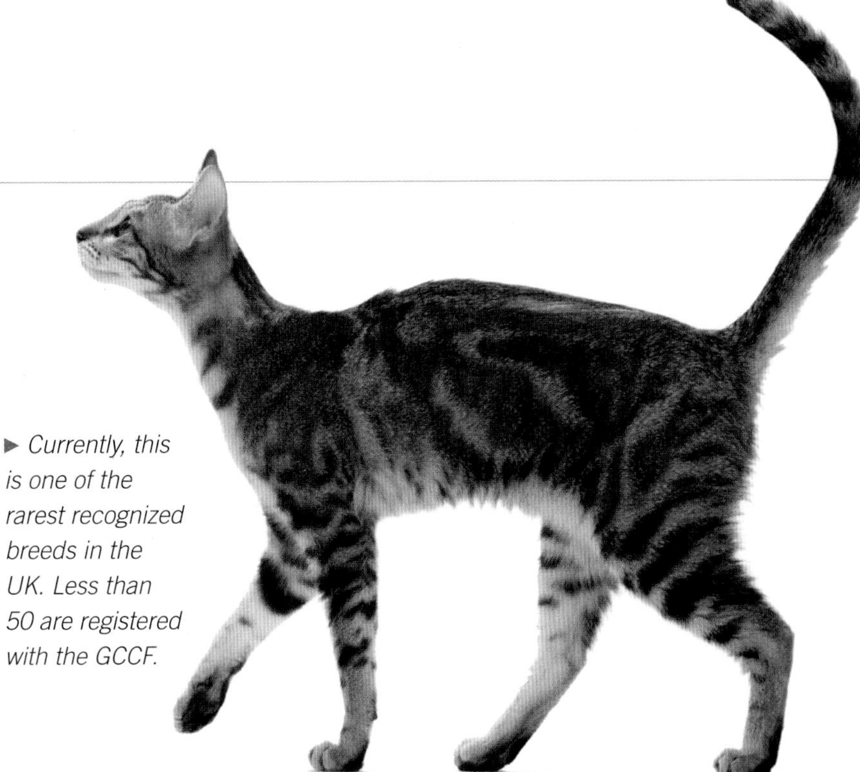

► *Currently, this is one of the rarest recognized breeds in the UK. Less than 50 are registered with the GCCF.*

Breed box

Coat: Close-laying, glossy shorthair with little or no undercoat

Eyes: Green, amber through to blue; almond-shaped

Other features: This cat is heavier than it looks

Grooming: Easy; brush weekly to increase gloss

Temperament: Athletic, intelligent and friendly

▲ *This breed reaches sexual maturity at or around eight to ten months.*

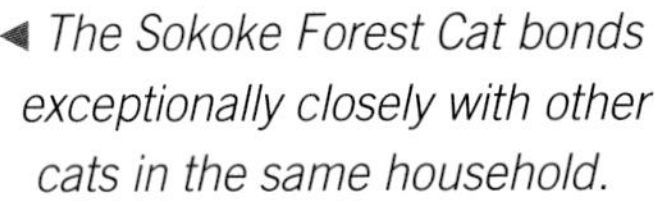

◄ *The Sokoke Forest Cat bonds exceptionally closely with other cats in the same household.*

Somali

► *An example of the Usual – or original colour – with an undercoat overlaid with rich golden brown and each hair tipped with black.*

The Somali is the semi-longhaired version of the Abyssinian cat. Although the Abyssinian is a shorthaired breed, semi-longhaired kittens have occasionally appeared in their litters over several decades. In the United States it was eventually realized that a new breed was appearing spontaneously. The long fur was the result of a naturally long-established recessive gene within the breeding population. It may have been introduced via ticked tabby cats of unknown parentage in the breeding programme. These cats would have been introduced to sustain the breeding viability of the early Abyssinians, for the gene pool was extremely restricted at the turn of the century – a state of affairs that lasted well into the 1920s and 1930s. Any fluffy Abyssinian kittens were initially regarded as below standard. Then an American breeder discovered that a longhaired Abyssinian at a humane society home had actually been sired by her own stud cat.

Breed box

Coat: Soft, fine, dense; lies flat along the spine
Eyes: Almond-shaped, slanting; outlined with a darker surround; amber, hazel or green, the richer and deeper the better
Other features: Smiling expression
Grooming: Easy if done regularly
Temperament: Intelligent, lively, alert, interested; may be shy; freedom-loving (must not be confined indoors)

▲ *The Somali's foreign ancestry is evident in its pointed face and almond-shaped, slanting eyes. Ideally, the eyes are beautifully defined by a dark outline surrounded by a ring of light fur.*

The coat pattern of the Somali is quite distinctive: it is ticked, with three two-colour bands on each hair, with the coat looking darker along the spine.

The ideal Somali is a beautifully balanced cat of medium build. Its body is firm, lithe and muscular with long legs and a long, bushy tail. It has tufts of fur between its toes. Ears are tufted, too, and are set wide apart, prominent and pricked. The head is slightly pointed and well-contoured.

▼ *The Sorrel Somali is rather paler than the Usual as the base apricot is ticked with cinnamon rather than black.*

Somali colours and patterns

Usual: Rich gold-brown, apricot ticked with black
Sorrel: Apricot ticked with cinnamon
Chocolate: Apricot ticked with dark brown
Blue: Mushroom ticked with blue
Lilac: Mushroom ticked with lilac
Fawn: Mushroom ticked with fawn

Also Red, Cream, six Tortie colours and Silver versions of all these colours

Sphynx

Hairless cats were supposedly bred by the Aztec people of Central America hundreds of years ago. The last pair of cats of this Mexican breed was presented to an American couple by Pueblo Indians in Albuquerque, New Mexico in 1903. Unfortunately, the male was savaged to death by a pack of dogs and so the breed did not survive. The modern Sphynx breeding programme began in 1966 in Toronto, Canada, when an ordinary short-haired, black and white domestic cat bore a hairless male kitten. An expert breeder bought mother and son and developed the breed from there.

The Sphynx is not exactly hairless; its skin is covered with a soft, warm down which feels like the furred skin of a peach. There may be visible fur on the brow, around the toes and at

► *The Sphynx is not hypoallergenic as it produces the same amount of dander as most other cats.*

► *A Black and White Bi-colour Sphynx demonstrates the breed's long, slender neck, very large ears and very short whiskers. The breed is sometimes referred to as the ET of the cat world.*

◄ *It is acceptable for a Sphynx to have wrinkled folds of skin around its neck and legs, but it should be smooth elsewhere, like this Brown Tabby.*

Breed box

Coat: A fine body suede
Eyes: Large, slightly slanted
Other features: Wrinkled skin at key points, few or no whiskers; big ears, whip-like tail
Grooming: Fairly easy; more sponging and wiping than combing and brushing
Temperament: Intelligent, very lively and playful

▲ *The face of a Black Tortie Tabby shows the high cheekbones, well-defined whisker pads, and backward-slanting, lemon-shaped eyes of the breed.*

the tip of the tail. Otherwise, it is a well-built, sturdy cat with a head slightly longer than it is wide, set on a long, slender neck. The large wide-open ears are tall and the outer edge is in line with the wedge of the face. Cheekbones are prominent, and inprofile there is a distinct break at the bridge of the nose. It has long, slim legs with elegant yet rounded paws – the toes are long, like little fingers – and a long, finely tapered tail.

The skin needs regular and careful cleaning, as the cat perspires and a greasy detritus can build up if neglected, which then has to be scraped or sponged away. The cat is also prone to skin allergies and to developing lumps. However, humans who are normally allergic to cats may find they can tolerate the furless Sphynx.

▲ *A very playful cat that was once described as 'part monkey, part dog, part child and part cat'. This is a cat that loves to be with people.*

The breed has been refused recognition by some registering associations on the grounds that its genetic constitution is a malformation. However, it does have official recognition from The International Cat Association as well as independent clubs in Europe, and there is a flourishing group of Sphynx breeders in Belgium and the Netherlands.

◄ *The breed can be prone to a condition called urticaria pigmentosa, which causes crusty sores on the skin.*

► *This Blue shows the remarkable, sleek bodyline of the breed. The cats are lithe and muscular, with accompanying energy and playfulness.*

Suphalak

This natural breed from Thailand is extremely rare, even though they have existed for at least 300 years. The Suphalak is mentioned in the ancient Thai manuscript *Tamra Maew*. Legend states that at the end of the Burmese Siamese war, in 1767, the Burmese king read the poem where the Suphalak is described as rare as gold and anyone owning one would be wealthy. He ordered the cats to be caught and taken back to Burma to increase his wealth. This story is used to explain their rarity but it is more likely that they interbred with other cats, making a pure bred a very rare find.

Often confused with the Havana Brown and the Burmese, the Suphalak is of Oriental type. The coat colour is very important and is described as a copper brown. When sitting in the sun these cats have a reddish glow as the light strikes the fur. Paw pads and nose leather are light brown with a pink tinge. The head is wedge-shaped. The Suphalak is a medium-sized cat with a lithe and athletic body.

To date, there are only a handful of Suphalaks outside their native Thailand. They are very people-orientated and not happy if left alone. This playful breed enjoys interactive toys. Dog-like in personality, they follow owners around the home. Highly intelligent, they can learn to open doors and cupboards and are best suited to indoor living due to their rarity and, therefore, value.

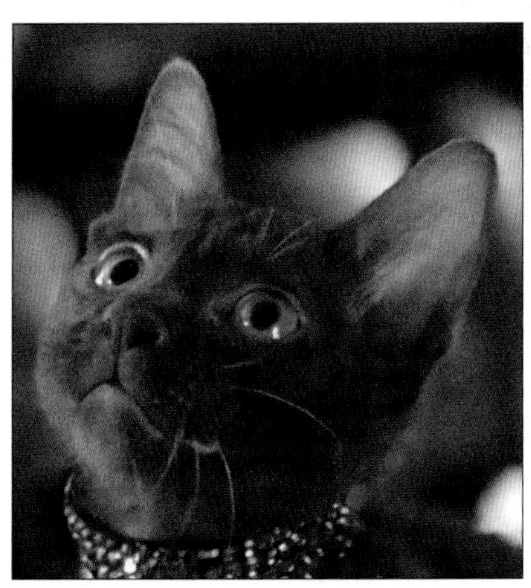

▼ *Outcrosses, using any non-Thai breed, are not allowed to be used in the Suphalak breeding programme.*

▲ *Also known as Thong Daeng, which roughly translates to 'copper', these cats are rarely seen outside Thailand.*

▼ *Thai breeders state that the coat should be the colour of the pulp of a tamarind fruit pod.*

Breed box

Coat: Shorthair laying close to the body
Eyes: Bright yellow-gold
Other features: Whiskers should be brown, complementing the coat colour
Grooming: Easy; brush weekly to maintain coat lustre
Temperament: Vocal, intelligent and affectionate

Thai

The Thai is variously called Wichian Mat, Classic Siamese, Old Style Siamese, Applehead or even Traditional Siamese. No single name of this breed is universally accepted. They are related to, but distinctly different to, the Modern Siamese cat (see pages 357–360). This is a natural breed that has descended from the landrace Wichianmat cats of Thailand. Wichianmat translates to 'moon diamond'. As such they are mentioned in the classic Thai book of cat poems, *Tamra Maew*. The first Thai cat brought to the UK was given as a gift to the royal family in 1886.

▼ *These attention-demanding felines are best suited to experienced cat owners and indoor living.*

► *Distinctive with a long, flat forehead, wedge-shaped muzzle, broad-based ears and striking blue eyes.*

This cat is more rounded and without the extremes seen in some breeds of Oriental type. Medium-sized, with a lithe body and whip-like tail, this is an athletic cat. Heads are wedge-shaped with a long, flat forehead. Cheeks are rounded. Ears are broad at the base and set relatively high on the head. The soft coat should never feel plush but must have a colourpoint pattern. Various colour-point colours occur including solid, tabby and tortoiseshell.

The Thai is a playful cat that equally enjoys life as a lap cat. An ideal family companion, but can be demanding. They are not afraid to use their voice to express their opinions and desires. The Thai will also communicate by tapping with a paw to gain attention. Owners must be prepared to spend time interacting with this feline. Thai cats that are deprived of the attention they crave may develop behavioural problems. They are curious and will investigate everything that they see.

Breed box

Coat: Shorthaired, flat-laying, single-coated
Eyes: Rounded, almond-shaped
Other features: Bodies are moderately long and substantial
Grooming: Easy; the occasional brush to remove shedding coat
Temperament: Social, talkative and clever

▼ *The Thai was part of the foundation of some modern breeds including the Himalayan, Havana Brown and Ocicat.*

Thai Lilac

This breed is confusing. It is not a colour variant of the Thai cat mentioned on the opposite page. In fact, it is the name given to cream-coloured kittens that are the progeny of crossing two Korat cats. Although Korats originate from Thailand they should be blue-grey in colour. In 1989 a Korat cat gave birth to pinkish coloured kittens and over the next few years other breeders reported similar incidents. Generally undesired traits, such as incorrect colouration, are bred out but in this case breeders are trying to preserve it. The Thai Lilac is acknowledged by the Korat Breed Advisory Committee but this cat has a long way to go before it is recognized as a breed in its own right.

The unusual colour is thought to occur when both parents carry a recessive gene for a white or pink coat colour. Cats of this colour did exist in the Thai ancient past and are recorded in the *Tamra Maew*. The adult Thai Lilac has a beige pink coat tipped with silver. Yellow or amber eyes change colour to green as the cat gains maturity. This can be as late as two years old. The face is heart-shaped.

This breed uses a wide range of sounds to vocally communicate. They like to involve themselves in everything that is going on and take part fully in family life. Some even enjoy going for rides in the car. Affectionate and loyal, this breed is an ideal companion for young and old alike.

► *This active cat loves its toys and owners should try to spend around 15 minutes a day in interactive play.*

▲ *Like most cats, the Thai Lilac likes a warm area to sleep and will appreciate a snug bed.*

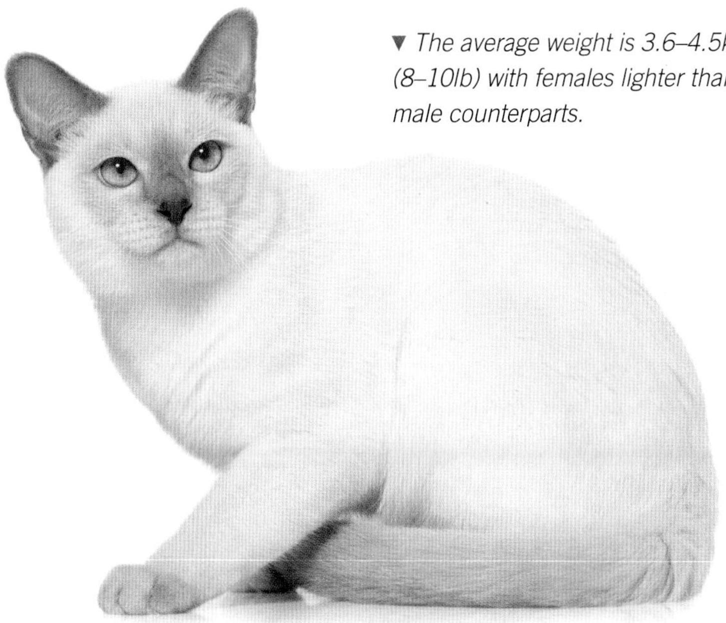

▼ *The average weight is 3.6–4.5kg (8–10lb) with females lighter than their male counterparts.*

Breed Box

Coat: Shorthaired laying close to the body

Eyes: Large, expressive and green in colour

Other features: Females have more dainty features than males

Grooming: Easy; remove dead hair weekly with a grooming glove

Temperament: Chatty, affectionate and curious

Tonkinese

For those who regard the modern Siamese as rather rat-like in its sleekness, and the American Burmese as too Persian and heavyweight, the Tonkinese is, perhaps, a compromise. The breed is also seen as having the points of the Siamese but with a more softly contoured body and a less assertive nature.

The Tonk is the product of mating Siamese and Burmese in America during the 1950s and the following two decades, although the type had occurred spontaneously for a long time. Such mixed parentage means no all-Tonk litters. The offspring from a Tonkinese coupling is likely to be two Tonks, one Siamese, and one Burmese. The Tonkinese cat type displays the mingled characteristics of the two breeds – of medium build, it has a gently wedge-shaped head rounded at the top, though slightly longer than that of the Siamese. Like the Burmese, there is an angle on its shortish nose, but it is not as pronounced. Tonkinese legs are slim but muscular, and its body is a perfect balance between the length of the Siamese and the tendency to stoutness of the Burmese. Ears are large with rounded tips. The coat pattern shades to a darker tone on the legs, ears, mask and tail. Coat colour too, is a compromise – paler than Burmese but darker than Siamese. The cat has a calm temperament but with a streak of mischief and the welcome addition of hybrid vigour.

It is very important for the point colour to be definitely darker than the main body colour on mask, ears, legs and tail, but without any sharp colour changes such as those seen in the Siamese. Underparts should be lighter than the upper body, which in turn should show gradation of tone rather than sudden changes.

The eye colour of the Tonkinese is neither the startling amber nor chartreuse green found in the Burmese, nor the deep sapphire of the Siamese. It can range from aquamarine blue to greenish-blue or bluish-green. It may take some time for eye colour to settle. Tonkinese generally mature slowly, reaching their final colouring and peak size at about two years of age.

▲ *Originally the result of a cross mating between Burmese and Siamese, the Tonkinese should not show too much of an inclination towards either of these foundation breeds, but be a happy medium of the two, like this Lilac.*

▲ *A Blue Tonkinese has the required light aquamarine eyes. Siamese blue or Burmese chartreuse are considered faults.*

▼ *This Blue Tabby is a typical example of the Siamese ancestry being too obvious in its extended limbs and slim line.*

Breed Box

Coat: Short, close-lying, fine, soft, silky with a lustrous sheen
Eyes: Almond-shaped, slightly slanted; aquamarine
Grooming: Easy; regular, gentle brushing
Temperament: Equable, lively, inquisitive, relaxed, very friendly

Toybob

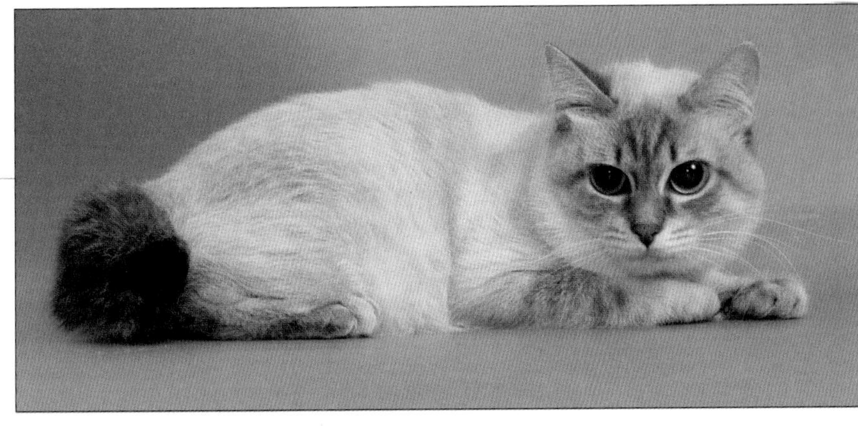

▲ *The feline equivalent of a Chihuahua, these cats are reputed to be able to mimic a dog's bark.*

The Skif-Thia-Toy-Don or Toybob originates from the Rostov region of Russia. It is thought to have originated from feral cats native to this region. The Toybob's diminutive size and short kinked tail are due to a spontaneous mutation. These cats first came to notice in 1983 but by the 1990s were very scarce. It was then decided to broaden the gene pool by using domestic cats within the breeding programme. In 2004 the first Toybobs were brought to the United States and quickly grew in popularity. The breed is now recognized by a number of registries worldwide.

A naturally small cobby cat, Toybobs have not been bred to reduce their size. An adult cat is roughly the same size of a three- to six-month standard kitten. Weight varies from 0.5–2.7kg (1–6lb). Coats are either short and plush or semi-long with various colours and markings permissible. The stumpy tail consists of several kinked vertebrae. This is a very social breed that is not happy if left alone for long periods. They are lively and energetic, enjoying the company of humans and other well-behaved animals. Toybobs are naturally healthy, have a good lifespan often reaching 15 years of age, and remain kitten-like for many years. These affectionate and loving cats make ideal companions for the elderly. Due to the Toybob's diminutive size care should be taken in households with small children who may inadvertently be too rough with this cat causing accidental injury.

Breed Box

Coat: Short and plush or straight semi-longhaired

Eyes: Large, almond-shaped

Other features: Exceedingly small with kinked tails

Grooming: Easy; use soft brush or massage glove

Temperament: Docile, friendly and playful

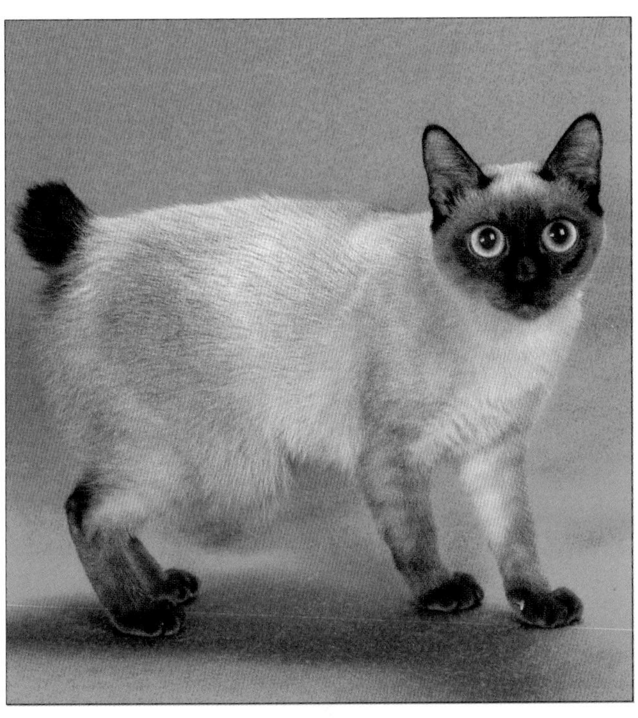

◀ *Tobybob breeders can be found in Russia, Sweden, UK, Denmark, France, Spain, Japan and United States.*

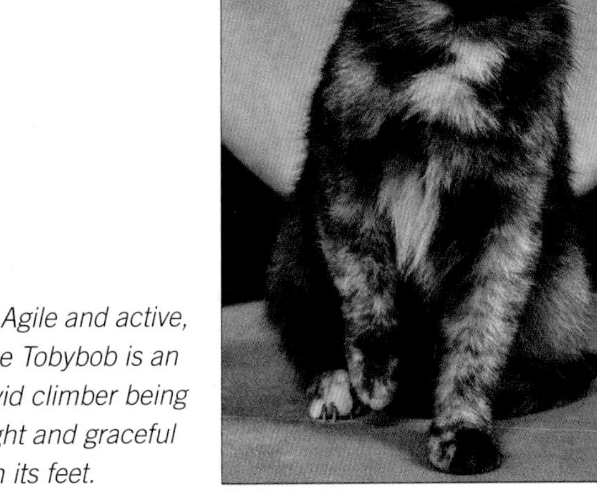

▶ *Agile and active, the Tobybob is an avid climber being light and graceful on its feet.*

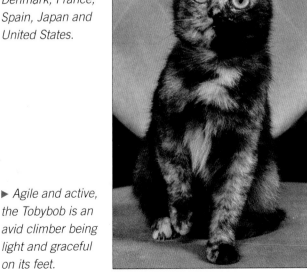

Toyger

The Toyger is a domestic cat breed formed to look like a miniature tiger. Foundation cats were domestic shorthairs and Bengals. Recently cat breeders have worked hard to produce a range of breeds that look like wild cats. The Toyger falls into this group but breeders hope that this cat will also help to highlight the plight of the Tiger. The breed was originally developed in the USA. Breeders can now be found in the UK, Europe as well as America. The Toyger gained Championship status with The International Cat Association in 2007.

This medium-sized cat has no wild cat blood in its make up, but the unique coat colouration of branching black or brown stripes on a vivid orange base mimic that of a tiger well. Visually, this is a stunning combination. The Toyger has a low-slung rectangular body and is well-muscled. They move with a rolling gait similar to the tiger. Adult males weigh 4.5–6.8kg (10–15lb), females are slightly smaller.

Toygers are climbers and love to play. Provide plenty of toys to entertain them and space for them to play. This is an intelligent breed and many owners teach them to walk on a harness and lead. They are happy to live as an indoor cat but if left alone for periods would benefit from a feline companion. Fairly vocal with a softer voice than some of the chattier breeds. They are generally a healthy breed and not overly fussy eaters.

◄ *The distinctive patterned coat with branching and broken stripes is unique to the Toyger cat.*

▲ *This is a rare breed; it is believed that there are less than 50 Toyger breeders worldwide.*

▼ *The International Cat Association describes this cat has having 'dark markings on a vivid orange background'.*

Breed box

Coat: Sleek shorthair with a sheen

Eyes: Round, medium-sized with hooding of upper inside

Other features: Face markings have a circular pattern

Grooming: Easy; weekly brushing to remove dead hair

Temperament: Active, confident and affectionate

Turkish Angora

When the Victorians launched their breeding programmes using longhaired Persians and white cats from Ankara in Turkey, the Persian type became dominant. While the Turkish cat was an essential ingredient in the creation of the longhaired Persian of today, its type did not catch on to the same extent as the Persian. The result was that by the early 1900s, there were no Turkish Angoras on the international show scene and the type was nearly wiped out. However, it has always been highly valued in its land of origin, and a handful of cats was kept at Ankara Zoo. They continued to breed there in relative obscurity until rediscovered by the rest of the world in 1963. A pair was taken to America and a breeding programme started, although it is still not recognized by the main United Kingdom cat fancy. The white version, in particular, is now highly prized in its native Turkey. The Turkish Angora is a graceful, small to medium-sized cat, with a neat and attractively tapered head. To begin with, only the white versions were recognized, but now there is a whole range of selfs, bi-colours, tabbies and smokes.

► *The Turkish Angora's pert and pretty profile and splendid plume of tail can be appreciated on this Black Tortie Smoke.*

Breed box

Coat: Fine, silky, medium length; wavy on stomach; no undercoat

Eyes: Large, almond-shaped; amber, blue, odd-eyed; green for Silver cats

Other features: Moults heavily in summer

Grooming: Relatively easy; daily brushing and combing

Temperament: Affectionate, intelligent, can be playful; enjoys peace and quiet

▼ *A Calico Turkish Angora shows the alert expression and high-set ears typical of the breed.*

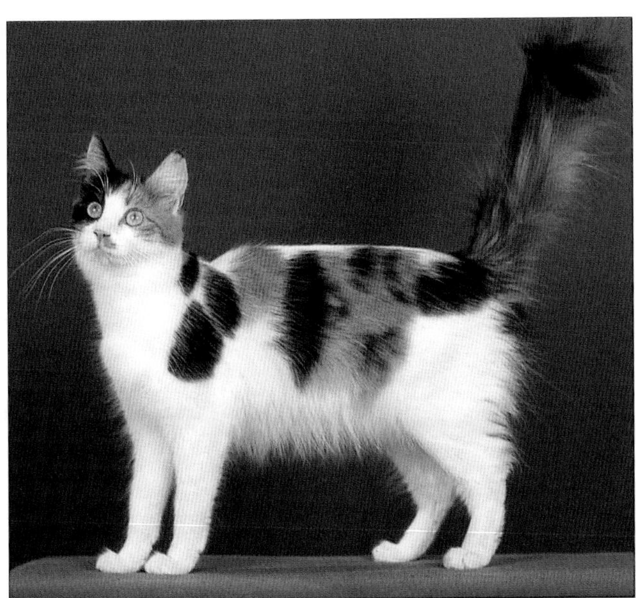

► *The pure white Turkish Angora is probably the closest to the first longhaired cat that was brought to Europe from Ankara, Turkey in the 1500s. This one, however, is a highly bred odd-eyed white with a definitely modern form.*

Turkish Van

Ancestors of the Turkish Van come from a rugged region in south-east Turkey, around the country's largest lake, Lake Van. This may be why this breed apparently loves water – and is sometimes called the Turkish swimming cat. It is not true that all cats hate water, but these cats will actually seek it out and seem to swim as a form of recreation. Turkey's domestic cats are predominantly white with auburn markings. Even today, in Istanbul, you will see many street cats of this colouring.

On a visit to the Lake Van region in the 1950s, two English women bought a stocky white female cat with flashes of head colour and a full auburn tail. Their Istanbul hotel manager told them of another cat – a male with very similar markings. They took both cats back to Britain, and after four years were successfully breeding consistently patterned kittens. The two women returned to Turkey and bought another male and female to add to the new gene pool. The breed was first officially recognized in Britain in 1969 as the Turkish Cat, the name later being changed to Turkish Van.

Despite its fine coat and white colouring, no link with the Turkish Angora breed has been established. The Van is the more muscular of the two breeds, deep-chested with a long, sturdy body. Its legs are medium in length with neat, tufted, well-rounded feet. The tail is a full brush in perfect proportion to the body and, of course, coloured and possibly faintly ringed. The cat has a long, straight nose and prominent, well-feathered ears.

▲ *The 'thumbprint' markings on the head of this auburn and white Van correctly (for the show standard cat) do not extend below the eyeline.*

▼ *A classically coloured auburn and white Turkish Van – this one has the unique distinction of winning the United Kingdom's Supreme Cat Show two years running.*

▲ *The creamy-white Turkish Van is one of the two colours accepted by the United Kingdom's cat fancy, the other being the classic auburn and white.*

The perfect coat is chalk-white with no trace of yellow, with coloured tail and head markings not extending below the eye line or the base of the ears at the back. There is a white blaze on the forehead and sometimes the occasional thumb-print of colour on the body. All colours are recognized (auburn and cream only in the United Kingdom).

Turkish Vans have reached the height of excellence, including the title of Supreme Exhibit at the United Kingdom's Supreme Cat Show.

Breed box

Coat: Long, soft, silky; no woolly undercoat

Eyes: Large, oval, expressive; light to medium amber, blue or odd-eyed

Other features: Enjoys swimming; not prolific (litters of about four kittens)

Grooming: Relatively easy; daily brushing and combing

Temperament: Affectionate, intelligent; not particularly lively; may be nervous

Ukranian Levkoy

This breed is a recent addition to the cat world. It was devised between 2000–2011 by Elena Biriukova who crossed Donskoy female cats with Scottish Fold males. Latterly, Oriental and domestic cats have been added to the mix. The Ukrainian Levkoy has two mutant genes in its makeup, one causing the ears to fold and the other responsible for the lack of coat. These cats are only recognized by cat registries in Russia and the Ukraine, so can only be shown in these countries. Social media has highlighted their unusual appearance with a subsequence surge in demand for the breed worldwide.

Bodies are not unlike that of a Sphynx, long, slender and muscular. The back arches slightly upwards and the chest is broad. Legs are long with elongated and mobile toes. The head is strikingly different to other cat breeds. In fact, it is more dog-like than cat-like. Ears are set wide apart on the top of the head with the top half to one-third folding forward and downwards. The breed is hairless with a soft supple skin.

Although affectionate, the Levkoy doesn't relish life entirely as a lap cat. They are active and very vocal, preferring to play than sit quietly. Happy to follow their owner around the house, this breed generally enjoys the company of another cat or well-behaved dog. They get on well with children, making them suitable as a family pet. As they suffer from both the cold and sunburn, the Levkoy would be best suited to indoor living.

The average weight for an adult male is 4.5–5.5kg (10–12lb), with females noticeably smaller.

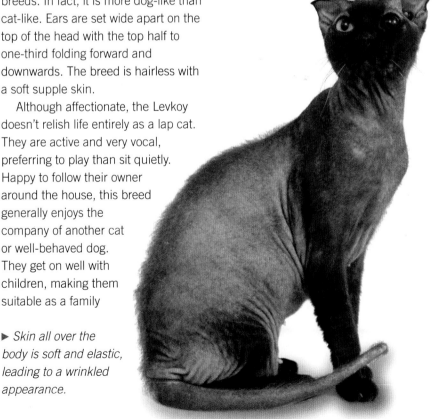

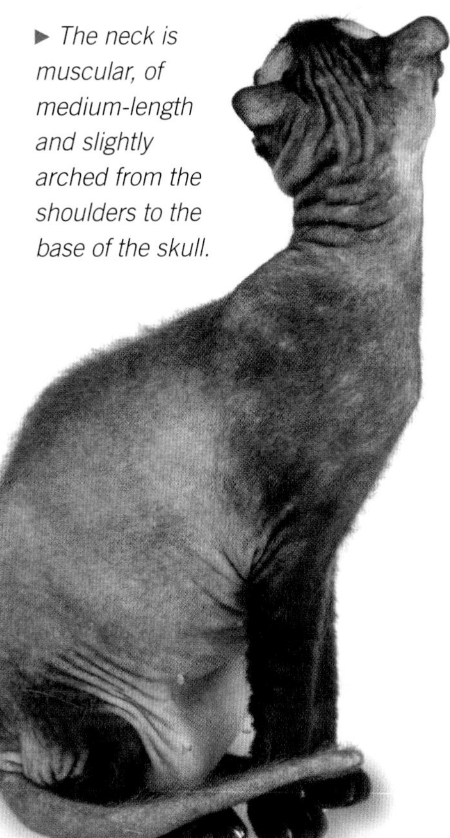

► *The neck is muscular, of medium-length and slightly arched from the shoulders to the base of the skull.*

▲ *Various faults result in disqualification, including too round heads, weak chins and crossed eyes.*

Breed box

Coat: Little or no hair

Eyes: Large, but not wide, almond-shaped

Other features: Whiskers must be curled

Grooming: Moderate; skin needs regular cleansing to prevent build-up of oil and dirt

Temperament: Sociable, intelligent and playful

► *Skin all over the body is soft and elastic, leading to a wrinkled appearance.*

Van Cat

▼ *Van cats have a chalky white coat, often with some coloration on the head, tail and hind quarters.*

The Van Cat is a naturally occurring landrace from the Lake Van area of Turkey. As such it is not a formalized breed. There is some uncertainty as to how long this cat has existed in the area but they are thought to have been in existence for thousands of years. Although still present in the Lake Van area, their numbers have greatly diminished. In 1993 a local university set an area on the campus to breed and preserve these cats. This is open to the public, charging a small entrance fee. Van Cats are believed to be the basis of the better known Turkish Van breed (see page 376).

The perfect Van Cat has a pure white semi-longhaired coat and odd-coloured eyes. The body is lean with long legs giving them a strong and graceful outline. The skin is shell-pink and ears are long with inner tufts and tufting on the tips. The Van Cat is large, exceeding the size of many other breeds.

▼ *Van cats can have either blue or amber eyes, but those with one of each colour are the most prized.*

Like its relation the Turkish Van, many, but no means all, Van Cats seem to love water. They can be seen swimming in their local area and one source records cats diving up to nine metres to catch fish. Domestic cats will play with their water bowls and dripping taps. This cat is an intrepid climber and will scale up curtains and high furniture. They are dog-like in behaviour and seem to enjoy having a canine companion.

Breed box

Coat: Semi-longhaired
Eyes: Blue, amber or odd-coloured; almond-shaped
Other features: Export of this rare breed from Turkey is prohibited
Grooming: Moderate; high shedding so regular brushing required
Temperament: Playful, alert and loving

York Chocolate

The York Chocolate, or York, is a recent American breed. Development started in 1983 on a goat farm with the mating of two farm cats. One kitten was an unusual chocolate brown and this caught the eye of the farmer, Janet Chiefari. She continued to try to produce cats of this colour and by 1989 had more than 27 chocolate brown kittens. With the help of other breeders, the cats were promoted and are recognized by many registries and given championship status by some.

This is a large cat that retains the substantial build of its farm ancestors.

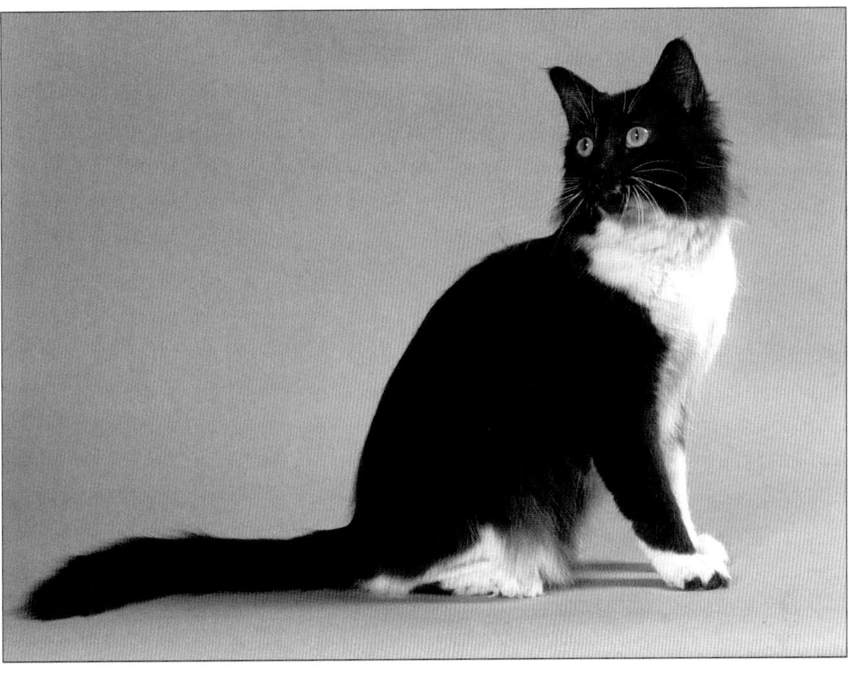

▲ *A solid, well-muscled breed that is much like a traditional farm cat in body shape.*

▼ *Medium-sized heads are wedge-shaped and should be longer than wide. The nose has a slight dip.*

Adult males can weigh up to 7.26kg (16lb) with females slightly smaller. Kittens are normally born with a lighter coloured coat which darkens over time. As the name suggests most are a rich chocolate brown but lavender is possible. The coat is lustrous with an undercoat that is matt-resistant. The coat is thicker round the neck and chest, forming a ruff. The tail is plumed. Feet are tufted between the toes and ears are feathered.

The York Chocolate has a very high prey drive, making them excellent rodent controllers. Those cats that don't have access to outdoors need a range of interactive toys that they can chase and hunt to satisfy this natural behaviour.

Loyal and loving towards their owners, the York enjoys being cuddled or sitting on a lap. They show their pleasure by purring loudly, often using a purr instead of a meow to greet and communicate with humans.

Breed box

Coat: Soft, downy semi-longhaired

Eyes: Almond-shaped, green, gold or hazel in colour

Other features: Ears have a light feathering

Grooming: Moderate; regular grooming to remove shedding coat and debris

Temperament: Independent, loving and playful

▼ *Although they crave attention from those they know, the Chocolate York can be shy with strangers.*

SHOWING YOUR CAT

A cat has no particular interest in whether it goes to a show or not, but its owner can gain a great deal of satisfaction from having a prize-winning animal and become part of the sociable cat-showing circuit. Shows provide an arena for the serious cat breeder or committed owner of pedigreed animals to display their stock. However, there are often more relaxed classes for ordinary household pets as well.

Be prepared to learn from those who have experience in the showing world. Most are happy to pass on tips and helpful advice. Always remember that, win or lose, the best cat is the one that you take home – your much-loved pet.

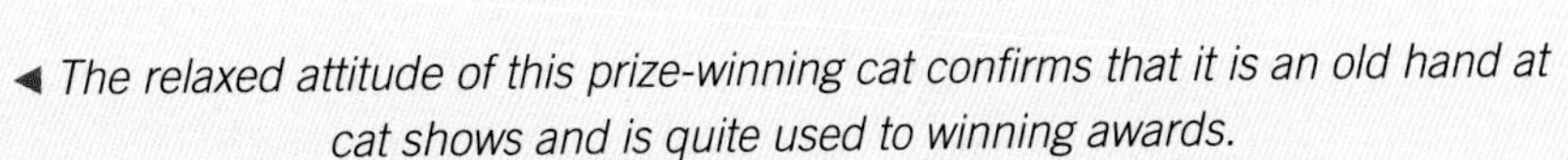

◄ *The relaxed attitude of this prize-winning cat confirms that it is an old hand at cat shows and is quite used to winning awards.*

The rewards of showing

Showing your cat is an expensive business, even if the animal has championship potential. The rewards are likely to be pride in your – and your cat's – achievements, a rosette and perhaps a silver cup or a supply of commercial cat food rather than prize money. Apart from the cost and maintenance of your pedigreed cat, there are equipment and travelling costs as well as high entry fees to consider. However, for the committed cat fancier – the person who is interested in breeding and showing pedigree cats – there are many other rewards. Cat shows present the ideal opportunity to find out about the various breeds. You can make valuable contacts with breeders and look out for your next new kitten, or for suitable mates for your queen. You will become part of the cat fanciers' network, check out the latest breeds and commercial cat products, make friends and fill in your social calendar with cat-related events. Whether your cat actively enjoys the show or not is debatable. Most cats are so adaptable they will tolerate being confined to a pen for the best part of a day. Others may have a shy or timid nature, or may be particularly active; in either case it would not be fair to subject them to the show scene. If you introduce a kitten to showing at an early age, it is more likely to adapt. Some cats even appear to relish the attention. If you are taking a cat to its first show, keep a close eye on it; if it is unhappy, it will let you know.

▶ *A White Persian at an American cat show sits with its rosettes in a decorated pen.*

▼ *Cat shows provide an opportunity for like-minded people to compare notes and make friends.*

▼ *The equipment inside a pen at a British show must be white, from the cat's blanket to the litter tray. However, now this Oriental Shorthair has been judged, he is allowed to have a toy in his pen.*

QUALITY CONTROL

It is through being judged at shows across the country that new breeds gain acceptance and established breeds are kept up to scratch. If a new breed does not make it through the various levels of judging, from the local show to national championship, it is unlikely to survive. When judges study a cat, they are making sure that it conforms with the standards set for that breed by the relevant governing council. If they spot signs of, for example, an aggressive temperament, or a deformity in an up-and-coming breed, the judges can disqualify the cat and stipulate that it should not be used for breeding.

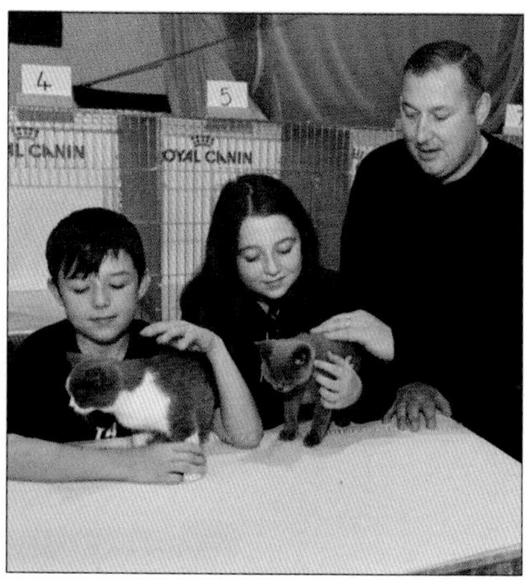

▶ *The whole family can be involved – and may prevent the cat from becoming too bored.*

A new craze for cats

A growing interest in the selective breeding of pedigreed animals and the arrival of exotic cats such as Persians and Turkish Angoras in the West led to the first official cat show in London in 1871. There is a record of a show being held in Winchester, England in 1598, but the 19th century London event had the cats in show pens, 25 classes for different breeds, and judging benches. Domestic shorthairs and Persians dominated the early shows, although there were some foreign introductions. The first benched cat show in America was held at Madison Square Garden, New York in 1895, in which Maine Coon Cats featured strongly.

These early events spawned a whole new leisure activity, and the breeding and showing bug soon spread to most parts of the world. Today, scarcely a day, and certainly not a weekend, goes by without a cat show being held somewhere, whether by a breed club for their specific breed, or for all breeds at local, as well as area and national levels.

► *The early cat shows at the end of the 1800s were dominated by Persians and domestic shorthairs in the United Kingdom.*

THE ORGANIZERS

Throughout the world, organizations register pedigrees and stipulate rules for running shows. Individual breed clubs and area clubs are affiliated to one or other of these authorities.

In the United Kingdom, The Governing Council of the Cat Fancy (GCCF), formed in 1910, is the main regulatory body. The Governing Council of the Cat Fancy in Ireland (GCCFI) licenses shows in the same way as the GCCF, although it is not affiliated to it, and has a close liaison with the GCCF. The Cat Association of Britain (CA), formed in the early 1980s, also registers pedigree cats; it is affiliated to the European Fédération Internationale Féline (FIFe) and runs shows under European rules.

FIFe, founded in 1949, is not just a European organization, but has member countries throughout the world (though not the major cat-fancying countries of the United States and Canada, Australia and New Zealand or Japan). The many independent clubs in Europe work as autonomous federations with their own registries, but many liaise with each other. Recently, more shows have been judged by both FIFe and independent judges. Organizational problems are shared, and judges from both systems can meet and discuss ideas and standards.

In the United States, the largest nationwide registering bodies are the Cat Fanciers' Association (CFA) and The International Cat Association (TICA), although there are many other organizations spread the length and breadth of North America. Some of them are regionally based, such as the American Cat Association (ACA) in California.

Your first step in showing is to contact your area or national organization for their schedule of shows, and show rules.

► *The author's mother, Yelva Willett, and her cream Persian Champion Woburn Monsieur after winning a Best in Show in 1957.*

Entering a show

There are rules and regulations surrounding entering a show and it is important to familiarize yourself with the process.

The organizing bodies usually publish an annual list of the shows under their jurisdiction, which you can buy for a small fee. These publications should have the name and address of a contact for each show to whom you can then apply for a schedule – allow about three months before the event. The schedule contains the rules under which the show is operating, the classes that can be entered, and qualification requirements for each. It is essential to read the rules carefully and go through the relevant class details before you proceed any further. You also need to check in the rules for such qualifications as the lowest age of entry for a kitten (usually 14 weeks), at what stage your animal should join an adult class (usually nine months), and what the restrictions are for neutered and entire animals. Any household pets over the age of nine months, for example, must be neutered.

There will also be an entry form with instructions on how to complete it, as well as details of the entry fees charged and how to pay them. Read it all meticulously. If you get something wrong, you could be refused entry on the day. If you are uncertain about any aspect, contact the show management.

If you are showing a pedigreed cat, you will need to refer to its registration details (obtained from the original breeder), and know its breed number, date of birth, parentage and breeder. Your breeder may be able to advise on which classes to enter if you are unsure.

PREPARING FOR A SHOW

Preparing your cat for a show will take more than just a quick comb-through. Longhaired varieties need to be bathed and groomed intensively for weeks preceding the show. Even shorthaired cats need in-depth preparation to ensure that they look and feel perfect to the touch.

Cat kit for a show

- Vaccination certificates
- Grooming equipment
- Blanket (white, if UK show)
- Food and water bowls (white, if UK show)
- Food and water (for the cat)
- Litter tray/pan (white, if UK show)
- Litter
- White ribbon (for the identification label)
- Cleaning materials
- Disinfectant (suitable to clean the cat's pen)
- String and scissors (to secure pen if necessary)
- Toy
- Decorations on a theme (if appropriate)

On the day of the show, make sure you have all the equipment you will need neatly assembled – keep it all together in a cat bag – and leave in good time. Many European shows last two days, the panel of judges taking different classes on each day. American and Canadian shows may even extend to three days, and therefore need a great deal of careful thought and preparation.

◄ *This well-prepared exhibitor and her cat are looking forward to an exciting day at the show.*

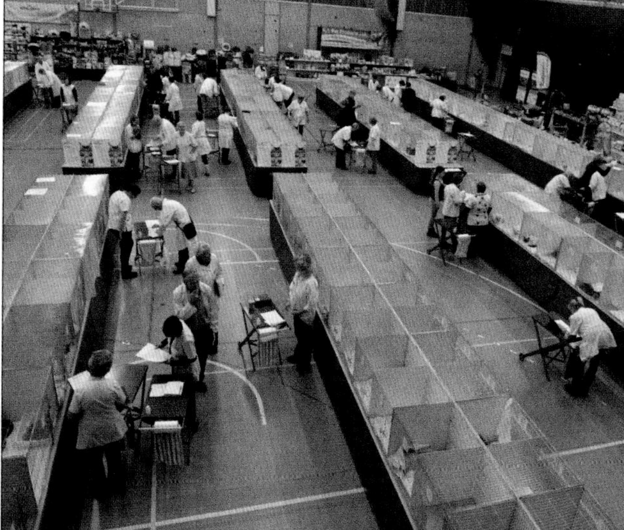

► *Judging is in progress. The hall is empty except for judges, their stewards, show officials and, of course, the cats.*

What happens at a show?

Show style and rules vary from country to country, and according to the size of the show. Individual breed clubs organize their own events, which tend to be small-scale, informal, friendly occasions. Others may be organized by major registering bodies, or may be compound affairs, with a number of separate shows running concurrently for different breeds or classes, each one presided over by a separate judge or team of judges.

Send off your entry and fee in plenty of time. When you receive the entry confirmation, check it carefully and if you spot any mistakes contact the show organizer quickly. Mistakes can lead to disqualification.

When you and your cat arrive at a British or European show you will need to have your cat checked by a vet (vetted-in). This is to check that your cat is healthy, inoculations are up to date and that the cat doesn't have a parasitic infestation. Some countries don't insist on a vetting-in but take on trust that the cat is fit to show. While queuing to see the vet, a show official will issue a pen number, identification label for the cat, a veterinary pass card and class check card. The latter is required to claim any prizes and rosettes that you may win. Providing the vet is happy with the health and vaccination status of your cat the next step is to find the pen in which your cat must stay for the duration of the show, except when it is being judged.

LAST-MINUTE ATTENTION

When you find your allotted pen, it is a good idea to clean it with the cat-compatible disinfectant you have brought with you. Check the security on the cage and make sure there are no loose or jagged ends. Attach the identification label (known as a tally) to some thin ribbon or shirring elastic and tie it loosely round the cat's neck. If it objects, as it almost certainly will, do not insist, especially if the cat is in a pen by itself; tie the label to the outside of the cage.

Setting the cat in the cage is termed benching, and all the information you need about this is in the show rules, including what you can and cannot put into the pen with the cat. You must have water in the bowl at all times and check the cat regularly. The rules even state when you are allowed to place food in the cat's pen. Toys are often only allowed after judging has finished.

Depending on the individual show style, either the judges go around the pens or the cats are taken to a judging arena where they are assessed. In Britain, the owners often have to leave their animals while they are judged. In Europe and America, however, owners remain in an inner showing square formed by the cat pens, and can be quite close to the judging table, while the rest of the public mill around outside the square.

The winners of each class are either announced or posted on a results board. At many shows the best cat in show is selected from the class winners by a panel of judges.

▲ *Cats are brought to the judge's table for examination. Note the toys on the table ready to attact the cat's attention.*

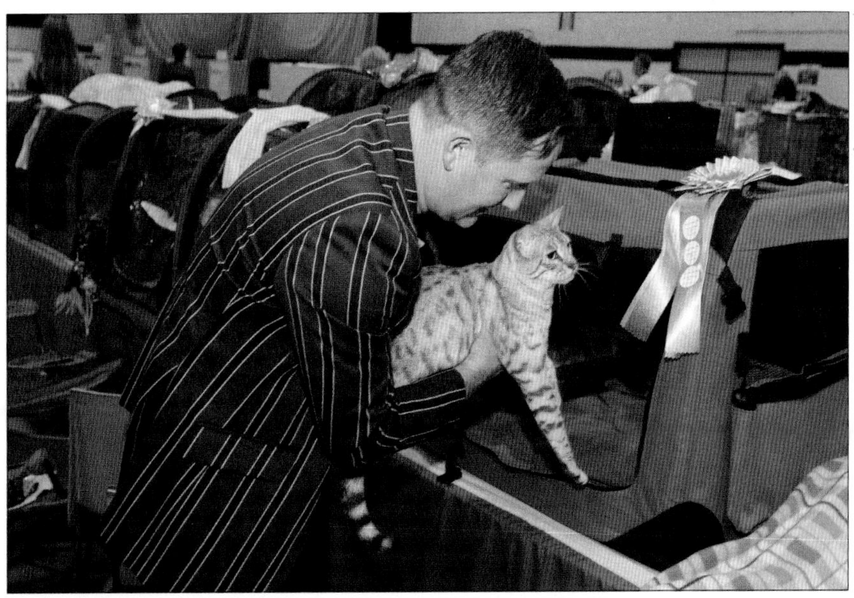

▼ *The bustle and noise of a cat show can be tiring. This winning cat will relish the security of the cat crate.*

What the judges look for

The judges check each pedigreed cat against the standard of points for its breed that have been set by the show's governing body. (These standards of points are published and can be bought from the relevant organizations.) A maximum mark is set for each aspect of the cat to be judged, such as the head, tail or coat. This will vary according to the breed and will often differ slightly between one registering body and another. For example, a perfectly textured and coloured coat of an Abyssinian cat could earn 40 points and ideal eyes 5 points, whereas on a Siamese the eyes rate more highly at 20 points, and the coat is worth 35 points. If you want to ask a judge about your cat, it is fine to approach them on the day after judging has finished. Judges are almost certainly very successful breeders in their own right and have a lot of sound advice to give; don't dismiss them just because they have not given a high award to your cat. Contrary to popular belief, judges hate down-marking exhibits.

▼ Here is an example of what judges would be looking for in a Blue-mitted Ragdoll under GCCF standards. They will also check the coat colour and pattern against the particular requirements for the breed, which in this case are worth 20 points.

TAIL (5 points) Long, bushy, slightly tapered towards the tip. Should at least reach the shoulder and be in proportion to the body.

COAT Length, texture and condition (10 points) Silky texture, dense, and medium in length; ruff and knickerbockers preferred on mature cats; short summer coat is acceptable.
Colour and markings (20 points)

BODY AND NECK (20 points) Long and muscular body with broad chest; short, heavy-set neck.

HEAD (20 points) Broad with flat plane, not domed, and width between the ears. Well-developed cheeks; rounded, well-developed muzzle; firm chin with level bite. Nose of medium length with a gentle dip, and slightly retroussé at the tip.

EARS (5 points) Medium in size, set wide with a slight tilt forward. Should be well furnished and rounded at the tip.

EYES (10 points) Large, well opened, slightly oblique and set well apart. Blue in colour, the deeper the better.

LEGS AND PAWS (10 points) Medium in length and substantial of bone; paws large, round, firm and tufted.

The British show scene

Anonymity is carefully guarded in the United Kingdom; there is little of the conviviality of the European or North American judging arenas, or the flamboyance of the decorated pens. At judging time, the owners are banished from the show hall and the judges visit each cat in turn. No identifying features are allowed on the pens, and all visible equipment in the pen must be white—the blankets, water, food bowls and litter tray.

There are three levels of show in Britain. Exemption shows are usually run by individual clubs. There are no major qualifying awards available, and some of The Governing Council for the Cat Fancy (GCCF) rules are relaxed. Sanction shows are run according to the rules but with no major awards.

Championship shows are strictly regulated and licensed by the GCCF. This is where qualifying awards, such as challenge certificates, for the country's top cat show, the Supreme, can be gained. To be awarded a challenge certificate, a cat – which must be an un-neutered adult over nine months old – must win its open class and then be 'challenged' against the set standard of points to see if it is good enough for the certificate to be awarded. A cat awarded three challenge certificates from three different judges qualifies for championship status and can enter classes for champions only. There is a parallel process for neutered adult cats aiming for premier certificates and premier status.

▼ *Decorated pens are more commonly seen in the United States. In the UK they are only used for exhibition cats.*

At most shows the best adult, kitten and neuter of each breed is awarded Best of Breed. The term 'neuter' refers to a desexed male or female cat. Neuter classes are specifically for cats that cannot breed or be bred from. At some shows, especially the smaller specialist breed shows, Best in Show is held. Judges each nominate their best adult, kitten and neuter, and those nominated cats are judged against each other to select the Best in Show Adult, Kitten and Neuter and, often, the Best Exhibit in Show. When Best in Show is held at an all-breed show, the 'Bests' are selected in each section – Longhair, Semi-longhair, British, Foreign, Burmese, Oriental and Siamese. The non-pedigreed cats also have their own Best in Show, but never compete against the pedigrees.

Open classes are open to all cats of a particular breed, regardless of whether they have previously won or not. They are split into male and female sections, neutered and entire cats, and kittens and adults.

There are also various miscellaneous classes for: cats bred by the exhibitor, cats under or over two years old, cats which have not yet won a first prize, and so on. Whether fun or serious, these classes give every exhibitor, however experienced, the opportunity to measure an exhibit's worth against the best of the rest; crucial if a serious show campaign is being planned. Most shows also have a section for non-pedigree cats.

If competition is not the aim, there is the possibility of placing the cat on exhibition. Here, the cat reclines in a splendidly decorated pen all day surrounded by evidence of past show glories. Often the full pedigree is on display and the cat does not have to face the indignity of being hauled out of the pen periodically.

The highest accolades for a British cat are won at the annual Supreme Cat Show. Here, judges provide a written resumé that the owners can see on the day. Only winners at lower-level championship shows are eligible to enter. The ultimate titles – Supreme Adult, Supreme Kitten and Supreme – are held for life. All three then compete for Supreme Exhibit, the ultimate prize.

The European show scene

Many European Shows last two days, as many exhibitors travel from other countries or even continents. The judges usually take different classes on the second day, so that any wins gained on the first day are not duplicated on the second.

Now that quarantine regulations have been relaxed, it is possible for animals to attend the majority of European shows provided that they have the required vaccinations, health checks and relevant paperwork. Certain differences in show style between Britain and the rest of Europe, however, will probably continue.

European shows are generally organized by Fédération Internationale Féline (FIFe). There has traditionally been a sound working relationship between FIFe and the British GCCF, although each organization continues to retain much of its independence in decision-making and rules. Europe's numerous independent cat clubs operate as autonomous federations with their own registries, but cooperate and usually accept exhibitors from other clubs at their shows.

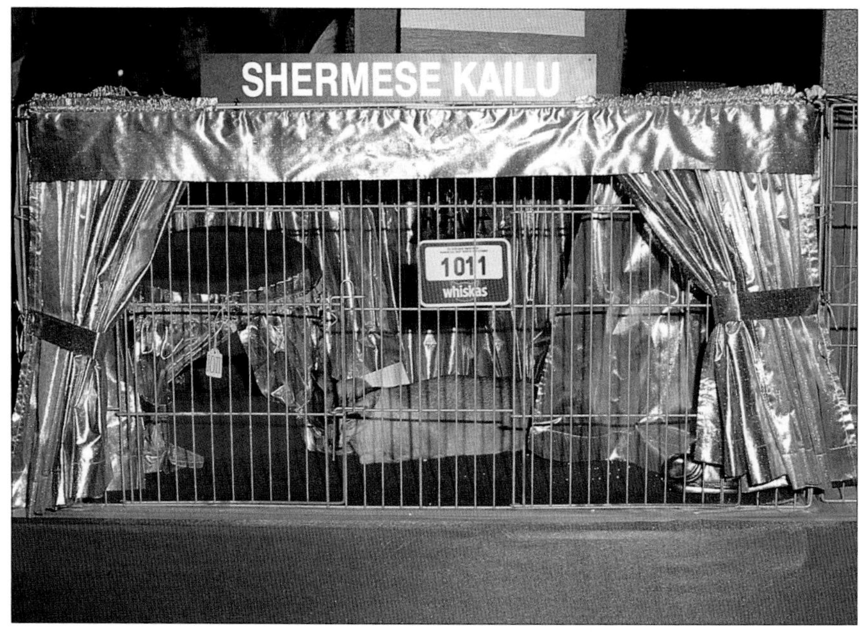

▲ *In European and North American shows, pens can be elaborately decorated (as shown above), although at British shows, only cats 'on exhibition' or at the Supreme Show can rest in splendour such as this.*

▼ *European Shorthairs have to reach the desired general standards of points rather than display a full pedigree to be eligible.*

Some of the shows run by independent clubs have two different judging methods going on at the same time. After vetting-in, the cats are penned, sometimes with other entries from the same household, in a large show pen which may be sumptuously decorated with pedigrees, photographs, previous wins and cattery cards on display.

The show pens are often arranged in squares, with the exhibitors inside the square having access to the animals, and the outward-facing side protected with perspex or heavy polythene so that the animals cannot be touched by the visitors on the outside of the square. Within the square of pens it is common for tables to be set up and laden with food, so that the exhibitors can have a good day with their friends.

Every cat is given a written report on how it conforms to the standard on that day, with the following ratings:

- Excellent: indicates that the animal has no physical defects; it conforms to standard, and is worthy of being bred from.
- Very good: indicates a cat of lesser quality relative to its standard of points, which is not good enough to gain a certificate.
- Good: indicates several defects or falling short of required standard.

All the cats are then judged for each award or qualification, and finally, Best in Section and Best in Show awards are decided.

The American show scene

Most shows in the United States, Mexico and Canada are full weekend occasions; some may even extend to three days. There may not be a preliminary vetting, on the assumption that no honourable exhibitor would take a sick animal to a show.

The holding pens at an American show are arranged like those in Europe, within a square (known as the ring) enclosed by the cages of the exhibitors. The owners can stay within the ring with their cats, and be fairly close to the judges when they give their verdict. The general public is on the outside of the square, and the outward-facing sides of the pens are usually protected from poking hands by heavy plastic sheets.

The judges remove each cat entrant in turn from its pen, to make an assessment against the required standards, accompanied by a simultaneous commentary. In virtually all North American associations, the judge is able to comment only on the favourable aspects of the animal, and not the negative points. Apart from brief notes for their own personal use, the judges make no written assessment of the cats.

► *Maine Coon Cats were major competitors at the very first American cat show held in Madison Square Garden, New York, in 1895.*

At the end of the show, the ten top kittens, adults and neuters in the Longhair, Shorthair and All Breed sections are taken to the ring for the Best Cat award. The placements are announced starting at tenth and working upwards. They are important, for promotion to championship status as the American system depends not only on points scored in class wins, but on how many top-five placements in the Best Cat stakes have been gained. It is not unknown, though rare, for a cat to become a Grand Champion at its very first show. There are classes for unaltered, pedigreed cats over eight months old, kitten competitions for animals of four to eight months, and provisional classes for breeds that have not been granted championship status (that is, registered as a distinct breed) by the registering association.

Various associations in North America promote the 'campaigning' of the very top cats. Exhibitors fly and drive huge distances to attend the shows where the greatest concentration of top cats will be found. Points are scored at every show attended in pursuit of championship or premiership status. The ultimate award is that of National Top Cat. Even to get into the National Top Twenty-five is a remarkable achievement.

◄ *Judges closely scrutinize all aspects of the cat and compare their findings to the breed standard.*

► *This beautiful Persian looks rather startled by its show success. Would have preferred a treat to a ribbon maybe?*

Breed standards

In essence, a breed standard is a written blueprint illustrating perfection. Many types of animal have a written standard for each breed. In the case of dogs and horses this blueprint may cover movement and working ability. With cats the emphasis is more on beauty and colour. Each cat breed has an individual breed standard. This is not always the case in the early days of the introduction of a new breed. Breed standards are used by breeders to try to ensure that they produce kittens 'as true to type' as possible. They are also used by judges as a guide to assessing both the good and not so good points of each exhibit.

In the early days of cat showing there was little difference between cat breeds, in fact few breeds were recognized, so a breed standard was mainly generic. One of the first is described in 1903 by Miss Frances Simpson in her *Book of The Cat*. In this, she states that cats should have 'a large broad paw' and when referring to eyes, she writes 'these ought to be round and large'. Nowadays, it is hard to see how the Sphynx with its elongated toes and the Modern Siamese with its almond-shaped eyes could fall into this category. But of course they didn't exist in their current form then.

▲ *If new to showing, join a relevant breed club. They will have information to help you understand the standard.*

Modern breed standards give a description of the important features of a breed. Each aspect does not have to be listed individually, but may be grouped together. These features are then given points. For example, the head would be allotted a range of points, according to the standard, but this would cover shape, ears, eyes, muzzle, chin, nose, profile and neck. Breeders work hard to produce kittens that conform to the description listed and judges have to assess how close the exhibit is to the standard.

Breed standards also list faults that would constitute a disqualification in a cat show. The most common of these is undescended testes in the case of an entire male, incorrect coat colour or texture and in some cases the cat's temperament.

Breed standards can be downloaded from most cat registries. There is sometimes a variation in breed standards according to the registry. The most common variant is permitted colour and coat markings. Study the applicable standard carefully to check your cat conforms.

◀ *A skilled judge is able to assess conformation by visual examination as well as feeling with their hands.*

▶ *Different registeries expect cats to be presented in different styles. This set-up would not be acceptable in the UK where the bedding must be white.*

Registrations and pedigrees

When pure-bred kittens are born it is the breeder's responsibility to register each kitten with the relevant registry. On application, the registry will satisfy themselves that the kittens are indeed 'pedigree' by checking through any relevant records that they hold. Then the registry will issue each kitten with its own registration certificate. These certificates will be in the breeder's name. When the kitten is sold, the registration document forms part of the sale and should be handed over to the purchaser. If, for any reason, the registration paper is not available at point of sale, a receipt, in lieu, should be issued by the breeder. The new owner is responsible for transferring the registration into their name. To do this, the document needs to be returned to the registry and a new one will be issued in the new owner's name. A fee may be applicable. A cat cannot be shown in a breed class without the appropriate registration documentation.

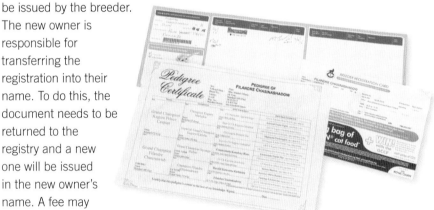

A pedigree is a written document detailing the lineage of a kitten. If one is available it is normally prepared and issued by the breeder. A pedigree is useful if an owner wishes to breed with their cat. It enables the breeder to research cats further back in the line. Using this information, a decision can be made as to the best mating to achieve healthy kittens that will conform to the breed standard. In the unlikely event of a registered cat not coming with a pedigree form, a search for one can be conducted using the information on the registration form. This can be done, either via the relevant registry or online where pedigree search sites can be found.

Unfortunately, not all breeders are reputable and pedigrees can be a work of fiction. The only way to be sure that a cat is of the breed advertised is to buy one with a registration certificate. Nevertheless, unregistered kittens will still make lovely pets and can be shown in pet cat classes.

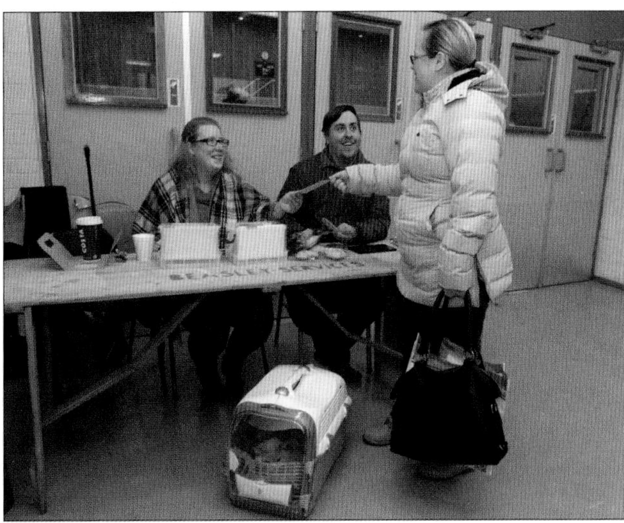

► *Before you leave for a show make sure you have any required documentation that needs to be presented.*

▼ *A registration document can be likened a little to a car logbook. It forms part of proof of ownership.*

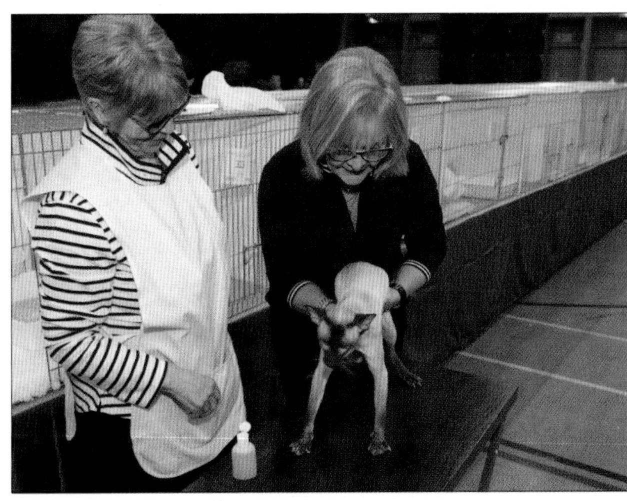

► *A judge examines a cat while the steward looks on. Note antibacterial hand spray on the table.*

Training for the cat show

Before commencing any pre-show training, careful consideration should be given to your cat's welfare and happiness. Cat shows are a strange and rather noisy environment. If your cat is of a nervous or shy disposition it may not be able to cope and become stressed. Early training can do much to help a cat feel more relaxed in a loud and busy situation, but there will always be cats that just can't cope. The person best able to assess their cat's possible reaction to a show is the owner.

▲ *Ask all your cat-loving visitors to handle or hold your cat so that it gets used to contact with strangers.*

WHEN TO START

Training, or socializing, should start at as early an age as possible. If you intend to show your cat it will normally have its first competition at four to five months of age, so preparation needs to be intensive. Much can be done in the home without disturbance to your daily routine. Training sessions should be fun for both cat and owner and of frequent but short duration. Training older cats for showing follows the same principles but may be more difficult as they are more set in their ways and will have established a behavioural response to noise and strangers.

Introduce your kitten to new noises such as loud radio or TV as soon as you can. Use the vacuum cleaner, washing machine or electrical kitchen equipment when the kitten is in the room. Recordings of noises, including thunder, can be bought or downloaded for free. These can be very useful. A common sound at shows is that of a water spray when cat coats are dampened as part of their grooming routine. Some cats are terrified of this noise. Often this is due to association with punishment, as spraying a cat with water is a common method of reprimand. If you intend to show, never use a water sprayer as a deterrent.

▼ *Start grooming your kitten when it is tiny. As it grows, extend the time of each grooming period.*

▼ *It may be boring to sit in a small pen at a cat show, but this display of rosettes shows that it can pay off.*

► *Start with short journeys in a well-ventilated car and gradually increase the journey length.*

Allow your kitten to meet all visitors to the home and to remain in the room when you are entertaining. Encourage willing guests to stroke and play with the kitten. Train your cat to be held and carried in the manner appropriate to the breed. Get all responsible members of the family, and friends unfamiliar with your cat, to handle the cat in this fashion so that it gets used to being handled by strangers. They should reward the cat with a treat each time.

Introduce your kitten to the grooming table as soon as possible. Always check that the table is stable before use. Lift them onto it and give them a treat. Repeat this exercise several times daily until the kitten considers being placed on the table as a rewarding place to be. Although a cat does not have to stand in a certain stance, like a dog, when shown, they should stand or sit with confidence. A cat cowering on the table doesn't present well to the judge. Teach the kitten to play with its toys in unusual places such as on your lap or on the grooming table. This will help build up their confidence.

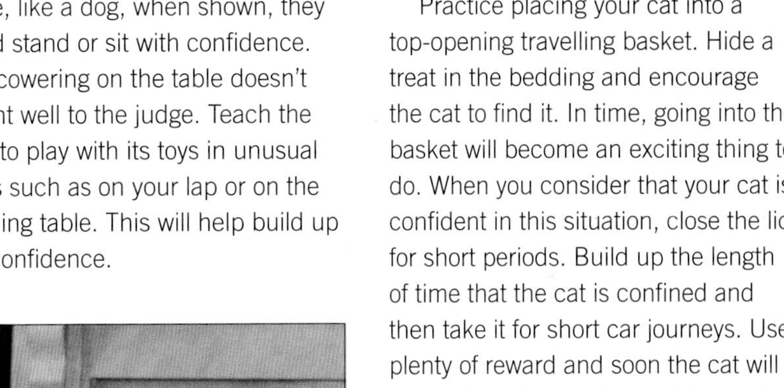

Practice placing your cat into a top-opening travelling basket. Hide a treat in the bedding and encourage the cat to find it. In time, going into the basket will become an exciting thing to do. When you consider that your cat is confident in this situation, close the lid for short periods. Build up the length of time that the cat is confined and then take it for short car journeys. Use plenty of reward and soon the cat will think of travel as a pleasurable event.

Some cats need a few shows to settle and find their feet in such a strange environment. If it is your first show you will be nervous too. The cat will pick up on these vibes and could become unsettled. Think of the first shows just as a continuation of the training that you have done at home. Turn each show into a happy experience by spending time rewarding and reassuring. This is the time to really pamper your feline friend. Your cat's comfort and welfare should always come in front of the hope of winning a prize.

▼ *Exposure to noise is important. Your cat should be confident around all forms of domestic appliance.*

Show preparation and grooming

If new to the cat fancy, the most important part of show preparation is to visit a cat show without a cat. Take time to see what is going on and familiarize yourself with the etiquette. It is also very instructive to have a clear idea of noise level, numbers of people attending, conditions and how the events are run. Watch the cats being judged so that you understand what will be expected of your cat. Look at the equipment needed and learn to understand schedules and catalogues. Observe cats of your breed being groomed and take note of the methods used. Talk to other competitors and breeders and generally soak up the atmosphere.

Differing cat breeds are presented, and in cases handled, in a different manner. For example, the grooming routine for a shorthaired breed will be vastly different to that of a longhaired breed. It is important to learn what is best for your breed. Specialist books and websites are helpful but the best source of information is the breeder of your kitten. Most have years of experience and a pride in their cats and their offspring. Generally, they are delighted to advise new owners. Breed clubs are another source of information. These offer information and advice on all aspects of the breed. Many have a members' forum and hold breed-specific seminars. Cat

► *Study the criteria of the classes in the show schedule. Contact the show secretary if you need class clarification.*

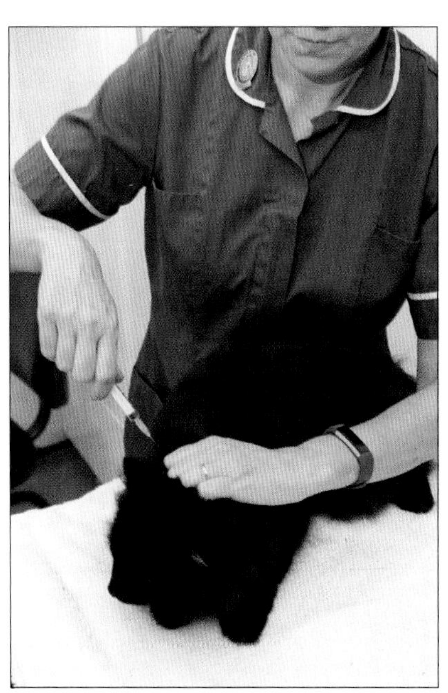

▼ *Vaccinations must be up to date. Some show societies will ask to see each cat's vaccination card.*

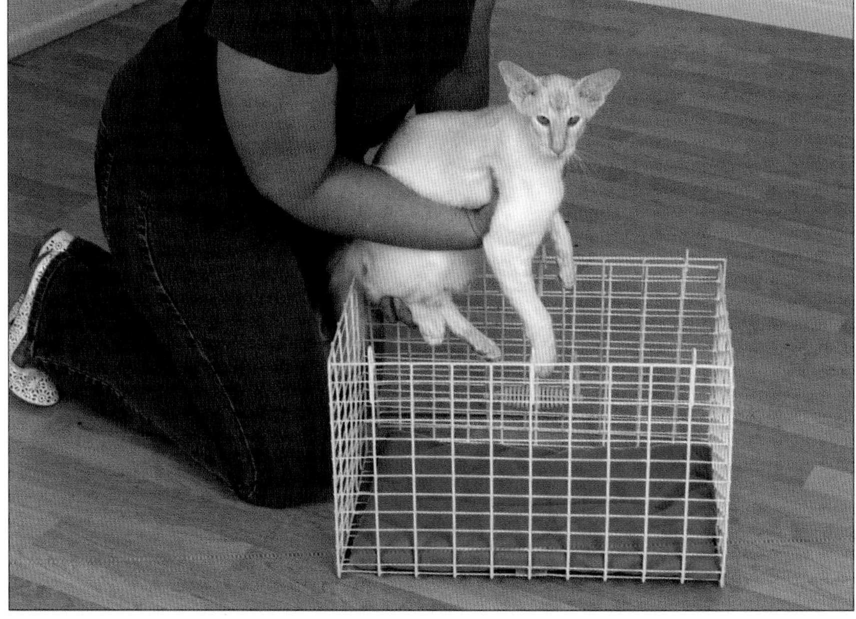

▼ *Make sure all your equipment is safe and scrupulously clean. Do not leave things to the last minute.*

registries also have websites, with pages concerning cat showing, but these are more breed-generic.

GROOMING

Regardless of breed, if you intend to show your kitten, show grooming should start almost as soon as you bring it home from the breeder. Appropriate equipment for coat type is vital and should be effective but gentle. Remember, especially in the case of longhaired breeds, brushes chosen for a kitten may not be adequate for a fully grown adult coat. Initially grooming sessions should be short. Make sure they are pleasurable experiences for the kitten and reward your pet at the end of each one. A grooming table should be introduced early on.

Bathing is an important aspect of show grooming and needs to start at an early age. However much you brush the coat, dirty, dusty or oily hair can only really be cleaned by shampooing. The frequency of, and the time between bathing and showing, is breed- and coat-type specific. Research and take advice on this aspect of show preparation.

Dental care is important for all cats but also forms part of show grooming. Not only should your cat be used to having its teeth cleaned but also having its mouth opened and teeth examined. The judge will need to look at the teeth as part of the judging procedure. Show visiting friends how to do this so your kitten gets used to having its mouth opened by strangers. Always reward afterwards.

A few days prior to a show, the tips of claws need to be trimmed. Don't remove too much or the claws will bleed and the cat will feel pain. Claw clippers should be sharp to prevent leaving ragged edges.

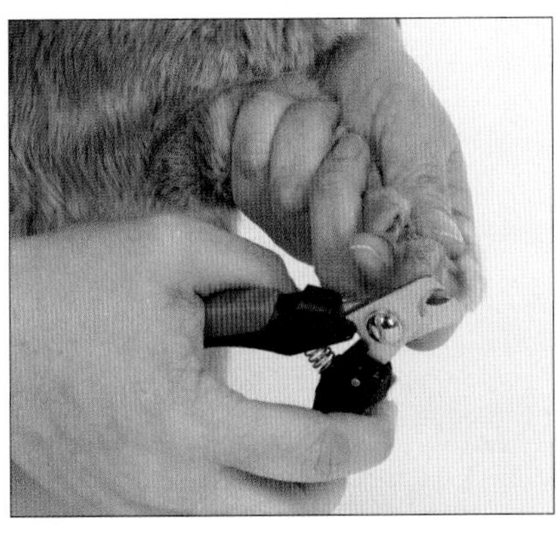

▲ *Trim claws a few days prior to the show so if the quick is accidentally caught, bleeding will have stopped.*

The day before the show check that the ears are clean. Any visible dirt and debris can be gently removed with either cotton wool moistened by liquid ear cleaner or the use of a pet ear wipe. Never scrub at the skin or poke anything into the ear.

It is a wise practice to prepare a checklist of all the items that you might require at the show and keep it in a handy place. This should include items that you need as well as those required for your cat. The evening prior to the show, tick them off as the items are packed in a suitable bag. Don't forget a change of travelling cat bedding in case of en-route accidents. If the weather is cold, additional clothing for you and a hot water bottle for your cat will provide comfort.

Plan your route before you leave home and allow plenty of time to reach your destination. It will not help you or your cat to arrive late and flustered. Early arrivals don't have to queue for so long for vetting, and have time to relax and acclimatize prior to judging. And above all enjoy the day and make sure your cat does too.

▼ *Ask your breeder how long it takes for the coat to 'settle' after bathing. Then do a dummy run yourself.*

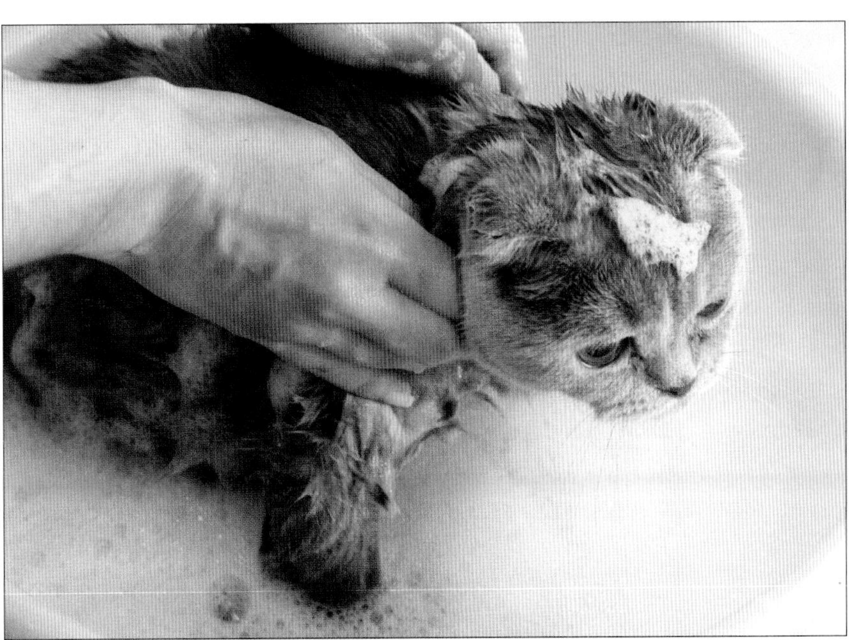

BREEDING FROM YOUR CAT

The vast majority of people are quite content to own a cat, or cats, and leave it at that. Their animals are neutered (altered) and live the life of non-reproductive felines that simply grace the lives and homes of their owner. There are other people who become deeply involved in breeding cats as a hobby – it is rarely a profitable business. The amateur cat breeder may be rewarded by a handful of exquisite and charming kittens that may or may not be perfect pedigrees, but he or she is also taking on an expensive, time-absorbing, and often frustrating commitment. Before embarking on a breeding programme make sure you equip yourself with all the facts.

◄ *An Abyssinian mother and her kitten in their beauty and character demonstrate the rewards of breeding.*

The rewards of breeding

Think carefully of the implications before you decide to let your cat have kittens. Whether you are giving your non-pedigree a chance to be a mother before having her neutered (altered), or planning to propagate a pedigree line, the process can be both time-consuming and expensive. Perhaps the most important consideration of all is to be sure that you will be able to find good homes for the kittens. If not, or if the prospective buyers change their minds, you must be prepared to give them a permanent home yourself.

Most people who breed from their cats are dealing with pedigrees rather than random-bred animals, with a view to continuing or improving on pure-bred lines. For the cat lover, the pedigree cat world is one of absorbing interest and beauty. It is also a stimulating environment where you will learn a great deal; your rivals will often become your best friends.

▼ *After a particularly awful day, with kittens into everything and apparently multiplying, many a cat breeder wonders, 'Why am I doing this?' One look at this trio of bi-colours would probably answer the question.*

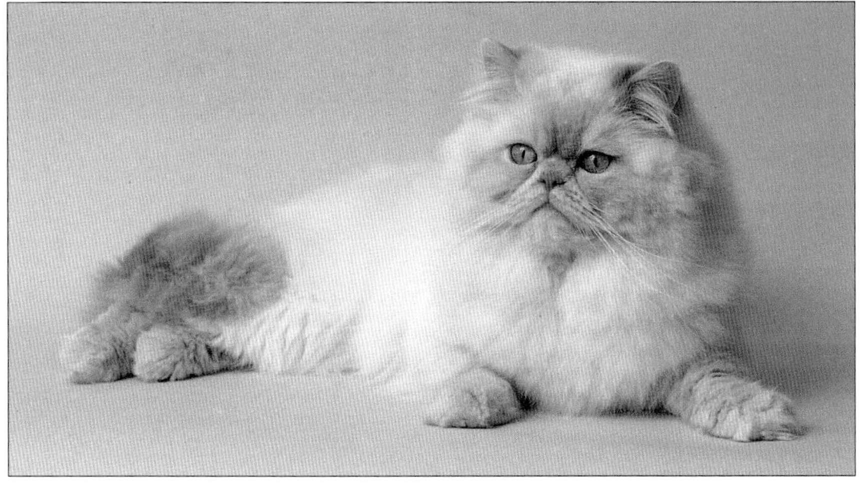

▲ *The ultimate reward for a breeder is to produce a pedigreed cat of such perfection of type and temperament that it becomes a national Supreme Grand Champion like the Cream Colourpoint Longhair, Rosjoy Rambo.*

THE COMMITMENT

Those who go into breeding pedigrees thinking they are going to earn a lot of money from selling them are going to be disappointed. Even the most experienced and reputable breeders are lucky to break even over the course of any financial year. There are veterinary bills to pay for both mother and offspring, stud fees, special diets for the pregnant and nursing mother, heating for the kittens, veterinary testing and inoculation, and registration and advertising costs.

A heavily pregnant and nursing cat needs attention. The queen may not deliver her kittens at a convenient time and place during the day. This may happen in the early hours of the morning, and she may need some help from you, especially if it is her first litter. There may be deaths to deal with, especially in a first litter, which will be extremely distressing for everyone concerned.

Kittens may be lovable and cute, but they can also be destructive and get in the way. They need to be watched and cared for, and prepared for going out into the world. You should raise a pedigree litter for love and interest rather than money, and preferably when you already have some experience as an owner.

HOW IT ALL BEGAN

Breeding pedigreed cats on a serious level did not take place until the 1800s. The first cat show, held in London in 1871, set a trend for exhibiting, which in turn led to a more

▼ *Diminutive yet powerful, Singapuras are the pedigreed version of the Singapore alley cat. The best examples were bred to produce a pedigree which is increasing in popularity.*

calculated approach to breeding. The organizer, an artist and author called Harrison Weir, set guidelines for breeding which became the basis for standards throughout the world, although different countries set their own rules. Most of the cats in the early shows were domestic shorthairs and Persians. It was not until the 1880s that Asian breeds were introduced to western Europe. The first Siamese cats were exhibited in Britain in 1885. By this time, breeders in Europe and America were setting up their own breeding programmes. They drew from the best British pedigreed stock and their own indigenous cats. The first American cat show was in New York in 1895.

A NEW BREED

There are now more than fifty internationally recognized breeds, and several others that are recognized as established and distinct breeds in some countries but not in others. The purpose of breeding may go beyond a desire to produce kittens for show or for sale, or even to keep a pedigree line going. Careful and well-informed selection of the queen and the stud can improve the type. Instead of waiting for the natural processes of evolution to select the fittest of a species, a breeder can speed up the process. Picking the healthiest and most well-formed examples of indigenous street cats, and mating them, for example, led to the development of standard types of British, American and European shorthairs. Breeders can also try to create a new variety of cat – a new colour variation of an established breed, or a new breed altogether. However, this is an area that should be left to the experts who have built up an in-depth knowledge of feline genetics, for mutations do sometimes occur. To establish a new breed takes many years. Only after several matings can a breed be proved to produce healthy offspring of consistent type, and only then be officially registered.

▼ *If your breeding programme produces a line-up of six-week-old Blue and Cream Persians, like this one, you should have no difficulty finding a home for them.*

Acquiring a queen

Choosing the breed and pedigree line you are going to use to found your breeding programme requires preparation and in-depth research. Gather as much information as you can about your chosen breed and study the genetics of breeding from specialist books, magazines and websites, and from the individual breed clubs.

Unless you are going to breed with a cat you already own, it is sensible to look for suitably pedigreed parents and book a female kitten from their next litter. This kitten will, after all, be the foundation of your breeding line. She should be of the best standard and pedigree that you can afford.

In any event, you should not select a kitten you are planning to breed from until it is at least three months old. By this time you will be able to assess its personality, and the colouring and patterns of its coat. The national cat-registering bodies, such as The Governing Council of the Cat Fancy in the United Kingdom and the Cat Fanciers' Association in the United States, publish set standards of perfection for each registered breed. These not only help you identify suitable parents for your own breeding female, but give you, as a breeder, clear guidelines to aim for.

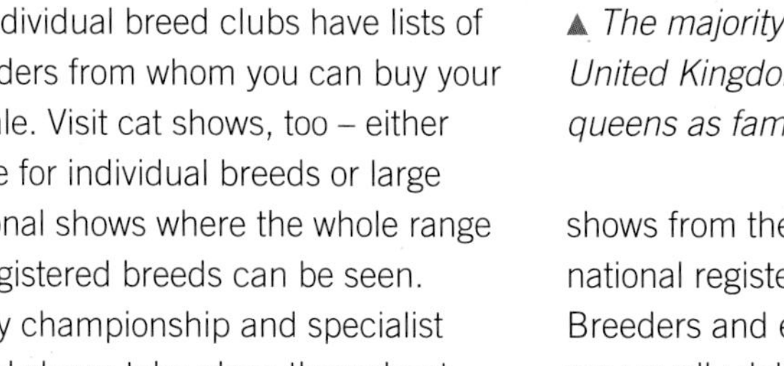

► *Think ahead when choosing a pedigree line to breed from. Maine Coons are splendid cats, but they are also one of the largest breeds.*

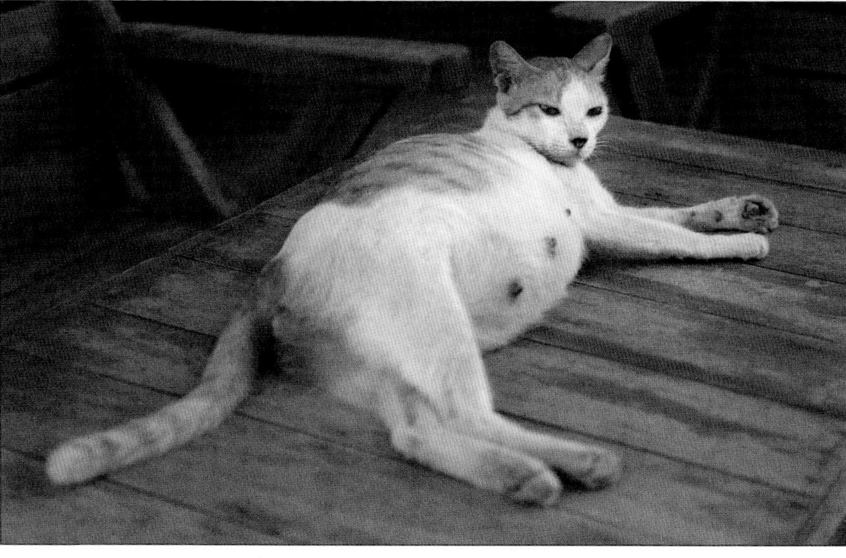

▲ *The majority of breeders in the United Kingdom keep their breeding queens as family pets.*

Individual breed clubs have lists of breeders from whom you can buy your female. Visit cat shows, too – either those for individual breeds or large national shows where the whole range of registered breeds can be seen. Many championship and specialist breed shows take place throughout the year. You can obtain details of shows from the breed clubs and national registering organizations. Breeders and exhibitors at cat shows are usually delighted to talk about their animals.

The early contacts you make at clubs and shows are vital first steps in joining the cat-breeding network. You may find not only the breeder from whom you will acquire your own potential queen, but also the one who might provide the stud she will mate with. The breeder of your choice may not have any kittens at the time you want one, but is likely to know of someone else who does.

BEYOND APPEARANCES

You will initially be attracted by the outward physical appearance of a particular breed or cat. However, when you are considering breeding, it is particularly important to look for animals with responsive and outgoing

◄ *It is not that unusual for queens to choose to share the care and feeding of each other's litter.*

yet calm natures. This generally indicates that they have been reared in a household where cuddles and good food are considered important, and that they have good character genes to pass on to their offspring.

If you are lucky, the cats you have marked out at a cat show will also be the ones the judges like. The parents of your kitten queen-to-be may be top show winners with great personalities, splendid condition and a helpful breeder/owner.

Before you commit yourself, visit the mother of your queen-to-be in its home, as this is very different from seeing her in the restricted atmosphere of a show. If other cats are there, such as her parents or siblings, you will be able to see how they interact with each other. These are the blood relations of your breeding queen.

Ask detailed questions about their pedigrees and breeding records. It is far better, for example, to acquire a female for breeding which comes from a long line of successful mothers that rear strong litters with no fatalities, than to go for a line of top-winning cats with only a marginally successful breeding record. Responsible breeders will also be assessing you as a future breeder in your own right, and note how their cats respond to you. Before releasing a kitten, they may even ask for references from your vet.

◄ *A Siamese demonstrates how to be a good mother. When you are choosing a kitten to found your breeding line, it is important to look at her mother, and how she reacts with her offspring. Good relationships can have a knock-on effect through the generations.*

COMING HOME

Finally, you have the new kitten; you have joined the breed club. The period between now and when she is ready for her first mating is a key preparation time. Your queen-to-be must have the best possible diet as recommended by her breeder. She must be played with and exercised until her muscular condition is superb, and generally handled with love and tenderness so that she bonds with you. When the time comes for her to have her kittens, she will then do so in the confident knowledge of the support of her owners.

▼ *An adventurous four-week-old Ocicat kitten is ready to explore, but mother is keeping close.*

Care of the stud cat

Three things are required prior to contemplating keeping a stud cat: experience, time and money. If an owner doesn't feel that they have these attributes then keeping a cat as stud is not for them.

Experience is required to decide if the little male kitten that you have bought is worth keeping as a stud cat. A good breeder should help you make this assessment, although it may be difficult to convince them that you are ready to own a stud cat. This is most definitely not a project for a novice to the cat fancy. It is important to check the registration document to ensure that no breeding restrictions are on the cat. Some registries have a policy allowing breeders to place 'not for breeding', or similar, on this document. The progeny of any cat thus registered would not be eligible for registration, defeating the object of using it as a stud cat. Consideration should also be given whether the stud cat will have enough 'work' to keep it happy. Most will require at least two queens to mate, per month.

▼ *Stud pants are similar in style to a nappy or diaper and are available in different sizes. There is a small hole at the back for the tail.*

◀ *Stud pants are not intended as a contraceptive but rather to prevent spraying while the stud is indoors. Some cats will not tolerate them, others are accepting.*

▲ *Ready-made outdoor cat chalets can be bought in sectional format.*

STUD CAT TEMPERAMENT

Keeping a stud cat cannot be compared to keeping a neutered male. Almost without exception, they do not make good family pets. They develop a strong territorial instinct and will spray urine to mark out their territory. Tomcat urine has a very strong pungent odour which is almost impossible to eradicate from the home. Defending territories involves fighting, which can be indiscriminate, including attacking other cats within the home as well as those that live in the locality. If a stud cat is let out, or escapes, they may be absent for several days while they seek out a mate, often returning home injured after fighting with another tomcat. For these reasons, a stud cat is best kept confined in quarters outside the home. This is where the money comes in. Outdoor stud houses can be bought, or a snug, watertight shed converted,

▶ *A roaming tom is likely to terrorize other local cats and may cause dissent between the owner and neighbours.*

to provide living accommodation. Purpose-built stud houses can be viewed and purchased online or at large cat shows. The building should have good ventilation, insulation and adequate space for exercise. Separate accommodation, within the stud house, will be required to house the queen safely away from the stud cat, but close enough so that they can 'talk' and get to know each other prior to the proposed mating. Electricity needs to be connected to the building to provide light and winter heating. As stud cats tend to be very vocal, consideration must be given to siting the building. Close neighbours will not appreciate the smell or noise of a howling tomcat. Veterinary costs include those for full vaccinations for cat flu, leukaemia and enteritis and all relevant boosters, plus testing and certificating negative against feline leukaemia. Top quality, suitable food is essential if a stud cat is to 'perform' to the best of his ability. The cost of care if you go away for a holiday must also be factored in. Most catteries will not take in a stud cat so the only alternative is to pay for a live-in carer from a reputable pet business.

The somewhat isolated life of the stud cat can lead to loneliness. Some will enjoy the company of an older cat but many are just too aggressive or harass companions by repeatedly trying to mate them. Owners must be prepared to spend significant time with their stud cat, playing, grooming and petting him. Time is also required to check and complete relevant paperwork, organise stud work, communicate with owners of queens and supervize each mating. Cleaning and de-odourizing the stud house is a daily necessity, whatever the weather.

Successfully showing off an entire cat will substantially increase stud bookings, especially if they gain a title such as Grand Champion or even Imperial Grand Champion. But to do this the owner will require a combination of time, money and experience plus a sprinkling of luck.

Unfortunately, if you decide not to continue using your cat at stud, neutering him is unlikely to return him to a placid family pet. Deciding to use a cat as a stud is a life-long commitment.

▼ *Prior to standing at stud the cat should be checked over by the vet and, if applicable, blood and DNA tests undertaken.*

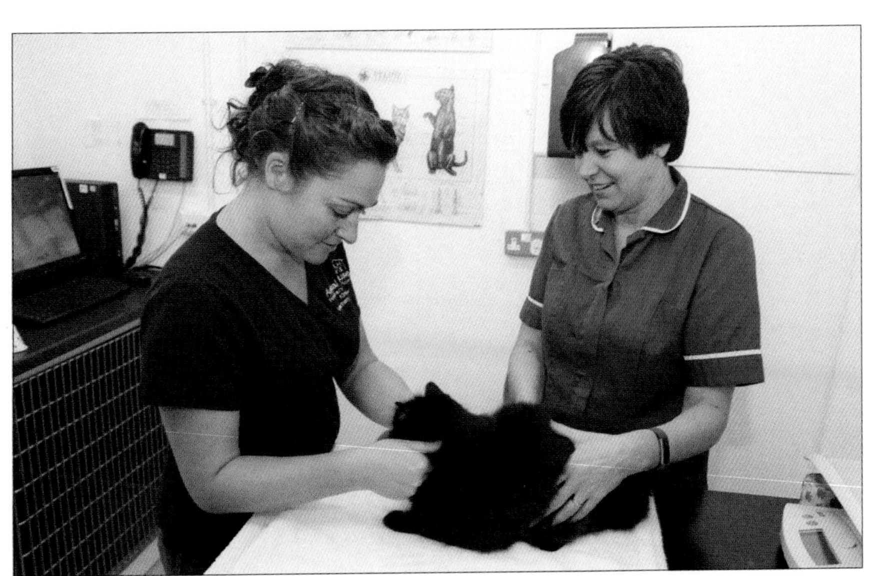

▼ *Plan to spend a proportion of each day with the stud cat to enrich his life and prevent boredom-related problems.*

Ready for mating?

It is quite obvious when a female is ready for mating. She starts what is known as 'calling' – although this can be more like shrieking or wailing in some breeds, such as Siamese. Some Persians content themselves with dainty little mews and miaows. The female displays some brazen behaviour, rolling and dragging herself around the floor, flicking her tail and raising her rump to expose the slightly reddened area beneath. She may also lose interest in her food. If her behaviour fools you into thinking she is unwell, try picking her up by her neck folds (as an interested tom would do) and stroke along her back. If she responds with pleasure, pads her feet and raises her tail, she is definitely in season.

The average age of sexual maturity in a female is around six months, but cats of Oriental origin such as Siamese and Burmese can be as early as fourteen or sixteen weeks. British Shorthairs and Persians do not start calling much before ten months. Generally, tomcats become sexually mature a month or two later than females of the same breed. The time of year also has an effect on the first call. If due in autumn or winter, it may be delayed until the warmer months of spring.

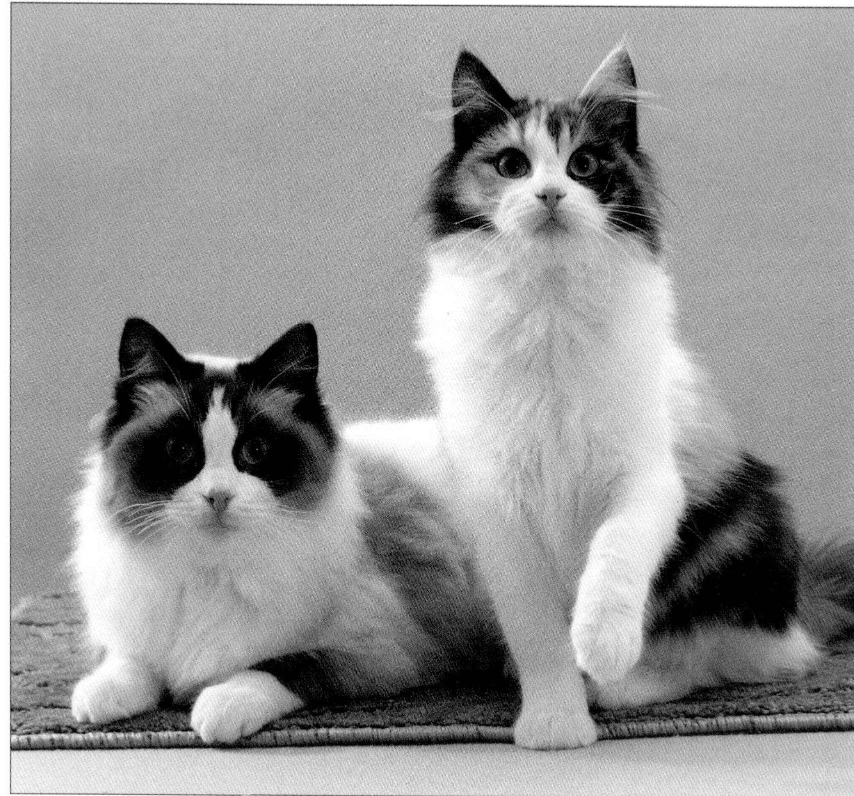

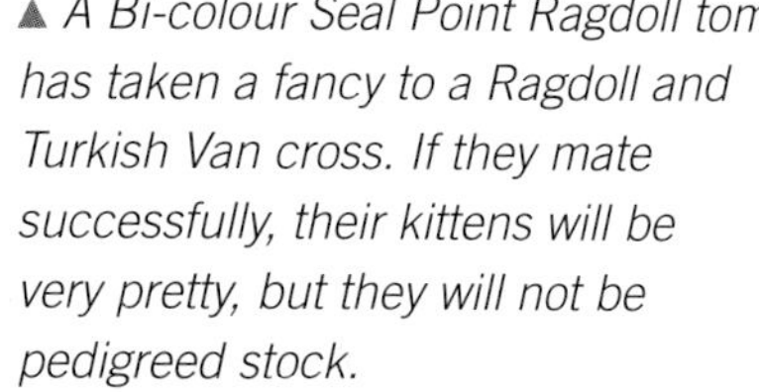

▲ *A Bi-colour Seal Point Ragdoll tom has taken a fancy to a Ragdoll and Turkish Van cross. If they mate successfully, their kittens will be very pretty, but they will not be pedigreed stock.*

▼ *A Siamese female in season rolls around and thrashes her tail. Siamese are notorious for announcing their sexual readiness with loud and strident calling.*

▶ *When selecting a stud, always look for the best example. While this Red Persian is a little out of coat, his type is superb, and he will no doubt father excellent kittens.*

▼ *Whatever the breed, it is important that the male is neither monorchid (one testicled) nor cryptorchid (hidden testicled): this Korat is fully endowed.*

The cycle is approximately 21 days and females may come into oestrus (on call) for about three to ten days. They continue to be fertile until at least 14 years of age.

It is best to let the young queen run through the first couple of cycles – until she is at least a year old – rather than put her to stud immediately. This gets the system going and reduces the risk of problems at birth.

CHOOSING THE MALE

Many breed clubs publish a stud list of proven males, but the breeder from whom you bought the female is likely to know of suitable mates. An experienced breeder is also likely to know about genetically compatible lines, and even if you have some ideas of your own, it is important to take expert advice.

If you go to a show to look for potential partners, do not be tempted to go for the stunning new male Grand Champion. Other breeders may be clamouring to use him, but the wiser choice would be his father. Not only has he proved himself to be the sire of outstanding stock, but with a maiden queen it is wiser to use an experienced stud for the first mating.

RENDEZVOUS

Before committing yourself to a particular stud, visit the breeder to check the conditions in which the maiden queen is to be kept. This is an opportunity also to ask vital questions about the number and the supervision of matings. Documentation on the participating animals that needs to be exchanged varies according to the conditions for entry to stud, but for your female include the following:

- Pedigree
- Registration and/or transfer
- Up-to-date vaccination certificate
- Current test certificates showing negative status for both feline infectious leukaemia and feline immunodeficiency virus (FIV).

The stud owner may require the tests to have been carried out within the last 24 hours, although others accept tests within the past five to seven days. The conditions and fees should be agreed before taking the queen to the stud. Conditions of the mating might include an agreement that no males from a resulting litter will be used for breeding, or for the pick of the litter to be substituted in lieu of a mating fee. It is usual for there to be another free mating should the queen fail to become pregnant first time round.

On an informal level, the stud owner should want to know the pet name of the cat and the diet she is used to.

► *The ideal Tabby stud should not only be of first-class type, but have clear, well-defined markings.*

The queen's reproductive cycle

There are five stages to a queen's reproductive cycle; anestrus, proestrous, estrus, interfollicular and diestrus.

Anestrus takes place during the shortest days of the year, usually in the winter months. During this period, she will not come into heat and will not attract male cats.

Proestrous is the term for the beginning of the cycle. During this period, she will exhibit all the signs of being ready to mate but, although males are attracted to her, she will not let them mate her. The time of proestrous varies from queen to queen. It can be as short as a few hours or last for a couple of days.

A queen is receptive to mating during estrus which can last for about a week. She may allow more than one tom to mate with her so it is possible the resulting litter of kittens may have more than one father.

If she has not been mated she will enter an interfollicular period; this is also called interestrus. At this point she will not be reproductively active or attract male cats. After about a week she will go into proestrous again and the cycle repeats itself.

▲ *The most obvious signal that a cat is in heat are behavioural changes. They will constantly rub against objects or their owner, demanding attention.*

If she was mated during estrus and ovulated, but did not become pregnant, she will go through a stage called diestrus. This lasts for 5–7 weeks and she will not be sexually active although she may show signs of a false pregnancy.

It is a common myth that a female cat should have at least one estrus cycle before having her spayed. There is no veterinary reason for doing so. The risk of pregnancy is high even in indoor cats who become avid escape artists at this time. Female cats are indiscriminate and will mate with a brother, their sire or any entire tomcat in the neighbourhood. There is also no evidence to back up the old wives' tale that having a litter of kittens will make a cat more friendly. If you do not wish to breed from your cat, and want to avoid accidental pregnancies early, surgical altering is advised.

▼ *The female cat in heat will urinate more frequently and may even spray on vertical surfaces.*

The mating

When the young queen starts to call, contact the stud owner. Both animals must be in good health, and have their nails clipped beforehand.

The journey to the stud usually takes place on the second or third day of the call. The stud's owner prepares for the arrival of the queen by thoroughly disinfecting the entire stud run and the queen's quarters. The queen is settled in her quarters within the stud run, where the stud can 'talk' to her. This enables the queen to become accustomed to the stud's presence, and prepares her for mating.

At a quiet moment, the stud's owner releases the queen from her quarters. If all goes to plan, she crouches ready to receive the male; he grasps her by the scruff with his teeth, and taps her rump with one of his back legs until she raises it and flicks her tail over. The first entry of the male induces ovulation in the female and may result in fertilization, though subsequent matings are more likely to do so. (Note that your queen is likely to remain fertile for several days, so keep her in when she returns home.)

When sexual climax is reached, the female utters a strange cry that is only ever heard at this time. As soon as he withdraws from the female, the male moves away as the female turns on him with tooth and claw. She then rolls around, washing furiously for a couple of minutes. Only after she has done this is she calm again. Several matings need to take place over two or three days to try to ensure that the female becomes pregnant.

▲ *The queen and tom go through preparatory rituals before mating takes place, but once the male has ejaculated, he moves out of the way to avoid a sharp cuff from his partner.*

The stud owner supervizes matings so that no harm comes to either stud or queen, but, in many cases, the male and female soon develop a bond. They are then allowed to run together and mating can take place freely. It is very common for the queen to take over the stud's bed and to assume matriarchal dominance. At the end of her stay, the stud owner will provide a certificate giving details of:

- The stud's pedigree
- Number of matings observed
- Dates of matings
- Expected date of litter arrival
- The agreed stud fee and conditions

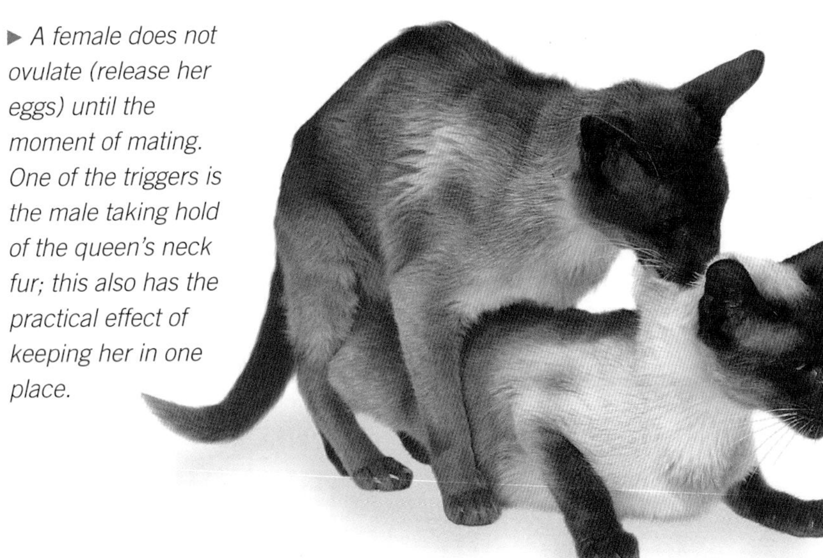

► *A female does not ovulate (release her eggs) until the moment of mating. One of the triggers is the male taking hold of the queen's neck fur; this also has the practical effect of keeping her in one place.*

The pregnancy

▲ *Towards the end of a pregnancy, most cats require more rest than usual, and this Persian is relaxing before her confinement.*

The average gestation period for cats is between 63 and 68 days. Occasionally, healthy kittens are produced even at 61 days. Kittens produced at or before this time usually require very specialized nursing, as key systems have not fully developed. Some females carry their kittens for as long as 70 days. In this event, the kittens may be larger than normal.

The first indication that a cat is pregnant (or in kitten) is when she does not come on heat two or three weeks after mating. Soon after this, there will be visible signs of pregnancy: the nipples become rather swollen and take on a deep coral-pink tone, a process that is called pinking up. Very experienced breeders may know a cat is in kitten a few days in advance of this, as there is sometimes a ridging of the muscles of the cat's stomach. A vet is able to confirm a pregnancy by feeling the cat's abdomen after three or four weeks.

ANTENATAL CARE

A pregnant cat should be encouraged to maintain a normal lifestyle. You can increase the amount of food you give her from about the fifth week of pregnancy, and introduce a vitamin supplement. In a feral state, a cat gorges itself as it does not know where the next meal is coming from. Your cat will let you know how much food she wants. Seek veterinary advice if you are in any doubt.

Climbing, jumping, running – and hunting if the cat is free-range – are all normal physical activities, even for a pregnant pedigree. Do remember, however, that allowing a pregnant female free range may expose her to other dangers. She may slow down a bit towards the end of her term, but regular activity ensures that good, strong muscle tone is maintained. This is essential for a natural, successful birth.

◀ *A kittening box is ideal for both mother and owner, but do make sure the cat is used to, and comfortable with, both the box and its location well before the birth.*

After about four weeks, the queen's stomach starts to distend, the nipples become very prominent, and she begins to look pregnant. By around 28 days, all the kittens' internal organs have formed, and the embryos are about 2.5cm (1in) long. The skeleton develops from about 40 days, and at 50 days, the kittens quicken – show signs of movement. Look for rippling, sliding motions along the mother's flank; they are most noticeable when she is resting.

About a week before the birth, the queen starts looking for a nesting place. It is a good idea to prepare a cardboard-box house for the queen with lots of plain paper inside for her to tear up. If this is not done, she will do her best to get into closets, drawers, airing cupboards – anywhere warm and draught-free.

Health problems in a queen

There are certain health problems that may affect a female entire cat of breeding age. The hormonal drive to reproduce is very strong and is repeated each time she comes into oestrus. It is thought that a hormone imbalance is a major cause of pseudo pregnancy (false pregnancy), although the exact cause is unknown. This is a distressing condition, for queen and owner alike, where a non-pregnant cat shows symptoms of pregnancy including abdominal bloating, enlarged mammary glands that excrete watery fluid, nursing non-existent kittens, lack of appetite, vomiting, nesting or restless behaviour, behavioural changes, self-nursing and depression. Often the symptoms will only be seen for two to three days but on occasion will last considerably longer. A veterinary examination is required to rule out true pregnancy and an infection. This may include blood and urine tests, plus an x-ray or ultrasound. Generally, once a diagnosis is reached, further treatment is not required. Wearing an Elizabethan collar to prevent self-nursing and using warm and cold packs on the mammary glands will help to minimize stimulus that promotes lactation. On rare occasions spaying or hormonal supplements will be recommended by the vet, to avoid repeated incidents of pseudo pregnancy.

Each time a queen comes into heat, her ovaries produce eggs. These eggs remain in the ovaries until fertilized. If a successful mating does not take place, after several heat cycles, the eggs become encysted. Any queen that has gone longer than a year between pregnancies is highly likely to have cystic ovaries.

▲ *There are many reasons for a vaginal discharge. Some are potentially life-threatening. All should be checked by a vet.*

NURSING ISSUES

When nursing kittens, some queens suffer from calcium deficiency. This condition is called eclampsia. It is most commonly seen when kittens are one to five weeks of age, when the queen is producing high quantities of milk. Symptoms include convulsions, fever, excessive panting, tremors, weakness and stiffness in the limbs, coupled with an inability to stand or walk normally. If any of these symptoms are seen in a nursing queen, prevent the kittens from suckling and seek immediate veterinary attention. Prompt diagnosis and treatment can lead to complete recovery, delayed treatment may not.

▼ *Frequent urination may be caused by the pregnancy or be a symptom of a urinary infection.*

▼ *An unkempt coat that looks dull and stands away from the body is a good indication that all is not well.*

The kittening

Birth is an exciting but messy business, which is why there should be a lot of padding in the kittening box and the area beneath and around the box should be easy to clean and disinfect without disturbing the inmates too much.

About 24 hours before the actual birth, the queen enters the first stage of labour. Outward physical signs are very few. There may be the odd faint ripple along the flank of the cat, and experienced breeders will note that her breathing through the nose has become shallow and rapid on occasion. Close examination reveals a flickering of the nostrils during these early, very faint contractions. Towards the end of this process, a small mucous plug may be found in the bedding, or adhering to the hair close to the cat's vulva.

▼ *A newborn kitten has just emerged and broken free from the protective sac of amniotic fluid.*

▲ *One week old, blind, deaf, hungry – and not at all domesticated.*

The next stage can take quite a long time, depending on the number of kittens. It is important not to panic: as long as the queen shows no signs of physical distress, all is going well. During this second stage, the classic signs of major contractions are clearly visible. The queen is breathing deeply and her whole abdomen seems to shudder and ripple downwards.

Eventually, a membrane sac containing a kitten and fluid starts to emerge from the queen's vulva and it may be possible to see the kitten's head within the sac. Sometimes the sac will burst at this point when it is said that the waters have broken. Often, the birth is so rapid that the kitten is born before the sac bursts.

▼ *Mother's first task is to take her newborn kitten and wash it thoroughly, especially around the nose and mouth to clear respiratory passages so that it can breathe – and utter its first cries.*

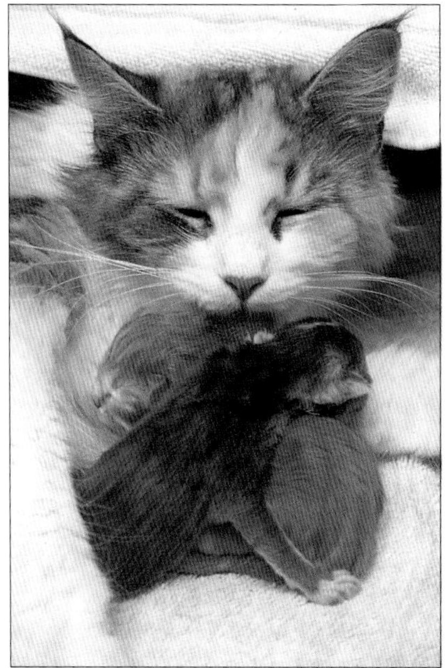

The queen clears the sac from around the kitten and immediately washes the newborn, particularly around the nose and mouth. This prompts the kitten to get rid of any amniotic residue from its respiratory system and it will often begin to cry. By this time secondary contractions have expelled the placenta (afterbirth), which the queen will instinctively eat. In a feral state, this would provide her with food and nutrients during the first couple of days after kittening when

Midwife equipment

- Disinfected, blunt-ended scissors
- Sterile surgical gloves
- Kitchen towels
- Hot water
- Ordinary towels
- Towelling face cloths
- Water-based lubricant

▲ *Three weeks old: eyes are open and mobility is improving. The kitten can now try some finely chopped cooked meat or kitten food to supplement the milk from its mother.*

she needs to recover. Hormones in the placenta promote milk secretion, and also help the uterus to contract, preventing a haemorrhage, which is a normal occurence after every birth. In the wild, such haemorrhaging could lead a predator to the kittens' nest. The queen also chews through the umbilical cord. In a straightforward birth, the queen, even a maiden queen, will usually cope with everything. However, it may be that you will have to assist on occasions. For this, a range of equipment should be within easy reach.

BREECH BIRTH

It is normal for some kittens to be born backwards, with hind feet being presented first. If the rump and tail rather than the stretched-out hind feet are presented first, this is a breech birth and can be a problem. It is so easy to become impatient and want to get your hands in the nest to help out, but the real need to do this should be very carefully weighed up.

If the queen is contracting strongly, it is likely that she will be able to birth the kitten quite normally. This way round is just a little more difficult, as the head is not widening the birth passage so that the rest of the body can slide through. However, if the waters have burst and the kitten is taking a very long time to be born, there is a risk of brain damage or stillbirth and the kitten should be helped out by the owner as quickly as possible.

If the legs are coming first, quickly slip on the surgical gloves and smear a little of the lubrication around the vulva. Never pull on any part of the kitten – it is an extremely delicate organism capable of being very easily damaged. As the queen's contractions push the legs further out of the vulva, use index and middle finger to "scissor" the legs right next to the opening of the vulva. As the contractions cease, the natural effect is for the legs to be drawn back into the vulva. The breeder's fingers will hold the legs in position until the next set of contractions. Then as more of the legs appear, use the index and middle fingers of the other hand to repeat the process. Generally, once the hips have emerged, the queen can do the rest by herself.

In the case of a rump or tail breech birth, you may need to gently insert a lubricated finger beside the kitten and hold it as a hook. But it must be emphasized that, in most cases, the queen knows what is best and can manage by herself.

▼ *A non-pedigreed litter has settled down after the trials of birth.*

◄ *The mother and her kittens need to be watched carefully at first, in case any complications arise. However, usually the mother is quite capable of looking after and training her kittens on her own.*

APPARENT STILLBIRTH

Sometimes a kitten will be born apparently lifeless. This may not be the case; it may not be breathing and be in a state of shock. If the queen does not immediately rasp away at the kitten's face, it is your job to do it. To clear any excess fluid from the nose and lungs, hold the kitten in your hand with index finger going over and supporting its head. Gently swing the kitten downwards two or three times and then wipe and stimulate the face around the nose and nostrils. At the same time, rub its body vigorously. If this doesn't get it going you may have to perform mouth-to-mouth resuscitation.

It may be that the kitten has suffered some form of foetal distress during the birth process and has, in fact, died. The cause may be more serious, and a dead kitten should be laid aside carefully for a post-mortem examination to establish the cause.

QUEEN DISTRESS

Even very experienced queens may become distressed and unable to birth their kittens. Because of this possibility it is wise to let your veterinarian know when the kittens are due. The most common form of distress is the lack of strong contractions. The vet may inject the queen with oxytocin, a hormone to improve contractions. If this does not work, birth by Caesarean section may be the only option. This is done very rapidly and with the minimum amount of anaesthetic, so that the queen is well able to look after her kittens after the operation.

One of the reasons why it is essential to examine the breeding record of the bloodline from which a queen is obtained is to check for any predisposition to the need for Caesarean sections.

POST-NATAL CARE

While it is rare for a healthy queen to encounter problems after pregnancy, a close watch should always be kept for the following conditions:

- Pyometra: an infection of the uterus characterized by a thick, off-white discharge. This condition is not serious if caught quickly and treated with antibiotics. In a serious form it will mean that the queen will have to be spayed.
- Eclampsia (milk fever): caused by a dramatic fall in calcium levels in the queen who will begin to convulse. An immediate intra-muscular or intravenous injection of calcium from the vet brings immediate recovery.
- Mastitis: the queen's mammary glands become hard, lumpy and hot due to an infection. Treatment is with antibiotics. Temporary relief can be given by the use of warm compresses on the affected area.
- Lack of milk: the queen's milk can dry up if she doesn't have sufficient wholesome food and drink; or the kittens are not suckling vigorously enough; or through mastitis. A homeopathic remedy such as Lachesis or hormone treatment may result in a return of the milk supply. If not, the kittens may have to be hand-fed until they are weaned. This means two-hourly feeds with a commercially available substitute milk. The vet may know of breeders who are specialists in the techniques of hand-feeding kittens.

Defects are rare. They include:

- Cleft palate or hare-lip
- Lack of eyes
- Heart defects including hole in the heart
- Umbilical hernia
- Intestines on the outside

When to call the vet

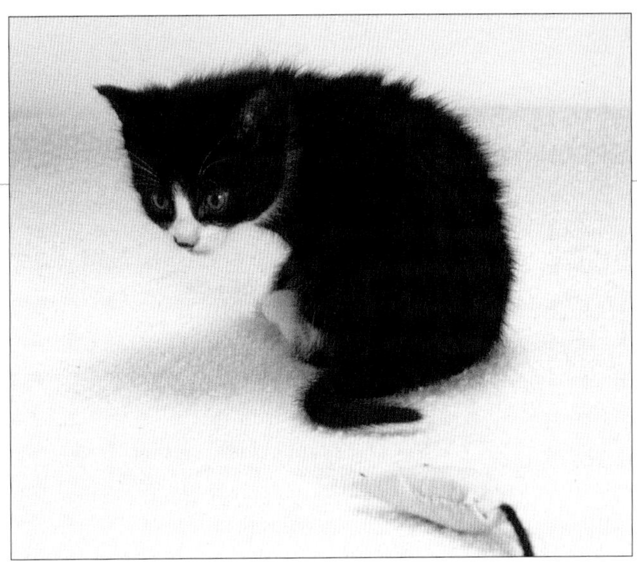

► *A kitten that is not interacting with its litter mates is a kitten in trouble. Place next to a teat to see if it will feed.*

New-born kittens need constant but non-evasive monitoring. Some mothers are uneasy if they are disturbed when nursing. Early observation is best undertaken from a distance or when she leaves the nest, either to eat or to relieve herself.

Healthy newborns should feel warm and have rounded bellies. They should suckle at least once every two hours and have a strong suckle reflex. Although they cannot walk, they are able to move around and find their mother or siblings. When not feeding, they will sleep quietly. During sleep, the kitten will appear to 'twitch'. This is a perfectly normal and healthy part of kitten development. These involuntary movements help the muscles and the nervous system develop correctly. They should also gain weight steadily. Weighing kittens twice weekly is important to ensure that this is happening and that they are thriving.

Unfortunately, not all kittens are strong and healthy. Statistics show that one in five will die in the early weeks. Sadly, some are just weak and may have a congenital defect. Newborn kittens are very fragile and not all can be saved, but prompt veterinary attention should be sought for any that are not following the normal pattern.

A kitten that doesn't seem to be able to hold on to a teat, and is constantly falling off and rolling away from the mother is a baby in trouble. Dehydration kills quickly. There can be many reasons for weak suckling including the possibility of a cleft palate. A kitten that is crying constantly may be hungry, cold or unwell. This is not normal behaviour and should be checked by a vet at the at the earliest opportunity. Providing the nesting area is kept clean, infections rarely occur in the site of the umbilical cord. Any stickiness or reddening in this area is an indication that all is not well and that antibiotics may be required.

Prior to eyes opening, check that this area is not swollen and that there is no discharge coming from the corner of the lids. A whiteish or yellow discharge should ring alarm bells and requires urgent veterinary treatment. Never try to prise the eyes open to have a look.

▼ *Healthy new-born kittens have a strong suckling reflex. A weak kitten will 'fall off' a teat easily.*

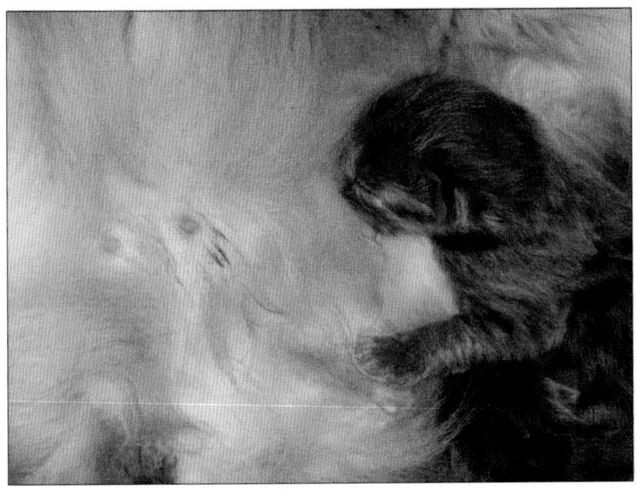

▼ *Kittens that are crying but active may be hungry. Check mum is able to feed them by gently trying to express a drop of milk*

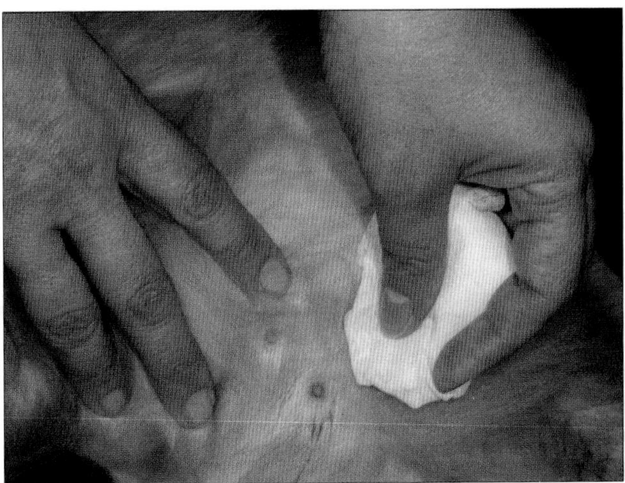

Hand-rearing kittens

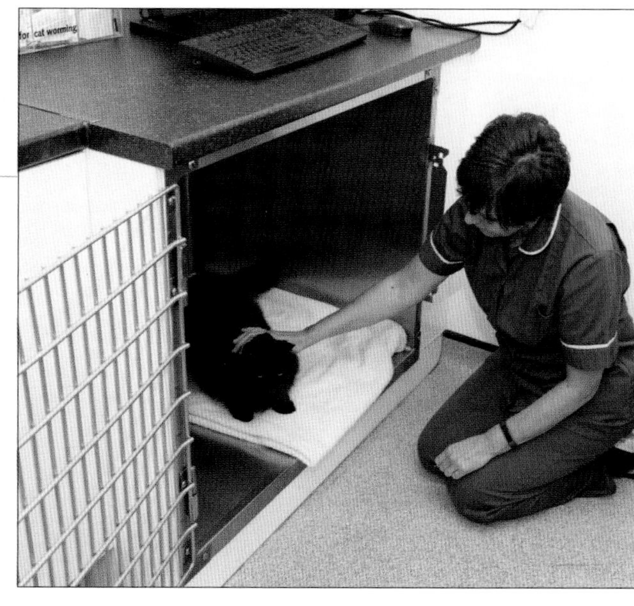

► *The majority of queens will be stressed to be separated from their kittens but there are times when this is necessary.*

There are many reasons why hand-rearing whole litters, or individual kittens, may be necessary. The mother might not have enough milk, or the litter is too large for her to cope with. Some queens are aggressive towards their kittens and may try to kill them or refuse to nurse them. The mother may have a medical condition and is either too unwell to nurse or be on medication that is unsafe for the kittens. The kitten itself may have a medical problem – either an illness or congenital defect such as a cleft palate. Hand-rearing is the only option if the litter has been abandoned, or if the mother has died.

Using a purpose-formulated milk substitute for kittens is essential. There are several on the market – your vet or an experienced breeder can advise you on this. Read the instructions carefully, work out how much you will need daily and divide this ration into the appropriate amount of feeds. Recipes for homemade substitutes are available but these are variable and may not provide all that a kitten needs. Kittens up to a week old should be fed every two to three hours, at two weeks of age this can be decreased to every three to four hours and at three weeks old, every four to five hours. This includes during the night as well.

Feeds can be administered via bottle and teat or by tube. Tube feeding is used when a kitten is very weak and unable to suckle. It is a skilled job and should not be attempted unless on the advice of a vet who will show you how to do it. Incorrect placement of the tube will result in the milk being discharged into the lungs. Bottles, kitten teats, bottle brushes etc., are readily available in pet shops and from your vet. Strict attention to hygiene is vital when feeding kittens. All equipment needs to be sterilized prior to use and cleaned immediately afterwards.

▲ *Vetbed bedding wicks moisture away from the top of the fabric to the base, leaving a dry surface to sleep on.*

▼ *The wise owner has kitten milk formula, feeding teats and bottles ready... just in case.*

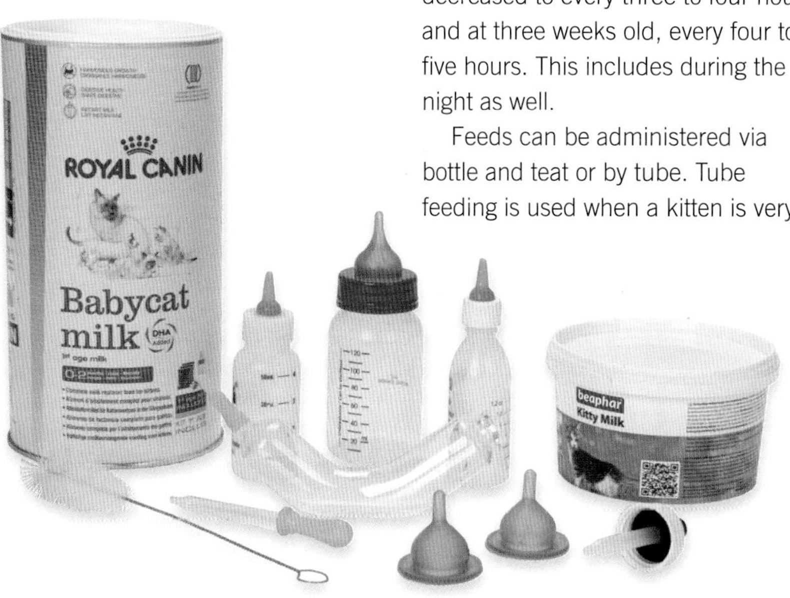

▼ *Some cats just do not make good mothers and completely abandon their offspring.*

▲ *Eyes should be discharge-free. Cloudy yellow or green discharge are signs of infection.*

► *Hand-reared kittens will need to be fed 10–12 times a day during the first two weeks.*

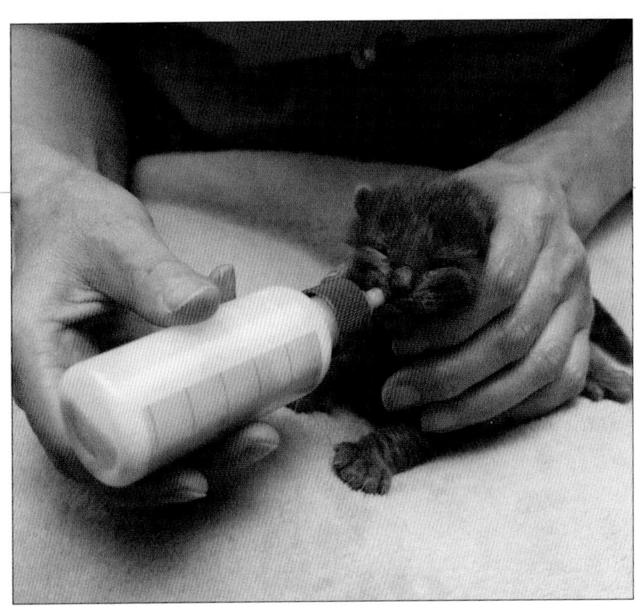

Hands must be carefully washed, and clothes clean, to prevent cross-contamination from other cats or animals. A loose cotton shirt, suitable to be worn over clothing and kept strictly for kitten feeding, is best.

FEEDING A KITTEN

Kittens should be fed when they are laying on their tummies, in a similar position as to how they would feed from their mother. Never force the milk down; allow the kitten to suckle at its own speed. Reluctant feeders can be encouraged by placing a small drip of formula milk on their lips, never into the mouth, or by experimenting with different teat shapes and sizes. The kitten may not take the full amount in one go, in which case leave for a short period and try again.

After feeding, the kitten will need to be burped, just like a human baby. While it is on its stomach, gently pat its back until you hear the burp. You may need to do this several times when feeding. After feeding, you must stimulate urination and defecation; kittens cannot do this themselves. Using cotton wool moistened with warm water, gently pat the anal area until the kitten relieves itself.

Kittens require a constant source of heat. The best way to do this is to heat the whole room. In the first week of life the optimum temperature is 29.5°C (85°F). This can be supplied by warm hot water bottles, checking that they are not too hot, or electric heat pads, if there is no alternative. Gradually reduce the heat by 5 degrees each week until a temperature of 21°C (70°F) degrees is reached.

Bedding can become a source of infection unless regularly changed. Blankets and material should not be used as it easily folds or wrinkles and kittens can get trapped underneath. Vetbed is ideal but if unavailable clean newspaper can be used.

The weaning process can begin when the kittens are three and a half weeks old. Gradually introduce solid food, initially presented as a soft mash. At this point, drinking water needs to be provided. Water bowls should be shallow so that the kitten can reach the contents, and small enough that it cannot get in and drown. Change water several times daily, ensuring it is always clean.

▼ *Clean the eye area with a cotton ball dipped in tepid water. Never use eye wash unless prescribed by a vet.*

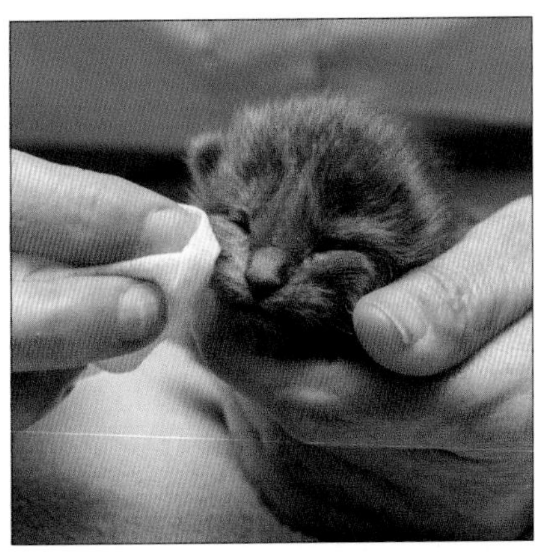

▼ *Use a damp cotton ball to stimulate a kitten to defecate and to keep the anal area clean.*

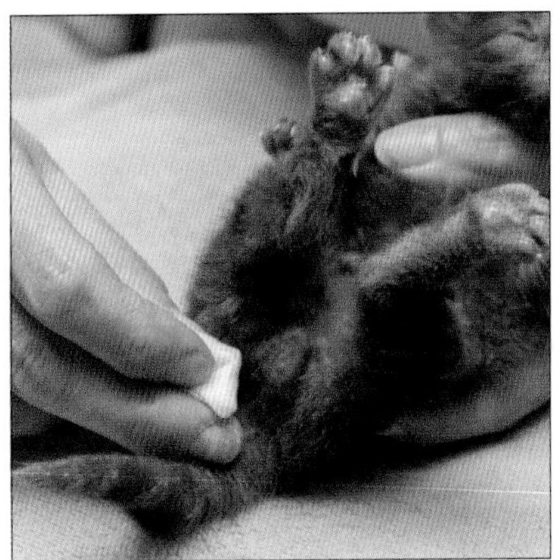

Growing up

If the litter is strong and healthy, the queen will require no assistance from you for the first two to three weeks. However, do change the bedding regularly (provided this does not upset the mother) and make sure the mother has plenty to eat: she may need three times as much as usual. The kittens' eyes open at around a week old and they will stop hissing at you every time you pick them up.

It is important to handle the kittens from the start. Encourage them to become used to the human voice and contact by picking them up and stroking them gently and regularly, and crooning to them. Experts used to advise that queens and their newborn kittens should be kept in a warm, dark, secluded place. However, this is just about the best way to make kittens nervous of people and activity. Once the kittens are weaned they can be introduced into the wider home environment and visitors, even if this is from within the sanctuary of a kitten pen. Social contact increases their confidence to tackle new situations when they leave home at 12–16 weeks of age.

▼ *Seven weeks old: these three look harmless enough, but at this age they will be learning to hunt and fend for themselves through play.*

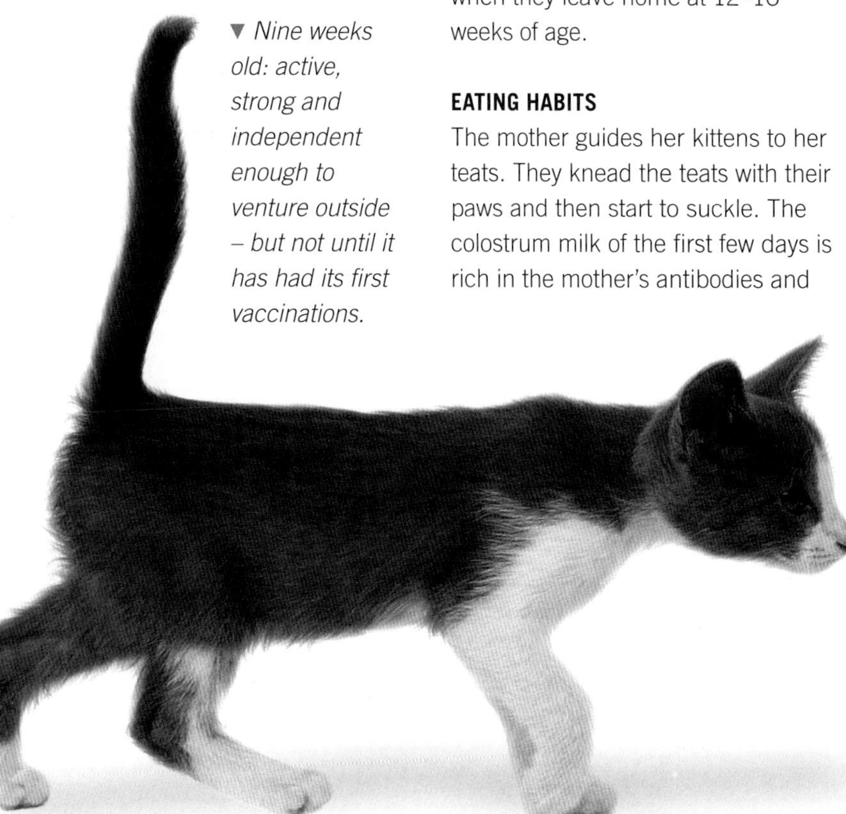

▼ *Nine weeks old: active, strong and independent enough to venture outside – but not until it has had its first vaccinations.*

EATING HABITS

The mother guides her kittens to her teats. They knead the teats with their paws and then start to suckle. The colostrum milk of the first few days is rich in the mother's antibodies and nutrients which protect the newborn kittens from infection. The kittens should be gradually weaned off their mother's milk. There is no specific time when this starts to happen, though they may begin to eat their mother's food at three to four weeks. It is not unusual for a kitten to remain on mother's milk for the first five weeks. Kittens must be fully weaned by 12 weeks, when they are ready to go to a new owner. They are actually capable of lapping water and of being on a solid diet by about six weeks.

The first solid food should be high-quality canned kitten food, finely minced cooked meat or poultry, or flaked white fish. Variety will encourage broad taste and good habits in later life as well as a balanced diet. Avoid dried food at this stage, and feed the kittens small quantities four to six times daily at three to four weeks of age, gradually reducing to three or four times daily from then on.

Until they begin eating solid foods, the kittens do not need to use the litter tray. The mother cleans them herself. You may find that the kittens simply copy their mother and use the tray

▲ *A Siamese mother shows her kitten exactly where, when and how to use the litter tray. It is unlikely that the kitten will need any extra training from its owner.*

without any help from you. If not, you can try placing the kittens in the tray immediately after each feed. The tray should be in a quiet spot where the floor and surroundings can be easily cleaned and disinfected. From this moment until the kittens leave to go to their new homes, your management of the environment is extremely important. Where there is a lack of hygiene, there is a risk of disease and infection. The kittens may also form bad habits which they will carry with them to a new home. Such a distressing situation would be a poor advertisement for a breeder.

Socialization is an important aspect of preparing a kitten for its new home. Potential purchasers have a strong preference for babies that are used to a range of noises and domestic activities.

▼ *Some are more interested than others in the prospect of solid food. One of these Siamese kittens may be reflecting on the warmth and comfort of its mother's breast.*

The basics of inheritance

Before you begin to breed from your cat, it is important to investigate her genetic inheritance and that of the stud you are mating her with. They are both the product of a vast number of generations of maybe 50 or more years of recorded breeding. A catalogue of cat show successes may also indicate a healthy genetic coding that a cat will pass on to their offspring. You can discover just how he or she acquired their particular colouring and characteristics, and work out what their kittens are likely to have.

◄ *In an attempt to breed out blue eyes in white cats, which seemed to coincide with a tendency to deafness, white cats were cross-bred with orange-eyed breeds. Sometimes the result was an eye of each colour.*

Quite how characteristics such as colour or pattern passed from one generation of cats to another was not understood until the second half of the 1800s. An Austrian monk called Gregor Mendel began to unlock the secrets of heredity and genetics in the 1850s, which made programmed breeding possible for the first time. Instead of random experimentation, breeders could select and cross-mate cats with the characteristics they wanted to promote and be passed on to the offspring.

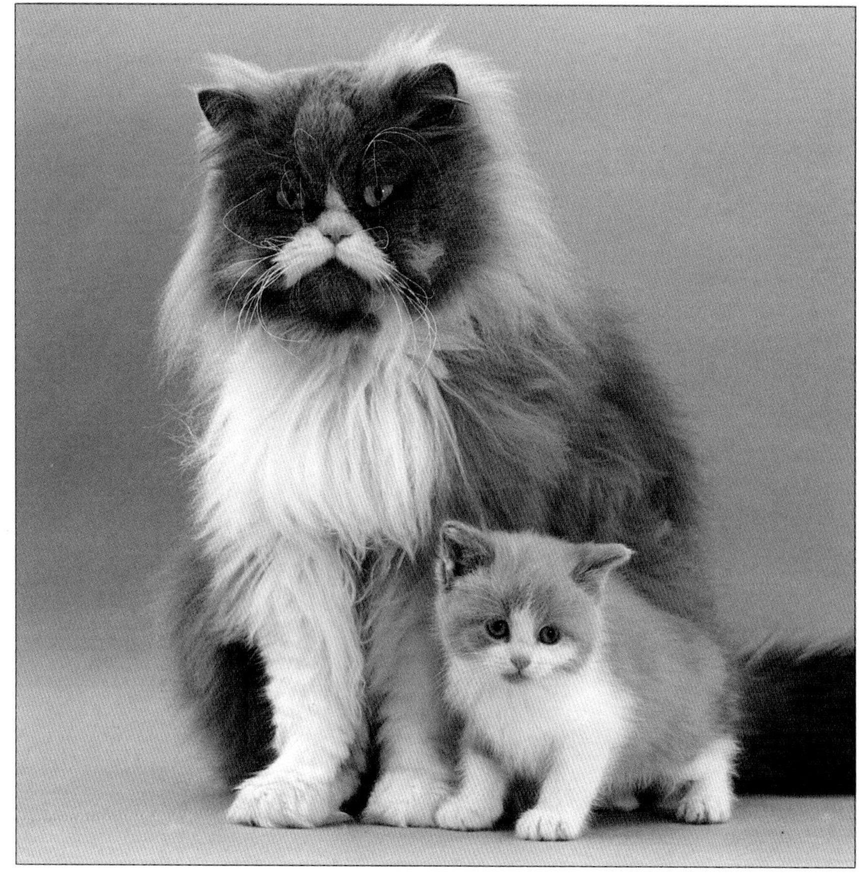

◄ *The blue colouring in a proud father – a Persian Blue Bi-colour – has diluted to lilac in his kitten.*

THE POWER OF THE GENE

The instrument of inheritance which controls particular features or behavioural traits is the gene. Genes are responsible for all inherited characteristics, from coat colour and pattern, length of tail or shape of ears, to health and character. A kitten inherits half of its genes from each parent. The arrangement of genes is different for each kitten in a litter, so each one is genetically unique.

There are certain genes carrying specific characteristics, such as the red gene, that can only be passed down through the generations by either a male or a female, but not both. These sex-linked genes are the reason why, for example, tortoiseshells are always female. A normal male cat cannot inherit both the red and the 'not red' gene.

Some genes are more powerful than others and are called dominant

▶ *The gene which causes folded ears in this Scottish Fold is dominant, but is a fairly recent mutation.*

genes. If one dominant colour gene and one recessive colour gene occur in a newly fertilized egg, the dominant gene determines the colour of the kitten. The recessive gene, however, could be passed on through several generations without coming out, or being expressed. Then, if it met up with a matching recessive gene, from the other parent, its particular gene characteristic would be expressed. What this means in cat terms is that there are certain dominant colour or pattern genes such as black or tabby, that override recessive colours and patterns such as blue or self. But at some point two black-coated parents may produce a blue or chocolate kitten and two tabby parents may produce a self kitten.

Sometimes the fundamental character of a gene is altered by an outside factor, such as radiation or other environmental situations. Japanese Bobtails and Manx cats both developed in isolated island communities which meant that they were forced to interbreed. A mutation gene occurred that resulted in the lack of a tail – which is, in fact, a malformation of the spine similar to spina bifida in humans. Some breeders have taken advantage of such mutations and developed new breeds from them. It is also true that a lack of socialization and introduction to the hurly burly of normal domestic life, which produces shy or nervous kittens, reflects poorly on the breeder.

▲ *In some breeds, polydactylism (excess number of toes) is a desirable trait and in others it is against the standard and thus a disqualification.*

▶ *Natural mutation has taken place in Manx breeds, probably as a result of enforced interbreeding on an island – in this case, the Isle of Man off the west coast of England.*

The art of selection

The colour range in a litter is determined by genes inherited from the parents, and whether those genes are dominant or recessive. Each kitten will inherit genes from both parents, but in a unique combination.

Genes are found in pairs. Black is dominant to chocolate and cinnamon, so a cat with one black gene will be black, whereas if it has no black genes it will be chocolate or cinnamon. Within this same pair, chocolate is dominant to cinnamon, so a cinnamon cat must have two cinnamon genes (a cat with one gene for chocolate and one for cinnamon will be chocolate in colour). The dilute gene, which dilutes the pigment of a cat from black to blue, chocolate to lilac, cinnamon to fawn, or red to cream, is recessive. In order for a cat to be a dilute colour it must have two dilute genes.

A tabby pattern is carried by the agouti gene which gives each hair a dark tip and alternate bands of light and dark colour. A non-agouti gene blocks the production of the light band in each hair, so producing a solid-coloured coat. White fur is the product of a gene which actually carries no pigmentation at all.

▶ *Top: Cinnamon is a recessive gene to black and is carried on the same gene locus as chocolate. Bottom: This Exotic Shorthair must be female as she is a tortoiseshell – a colour produced by the presence of one red and one 'not red' gene.*

Colour mutations

Black The first colour recessive mutation from the ancestral grey/brown agouti. Produces an extremely dark, solid colour perceived as black.

Chocolate Recessive gene to black creating a dark brown.

Cinnamon Recessive gene to black and chocolate. Carried on the same gene locus as chocolate, producing a light-brown colour with a warm (almost red-tinted) tone.

Orange Sex-linked gene (carried on the X chromosome, so females XX can have two such genes, males XY can have only one).This alters black, chocolate and cinnamon to an orange (red, auburn, ginger) colour. Females are not sterile.

Dilution Very often known as the 'blue' gene as the presence of the recessive dilution with black creates a grey (lavender-blue) individual. Also affects other colours. Alters the structure of the pigment cells.

Dilution + black = blue
Dilution + chocolate = lilac
Dilution + cinnamon = fawn
Dilution + orange = cream

Tortoiseshell The presence of the orange gene plus black and its recessive colours of chocolate and cinnamon creates the two-coloured tortoiseshell female, i.e. black, chocolate and cinnamon tortoiseshells. In combination with the dilution gene the pastel blue-cream, lilac-cream and fawn-cream are created. The rare occurrence of the tortoiseshell male is probably due to the presence of an extra X chromosome. The males are usually sterile.

Inhibitor Dominant and, as its name suggests, inhibiting – this gene reduces ground colour, e.g. the rufous colour of the brown tabby to the pewter ground of the silver tabby, or converting a self cat to a smoke.

Dilute modifier Dominant gene, the presence of which is still disputed. Creates a rather dull brownish-grey colour known as caramel. It has no effect on the dominant colours black, chocolate, cinnamon or red. It is to be found in several breeds of pedigreed cat.

Full colour and its recessives
Recessives to full colour are Burmese, Siamese, and blue-eyed and pink-eyed Albinos.

Burmese affects black, reducing it to a lustrous brown, or sable. In the Siamese cat, black becomes a warm-toned seal.

Albinos are almost completely lacking in pigmentation (the blue-eyed version) or entirely without pigmentation (the pink-eyed version). Both may be completely or incompletely light-sensitive. Extremely rare in cats, although a race of Albino Siamese was discovered in America.

Pattern mutations

Agouti The dominant ancestral pattern of the domestic cat in which the individual hairs of the coat are banded with colour. Normally light or grey at the roots of the hair with the darkest colour at the tip.

Tabby A range of pattern genes which is not seen unless in conjunction with the agouti gene or the orange gene. The mackerel tabby has thinly striped markings like those along the sides of the mackerel fish. The spotted tabby, in which the thin lines are broken down into clearly defined spots, may be a recessive to the mackerel tabby or created as the result of the effects of polygenes. Abyssinian or ticked tabby markings are reduced almost entirely or restricted to face, legs and tail. This is the dominant pattern.

Blotched, marble or classic tabby markings include a bulls-eye on each flank and further marbling of colour on an agouti-based ground colour. The gene causing this is recessive to the other forms of tabby marking.

Tipping or shading It seems likely that the fairly recently discovered wide band gene combined with the agouti gene affects the degree of colour shown towards the tip of each hair. The effect of the gene varies from the lightest of tipping, as seen in the chinchilla, to quite heavy shading, where as much as half the hair may be dark. This effect may be mimicked by a very heavily silvered smoke, although never to the lightness seen in the chinchilla. The presence of the wide band gene appears to be confirmed by the existence of the golden chinchilla or shaded cat, which is rufous with dark tips to the hair. The ground colour has not been inhibited.

White Dominant gene which covers all other colours in an 'overcoat' effect to create an all-white coat. In its pure form, in which all offspring produced are white, blue-eyed or odd-eyed cats, may well suffer from hearing loss, either partial or total. This is less likely to happen where one parent is white and the other coloured.

White spotting A dominant gene that results in areas of colour being suppressed by areas of white, creating the bi- or tri-coloured cat. White spotting can range from a few white hairs creating a chest mark or a spot on the belly, to an almost complete absence of colour. The van pattern suppresses colour to form flashes on the head and a solid-coloured tail, whereas the harlequin shows a more spotted pattern of colour on the body and legs as well.

Himalayan or Siamese A recessive gene in which the colour is restricted to the 'points' of the cat, these being the face (mask), legs and tail. This pattern is usually associated with intense blue eyes.

Burmese A recessive gene to full colour, but incompletely dominant to Siamese. The body appears to be a solid colour, though of reduced intensity.

Tonkinese A slightly pointed hybrid pattern created by a cross between Burmese and Siamese cats.

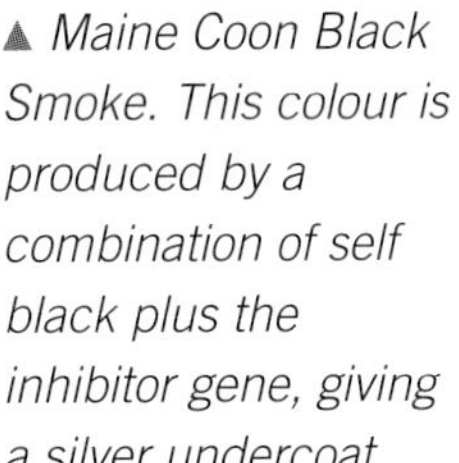

▲ *Maine Coon Black Smoke. This colour is produced by a combination of self black plus the inhibitor gene, giving a silver undercoat.*

▲ *A Siamese Blue Point has one black, two dilute and two Siamese genes. Selective breeding has reduced the incidence of squints and kinks in Siamese tails.*

▶ *An Oriental Classic Tabby has tabby markings on an agouti background.*

Coat quality and length

Shorthair Dominant gene restricting coat length. Strong guardhairs give impression of a crispness or sleekness of texture.

Semi-longhair Recessive gene basically producing a long-coated cat but with more noticeable length on neck, chest, rear legs and tail. Coat generally self-maintaining.

Longhair Produced by the same recessive gene as the semi-longhair, but bred to produce a coat of extreme length, softness/silkiness of texture and requiring much human intervention to maintain it.

Wirehair Dominant gene producing crimped, wiry, upstanding coat.

Rexed coat Recessive group of genes, not always genetically compatible, producing a mostly tightly curled, soft-textured coat.

Selkirk Rex coat Dominant gene which is the exception to the general Rex group, producing a shaggy, plush-coated cat.

Sphynx Recessive gene officially designated hairless but, in fact, producing a peach-skin-like coat which is quite different in quality and texture from the truly hairless individuals still sometimes produced in Devon Rex cats. A hairless cat produced by a dominant gene is seen in Russia.

▼ *A strange, curly kitten from Oregon proved, on first mating, to have a previously unknown dominant gene which gave it and its kittens curly hair.*

▼ *The recessive gene for hairlessness has been discovered and lost many times. When a hairless kitten was born in Canada, in 1966, breeders started to develop the breed known as Sphynx.*

▶ *A longhaired coat needs two recessive genes for long hair, but in Persians generations of selective breeding have lengthened the coat of the non-pedigreed longhair to the magnificent coat seen here.*

▶ *An ordinary ginger tom looks perfectly contented with his non-pedigreed lineage, and is probably allowed more freedom to roam than his high-bred equivalent would be.*

In recent decades, there has been an explosion in new cat breeds. Many of these involve the production of a cat that varies from what could be considered a standard domestic feline. There is much talk of mutant genes but these are not all necessarily bad. The definition of the word mutation means 'major or significant change'. Assuming we use, as a base line, an ancient landrace of cat, then almost all breeds are, in some way, mutants. In the wild those cats that carry a harmful or defective gene would die out. In the domestic situation, this is not automatically the case. Some cat breeds are so recent that it is not yet possible to totally analyze, and act on, any long-term health problems. The Scottish Fold is one such breed. The gene (Fd) that causes the ear to fold forward is also associated with bone and cartilage defects. Breeding two cats carrying this gene together was seen to cause severe osteochondrodysplasia. To avoid this, breeders only bred fold ear cats to those that were non-fold, believing this would avoid the problem. Unfortunately, it is now found that the progeny may still develop osteochondrodysplasia.

The Sumxu, or Chinese Lop Eared Cat, may have carried a similar gene, resulting in the ears folding completely over, like those of a spaniel, demonstrating that this is not a new phenomenon. Although there is documentary evidence to prove that this cat was in existence during the 1700s, the last known Sumxu died in

▼ *There is a 65–85 per cent chance of deafness in an all-white cat with two blue eyes, reducing to 40 per cent if only one eye is blue.*

▼ *Ragdoll kittens will grow into calm, good-natured adults that should adapt happily to an indoor lifestyle.*

▼ Calico-coloured cats are 25–75 per cent white with large orange and black patches. They are nearly always female.

▼ True black cats need to have both parents who are carrying the dominant black colour gene.

1938. There is, however, a taxidermy specimen of this extinct breed in a German museum, so it is possible that a DNA sample may be taken to assist breeders in the future.

Genetic variants influence more than just conformation, structure and looks. They also impact on reproduction and longevity. Again, this can be both good or bad. Some breeds are known for their large litter size or living to a good age. On the other side of the coin, the breeding together of two cats carrying a particular genetic mutation can result in unviable embryos or, in some cases, living offspring may be sterile.

CAT REGISTRY CONTROL

Cat registries are taking an active part in monitoring and safeguarding the genetic health and conformity of the breeds that they recognize. Good health is the overriding factor in breeding programmes. Most publish information, or run seminars, to help breeders make wise decisions when planning cat matings. They have worked hard to promote an understanding that a doubling up of good traits will also result in a doubling-up of the bad traits as well. Close matings, such as mother to son, father to daughter and full siblings to each other, is now frowned upon unless there is good reason. These matings are called 'line breeding' and at one time were extensively used in the belief that they would increase the likelihood of the positive aspects of a cat breed. In many cases restrictions have now been put in place to reduce the occurrence of line breeding. The Governing Council of the Cat Fancy requires the progeny of any of these matings to be placed on the non-active register.

▼ *The chance of deafness in blue-eyed cats decreases dramatically if the coat is not totally white.*

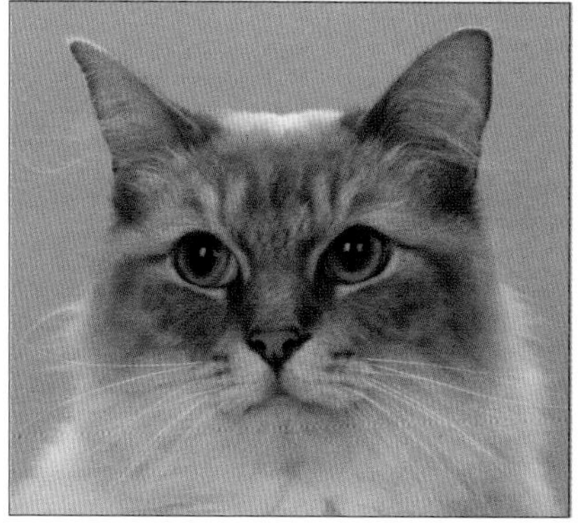

The offspring of cats on a non-active register are not eligible for registration. This action will prevent the inheritance of detrimental genetic traits in future generations. There are exceptions to this rule. These are strictly monitored and can only take place on the advice of a veterinary surgeon or genetic counselling and must be supported by the relevant Breed Advisory Committee (BAC) or Genetics Committee.

OUTCROSSING

Outcrossing is the opposite to line breeding and is where new genetic material is introduced into a breeding line. Often this involves introducing a cat of a different breed to improve the genetic health of another breed. This may be used to dilute a bad genetic aspect or to introduce a new trait into a breed. Outcrossing is a long-term project that requires knowledge and the breeding of several generations to assess the possible benefit to the breed.

▲ *Polydactylism is caused by an incomplete dominante gene. If one parent is polydactyl 40–50 per cent of the kittens will have extra toes.*

It is hard for a novice breeder to understand how a gene that produces one visible trait can also affect the overall health of an animal. This is the case in white cats. In a study that took place in 1997, it was found that 72% of white cats suffered from some form of hearing loss. This was seen to be more prominent in white cats with blue eyes. Interestingly, cats with one blue eye and one of another colour were more likely to be deaf in the ear on the side of the blue eye. It should be noted that not all white cats, or white cats with blue eyes, will suffer from hearing loss. Once this genetic trait was realised cat registries acted to help alleviate the problem. Since 1st June 2016, The Governing Council of the Cat Fancy requires certificated proof that any white cat, regardless of breed, has bilateral hearing for it to be placed on the active register.

DNA KITS

An interest in genetics, or the 'origin of your cat', is not solely restricted to owners and breeders of pedigree animals. Recently there has been increased curiosity from owners of mixed breed cats, and those that own a cat of unknown parentage, to understand which breeds make up their pet cats. It is now possible to buy online DNA kits that can tell you which race a cat shares most variants with. The kits cost around £95 ($130) each and are very simple to use. They contain a cytological brush, similar to a cotton wool bud, that is used to take a swab from the inside of the cheek. Once returned to the laboratory, a result will be obtained within a couple of weeks. Initially there was some doubt as to the authenticity of the outcome but, with an increase in companies offering this service, there is more certainty in the outcome.

▲ *If two wirehaired cats are bred together only part of the resulting litter will be wire-coated.*

Our understanding of genetics has come a long way since the early experiments of Gregor Mendel, but breeding is still a huge responsibility. All breeders must ensure that kittens are healthy and that new owners are not going to suffer the heartbreak that comes from owning a cat that is not vigorous in every aspect.

► *The LaPerm cat is genetically unique and so differs from the other curly coated cat breeds.*

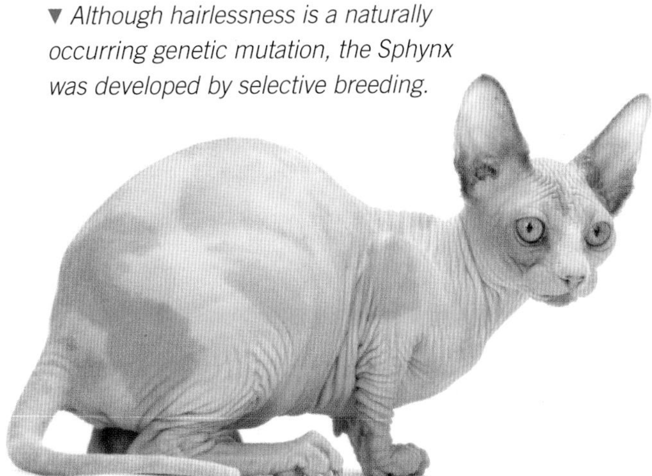

▼ *Although hairlessness is a naturally occurring genetic mutation, the Sphynx was developed by selective breeding.*

NATURAL CAT CARE

From ancient times it has been recognized that there is an intimate relationship between the activity and life of animals and their natural environment.

The Yellow Emperor's Classic of Medicine, 250BCE

We would all like to give our cats as natural life as possible and strive to achieve this goal with the living conditions we create for them, as well as the products that we buy for their care. But in reality if the cat was truly living naturally it would be hunting its own food, frequently increasing the feline population and suffering greatly, without veterinary intervention, if unlucky enough to receive an injury or illness. Clearly this is not what we want for our cat either. So, we have to learn to walk the middle line and explore all-natural possibilities as well as incorporating 'less natural' aspects of cat care when this is appropriate.

◄ *Kittens are genetically engineered to play as a preparation for hunting. Normally the mother would teach them this skill.*

Harmony and balance

Achieving harmony and balance is the goal of all natural healing therapies. All living organisms – whether human or animal – exist in an inter-dependent relationship with one another in nature. When this balance is disturbed, the result can lead to illness and disease.

CONVENTIONAL V HOLISTIC

Orthodox veterinary medicine is primarily concerned with treating physical symptoms of disease. Medical science is geared towards trying to understand in greater and greater detail how the physical body works, and there is now an incredible wealth of knowledge about the body's physical make-up and structure. This knowledge forms the basis of both human and animal medicine.

Science is reluctant to acknowledge the existence of things that cannot be measured. Because it is difficult to assess invisible emotional and psychological states, orthodox veterinary science largely ignores the effects of these when considering the health of an animal. Holistic medicine, on the other hand, whether for humans or animals, is not only concerned with the visible, physical body, but also with the intangible mental and emotional world of the patient. It maintains that true health is the harmony that is achieved when the mind, body and spirit are healthy and in a state of balance with one another.

Conventional scientific opinion is more prepared to accept those holistic therapies with a physical or medicinal basis than the invisible energy-based therapies, which often defy rational explanation.

A DEEPER LEVEL

Energy therapies are based on the idea that the body contains a subtle energy system, radiating out as an aura. Imbalances in this system create disturbances which first show up on a mental and emotional level before they become physical reality and disease. There is some evidence to suggest that the body may be surrounded by such a system.

◄ *A healthy cat is happy and alert. It is active, curious about its surroundings and reacts to all stimuli quickly and appropriately.*

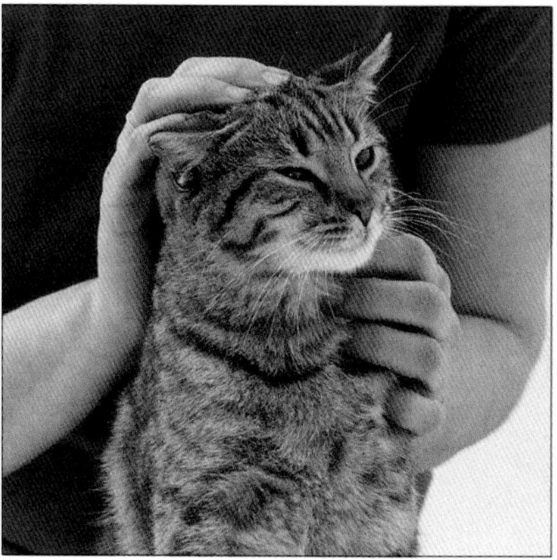

▲ *Cats enjoy being stroked behind the ears because the scent glands in this area anoint their owner.*

Kirlian photography demonstrates that the electromagnetic field of the body extends beyond its physical form. Some people believe this to be a reflection of the aura. Sequential images, taken during holistic sessions with human patients, show that the aura becomes more well-defined as the session progresses. Kirlian photographs taken of diseased and healthy parts of the body allow for a comparison of the auras, with diseased areas showing a weaker aura than healthy parts.

If we could measure the body's aura – to show when the body is working efficiently and alert us to imbalance and disease – magnetic vibrations could be fed back to the weak body, and a self-healing process could then be initiated.

DEFINING HEALTH

Western culture usually defines health in terms of soundness of the mind and body, and disease as its opposite: an illness of the body and/or the mind. Health and disease are defined in

▲ *Cats will enjoy being stroked by humans they trust, provided their independence is not compromised.*

terms of each other: good health is an absence of illness.

A holistic approach takes a different view. The distinction between health and disease is not so black and white, but is seen in terms of a continuum, with optimum health at one end of the scale and serious illness or even death at the other. Good health is regarded as a natural, balanced state of being, at one with the world. When this state is broken, a state of dis-ease is created in which mental and physical abnormalities can develop.

NATURAL LIFESTYLE

For animals and humans alike, the move towards increasing levels of health and vitality involves taking into account the environmental and lifestyle factors.

When you take a cat into your home as a pet, you artificially restrict its interaction with nature and the world. This means that you become responsible for making sure your cat can lead a healthy life. A cat's basic needs are very similar to your own. It requires a good, clean place to live and the right sort of food to eat. It needs enough exercise to keep its body fit and healthy, and it needs protection from any form of prolonged or excessive stress. Most importantly, your cat needs to be treated in a kind and loving way. Emotional contentment is recognized universally as the foundation for good health and resistance to disease. This section is designed to help you achieve that state for your cat.

▼ *In spite of all our efforts to domesticate it, the cat remains close to nature, and it enjoys the opportunity to walk by itself in open countryside.*

Holistic medicine

The approach taken by the medical profession, and by veterinary specialists, is based on the scientific method of examining the world in order to understand it. A patient's symptoms are examined in minute detail, sometimes to the exclusion of everything else. Drugs are selected for the effect that they have on the system, organ or tissue that is thought to be causing the illness. The problems that the drugs may inadvertently cause in other parts of the body are accepted as inevitable side effects which have to be tolerated. All patients are treated in the same way and are expected to respond to treatment in a similar fashion, with little allowance made for individuality.

A holistic approach is more broadly based and endeavours to treat the patient (human or animal) and their unique needs, rather than the disease itself. Emotional, mental and physical characteristics all have a part to play in the development of illness and these are taken into account during treatment. One of the main difficulties in transferring a holistic approach from humans to animals is that an animal cannot tell you what it feels or thinks. If you are interested in complementary treatment for your cat, you need to pay close attention to its behaviour and notice any marked changes or mood swings. The vet and any other practitioners involved will be relying on you in much the same way as a doctor treating a young child relies on its parents for information.

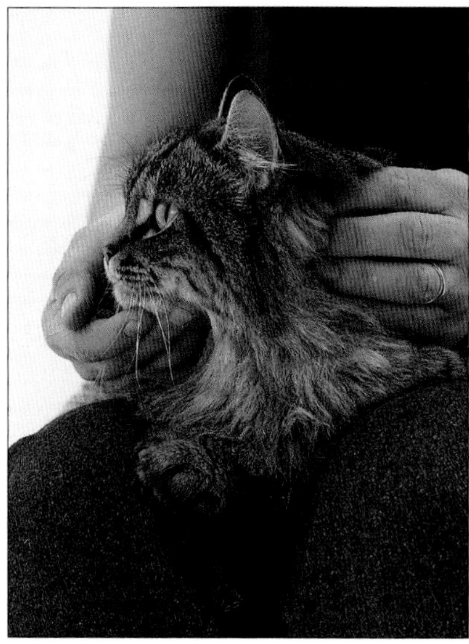

▲ *A quiet moment spent stroking your cat can be beneficial when minor strains occur.*

Sometimes, a course of treatment using only one method or therapy will not prove to be totally effective. In such a case, you or the vet may suggest trying other approaches. It is important that the vet and other therapists involved in the case talk to each other and explain how their treatment works and how it interacts with any other treatment: aromatherapy can inhibit the action of homeopathic remedies, for example, while massage is compatible with all therapies.

The prime concern of any form of veterinary care is how it will affect the quality of the animal's life. The holistic approach does not ignore conventional science but tries to work alongside it. Natural forms of treatment can promote wellbeing in a healthy cat and can be used in order to alleviate the distress of illness, but if modern drugs are needed for chronic cases of disease then they should be given.

In the past, holistic medicine and therapies were often labelled as

▲ *The sensitivity of cats enables them to respond well to the gentle Bach Flower remedies.*

◄ *A sick cat will instinctively be attracted to the aromatherapy oil that can help it when unwell.*

▲ *Some herbs are a healthy addition to a cat's diet, but others are toxic. Take advice before adding to the meal.*

▼ *Massage beneficially stimulates muscles, circulation, nerves and the lymphatic system.*

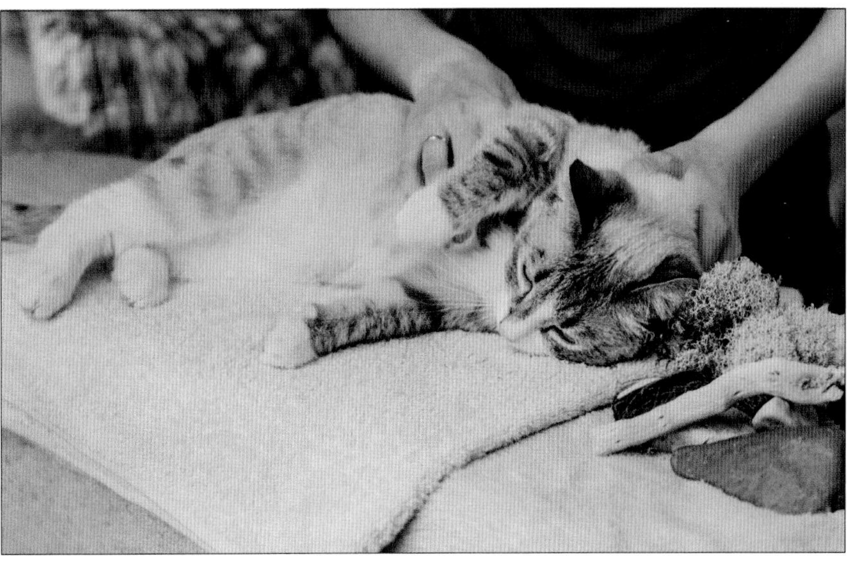

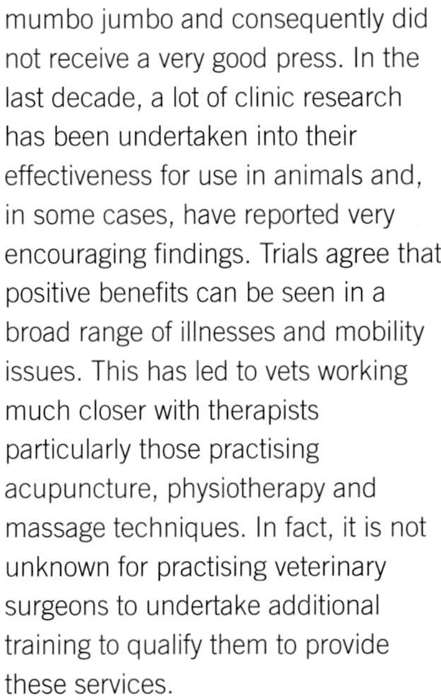

mumbo jumbo and consequently did not receive a very good press. In the last decade, a lot of clinic research has been undertaken into their effectiveness for use in animals and, in some cases, have reported very encouraging findings. Trials agree that positive benefits can be seen in a broad range of illnesses and mobility issues. This has led to vets working much closer with therapists particularly those practising acupuncture, physiotherapy and massage techniques. In fact, it is not unknown for practising veterinary surgeons to undertake additional training to qualify them to provide these services.

If you decide to follow the holistic approach for your cat some caution is advised. In every walk of life charlatans abound and qualifications vary. Your vet will be able to recommend trusted practitioners in some of the aspects of holistic medicine. Many countries have a governing body of homeopathic vets. They will be able to provide you with contact details for services in your neighbourhood. Alternatively, your own vet may choose to refer your pet to a veterinary practice that specializes in homeopathic or holistic treatments.

Beware of adverts selling homeopathic medication on the internet. Never use these products without express permission from your vet or holistic practitioner. Some so-called cures are not what they seem and could be, quite simply, unsafe to use. It is never wise to self-prescribe, for either yourself or your pet, and in some cases, is illegal.

The holistic approach covers every aspect of life and this includes diet, fitness and wellbeing. There is much that an owner can do to embrace this. Monitoring weight, activity levels and stress in their pet can help prevent illness and distress. Simple activities such as checking that a bed is comfy and draught-free or that a cat is able to reach its drinking water are all holistic actions. Owners may like to consider learning animal massage techniques for use on their own cat. This is an aid to relaxation and encompasses overall wellbeing.

► *Touching noses is a way of sharing scents and shows that both cats are on an equal social footing.*

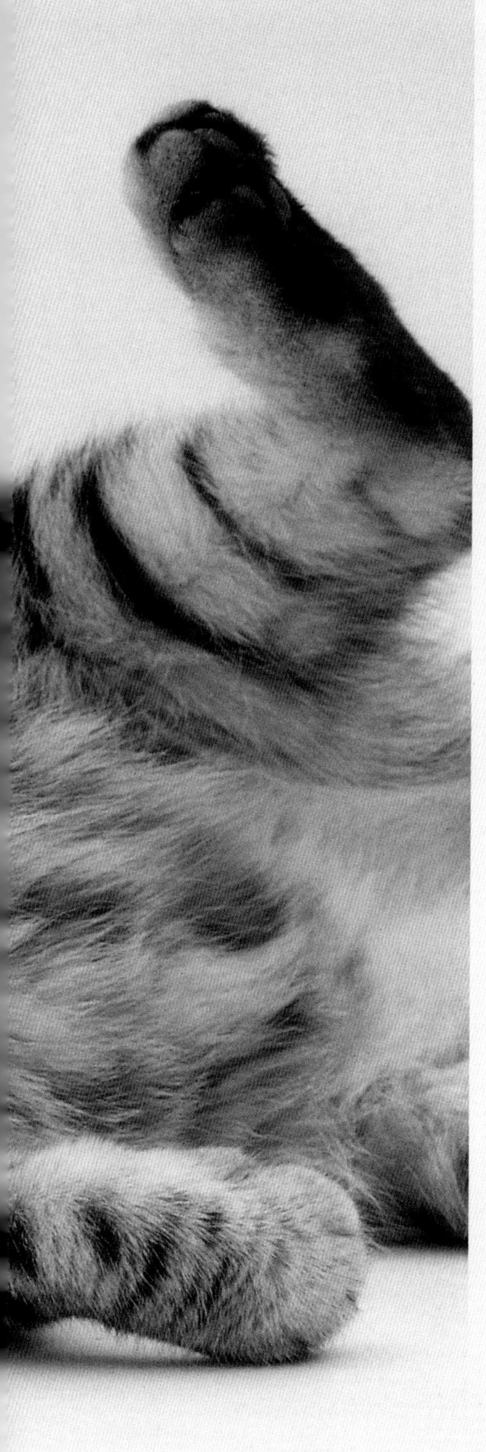

HOLISTIC THERAPIES

When internal energies are able to circulate freely, and the energy of the mind is not scattered, but it is focused and concentrated, illness and disease can be avoided.

The Yellow Emperor's Classic of Medicine, 250BC

Holistic therapies are also referred to as alternative therapies. Many have been practiced for thousands of years, particularly in the Far East. Despite this, until relatively recently, they have been treated with an element of suspicion in the West. Of late there has been a change of attitude and holistic treatments have become a more popular choice. Many vets now offer acupuncture, physiotherapy, massage and chiropractic treatment as standard. Even if these services are not available in the surgery, vets are happy to refer owners to tried and trusted practitioners nearby.

◄ *Holistic treatments can be wonderful aids to promoting or restoring health. Equally they can be potentially dangerous if incorrectly used.*

An alternative view

The basic philosophy underlying holistic medicine is a concern for the living totality of the patient. Its aim is to treat the patient as a whole and not the disease in isolation.

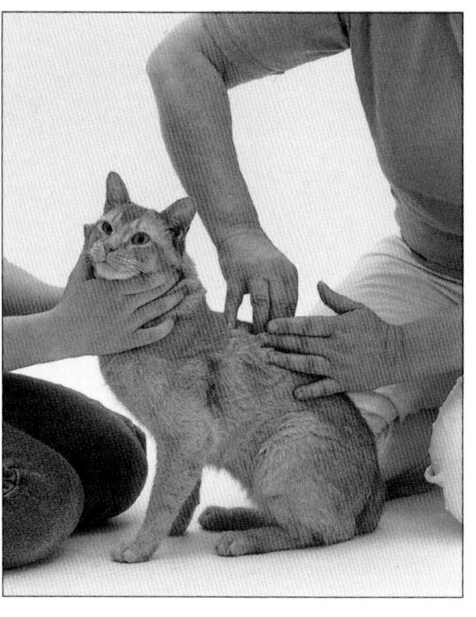

▲ *Osteopathic and chiropractic manipulation can help back and limb problems.*

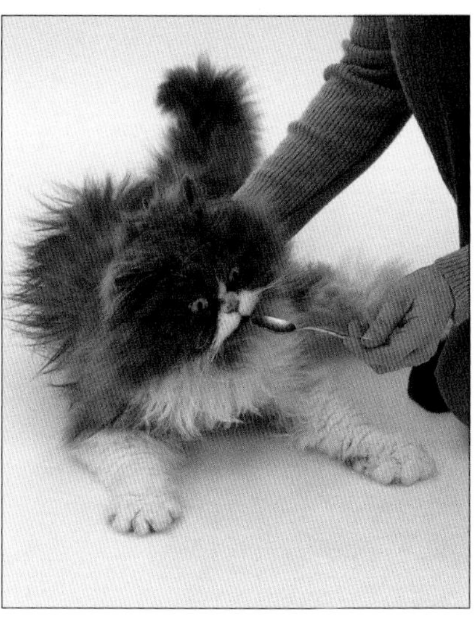

▲ *Homeopathic remedies can usually be given easily to cats, and can be helpful for injuries and chronic disease.*

THE WHOLE CAT

Holistic treatment is not aimed at the cause of infection or the suppression of symptoms, but at all aspects of the cat's life, including its mental and emotional state, co-existing physical complaints, lifestyle stresses and nutritional status. Western medicine looks for the name of the disease (the diagnosis) and for the one correct treatment to cure the symptoms. Holistic medicine looks at a wider concept of dis-ease. It recognizes that a number of treatments may be needed, from simple lifestyle changes to surgery and conventional medicines. It also accepts that therapies that cannot be explained by science can affect the whole organism, and are often needed to achieve a cure.

WHERE TO GET TREATMENT

In human medicine, there are now many holistic clinics where patients are treated by teams of therapists under the supervision of a doctor. In the veterinary field, things are not so sophisticated. There is a growing number of veterinary practices worldwide offering holistic therapies, but the range of services available is still very limited.

There are also legal restraints in holistic practice for animals. The law recognizes that humans understand the risks involved in seeking non-medically qualified treatment. Because an animal is incapable of assessing risk, the treatment of disease in animals is restricted to veterinary surgeons only. Vets are allowed to work alongside qualified, animal-trained physiotherapists, osteopaths and chiropractors, but the more esoteric therapies can only be carried out by the cat's owner, or by vets who are suitably qualified – and of these there are very few.

If you wish to use holistic therapies on your cat, discuss the matter first with your vet. This way, any essential conventional care can be given before a holistic treatment plan is worked out between you.

▼ *The most used alternative therapy for animals is acupuncture. It is considered very beneficial for cats.*

▲ *Taking care of your cat or kitten means providing it with the lifestyle that suits its needs. Start this approach early in your cat's life and you should be rewarded with a lively, healthy pet*

THERAPIES FOR CATS

Of the therapies suitable for cats and other animals, homeopathy and acupuncture are the most common. These are complete systems of medicine, and each has its own philosophy. Both see disease as an imbalance of energy. Homeopathy recognizes a 'vital force' in the body which attempts to keep the body in good health. Disease is seen as a disturbance of that force, and the symptoms as the body's attempt to regain equilibrium. Homeopathy believes that problematic lifestyle circumstances may predispose us to disease, and that these must be eliminated if a true cure is to result.

Acupuncture is a branch of Traditional Chinese Medicine (TCM). This system sees energy as flowing round the body along channels known as meridians. Disease occurs when this energy flow is disturbed. Stimulation of specific points on the body's meridians restores balance to the system and health to the body.

Ayurvedic medicine is an Indian holistic system with its own philosophy of disease. It recognizes a flow of energy, which it calls prana through channels known as nadis. The major nadis have energy vortices or chakras. Treatment is based on herbal medicine and diet. Ayurvedic medicine is far less common in the Western world than acupuncture and homeopathy.

Complementary therapies which work at the energy level include the Bach Flower remedies and crystal therapy. The Bach Flowers are chosen on the basis of the cat's emotional state. Crystal therapy attempts to use the energy given off by crystals to restore balance to the energy field of the body. Other widely practised holistic therapies include herbalism, aromatherapy, massage, physiotherapy, osteopathy and chiropractic. Orthodox science, in general, is more ready to accept therapies with a physical basis.

If you wish to use holistic therapies on your cat, discuss the matter first with a vet.

Pharmaceuticals

Even when adopting a holistic approach to health, conventional Western medicine has its place. Acupuncture, herbalism and homeopathy are complete systems of medicine in their own right, but this does not necessarily mean that these systems are equally effective 100 per cent of the time. Each individual is unique, with their own particular response to treatment. Every cat will respond in a different way to the same treatment. Complementary treatments can and do work, and sometimes they will effect a complete cure. There are also times, however, when modern medicines are needed, forming part of an approach using a well-chosen combination of several therapies.

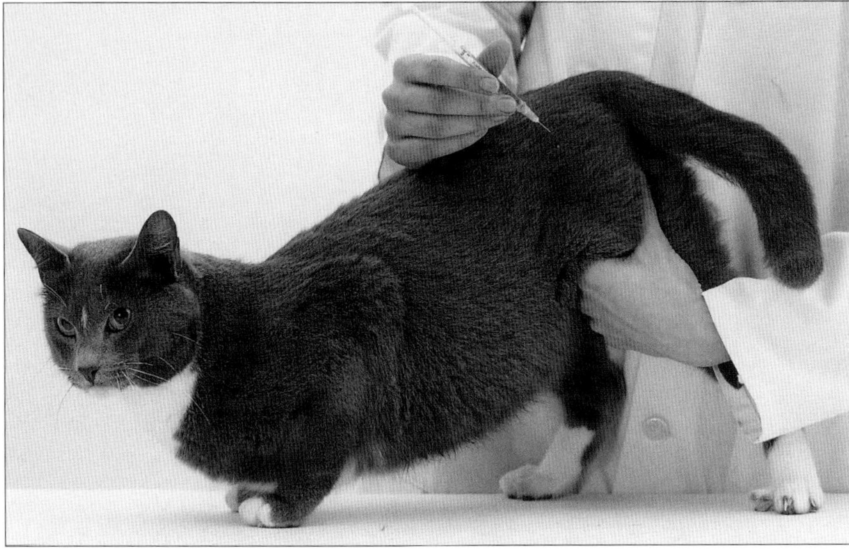

▲ *Injections are given into the muscles of the front of the thigh to avoid the nerves and blood vessels, which are situated towards the back.*

WHAT ARE PHARMACEUTICALS?

Many modern medicines are derived by isolating the active ingredient found in herbal medicines. Having isolated and identified the chemical structure of the active ingredient, attempts are then made to synthesize medicines that have a similar structure and a stronger action. These tend to have more pronounced side effects as well. The first antibiotic, penicillin, was isolated from a fungal culture. Since then, other natural antibiotics have been found, and synthetics based on the chemical structure of the natural products have been manufactured. However, the side effects of synthetic drugs usually become more serious as new generations of antibiotics are developed. Scientists have also manufactured synthetic hormones and vitamins, but some of these are less effective than the natural product.

HOW THEY WORK

Modern Western medicine is based on an accurate diagnosis. After the illness has been correctly identified and named, the aim is to find and administer the best medicine which will hopefully cure the condition. It is worth noting that some medicines can have more than one, simple action in the body. Unwanted actions are the side effects of the drug. When medicines are given in short courses of small doses, the body is able to correct any damage which may have been done, inadvertently, by the medicine whilst it heals the disease it was sent to cure. In chronic disease, where medicines are given over long

◄ *Pharmaceutical preparations come in many forms. They are standardized so that every dose should have the same effect on every patient.*

► *If you tickle your cat's throat when giving tablets or medicine, it will encourage the cat to swallow.*

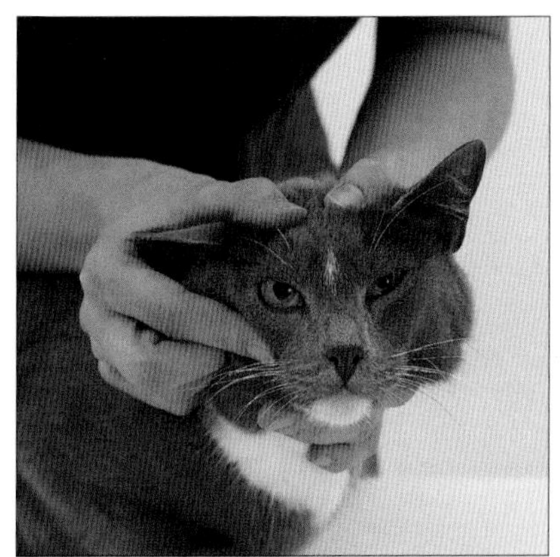

► *Hold your cat's eyes open with gentle pressure of your thumb and forefinger, so that you can put drops in accurately.*

► *Hold the cheekbones with one hand, tilt the head back and pull down gently on the jaw: the cat's mouth will then open.*

periods of time, the side effects can overcome the body's ability to deal with them. The original natural disease is now worsened by medicine-induced disease. It might be argued that chronic disease is itself an indication that medicine has not brought about a cure but has simply suppressed the original symptoms, thereby giving a false impression of a cure.

WHEN TO USE PHARMACEUTICALS

Modern medicine is at its best in cases where the cat has a mineral or hormonal deficiency. Injections or tablets will replace the missing nutrient or hormone, although dietary changes will be needed to prevent a recurrence. For example, in diabetes, which is becoming increasingly common in cats, replacement of the necessary hormone with insulin injections will correct the deficiency and restore normal glucose metabolism. Properly supported by an appropriate complementary therapy, the amount of insulin needed can be reduced, and sometimes the need for replacement therapy disappears altogether.

In acute bacterial infections, antibiotics are very useful, but good complementary medicine, used alongside the drugs, will often allow the use of shorter courses of antibiotics than would otherwise be needed. Such a holistic approach will reduce the number and the severity of the side effects experienced by the cat. It will speed convalescence and correct the weakness that allowed the infection to occur in the first place. Steroids are useful when your cat has a severe inflammatory condition (they should only ever be used in short courses) but good complementary support used alongside antibiotics can provide similar benefits without the need for steroids. With certain cancers, chemotherapy is a valid treatment, although its extremely painful and distressing side effects can be reduced if a sensible holistic treatment plan is used in support.

Modern medicine has a genuine place in the treatment of disease. Ideally, however, it would form just one part of a holistic approach to your cat's health.

Massage

Massage is probably one of the oldest and simplest therapy techniques of all. When a child hurts itself, a parent's instinctive reaction is to 'rub it better'. In the womb, the skin develops from the same cell layer as the nervous system and the two are closely connected. This may explain why massage calms the mind as well as the body.

POSITIVE EFFECTS

Cats, in general, like to be rubbed, stroked and massaged, and will often seek out their owners for this kind of attention. A cat will convey pleasure by purring and kneading its claws. When you massage your cat, you are establishing a non-verbal communication that conveys an attitude of loving care. This strengthens the bond that exists between you and your pet, and increases trust. The resulting feeling of harmony is not only physically soothing, but it will promote mental and emotional strength which will help to guard the cat against disease.

Massage has many beneficial effects on the physical body. By stimulating the circulation, it relaxes the muscles, helps to balance joint action and muscle function, and speeds the dispersal of scar tissue. The improved circulation also speeds up the rate at which the lymphatic system detoxifies the body. Finally, massage will increase the production of the body's natural painkillers (endorphins), which optimize a feeling of wellbeing. The act of giving a massage can also help to reduce the stress and blood pressure levels of the masseur, in addition to the effect on the patient.

A BASIC ROUTINE

Begin with a few long, gentle strokes of even pressure along the body and limbs, in the same direction as the hair growth. The strokes should be slow and rhythmic and will help to relax the cat. They also allow you to locate any tender spots. Lubricants are not normally necessary. If lubrication is needed, use baby powder and not one of the vegetable-based oils used in human massage. Oils make the fingers slide too quickly over the skin for the massage to be effective. They are also very messy on fur, and will penetrate easily into the skin, which in a cat is highly absorbent.

Cats are private, sensitive creatures who do not like attention forced on them, and they may be suspicious of your first attempts at massage. If this is the case, do not persist, but stop as soon as the animal indicates that it has had enough.

If the cat allows it, increase the pressure of each stroke and change the direction towards the heart to stimulate venous and lymphatic drainage. Ideally, the massage should start at the feet and move upwards towards the head. Cats which

When to use massage

Massage is an aid to keeping a healthy cat fit. It should not be used on sick cats unless they have first been checked by a vet. Do not use in cases of acute muscle injury or severe joint pains, or where the skin is damaged or infected. Don't use massage if the cat has recently had a high temperature and is recovering from an acute infection, or if it is known to have high blood pressure. If you are in any doubt at all, consult a vet.

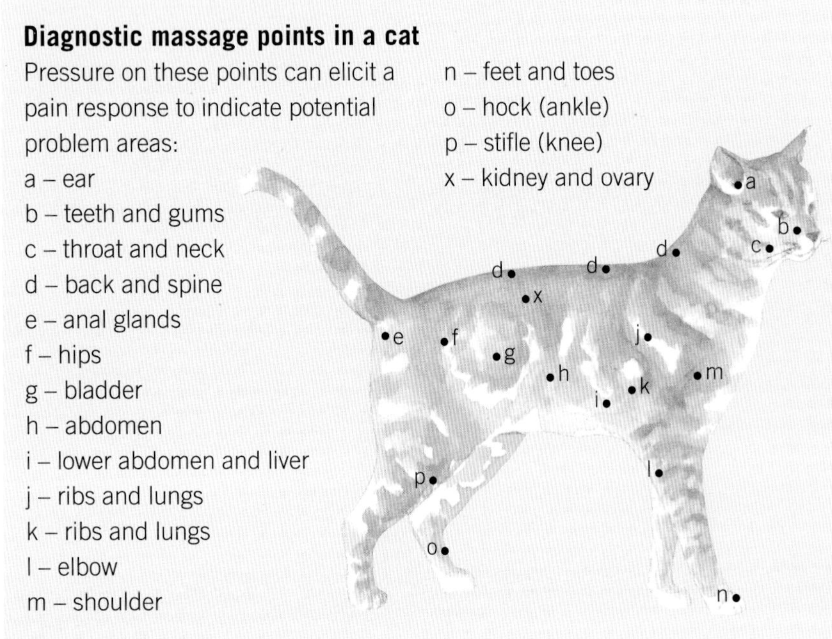

Diagnostic massage points in a cat

Pressure on these points can elicit a pain response to indicate potential problem areas:

a – ear
b – teeth and gums
c – throat and neck
d – back and spine
e – anal glands
f – hips
g – bladder
h – abdomen
i – lower abdomen and liver
j – ribs and lungs
k – ribs and lungs
l – elbow
m – shoulder
n – feet and toes
o – hock (ankle)
p – stifle (knee)
x – kidney and ovary

have particularly sensitive feet may resent having them handled. In this case, start the massage at the head and work down the body, stroking upwards all the time.

If you can start at the feet, massage slowly and gently, putting your fingers in the spaces between the toes. Then use your fingers to massage the legs, upwards towards the body, beginning just above the paw. If the cat will allow it, get it to roll over and massage its tummy, using a circular motion. If not, turn your attention to its back and chest, using your palms, if possible, or your fingers. Starting at the tail-end and using circular movements, massage along one side, working forwards to the head, before moving to the other side.

Never massage directly on to the spine. Instead, use your fingertips on the muscle groups on each side, where muscle trigger points may exist. These points cause the surrounding muscles to contract or go into spasm as a protective reflex. The bands of tight muscle can be felt with skilled fingers. They should be lightly massaged so as to reduce the reactivity of the point and relax the tight muscles. Firm finger pressure on the point itself can deactivate it, but any vigorous massage can increase pain.

Finally, move to the head and neck. You can massage all parts of the head, including around the eyes, nose, mouth and ears. Touch gently with your fingertips, paying particular attention to any region that seems to give the cat extra comfort. The neck should be treated as an extension of the back, and massaged on each side of the spine. End the sequence with a few light strokes from head to tail.

SIMPLE MASSAGE

Cats are tactile creatures and usually enjoy receiving the attention that goes with a massage. The experience may bring therapeutic benefits to you as well, and a regular massage will help to strengthen the bond between you and your cat. Add the massage to the end of the daily grooming session.

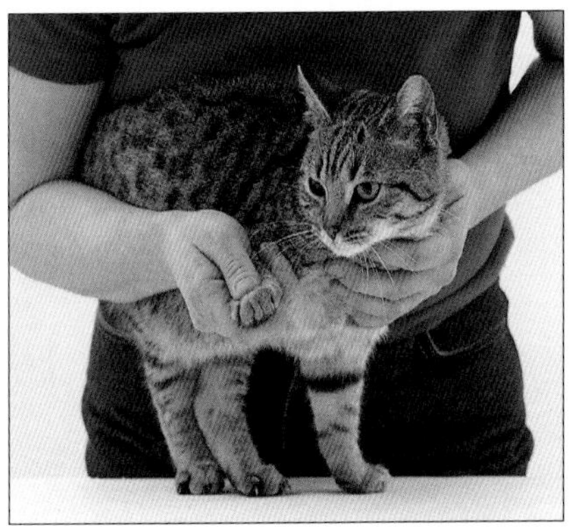

1 Try to start with the cat's feet and legs. This will stimulate the flow of blood and lymph back to the heart. Be smooth and gentle, and work carefully into the spaces between the cat's toes.

2 Work up the hind legs to the hip and up the front legs to the shoulder. Keep the movements firm but smooth, using your fingers or palm.

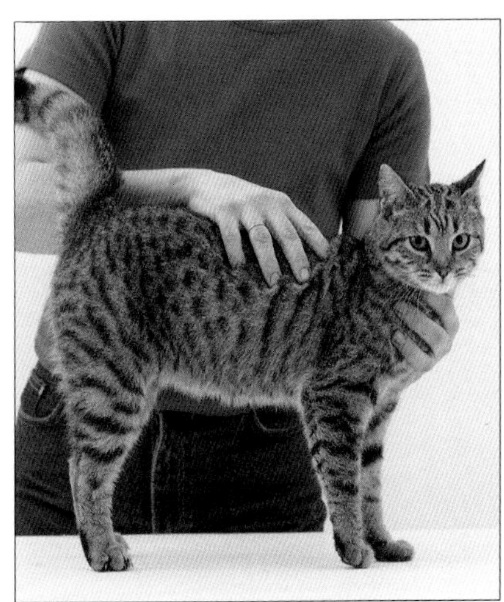

3 The back muscles often contain trigger points that cause the surrounding muscles to go into a reflex spasm. Any tight band of muscle should only be massaged lightly to help relax it; vigorous massage will increase the contraction and cause pain.

4 End the session with gentle strokes over the whole head area. This part of the session is usually greatly enjoyed by the cat.

Physiotherapy

This therapy supplements the medical and surgical treatment of conditions that have a major impact on the musculoskeletal, or locomotor, system and the circulation. It plays an important part in mainstream medicine and is also a vital component of holistic medicine.

◄ *Stroke your hands down the cat's back to relax your pet with a massage. Relaxation of the damaged area will encourage the reduction of swelling, pain and tension.*

WHAT IS PHYSIOTHERAPY?

Physiotherapy aims to regain the strength and full range of movement of an injured area by manual manipulation or by a series of controlled exercises. It can help to control pain, speed up healing, and preserve the function of injured tissue. It can be used alongside surgery, pharmaceutical medicines and all complementary therapies. Veterinary physiotherapy is routinely performed on professional sports animals, such as racehorses and greyhounds, and is slowly becoming more widely used in general veterinary practice.

Simple massage may be tried by owners as self-help treatments at home. However, the more specialist physiotherapy techniques can inflict further injury if misapplied, and these should only ever be used by a qualified physiotherapist.

HOW IT WORKS

Treatment is achieved by manual manipulation or by a series of controlled exercises. The treatment is supported by the use of cold and heat, electrical stimulation and laser therapy. It is particularly useful with cats who have been involved in severe road traffic accidents, although in general cats are not used to being exercised and will not tolerate much in the way of manipulation.

The therapeutic use of coldness is applied as quickly as possible after an injury, in the form of a cold compress to reduce the seepage of blood and other fluids into the surrounding tissue. This will also decrease muscle spasms and reduces nerve pain. A plastic beaker filled with water and frozen, or a packet of frozen vegetables, could both be used at home as a cold compress on large areas and surgical wounds. The compress should be used 2–4 times a day, for up to 20 minutes at a time.

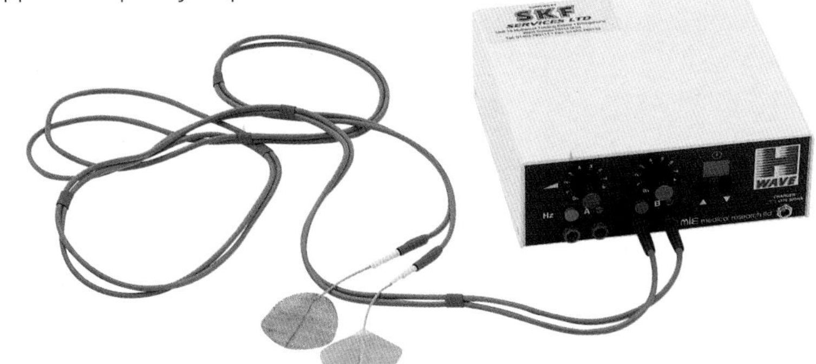

▲ *The H Wave machine passes warm currents of heat to the injured area to energize the tissue and encourage relaxation. As the muscle tissue relaxes, tension is released and pain is reduced.*

▼ *Lasers uses light energy to stimulate tissue circulation in muscle. Increasing the circulation relaxes muscle tension, to speed healing.*

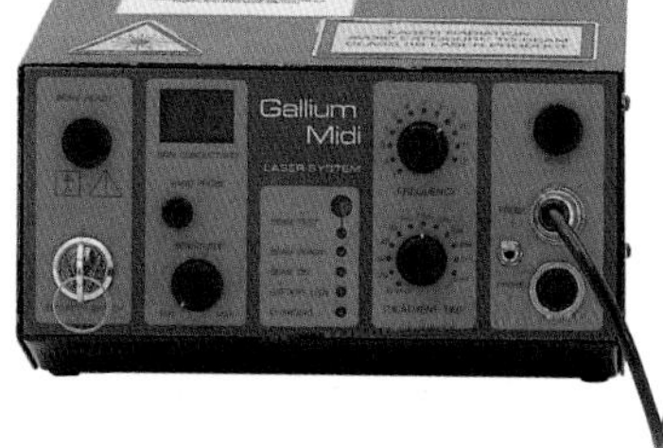

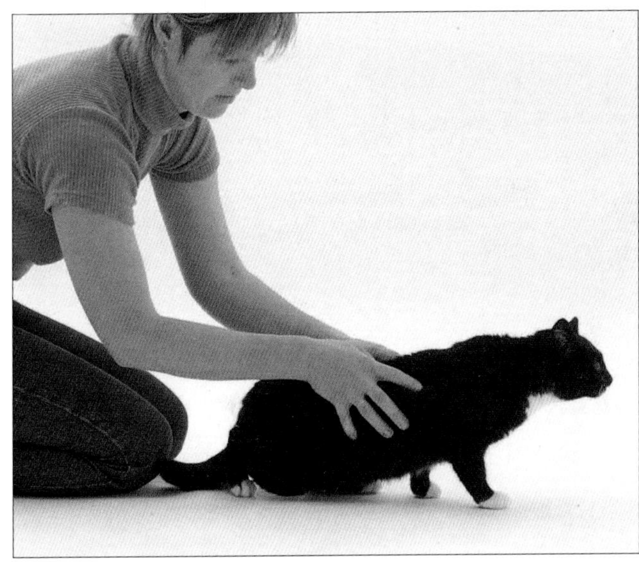

◀ *Pressure point work, using the thumbs, can be done at home. Work on musculature to relieve pain and tension by enhancing the blood circulation.*

Therapeutic warmth is used 72 hours after an injury to increase blood circulation in the damaged tissue. Warmth also helps to remove waste products and increases nourishment of the area, speeding up the healing, and relieving tension and pain.

Electrical stimulation has a variety of benefits. Special equipment can be used to help with pain relief and to stimulate muscle contractions. The latter can help to counteract muscle wastage, reduce spasm pains and increase muscle strength. It can also improve blood flow in damaged tissue and where there are certain forms of circulatory disease. This aids healing.

Ultrasound is used to provide heat therapy by using the energy of ultrasonic vibrations to warm the tissues beneath the skin, which helps to increase the amount by which scar and other fibrous tissue can stretch. This allows the remodelling of scar tissue and helps to reduce the amount of scar tissue that does form. It can also help to deactivate painful muscular trigger points when used by trained operatives. Ultrasound treatment must never be used after exercise: it can have the opposite effect of increasing pain by overheating the tissue, causing further damage to the area.

As part of their treatment, a physiotherapist will normally suggest suitable exercises to help the cat's recovery. However, it can be difficult to use controlled exercise with cats, although stretching is useful when the cat is recuperating from injuries. Physiotherapists will use their knowledge of the cat's anatomy to perform manually assisted stretches once the cat's muscles are warm.

AVAILABILITY

Qualified physiotherapists are registered and legally recognized. Once a medical diagnosis has been made by your vet, the physiotherapist will treat the cat under the vet's direction. In order to practise on animals, some physiotherapists undertake additional veterinary training. If you or your vet think that physiotherapy would be beneficial for your cat, try to enlist the help of a qualified veterinary physiotherapist: they will be more familiar with the cat's anatomy and will be more able to handle the animal.

▲ *Pull your cat's hind leg backwards to gently stretch the injured limb. This maintains the range of movement and will help to prevent stiffness.*

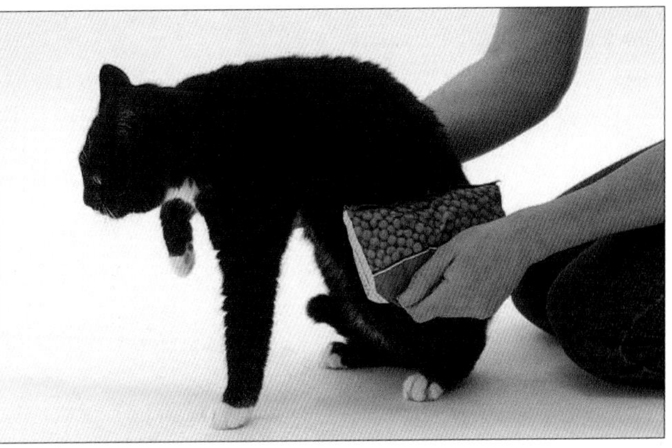

▲ *Hold a packet of frozen vegetables against the injured area as a cold compress to reduce damage in the area immediately surrounding the injury.*

Osteopathy

This is a form of treatment based on the manipulation of the body's bony skeleton. Its basic premise is that imbalance and disharmony will result from the changes that occur in all parts of the body when one part of its structure is altered. Osteopathy is not a complete system of medicine.

WHAT IS OSTEOPATHY?

Osteopathy was developed in the late 19th century by an American, Dr Andrew Taylor Still. He saw the skeleton as having a dual purpose. The commonly recognized function was that it provided the physical framework for the body. By the action of the muscles that were attached to it, it allowed the mechanical movement of the body. Its other, equally important, function was to protect the body's vital organs. Dr Still theorized that if the skeleton were out of alignment, the body it supported and protected would not be able to maintain a state of good health. The basis of osteopathy is that structure governs function.

Osteopathy is used alongside orthodox Western medicine. Osteopaths are trained to treat each patient as a complete structure, paying close attention to the relationship between the musculo-skeletal system and the function of the body. They look at a patient's history to decide if osteopathy is a suitable treatment. A thorough physical examination enables them to observe the ease and range of movement in the limbs and spine. By feeling the muscles and bones, the osteopath can locate painful areas and identify any misalignments of the skeleton. The osteopath is then able to make a diagnosis and develop a treatment plan.

HOW IT WORKS

Osteopathy on cats uses soft-tissue massage techniques and joint manipulations to make adjustments to the damaged neuro-musculoskeletal structure. The techniques used on cats and humans are very similar. Manipulation techniques make corrections which repair the damage and allow healing to occur. After the initial treatment, the osteopath will monitor improvements by sight and by feeling the changes that occur in the diseased area and in the body.

Osteopathic massage increases blood flow, which helps to speed up the elimination of toxic waste products that build up in the damaged areas. It increases the oxygenation of the tissues to relieve pain and stiffness.

The most common joint-manipulation technique used in osteopathy is the high-velocity thrust. Contrary to popular belief, although this causes popping noises, it does not realign bones and joints. It does, however, slightly separate the joint surfaces momentarily. This separation stretches the joint capsule and gives it greater freedom of movement. As the

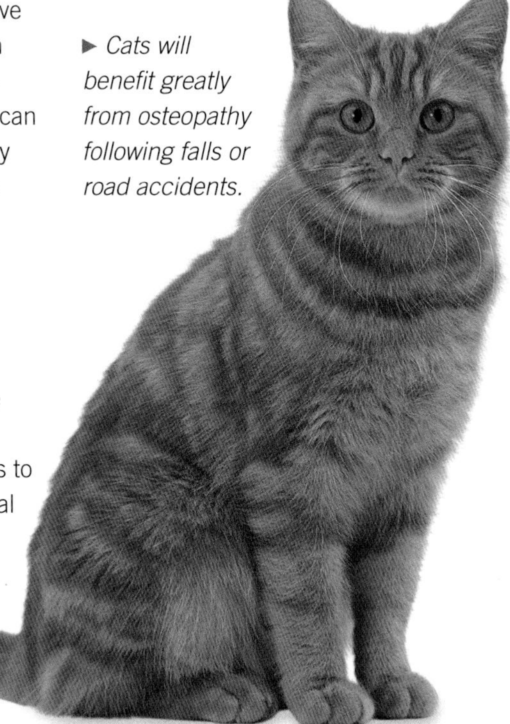

► *Cats will benefit greatly from osteopathy following falls or road accidents.*

When to use osteopathy

In the absence of scientific research it is difficult to evaluate the value of osteopathy in cats. However, where vets have referred cats for osteopathic treatment, the results have been encouraging. Osteopathy seems to be particularly useful to alleviate any joint pain arising as a result of road traffic accidents and degenerative diseases.

Although the theory of osteopathy is valid for all species, it is important to remember that cats, generally, do not like being handled by strangers. Their reluctance to co-operate with osteopathic treatment is a great drawback to its use, except when the cat is trusting enough to relax and allow manipulation, in which case good results can be obtained. However, if the cat refuses to co-operate, do not force it, but postpone the treatment session to another date. Alternatively, you may wish to consider a different therapy after discussing the options with your vet.

joint capsule is stretched, tiny bubbles of carbon dioxide come out of solution from the joint fluid and these are responsible for the popping sound.

The other techniques used are passive movement and articulation. These gently and painlessly stretch the soft tissues to result in greater joint and limb mobility. Passive movement involves the osteopath moving the cat's limbs while the cat relaxes and makes no physical effort. Articulation takes this a stage further, and uses the cat's limbs as levers to stretch the soft tissues. In all techniques, the osteopath monitors the cat's response and makes adjustments to its treatment plan accordingly.

AVAILABILITY

Osteopathy is now recognized as a valid treatment for animals, although there are as yet no recognized schools of veterinary osteopathy. If you wish to have your cat treated osteopathically, it must first be examined by a vet. If the vet also thinks that treatment would be beneficial, a qualified human osteopath will work on your cat under the vet's direction.

It is important that the vet and the osteopath co-operate with each other. The vet's notes, diagnosis and schedule should be made available to the osteopath, and the osteopath should discuss the treatment, benefits and outcome. Failure to liaise effectively can result in an inappropriate treatment being given. Osteopaths may use other therapies in their treatment of human patients, but by law they are not allowed to use techniques other than osteopathy on your pet without the permission of the vet.

GENERAL OSTEOPATHIC TREATMENT

The initial stage of any osteopathic treatment is a total examination of the animal. The osteopath will work through a sequence of movements to manipulate the cat's limbs so as to identify a suspected misalignment. Note the gentleness of the techniques: this cat did not even need to be held.

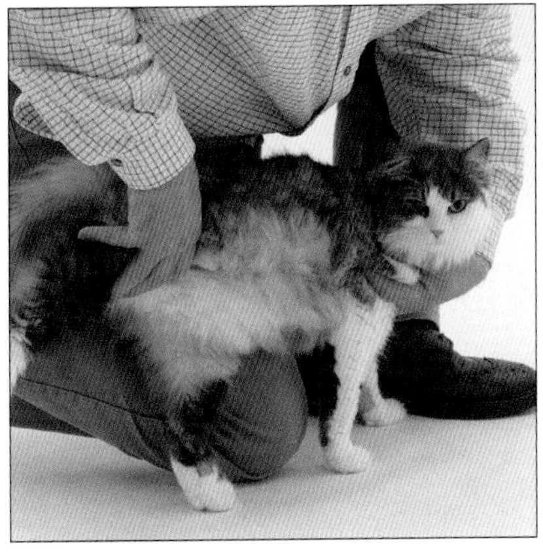

1 Examination and articulation of the cat's pelvic bones. Each hind leg is extended to stretch the muscles.

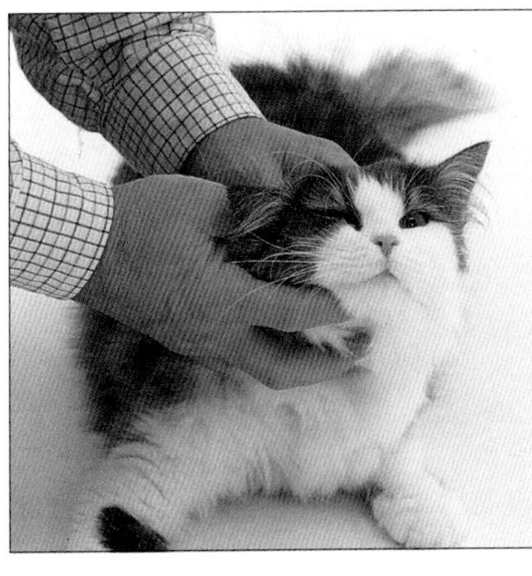

2 Examination and articulation of the neck. The head is gently rotated clockwise to stretch the muscles in the neck and shoulder.

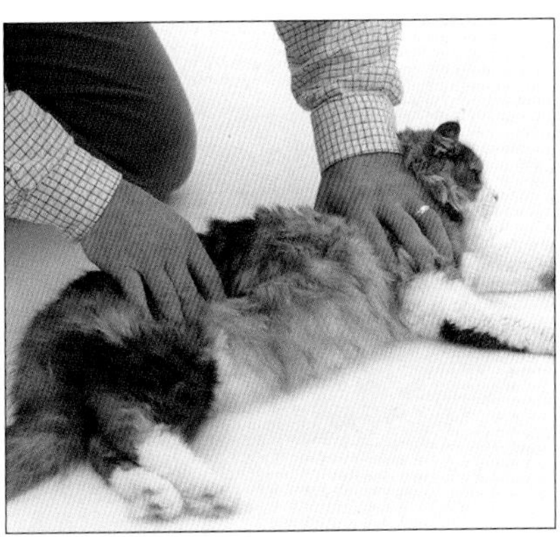

3 Examination of the front leg. The cat lies on its side with its muscles relaxed, while the positions of the skeletal structure are examined.

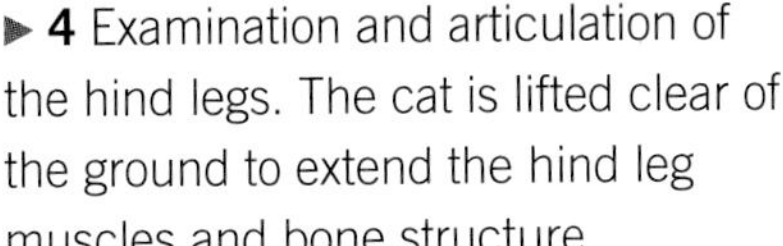

▶ **4** Examination and articulation of the hind legs. The cat is lifted clear of the ground to extend the hind leg muscles and bone structure.

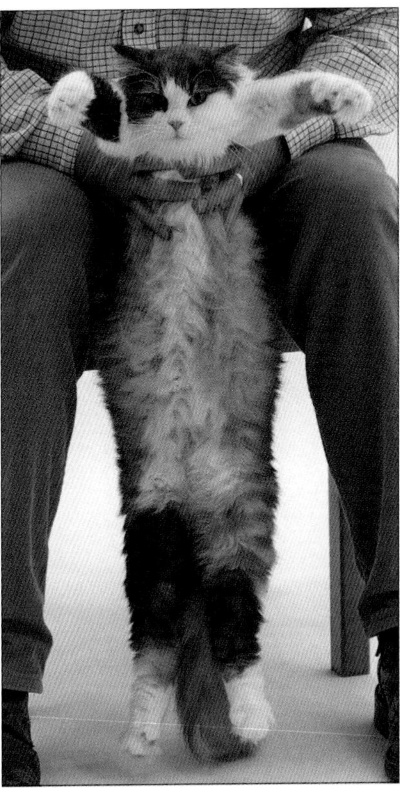

Chiropractic

Like osteopathy, chiropractic concentrates on the anatomy and physiology of the cat's musculoskeletal and nervous systems, and on the safe manipulation of the spine. The difference between the two therapies lies in their basic philosophy of disease.

WHAT IS CHIROPRACTIC?

Chiropractic theory says that if vertebral segments of the spine are misaligned, there will be undue pressure on the spinal cord or spinal nerves. This can cause interference with nerve transmissions, which may result in abnormal function and disease. If the malfunctioning vertebral segment can be repositioned by manipulation, the pressure on the spinal nerve roots is relieved and normal nerve function is restored.

HOW IT WORKS

The first stage of chiropractic treatment with a human patient involves taking a detailed case history, and an examination of the nerves (neurological examination) and bones (orthopaedic examination). These same tests are carried out on a cat. The neurological examination includes reflex and nerve stretch testing; the orthopaedic examination tests the range of movement of the various regions of the spine. At the same time, positions that cause pain are noted, as are abnormal movements of the joints of the spine. The chiropractor will consult with a vet to take x-rays (radiography), which are used to check for the existence of spinal disease that might cause a similar clinical condition, and to rule out the possibility of serious spinal damage, such as fractures after recent accidents.

The chiropractor is concerned with the physical effect of restriction of movement of the spine, however small and subtle. A change in alignment of the surfaces of the small vertebral joints, together with an associated nerve dysfunction, is known as a subluxation, a term used to describe partial dislocations. Chiropractic diagnosis aims to recognize such restrictions and gives the appropriate treatment to adjust them. The adjustment itself seldom results in total correction but initiates the body's natural healing processes, which will complete the realignment.

Chiropractic adjustment involves applying a high-velocity, short-amplitude thrust to the appropriate small facet joints of the vertebrae. It is the aim of the adjustment to correct the mechanical function of the joint and restore normal nerve function in the area.

Chiropractic is a non-invasive therapy, and while the hand movements are fast, they are subtle and extremely gentle. In severe or long-standing cases, chiropractic treatment may be given in a series of adjustments to give a gradual return to normal function, rather than in one or two more traumatic ones. Chiropractors are also taught deep-tissue massage techniques. These are used to support their manipulations, particularly in chronic cases. Drugs are never used in chiropractic treatment.

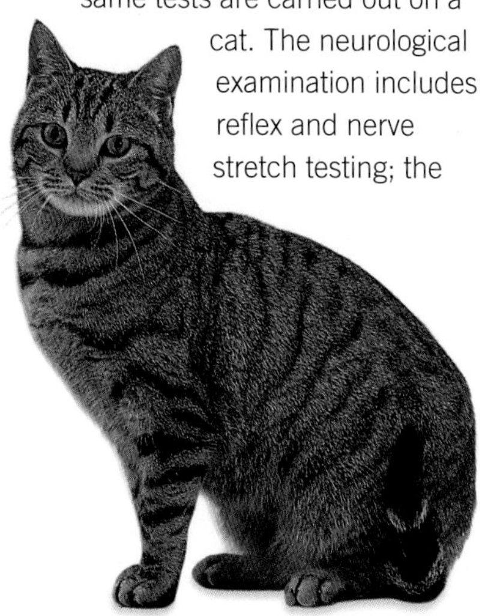

◀ *Monitor your cat's response to treatment and stop treatment if the cat seems uncomfortable. Not all cats enjoy being manipulated.*

When to use chiropractic

Chiropractic is not for home use. Because treatment involves manipulation of the spine, the consequences of misapplied techniques can be severe and could lead to paralysis. Even after observing the actions of a trained chiropractor during treatment sessions with your cat, never attempt to treat it yourself.

If you are having your cat treated, pay attention to its instinctive response to the practitioner. On subsequent visits to the clinic in particular, watch for any signs of reluctance, the need to escape, or defensive aggression. This may be your cat's way of telling you that it dislikes the treatment. No matter how beneficial you, your vet and/or chiropractor think the treatment can be for your cat, if the cat does not feel comfortable with what's happening, you need to put an end to the sessions and reassess the alternatives. Resentful cats cannot be treated successfully.

In spite of the difficulties involved with treating cats, chiropractic is a valid form of holistic treatment for cats who suffer the equivalent of back pain. Because drugs are not involved, the treatment is non-toxic. Adverse effects can occur after treatment, although rarely. Discuss the possibility of things getting worse before they get better with both the vet and the chiropractor before starting the treatment.

AVAILABILITY

In the United Kingdom, the McTimoney Chiropractic Association runs courses in chiropractic work on animals. The qualified practitioners treat animals referred to them by a vet. In the United States and Canada, the American Veterinary Chiropractic Association runs courses both for vets and human chiropractors who want to work on animals. Chiropractic treatment on animals is permitted by law only under the direction of a vet; only an animal-trained chiropractor is allowed to treat a cat. The practitioner is trained to handle different animals, but treating a cat can be made more difficult because of the cat's natural dislike of being examined. There should be good communication between the vet, the chiropractor and the owner.

McTIMONEY CHIROPRACTIC

The following sequence shows the checking procedure that is done before the problem can be diagnosed and treatment given. All types of ailments are treated by McTimoney Chiropractic, from strains and lameness to the animal's inability to move normally – for example, when running or jumping over a hurdle. Treatments can be given weekly or each month until the problem has cleared. In general, six-monthly check-ups are advised after a course of treatment has been completed.

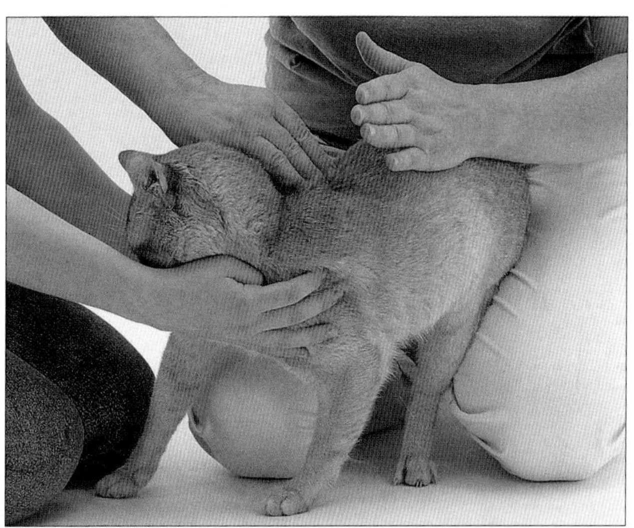

► **1** The hands move along the cat's cervical and thoracic spine as the practitioner makes an adjustment to the thoracic vertebrae, which lies between the cat's shoulder blades.

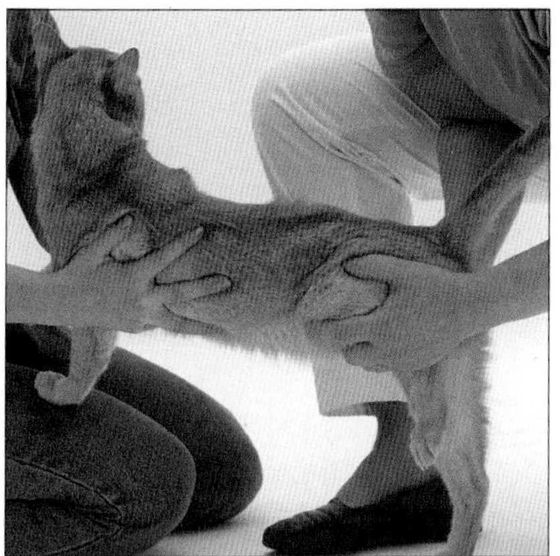

2 The practitioner positions the hind legs to check for subluxations in the pelvis area and the stifle (knee) joints.

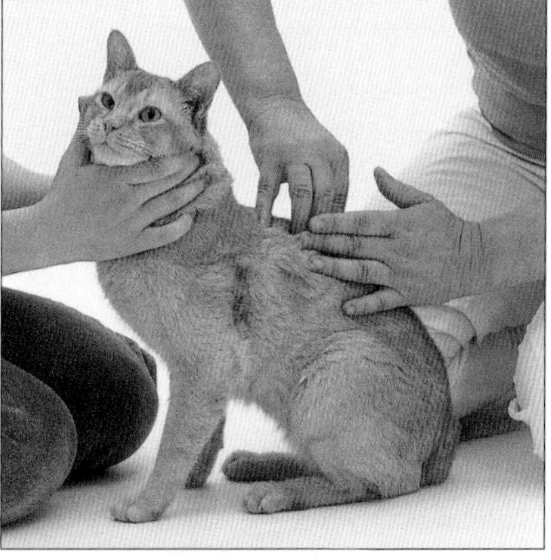

3 Here, the McTimoney practitioner checks the thoracic spine. There is a chiropractic checking procedure for all animals. If a subluxation is located, the hand movements are adjusted.

4 The forelegs are then checked for signs of subluxations in the joints and elbows, which could be the cause of lameness.

TTouch

The TTouch technique is very similar to massage, the difference being that it affects the skin only and not the underlying tissue. Gentle, rhythmic finger touches are applied to the cat's body to calm and relax it and to improve its capacity for training. TTouch is particularly useful for frightened cats.

WHAT IS TTOUCH?

The therapy was developed by a Canadian physiotherapist, Linda Tellington-Jones, who first worked with horses. Tellington-Jones developed her ideas from the work of Dr Moishe Feldenkrais, an Israeli writer who taught physical body awareness to humans. The theory is that non-habitual movements, combined with gentle manipulations, can promote body awareness, which in turn affects behaviour. The system is known as the Tellington-Jones Every Animal Method (TTEAM), and the individual strokes as TTouch.

▼ *Spending a quiet moment practising TTouch at home with a nervous cat can be beneficial. Start with a single stroke and repeat it over the cat's body.*

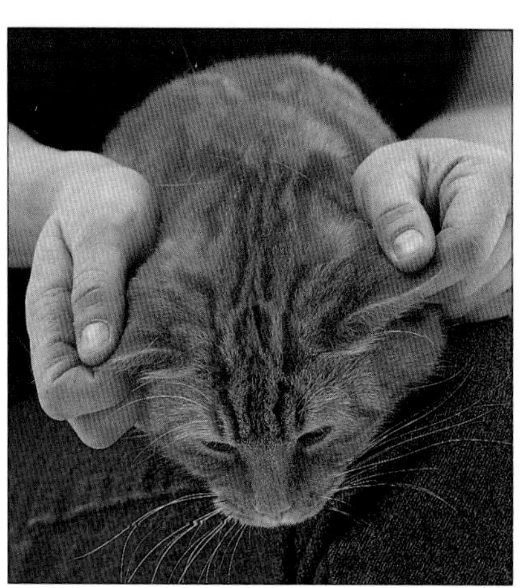

▲ *The gentle TTouch movements can help where a cat's behaviour has deteriorated due to the stress and pain of an injury.*

HOW IT WORKS

The principle behind TTouch is that the skin is moved in a circular motion through just over 360 degrees. If you imagine a clock face on the skin, the movement is clockwise from 6 o'clock through 12 o'clock, down 6 o'clock to end up at 9 o'clock position. TTouch stimulates the nervous system, and benefits the mental and emotional states. One effect of the technique is to change brain activity. Changes have been seen in the alpha, beta, delta and theta waves of horses.

Skin manipulation is done with one, two or three fingers, depending on the size of the cat. The thumb and the heel of the hand rest on the body, while the relaxed fingers move the skin. Only one circle is made in any one position. The hand is then slid to an adjacent area of skin and another circle is made, with the sliding action connecting the two circles. Whilst one hand makes the circles, the other hand rests on the cat's skin for balance and to complete the connection between owner and cat.

There are 15 individual TTouch movements, each using different parts of the hand, and different pressures and speeds. The techniques include back and belly lifts, crossways movements across the belly, manipulation of the ears from base to tip (to stimulate the acupuncture points in the ear) and, if the cat will allow it, circles made in and around the mouth, lips and nose.

AVAILABILITY

You can practise TTouch on your cat at home. Light, flexible wands, or even feathers, can be used on cats that resent being touched. TTouch relaxes nervous animals, often allowing them to be handled safely in due course. It is a valuable technique for relaxing stressed or frightened cats that are in pain through injury. Regular sessions can also help to strengthen the bond that exists between owner and cat.

▼ *You will gain the cat's trust quicker by paying close attention to its likes and dislikes as you build on your repertoire of strokes.*

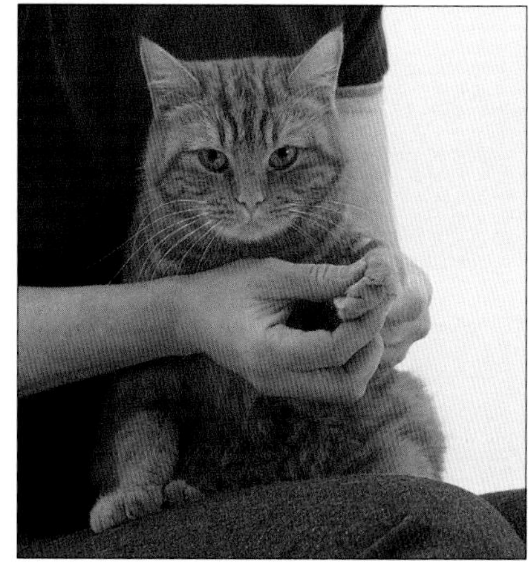

TTouch hand movements

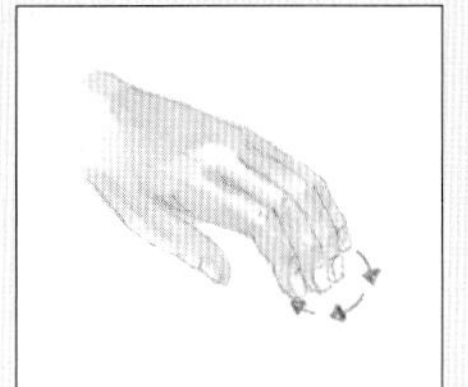
1 the clouded leopard

2 the lying leopard

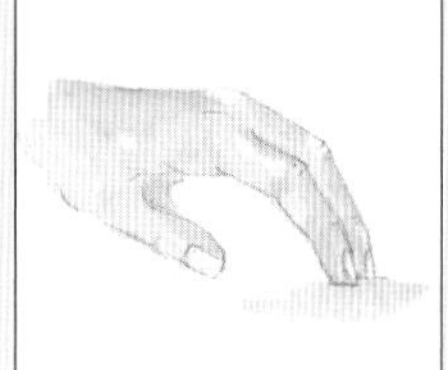
3 the racoon

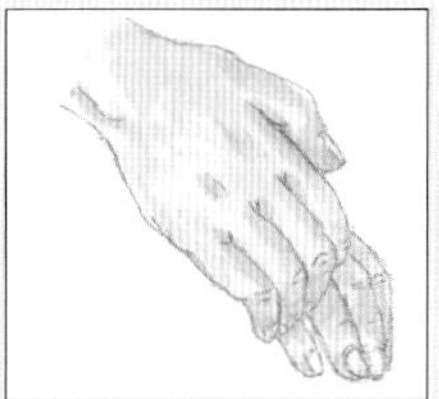
4 the snail's pace

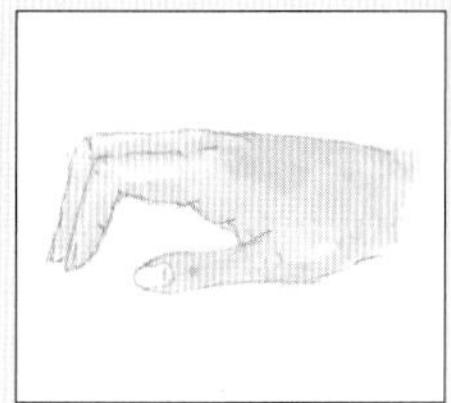
5 the bear

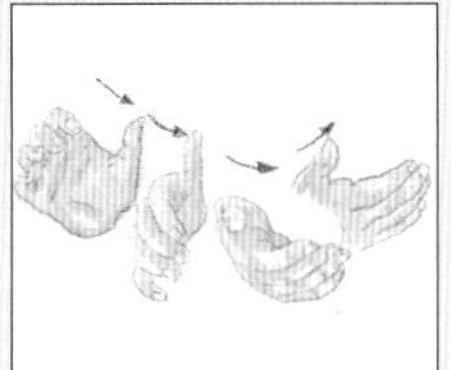
6 feathering

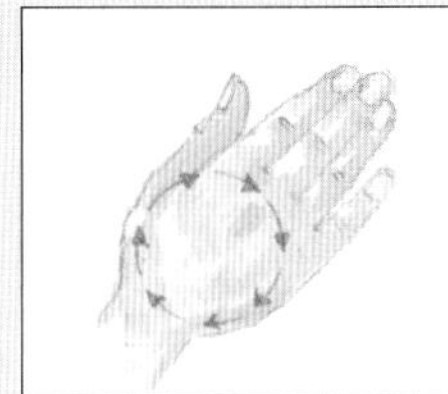
7 the abalone

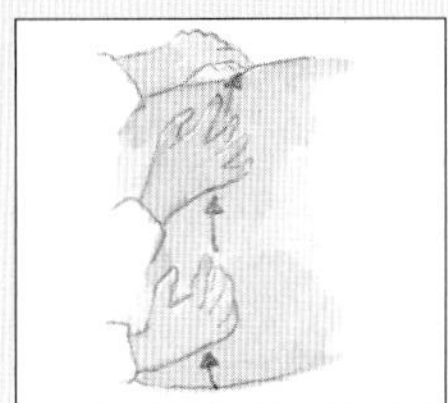
8 the lick of the cow's tongue

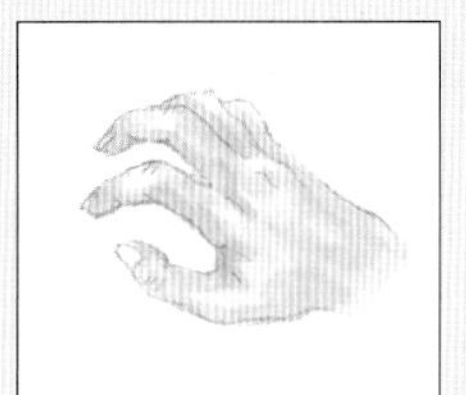
9 the tiger touch

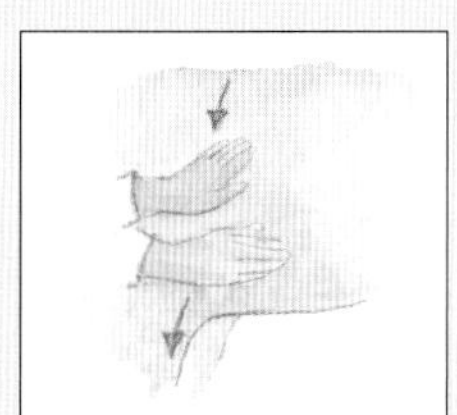
10 Noah's march

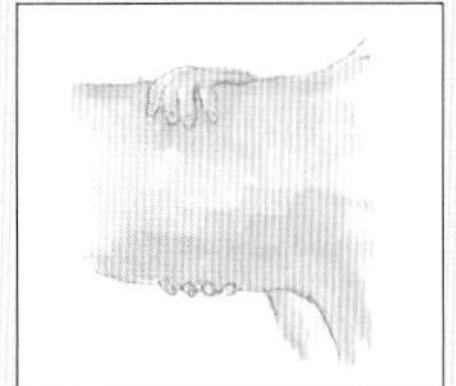
11 the python lift

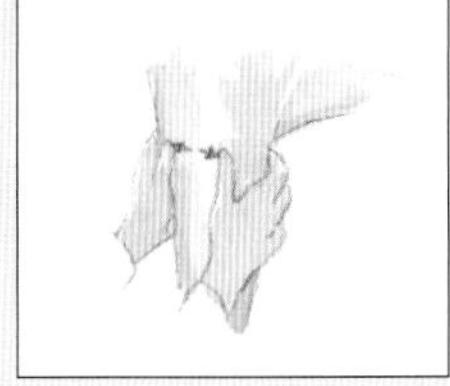
12 the butterfly

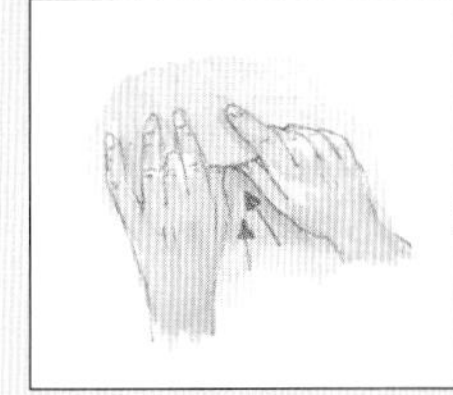
13 tarantulas pulling the plough

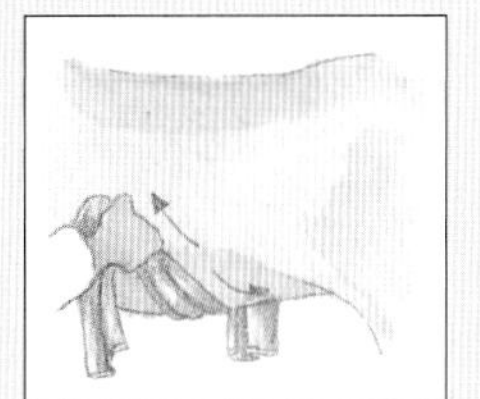
14 belly lifts

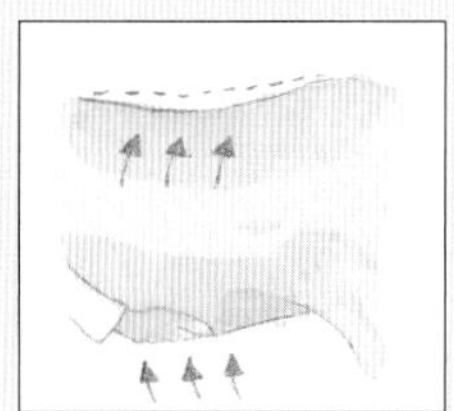
15 back lifts

The Leopard The 'Clouded Leopard' has a light and stealthy hand contact. The 'Lying Leopard' uses a firmer pressure. They are used to focus an excitable cat.

The Racoon Use on cats for more delicate work; for working around wounds; to speed healing; to increase circulation and activate neural impulses in the lower legs; to reduce swelling without causing pain.

The Snail's Pace The slow contractions and extensions of the fingers are used to relax back and neck muscles, to improve breathing and to reduce stress.

The Bear For areas of heavy muscling, such as the shoulders, back and flank.

Feathering For cats who are frightened of being touched, in place of the Bear.

The Abalone This mimics the slow circular motion of the sea abalone. It is not so much a movement as a firm pressure that pushes the skin around the circle.

The Lick of the Cow's Tongue A gentle swiping movement upwards from the belly to the back to soothe and calm a nervous or anxious cat. On very sensitive animals, the skin may twitch. If this happens, stop the movement and make a light Abalone circle before moving on to the next area.

The Tiger Touch A movement for physically strong cats, and for itch relief. The fingernails are the point of contact, and because the fingers are raised and apart, the nails almost make their own circles.

Noah's March Use these long, firm strokes to close a TTouch session: after the experience of revivification that the TTouch has brought to individual parts of the body, this will bring back a sense of wholeness. Using both hands, begin at the cat's head and make long, smooth strokes over the entire body.

The Python Lift Use on the shoulders, legs, neck and chest areas to relieve muscular tension and spasms. Place both hands on either side of the cat's body or leg and slowly lift upwards for 1–2cm (½–1in). Hold for 4 seconds, come back down, then slowly release.

The Butterfly Use this light movement alongside the Python Lift to increase circulation. The thumbs are pointed upwards with the fingers wrapped around the cat's leg. Lift the skin and muscle of the cat, as for the Python Lift.

Tarantulas Pulling the Plough Use light, nimble movements to gently roll the skin, working in a smooth pathway across the cat's shoulders, back and sides.

Belly Lifts Start behind the front legs and lift the cat's abdomen. Hold for 10–15 seconds, depending on the reaction. It is important that the pressure is released slowly and takes more time than the lift. Move gradually along the body towards the flank and repeat. Go as close to the flank as is comfortable for the cat.

Back Lifts With fingers apart and curved upwards, start on the far side of the belly in the middle. In a raking motion, bring both hands across the belly and partway up the barrel of the body. Start gently and increase pressure if the cat doesn't respond.

Reiki

Like massage and TTouch, Reiki is a hands-on therapy. However, this technique also bridges the gap between the physical therapies and the energy therapies. Its hand-placements and movements on the surface of the body are designed to direct healing energy to an injured area and to strengthen the spirit, rather than to stimulate the skin and underlying tissues themselves.

◀ *Reiki hand placements channel the healing energy to where it is best absorbed. The cat's chakra at the sides of its face is very receptive to the positive life-force.*

WHAT IS REIKI?

The origins of Reiki are not certain. Some people believe that it was first used in India by the Buddha and, later, in the Middle East by Jesus. Its secrets were lost over the years but were more recently discovered by a Japanese doctor, Dr Mikao Usui. When the doctor was close to death from cholera, he joined a Zen monastery and was introduced to the theory of Reiki. In a vision, he was shown healing symbols from the holy texts (sutras) and was taught how to use them. He was also given the ritual of attunement which allows Reiki knowledge to pass from the initiated master to the uninitiated student. These rituals are still in use today.

The name Reiki is thought to originate from two Japanese symbols, 'Rei' meaning universal and 'Ki', the non-physical life-force. Ki is similar to the concept of Q'i in acupuncture, and the vital force of homeopathy. Ki is a powerful healing energy and is available to anyone who is willing to learn how to use it. The pressures of

▼ *The healing energy of Reiki can be used to heal a cat that is suffering an emotional upset.*

Some hand positions for treating cats

Choose one of the following to give your cat the benefit of a Reiki treatment at home whenever it is needed. If your cat is suffering physical or emotional distress, be sensitive to its response; if the cat shows signs of resentment, stop the treatment immediately. For cats suffering recent physical injury, do not place your hands directly on areas of acute inflammation, but hold your hands parallel to, and just above, the damaged area, so as to be able to focus the healing energy where it is needed.

- With the cat seated on your lap or on the floor in front of you, hold your hands on either side of the cat's ribcage. This will treat the cat's whole body and the Reiki will reach the central parts immediately.
- Put one hand on the head of your cat as though you are going to stroke its ears, and one hand very lightly on the middle of the cat's back.
- Hold the cat between your hands, with one hand at the top of the spine and the other at the base, by its tail. All hand movements should be slow.

modern society mean that most of us have become disconnected from Ki in our everyday life. Reiki aims to reconnect people to this universal life-force, giving them the capacity to heal themselves, their families, their friends and their pets.

▶ *Giving the cat a whole body treatment will direct the flow of energy where it is needed. Start with your hands over the bud chakra at the base of the cat's ears and work towards the feet.*

HOW IT WORKS

There are three degrees of Reiki. In the first, the student is attuned to the life-force and can begin to channel the healing energy where it is needed. The student is taught the hand placements and movements that are needed to direct the energy to the patient. In the second degree, the student is taught the symbols and healing sounds (mantras) that focus the energy on the patient. The student is also taught how to use Reiki for distant healing. The third degree, or Reiki Master level, is the teaching level. The knowledge of this degree is passed from master to student during a private, sacred ceremony.

USING REIKI

Reiki energy is a universal life-force that connects all life forms, and it can be used to treat animals in the same way as humans. Reiki can provide an uplifting tonic or pick-me-up, or it can ease physical pain and suffering. It can also be used to reassure cats who are emotionally upset.

When treating an injured cat, place your hands parallel to and above the wound. The cat will move away or will appear restless when it has received enough of the healing energy.

It is not recommended to use Reiki as the only method of treating a sick animal. If your cat is injured or appears to be ill, consult the vet as normal, then use Reiki as a support to any prescribed treatment. The best use of Reiki is preventative, to help keep your cat in a state of good health and to prevent serious disease from becoming established.

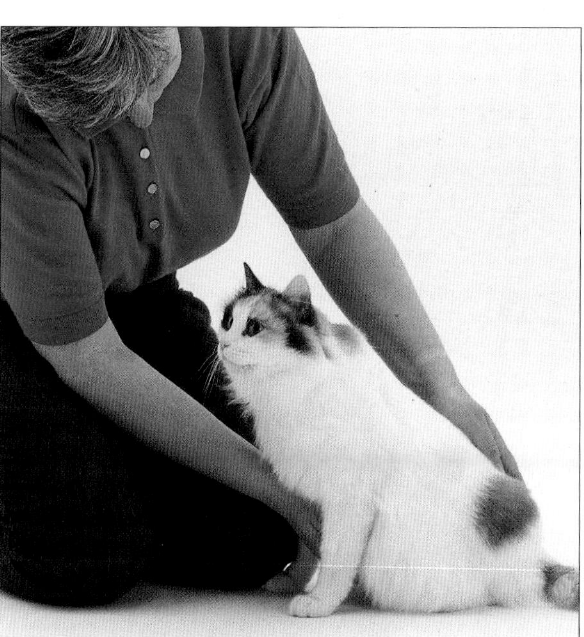

◀ *Reiki can be used on an unwell cat to support conventional veterinary treatment, and can help to soothe physical or emotional pain.*

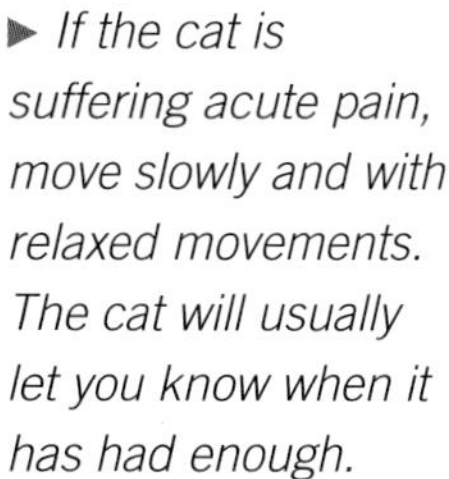

▶ *If the cat is suffering acute pain, move slowly and with relaxed movements. The cat will usually let you know when it has had enough.*

Herbalism

Medicine is the art of restoring and preserving health using remedial substances and dietary regulation. It is also the name given to the substance used in this art, which is usually taken internally. Medical substances fall into three categories: herbals, which are simple plant extracts; synthetic drugs, which are produced commercially by the pharmaceutical industry; and volatile plant oils, which are used in aromatherapy.

WHAT IS HERBALISM?

This is probably the oldest form of healing still in use today. Herbal medicines play an essential part in both Traditional Chinese Medicine (TCM) and the Indian Ayurvedic system. Western herbalism dates back to the ancient Greeks. It was the mainstay of English medicine until the early 1930s, when the group of medicines known as sulphonamides, the precursors of modern antibiotics, were first introduced.

Herbalism is now making a resurgence, caused in part by an increasing suspicion that the long-term effects of some modern drugs may not be totally beneficial to the patient. This suspicion is prompting a reappraisal of all medical therapies and is encouraging an interest in holistic medicine and a desire for effective natural treatments, for both humans and animals, which do not involve toxins or side effects. The fact that cats and other animals actively seek out and eat plants that are known to have medicinal properties supports the view that herbalism should have an established and widespread place in orthodox veterinary medicine.

Many people take the view that, almost by definition, natural is synonymous with safe; as herbal medicines are natural, they must therefore be safer than manufactured ones. However, this is not necessarily the case and herbal medicines should be treated with the same respect as pharmaceutical drugs. Some plants are poisonous in their natural form and herbal medicines derived from an original plant source can be toxic if given in too high a dose. Always check the toxicity of your chosen plant.

When to use herbalism

Condition	Herbal therapy
Cancer protection	barberry bark; comfrey leaf; echinacea root; fenugreek seed; lemon balm; mistletoe leaf; Roman chamomile flower
Diarrhoea	garlic; marshmallow root; slippery elm bark
Itchy skin	burdock root; fenugreek seed; German chamomile flower; liquorice root
Liver disease	barberry; dandelion milk thistle
Kidney problems	cleavers; goldenrod; parsley
Skin abrasions	comfrey leaf; peppermint; turmeric root; yarrow
Urinary tract disorders	bearberry leaf; couch grass; cranberry; field horsetail; juniper berry; marshmallow root

◄ marshmallow

▲ *Preparations of marshmallow root soothe the bowel lining and can be useful in cases of chronic vomiting, diarrhoea and colitis.*

Some pharmacists object to the use of herbalism on the grounds that the chemical composition of individual plants of the same species may vary according to the soil they are grown in and the time of the year they are harvested. This means that medicines derived from plants cannot be standardized, unlike manufactured drugs. This is compounded according to which part of the plant is used and the method of extraction. Pharmacists would prefer to isolate the part of the

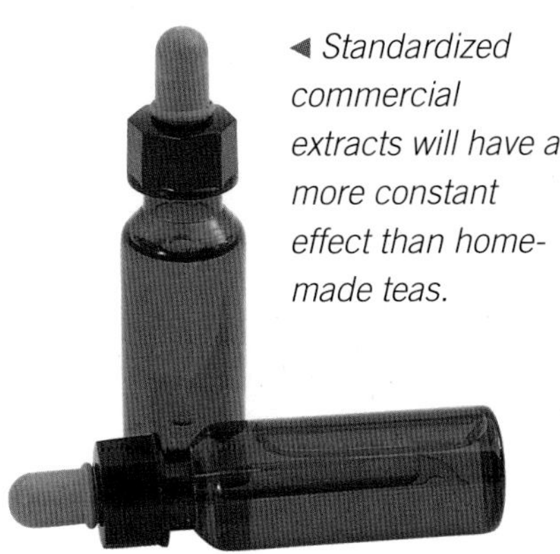

◄ *Standardized commercial extracts will have a more constant effect than home-made teas.*

plant that they consider to be the active ingredient, and use only that ingredient in a purified form. This is the only way to know in advance exactly what effect a single dose of medicine will have on the body.

Unfortunately, few active agents have only one effect. They also tend to have other unwanted actions or side effects. Herbalists believe that the active ingredients of herbal medicines work together to counteract harmful side effects. This allows a safe, effective dosage to be made.

USING HERBALISM

Herbal medicines can be administered in many ways. The traditional method is in the form of herbal infusions or teas, which are made from bulk herbs sold loose by weight. Like all herbal preparations, bulk herbs should always be purchased from reputable firms. Herbal teas for cats are made in the same way as they are for humans, with hot water poured over herbs in a strainer. The difference seems to be that cats appear to need more than humans in relation to their body weight. A dose of 15ml (3tsp) twice a day is accepted as suitable for a cat weighing 5kg (11lb). Good-tasting bulk herbs can be fed directly to the cat if mixed with its food.

Commercial herbal extracts in the form of glycerine/water and alcohol/water tinctures are also available, and these can be given directly into the mouth, if your cat will tolerate it. Here, the dose rate is one drop per 1kg (2¼lb) of body weight. Herbal capsules and tablets are available for cats, but some authorities believe that capsules of powdered herbs are not suitable for carnivorous animals. If using these, follow the instructions carefully. Bulk herbs can also be used to make poultices and compresses. Do not use toxic herbs in this way as a cat may lick the dressing and poison itself.

There are very few practising veterinary herbalists. Some vets undertake courses in herbalism to combine it with scientific knowledge. When treating animals, the vet will monitor the response to treatment and will amend the dose accordingly. As experience of veterinary herbalism grows, so dosing regimes become more accurate.

In cases of minor illness, you can treat your cat at home. Keep up the treatment for one week before rejecting it, if it seems to be ineffective. It can take longer to see improvements in chronic cases, although in these situations, herbalism is best used to support conventional care. If ever the cat's condition appears to deteriorate at all, stop the treatment and consult your vet.

▲ *Diluted eyebright tincture can be used to bathe inflamed eyes, while diluted calendula lotion can be used on mild infections.*

▼ *Suspicious cats may be willing to take commercial extracts if they are added to favourite foods.*

Aromatherapy

Aromatherapy is the use of volatile aromatic oils, which are derived from plant material, to cause physiological and psychological changes in the patient. The molecules of these essential oils are able to enter the body and the bloodstream by absorption either through the lining of the nose and lungs, or through the skin. This means that essential oils used for aromatherapy should always be handled with care and the same respect as any other medicinal substance.

ESSENTIAL OILS

Fragrant essential oils have been used medicinally in Egypt and the Middle East for thousands of years. Their use is not taught in medical or veterinary schools at the present time, although many holistic veterinary clinics employ qualified aromatherapists, as do some human hospitals.

Several parts of the plant are used as a source of the essential oil. Flowers, leaves, twigs, roots, seeds, bark and heartwood may all be used, depending on the plant. There are several methods of extracting the oils, the commonest being steam-distillation. This yields an oil and water mix that is cooled and separated into its two components. Pressing is used to squeeze the oil out of plants containing non-volatile oils. Carbon dioxide extraction can also be used but is more expensive. Enfleurage is the traditional method of oil production, and involves laying petals on layers of fat for up to three weeks. During this time, the oils seep into the fat, from which they are then separated by extraction with alcohol. This method is used for extracting delicate flower oils, such as rose and jasmine. It produces fine quality oils which are very expensive. Solvent extraction produces oils known as absolutes, which may contain traces of the solvent. For this reason they are disliked by some therapists. Synthetic oils are also produced. Although these are a standardized product, they are unlikely to contain as many components as the natural oil, and this may reduce their therapeutic effect. Some aromatherapists believe the reason synthetic oils are not as active as the natural oils is because they have an artificially produced chemical source, which is devoid of the vitality of living materials.

There are hundreds of component oils in every extract of essential oil. The final contents are governed by the geographical area and the soil in which the plant is grown, the climate, and the methods used in cultivation. Some people prefer those oils produced from organically grown plants, as this eliminates any contamination with agrochemicals. Whichever type of essential oil you choose, always buy from a reputable supplier; regard cheap oils with suspicion, but bear in mind, too, that expense does not necessarily indicate quality.

► lavender

◄ *Lavender oil is non-toxic but should never be used on damaged skin.*

▼ *All essential oils should be blended with a carrier oil if they are to be used for massage on a cat. Essential oils containing phenolic oils should never be used on cats.*

USING AROMATHERAPY

Cats have a highly developed sense of smell, providing it has not been reduced by cat flu or similar diseases. Cats use the secretions of their anal sacs, and the glands in their cheeks and tails, along with saliva, urine and faeces, as a means of communication and to mark their territorial boundaries.

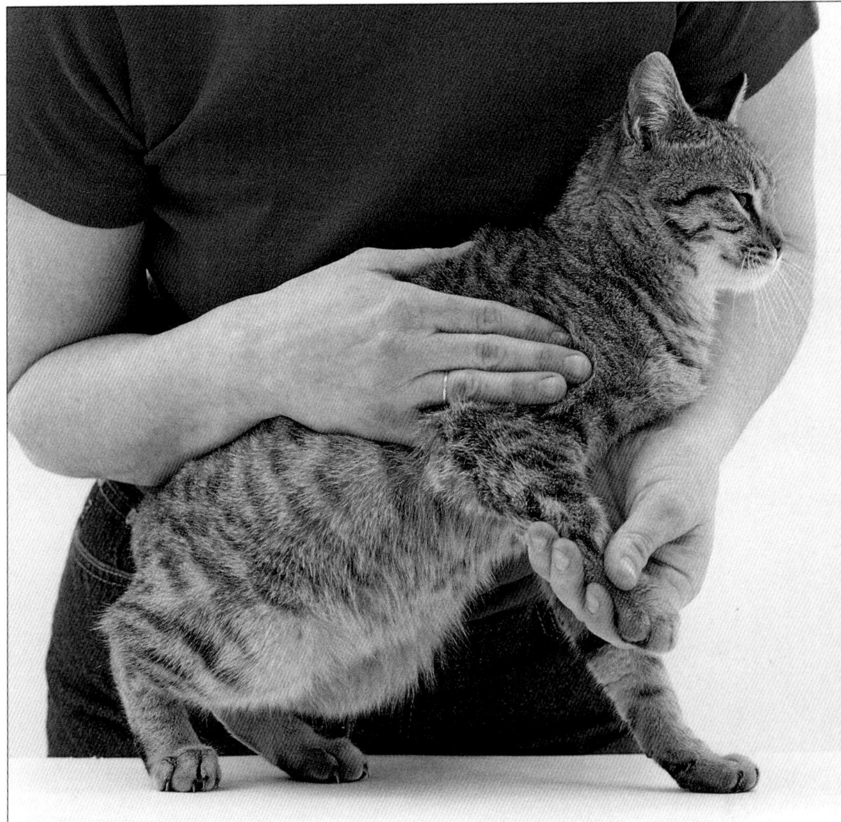

Because their sense of smell is so refined, most cats will respond well to aromatherapy. However, you should never force your cat if it appears unwilling to co-operate.

Essential oils are not to be taken internally by cats because of the risk of toxicity. For the same reason, it is not advised to massage a cat with oils because of the absorbency of the skin. Baths are obviously unsuitable for animals. The most effective way of using aromatherapy with your cat is in a diffuser. In this method, five to ten drops of oil are floated on water which is heated by a candle; electric vaporizers are also available. The heat will cause the oil/water mixture to evaporate, and the fragrant vapour fills the room, where it is inhaled by everyone, people and pets alike. This is ideal for home.

Essential oils are chosen according to the cat's symptoms. Combinations of up to four oils can be burned at one time, and blends for use in a vaporizer can be prepared at home. Essential oils are concentrated chemicals and can be highly toxic in their neat form: never use them undiluted on an animal's skin. A cat will try to clean the oil off and may ingest toxic amounts by doing so. Remember, too, that a cat's nose is very sensitive. What smells beautiful to you may be unbearably strong for your cat, and if so, the treatment will not work.

Aromatherapy can be used to support any mainstream or complementary therapy with the exception of homeopathy, because homeopathic remedies can be deactivated by highly aromatic substances.

▲ *Essential oils should not be rubbed into the cat's fur. If they must be rubbed in, dilute 2 drops of the essential oil in 15ml (1tbsp) of a vegetable-based oil, and use the bald areas of the groin and armpit.*

▼ *Vaporizers are efficient but they should only be placed where they cannot be overturned.*

When to use aromatherapy

Condition	Essential oil
Lack of confidence, anxiety, panic	Sandalwood; ylang-ylang
Loneliness, fear of being alone	Basil; bergamot; orange blossom
Restlessness, frustration	Chamomile
Liver problems	Rosemary
Kidney and bladder problems	Juniper
Skin allergies	Lavender; pine; terebinth
Respiratory problems	Cedarwood; eucalyptus; lemon; tea-tree
Minor skin wounds, bites and stings	Lavender; tea-tree
Toothache	Clove

Acupuncture

Acupuncture forms part of Traditional Chinese Medicine (TCM), which was first developed by the Chinese more than 3,000 years ago and is still practised today.

WHAT IS ACUPUNCTURE?

Acupuncture is based on a principle of the flow of energy, or Q'i (pronounced chee), around the body through non-anatomical channels known as meridians. If the flow of Q'i passing through any of the channels is disturbed, the health of the body will be impaired, which leads to disease.

The body's energy flow increases and decreases in each meridian in a fixed cycle. The meridians also govern the function of anatomical units, although their function in TCM is different to Western medicine.

Q'i has two opposite, complementary components: yin and yang. Everything in the universe contains yin and yang, but some things contain more yin than yang and vice versa. The solid organs of the body – liver, spleen, kidney, heart, lungs and pericardium – are yin, while the hollow organs – stomach, small and large intestines, gall bladder and urinary bladder – are yang. One pair of meridians governs each organ, and there are two other non-paired meridians, the Governing Vessel and the Conception Vessel. These meridians run in pathways up the front and down the back of the body.

Acupuncture theory states that everything in the universe is made from five basic philosophical elements: wood, fire, earth, metal and water. These elements relate in a positive or negative way to one another, so that wood produces fire, but restrains or destroys earth. Each element can change to the next in the course of a creative cycle.

Chinese acupuncture recognizes six environmental factors as the reasons for disease: wind, cold, summer heat, dampness, dryness and heat; each is associated with certain forms of disease. It also recognizes eight conditions composed of four pairs of opposites: yin and yang, heat and cold, internal and external, excess and deficiency. The theory is that disease can be expressed by a combination of these eight conditions.

▼ *Fine surgical steel needles have replaced the slivers of bamboo or bone that were first used in acupuncture to stimulate the meridian points.*

HOW IT WORKS

No medicines are given, although Chinese herbs may be used to support treatment. Treatment is by the stimulation of precise anatomical points on the meridians; the knowledge of these points is based on results recorded over thousands of years. Today, fine surgical steel needles are inserted into underlying tissue. The relationships between the elements, environmental factors and conditions of opposites indicate which points on which meridian should bring Q'i back into balance and allow the body's own healing forces to complete the cure.

There is no anatomical structure or organ recognized by Western medicine that is penetrated by the needles and which could be responsible for the physical and physiological changes that can result from treatment. The effects of acupuncture cannot be explained in either physical or biochemical terms, which suggests that they occur at a different level, in the invisible, energetic bodies that surround the physical body. For many conventional, Western-trained physicians, acupuncture and its approach lo treatment is hard to evaluate. A form of acupuncture has been developed in the West which uses fixed combinations of points for

Conditions that best respond to acupuncture

- Back pain and paralysis from injury and disc problems.
- Conditions: allergies and dermatitis; epilepsy; non-spinal origin paralysis; chronic gastro-intestinal conditions, such as diarrhoea or vomiting.
- Respiratory diseases and asthma.
- Painful neuralgic type conditions and general pain relief.

each diagnosis. It is empirical, but the essential art of TCM has been lost. Western acupuncture cannot be used on as many conditions and the results are inferior. References in this book are to Chinese acupuncture.

TREATMENT FOR CATS

Q'i, the philosophical elements, the environmental factors and the conditions of acupuncture are universal, which means that acupuncture can be used as easily on animals as on humans. The position of the meridians and acupuncture points varies from species to species, but the techniques are just the same. Your cat will not tolerate over-stimulation and will always let the practitioner know when it has had enough.

Acupuncture is not as effective as antibiotics at treating acute infections, but it is very good with chronic diseases, including diseases of the immune system.

◀ *A thorough clinical examination of the cat should be made, and a Western diagnosis given, before a course of acupuncture is begun.*

This therapy is not for home use: the untrained use of needles can be dangerous. Your vet will refer you to a practitioner if you are interested in using it on your cat.

ACUPRESSURE

By law, only qualified vets are allowed to use acupuncture needles on animals. However, if you wish to provide back-up care for your cat, simple training from a qualified practitioner will allow you to perform finger pressure, or acupressure, at home in support of any conventional treatments your cat may be having.

Like acupuncture, acupressure is based on the theory of Q'i, and is said to reduce pain by relaxing muscles. It is applied with very light fingertip or pressure on the acupuncture points; some styles of acupressure also involve rubbing, kneading and rolling. Acupressure done incorrectly can increase pain. As with any therapy, do not continue if your cat resents it.

▼ *The points that are stimulated are chosen on the basis of the examination, the cat's case history and the experience of the practitioner.*

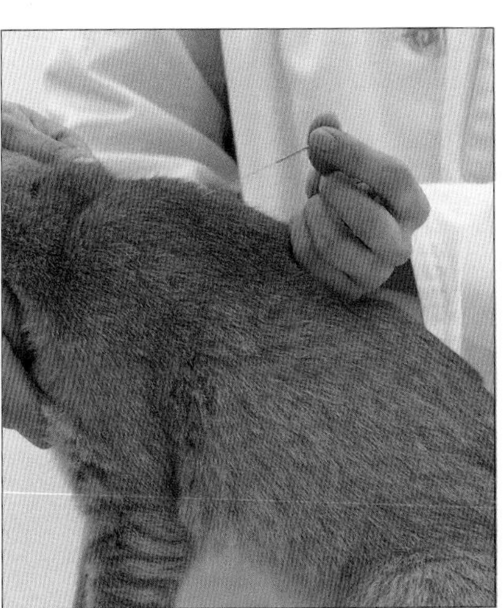

▼ *Cats will usually tolerate acupuncture reasonably well when they are ill, but they will always let you know when they have had enough.*

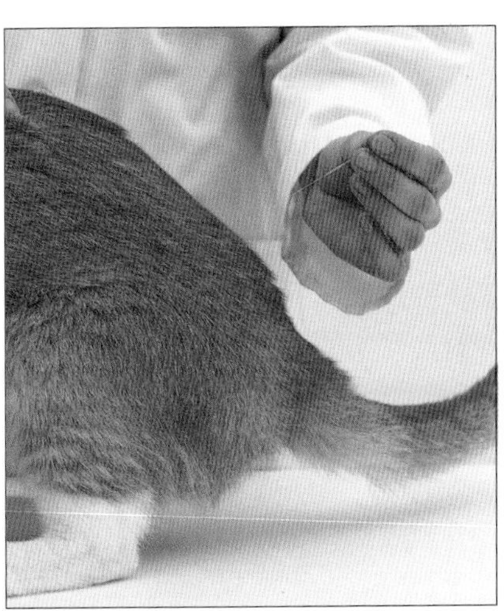

▼ *The cat's acupuncturist can show you the correct acupressure points so that you can continue the treatment at home.*

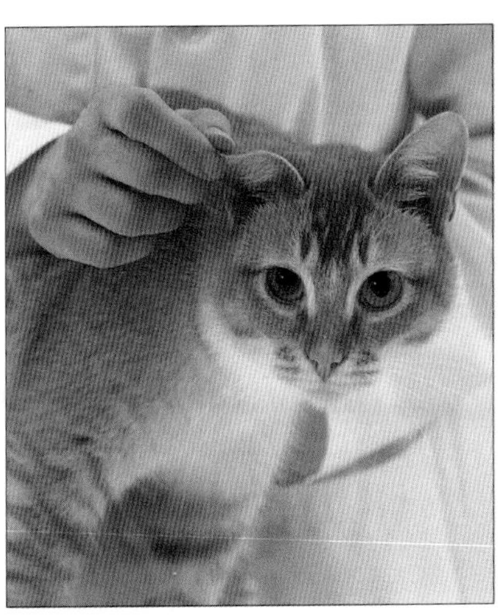

Homeopathy

Homeopathy was the first holistic system of Western medicine to be developed. It can be very effective both on its own and in support of conventional medicine and, like acupuncture, it is at its best where conventional medicine is weakest.

WHAT IS HOMEOPATHY?

The body has a natural healing force, which comes to the fore in cases of ill health: minor cuts and grazes heal on their own, and we quickly recover from mild coughs and colds. Science calls the healing force homeostasis, and homeopaths believe that their medicine stimulates it.

Samuel Hahnemann, an 18th-century German doctor and the originator of homeopathy, called the body's basic impulse towards self-healing the vital force. He saw it as an energetically active, living force, which is essential to life. From his observations he deduced that a non-lethal quantity of a poison can stimulate healing of any disease where the symptoms are similar to the effects of that poison.

▼ *Homeopathic remedies come in the same forms as conventional medicines. To the casual observer, there is no difference in appearance between any of the homeopathic remedies.*

The idea that 'like cures like' dates back to the ancient Greeks, but had never before been used as the basis for a medical therapy. Hahnemann tested his substances on himself and his friends, and recorded the results in a volume he called the *Materia Medica*.

Hahnemann used small, material doses, and noted that some patients got worse before they got better, a phenomenon he called homeopathic aggravation. To lessen the aggravations he reduced the dose, but although dilution made the aggravations less severe, it also lessened the benefits. Next, liquid medicines were shaken after dilution in a method known as potentizing. This reduced the aggravations while, at the same time, it enhanced the healing property of the medicines, or potencies.

The use of highly diluted medicines has led to two main misconceptions. First, that the essence of homeopathy is the use of a very small dose rather than the use of a 'similar'. Second, that because there are no molecules left in the highly-diluted potencies (above *24X* or *12C*) the medicine could not possibly work. However, observations over the last 200 years have shown that these medicines do affect the living body. The phenomenon is under scientific study, but the method by which homeopathy achieves results will probably prove to be at a sub-atomic level. Homeopathy is as relevant to animals as it is to humans.

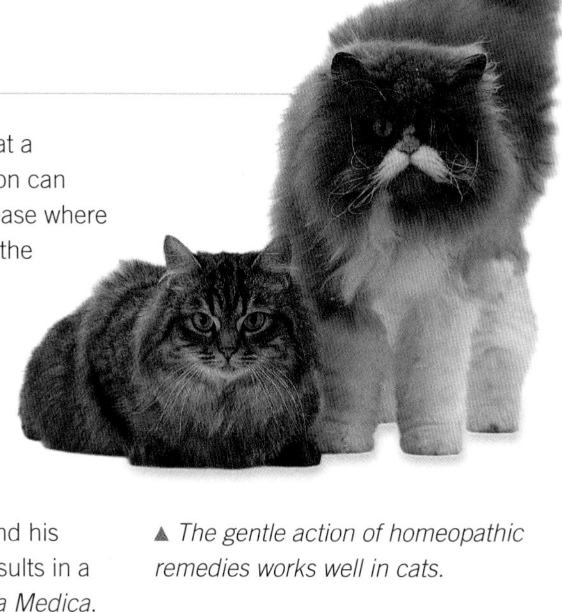

▲ *The gentle action of homeopathic remedies works well in cats.*

POTENTIZATION

This process is unique to homeopathy. There are two procedures: the dilution in a fixed ratio of 1:9 or 1:99, and the succussion of the diluted solution by vigorous shaking. This is essential if the medical effects of the solution are to be enhanced, or potentized, as the concentration is reduced.

The starting point of any potency is the saturated solution of a soluble chemical, or the alcoholic extract of plant material, known as the mother tincture. Each succeeding potency is given a number for the number of dilutions made, and a letter for the Latin number of the degree of dilution,

X or *D* standing for 10, *C* for 100 and *LM* for 50,000. For example, if you put one drop of the mother tincture of *Belladonna* with 99 drops of alcohol/water and succuss it, you get a *1C* potency. One drop of the *1C* potency mixed with 99 drops of alcohol/water gives a *2C* potency, and one drop of a *2C* potency mixed with 99 drops of alcohol/water gives a *3C* potency, and so on. Potencies up to *30C* are still made by hand, and to these is added the suffix H for Hahnemann. Potencies from *30C* to *10M* are usually produced by mechanical methods.

When to use homeopathy

Remedies are available in different potencies, of which the most common are *6C* and *30C*. Use *6C* for chronic or long-standing conditions, and *30C* for emergencies and acute conditions.

Condition	Remedy
Panic attacks and sudden emotional stress	Aconite
Prolonged grief, bereavement	Natrum mur.
Flea bites and insect stings	Apis mel.
Bruising and other trauma	Arnica
Flatulence and digestive disorders	Carbo veg.
Skin grazes and superficial wounds	Hypericum; Calendula
Physical exhaustion	Arnica

When to use tissue salts

Condition	Remedy
Neurological disorders	Kali phos.
Allergies	Nat. sulph.
Chronic infections	Silica
Dental problems	Calc. fluor.

HOMEOPATHIC TREATMENT

A 'similar' is the medical agent which produces symptoms closely resembling those of the cat; if the symptoms match completely, it is a similimum. When a cat is treated, its physical, mental and emotional reactions to the world are used to identify the disease. The totality of the animal and its condition is treated, and the more you know about your cat when it is healthy, the more you can help when it is ill. The smallest dose of the similimum that will stimulate the healing process is given. In acute cases, doses are repeated until benefits are seen. In chronic cases, each dose is left to have its full effect before it is repeated.

The second branch of homeopathy is the removal of obstructions to a cure. This relates to the holistic idea that unless there are suitable nutrition and lifestyle changes, a permanent cure cannot result.

Tissue salts make up the third branch of homeopathy. In the 19th century, a German homeopathic doctor, Wilhelm Schüssler, identified 12 basic salts present in the body. He thought that all diseases, if caught early, and without complex symptoms, could be cured by the correct combination of these salts. Biochemic tissue salts are prescribed in a low, *6X* potency to alleviate mild disease or emotional conditions, which may be caused by a mineral salt deficiency. Nutritional advice will usually be given as part of the treatment.

▼ *If you experience difficulty in giving your cat a homeopathic tablet, it can be crushed and mixed in with the cat's food.*

Bach Flowers

Plants and flowers play an essential part in many traditional healing systems. The Bach Flower remedies, prepared from the stalks, petals and leaves of plants, can be used to treat mental and emotional states.

WHAT ARE FLOWER REMEDIES?

The 18th-century German homeopath, Dr Samuel Hahnemann, used the vibrational energy of plants to stimulate natural healing processes in his holistic system of homeopathy. A British bacteriologist, Dr Edward Bach, took Hahnemann's ideas one stage further. His experience as a homeopathic doctor had convinced him that physical disease was the body's reaction to a non-material cause. Changes in the body's fundamental vibrational energy (an acupuncturist's Q'i and a homeopath's Vital Force) resulted in a pathological change of mental state that could eventually lead to physical disease.

To Dr Bach, mental attitude was more important than physical symptoms when choosing a medicine. He believed that the mind showed the onset and cause of disease before the body. In 1930 he set out to seek a means of healing that used non-toxic materials.

Dr Bach was a sensitive, spiritual man who noted that his own moods could be strongly influenced by the plants he came into contact with. He looked to individual plants for his remedies, and his theory was that the natural vibrations of certain plants seemed to match the vibrations associated with certain mental states. Therefore, if these plants were appropriately prepared, they may be able to help correct distorted vibrations by the principle of resonance.

Bach intuitively discovered 12 plants which could affect pathological mental states. He later increased the range to 37 plants, and added *Rock Water*, which is water from a natural spring (preferably one reputed to have healing properties). He also sanctioned the use of a combination of five remedies in a preparation he called *Rescue Remedy*. *Rescue Remedy* is the most popular, general-purpose Bach Flower remedy for both humans and animals. It is used in emergency situations as a calming treatment for all types of panic, shock and hysteria.

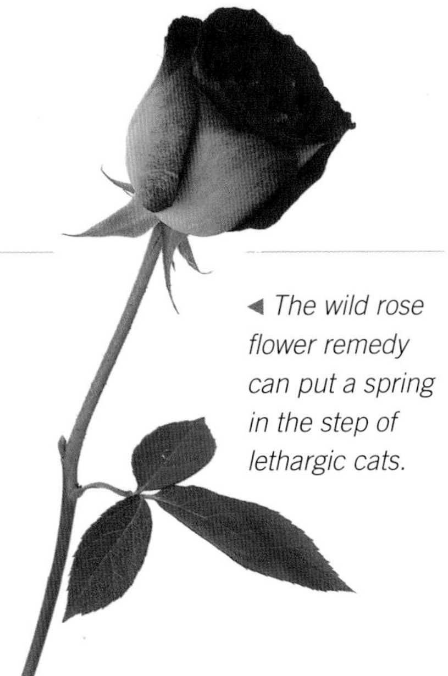

◄ *The wild rose flower remedy can put a spring in the step of lethargic cats.*

TRADITIONAL PREPARATION

Bach chose two methods of preparation for his plants, based on seasonal availability. Flowers that bloomed in the late spring and summer were picked at 9 a.m. on sunny days. The flowers were floated on 300ml (½ pint) of spring water in a

◄ *Dr Bach's remedies covered all the emotional states of his era. More remedies have been developed in recent years to cope with modern life.*

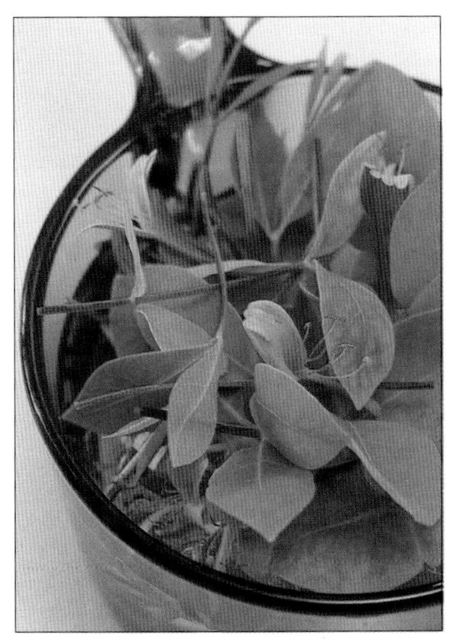

► *The boiling method is used to provide the mother tincture of those plants that bloom in winter or the early spring.*

When to use Bach Flowers

Choose the remedies according to the cat's mental state, using human emotions as a guide.

State of mind	Flower remedy
Shyness	Mimulus
Apathy	Wild Rose
Hormonal imbalances	Scleranthus
Lack of self-confidence	Larch
Maliciousness	Willow
Aloofness	Water Violet
Excessive desire for company	Heather
Possessiveness	Chicory
Dominance	Vine

▲ *Flower essences can be added to the cat's drinking water to help treat emotional problems.*

glass bowl and left in sunlight. If the sun clouded over, the batch would be discarded. The flowers were removed using stems of the same flower so that the energized water was not contaminated by human touch. The energized water was used to fill bottles half-full of brandy. This was the mother tincture. Two drops of this added to 30ml (2tbsp) of brandy gave the stock solution.

Plants that bloom in the late winter and spring were prepared by the boiling method. Flowers and stems were picked on sunny mornings. They were collected in a pan, and when the pan was nearly full, the lid was fitted and the material was taken home. The flowers and stems were covered with 1.2 litres (2 pints) of spring water and simmered for 30 minutes, uncovered. The lid was then replaced and the covered pot put outside to cool. When cool, the stems were removed, and the liquid filtered and used to make the mother tincture, as before.

The plants used in the remedies should be wild ones, growing in unpolluted areas. If cultivated plants are used, they should be organic and free from any chemical contamination. *Rock Water* should also be free from agrochemicals. Flowers from several plants are used.

Stock solutions of single Bach flower remedies are now widely sold ready-prepared, in health food stores and large chemists (drug stores). These remedies may be given alone or combined with up to five essences at one time to make a medicine. To prepare a medicine, add two drops of each essence to 30ml (2tbsp) of spring water.

USING FLOWER REMEDIES

Flower remedies are particularly valuable for emotional problems and, while clinical tests have proved inconclusive in explaining how and why they work, positive results have been seen in humans and animals. The cat's temperament is the key, so the better you know your cat, the more you can help it. Treatment is based on the cat's usual temperament and not on any innappropriate behaviour as a result. The simplest way to treat your cat is to add 3–4 drops of essence to its drinking water.

Dr Bach believed his remedies covered all known emotional states, and it probably is true that they addressed the most widespread symptoms of his era. More recently, however, other series of flower essences have been developed, such as Californian and Australian Bush flower remedies. These have been developed with modern life in mind, and offer treatments for such factors as the ill-effects of pollution and stress. These remedies are prepared and used in the same way as the Bach Flowers, and although they can be used on cats, they are perhaps less relevant for animals than for humans.

▼ *Bach flower remedies are taken in a very dilute form. Two drops of stock solution make 30 ml (2 tbsp) of medicine, which is diluted further when taken.*

Crystal therapies

Crystals have been used for healing purposes for thousands of years. Empirical studies indicate that through harmonic resonance, the vibrational energy of a crystal can affect the basic energetic vibration of both humans and animals.

▶ citrine

▼ tiger's eye

◀ amber

◀ iron pyrites

◀ tiger's eye

◀ rutilated quartz

◀ *Yellow stones relate to the chakra that governs the nervous, digestive and immune systems. Stress, fear and happiness are all linked to this colour.*

WHAT IS CRYSTAL THERAPY?

Crystals have a fixed, atomic structure, as opposed to the chaotic arrangement of atoms in non-crystalline material. The natural energy of the atoms is harmonized by this structure and every crystal has a natural frequency of vibration.

The energy of the crystal is believed to enter the body through the chakras of Indian Ayurvedic medicine. Each chakra is related to a hormone-producing gland in the body, and each has its own harmonic colour vibration. In turn, these correspond to seven layers or energy bands in the aura – the invisible energy field surrounding the physical body. Because of the universality of life-energy, these factors are as valid for animals as they are for humans. The only difference is the location of the chakras within the physical body. They have been accurately mapped in humans, but the corresponding chakras are not identical for animals. There is some controversy over the location of the minor and bud chakras in cats, although there is general agreement about the major chakras.

The chakra system for cats

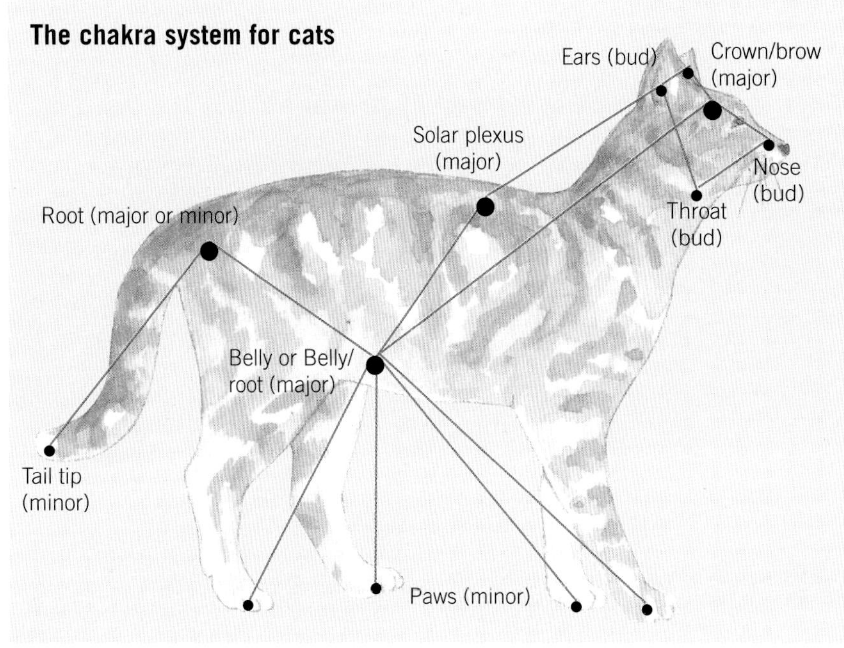

USING CRYSTALS

As with Bach Flower remedies, the mental state of the patient is the major factor in choosing which crystals to use. Some crystals have an affinity for certain body systems or symptoms. The factors quoted for crystal selection for humans can be applied to cats and other animals.

Once the appropriate crystals have been selected, they are placed on the patient's resting body in set patterns. For a cat, the crystals can be taped to its collar or an improvised harness if the cat will tolerate it. It is also possible to use liquefied crystal essences, which are produced in a similar way to the flower essences and can be successfully used to treat both mental and emotional problems.

Crystals can also be used in light therapy. Light is shone through coloured crystal filters in a darkened room on to the cat's body; the light is directed either on to a chakra, acupuncture point, or the region of the affected organ. Colours have long been known to affect the human mind and this phenomenon is used when choosing colour schemes for high-stress areas such as hospitals and police cells. It may be that animals are similarly affected by colour.

Crystal healing is helpful for cats whose illness is due to mental and emotional problems, and it can be used to support all physical and medical therapies. Do not use crystal therapy on unset broken bones, or before surgery, as it can interfere with the anaesthetic. Ensure you discuss crystal therapy with your vet before treatment is started and only proceed with the vet's approval.

HOW CRYSTALS WORK

Crystals contain metallic ions which can benefit the body's metabolic system. These are slowly absorbed by the body through the skin, if the crystal is placed in contact with it. This is similar to the use of essential oils in aromatherapy.

It has been demonstrated that if a human holds a crystal in the hand for more than 30 minutes, the brain waves change from the alert beta waves to the more relaxed alpha waves. The deep relaxation pattern associated with theta and delta waves will increase even further if the crystals are held for periods of more than half an hour.

► *The vibrations of crystals can restore balance to a cat's energy field. Every crystal has a vibrational rate which governs its therapeutic use.*

While crystals emanate positive healing vibrations, they also absorb negative and pain vibrations from the patient. To maintain the healing potential of crystals it is necessary to cleanse them regularly. They can be left outside for a 24-hour period when the moon is above the horizon: it is said that the dual action of sunlight and moonlight over this period will cleanse the crystal. Alternatively, the crystal can be left to stand in salt-water for 24 hours and then taken out of the water and left, pointing downwards, for eight hours to dry. Iron-containing crystals can be cleansed using spring water in the same way. Porous crystals, such as lapis lazuli and moonstone, should not be washed. These should be buried outside in the ground for 24 hours and then wiped clean with a paper towel, using a little spring water, if necessary, to remove all traces of dirt.

Choosing crystals

Amethyst	A healing stone to calm the mind
Bloodstone	To heal and energize the physical body
Blue lace agate	A cooling, calming stone to lighten thought
Citrine quartz	An energizing stone, physically and mentally
Clear quartz	For general wellbeing
Lapis lazuli	Releases stress to focus and calm
Moonstone	Clears tension from the emotions and abdomen
Rose quartz	To balance the emotions
Smoky quartz	A grounding stone and a deep cleanser
Tiger's eye	A stable and stimulating energy

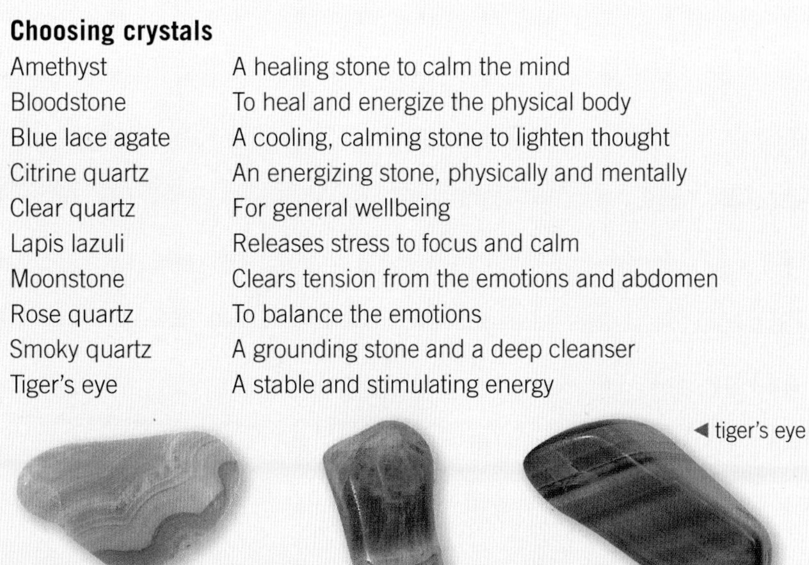

◄ tiger's eye

▲ blue lace agate

◄ amethyst

HOLISTIC CARE

Look in the perfumes of flowers and
nature for peace of mind and joy of life.
From the writings of Wang Wei, 8th century

Holistic care involves giving equal importance to physical and mental care, environmental needs and emotional requirements, as well as any past health challenges. All aspects must be considered for a well-balanced lifestyle. A happy contented cat is less likely to become unwell. The same theory applies to the owner too.

A holistic practitioner will evaluate the entire situation and consider symptoms as an indicator of a deeper problem. Holistic veterinary treatment combines conventional medical treatment with complementary therapies. Ideally the emphasis is on prevention as opposed to cure.

◄ *An ancient myth suggests that if you look into a cat's eyes it can see into your soul when it stares back.*

Treating your cat

Cats can bring us great pleasure when we keep them as pets. In return, it is up to us to make sure that they are properly looked after, and that if they become ill, they receive the best possible treatment.

WHO CAN TREAT YOUR CAT

As the cat's owner, by law you have the right to treat minor ailments yourself, but serious conditions can only be treated by, or under the supervision of, a vet once the cat has been examined and a diagnosis made.

Only a vet is qualified to prescribe medical drugs. Likewise, the practice of treatments such as acupuncture, chiropractic and osteopathy must be left to animal-trained therapists. The borderline case is herbalism. Using proprietary medicines available from chemists (drug stores), Western herbalism can be used at home. On the other hand, herbalism that forms part of Traditional Chinese Medicine (TCM) is only for qualified practitioners. If you are ever in any doubt about holistic treatment, consult your vet.

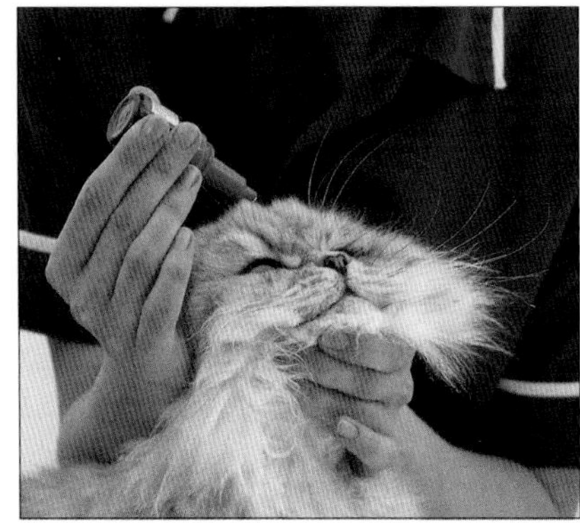

▲ *Both the homeopathic and Bach Flower remedies are tasteless and easy to administer.*

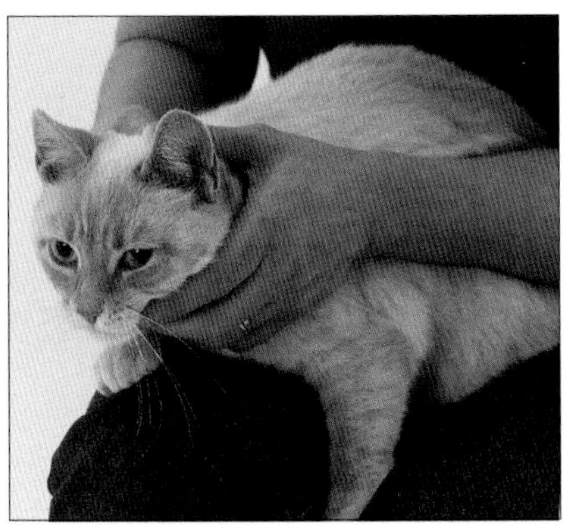

▲ *The close contact involved in the massage therapies will strengthen the owner-cat bond.*

USING HOME TREATMENTS

If your cat is showing signs of being mildly unwell, some of the therapies discussed in this book can be used at home with a basic self-taught knowledge of the therapy.

If you are interested in holistic treatment for your cat, it might be worth taking an introductory course in the therapy which most appeals to you. Veterinary courses are available in TTeam, TTouch, homeopathy and the Bach Flower remedies. It is more difficult to find animal-based courses for crystal therapy, massage or Reiki. One of the good things about holistic therapies, though, is that they are energetically rather than anatomically based, and the species of the patient does not seem to matter. It is possible to adapt knowledge of the therapy as it applies to humans over to cats – if you use a little common sense.

Mood swings, emotional distresses, or early signs of behavioural problems can all be treated in the first instance at home. Similarly, if the cat has only mild physical symptoms, such as diarrhoea and vomiting, a cough or muscular stiffness, you can try the therapy of your choice. When the cat is in severe pain, has blood in any of its bodily discharges, or if it does not respond to home treatment, you should see a vet. Similarly, if your cat suffers from the same minor symptoms again and again, you should consult your vet, who will check for an underlying cause. This is why conventional medicine is such a necessary part of holistic care.

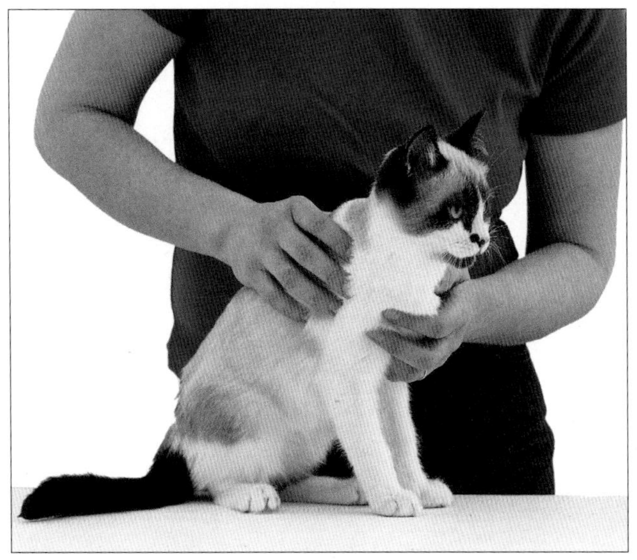

◀ *Massage is one of the simplest ways to help your cat at home. You don't need equipment or training, just an understanding of your cat.*

▼ *Cats do not all appreciate being dosed with medicine or manipulated by strangers, so consider your cat's usual likes and dislikes when choosing a therapy.*

A SUPPORTIVE ROLE

If your cat is seriously ill, holistic therapies may be used in a supportive role alongside conventional treatment, with the vet's agreement. Medical conditions, such as diabetes, will often respond quickly to conventional veterinary treatment. The correct use of complementary medicines, however, can reduce the amount of drugs needed, and may even give a complete cure. Similarly, after surgery, holistic support can help recovery.

WORKING TOGETHER

The veterinary profession the world over is beginning to take an increasing interest in holistic medicine, but as yet few vets have much experience of using it. The next time you visit the vet, tell him or her of your interest. Ask what the prescribed treatment is designed to do and, if there are any side effects, if there is a complementary therapy that would help your cat. Let the vet know that you want to work together for the benefit of the cat – it is extremely important that conventional and holistic medicines are used in a complementary way. In the end, the aim of both is to make sure the animal enjoys a long and happy life.

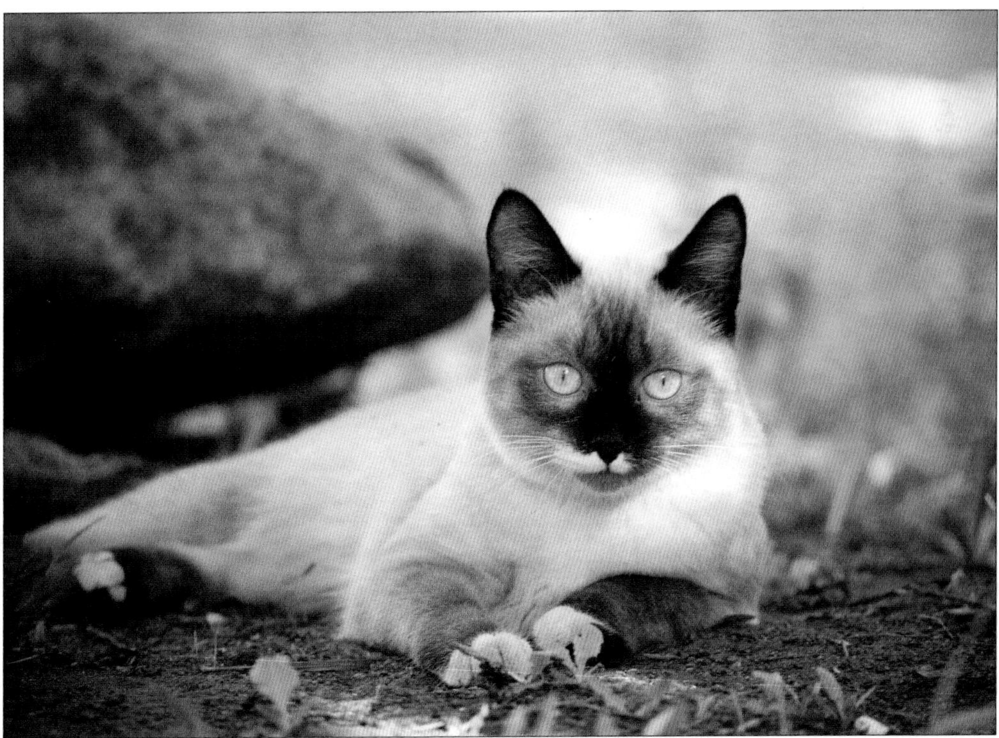

▶ *The use of home alternative remedies should only be used with extreme care. Check products are safe to use on cats and that physical treatments will not painfully aggravate a hidden underlying problem. If your cat is physically unwell always seek veterinary advice. Do not risk serious health issues by wasting time with home dosing.*

House-training

The inappropriate elimination of urine and faeces is the commonest behavioural problem in cats, and the one most likely to create difficulties for its owner.

Kittens are still very young when they develop their preference about where to eliminate their waste. Problems with this will arise because of one of three situations: in the adoption of an untrained (usually feral) cat, when a trained cat suddenly loses its house-training, and when the cat starts to deliberately use its urine and faeces as a means of marking out its territory.

If you decide to take in a feral cat, the normal house-training routine should be started immediately. Put the cat on to the litter tray or outside after meals, and when it looks as if it wants to go. Try different substances in the tray until you find one that the cat finds acceptable. Remember also that cats are very private animals and that its tray should be well away from the busy part of the house, its eating utensils and its sleeping area. If there are other cats in the home, it may be necessary to provide separate trays for each cat. Close-confining a cat with a litter tray may speed things up but it can be so stressful to a cat that has been used to free-roaming, that the stress can outweigh the benefits.

Sometimes a cat that has always had clean habits will start to mess in the house; this behaviour may have physical and/or mental origins. If a cat has a bowel or urinary tract infection, it may be unable to control itself long enough to get to a tray or outside. If this happens often enough, the cat may persist with inappropriate elimination even when it gets over the infection. If the cat has started to habitually use another part of the house, that area should be cleaned with an enzymatic odour-removing product. These are available from veterinary surgeries and good pet shops. A second tray can be placed in that area on several thicknesses of paper, on top of a layer of thick polythene to prevent any soiling going through to the floor covering. Alternatively, the cat and a suitable litter tray can be kept in a small room – usually the bathroom – to encourage it to use the tray. Cats are very particular, and many dislike reusing a soiled tray, so regular cleaning is a good idea.

Mental and emotional causes, however, are probably the most usual reasons for a loss of house-training. Fear is a frequent cause of loss of training. The most common fear is of being attacked by another cat or a dog that has moved into your cat's territory. If the cat has been involved in a road accident, this can also deter it from going outside. Fear can also develop if

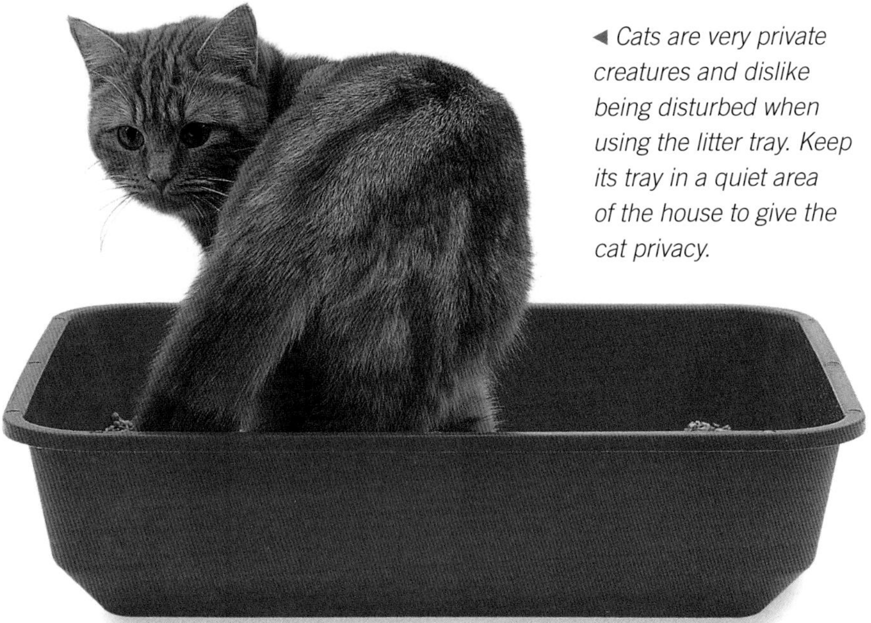

◄ *Cats are very private creatures and dislike being disturbed when using the litter tray. Keep its tray in a quiet area of the house to give the cat privacy.*

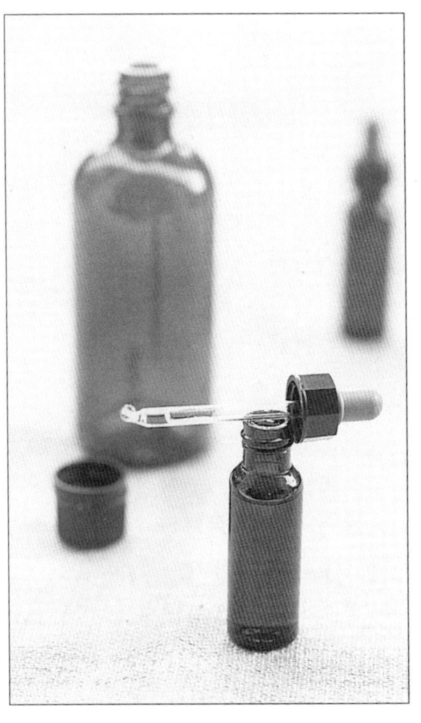

◄ *The Bach Flower remedies can help in cases where a loss of house-training is the result of an emotional disturbance of some kind.*

▼ *Covered trays such as this are favoured by the more timid cat. The top is removable to facilitate cleaning.*

the cat associates using its tray with an unpleasant experience, such as accidentally having things dropped on it, being attacked by the family dog, or being disturbed by very loud noises, such as smoke alarms and children's noisy toys, for example.

COMPLEMENTARY TREATMENT

If you think that fear may be the underlying cause of your cat's distress, use the Bach Flowers *Mimulus*, *Cherry Plum* and *Rock Rose* to support a retraining plan, or try the homeopathic remedy *Aconite*. Give TTouch to help reassure the cat, and the aromatic oils basil, chamomile and lavender can be used in a diffuser. If you want to try these oils in a massage, dilute 2 drops of oil first in 15ml (1tbsp) of a vegetable-based carrier oil. Use an oil massage no more than once or twice a week. Herbal infusions of chamomile or vervain can help; the tissue salt *Mag phos.* may act as a nerve tonic.

▼ *Make sure that the tray is large enough for your cat, and that it contains a litter of your cat's liking.*

Feelings of resentment closely follow those of fear. Resentment can happen when a foreign cat comes into the house, eats your cat's food and uses its litter tray. Or it could arise when your cat has been sent away to a cattery or when a new pet or baby comes into the home. In such cases, try the Bach Flowers: *Centaury* for lack of assertiveness, *Elm* for feelings of inadequacy, or *Willow* if the cat is showing concurrent destructive behaviour out of spite, perhaps to pay you back for being sent away from home or ignored. Homeopathic *Staphysagria 30C* can be given twice daily for resentment, and herbal infusions of passiflora and vervain may also help. TTouch will help to restore the cat's confidence.

The extreme case of territory marking by spraying or defecating in the house will often be done as a response to an outside threat, as above. When a cat sprays to mark its territory it aims at a vertical surface 30–45cm (12–18in) from the floor. It does not squat in the way that it does when it urinates. Try the Bach Flower

Rescue Remedy and homeopathic *Staphysagria*. If circumstances permit, it's also a good idea to treat the invading cat, using the Bach Flower *Vine* or the homeopathic remedy *Lachesis*. If the aggressor is an exceptionally strong bully, homeopathic *Platinum 30C* given twice daily for five days may help. If your cat is an un-neutered tom who is spraying, then it is most likely due to hyper-sexual behaviour. In such a case, the homeopathic remedy *Ustilago maydis* may be of some help.

If your cat does not show any sign of improvement in its house-training, or if the behaviour seems to get worse, you should see the vet, who will check for signs of physical abnormality or disease. He or she will either prescribe treatment or, in the absence of any disease, he or she may suggest pheromone sprays to put around the house on the furniture and walls to inhibit spraying. The vet may also prescribe anxiety-reducing (anxiolytic) drugs for the cat. A referral to a behavioural specialist may be suggested in particularly stubborn cases.

Aggression

Aggression in cats is not usually a serious problem for their owners, and cats rarely need to be referred to animal behaviourists for treatment.

Cats may still show isolated signs of aggression towards other cats and/or humans. Inter-cat aggression, as its name suggests, is shown only to other cats; assertion or status-related aggression is shown only to humans. There are many other types of aggressive behaviour which are shown towards both cats and humans.

INTER-CAT AGGRESSION

The classic, violent cat fight usually occurs between two toms wanting to mate with the same queen. This is the most common example of inter-cat aggression. To reduce the likelihood of your tom being involved in too many fights, he is best neutered before he is six months old. This will control his testosterone levels, which may otherwise cause him to fight. The other treatment is to keep him shut away from other cats, except when he is needed for stud purposes.

Inter-cat aggression is not restricted to tomcats, however. It can also be male-to-female and female-to-female, particularly in households with three or more cats. The dominant cat will take up an aggressive stance and the other will try to defuse the situation and avoid physical injury, its body language suggesting a deferential pose.

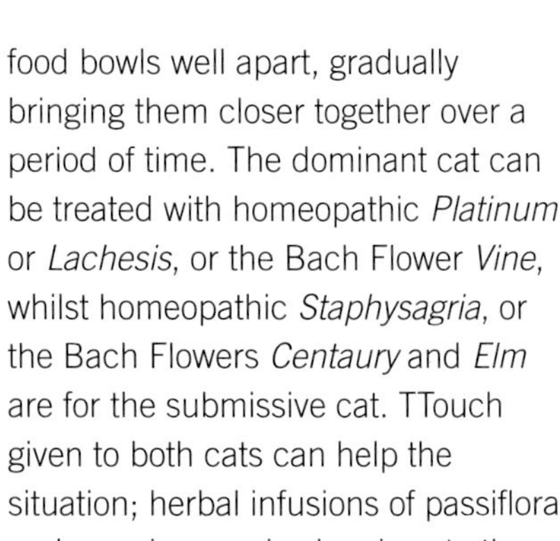

► *Cats have no 'natural handles'. The scruff of the neck probably gives the safest hold on a cat of uncertain temperament.*

It is only when two cats feel of equal status that the trouble starts. In this case, the cats have to be housed in separate rooms, the more aggressive cat being given the smaller, less attractive room. When their owner is present, however, the cats can be in the same room. If the dominant cat shows aggressive behaviour it should be startled, using a rattle or horn, and gently moved back into isolation. If there are no signs of aggression, give both cats a treat.

When the cats can be in the same room without fighting, they can be brought closer together using harnesses and given treats as rewards for good behaviour. Try feeding the cats in the same room but with their food bowls well apart, gradually bringing them closer together over a period of time. The dominant cat can be treated with homeopathic *Platinum* or *Lachesis*, or the Bach Flower *Vine*, whilst homeopathic *Staphysagria*, or the Bach Flowers *Centaury* and *Elm* are for the submissive cat. TTouch given to both cats can help the situation; herbal infusions of passiflora and vervain can also be given to the inferior cat.

◄ *When fighting breaks out regularly, treat both cats. Try to subdue the dominant cat whilst strengthening the weaker one.*

CAUSES OF AGGRESSION

Lack of socialization with humans arises when kittens have not had enough human contact in the first seven to ten weeks of life. These cats tend to grow up displaying aggressive behaviour towards humans and are difficult to treat. Not interfering with the cat is usually the best approach to take. The Bach Flowers *Beech* or *Rock Rose* can be tried, as can homeopathic *Stramonium* for fear of being attacked. TTouch, using a wand, can be helpful. The burning of the essential oils sandalwood and ylang-ylang has also helped in some cases.

When a cat is in a situation of perceived danger and it cannot escape, it is likely to become aggressive through fear. Recognize that the cat is frightened and under stress; do not advance, but back off and give the cat its chance to run away. TTouch is good, as are the Bach Flowers *Aspen*, *Cherry Plum* and *Mimulus*, and *Stramonium* can be tried. If these do not help, the vet may prescribe a tranquillizer. If the situation is a recurring problem, refer your cat to a behaviourist. Aggression may be caused by pain resulting from various issues, such as disease, accidents, surgery or a course of painful injections. In such cases, the cat needs sensitive handling, while its pain can be treated with homeopathic *Arnica*; an appropriate Bach Flower remedy can be used for emotional disturbance.

The cat's major facial expressions

calm: face relaxed, teeth covered, ears pricked

worried: ears back, pupils dilated with fear

ready to attack: ears back, eyes narrowed

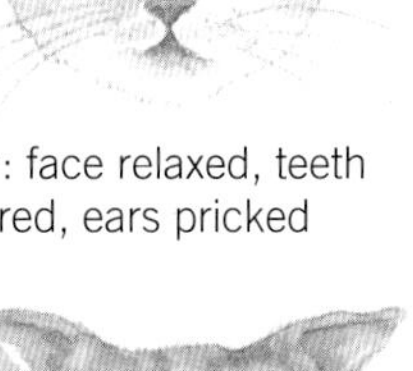
reconsidering attack: ears back, eyes widened

warning: ears back, eyes narrowed, teeth shown

ready to attack: ears down, mouth open, teeth bared

The cat's major tail positions

calm

defensive

affectionate

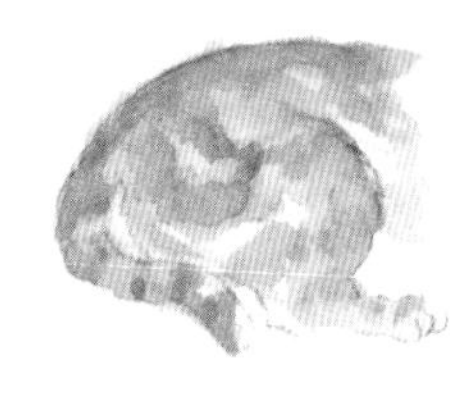
submissive

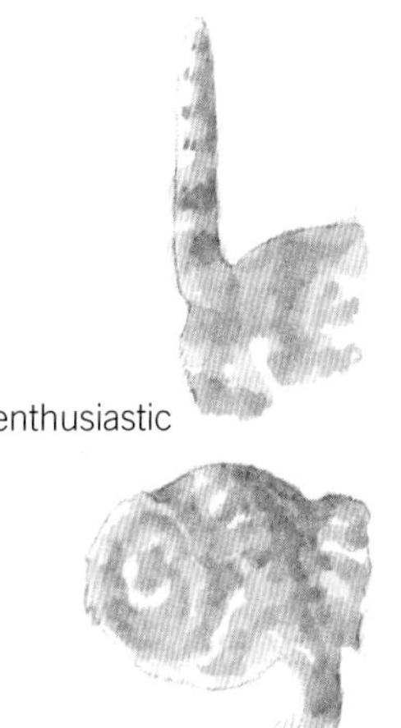
enthusiastic

stalking prey

Complementary treatment

TTouch is good for calming anxious cats. Wands may be necessary for safety reasons. This can be tried on rehomed cats and kittens that are not properly socialized to humans. Aromatherapy, using the essential oils of sandalwood and ylang-ylang can be helpful if used in a diffuser. Herbal preparations can be helpful. Infusions of chamomilla relax cats that become angry and bite from impatience. The proprietary *Skullcap* and *Valerian* tablets have a calming effect.

Bach Flower remedies can be successful where negative emotional states cause aggression. They may be used singly or in combinations of up to five essences. If pain is causing the cat to bite, *Star of Bethlehem*, *Sweet Chestnut* or *Rescue Remedy* can be given.

Homeopathic remedies should be given singly, using a *30C* potency twice daily for up to five days. They should be reduced or stopped if an improvement is seen. If there is no improvement, consult a homeopath: some remedies are developed for specific situations. *Belladonna* helps cats that explode with anger; *Nux vom.* helps those that are irritable, sensitive to noise and have bowel troubles.

Crystal therapy, using liquid-gem oral remedies, can modify behaviour by stabilizing the emotions.

Pining

Ask any cat-owner and they will almost certainly be able to think of a time when their cat showed signs of upset after being left or sent away. Cats are more emotional creatures than many people think.

Pining is a form of separation anxiety, mixed with sadness or resentment. It is commonly seen in cats whose owners have died, but it can also show itself when the cat is put in the cattery, if it has to be rehomed, or when its greatest friend leaves home. Typical signs of bereavement in the cat are a loss of interest in life and a withdrawal into itself. This may progress to a loss of appetite and thirst.

It has been known for cats to starve and dehydrate themselves so badly when put in quarantine or even in a cattery, that intravenous feeding was needed to keep them alive until they could go home. Treatment with vitamins and anabolic steroids does not unfortunately stimulate the appetite of these cats.

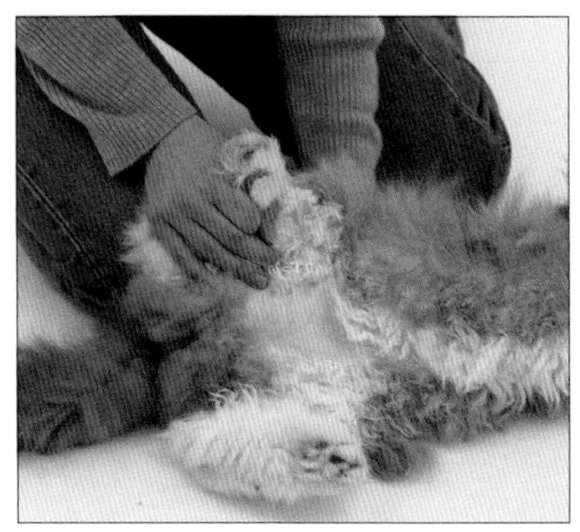

▲ *Massage with the essential oils of basil, bergamot and orange blossom, diluted in a vegetable-based oil, on the bald groin area can help to relieve emotional stress.*

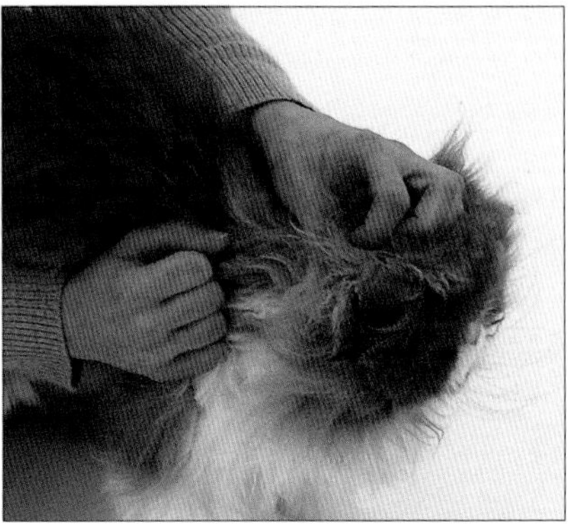

▲ *Large flakes of scurf around the neck can indicate resentment and the need for the homeopathic remedy,* Staphysagria.

Resentment can appear as physical symptoms. In extreme cases, the cat's coat becomes greasy, clumps form in the fur, and the skin is scurfy. The skin of the belly and groin may also become dry, red and itchy, with flakes of scurf around the neck. Some cats develop incontinence and/or cystitis, and may have blood in their urine.

Orthodox treatment for both skin and bladder problems is with antibiotics and steroids. However, if these problems are emotionally based, then the treatment is rarely successful. Typically, there will be an initial positive response to treatment which then slips back, and a chronic condition will often become established.

Complementary therapies, which tackle the underlying emotional problem, are more effective in producing a permanent cure in these cases. Conventional and holistic therapies can also be used together.

Complementary treatment

TTouch can be given both at home and in a cattery to help the cat feel loved. Aromatherapy with basil, bergamot and orange blossom can all be useful and you can try the Bach Flowers: *Heather* for loneliness, *Honeysuckle* for homesickness, and *Walnut* to help the cat adjust to the change in its circumstances. Homeopathic *Ignatia* is used for the mood-swing type of grief, whilst *Natrum mur.* is used when the coat is greasy and there is a loss of fur that starts at the base of the tail and works its way back towards the head, a bit like an arrow-head.

Resentment that shows itself by a loss of house-training, cystitis (possibly with blood in the urine), or a dry red itchy skin that begins in the belly and groin region, can be helped by homeopathic *Staphysagria.* Greasy fur with dandruff at the base of the tail is often the first sign of separation anxiety. Homeopathic *natrum mur.* will often help to acclimatize the cat to its new situation.

Young kittens are understandably likely to miss their mother when they are first rehomed. They can be given the Bach Flower remedy *Honeysuckle* for their homesickness. If the stress is so great as to cause physical illness like diarrhoea, the homeo-pathic remedy *Capiscum* may help.

Destructiveness

Destructiveness in the house usually takes the form of scratching at the furniture. Carpets, doors and soft-furnishings can also be favourite scratching places. If left unchecked, the scratching can eventually cause unsightly and expensive damage to items around the home.

Cats like to scratch solid objects for two reasons: as part of a grooming routine and as a way of marking their territory. In grooming, cats often develop a preference for a particular type of material. Cats which are allowed to roam outdoors will mark their territory with secretions from the glands between their toes, as well as with the visual signs of their scratch and nail shreds. Outdoors, cats have access to many types of materials and this reduces their need to scratch indoors. These cats are not likely to cause problems until they become elderly, when they spend less and less time outside and may start looking for suitable objects to scratch at indoors.

▼ *A fine nail file or emery board can be used to trim the nails of kittens and younger cats.*

▲ *Trim claws to reduce the damage caused to furniture as the cat uses its foot glands to mark its territory.*

Cats kept entirely indoors need a scratching post of some kind. Most cats prefer a vertical surface, about 1m (3ft) high, which will give them a good stretch as they scratch. These poles may be covered by thick sisal rope or carpet, or they may be left bare. Young kittens can sometimes be trained to scratch on a specific surface by gently dragging their toes and nails over the material, particularly if this is introduced as part of a nail-cutting session.

The need to scratch can be controlled if the cat can be persuaded to let you trim its claws regularly, using clippers or a nail file. This should be started early in its life to accustom it to having its feet handled. When clipping claws, you may find it easier for both of you if you turn the foot backwards to expose the under-surface of the foot, in the same way as a blacksmith does when lifting a horse's hoof.

Destructiveness in the house can also take the form of territorial marking, as exhibited by scratching and/or spraying. If your cat is an only one, then this will not usually be a problem. However, if a second cat is introduced into the household, it can prompt the first cat into an orgy of scratching and spraying as it asserts its right to control the whole house.

The second cat does not even need to be a member of the household to cause problems. A dominant cat may have moved into the area, and be trying to take over not only your cat's territory, but also its house, feeding bowl and litter tray. This will cause your cat to mark inside its home with even more enthusiasm. You can discourage the intruder by using a startler rattle, water pistol or similar whenever you see it. At the same time, try startling your own cat if you see it about to mark indoors. Your vet can prescribe a pheromone furniture spray, which will further deter your cat.

Complementary treatment

You can encourage your cat to stand up for itself by using the Bach Flowers *Centaury* for submissiveness, and *Walnut* to help the cat to adjust to new circumstances. Use the homeopathic remedy *Staphysagria* if the cat seems a bit resentful and *Colocynth* if it seems angry. Give reassurance and support with TTouch. The essential oil of chamomile, used in a vaporizer, will help to relieve the cat's anxiety and calm it down.

Jealousy

Jealousy is an emotional state that many scientists believe only exists in human beings. However, there are indications that cats are also subject to this emotion. In a jealous state, the cat will become over-conscious of its rights and privileges and tries to retain them if it considers them to be under attack. These rights extend to territory, food and people.

The arrival of another cat, the birth of a baby, or even the presence of a friend or partner are situations in which the owner's attention is diverted away from the cat, triggering it into jealous behaviour.

◀ *Cats and young children usually get along well together. However, this child is immersed in his toy, and the cat is mildly jealous, vying for the child's attention.*

Complementary treatment

Give regular TTouch sessions to restore confidence and balance to a disturbed cat. Aromatherapy diffusions with ylang-ylang and sandalwood essential oils can also help to make cats feel more secure in the home. The Bach Flowers can be tried: *Chicory* for a possessive cat, *Red Chestnut* for being overprotective, and *Vine* for territorial aggression. Use homeopathic *Lachesis* for aggressively jealous cats, and *Pulsatilla* for the normally gentle cat who has a tendency to push and nudge between humans to claim its rightful place. *Pulsatilla* is particularly appropriate if the cat produces bland, yellow discharges and suffers any infection, particularly of the eyes and/or nose.

If a kitten is introduced into the house it may seem to get on well with the existing cat. Well-adjusted cats will partition their home with invisible boundaries and each animal will have its own share of the house without too much fuss. Trouble may not start until the younger newcomer attains social maturity at about two years old.

Following the birth of a child, some cats can take a dislike to the new baby. If jealousy is suspected, it is wise to keep the cat away from the child, and to pay as much attention as is practical to the cat, to make it still feel loved and part of the home.

Where adults are concerned, cats may try to push their way between their owner and a close friend or partner. Some cats will attempt to drive the other adult away by force, and others will try attention-seeking behaviour, such as continuous vocalization or self-mutilation by over-grooming. All of these behaviours are designed to draw the owner away from visitors and friends. The conventional treatment for such behaviour is for the vet to prescribe some form of tranquillizer that will reduce tension in the cat and allow its normal behaviour to return. Training cats to accept a situation can be difficult; this may require the help of an animal behaviourist.

▼ *Jealously can lead to the cat trying to draw attention to itself by displays of bad behaviour. Complementary treatment is more rewarding than chemical sedation when the problem gets out of hand.*

The eyes

Perhaps one of the most striking features of a cat is its eyes. In a healthy cat, these are clear and bright and can vary in colour enormously – beautiful shades of amber, green or blue are all common. The pupil should be black; its shape varies according to the light conditions: in bright light it narrows to a slit, but as it gets darker the pupil becomes rounder and larger. At times of extreme fear, the pupils dilate and the iris almost disappears.

Although a cat can see extremely well in the dark, it takes at least half an hour for its eyes to adapt to a sudden loss of light. In the wild this does not matter, but a cat leaving a well-lit house at night will effectively be blind for a while whilst its eyes adjust. This may be why most of the road traffic accidents involving cats take place shortly after the cat has gone outside at night. It is a good idea to check your cat's eyes as part of its daily grooming routine. Good eye condition is an indication of good health.

DISCHARGES AND INFLAMMATION

Cats have a third eyelid that moves across the surface of the eye, from the inside corner towards the outside. The third eye is clear and membranous, and under normal circumstances it is barely visible. However, if the eye looks painful, or if the pad of fat on which it rests disappears, this membrane becomes more obvious. If it comes into view and remains visible for more than 48 hours – even if there is no sign of inflammation or discharge – consult the vet in case it is the first sign of a more serious disease.

Any discharges from the eyes should be noted as these can occur for several reasons, some minor and some more serious.

The tear duct is responsible for draining tears into the nose. If this becomes blocked or is absent for any reason, it may result in a mild tear overspill on to the face. Tear duct problems are more common in the flat-face breeds, such as Persians. If the discharge is mild, the eye can be cleansed with warm salt-water or a cold tea solution. If the problem persists, your vet can check to see if the tear duct is working properly. If it isn't, the cat may need a small operation to clear the duct under a general anaesthetic.

Thick purulent discharges from the eyes are generally more serious. These may be a sign of cat flu, or that a foreign body, such as a grass awn, may have worked its way behind the third eyelid and become stuck.

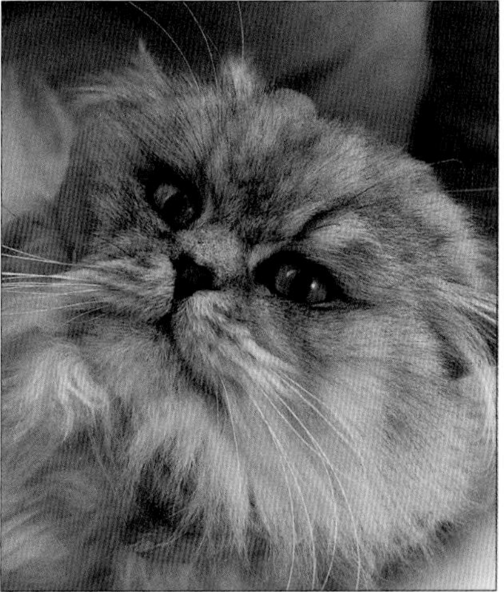

▲ *Regular cleaning of eye discharges, particularly in the longhaired breeds, helps to keep the facial fur free of unsightly stains.*

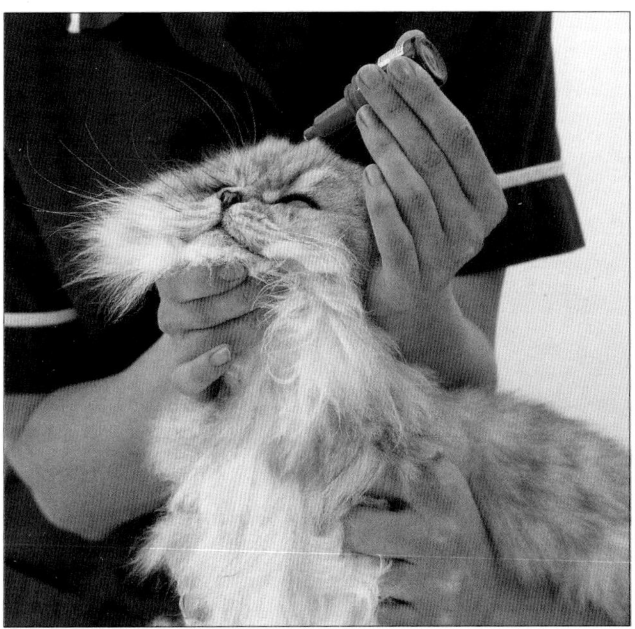

◀ *Many cats resent being treated. An extra pair of hands is often needed to get drops into the eyes of an uncooperative animal.*

CONJUNCTIVITIS

The conjunctiva is the peachy-pink membrane that lines the lids and surrounds the white of the cat's eye. An inflamed conjunctiva is known as conjunctivitis. If there is inflammation but no discharge, you can try bathing the eye with a solution of homeopathic *Euphrasia* tincture diluted 1:10 with water, or a herbal infusion of *Golden*

► *If your cat rubs its eyes a lot, it may be necessary to clip the dew claw to prevent it making things worse by inadvertantly scratching the eye.*

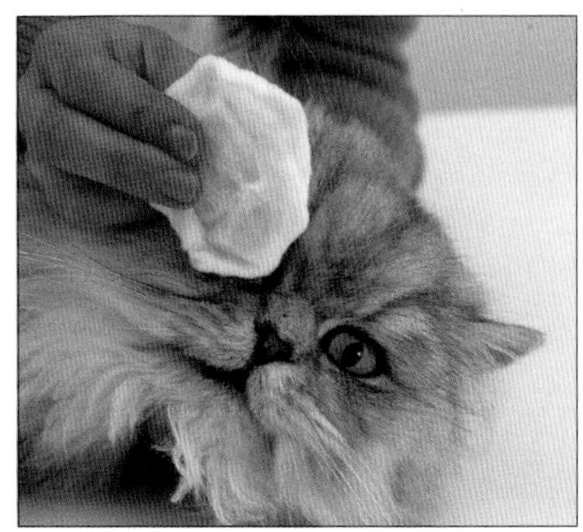

▲ *Diluted euphrasia tincture, or a herbal infusion of goldenseal, will soothe inflamed eyes. Apply with a soaked wad of clean cotton gauze or cotton wool or cotton balls.*

Seal. Homeopathic *Apis mel.* may be indicated if the eye is red, the conjunctiva very swollen and there is marked weeping of the eye. This can be given every two hours. If the cat shows no improvement after six hours, you should contact the vet.

If the conjunctivitis is accompanied by discharges, the eyes can be bathed as above, and the following homeopathic remedies may be tried: *Arsen. alb. 6C* if the discharge is watery and scalding the fur off the cat's face; *Kali bich.* if the discharge is thick, green and stringy; or *Pulsatilla* for a creamy yellow discharge.

If the symptoms don't improve in 36 hours, or if the condition keeps recurring, the cat should be checked for a more serious underlying condition. If none is found, a homeopathically-trained vet may prescribe a constitutional remedy to help your cat. Alternatively, try to improve the cat's resistance to infection, using *Ferrum phos.* in the absence of discharges; *Kali mur.* for white discharges; or *Natrum phos.* for sticky yellow ones.

◄ *When using dropper bottles, make sure the dropper does not touch the eye or any of the discharges: this is the surest way to spread infection.*

CORNEAL ULCERS AND GLAUCOMA

The delicate, transparent part of the eyeball is known as the cornea. It is frequently damaged in fights, but grass awns and other foreign bodies can also scratch the eye. Left untreated, scratches can develop into corneal ulcers. As these deepen, the cornea can burst and the eyeball loses its fluid and collapses. Sight is then permanently lost in that eye.

If you suspect your cat has damage to its cornea, it should be seen urgently by a vet, who will test the eye for ulcers. If ulcers are found, you can support the vet's treatment by bathing the cat's eye with goldenseal or diluted euphrasia and the following homeopathic remedies: *Argent. nit. 6C* if the cat is anxious; *Acid nit. 6C* if it is irritable or aggressive; *Merc. cor. 6C* if the eye is very sore, the cat dislikes the light and the discharge is greenish; and *Kali bich.* in the unusual case where the eye is painless. *Silica 30C* can be given when treatment is already underway, to help with the final stages of healing.

Sometimes the iris, or even the whole of the eyeball, can become infected, usually as a result of a deep infection after a bite. In such a case, the cat must be seen by a vet immediately. You can support the prescribed conventional treatment plan with homeopathic *Hepar sulph. 30C* and infusions of greater celandine to bathe the eye and to soothe it.

Infection and damage to the eye's inner structures can result in a build-up of fluid within the eye. The eyeball becomes swollen and red, and the cornea turns a cloudy white colour, with a red fringe around the edge. This condition is known as glaucoma and is extremely painful and serious. It can lead to damage of the retina, loss of vision and, sometimes, to a loss of the eye itself.

If you suspect your cat has glaucoma, it should be taken to the vet

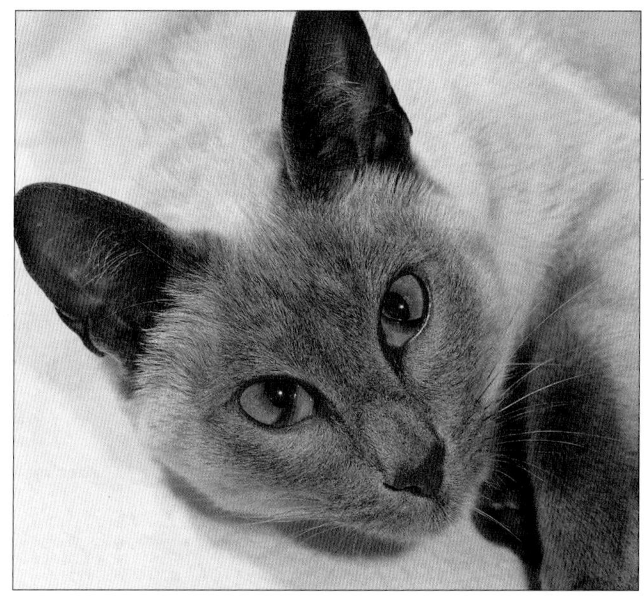

◄ *When the third eyelids, or haws, come across the eyes it usually means that there is some damage that requires veterinary attention.*

immediately. The vet's treatment can be supported by bathing with euphrasia and trying homeopathic remedies: *Phosphorus* for the very active, demonstrative cat who is afraid of thunder, and *Spigelia* if the eye is extremely painful. Begin by giving the appropriate remedy hourly and reduce the frequency when you see signs of improvement.

▼ *Euphrasia, otherwise known as eyebright, is used as both herbal infusions or as a diluted homeopathic tincture for sore eyes.*

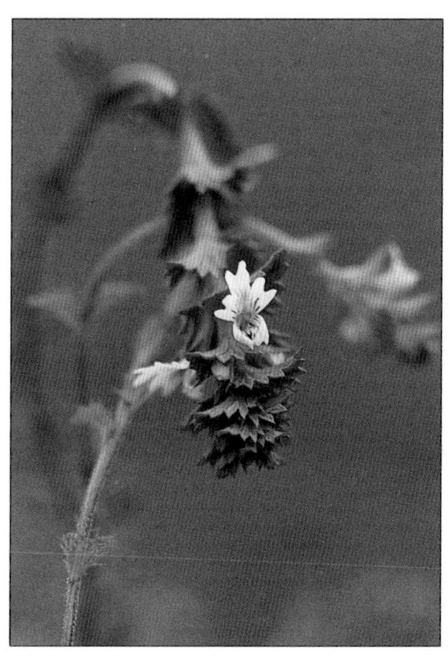

CATARACTS

If you notice any white spots in the cat's pupil it may be an early indication of cataracts. These spots can grow to make the entire pupil look a milky-white colour and the clear lens of the eye becomes cloudy. These opacities prevent light from reaching the retina (the light-sensitive tissue at the back of the eye) and cause blurred or partial loss of vision. Eventually they may lead to a total loss of sight.

Cats can be born with cataracts (congenital) or they may develop later in life as a result of poisoning, ageing or the effects of diabetes. If you suspect your cat has cataracts, you should seek your vet's advice urgently.

Unlike the more traditional surgical methods, which need the cataract to grow to a certain size before it can be cut out, laser surgery techniques can be used very successfully to treat cataracts at a very early stage.

The main drawback of laser surgery is that it can be expensive and may not be appropriate in every case. If laser surgery is unavailable, bathe the eye twice daily with the homeopathic *Cineraria* tincture diluted 1:10 with water. This needs to be kept up for several months.

Alternatively, it can help if the cat's eyes are bathed with a fresh herbal infusion of greater celandine. This can be supported with the tissue salts *Natrum mur.* for cataracts in their early stages, or *Silica* for longer standing cases.

In addition, the following homeopathic remedies can be tried: *Calc. carb. 6C* for overweight cats; *Phosphorus 6C* for thin, nervous cats; and *Silica* for naturally large-bodied cats with thin legs.

The diet can also be supplemented with a daily dose of 100 I. U. of Vitamin E (d-alpha tocopherol) in the form of wheatgerm oil, and a daily tablet of Selenium 25 mg, as these may slow the growth rate of cataracts.

A blow to the cat's eye, such as from a road accident or from a thrown stone, can be helped with homeopathic *Symphytum*, when there is marked pain but little bruising, and *Ledum*, when the bruising is severe, even to the point where there has been bleeding into the front chamber of the eye. *Ledum* is also recommended when the cat's eye has been punctured by a sharp object, such as another cat's claw, but there has been little or no fluid lost from the eye.

▼ *Tablets of Vitamin E can be given if wheatgerm oil is not readily taken. The taste of the tablets is usually acceptable to the cat.*

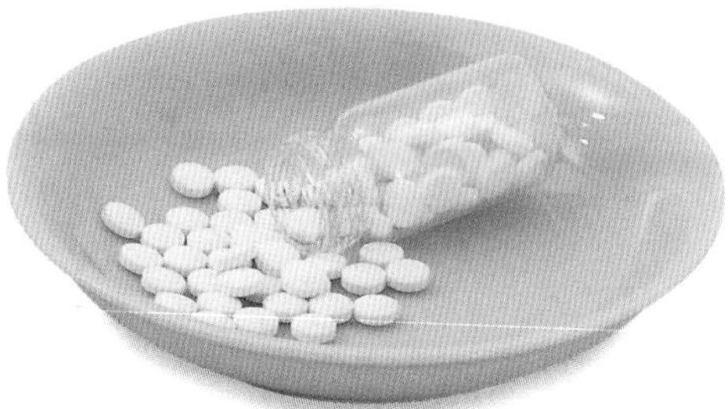

The ears

Ear problems in cats fall into either one of two categories. Either they arise as a result of a problem with the metabolism, or else they are the result of infections following bites to the head during cat fights.

The ear canal is lined with glands that produce natural wax in controlled amounts in a healthy cat. These glands are also capable of excreting mineral salts and other toxins if these are allowed to build up excessively in the body. Excess abnormal secretion, however, changes the micro-climate within the ear canal, which then allows unfriendly bacteria and parasitic insects to live and flourish in the ear. The presence of these organisms can cause unnatural and foul-smelling discharges. Similar changes in micro-climate also occur when foreign bodies, usually grass awns, find their way into the ear.

There are two things to check when examining your cat's ears: their colour and their smell. A healthy cat's ears should be a light pink colour on the inside. Some cats, however, have white, unpigmented ear flaps and are prone to developing cancer of the ear. This can be prevented by the use of a sunblock when there is bright sunlight.

◄ *Sunblock can be used to help prevent bright sunlight causing cancer of the ear flap in cats with unpigmented earl flaps.*

If the edge of the flap becomes crusty and thickened, see a vet straight away as surgery may be necessary.

Your cat's ears should smell clean and healthy, with very little odour. If the ear starts to smell it is a sign of infection. The Indian herbal cream *Canador* is useful in the early stages, and *Echinacea 6X* will help to detoxify the cat and support its immune system. Before the infected stage really takes hold, try cleaning with the homeopathic remedy, *Hypercal* tincture, diluted 1:10 with water. Alternatively, two drops of lemon juice in 5ml (1tsp) of water, or a mixture of three parts rosemary infusion added to one part of witch-hazel lotion can be used to clean wax from the ear. If you know your cat's homeopathic constitutional remedy, a dose should help with the underlying cause of the problem.

A dark, dry, crumbly wax usually points to the presence of otodectic mites. In this case, it is worth trying a mixture of one part each of rosemary, rue and thyme mixed with three parts of olive oil to clean the ear.

If an offensive smell or discharge starts, or if there is no improvement in five days, then you should take your

► rosemary

◄ *Regular rosemary infusions can help get rid of ear mites.*

◄ *A mixture of rosemary, rue and thyme diluted with olive oil is better than rosemary alone when there is a lot of wax present in the ear.*

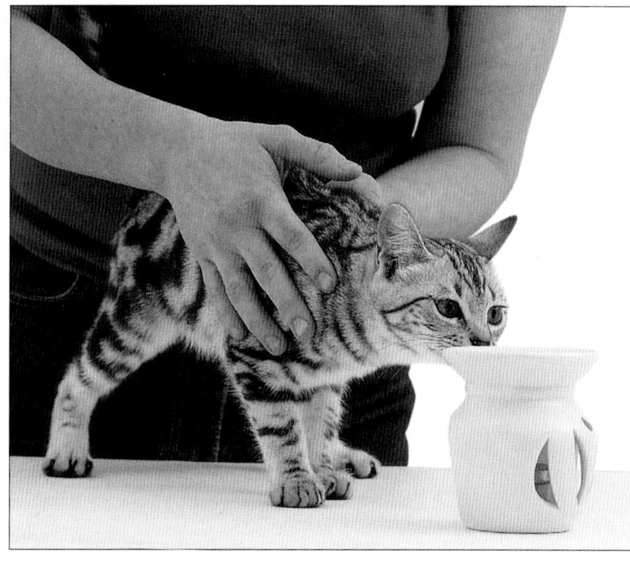

◄ *Emotional issues can underlie chronic ear infections as well as behavioural problems. Advice from an aromatherapist may be helpful.*

cat to the vet. Depending on the case he or she may give an antibiotic and steroid drops, or else may suggest a general anaesthetic so that he or she can clean the ear and search for any grass awns.

Both of these measures can be supported with holistic treatments. Homeopathic *Graphites 6C* can be given four times a day if the discharge is very sticky (similar to glue ear in children) and *Hepar sulph. 30C* every two hours if the ear is hot, painful and sensitive, reducing the frequency as the ear improves. *Sulphur 30C* and *Psorinum 30C* can be given twice daily for up to three days to help the internal disturbance. Use the former on itchy cats that like to be cool, and the latter on itchy cats that hog the fire. Cats that need these remedies are usually dirty and scruffy-looking.

If grass awns are removed from the ear, diluted *Hypercal* tincture will be sufficient, or else an infusion of thyme can be used to bathe the ear.

◄ *Homeopathic* Hamamelis *is useful for injuries like haematomas which are painful and where there is passive venous bleeding.*

URAL HAEMATOMA

If your cat is a fighter, it runs the danger of breaking the tiny blood vessels in its ear. The cat's ear flap is essentially a bag of skin, attached to an inner sheet of cartilage. The blood vessels of the ear lie on the inner side of the cartilage. If these vessels bleed, the blood fills and distends the bag to produce a swelling known as a haematoma.

The conventional treatment consists of cutting the inner surface of the ear, draining the blood clots and sewing it up like a mattress so that it can't swell up as it heals. An alternative method is to drain the blood through a wide-bore needle and then inject a small amount of a steroid into the ear through the same needle. This procedure sometimes has to be repeated two or three times before it is successful.

If the haematoma is caught in the early stages, homeopathic *Arnica 6C*, given four times a day for two days, may stop the bleeding, and *Hamamelis 12C*, twice daily, may help to reverse the process. *Hamamelis* cream or lotion can be applied to the ear flap. Sometimes *Pulsatilla 6C* is better for gentle affectionate cats and *Phosphorus* often works in cats that hate thunder. The tissue salt *Ferrum phos.* can be given for a few weeks if the problem has a tendency to recur.

MIDDLE AND INNER EAR INFECTIONS

If your cat has an ear infection, it must be treated. If infections are neglected, they can spread to the deeper parts of the ear. If this has happened, there will most likely be an awful discharge and the cat may start tilting its head to the affected side to compensate. Untreated ear infections can eventually lead to loss of balance.

These cases will all need vigorous orthodox treatment, but referral to a homeopathic vet will result in the treatment of any underlying causes. Any nutritional imbalances and/or stress factors would also be addressed. Emotional problems can be supported by the Bach Flower remedies, or possibly by aromatherapy, if homeopathy is not available.

► *Cats' ears are often injured during fights. The majority of such injuries do need conventional treatment but holistic support will help the cat during recovery.*

The nose

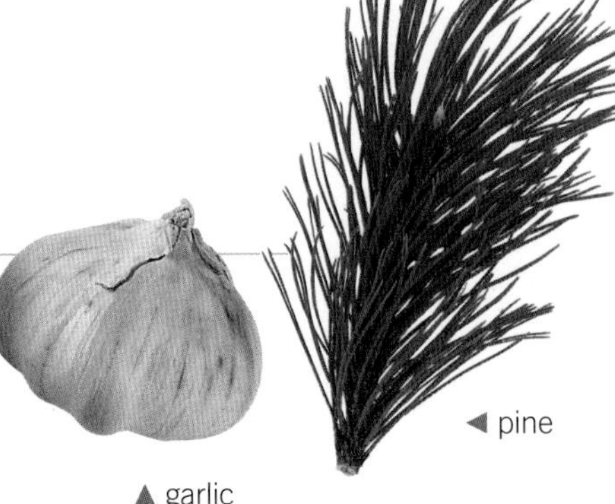

▲ *The essential oils of both pine and garlic, burned in a vaporizer, can provide relief from some of the more chronic symptoms of cat flu.*

Nasal problems are very common in cats, the most likely cause being infection, either from one of the cat flu viruses, organisms such as chlamydia, or bacteria.

CAT FLU

Vaccination gives some protection against cat flu but it does not always give 100 per cent immunity. Many cats are then left with a continuous snuffle, or a snuffle that reappears when the cat is stressed, as is often the case when it goes into a cattery.

The discharges of cat flu are usually thick and purulent, and interfere with the cat's sense of smell and its breathing. There is usually a lot of sneezing, accompanied by a loss of appetite and thirst. Since the infections are mainly viral, antibiotics are not a satisfactory solution: they can only prevent secondary bacterial infections and cannot kill the virus. Instead, the virus has to run its course and the cat may need intravenous fluids and nourishment to survive. The inflammation can also spread to the trachea and cause coughing.

Complementary therapies can be successful with both the acute and chronic forms of cat flu. Homeopathic *Natrum mur.* is useful if the discharge looks like egg white, the skin is greasy and the flu started in the cattery. *Pulsatilla* helps the soft, gentle cat who has a bland yellow discharge, and *Kali bich.* if the discharge is yellow, tough and stringy. These remedies can be given in the *30C* potency twice daily. For chronic cases, *Silica 30C* can help where the infection has spread to the sinuses. If known, try the cat's constitutional remedy.

Where there may be a strong emotional component to the condition, caused by being in quarantine or in a cattery for example, you could try the Bach Flower *Heather* for loneliness, *Honeysuckle* for homesickness, and *Walnut* for difficulty in adapting to new circumstances.

Aromatherapy can also help to alleviate chronic symptoms, provided the cat can breathe fairly easily: eucalyptus, pine and thyme can be used in a diffuser. Otherwise, try herbal infusions of garlic, goldenseal or liquorice.

Tissue salts can also help to strengthen the cat in chronic cases: try *Kali mur.* if the discharge is white; *Kali sulph.* if it is yellow; or *Natrum mur.* if it is watery.

▲ *It is important that the cat's nose is kept clean. Cats find mouth-breathing difficult, and the loss of smell causes a loss of appetite.*

▼ *Catmint, or catnip, is used mainly as a feline stimulant, but a herbal infusion is helpful for catarrh.*

FOREIGN BODIES

Grass awns stuck in a cat's nose may cause discharges. Cats have small noses, and it can be difficult to remove foreign bodies, even under anaesthetic. Consult your vet about suspected nasal obstructions. A rhinoscopy examination may be necessary as foreign bodies do not show up well on X-rays.

NEOPLASIA

Nasal and sinus tumours may be a problem for older cats. Holistic therapies can be used to support conventional treatment.

The mouth and throat

Mouth problems in cats are common and can be caused by any number of reasons. Some problems can be prevented with due care, and most can be treated if caught in good time.

► *Cats need to be fit to catch their prey, and obesity will seriously affect hunting success.*

TOOTH CARE

The biggest problem seen in cats' mouths is neglected tartar, which can result in severe gum infections, and abscesses developing in gums and sinuses. The affected teeth will need descaling and possible extraction under anaesthetic. Use homeopathic *Merc. sol.*, before and after dentistry, to support the antibiotic prescribed by the vet.

A good natural tooth-cleaner is for your cat to chew on raw bones, as these seldom stick in its mouth. If your cat will not chew bones, then cleaning with special small brushes, or finger brushes is called for. Homeopathic *Frageria 6C*, given daily for several months, may assist in discouraging the development of tartar.

ULCERS

Some cats develop ulcers on the lips and in the mouth which are not always associated with dental problems. The conventional antibiotics, steroids and female hormones are not very successful long-term. Homeopathic *Acud nit.*, given as a *30C* tablet twice daily for up to three weeks, can be more useful.

FOREIGN BODIES

Problems concerning objects stuck in the cat's mouth usually involve soft-cooked cartilage and bone sticking between the teeth. This results in excessive salivation and licking or chewing. Checks inside the cat's mouth while grooming can prevent this. Sewing needles are also a problem: the cat licks a piece of thread, and the spikes on its tongue mean that it has to swallow it. The needle is regurgitated, and impales itself on the back of the tongue. The needle can be removed under anaesthetic.

NEOPLASIA

These may occur in the mouth and throat. Some are operable but if not, seek a referral to a holistic vet. Tumours are increasingly common in the thyroid gland of cats over 12 years old. The symptoms can look like renal failure – high thirst and weight loss in spite of a good appetite – but diagnosis is easy with a blood test. They can be treated by surgery coupled with holistic support.

◄ *Feeding raw bones to your cat will help to keep its teeth clean. Most cats are quite happy to source their own raw bones.*

▼ *Give infusions of liquorice for coughs, while the essential oil of thyme can be massaged into sore throats.*

◄ thyme ◄ liquorice

The chest and lungs

If your cat has a persistent cough, however mild, it should always be checked by the vet. It could be an indication of a more serious disease of either of the two major organs of the chest: the heart or the lungs.

If the cat has a persistent dry cough, which is brought on by exercise, it may be connected with its heart. If the heart is not working properly, body fluid can seep into the tissues causing swellings (oedema), and into the body cavities, causing dropsy. As the lungs fill with fluid, the cough gets worse, becoming soft and moist. Dropsy can also result from liver troubles; your vet will be able to tell you which organ is at fault.

If the cough is connected with its heart, the vet will prescribe diuretics to remove excess fluid from the body and drugs that stimulate the heart and/or dilate the small blood vessels.

Complementary treatments can also work well and may reduce the amount of prescriptive drugs needed. The cough may have an emotional cause, with the cat suffering some upset or distress before it started. In this case, try the Bach Flower remedies *Heather* for loneliness, *Star of Bethlehem* for emotional shock, and *Walnut* for difficulty in coping with changes.

▼ *The Bach Flower remedies can help illness caused by stress. Coughing in rehomed or kennelled cats responds to* Walnut, *in particular.*

A homeopathic vet may prescribe low-potency herbals or traditional herbals. Both of these can be very effective in well-chosen cases. A constitutional remedy may also be suggested to treat the underlying causes of the condition.

For home treatment, you can support conventional medication with homeopathic *Rumex crisp 6C* for dry coughs that are worse by day, and *Spongia 6C* for coughs that are worse at night. Give both remedies four times a day. If the pulse is very slow try *Digitalis 30C*, or *Carbo veg. 30C* when the slow pulse is accompanied by a desire for fresh, cool air. If the cat seems to have great pain in its chest, try *Cactus Grandiflora. Arsen. alb.* is often indicated if the cough causes restlessness around midnight, but *Lycopodium* is better for coughs that are worse between four and eight a.m.

If the cat's limbs show signs of dropsical swelling, this can often be helped by *Apis mel.* The tissue salts *Calc fluor.*, given twice daily, can strengthen the heart muscles, and *Kali phos.* will help to stabilize abnormal heartbeats. Herbal infusions of dandelion or hawthorn may also help.

SPECIAL DIETS

Cats with a heart condition should follow a low-salt diet. Special 'heart diets' are available, containing less salt than normal foods; these are generally less appealing to choosy cats. Conventional diuretics can result in a loss of potassium from the body. To compensate, sprinkle seaweed powder (kelp), rich in vitamins and minerals, over food, or give the tissue salt *Kali phos.*

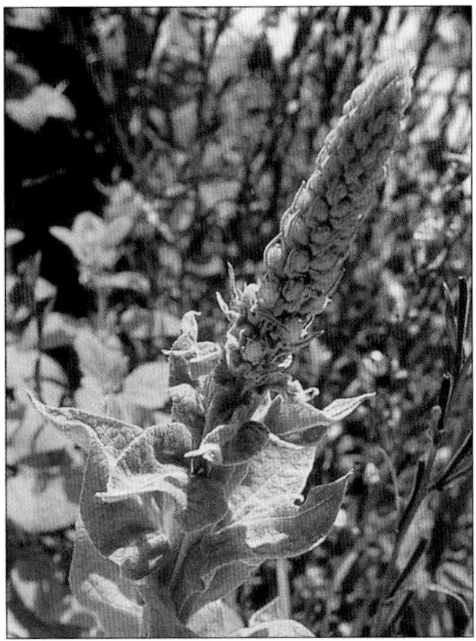

▲ *Herbal infusions of mullein can soothe night-time coughs, whilst thyme, sage and liquorice are useful for most coughs.*

LUNGS

Bronchitis is inflammation of the airways in the lungs. If this spreads to the actual lung tissue itself it can become pneumonia. The commonest cause is from cat flu, but deep wounds from fights or accidents, or wounds from air-gun pellets, can also develop into purulent pneumonia.

FIP is a viral infection in which the cavity surrounding the lungs fills with thick pus, whilst tumours of the chest may also occur in cats. X-rays and blood tests may be needed to identify these conditions as their symptoms are similar: both display a difficulty in breathing, with little coughing.

Homeopathic aconite 6C can be given in the early stages of a cough, while the cat's temperature is still rising.

Many cats enjoy the snow, but chilling can affect their chests, lowering resistance and opening the way for infections to set in.

Antibiotics, coupled with steroids to control the inflammation, is the conventional treatment for chest infections. In the case of FIP it is often essential to drain pus from the cat's chest with a wide-bore needle to give the cat's lungs room to expand and reduce the workload of the antibiotics. In the short term, it may be necessary to use these drugs, but if long or repeated courses are prescribed, it may be worth considering holistic treatment.

For mild infections try aromatherapy inhalations of eucalyptus if there is a lot of mucus on the chest, and tea-tree or thyme where pus is suspected.

If you prefer a homeopathic approach, *Aconite 6C* given frequently in the early stages of an infection is helpful, particularly where the cough is accompanied by a rise in temperature. *Belladonna* can be given if the cat becomes very fevered and its eyes dilate widely. Once the temperature begins to drop, try one of the following remedies, given four times a day: *Bryonia 6C* if the cat seems in pain when it moves, does not want to be touched and drinks a lot at long intervals, *Phosphorus* if there is blood in the sputum; *Kali carb.* if the cough is worse about 3 a.m.; *Rumex crisp* if the cough is dry and worse by day; *Spongia* for a dry cough that is worse at night; and *Antimony tart* if there are rattling sounds in the chest.

Cats can be given medicine in food or water, provided that the cat can feed without getting the medicine on its nose.

Tissue salts can also help: try *Ferrum phos.* for harsh dry coughs; *Kali mur.* if the phlegm is white; and *Kali sulph.* when yellow phlegm is coughed up.

Herbal infusions of mullein are good for night coughs, and thyme and liquorice are good for coughs in general. Garlic helps the immune system to combat infections but it may antidote some homeopathic remedies, so it is best avoided if the cat is having homeopathic treatment.

Asthma is becoming more common in cats. This is a chronic condition which is caused by a malfunction of the cat's immune system. A referral to a holistic vet would be beneficial. Homeopathic *Arsen. alb. 6C* or eucalyptus essential oil may help in the interim.

The abdomen

Severe pain, vomiting and diarrhoea are likely to indicate a problem with one of the organs of the abdomen: the stomach, intestines, liver, pancreas, kidneys, bladder, or the sex organs (ovaries/uterus or prostate).

General abdominal pains will indicate intestinal or pancreatic troubles. Pain that is just behind the ribs is probably related to liver disease, and if it is in the triangle between the ribs and the back muscles, it probably relates to either the kidneys or the ovaries. If there is discomfort in the rear of the abdomen this may be a sign of bladder or prostate problems.

VOMITING AND/OR DIARRHOEA

Physical symptoms such as vomiting and/or diarrhoea may result from either a primary or secondary inflammation of the stomach (gastritis), the small intestines (enteritis), or the large intestine (colitis). Primary gastritis and enteritis can be caused by food and other poisoning, eating too much rich food, foreign bodies or tumours. Foreign bodies in the stomach are very rare in cats – they usually eat too slowly and carefully to swallow anything that might block their intestines.

Worms are always present in kittens but sometimes these may become a problem. The small intestine becomes very active to rid the body of the worms and part of the bowel can get pushed out of place, which causes a blockage that may need surgery. This involution is called an intussusception.

Pains in the stomach or intestines, as well as vomiting and diarrhoea, may arise as a by-product of more serious diseases in the liver, kidney, or pancreas.

You should consult your vet if symptoms persist for more than 24 hours or if blood is present in the faeces. The vet will probably examine the cat for any foreign bodies or tumours and may take X-rays, especially if the vomiting is first thing in the morning. He or she may also take blood samples to see how the other organs are working, or take swabs for bacteriology tests.

Conventional treatment uses antibiotics to control infections, and steroids to dampen down the inflammation. Anabolics may be given for weight loss, insulin if the cat is diabetic, and intravenous fluids if the cat has lost a lot of fluid and is dehydrated. Dietary changes, vitamin and mineral supplements, and proprietary medical diets may also be suggested.

▲ *At the vet's surgery, careful palpatating of the abdomen of an ailing cat can reveal the organ that is most likely to be affected.*

For complementary home treatment, an immediate first-aid step is to stop feeding the cat. If there is vomiting, add a little salt to its drinking water and bicarbonate of soda if there is diarrhoea. If emotional factors could be involved, try the Bach Flowers: *Aspen* for fear, *Chicory* for separation anxiety, and *Impatiens* for the irritability associated with Irritable Bowel Syndrome.

Slippery Elm and *Arrowroot* soothe the intestines. These are available as powders which can be sprinkled on to the cat's food. Herbal infusions of gentian, St John's wort and peppermint will also ease the stomach.

► *The amount and manner in which a cat drinks can be an important guide to the appropriate homeopathic remedy.*

Homeopathic *Arsen. alb.* is probably the first remedy to think of for vomiting and diarrhoea, particularly if it's been brought on by food poisoning. Symptoms are worse around midnight, the cat is restless and will sip a little water at frequent intervals. *Phosphorus* can be tried for thirsty cats who drink a lot but then regurgitate it after 15–20 minutes. If the vomiting starts after too much rich food, *Nux vom.* is useful. *Ipecacuana* is for persistent vomiting and diarrhoea that comes on after eating indigestible foods, when there is often blood and mucus in the faeces. Try *Aloes* for diarrhoea with flatulence and *Podophyllum* if the stools are watery. *Chamomilla* helps teething kittens, especially if the stools are a greenish colour, and *Capiscum* helps rehomed kittens suffering from recurrent bouts of pale-coloured diarrhoea. In all cases the *6C* potency can be used at short intervals, lengthening the time between doses as the condition improves.

Tissue salts can also be tried: *Ferrum phos.* if the cat is bringing back undigested food; *Kali mur.* if the vomit is thick mucus; *Natrum phos.* if it is sour and acidic; and *Natrum sulph.* for yellow green bile. Give *Kali phos.* for diarrhoea due to anxiety; or *Natrum mur.* if diarrhoea alternates with constipation. As the cat shows signs of recovery, start feeding it with small bland meals of cooked fish or chicken (off the bone), together with rice or pasta.

LIVER AND KIDNEYS

If your cat has lost its appetite, is bringing up bile and has pain around its ribs it may have problems with its liver. Jaundice is also caused by liver disease. Kidney trouble can show either as an absence of thirst or else a great thirst with vomiting. If the trouble is chronic it can lead to loss of appetite, high thirst and vomiting, increased urination, weight loss and dehydration. All of these symptoms need referring to a vet in the first instance before commencing any holistic therapies.

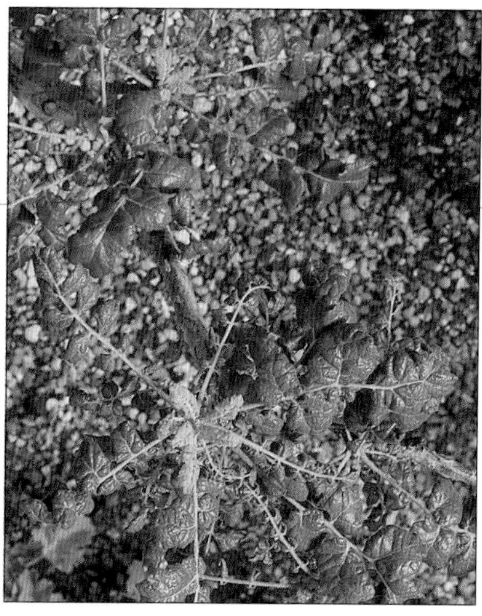

▲ *Homeopathic* Capiscum *(red pepper) will resolve the diarrhoea of newly-rehomed kittens.*

The Bach Flower *Crab Apple* will help to detoxify the body and should be given in the first instance for problems with the liver and kidneys. Herbal infusions of barberry are also good for both organs, whilst infusions of dandelion are good for the liver and bearberry for the kidneys. Try aromatherapy inhalations of rosemary for the liver, and juniper for the kidneys and bladder.

In homeopathic terms, give *Lycopodium* for liver problems which are worse around 4 p.m. If jaundice is caught in its early stages, and where there is vomiting, give *Chelidonium.* Try *Carduus marianus* for dropsy and jaundice if there are hard dry stools. Kidney problems with intense thirst, weight loss and greasy fur usually respond to *Natrum mur. Merc. sol.* helps if the cat has excessive saliva and ulcers have begun to form in its mouth, and *Kali chlor.* helps if its breath is putrid and the ulcers are a greyish colour.

▲ *Not all cats dislike water. However, if the temperature of the water is too cold it can bring on cystitis. When your cat is outside, you will have very little control over its movements.*

PANCREAS

Both inflammation of the pancreas and diabetes need veterinary diagnosis and treatment. Homeopathic *Iris ver.* can be tried but constitutional treatment from an expert is really needed.

BLADDER

Veterinary tests are needed to differentiate between infections, gallstones and simple incontinence. Complementary therapies are very useful once the cause is known. Homeopathic *Cantharis 6C* or *Merc. sol. 6C*, given every hour, can help if there is a sudden onset of straining to pass blood-stained urine. If stones are present, try *Berberis 6C*, and *Thalaspi Bursa 6C* if there are lots of crystals. Incontinence of old age often responds well to *Caustisum.*

The skin

The skin is the biggest organ of a cat's body. It forms a barrier against the outside world, protects the body against the elements and helps to control the body temperature. Sweat and sebum are waste matter produced in the sebaceous glands of the body which are excreted via the skin. The skin is usually the first place where signs of any inner disease are detected.

In disease, the body's metabolism becomes disturbed and the secretions from the sebaceous glands are changed. This is followed by changes in the skin's micro-climate that allow the development of infections and other skin diseases.

Orthodox skin treatments are excellent at reducing the pain and inflammation that accompanies acute skin conditions, but, unfortunately, they rarely correct the underlying imbalance. In fact, prolonged or repeated skin treatment can suppress symptoms, which can lead to chronic, and sometimes drug-induced, disease.

Chronic skin conditions are based upon malnutrition, hormonal imbalances, and emotional problems that stress the immune system and open the way for bacterial or fungal infections, parasitic infestations and allergies. All chronic skin conditions can be helped by complementary treatment.

PARASITES

The main external parasites of cats are fleas, lice, harvest mites, ticks and burrowing mites. Fleas are small reddish-brown insects that move and jump through the fur. Lice are small, slow-moving grey insects, normally found on the ear flaps. Tiny red or orange harvest mites can be found on the ears and between the toes in late summer and autumn. Ticks bite the skin and then suck the cat's blood for several days; burrowing mites are found on the cat's head.

Almost every cat owner will know the nuisance caused by one or other of these parasites. Apart from the fact that they are unpleasant and annoying for both cat and owner, the main significance is that some parasites can transmit disease to humans. Fleas can spread the bubonic plague in areas where the disease still exists in wildlife, and ticks commonly spread blood parasites, the cause of tick-borne fevers in humans.

◀ *The cat's coat should be sleek. Signs of stress or chronic disease will often appear in the skin and the coat.*

▲ *The essential oil of lavender can be used as an insect repellent if well diluted with water. It also has a sedative effect.*

Conventional treatments involve the use of chemicals to kill the insects, both on and off the animal. Always follow the instructions with care as overuse can cause problems.

Complementary treatments aim to repel the insects rather than kill them. Plastic hooks are available from your vet that will safely remove ticks. *Xenex* is a herbal product that has been demonstrated to repel fleas for up to 40 days. Herbal garlic given daily and homeopathic *Sulphur 30C* used weekly are also reputed to repel insects; use one or the other but not both. Three drops of one of the essential oils of cedarwood, eucalyptus, lavender, lemon, mint, rosemary or terebinth added to 150ml (¼ pint) of water can be brushed into the coat, although the cat probably won't like the distinctive smell on its fur.

Ringworm is hard to detect in cats. There may be no outward signs at all, as it does not cause the red round

▶ *Check for signs of parasites when grooming your cat. Small black specks are far more likely to be flea dirt than coal dust.*

itchy spots and rings in cats that it does in dogs. Sometimes the cat may have a little mild dandruff and some cats get a very scurfy coat. Cats can pass ringworm on to humans. The treatment is applications of conventional lotion supported by homeopathic *Baccillinum 200* weekly or *Tellurium 30C* weekly. Again, the essential oils of lavender or tea-tree can be tried.

Complementary support for all skin troubles can be given. Try homeopathic *Sulphur* for cats that dislike the warmth, or *Psorinum* for those that hate the cold. Herbal garlic tablets have a beneficial effect on the skin but can antidote homeopathic remedies. The tissue salt *Calc. sulph.* is usually good for skin disorders, and the essential oils of lavender, lemon and wild marjoram can be used in a diluted form in the same way as for skin parasites above.

◀ *A compress made from an infusion of oak bark can help to relieve hot, red skin lesions.*

ALLERGIES

Eczema and skin allergies are usually skin manifestations of an internal disorder, often with an emotional basis. The removal of the allergy-provoking trigger (if known) will obviously keep the cat's symptoms at bay, but if it comes into contact with the substance again in the future, the allergic reaction will most likely recur.

A good holistic treatment could cure the underlying problem. If you can't get a referral to a suitable practitioner, some home treatments can be tried. If emotional factors are involved, try the Bach Flowers *Agrimony* where there is underlying anxiety; *Crab Apple* if the cat is toxic with matted fur and secondary skin infections; and *Holly* to help allergies in the more malicious cat.

Aromatherapy with rosemary and lavender, or lavender, pine and terebinth does help, but the oils should be diluted and kept away from the affected areas of skin. Burning the same oils in a diffuser in the room where the cat has its basket can also help. The indications for homeopathic *Sulphur* and *Psorinum* have been discussed above, but homeopathic *Apis mel.* is useful for allergies where the skin is shiny, red and better for cold applications, and *Urtica urens* if the skin is better for warmth. *Natrum mur.* can be indicated when there is a possibility of long-standing grief: the skin looks greasy and the fur seems clumped together like a paintbrush. Herbal infusions of oak bark or decoctions of mallow can be applied as compresses to soothe hot, red skin; *Aloe vera* gel can also help to soothe and calm inflammation. Nutritional support with evening primrose oil and fish oils also helps; continue this even when the skin improves.

The female system

Because of the modern-day tendency to neuter female cats, problems of the female reproductive tract are far less common now than in the past. Today, ovarian infections are rare, although ovarian cysts can occur and lead to infertility or abortions. These conditions are difficult to treat by any system, whether orthodox or complementary.

The Bach Flower remedy *Scleranthus* can help to restore balance to a disturbed system and may help if the cat has a history of regular abortions. Herbal infusions of raspberry leaf can also be tried. Ideally, a homeopathic consultation would help. *Sepia* and *Pulsatilla* are the remedies most concerned with female hormone balance, but there are others. *Viburnum 30C* given weekly during the first three weeks after mating, and *Caulophyllum 30C* given weekly during the last three weeks, have helped some queens who have problems with miscarriage.

▼ *It can be difficult to tell a diseased uterus from a healthy one by feel alone, even for experts at the vet's surgery.*

Metritis is when the uterus becomes inflamed, usually from infections that arise during abortions or after giving birth. If neglected, the condition can worsen and the uterus fill with pus (pyometritis). Pyometritis may also result from a hormonal imbalance. The uterus becomes cystic and then fills with the cysts' contents as they rupture.

The result of both metritis and pyometritis is an unhappy cat with a messy vaginal discharge. In rare cases, the cervix remains closed and the cat's belly swells as the pus builds up inside. She may develop a high temperature and a high thirst. If the condition develops rapidly, surgery may be necessary to remove the ovaries and uterus. If the condition is in the early stages, complementary treatment may stop the disease and prevent the need for surgery.

The Bach Flower remedy *Scleranthus* can be tried to restore normal hormone balance. Homeopathic remedies can be given in the *30C* potency, up to four times a day. The choice of remedy is based mainly on the type of discharge: *Sepia* for brownish discharges; *Caulophyllum* for chocolate brown ones; *Pulsatilla* for bland creamy yellow ones; *Hydrastis* for a white mucoid one; and *Sabina* if fresh blood is present. Herbal infusions of goldenseal and hyrrh may help, and the tissue salt *Calc sulph.* can also be given.

▲ *A herbal infusion of myrrh has both antiseptic and anti-inflammatory properties. It can help in cases of abnormal discharges.*

▼ *Further investigations, such as blood tests and X-rays, may be needed if the cervix is closed and there are no discharges.*

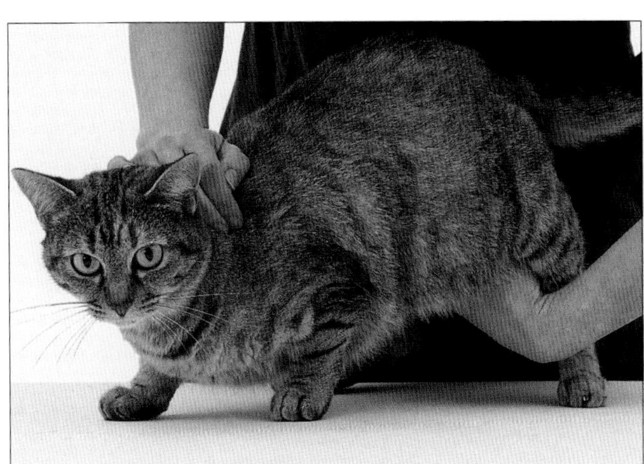

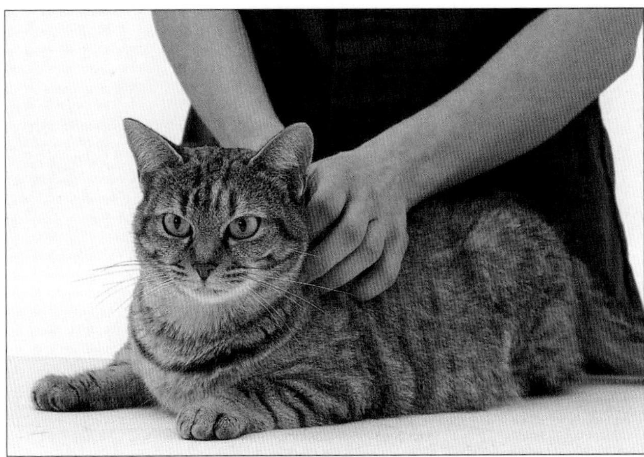

The male tract

The male tract of the cat comprises the testicles and penis. Cats do not have a prostate gland. Since the vast majority of tom cats are castrated before they are six months old, medical conditions of the male reproductive tract are relatively rare.

The most common cause of problems in the testes is through injuries gained while fighting. This area is the prime target during cat fights, followed by the eyes and ears. This accounts for the large number of bite wounds typically seen around the base of a tom's tail and on its head.

The result of cat bites is usually an infection causing pain and swelling. These bites should always be seen by a vet, and the treatment should be supported by homeopathic remedies. In the first stage, when the cat is running a high temperature, *Belladonna 30C* can be given every hour for four doses. The cat's pupils will be dilated and the area around the testes will be red, hot and painful. If pus is present or an abscess is developing, *Hepar sulph. 30C* should be given. If the pus is a greenish colour, try *Merc. sol. 30C.*

► *The Bach Flower remedy* Scleranthus *can often help to stabilize the behaviour of over-sexed tom cats.*

The testes can also suffer bruising from road accidents, a misjudged jump or from being kicked. Such a situation is best treated with *Aconite 30C* (for the shock) and *Arnica 30C* (for the bruising) in the first instance.

Persistent painful bruised testes can be treated with *Spongia 30C*, but if the testes are swollen and harder than normal, *Clematis* may be better. The Bach Flower *Rescue Remedy* should be given for all testicular trauma and the tissue salt *Ferrum phos.* can also help.

If the scrotum is ruptured in an accident, leaving the testes exposed and hanging free, surgical removal is the best option. Only if the tom is a valuable stud cat would it be worth having the damage repaired.

Some toms may develop hyper-sexual behaviour due to an overproduction of male hormones. Unless the cat is wanted for stud purposes, castration is strongly recommended. Alternatively, the Bach Flower remedy *Scleranthus* may bring hormonal production under control, and homeopathic *Ustilago maydis* or *Pulsatilla* may help to a certain degree to subdue the cat. Holistic treatments for aggressive behaviour may also be useful to administer before serious fighting breaks out.

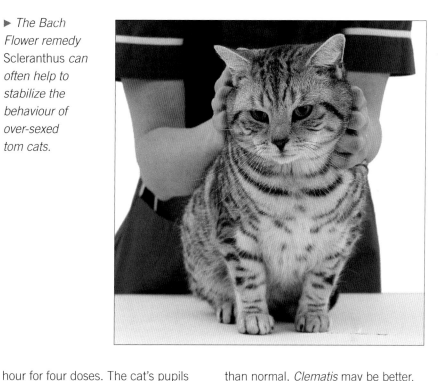

◄ *Fighting and accidents cause more damage to the tom cat's reproductive system than primary diseases of the organs themselves.*

The hormone system

Hormone production plays an important role in keeping the body working healthily and efficiently. Hormones are produced by the endocrine glands and are then secreted into the bloodstream and carried round to the body's tissues and organs.

The pituitary, adrenal and ovaries are three glands which together control the female reproductive system. The body's metabolic rate is controlled by the thyroid gland, while the pancreas controls glucose metabolism as well as producing digestive enzymes. The adrenal gland, in addition to its reproductive role, produces many steroids (including cortisone) and these control many functions. Cushing's disease is when the body is producing too much cortisone. This may be due to tumours of the pituitary gland or of the adrenal itself. Addison's disease is an under-production of cortisone. This can result from the adrenal gland's capacity being suppressed by overuse of steroid drugs, or by tumours of the adrenal gland. Both these diseases and diabetes can lead to weakness, lethargy and great thirst in the cat. Loss of fur may be seen in Cushing's disease and in under-activity of the thyroid (hypothyroidism).

▼ *Homeopathic sarcodes can help to restore the function of diseased endocrine glands. These are not available as over-the-counter products, and should only be used under the supervision of a vet.*

An overactive thyroid gland (hyper-thyroidism) is characterized by a high thirst, weight loss, a rapid heartbeat and marked hyperactivity and irritability.

If any hormonal imbalance is suspected in your cat, you should see a vet who will carry out blood tests to find out exactly what is wrong. Hormonal deficiencies are best treated by replacement therapy, using insulin for diabetes and thyroid extract for hypothyroidism. An overactive thyroid is best treated by surgery.

Holistic support can improve the quality of the cat's life and reduce the amount of conventional treatment needed. Therefore, you should let the vet know if you are giving remedies and the cat's blood hormone levels should be monitored regularly to check their effect.

The Bach Flower *Scleranthus* can support any endocrine gland, as will the tissue salt *Natrum mur.* Homeo-pathic preparations of normal healthy glands (sarcodes) can help if given as a *30C* potency every week: *Pancreatinum* for the pancreas; *Thyroidinum* for the thyroid; *Cortisone* for the adrenals; and *Pituitin* for the pituitary. In addition, *Iodum* or *Natrum mur.* may benefit hyperthyroidism; and *Iris ver.* the pancreas. Use both remedies in the *30C* potency, weekly. *Syzygium 6C* helps to stabilize insulin production and *Thyroidinum 6X* can help as a replacement for thyroid extract.

Herbal tablets of seaweed and garlic are used for hypothyroidism, and dandelion, nettle and parsley infusions have been used for adrenal problems.

► *Homeopathic* Iris ver. *30C plus* Aloe Vera *gel can help reduce the need for insulin in cats with diabetes.*

◄ iris

▼ parsley

▲ *Herbal infusions of parsley have a diuretic effect that can help to control the dropsy seen in both Cushing's and Addison's disease.*

The nervous system

A network of nerves runs throughout the cat's whole body. These nerves carry instructions to and from the brain, and they branch off from the spinal cord. It is the brain, nerves, and spinal cord which make up the nervous system.

Convulsions in cats are usually due to poisoning, particularly from slug-bait or anti-freeze. They can also be caused by epilepsy, diabetes, physical injuries, brain tumours and chronic infections. A cat may begin to shake, go rigid, lose its balance, fall over and have violent muscle spasms when it is having a convulsion. Although these may be violent, they are not painful. The cat should be left in a cool, dark, quiet place to recover, and taken to the vet when the convulsions stop. If, however, the convulsions continue for more than ten minutes, or if they recur, then the cat should be put in a padded box and taken to the vet as an emergency.

Other effects of inflammation of the brain and its membranes are behavioural changes, pain, loss of balance and limb paralysis. These can result from infections – including a feline form of mad cow/variant CJD disease – and tumours. Uncontrollable twitching (chorea) can also result from brain disease.

All these conditions will need urgent investigation by a vet, who may prescribe anti-convulsants and antibiotics. Holistic care can be used in support.

The Bach Flower *Rescue Remedy* can be given at the onset of symptoms and this can be followed by *Cherry Plum* to restore control of 'crazy' behaviour in the cat. Aromatherapy, using diffusions of lavender and chamomile oils, can help. The homeopathic remedy *Belladonna* is good for fitting cats with dilated eyes, and *Stramonium* helps those who fall to the left. Both can be given in the *30C* potency every 15 minutes to begin with. *Cocculus 30C*, given weekly, has been used as a long-term preventative of fits, while *Cuprum met.* or *Zincum met.* will help to control chorea if given daily as *6C*. Herbal infusions of skullcap and valerian may also help as they have a sedative effect.

Neuralgia is a painful condition when the nerves themselves become inflamed. It can cause self-trauma from scratching or biting at the affected area. Nerve pain, following heavy blows and crushing injuries, will respond well to homeopathic *Hypericum*, teething pains to *Chamomilla*, and other neuralgias to *Colocynth* if the pains are on the left side or *Mag. phos.* if they are on the right. The tissue salt *Mag. phos.* can be used for all neuralgias. Lavender oil, diluted in a carrier oil, may be massaged into the area if the skin is undamaged, and herbal infusions of passiflora may help.

◀ *Chamomile is used as a herbal infusion for anxiety, colic and convulsions in aromatherapy, and for teething pains in homeopathy.*

▶ chamomile

◀ *Skullcap is used mainly with valerian, in the form of herbal infusions or tablets, as a sedative.*

▶ skullcap

▼ *The Bach Flower remedy* Cherry Plum *is often used following epileptiform convulsions, usually in conjunction with aspen.*

The locomotor system

Cats are renowned for their agility and dexterity. Most of us have probably been impressed to see a cat jump from a high spot and land lightly on its feet, or have held our breath as we watch it pick its way across a narrow shelf, nonchalantly stepping over precious china.

The strength and mobility of the cat are dependent on the healthy functioning of the locomotor system – the joints, muscles and bones of its body. Malfunction of any of these parts is usually accompanied by pain, which may be acute or chronic. The onset of severe, sudden pain is usually the result of accidents or acute infections, whilst a more continuous, low-grade pain is the sign of a chronic condition.

ACUTE CONDITIONS

Cats falling from heights above 5m (15ft) will land on their feet but not always safely. They can suffer compression fractures of their limbs, and may suffer injuries of their mouth, chest and abdomen as their legs unfold. The number and severity of the injuries will get worse with heights up to 15m (45ft); above this height the injuries will be on a similar level of seriousness.

▼ *It is not always obvious that a cat has suffered internal injuries in an accident. The cat should be checked over by a vet.*

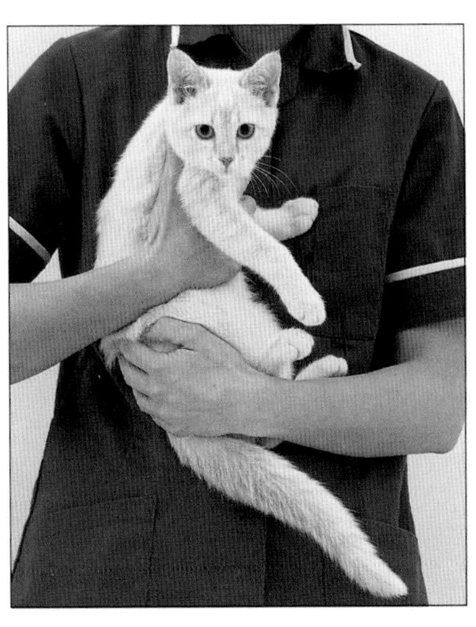

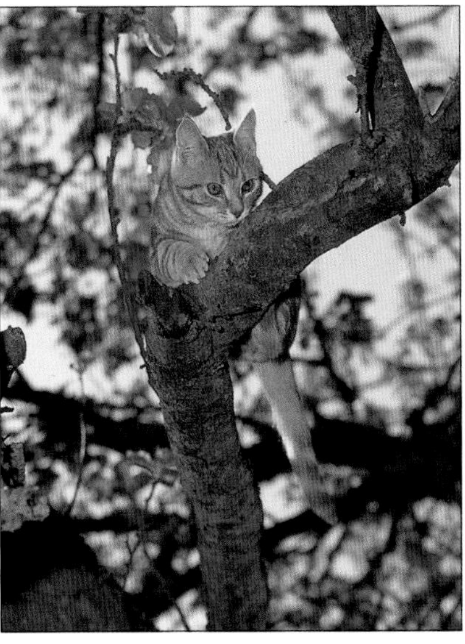

▲ *Cats seldom fall, and when they do they usually land on their feet. The impact, however, can be too great for their limbs to withstand.*

If your cat is involved in an accident and is in great pain, is showing signs of lameness, or is unconscious, then it should be seen by a vet as soon as possible. Low-grade pain and stiffness that lasts for more than five days should also be checked at the veterinary surgery, so that any necessary X-rays can be taken.

All fractures and dislocations will need surgical treatment. The conventional treatment for pain relief is either by a course of non-steroidal, anti-inflammatory drugs or by steroids. Cats, in general, do not respond well to non-steroidal drugs, and aspirin is particularly toxic to them – the dosage recommendation is one-hundredth of that for an adult human.

Acute infections may also bring on pain which is sudden and severe. Cat bites should always be taken seriously. Typically, the wounds are deep and penetrating and can cause painful infections of both the muscles (myositis) and the bones (osteitis). Acute infections will usually need treatment by antibiotics, and these should be prescribed by the vet.

The Bach Flower *Rescue Remedy* or *Aconite 30C* should be given for shock as soon as possible after any accident. This can be followed by *Arnica 30C* to help with bruising and for pain relief. If the vet has confirmed that there are no fractures and dislocations, then acupuncture, osteopathy or chiropractic can be tried. These may be supported by physiotherapy, TTouch or simple massage. Reiki can also be helpful. If the skin is unbroken, you can try essential oil of rosemary in a cat massage.

Although homeopathic *Arnica* is the standard remedy for bruising, *Bryonia* may also be indicated when the cat refuses to use its injured limb. Both of these can be followed by *Ruta grav.* and *Rhus tox.* as the cat improves. Use *6C* up to four times a day.

Antibiotic treatment can be supported with *Hepar sulph. 30C* for muscles and joint infections, but a higher potency, such as a *200C*, may be better if the bones are involved. If it does not help you can try *Calc. Fluor. 6C* until the pus finds a way to the surface. All bone and joint surgery should be supported with *Arnica 30C*,

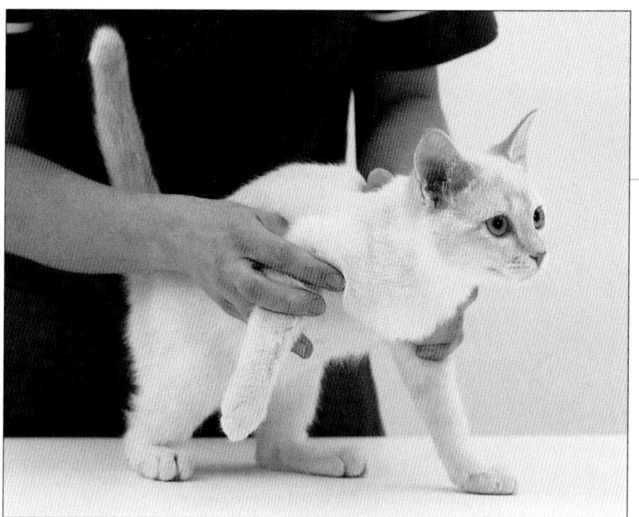

▲ *Gentle manipulation of the limbs will usually indicate the existence of any fractures or dislocations. Comparing the limbs on both sides of the cat's body will show its original range of movement.*

▲ *Simple, manipulative physiotherapy by a trained therapist has its place in treatment if there is no bone damage present.*

at the time of the operation, and *Arnica* or *Bryonia* afterwards, depending on the cat's attitude to movement. Further support can be given with weekly doses of *Calc. phos.*, to balance calcium metabolism, and *Symphytum*, to stimulate the activity of the cells that repair the bones.

CHRONIC CONDITIONS

Rheumatism and arthritis are chronic conditions which cause low-grade pain in either the muscles (rheumatism) or joints (arthritis). In general, cats are not as prone to these diseases as larger animals, as their relatively small size puts less strain on their limbs. These diseases are sometimes seen, however, in older cats.

Under the guidance of the vet, acupuncture, physiotherapy and the various massage therapies can help a cat suffering from rheumatic pains. The Bach Flowers can also help. *Beech* is indicated for cats that are rigid and stiff with pain; *Impatiens* for those that are tetchy and irritable; and *Rock Water* can help to restore physical flexibility to cats that have become mentally rigid and need a fixed routine. Homeopathic *Rhus tox.* is useful for restless cats suffering from the classical rheumatic stiffness that is worse in cold damp weather and better for gentle exercise; *Causticum* helps those who are prematurely stiff, particularly if they are prone to cystitis; *Caulophyllum* will help when the small joints, such as the knee and hock, are involved. Use these remedies as a *6C* daily. *Calc. fluor. 30C* given weekly, can help to resolve boney changes.

Dietary supplements of evening primrose oil, royal jelly and a weekly dose of 300mg of cod liver oil can all help to maintain joint flexibility. Glucosamine, chondroitin sulphate and green-lipped mussel extract are all useful for arthritis in humans; cats need about half the dosage, but check these with your vet before feeding to your cat. Magnetic collars also seem to be helpful for cats suffering from pains in the joints.

Bone tumours can occur in cats and they are always painful. These tumours are not as aggressive in cats as they are in dogs and other animals, and surgery is very often successful if the tumour appears on one of the limbs. While conventional treatment is advised for tumours, holistic care can be used in a supporting role (see pages 492–493).

◄ arnica

◄ *Herbal creams and ointments are available for external use on bruises. Homeopathic preparations can be taken by mouth for internal damage.*

▼ *Brewer's yeast and evening primrose oil can benefit cats as much as humans.*

▲ brewer's yeast

▲ evening primrose

Neoplasia

For reasons we don't yet fully understand, the cells of the body can begin to multiply uncontrollably, forming new growths (neoplasia). These growths are commonly referred to under the umbrella heading of cancer, although, strictly speaking, the term tumour is used for benign neoplasms, whilst cancer applies to neoplasms which are malignant.

CAUSES OF NEOPLASIA

Benign tumours are considered non-life-threatening: they do not spread to other parts of the body and usually have a clearly defined edge. Because of this, they are relatively easy to remove in surgery. Sometimes, however, they are difficult to remove and can become life-threatening, either because of their size or because of the impact they have on other organs. For example, a small brain tumour can cause problems because of its location.

Malignant growths, on the other hand, are not so clearly defined. These growths send tentacles of abnormal cells into the adjacent tissues and it becomes impossible to tell the difference between what is healthy and what is abnormal. The growths can also spread around the body through the blood or lymphatic system. These two factors make surgery less successful.

Neoplasms range from harmless warts (papillomas) at one end of the scale to highly malignant cancers that can kill a cat in a few weeks. Current medical science recognizes that neoplasms can develop after exposure to cancer-inducing agents, known as carcinogens. Inhaling tobacco smoke, the effect of sunlight and radioactive materials, some chemicals and certain infections, for example, are known to increase the risk of cancer in humans, and the same factors also seem to apply to cats.

There is a tendency for some cats to develop cancer of the ear. This is caused by overexposure to bright sunlight on the often pale and delicate skin in this area. Cats are also susceptible to specific viral infections that can cause cancers. The two most important are Feline Leukaemia (FeLV) and the Feline Immunodeficiency Virus (FIV). Both of these diseases are, at present, incurable.

Although cats can be vaccinated against FeLV, as yet there is no vaccine against FIV. FIV affects the cat in a similar way to the human AIDS virus; it is not transmissible to humans. Both of these diseases cause a wide range of symptoms, often including swollen lymph glands. Cats with strange symptoms, especially with gland enlargement, should be tested by the vet as soon as possible.

◀ *Holistic treatment of cats with cancer reduces the side effects of conventional therapy and improves the quality of the patient's life.*

◀ *Herbal infusions can be of help. Red clover has an effect on cancers in general, and autumn crocus relieves their pains.*

TREATMENT OPTIONS

Conventional knife surgery, laser surgery, chemotherapy and radiotherapy are all used in the treatment of malignant tumours. The holistic viewpoint sees the cancer as the body's attempt to store potentially toxic material – produced as a result of a reaction to carcinogens – which it is unable to excrete. Malignant neoplasms represent the end point of a disease process that may have been going on for weeks, months or years.

We do not know exactly why neoplasms occur in the first place, but it seems certain that they are likely to grow when early and apparently minor symptoms are ignored, or when the animal's vitality is weak and it is unable to respond to therapy.

Sometimes treatment is unsuccessful and the cancer continues to grow, or else returns soon after a reprieve.

The body's attempts to cope with cancer are affected by physical and mental stress factors. Good complementary therapy will help to strengthen the animal's immune system, and may even halt or reverse the disease process. Several veterinary practices have reported a decrease in the number of cancer cases they see after having introduced holistic methods into the practice. They have also noticed long-lasting remissions following complementary treatment in cases that would, otherwise, have almost certainly been terminal.

If your cat has cancer, deciding which therapies to try is a personal choice and all options should be discussed with the vet. The best approach is usually a combination of conventional and complementary methods. If the cat is too weak to undergo orthodox treatment, such as radiotherapy, complementary treatment may help to build up the cat's vitality to facilitate its use later on. Surgery should always be supported by complementary remedies to help with the trauma, while the side effects of chemotherapy or radiotherapy can be reduced with natural remedies. Once the active treatment is over, an holistic attempt can be made to treat the underlying cause of the disease.

It is difficult to assess the outcome of the various treatments for cancer objectively. Most people would consider the disappearance of the neoplasm a success, particularly if it doesn't return over a reasonably long time period. This result may be obtained by both conventional and complementary treatment. Many owners would consider the treatment successful if it helps their pet to have a calm, relatively pain-free, natural death, as opposed to the end of its life being one of suffering. Holistic treatment is certainly beneficial in this respect.

HOLISTIC CARE

The Bach Flowers *Agrimony, Gentian, Gorse, Impatiens, Mustard, Oak*, and *Olive* have all been found to help in cancer cases, the selection being based on the cat's mental state at the time. Reiki, TTouch, various massage techniques and acupuncture have been used to bring calm and balance to the cat, and to relieve pain.

Homeopathy is useful to support and reduce the side effects of conventional medicine and will treat the underlying cause of the cancer. *Arnica* helps to reduce bruising and pain and both *Hypericum* and *Calendula* can help the skin to heal after surgery. *Calc phos.* and *Symphytum* are useful if bone tissue is affected. *Uranium 30C* is useful for the side effects of radiotherapy as it helps with radiation sickness. Non-specific support can be given by *Viscum album, Echinacea*, which strengthens the immune system generally, and *Hydrastis* or *Eupatorium perfoliatum*, which both help to relieve pains. *Arsen. alb.*, given in rising potencies, can remove the fear of dying from a terminally ill cat, and will allow a peaceful transition from life to death.

The tissue salt *Calc. phos.* is useful for stimulating the body's metabolism, whilst *Echinacea* may be given to the cat as a herbal infusion, rather than homeopathically, if preferred. Other herbal infusions which are helpful are *Red Clover*, as an all-purpose anti-cancer treatment, and *Autumn Crocus* for pain relief. The infusions should be given twice daily.

Anthroposophical preparations of herbal mistletoe (*Viscum abnova* and *Iscador*) are used successfully for human sufferers. This is expensive and not widely used at present, but it is a valid therapy, and it should form part of the discussion with your vet.

Dietary changes will also help. Adding antioxidant-rich vegetables, plus vitamin supplements, royal jelly and garlic to the diet can benefit cats as much as humans.

Holistic medicine may not cure cancer, but it will help to reduce the suffering, and can extend the period of quality life for you and your cat.

▼ *The Bach Flower remedies are useful in treating cancers. Base your choice of remedies on the cat's emotional state.*

Natural first-aid treatments

Many complementary therapies are suitable for first aid in the home and it is probably worth investing in a few to create your own natural remedy first-aid kit. However, although it is valid for a cat's owner to give their pet first aid for minor conditions, any animal involved in a serious accident must always be checked by a vet.

ARTIFICIAL RESPIRATION

In an emergency situation where your cat is injured and not moving it is worth trying artificial respiration while you wait for the vet. Begin by checking to see if the cat is conscious by pinching the web between its toes. If the cat is awake it will quickly pull its paw back. If it doesn't, look to see if its chest is moving. Movement in the chest shows that the cat is breathing. If there are no signs of movement, make sure that nothing is stuck in its throat and/or nose – blood, mucus or foreign bodies can get stuck in these places. If the airways are clear and the cat still does not breathe, close its mouth with one hand and very gently blow down its nose. Its chest should rise as air enters its lungs. Keep the lungs inflated for a count of three, then let the air out naturally. Repeat this at five to ten second intervals.

Between puffs, feel for the heartbeat by touching the ribcage. If there is no heartbeat, cardiac massage can be given by squeezing the chest between the fingers and thumb of one hand once or twice every second. Alternate the blowing and squeezing every 15–20 seconds. If the heartbeat restarts, artificial respiration can be kept up for 20 minutes. If the heartbeat does not restart within four minutes, the cat has died.

BLEEDING

If your cat is bleeding heavily try to put a layer of wadding (batting) material over the wound and bandage it firmly. Many cats may resist this, in which case wrap the cat in a blanket or towel, put it in a suitable carrier and get it to the vet as quickly as you can. If possible, let the vet know you are coming. The first-aid treatment for the shock that accompanies any accident is two drops of the Bach Flower *Rescue Remedy* or homeopathic *Aconite 6C* or *30C*. These medicines can also be given to unconscious cats because they will be absorbed through the lining of the mouth.

TREATING WOUNDS

Fight wounds and road accidents are always accompanied by a degree of shock. Always give either *Rescue Remedy* or *Aconite* before doing anything else. Minor wounds can be cleaned and dressed before seeing a vet. If there is a lot of bleeding, use thick padding and bandage as firmly as the cat will allow.

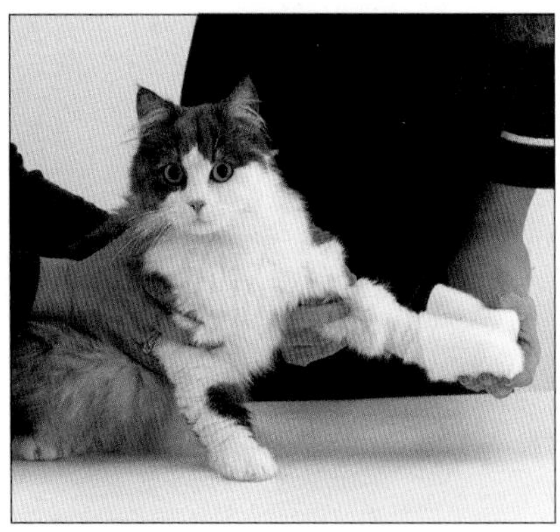

1 Having removed any objects from the wound and after cleaning it, apply a bandage to cover it, using a non-stick dressing and a soft cotton bandage. It may need two people: one to comfort the cat, the other to treat it.

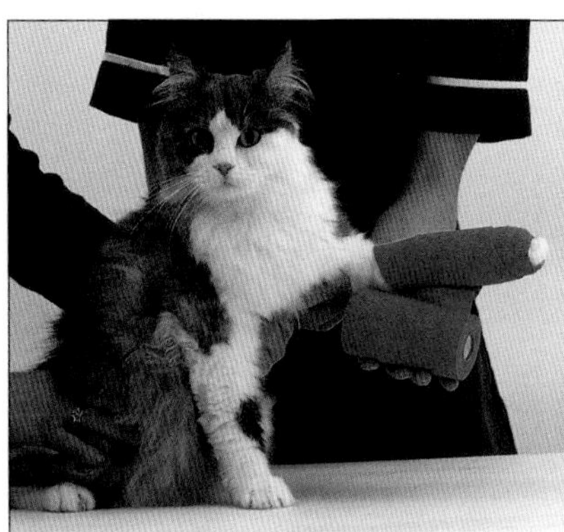

2 In an emergency, masking tape or adhesive tape may be used instead of elastoplast to hold the dressing in place. Take the adhesive bandage 2.5cm (1in) up the fur to prevent it from slipping off.

WOUNDS

Serious wounds must always receive professional help. Cuts and bruises can result from many causes, such as traffic accidents and cat fights. If necessary, treat the cat for shock and bleeding, as above. This can be followed by homeopathic *Arnica 30C*, the ideal first medicine for all cuts and bruises. If the bruising is severe, a change to *Bellis perennis* may be needed after a couple of days. *Hypericum 12C* helps all crushing injuries of the legs and tail, and *Calendula 6C* helps minor cuts and grazes to heal. If blood spurts from the wound, *Phosphorus 30C* will help, if it flows more smoothly from the wound use *Ipecacuana*, and if there is dark-coloured blood use *Hamamelis12C*. A tablet of the tissue salt *Ferrum phos.* can be crushed and sprinkled on to bleeding wounds. Minor wounds can

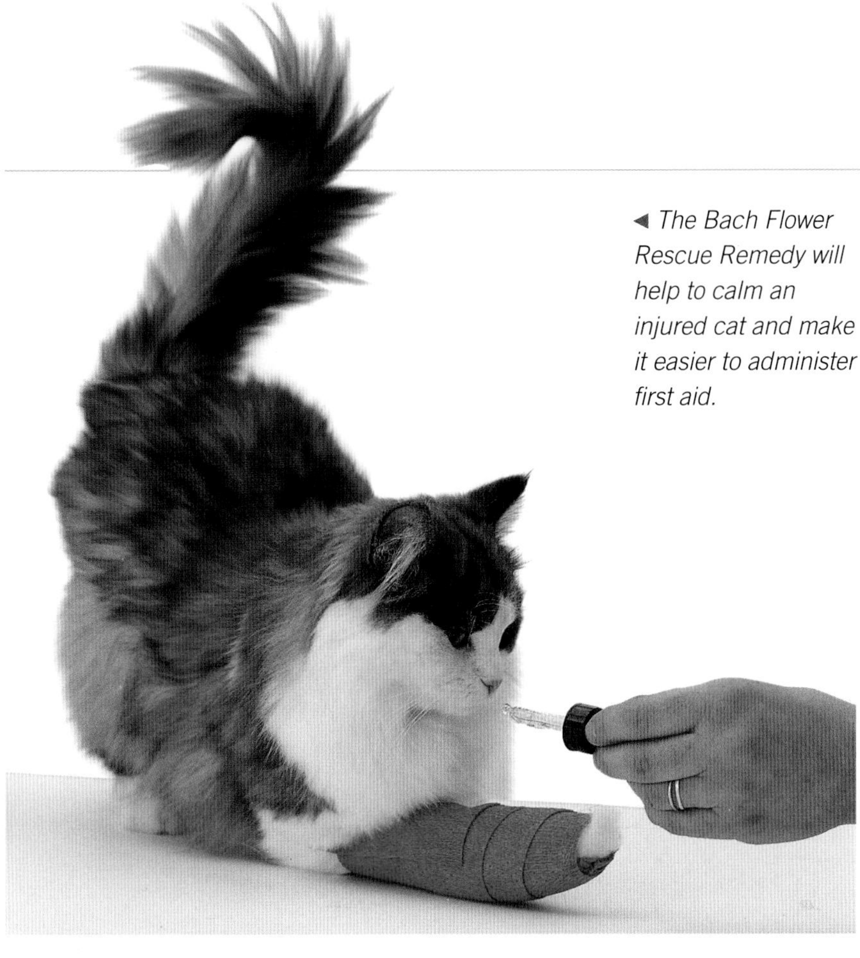

◄ *The Bach Flower Rescue Remedy will help to calm an injured cat and make it easier to administer first aid.*

be cleaned with *Hypercal* tincture diluted 1:10, and *Hypercal* cream can be used as a dressing. Essential oils of lavender or terebinth may be massaged gently around the injury, but do not use them directly on the injured part.

BURNS AND SCALDS

A burn is caused by dry heat and scalds by moist heat or steam. The kitchen is usually where these kinds of injuries occur. The cat's curiosity may lead it to jump on to a still-hot ring on the hob, for example.

Do not put grease on burns but bathe them with cold water. If fat has been spilt on the fur it may be necessary to trim some of it away. *Rescue Remedy* or homeopathic *Aconite* should be given as for shock. If there is blistering, *Cantharis* will help, while the essential oils of lavender and rosemary may be massaged around, but not on, the actual area.

BITES AND STINGS

Cat fights are common and the bites received frequently turn septic. *Rescue Remedy* and *Aconite* can be given for shock. This should be followed by *Ledum 30C* for penetrating wounds that are more painful than they look. One or two doses at ten minute intervals can be given. If the bites develop into painful abscesses, give homeopathic *Hepar sulph. 30C* every two hours. Chronic non-painful ones should be treated with *Silica 30C* daily until they heal. Herbal tablets of garlic or echinacea will aid the healing. Dog bites tear the skin and muscles, and should be treated in the same way as any other wound.

Insect bites and stings are very common because of the cat's habit of chasing after bees and wasps. These wounds are best treated with *Apis mel. 30C* every 15 minutes if they appear swollen, red and better for cold bathing, while *Urtica urens* works well on those that are better for warmth.

POISONING

If you suspect poisoning, contact the vet immediately. It is unusual for a cat to swallow human tablets, but if you think it has, let the vet know the name and quantity. Poisoning by slug-bait is common. Do not try to make the cat vomit, unless advised to do so by the vet. *Rescue Remedy*, followed by *Crab Apple*, will detoxify the cat.

Homeopathic *Nux vom. 30C* is also a good detoxifier. *Veratrum alb. 30C* can be given every 15 minutes if the cat is cold, collapsed and has diarrhoea. If oil has been spilt on its fur, the fur should be cut away or washed, if the cat will allow it.

▼ *Clean any oils or creosote from the fur quickly. They are absorbed through the cat's highly-absorbent skin and can poison its liver.*

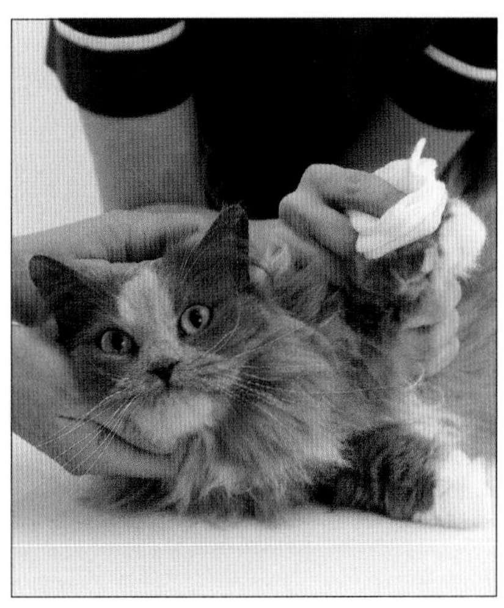

Glossary of terms

Terms in ***bold italic*** type within the main text refer to separate entries.

Abscess – pus filled cavity.
ACF – Australian Cat Federation.
ACFA – American Cat Fanciers Association.
Acute disease – rapidly progressing illness.
Adenoma – benign tumour of the glandular tissue.
Adult – a cat over the age of nine months.
Affix – a cattery name placed at the end of a cat's registered name denoting the owner but not the breeder.
Agouti – a coat pattern where each individual hair is banded with two or three colours.
Ailurophile – a person who loves cats.
Ailurophobe – a person who hates, or is frightened of, cats.
Allergen – a substance that can produce an allergic reaction.
Albino – a genetic term referring to a lack of pigment in the skin and hair, resulting in an abnormally white animal with pink eyes.
All Breed Show – a show catering for all breeds of cats.
Alopecia – hair loss due to any reason, often commonly associated with an allergy to flea bites.
Altering – American term for neutering
Analgesic – a drug that offers pain relief without producing anaesthesia.
Anaphylactic shock – a violent allergic reaction. Can be life-threatening.
AOC – any other colour.
AOV – any other variety.
Applehead – describes a flattened head shape, usually referring to old-fashioned Siamese.
Arthritis – a condition involving inflammation of the joints. Signs include reduced movement of the joint, lameness, pain, joint swelling, inability to jump up and a reluctance to move around.
Ataxia – shaky, staggering or unsteady movement, often associated with lack of voluntary muscle coordination.
Awn – the middle of three layers of coat. Acts as an insulator. Not all cats have three layers of hair.
Back-cross – the process of mating a cat to one of its own forebears, including its parent.
Barring – tabby striped markings.

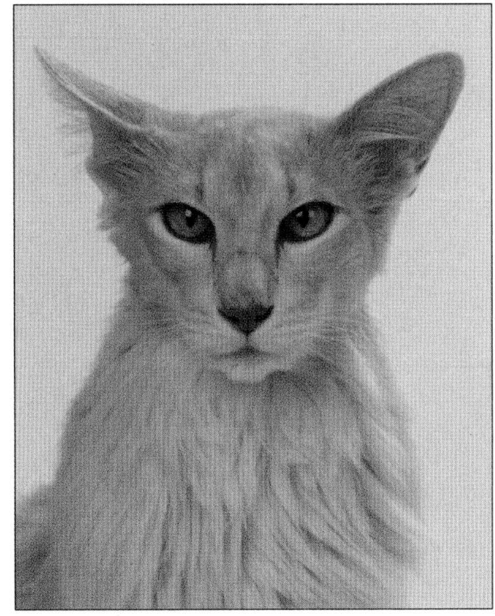

▲ ***Almond*** *– referring to the shape of a cat's eyes that have a slight upward lift at the outer corner. Commonly seen in oriental breeds..*

► ***Bloodline*** *– a record or pedigree of parentage, equivalent to a cat's family tree.*

Benching – area used to place a cat's cage at a show when not being judged.
Bi-colour – a white cat with solid patches of another colour in its coat.
Bite – referring to the way a cat's teeth meet. If the teeth meet evenly this is called an 'even' or 'level' bite.
Blaze – inverted V-shaped white marking on the face.
Bloodline – pedigree of a cat, similar to a family tree.
Blue – coat colour being the ***dilute*** version of black.
Booster – top-up vaccinations, usually given annually by a veterinary surgeon.
Break – the indentation of a cat's nose.
Breeches – term used to describe the longer hair on the back of the upper hind legs.
Breed – a particular and consistent type, colour and size of cat that is officially registered by one of the cat associations or registries.

▶ ***Close-lying** – describing a coat that lies close and flat to the skin. Often with little or no undercoat.*

Brindled – where there are hairs of different colour, usually white, in a ***solid*** coloured part of the coat. This can be very noticeable on the ***mask*** of a Seal Point Siamese.
Brush – referring to the tail of a longhaired cat.
Butterfly – pattern around the shoulders of a classic tabby that resembles a butterfly.
Calico – American term for a tortoiseshell and white cat.
Calling – when a female is ready to be mated; so-termed because of the noise she makes.

Cameo – describes a white or silver coat subtly ***tipped*** with red, cream or tortoiseshell.
Carpal pads – pads on front wrists of a cat that stop it slipping or sliding when jumping.
Castration – the removal of the male reproduction organs.
Catalogue – booklet produced by each cat show that forms the official record of the cats entered at the show.
Cataract – clouding of the natural lens of the eye.
Cat Fancy – the selective breeding and exhibiting of cats.

Catnip – a herb (*Nepeta cataria*) that many cats are attracted too, although some hate it. Can be bought dried and is often added to the stuffing in cat toys.
Cattery – 1. A registered cat breeder. 2. A place to board cats.
CCA – Canadian Cat Association/ Association Féline Canadienne.
CCCofA – Co-ordinating Cat Council of Australia.
CFA – the Cat Fanciers Association, the main registration body for cats in the United States.
CFF – Cat Fanciers Federation.
Chinchilla – a white cat whose coat has the lightest form of ***tipping***, with dark tips at the very top of each hair shaft.
Chintz – another term for a ***calico*** or ***tortoiseshell*** and white cat.
Chocolate – coat colour that ranges from milk chocolate to chestnut brown.

▼ ***Conformation** – the physical visual make-up of the cat to include type, bone structure, facial shape, eye colour and coat length and colour.*

▼ ***Cornea** – the outside transparent window of the eye that covers the iris and pupil.*

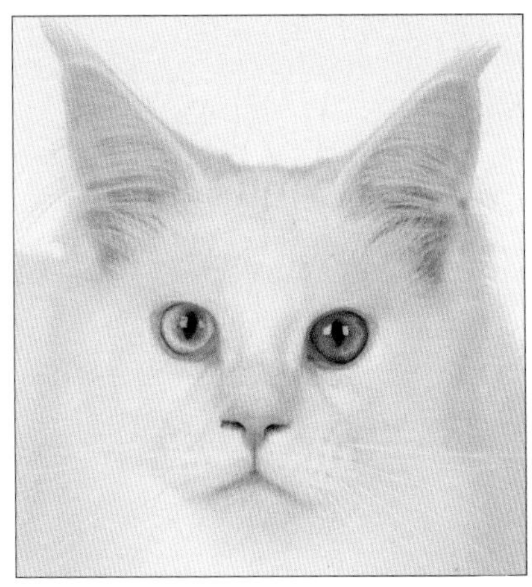

▲ ***Ear tufts*** *– hair that grows from the tips of the ear, thought to help filter sound into the ear.*

▲ ***Ear shape*** *– an important criteria in breed standards. Persians should have small, rounded ears.*

▲ ***Ear furnishings*** *– hair found in the inner portion of the ear. Seen on many cats regardless of the breed.*

Cinnamon – reddish brown coat colour, seen in Abyssinians and some other ***breeds***.
Classic tabby – a cat with ***tabby*** markings that swirl on the side of the body to look like a 'bull's eye'. Surrounding bands of colour should be bold and wide. There must be no lines going down the side of the body.

▼ **Felis silvestris catus** – *scientific name for the genus, species and group that contains all domestic cats.*

Cobby – describes a short-legged, sturdy-bodied build.
Coital crouch – squatting position displayed by a female in heat when she is ready to be mated.
Coitus – mating.
Colourpoint – description of cats with darker faces, ears, feet and tails.
Colostrum – the first milk produced by a ***queen***. Contains antibodies that help to protect kittens from infections and is rich in nutrients.
Cow hocked – describing the hind legs when the feet turn outwards and the legs bend inwards.
Cream – a dilution of the red coat colour giving a pale beige or buff colouration. This is a sex-linked (X chromosome) colour.
Cross breed – the progeny resulting from a mating of two different ***breeds***, for example Cornish Rex x Siamese.
Cryptorchid – adult male whose testicles have not descended into scrotal sac.
Dam – the female parent/mother of a kitten or cat.
Dander – tiny flakes or particles of skin and hair.
Declawing – the practice of surgically removing a cat's claws to prevent damage to people and furnishings. It is illegal in some countries unless for necessary veterinary treatment following an accident, for example.
Dew claw – a small digit on the inside of the foot. Wild cats use the dewclaw in hunting, where it provides an additional claw to catch and hold prey.
Dilute – a genetic term referring to a paler version of a basic, ***dominant*** dark coat colour, for example, the dilute version of black is ***blue***.
Dome – the rounded part of the head between the ears.
Dominant – 1. The base colour of a breed, usually black or brown. 2. Genetic term for a gene that overrides another, so that its particular characteristics are expressed in the offspring.
Ebony – a black-coloured coat.

Elizabethan collar – a specially designed plastic or card cone that is placed over a cat's head. Often secured to the collar. Used to prevent licking or biting over a wound thus allowing healing to take place.
EUR – European Shorthair.
Exhibition Only – relating to cats or kittens that are displayed at a show but are not scheduled for judging.
EXO – Exotic Shorthair.
Feral – a once-domesticated cat that has been left to wander and has reverted to its wild nature.
Feral colony – a group of ***feral*** cats that live together in one territory, this is often near a source of food or shelter, for example, a town or village.
FIFe – Fédération Internationale Féline, the major European cat registration body.
Flehman Reaction – the sneer-like action that makes use of the taste-and smell-sensitive Jacobson's organ in the roof of a cat's mouth. It is a means of receiving messages from other cats.
Frost – another name for the colour ***Lilac***.
Foreign – a term to describe a cat of more elongated type compared to ***cobby*** British or Persian type.
Gastric – relating to the stomach.
GCCF – The Governing Council of the Cat Fancier's Association, the major registration body for cats in the United Kingdom.
Gene pool – the variety of genes available within a breed after several generations of breeding. If all cats within a breed are descended from a single mating, with no further ***outcrosses***, the breed has a very limited gene pool.
Genotype – the genetic make-up of a cat, as distinct from the outward appearance (see also ***phenotype***).
Gestation – the period taken from conception to kittening, most usually 65 days.
Gingivitis – inflammation of the gums often associated with dental disease.
Guard hairs – the topcoat of hairs over the ***awn*** (undercoat) and soft down hairs. Not all cats have three levels of coat.
Ground colour – the colour of the hair that is closest to the body.
GRX – German **Rex**.
Harlequin Bi-Colour – descriptive term of a white coat with patches of colour randomly scattered on the body.
Haws – see ***nictitating membrane***.
Heat – see ***oestrus***.
HHP – Household Pet
Himalayan – 1. A breed. 2. A genetic characteristic expressed in dark ***points*** on ears, face, legs and tail cn an otherwise pale-coated cat.
Hip dysplasia – a malformation of the hip socket that causes crippling pain and lack of mobility. Has a hereditary factor.
Hot – term used to describe incorrect reddish tinges on a cream coat.

▼ ***Hock*** – *the joint on the rear leg roughly equivalent to the ankle. Hock injuries can result in hind leg lameness.*

▲ ***Heredity*** – *traits that are inherited from parents by progeny ensuring a biological similarity.*

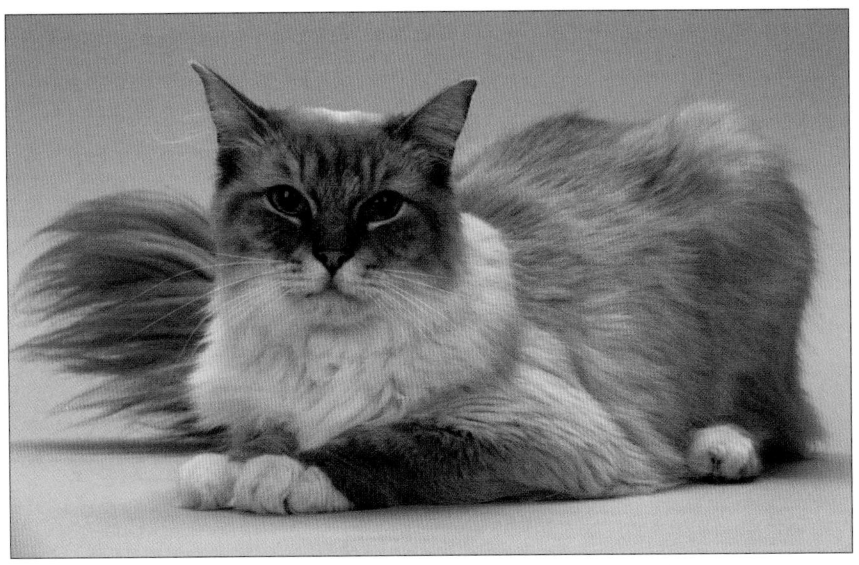

▲ ***Junior*** *– classification term for a cat that is over nine months of age but less than two years old.*

Hybrid – progeny of a cross between two different ***breeds***, the first three generations are labelled F1, F2 and F3 showing how close they are to the initial crossing.
Hypoallergenic – unlikely to cause an allergic reaction
Inbreeding – the mating together of two related cats.
Intact – a male or female cat that has not been either ***spayed*** or ***neutered***.
Intramuscular – into the muscle. Term used with reference to injections given into the cat's muscle.
Intravenous – into the vein. Usually used with reference to injections given into a cat's vein.
JAV – Javanese.
Kink – Misshapen vertebrae in the tail.
Kitten – a young cat of less than nine months old.
KOR – Korat.
Lactose – a milk sugar that cats find hard to digest. Giving cats cow's milk to drink can cause diarrhoea because of this and should be avoided.
Landrace – a species of animal that is traditional and has developed naturally to suit its environment.
Lavender – grey coat colour with a pinkish cast.
Lilac points – grey-pink coloured points.
Litter – 1. Collective term for kittens born to a ***queen*** in one pregnancy.
2. Substance placed in a litter tray to absorb fluids and reduce odours.
Locket – a spot of white hair at the base of the throat that is often a fault.
Locus – the specific location of a gene or other DNA sequences on a chromosome.

▶ ***Melanin*** *– produced by melanocytes cells – provides colour pigmentation to coat, skin and eyes.*

Lynx tufts – hair furnishings on the tips of the ears similar to those seen on a wild lynx.
Mackerel – vertical stripes in some ***tabby*** coats that look similar to the bones of a fish.
MAN – Manx.
Marbling – term describing a coat pattern as seen in the Bengal.
Mask – the facial marking of a cat.
Matt – knotted or felted hair, usually seen in longhaired or semi-longhaired cats that have not been regularly groomed. Matts can form close to the skin and be difficult to comb out or cut off. In extreme cases, the cat may have to be sedated and have the matt shaved off.
Monorchid – male cat with only one testicle.
Mutation – genetic accident that alters some genetic characteristics.
Natural breed – a ***breed*** without the interference of selective breeding.
NFO – Norwegian Forest Cat.
Neuter – a desexed male or female cat.
Neutered –a castrated or spayed cat.
Nictitating membrane – a membrane that is also known as the ***haw*** or third

▲ ***Modified wedge*** *– a term used to describe the shape and length of the face from ears to the chin.*

eyelid (nictitating means blinking). It moves horizontally and is most usually seen when a cat is ill or has a foreign body in the eye, and is therefore cause for concern.
Nose leather – the leather-like nose area.
NZCFA – New Zealand Cat Fanciers Association.
Odd Eyed – each eye is a different colour. Depends on breed as to whether this is a desirable or negative trait.
OCI – Ocicat.
Oestrus – the state of a female cat on ***heat*** or in season, when she is sexually receptive.
ORI – Oriental Shorthair.
Oriental – cats typified by long limbs, svelte bodies, wedge-shaped face, almond eyes and pointed ears.
Outcross – the breeding of two cats together that don't have ancestors in common for at least three generations.
Overshot jaw – lower jaw that protrudes abnormally past the upper jaw.
Parasite – an organism that lives off another.
Parti-colour – one or more colours or patterns on a white coat, as in ***tortoiseshell*** and white.
Pasturella – a bacteria found in a cat's mouth. Can cause abscesses in bite wounds received after a fight with another cat. If a cat bites a person may cause the wound to become infected.
Paw pads – the leathery underparts of the paws.
Pedigree – a written record of a cat's ancestry, showing its parentage over several generations.
Peke-faced – a term used to describe a cat, typically a ***Persian***, with a very short-nosed, flat face.
Periodontal disease – a disease in the tissue that supports a tooth. May result in loosening of the tooth and allow bacterial infection to enter the blood.
PER – Persian.
Persian – longhaired cat of Persian type, quite distinct from the members of the semi-longhaired group.
Phenols – a component found in some disinfectants. Poisonous to cats if ingested, either by drinking but more commonly by licking paws or washing fur that has been in contact with the solution. Symptoms include burns or sores on the lips and colic. May also induce fits and can result in death.
Phenotype – the outward, physical appearance of a cat, as distinct from the genetic make-up, or ***genotype***, which is quite different.
Pica – the habit of eating non-food items. Some cats will eat fabric, particularly wool, and this behaviour is believed to have an inherent factor. Seen in Siamese and Siamese crosses, as well as other breeds.
Pinnae – ear flaps, sometimes referred to as ear leather.
Points – the cat's face, ears, lower legs and tail, which may be a darker colour than in the main body as in a ***Colourpoint*** or Siamese.
Platinum – silver-beige coat colour.
Polydactyl – extra toes, often on the front feet. Not uncommon in cats.
Polydipsia – excessive thirst. May be a symptom of disease including diabetes and kidney problems.
Prefix – a name registered by a breeder and placed before any particular name of the cat, denoting the breeding line of the cattery. Similar to a brand name.
Prey drive – the instinctive inclination of a carnivore to find, pursue and capture prey.
Puberty – the age of sexual maturity. In a cat, this can be as young as four months but generally occurs between five and eight months of age. Females reach puberty sooner than males.
Quarantine – a period of isolation from other cats, and at times other animals, to prevent the possible spread of disease.
Queen – a female cat, over nine months of age, that has not been ***spayed*** and is capable of breeding

▼ ***Mitted*** *– white feet markings seen on breeds such as the Snowshoes, Ragdolls and Birmans.*

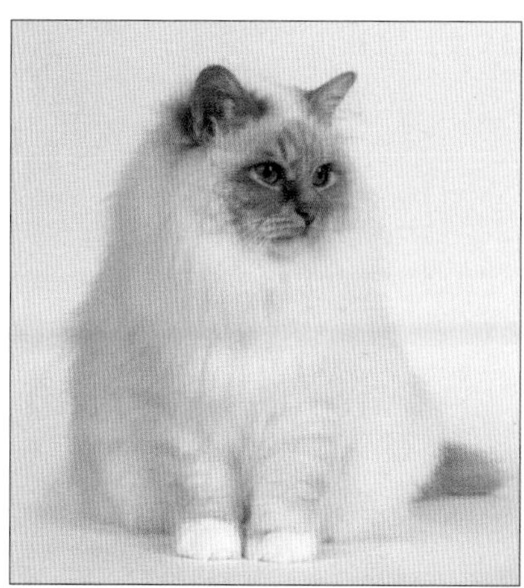

when she is in ***oestrus*** or on ***heat***.
RAG – Ragdoll.
Rangy – a long body.
Recessive gene – a gene, that on its own, is usually over-ridden by the ***dominant*** gene and therefore not expressed in physical characteristics. Two such genes, one from each parent, must be present in a kitten for the characteristic caused by this gene to be displayed. Examples of this gene are those for ***blue*** or ***chocolate*** coat colour.
Renal – to do with kidneys.
Rex – a soft coat, without ***guard hairs***, that is curled or kinked as seen in the Cornish Rex or German Rex.
Roman nose – descriptive term for a nose type with arch and low set nostrils.
Ruff – the distinctively longer fur as seen round the neck of many semi-longhaired cats.

▼ ***Set type*** *– the process of breeding several generations with a particular trait hoping it will be passed on.*

▶ ***Recognition*** *– acceptance by a registry of a cat breed for registration and showing purposes.*

RUS – Russian Blue.
Rust – traces of reddish brown hair seen on a black coat.
SBI – Birman.
Sclera – the white part of an eyeball.
Seal Point – dark ***points***.
Selective breeding – term relating to the intentional mating of two cats to achieve or eliminate a particular trait.
Self – a ***solid***-coloured cat with no pattern or shading on the coat.
Shaded – a ***tipped*** coat, midway between the ***chinchilla*** and the ***smoke***.
SIA – Siamese.
SIB – Siberian.
Sire – the male parent/father of a kitten or cat.
Smoke – the effect of the inhibitor (silver) gene on a non-***agouti*** coat. Each hair is dark for 30–60% of its length and silver at the base.
Socialisation – a process of introducing a ***kitten*** to sounds, people, sights, smells and textures so that they accept them as normal. The 'socialisation period' is between two and eight weeks of age, after eight weeks old ***kittens*** tend to be fearful of new experiences. The socialisation period during a time that the ***kitten*** will generally be with the breeder so it is important that they introduce them to a domestic environment during this time.
SOK – Sokoke.
Solid – see ***self***.
SOM – Somali.
Spaying – the surgical removal of the reproductive organs of a female cat.
Spraying – territorial marking of the home and garden with urine.
SPH – Sphynx.
Spotting – white markings in the coat.
Standard of points – the standards of size, colouring, markings, and other characteristics for pedigree ***breeds*** that

▼ ***Stroma*** *– the thickest part of the cornea, made up of densely packed layers.*

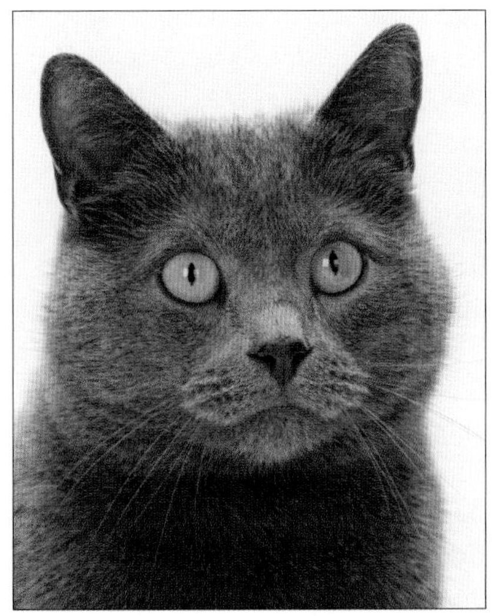

are laid down by cat-registering bodies. Judges assess each cat against the standard of points for its particular ***breed***.

Starey – the coat of a sick animal when the guard hairs are dull and standing on end.

Stud – an entire male cat that has not been ***neutered*** (***altered***). A breeding male.

Subcutaneous – under the skin. With reference to injections given under a cat's coat.

Suffix – see ***affix***.

Tabby – striped, blotched, spotted or ***ticked*** markings that in the wild give the optical illusion of breaking up body shape by camouflage.

Tartar – a substance that builds up, over time, on a cat's teeth.

Taurine – a nutrient required by cats. Most animals manufacture this nutrient themselves but a cat is unable to do so and must gain taurine from their diet. Taurine is added as an ingredient to commercial cat food.

Ticked – 1. When applied to hairs, another term for ***agouti***. 2. When applied to pattern, the ***tabby*** pattern as seen in the Abyssian cat.

Ticks – small, bluish-grey blood sucking ***parasites***. Often mistaken for a wart or lump when attached to a cat. Some flea products also control ticks or they can be removed with care. Mainly seen in spring or autumn months.

TICA – The International Cat Association.

TIF – Tiffany.

Tipped – the colouring of a cat's fur at the very tip of each hair shaft, the remainder of the hair being pale.

Tom – adult male cat.

Torbie – an abbreviation for a ***tortoiseshell-tabby***.

▶ ***Whip tail*** *– tails that are broad at the base and taper to a point at the end. Seen in breeds such as the Sphynx.*

Tortie – an abbreviation for a ***tortoiseshell***.

Tortoiseshell – sex-linked colour variant. Most cats of this colour are female, it is very rare to find a male tortoiseshell cat.

Tri-colour – another term for ***calico***, ***chintz*** or ***tortoiseshell*** and white.

TUA – Turkish Angora.

Tufts – hair on the tips of the ears or between a cat's toes.

TUV – Turkish Van.

Tuck up – where the underbelly of a cat curves up into the haunches.

Type – the ideal head and body shape of a cat as laid down in the ***standard of points***.

Undershot jaw – upper jaw protruding abnormally over the lower jaw.

Van – 1. A breed 2. a type of coat pattern consisting of a white body with a coloured tail and coloured spots on the head.

Vetting in – term for the veterinary inspection conducted prior to allowing a cat into a show.

Vibrissae – whiskers.

Wedge – a head shape that appears triangular.

White – a coat colour that lacks pigmentation.

X chromosome – the female chromosome. This is present in both male and females. To get a female two X chromosomes are required.

XLH – Longhaired cat of no particular breed.

XSH – Shorthaired cat of no particular breed.

Y chromosome – the male chromosome. To produce a male, you need an X and a Y chromosome.

Zoonosis – infections that can be transferred from animal to human and vice versa, such as rabies and ringworm.

Zygomatic Arch – cheekbones.

▼ ***Whole*** *– a male or female cat that has not been neutered or spayed and so is entire.*

Useful Addresses

CAT REGISTRIES

The Governing Council of the Cat Fancy
5, King's Castle Business Park
The Drove
Bridgewater TA6 4AG
Tel (0) 1278 427575
email: Info@gccfcats.org
www.gccfcats.org

The International Cat Association
PO Box 2684
Harlingen
Texas 78551
Tel (1) (956) 428-8046
email: inquiries@tica.org
www.tica.org

The Cat Fanciers' Association, Inc.
260, East Main Street
Alliance OH 44601
Tel (1) (330) 680-4070
email: aganni@cfa.org
www.cfa.org

The Governing Council of the Cat Fancy Australia and Victoria
PO Box 429
Craigieburn, Victoria
Australia 3064
Tel 0408 300 392
email: gccfvic@gmail.com
www.catsgccfv.org.au

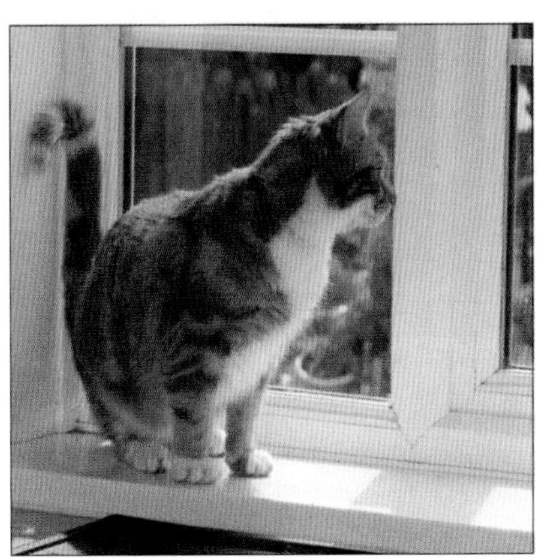

New Zealand Cat Fancy
34 Second Avenue
RD 3
Te Aroha 3393
New Zealand
Tel (07) 884 9358
email: secretary@nzcf.com
www.nzcf.com

Canadian Cat Association/Association Féline Canadienne
Unit 118
1 Centre Street
Toronto, ON M1J 3B4
email: office@cca-afc.com
www.cca-afc.com

The Governing Council of the Cat Fancy of Ireland
Tel (353) 53 942 4528
email: secretary@gccfi.com
www.gccfi.com

The Southern Africa Cat Council
PO Box 287
Oudtshoorn
Western Cape 6620
South Africa
Tel 011 616 70174
email: sacatreg@iafrica.com
www.tsacc.org.za

Fédération Internationale Féline,
Consult website for representatives in your own country.
www.fifeweb.org

American Cat Fanciers Association
PO Box 1949, Nixa
MO 65714-1949
Tel (417) 725-1530
email: acfa@aol.com
www.acfacat.com

American Cat Association
20403 Lake Pleasant Road
No 117-458
Peoria AZ 85382
Tel (1) 623-977-4959
email: AmericanACA@yahoo.com.
www.americancatassociation.org

EDUCATION AND WELFARE

National Cat Centre
Chelwood Gate
Haywards Heath
Sussex RH17 7TT
United Kingdom
Tel () 1825 7411 330
email: cattery.reception@cats.org.uk

International Cat Care
Place Farm
Tisbury,

Wiltshire SP3 6LW
United Kingdom
Tel (0) 1747 871 872
email: info@icatcare.org
www.icatcare.org

American Society for the Prevention of Cruelty to Animals
424, E 92nd Street
New York
NY 10128-6804
Tel (212) 876-7700
email: publicinformation@aspca.org
www.aspca.org

Royal Society for the Prevention of Cruelty to Animals
Wilberforce Way
Southwater
Horsham
West Sussex RH13 9RS
United Kingdom
Tel (0) 300 123 0346
email: Email link on website
www.rspca.org.uk

EU Dog and Cat Alliance
Tel (0) 7920 658685
email: info@dogandcatwelfare.eu
www.dogandcatwelfare.eu

VETERINARY

British Veterinary Association
7 Mansfield Street
London W1G 9NQ
United Kingdom
Tel (0) 2076 366 541
email: bvahq@bva.co.uk
www.bva.co.uk

American Veterinary Medical Association
1931 North Meacham Road,
Suite 100
Schaumburg, IL 60173-4360
Tel 800-248-2862
email: Contact email form on website
www.avma.org

International Association for Veterinary Homeopathy
Unit 5 Pelham Court
Marlborough SN8 2AG
United Kingdom
Tel (0) 1672 514 875
email: office@iavh.org
www.iavh.org

American Holistic Veterinary Medical Association
PO Box 630, Abington MD 21009
United States
Tel (1) 410-569-0795
email: office@ahvma.org
www.ahvma.org

International Veterinary Acupuncture Society
PO Box 271458
Fort Collins, CO 80527
Tel (1) 970-266-0666
email: office@ivas.org
www.ivas.org

British Association of Homeopathic Veterinary Surgeons
15 Algarth Rise
Pocklington
Yorkshire YO42 2HX
Tel 07768 322075
email: sec@bahvs.com
www.bahvs.com

Index

P

Q

R

S

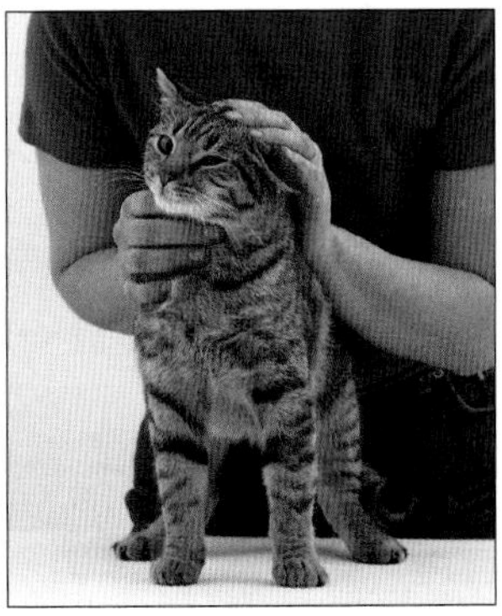

ACKNOWLEDGEMENTS

This edition is published by Lorenz Books
an imprint of Anness Publishing Limited
info@anness.com
www.annesspublishing.com

@ Anness Publishing Limited 2021

All rights reserved. No part of this publication may be reproduced, stored in a retrieval system, or transmitted in any way or by any means, electronic, mechanical, photocopying, recording or otherwise, without the prior written permission of the copyright holder.

A CIP catalogue record for this book
is available from the British Library.

Publisher: Joanna Lorenz
Editorial Director: Helen Sudell
Photography: Robert and Justine Pickett
Additional photography: John Daniels
Additional text: Alan Edwards (breeds), Trevor Turner (breeds consultant) and John Hoare (holistic care)
Index: Elizabeth Wise
Designer: Nigel Partridge

Parts of this book were previously published as *The Ultimate Encyclopedia of Cats, Cat Breeds and Cat Care* by Alan Edwards and *Natural Cat Care* by John Hoare.

The publisher would like to thank the many cat owners and breeders who provided animals for photography.

We would also like to thank the following for allowing their photographs to be reproduced in this book (l=left, r-right, t=top, m=middle, b-=bottom). Alamy: 198 br, bl; 317 br, bl; 345t. American Exotic Cats, Cathleen O'Hare: 164 tl, b. Animal Photography: 165 t, br; 169 all; 172 br; 173 t; 181 all; 197 t, m; 206 all; 214 all; 220br; 221 b; 226 m; 227 tr, tl; 228 t, br; 230 m; 231 all; 233 t, bl; 238 all; 242 all; 246 all, 247 t, b; 252 all; 273 all; 280 t, m; 287 all; 303 all. TAnthony: 228 br. Big Spots Cattery (Rachel Wyate): 164 tr; 212 all. Catskills Cattery (Anne Mae Ullman): 245 all; 306 t. Chanan Photography: 204 all. ChocolateGemSuphalak: 293 all. DK Images: 159 br; 165 bl; 172 bl, t; 173 m b; 176 all; 205 tr, tl; 207 tr tl, m; 221 m; 226 t; 234 all; 276 all. Giselle Guerriero: 297 all. Ricck Martinez (breeder H and L Cattery): 215 all. Natural Picture Library: 182–186 all; 227 b; 230 b; 277 all, p396. Rosie Pilbeam: 311 b. Russmik Blue Cattery: 269 br; 272 b. Arnos Tessers: 202 all. Warren Photographic 272 t.

PUBLISHER'S NOTE

Although the advice and information in this book are believed to be accurate and true at the time of going to press, neither the authors nor the publisher can accept any legal responsibility or liability for any errors or omissions that may have been made nor for any inaccuracies nor for any loss, harm or injury that comes about from following instructions or advice in this book.

The reader should not regard the recommendations, ideas and techniques expressed and described in this book as substitutes for the advice of a qualified vet or cat behavioural professional. Any use to which the recommendations, ideas and techniques are put is at the reader's sole discretion and risk.

Rosie Pilbeam: Applause for Paws Dog Agility Club
Robert and Justine Pickett: www.robertpickett.com